Four Economic Topics for Studies of Antiquity

Agriculture, trade, population, and the behavior of aggregate economies

Donald W. Jones

BAR INTERNATIONAL SERIES 3018 | 2021

BAR
PUBLISHING

Published in 2021 by
BAR Publishing, Oxford

BAR International Series 3018

Four Economic Topics for Studies of Antiquity

ISBN 978 1 4073 5768 3 paperback
ISBN 978 1 4073 5769 0 e-format

DOI https://doi.org/10.30861/9781407357683

A catalogue record for this book is available from the British Library.

COVER IMAGE *Shutterstock*

BAR
PUBLISHING

BAR titles are available from:

BAR Publishing
122 Banbury Rd, Oxford, OX2 7BP, UK
EMAIL info@barpublishing.com
PHONE +44 (0)1865 310431
FAX +44 (0)1865 316916
www.barpublishing.com

Of Related Interest

The Resilience of the Roman Empire
Regional case studies on the relationship between population and food resources
Edited by Dimitri Van Limbergen, Sadi Maréchal and Wim De Clercq

Oxford, BAR Publishing, 2020 BAR International Series **3000**

Economia e Territorio
L'Adriatico centrale tra tarda Antichità e alto Medioevo
Edited by Enrico Cirelli, Enrico Giorgi and Giuseppe Lepore

Oxford, BAR Publishing, 2019 BAR International Series **2926**

Economy and Cultural Change in the Pre-Roman Iron Age in Northern Central Europe
Tracing the La Tène factor by the River Oder
Joanna Ewa Markiewicz

Oxford, BAR Publishing, 2019 BAR International Series **2933**

The Archaeology of the Roman Rural Economy in the Central Balkan Provinces
Rural settlements and store buildings
Olivera Ilić

Oxford, BAR Publishing, 2017 BAR International Series **2849**

The Scale and Nature of the Late Bronze Age Economies of Egypt and Cyprus
Keith Padgham

Oxford, BAR Publishing, 2014 BAR International Series **2594**

Acknowledgements

I record my long-standing debt to Elizabeth Lyding Will (Betty) for urging me to undertake the project of which these chapters are a portion, some twenty years ago. I've gotten distracted. And throughout, Geraldine Gesell, of the University of Tennessee, has been a constant supporter and encourager. More recently, Henry Colburn and Charlotte Maxwell-Jones continued to encourage me to push this material to completion. Two readers from BAR offered helpful suggestions. Michael Leese allowed me to read and cite his forthcoming book, and Alexander Conison helped me with some important Roman references. Anastasios Malliaris generously pointed me to, and provided me with, useful recent economic research on the Classical Athenian economy. In the final push, Salam Al Kassar has helped with the graphs, and Bharat Hazari has read and commented on the sections on nontradable and intermediate goods in Chapter 3. And finally, my editor at BAR, Ruth Fisher, has been helpful, supportive, and encouraging, as has my production editor, Lisa Eaton.

Chicago, October 2020
Loyola University Chicago, Department of Economics
University of Tennessee, Department of Classics

Contents

List of Figures

List of Tables

1

Four Topics of Consuming Interest

My 2014 book (Jones 2014) offered a combination of a tutorial or textbook treatment of the basic principles of contemporary economic theory as they could be applied to the world of the Ancient Mediterranean, including the Ancient Near East, and a series of special topics that were of pressing concern to scholars of that region's antiquity, both long-standing and emerging. The book was unable to include four other topics of long-standing and equally emerging concern to those scholars: agriculture, trade, population, and the behavior of aggregate economies. The concerns in the literature dealing with agriculture, trade, and population are readily recognizable. The behavior of aggregate economies is most likely a foreign expression to archaeologists and ancient historians, but the subject addresses various interests in the short-run behavior of economies such as those of Athens during the Peloponnesian War and that of Republican and Early Principate. This book fills those gaps.

1.1 Interests and Developments in Agriculture, Trade, Population, and the Behavior of Aggregate Economies

The chapters I sacrificed in the 2014 book dealt with the economics of agriculture, international trade theory, the economics (and demography) of population, and the behavior of aggregate economies – which passes in contemporary economic curricula as macroeconomics. Both agriculture and international trade – the latter frequently under the rubric of "exchange" to avoid modernization – have been perennial interests of both archaeologists and ancient historians, and there has been extensive interest in recent decades in the demography of ancient populations. While the behavior of aggregate economies has received little attention by ancient historians, a number of efforts have been made by both ancient historians and economic historians to measure the gross domestic products (GDP) of the Roman Empire, Classical period Athens, and the Seleucid Empire. And there remain financial panics in Republican and Early Principate Rome to be explored.

Most ancient economic activity was agricultural or refashioned agricultural products.[1] For Greek prehistoric periods, Paul Halstead has offered sophisticated and interesting hypotheses regarding both archaeological remains and the at-least quasi-literary information in Mycenaean Linear B texts (e.g., Halstead 1999). In palatial situations, storage of agricultural products has been a topic of long-lasting interest. Thomas Gallant (1991) has studied how Classical Greek farm households managed the uncertainties involved in agricultural production. Both topics, among others, are discussed in the chapter here on agriculture. And throughout antiquity and the ancient Mediterranean regions, farm tenure conditions have interested ancient historians and even philologists when relevant texts survive, as was the case with Matthew Stolper's translation of Babylonian sharecropping texts analyzed in my 2014 book (Jones 2014, 25–26). Central to all of these issues are the uncertainties involved in agricultural production. These conditions are not restricted to antiquity, but face agriculturalists today, and agricultural economics has studied many problems involving multiples of these circumstances which clearly faced ancient agriculturalists, even if only individual aspects of these multifaceted problems are addressed in the archaeological and ancient historical literature to date.

Regarding international trade, the appearance of non-local objects in excavations has long intrigued archaeologists, in addition to underwater excavations of shipwrecks over the past half-century. More highly organized international trade during historical periods long has attracted the attention of ancient historians. Archaeologists dealing with exchange or trade have been heavily, although not exclusively, influenced by the interests of anthropology – cultural transmission, meaning, prestige, physical mechanisms of exchange.[2] Ancient historians have been interested in identifying trading partners and in quantifying magnitudes – quantities and values – and in understanding institutions involved in executing these trans-national transactions.[3] Economic interests in trade have extended to those transactions' motivations and their consequences for incomes and activity in trading partners. During historical parts of antiquity, data are often available to shed at least partial light on these interests. For prehistoric periods, the models of international trade theory can help discriminate among hypotheses regarding interpretations of artifacts by archaeologists. Trade models are general equilibrium models, modeling hypothetical "complete worlds" – two countries, two industries, and two factors of production - under varying circumstances. This makes them more intricate than partial equilibrium models of single markets. Keith Hopkins' (1980) article on taxes and trade in the

[1] In an interesting and possibly path-breaking study of the wool products industry, Mazow (2014) has reported distinct, non-complementary production processes from an agricultural activity. Wool could be boiled to extract lanolin for use in various subsequent products, but the remaining wool was unsuitable for spinning. This is an example of activities within an industry which competed for inputs.

[2] For a few early examples and a relatively recent one: Kohl (1975); Renfrew (1975; 1978); Oka and Kusimba (2008).

[3] For a recent, well researched example, Wilson (2012).

Roman Empire seemed counterintuitive to many scholars of antiquity at the time, and even later,[4] but Hopkins had intuited what international economists had discovered as the "transfer problem," whereby an international capital transfer must be accompanied by an outward flow of goods (exports) of equal value. Think about it this way: when you send your gold overseas, the recipients can't eat it or wear it, but they can use it to buy your products that they can eat and wear.

Moving to population and demographics, studies in particular of historical periods of ancient Greece and Rome have emphasized the importance for historical analysis of the sizes of these regions' ancient populations. For both archaeologists and ancient historians, population growth rates have been of particular interest. From the question of 8th century B.C.E. Greek regional population growth rates to the growth of the Roman population during the Late Republican period those subjects have interested archaeologists and historians of those periods. Roger Bagnall and Bruce Frier (1994), in their magisterial analysis of Egyptian demography in the Roman period, found a fertility regime in correspondence with the implications of natural fertility, a concept which excludes effective birth control actions but allows for culturally determined practices limiting births. Walter Scheidel (2001) also has applied model life tables to population data from Egypt. And De Ligt (2012) and Hin (2013) have studied the Roman censuses, and Hin in particular has brought demographic principles into her assessment of the population of Roman Italy in the last two centuries B.C.E. (De Ligt 2012; Hin 2013). Ancient historians have become comfortable and quite adept at using model life tables to study ancient populations, while recognizing the importance of data limitations. One issue that these excellent studies have not addressed clearly is the motivations of families to have children and the constraints they faced in reaching their desired family size. The natural fertility concept has been an obstacle to addressing these issues. The chapter dealing with demography and the economics of population characteristics and dynamics examines this hypothesis, introduces a number of demographic principles and applies some of the principles to problems of ancient demography, presents economic models of fertility and intergenerational economic behavior, and relationships between population growth and economic growth. The microeconomics of fertility decisions – the "demand for children" – integrates fertility decisions with other decisions families and households must make.

Models of aggregate economies are general equilibrium models, but they study different variables from most price-theoretic general equilibrium models. "Macroeconomic" models deal with aggregate output, the quantity of money, price levels and inflation, employment, and interest rates. Finance is central to macroeconomics. It has been recognized that private banking which could expand the money supply was practiced in Classical Athens. Financial panics were not unknown in ancient Rome. What would the unnoted concomitants of such financial market meltdowns have been? Theory might fill in some blanks in the historical record. Historians of ancient Roman money have identified periods of sharp and sustained increases in the price level as lower-value, base-metal coinage flooded the market. Lack of understanding of the behavior of interest rates led to widespread bankruptcies of lenders during these inflationary periods. Archaeological bits of evidence regarding the overall condition of a country's or a region's economic circumstances are likely to be snapshots in time, or even "time series" of snapshots. Annalisa Marzano provides an interesting case of such a "time series" of observations of investment activity as well as on-going production in her study of olive and wine presses in Gaul, the Iberian Peninsula, and the Black Sea region between the 1st century B.C.E. and the 4th–5th centuries C.E. Although the investment activity began at different times in the three regions, it began to decline roughly synchronously, which suggests systemic economic factors at work raising interest rates, with possible contributing factors ranging from the Antonine Plague to invasion by the Mauri from North Africa, and barbarian incursions during the 3rd century CE (Marzano 2013, 126, 134–135, n. 105). Historically reported sequences of circumstances are better suited to yield something roughly equivalent to a time series of observations on key variables whose progress marks out how a national economy behaves over relatively short periods of time.

1.2 How Economists Study Problems

Economists typically specify people's decision problems – what economics is all about – as either maximization or minimization problems. Demand functions,[5] one of the fundamental relations of economics, can be derived as solutions to either a utility maximization problem or an expenditure minimization problem. The utility maximization problem is constrained by income, and the expenditure minimization problem is constrained by utility – i.e., finding the characteristics of the lowest expenditure that will yield a target level of utility. These constrained, static optimization problems are solved with calculus tools called Lagrangean functions, which are simply single equations containing the objective function (what the individual wants to maximize or minimize) and terms defining the various constraints (there can be quite a few constraints, depending on the problem), with each constraint multiplied by its own "Lagrange multiplier," which tells how much the objective function could be either increased or decreased by a small relaxation of the constraint. There are other techniques for optimization, particularly optimization over time, but I do not get deeply

[4] For continuation of the controversy over Hopkins' discovery, Bowman and Wilson (2013, 26) say, "Whether or not we accept the 'taxes-and-trade model' for Egypt or anywhere else. . . "

[5] Sometimes called demand curves, after the typical graphical representation typical of textbooks, relating how purchases of a good fall as the price of the good rises. See Jones (2014, Chapter 3) for further details).

into any problems requiring those techniques in these chapters. But back to calculus, it's not terribly different from the slopes of lines we studied in 9th grade plane geometry in the United States (the 9th grade in the United States is equivalent to the 3ème in France, 9 Klasse in Germany, Year 10 in England and Wales): it's how many vertical units we increase or decrease as we increase a horizontal unit (move from left to right) on a graph.

Once a Lagrangean function is set up with its objective and constraint function(s), it is maximized or minimized by differentiating (a simple calculus operation – you just increase the magnitude of a variable by a very small amount and see what happens to the function) the entire function with respect to the variables under the control of the agent owning the problem. This operation is called differentiation, and the resulting calculation is called a derivative. This differentiation to find an optimal value of a choice variable is called "taking the first-order conditions (FOCs)." What this operation does is find the value of the choice variable, holding all other choice variables constant, that will yield either the maximum or minimum value of the entire Lagrangean function. If you think of a curve that looks like a hill with a top and a downslope, the FOC finds the value of the variable that yields a tangency to the top of the hill, where it has a slope of zero. For a minimization, instead of a hill, we have a dip, and the tangency still has a slope of zero, only at the bottom of the dip. In calculus terms, the FOC finds a derivative (the slope of a function of one variable) or a partial derivative (the slope of a function of several variables) equal to zero, indicating a tangency to a maximum value or a minimum value. Marginal utility – the increment to utility of a small increase in the consumption of one good that is in an individual's utility function – is one such partial derivative. Partial derivatives are commonly denoted by a variable with a subscript, e.g., MU_x, where x may represent a consumption good like apples or shoes, or MP_L, the marginal product of labor time in a production process – similarly to marginal utilities, a marginal product is the increment that a small increment in an input such as labor time, all other inputs held constant, contributes to output. For functions of one variable, a "prime" symbol is typically used to denote the derivative with respect to the variable in the function, such as f', where f is the function, say, of the value of women's dowries as a function of eligible bachelors, and f' represents what happens to the value of dowries when one more bachelor (out of many) is added. In expressing the forms of derivatives in the chapters, I have avoided the dx/dy form, substituting Δ for d, in anticipation that the Δ is commonly used in junior high school or middle school in mathematics lessons involving Cartesian graphs and hence may be less foreign than the "d" for people who left the study of mathematics early.

The agriculture chapter is replete with Lagrangean expressions in its models of various circumstances because there were so many missing, incomplete, and imperfect markets in ancient peasant agriculture – and surely many even in more industrial agriculture such as was practiced in Egypt and North Africa during the Roman period. Each of these missing or incomplete markets requires a separate constraint in a Lagrangean function to determine how well those activities were doing despite their constraints. The other three chapters deal much less with constrained optimization problems.

Other mathematical tools are used for intertemporal optimization problems – optimal control (a generalization of the calculus of variations) and dynamic programming. The population chapter, as might be imagined, contains intertemporal optimization problems[6] formulated as optimal control problems. Both optimal control and dynamic programming use the concept of the first-order condition to determine the optimality of the magnitudes of variables subject to choice by the maximizing agent. In optimal control problems, the Lagrangean function is replaced by a Hamiltonian function, which maintains the optimality of the magnitudes of variables under the control of the optimizing agent in different time periods as the first-order conditions are found. The first-order condition of a dynamic program is called a Bellman equation, after the developer of dynamic programming. It differs considerably from the FOCs of the Lagrangean and Hamiltonian functions. The first-order conditions of all of these optimization methods accomplish a common goal: to find the form of the derivative of the choice variable whose value is zero, implying that it has found the "top of the hill." Only one instance of a Bellman FOC is encountered, in the agriculture chapter. Hamiltonian functions are encountered several times in the population chapter.

A constant interest economists have regarding the behavior of variables to exogenous forces is how sensitive the responses are. The usual measure of sensitivity in economics is a measure called the elasticity, the percent change in an endogenous variable divided by a one-percent change in an exogenous variable. A typical value of an elasticity could be -0.4: a one-percent increase in the forcing variable causing four-tenths of a percent decrease in the dependent variable. Commonly cited elasticities are price and income elasticities of demand, supply elasticities, output elasticities (the percent change in the output of a production process for a one-percent increase in one of the inputs to the process, holding the quantities of all other inputs constant), and elasticities of substitution between various consumption items and between factors of production. Various elasticities are cited throughout the chapters.

So, to end this brief section on the methodology of these chapters, a reader might ask, "Can I get anything out of this book without being a mathematician?" Yogi Berra, the late, famous, American baseball catcher for the New York Yankees once said, "A lot can be observed just by watching." A lot can be learned just by reading the mathematical symbols and expressions (equations) as

[6] Developing a series of optimal magnitudes of the variables of interest over time – for example, what would be the optimal time path of consumption and savings over an anticipated number of working years and post-working years before death?

text – possibly like reading *Moby Dick*, but nonetheless reading like text. Mathematical symbols generally compact a phrase or a sentence worth of information into a single symbol. Once you understand what the symbol means, it saves you a lot of words. Sometimes some contemplation of a first-order condition or a base equation will reveal useful and intuitively interpretable information to a non-mathematical reader. Knowledge of the rules of differentiation is not necessary.

1.3 Rationality, Preferences, Markets, Capitalism, and Modern Economic Theory

Rationality, in economics, is very simple, if austere. It involves only three logical operations: completeness, transitivity, and "revealed preference." Completeness: you either prefer one offering to another or are indifferent between the two. Transitivity: if you prefer choice A to choice B and choice B to choice C, you'll prefer choice A to choice C. Revealed preference: if you choose set A out of set Δ, you prefer set A to all other possible combinations of sets from group Δ. So we are not talking about the rationality of religious beliefs – suppose that during a hard-fought war, one side is afflicted with a plague of some sort and the affected population believed that they had displeased the gods, so they began sacrificing their livestock in appeasement, were they irrational? Absolutely not. They didn't have the information set regarding the infection that we have some twenty-five hundred to three thousand years later, but given the state of their science and religion, they are behaving completely rationally . . . even if they went overboard and happened to sacrifice too large a proportion of their animal power and protein.[7]

Preferences can involve a complicated set of beliefs regarding what makes a good life. Neighbors may have different preferences. That just means that they would sacrifice more for choice X than for choice Y than their neighbors would. People at different times and places may have been willing to spend more for an amount of Y among their own family than for that same amount from another family, because of what could be side-conditions, but that is another matter that may involve budget constraints. I don't want to dig too deep a hole on such side conditions, but each economist's utility maximization exercise, whether with historically or archaeologically identified constraints, takes these limitations explicitly into account.

Markets are one method of allocating resources. Contemporary industrial economies rely extensively on both market and non-market allocation systems: think of the extent of government activity in most of these countries. But back to, say, the ancient Near East and Egypt, where it is clear that large organizations such as temples and crown activities paid their employees predominantly or wholly in "rations." Those employees wore clothes. How did they convert barley into cloth? Some scholars like to call the process "exchange," but markets – which furnish knowledge of valuations to participants – would help keep the exchange rate between barley and cloth within a range that people could anticipate with little effort. In fact, Morena Garcia (2014, 68–69) contends that enough gold and silver had been robbed from tombs by the second millennium that laundering those precious metals through markets was routine, and Tenney (2017, 750) notes that LBA Babylonians would exchange rationed grain for oil and clothing.

Capitalism is a touchy subject for many people these days, with the extensive roll-backs of regulatory safeguards in the past several decades, even as the appeal of Marxism as a social allocation system may have waned. Much has been written about capitalism, but at its core, it is a social system in which individuals own various means of production and operate so as to try to do better than just break even – i.e., make a profit. In doing so, they typically contract with owners of other means of production who also want to make a profit. One way to think about making a profit is this: if you keep making a loss (produce less than you expend) period after period, eventually you'll starve. So trying to make a profit can be thought of as a reasonable goal held by reasonable people over long periods of time.[8] Now, returning to the subject of economics, it is not capitalism. Activities undertaken in societies organized as largely capitalist enterprises are common subjects of contemporary economics, but so are activities undertaken in heavily regulated societies and even within the confines of families. There is no reason to conflate contemporary – or 18th or 19th century – economics with capitalism.

Modern economic theory is inappropriate to antiquity, I occasionally read in scholarly commentary on its applications. Straight out of the textbooks, it's also inappropriate to today's circumstances, which is why textbook treatments have to be so extensively modified in both purely theoretical and empirical research. One Nobel Prize in economics has been awarded for the development of a statistical procedure for dealing satisfactorily with non-random samples.[9] Statistical (econometric) analyses of economic relationships routinely hold constant multiple factors that could spuriously influence the relationship between the variables of interest. This is no different from accounting for other factors in ancient behavior.

Some prominent scholars of ancient economic behavior I've neglected in this work: Karl Polanyi, Moses Finley, and Marcel Mauss. All three of these men have been and continue to be influential among some

[7] Foxhall (1990, 99, n. 16) laments the interpretation of rationality by Polanyi, Finley and de Ste. Croix. Leese (2015 and forthcoming) has conducted empirical analyses of economic rationality in Classical Greek contexts.

[8] Monroe (2009, 283–285), in his study of Late Bronze Age Near Eastern international trade, offers a calming assessment of capitalism and profits in a section titled, "Capitalism and its contents."

[9] https://www.nobelprize.org/prizes/economic-sciences/2000/heckman/facts/

contemporary scholars of ancient economies.[10] Polanyi had the misfortune, in my assessment, of being the early bird who arrived before the worm: the extensive evidence of market activity with or without identified locations. Why do I not pay more attention to him? Long-term, traditional terms of exchange (prices to a contemporary economist) don't make sense. Costs change over short periods of time: the weather changes, people get sick, some die unexpectedly and prematurely . . . all of which can change costs. Why would individuals stick with "traditional" exchange rates from which they would lose the ability to stave off hunger? In recent decades, historians relying on ancient texts, particularly Latin, have dipped behind the curtains of ideology purveyed by many of those writers. What was the ideology of ANE writers who thought of wealthier individuals and families as corrupt (Dale 2013)? As I suggested above, as an economist, I have a very catholic view of markets. No fixed site is needed, no auctioneer, simply word of mouth about costs and willingness to pay. Shoes per volume of barley should stay in a narrow range in a village or town. Finley was an inspirational figure among his students, but he accepted the blasé statements of upper-class ancient Greeks regarding their aversion to seeking net benefits from their economic transactions. But that was after their wealth had been accumulated and probably stabilized through formal and informal laws. Mauss, who preceded both Polanyi and Finley, introduced the gift-exchange concept, which archaeologists and historians have been willing to accept in various situational capacities. Royal "brothers" sending gold or daughters to "brothers" as attested in the Amarna Letters, or Vladimir Putin giving Donald Trump a signed soccer ball, clearly fit this concept. Aegean drinking sets on Cyprus or Naue II swords in the Peloponnese as gift exchanges rather than quid pro quo . . . I see no compelling logic to favor one account over the other. As an economy-wide organizing principle for resource allocation in, say, the Greek Dark Age, gift exchange strikes me as insubstantial, and in the ANE during the Late Bronze Age as even more so. Could some archaeological remains be evidence of gift exchange? Why not? At any rate, these are inclinations I bring to the present work.

References

Andreau, Jean. 2002. "Twenty Years after Moses I. Finley's *The Ancient Economy*," in *The Ancient Economy*, edited by Walter Scheidel and Sitta von Rede, 33–49. Edinburgh: Edinburgh University Press.

Bagnall, Roger S., and Bruce W. Frier. 1994. *The Demography of Roman* Egypt. Cambridge: Cambridge University Press.

Bowman, Alan, and Andrew Wilson. 2013. "Quantifying Roman Agriculture: An Introduction," in *The Roman Agricultural Economy: Organization, Investment, and Production*, edited by Alan Bowman and Andrew Wilson, 1–32. Oxford: Oxford University Press.

Dale, Gareth. 2013. "'Marketless Trading in Hammurabi's Time': A Re-appraisal." *Journal of the Economic and Social History of the Orient* 56: 159–188.

De Ligt, Luuk. *Peasants, Citizens, and Soldiers; Studies in the Demographic History of Roman Italy 225 BC – AD 100*. Cambridge: Cambridge University Press, 2012.

Gallant, Thomas. 1991. *Risk and Survival in Ancient Greece*. Stanford: Stanford University Press.

Halstead, Paul. 1999. "Surplus and Sharecropper: The Grain Production Strategies of Mycenaean Palaces," in *Meletemata: Studies Presented to Malcolm Wiener as He Enters His 65th Year*, Aegaeum 20, Volume I, edited by Philip P. Betancourt, Vassos Karageorghis, Robert Laffineur, and Wolf-Dieter Niemeier, 319–326. Liège and Austin: Histoire de l'art et archeology de la Grèce antique, and Program in Aegean Scripts and Prehistory, University of Texas at Austin.

Hin, Saskia. 2013. *The Demography of Roman Italy: Population Dynamics in an Ancient Conquest Society*. Cambridge: Cambridge University Press.

Jones, Donald W. 2014. *Economic Theory and the Ancient Mediterranean*. Malden, Mass.: Wiley-Blackwell.

Kohl, Philip L. 1975. "The Archaeology of Trade," *Dialectical Anthropology* 1: 43–50.

Leese, Michael. 2016. "*Kapêloi* and Economic Rationality in Fourth-Century B.C.E. Athens," *Illinois Classical Studies* 42: 41–59.

Leese, Michael. Forthcoming. *Making Money in Ancient Athens*. Ann Arbor: University of Michigan Press.

Mazow, Laura. 2014. "The Root of the Problem: On the Relationship between Wool Processing and Lanolin Production," *Journal of Mediterranean Archaeology* 27: 33–50.

Marzano, Annalisa. 2013. "Capital Investment and Agriculture: Multi-Press Facilities from Gaul, the Iberian Peninsula, and the Black Sea Region," in *The Roman Agricultural Economy: Organization, Investment, and Production*, edited by Alan Bowman and Andrew Wilson, 107–141. Oxford: Oxford University Press.

Monroe, Christopher Mountfort. 2009. *Scales of Fate: Trade, Tradition, and Transformation in the Eastern Mediterranean, ca. 1350-1175 B.C.E.*, Alter Orient und Altes Testament, Bd. 357. Münster: Ugarit-Verlag.

Oka, Rahul, and Chapurukha M. Kusimba. 2008. "The Archaeology of Trading Systems, Part 1: Towards a New Trade Synthesis," *Journal of Archaeological Research* 16: 339–295.

[10] Dale (2013) assesses Polanyi's continuing influence, and Andreu (2002) considers Finley's to some extent more waning influence.

Renfrew, Colin M. 1975. "Trade as Action at a Distance: Questions of Integration and Communication," in *Exchange Systems in Prehistory*, edited by J.A. Sabloff and C.C. Lamberg-Karlovsky, 3–59. New York: Academic Press.

Renfrew, Colin M. 1978. "Alternative Models for Exchange and Spatial Distribution," in *Exchange Systems in Prehistory*, edited by T.K. Earle and J.E. Ericson, 71–90. New York: Academic Press.

Wilson, Andrew. 2012. "Saharan Trade in the Roman Period: Short-, Medium- and Long-Distance Trade Networks," *Azania: Archaeological Research in Africa* 47: 409–449.

Hopkins, Keith. 1980. "Taxes and Trade in the Roman Empire (200 B.C.-A.D. 400)," *Journal of Roman Studies* 70: 101–125.

Scheidel, Walter. 2001. *Death on the Nile; Disease and the Demography of Roman Egypt*, *Mnemosyne* Supplement 228. Leiden: Brill.

2

The Economics of Agriculture

2.1 Introduction

I introduce this chapter with a justification for a treatment of agriculture separate from simpler supply-and-demand analyses in Jones (2014) since some readers might think further discussion of agriculture little more than a rehash of previously treated principles. Next, since the issue of markets, particularly in ancient agriculture, continues to be a subject of debate – often more conceptual than empirical – I describe my attitude toward agricultural markets in antiquity. Finishing off this section is a guide to the remainder of the chapter.

2.1.1 Why a Chapter on Agriculture?

With the wide applicability of the economic models presented in Jones (2014), one is tempted to ask why should an entire chapter be devoted to the economics of a single industry? And why agriculture in particular, since there are a number of interesting activities in the economies of the ancient world: construction, metallurgy, shipping, to name just a few. I can offer several reasons, none of which should be surprising.

First, agriculture was the dominant industry and occupation in the ancient world. While precise percentages elude us, probably 90–95% of ancient societies' populations worked in agriculture, and agricultural production accounted for only a slightly smaller share of the total value of most societies' production. Agriculture was important economically, so why not address it in more detail?

Second, while the principles of supply and demand certainly apply to economic issues in agriculture, and the more applied principles dealt with in Jones (2014, Chapters 6–13) find ample scope of application in agriculture, many of those topics dealt with separately heretofore are found in combination with one another in agriculture. For example, while basic supply and demand analysis can both explain and predict many phenomena in the long run, farmers' responses to external changes are often complicated by (1) the lag between beginning a farm production activity and reaping its rewards, (2) the fact that many agricultural products represent both consumption goods and capital goods, and of course (3) the omnipresence of risk. Third, add to these complications of basic supply and demand analysis the frequency of weak or absent markets for some critical goods and services important to agriculture such as insurance and credit, and important transactions whose evidence remains to be studied were sometimes striving to solve multiple problems. Unless the full array of the problems being solved is in the student's mind, the solutions ancient farmers found may seem counterintuitive or downright confounding.

2.1.2 Markets and "Markets"

Throughout this chapter, I will make reference to this market or that market, and such a routine reference to markets may seem anachronistic or otherwise jarring to some readers. I am aware of the extensive literature in ancient history regarding the existence or non-existence of markets, and even of the applicability or inapplicability of market principles to understand behavior in ancient societies. A word on the subject, which I can't find a better way to express than P.K. Bardhan (1980, 83) has: "In the institutional setting of a poor agrarian economy, the term 'market' is to be interpreted somewhat loosely. "

It is not necessary that a market be formal or organized impersonally or monetized for its transactions to be based on economic principles. As long as extra-economic coercion, such as legally compulsory labor service, is not involved, the the transaction can be studied with market principles.[1] Long-term relationships are not excluded from such analysis, because workers' needs for employment and employers' needs for a dependable source of labor can be met with such relationships under a variety of conditions. Workers may look attached, but the attachment is the consequence of a predominantly market relationship, and indebtedness to one's employer or landlord doesn't make one a bonded laborer, as will be explained at length in subsequent sections. Personalized transactions or the absence or infrequency of arms-length transactions do not indicate the inapplicability of market principles. There may indeed have been situations in which individual-gain-oriented exchange was not the mainstay of economic organization, but applying the principle of seeking the simplest explanation of a phenomenon, in this chapter I restrict myself to use of market economic principles. That said, in many circumstances in the archaeological and ancient historical records, it will be a matter of judgment whether the modes of transaction used to arrange the allocation of resources, the organization of work, and the disposition of products resemble those of a market or some other social arrangement will remain a matter of some judgment (Bardhan1980, 83-85).

[1] The consequences, as well as origins, of coercion such as warfare, piracy or slavery certainly can be studied with economic theory although many of the actions involved in these activities are not voluntary transactions.

While it is restricted to a single, relatively well-developed region, and although its observations span some 600 years, Temin's econometric analysis of Alice Slotsky's Babylonian agricultural commodity prices reveals a number of patterns that should occur in market determined prices (Temin 2002, 46–60; Slotsky 1997). The long-term unpredictability of these prices, the general covariation among prices of different commodities, and their response to known external events, such as the death of Alexander in 323 B.C.E. and the ensuing increase in money supply, parallel the behavior of agricultural commodity prices Temin reports from Europe from Medieval to Early Modern times, when regional and interregional markets are known to flourished. Temin's null hypothesis, or counterfactual, is that these prices were administered, and the null is rejected on every point. I will not attempt to extrapolate these results to earlier times in the region, or to even the same time in different regions. Few, if any, other regions and times provide the luxury of such extensive price data series that are amenable to systematic statistical analysis. Janssen's prices from Ramessid Egypt are much spottier in temporal coverage and span a far shorter time period, but cover prices of many items other than agricultural commodities, including wages, and to my knowledge they have not been subjected to any corresponding analysis (Janssen 1975). Babylonia during this time period was well urbanized, and many, if not most, farmers apparently sold some of their production off-farm, as is allowed for in the agricultural household model discussed below, even if the associated markets are imperfect and some missing.

2.1.3 Guide to the Chapter

The two primary sources of models used in this chapter are the fields of agricultural economics and development economics. Both have much to say about the problems ancient farmers endeavoured to solve, although some picking and choosing has been necessary among the offerings of both fields. Much of agricultural economics is aimed at issues in contemporary farming and the post-farming industry of agriculture. Consequently, technological specifics and markets written about in many papers and books are clearly anachronistic; expensive, complicated capital equipment, R&D, and futures markets are clear cases, while fertilizer markets may at least remain a useful construct even if off-farm purchases may have been infrequent or rare in many ancient settings. Development economics has generated a rich offering of models invoking transactions in highly constrained market situations, sometimes even in non-market situations, and I have drawn widely upon many of these. Again, with that field's contemporary focus, a number of issues, such as potential government policies to hasten development, encourage technological innovation, and generally raise incomes are likewise anachronistic, and I have striven to avoid those aspects of models.

While there is a long and rich anthropological literature (several literatures, in fact, one could be tempted to say, recalling the lengthy formalist-substantivist dichotomy) on peasant economic activity and behaviour, I have not drawn upon it directly, for several reasons. While I have some familiarity with that literature, many development economists, and agricultural economists who have worked with problems in developing countries are familiar as well and have made use of many of the anthropological literature's findings in developing their own models, so a good bit of that literature forms a backdrop, if not highly visible, to the models presented here. Where the theories the anthropologists have developed to explain their observations largely parallel separately developed economic models, the chapter focuses on the economic models simply because introducing the economic modeling is the purpose of the chapter. Where completely alternative theories have been developed by the anthropologists, I decided that retaining the exclusive focus on the economic models was useful in conserving space and the readers' time as well as in avoiding potentially contentious evaluation of competing models, often from disparate paradigms, since that also is outside the purview of the chapter.

Now, for what the chapter does, as opposed to what it doesn't do. The substantive sections of the chapter begin in section 2.2 with further detail on the farm household model (alternatively called the agricultural household model, or AHM for its acronym; it shouldn't cause much confusion if I use one name or the other now and then). The AHM provides the farm- or firm-level setting of decisions analyzed in subsequent sections. The property called separability (of production decisions from consumption decisions) is important in highlighting what is to be gained by venturing beyond straightforward application of supply and demand analysis to ancient agricultural issues. One of the more important lessons is that, frequently, understanding production decisions may need a wider context than is availed by direct and exclusive focus on what goes into and comes out of a single activity. Missing markets and restrictions in existing ones create linkages between consumption and production decisions. The concept of the transaction cost has been used to give substance to what constitutes market restrictions that can cause non-separability. Transaction cost models are useful in illuminating major choices such as decisions to participate or not in an existing market.

Section 2.3 addresses agricultural production's inherent complexities. Timing is a more central feature than it is in most other economic activities. The first sub-section formalizes the temporal and sequential structure of agricultural production. The second sub-section addresses the supply of agricultural output, showing the impact uncertainty can have on supply. The typical ancient farm supplied a large share of its own consumption and consumed a large share of its production. While the production of a good implicitly may be equated with its supply in many instances, the agricultural output reaching the market (possibly in a city) in antiquity would not have been total supply, but only the part of supply that the family decided to not hold back for its own consumption, called marketed surplus. In the third sub-section, the complication is considered that many agricultural products have elements of both consumption goods (they're intended to be eaten) and capital goods (they can be used to produce something else later, most commonly more of the same good). The fact that part of a crop had to be held back to provide seed for the next year's production (wheat is an example, although a famous, more recent example is the potato at the center of the mid-19th century Irish Potato Famine) would have made producers solve a consume-or-save problem. Similarly with animals, although with a longer holding period than for crop seed. In both cases, interruption of longer-term, or customary, plans can cause short-term supply responses that appear to respond irrationally (i.e., negatively) to price increases, although without any irrationality at all involved.

Section 2.4, on farm operation, addresses tenancy choice and interlinked transactions. First, the opening sub-section discusses how broad environmental circumstances can affect a number of operational choices. The second sub-section discusses the contract choices available for operating a farm: owner operation, possibly with hired wage labor; rental for a fixed amount established in advance, called fixed rental; and rental for a share of the output, called share tenancy or sharecropping. The third sub-section goes into detail on explanations of sharecropping. This section implicitly deals with conditions leading to choices of owner operation and fixed rental as well since they are alternatives. The fourth sub-section presents models of interlinked transactions. The topic is addressed in this section because these interlinkages and the market conditions that lead to them affect farm operation.

Storage of agricultural products, the subject of section 2.5, has had a prominent place in the archaeological and ancient-historical literature. A number of architectural remains, frequently circular pits sunk into the ground, have been interpreted as centralized (public, or royal) storage facilities for agricultural products, generally grains. Similarly, some texts, both cuneiform and Linear B, have been interpreted to infer the existence of centralized agricultural storage. In remains of private houses, especially in rural areas but in some urban cases as well, structures have been interpreted as private storage facilities. Based on volumes of identified storage pits and calorie counts of contemporary grains, much has been made of the ability of these structures to feed a local population over a crop year and to provide risk buffers. This section presents the theory of agricultural commodity storage to pinpoint more precise decisions ancient decision-makers might have made in their decisions to store part of a year's crop for consumption at a subsequent time and to assess the impact of the stored volumes on risk reduction.

Section 2.6 presents A. K. Sen's theory of famines, based on the concept of entitlements, defined positively rather than normatively, to food in contrast to theories based on availability of food.[2] Notice of this model has found its way into the ancient history literature on agriculture. The discussion here may enhance the understanding of, and widen the familiarity with, this model.

The final section is a logical continuation of Jones (2014 section 13.2.4), the theory of how a resource to which access cannot be controlled will be over-exploited, sometimes to exhaustion or extinction. Common property is a form of managing resources over which it is difficult if not impossible for a single agent to enforce ownership rights. The management fosters more productive use of the resource than does the non-management found in the open-access situation. Understanding of animal grazing practices in ancient times may be enhanced by consideration of management practices. Analysis of other ancient resources, such as allocating river water for irrigation and exploitation of forests for wood and hunting may also be sharpened by heeding the distinction between open-access and common property.

2.2 The Farm Household Model

The farm household model, in which a family firm maximizes utility rather than profits, is central to thinking about economic behavior in non-industrial, agrarian communities, both their production choices—farming as well as other activities—and their consumption decisions. The first sub-section below recapitulates its basics and discusses household responses to price and income changes, the concept of shadow prices, and the effect of the absence of an important market—that for labor—on farm production decisions.

One of the most important concepts the farm household model brings to the analytical table is the separability or non-separability of production and consumption decisions. Separability of the two—the ability to make production decisions independently of consumption decisions (but not the reverse, since what one produces determines one's income, which affects consumption)—is a hallmark of the complete array of markets that typically characterize contemporary industrialized economies.[3] Non-separability is a hallmark of traditional agrarian communities with poorly developed or missing markets for important inputs and outputs. The second sub-section addresses causes of non-separability. The last sub-section explores the consequences of non-separability.

[2] The positive-normative distinction refers to simple statements of fact (or logical results that someone believes strongly enough to consider a "fact" of how things work) versus a value judgment of whether an outcome is better or worse than another outcome according to some defined criteria.

[3] This is an overstatement, since contemporary industrialized economies are indeed without markets for a number of goods, services and contingencies, some of which are the cause of important externalities, from beach pollution to global climate change. However, the typical household in most of these economies is largely unaffected in its daily activities by the absence of markets for activities they conduct routinely, such as earning their incomes in an office or a factory and buying their groceries in stores that are in contact with agricultural markets throughout the world.

2.2.1 Overview of the Farm Household Model

The section begins with a brief description of the model, followed by some exercises with it. First, I address a farm household's responses to price and income changes. This discussion raises the issue of shadow prices, which are discussed in a succeeding section. The last topic of the section addresses a household's responses when no labor market exists.

The Model. The farm family maximizes its utility[4] as a function of its consumption of goods and leisure, $U = U(X_1, \ldots, X_L)$, where the X_i are consumption of various goods and X_L is leisure, subject to a full income constraint and its production technology. On the expenditure side, $Y = \sum_{i=1}^{L} \cdot p_i X_i$, where Y is full income. On the sources side, full income is defined as $Y = p_L T + \sum_{j=1}^{M} q_j Q_j - \sum_{i=1}^{N} q_i V_i - p_L L + E$, where p_L is the market wage rate, T is the household's total time endowment, the Q_j are outputs of goods produced on the farm and the q_j are their prices, the V_i are quantities of variable inputs used in the farm's production operations and the q_i are their prices, L is total labor used (labor demand) in the farm's production operations including family and hired labor, and E is outside income. For simplification, I'll define Q_c and q_c as the quantity of a cash crop the farm produces and its price and X_m and q_m as the quantity of a consumption good the household purchases on the market and its price. The production technology that relates inputs to outputs is represented by an implicit production function $G(\mathbf{Q}, V, L, \mathbf{K}) = 0$, where the bold font indicates vectors containing arrays of outputs and variable and fixed inputs. The farm household maximizes its utility, subject to the full income constraint and the technological constraints embodied in the production function by choosing the best levels of consumption, labor inputs and variable inputs in production, and the outputs of goods consumed at home and sold off-farm.

As long as all the markets exist and work well, the household's maximization can be accomplished sequentially, first maximizing the revenue side of this system subject to the technology constraint, then maximizing utility through its consumption decisions subject to the full income constraint. The prices of consumption goods, household preferences, and income do not affect production decisions. This condition is referred to in the literature as recursiveness in the AHM. The farm's supply (output) of the goods it produces responds positively to own-prices, and the price of the cash crop, q_c, will be related to the household's consumption of market-purchased goods, X_m, through changes in income. Changes in the quantities of fixed inputs will affect income and hence the consumption of X_m.

Household Responses to Price and Income Changes. The general form of the farm household's demand function for a good is $X_i = X_i(p_m, p_a, p_L, Y)$, which simply says that demand depends on prices and income. A farm household's income, however, is determined by its production activities, so factors influencing production will affect full income Y, and consumption behavior is not independent of production activity. There is a profit effect in consumption that can be large enough to outweigh the normal negative effect of price on consumption of a good. The effect of a change in the price of the cash crop on the household's consumption of the cash crop is given by $\Delta X_a/\Delta p_a = \Delta X_a/p_a + (\Delta X_a/\Delta Y)(\Delta Y/\Delta p_a)$,[5] the first term of which is the standard substitution effect of consumer theory and is negative for a normal good. The second term captures the profit effect as an increase in the price of the cash crop increases the farm's profits and hence its full income: $\Delta Y/\Delta p_a = (\Delta\pi/\Delta p_a)\Delta p_a$. By duality, a change in the value of the profit function π caused by a change in the price of an output is the farm's supply function for that product, so $\Delta\pi/\Delta p_a = Q_a$, so $\Delta Y/\Delta p_a = Q_a \Delta p_a$, hence the potential magnitude of this positive profit effect on consumption. Because the household consumes some of the good, the profit effect is actually composed of the net sales: $\Delta X_a/\Delta p_a = \Delta X_a/\Delta p_a|_u + (Q_a - X_a)(\Delta Y/\Delta p_a)$, where the notation $|_u$ indicates that u (utility) is held constant when calculating the effect of a change in price p_a on consumption X_a. For a household that sells net to the market, the profit term is positive, but for a net buying household it is negative.

Shadow Prices. When some markets do not exist or function imperfectly, the resource values the farm household perceives and to which it responds will not be market prices, if those exist, but shadow prices, sometimes called virtual prices in the literature. The absence of a market, or imperfections in a market, impose restrictions on the consumption or supply of a good (think of labor supply as the negative of leisure consumption). Under conditions of such a restriction (or restrictions), a shadow price is the price that would induce a household to choose the restricted consumption in an unconstrained setting. In general then, when a restriction limits a household to a lower consumption level than it would choose in an unconstrained setting, a shadow price is higher than the market price, if it exists, and vice versa. Shadow prices will be household-specific and endogenous to that household and are functions of both household preferences and the farm's production technology. Because these prices help determine both consumption and production choices, the farm's demand for household goods depends on production technology, through both the shadow price and full income. Output supplies and input demands depend on preferences through the shadow price. But if a household faces only market prices, or if it faces a shadow price for a good that it

---

[4] Another literature has studied how to specify the distribution of utilities within a group such as a family, but for simplification here, just consider that one and all household members fare the same.

[5] The market price of the cash crop has been denoted q_c above, but the price facing the farm household in its consumption of some of that crop is denoted p_c. Assume that p_c here is the same as q_c above.

consumes but doesn't produce (or vice versa), production choices will not depend on household preferences, but consumption choices will depend on production technology through full income, and the model becomes separable and can be solved recursively, i.e., one part at a time.

Output Responses in the Absence of a Labor Market. Consider first a crop, Q_c, the entire output of which the farm sells. If labor is the only variable input, the sign of a farm's output response to the output price must be opposite to its leisure response (work and leisure add up to total labor endowment). We can write output supply as $Q_c = \Delta\pi/\Delta q_c(q_c, p_a, p_L^*, q_v, K)$. Then the response of supply to output price (the slope of the supply curve) is $\Delta Q_c/\Delta q_c = \pi_{cc} + \pi_{cL}\Delta p_L^*/\Delta q_c$. The first term is the output-supply response with an unchanged shadow wage, and it's positive. If output responds negatively to the shadow wage ($\pi_{cL} < 0$), the second term is negative, and the sign of the entire term is indeterminate. However, if household utility is held constant, the response is positive. To see this, substitute from the relationship between the compensated and uncompensated shadow prices of labor to get $\Delta Q_c/q_c = (\pi_{cc} + \pi_{cL}\Delta\bar{p}_L^*/\Delta q_c) + Q_c(\Delta p_L/\Delta q_c)$. The first two terms of this expression are the responses of output supply when utility is held constant. The last term is an income effect, which is negative if $\pi_{cL} < 0$. The second term is $\pi_{cL}^2/(e_{LL} - \pi_{LL}) < 0$. However, the sum of that term and π_{cc} is non-negative by virtue of the shape of the expenditure function in prices. The magnitude of π_{cL} and the attendant likelihood of a negative output response is influenced by the number of variable inputs and the substitutability between labor and those inputs. The larger the number of variable inputs and the more substitutable they are with labor, the smaller negative π_{cL} will be and the more like a positive response of supply to output price. The output responses are unambiguously positive when the shadow price of labor is exogenous to the household and is larger than a positive response with an endogenous shadow price of labor.

Now suppose that the household consumes some of the output whose price is changing. (Consequently, we study Xs, which represent consumption, rather than Qs, which represent production.) In this case the relationship between consumption and the price has an additional substitution effect, and the income effect is weighted by net output sold (marketed surplus) rather than by total output. Thus the response of the demand for a consumption good (where the subscript i could represent leisure, the market-purchased good, or the household-produced good) is $\Delta X_i/\Delta p_a = \Delta X_i^c/\Delta p_a + (Q_a - X_a)\Delta X_i/\Delta Y$, where the consumption subscripted by i can be of leisure (L), the market-purchased good (M), or the household-produced good (A). When i = L or M, the analysis examines cross-price responses; when i = A, it is an own-price response. So the full change in the demand for one of these consumption goods as p_a changes operates through two routes: the substitution effect of p_a on the compensated demand for the good and an income/profit effect, which is weighted by the amount of the good sold.

2.2.2 Causes of Non-Separable Production and Consumption Decisions

There are many routes to non-separability, missing or grossly imperfect markets and transaction costs being two of the most prominent. The first sub-section addresses missing or imperfect markets very briefly, since transaction costs, the subject of the second sub-section, are a cause of many market imperfections. There is an extensive literature on transaction costs in agrarian comunities. Beyond these two major causes of non-separability, a plethora of other sources exist which do not lend themselves to easy classification. The final sub-section illustrates some of these.

Missing or Imperfect Markets. Many households in a community tend to be net buyers or net sellers in the same year. For example, with a good harvest, a household could become a net seller. The market prices at which they buy or sell will differ from either their full acquisition cost or their net sales return, resulting in a spread of what might be called an effective price band around the market price. These spreads are household-specific since households may face different acquisition and selling costs, to be explained more thoroughly below. As household supply shifts, say after a good harvest, the lower bound of the effective price (the net return) falls, reducing the likelihood that the shadow price of a particular household will fall below the sale price and make it a net seller. Conversely in a bad year, the upper bound of the band (the full acquisition cost) rises, preventing households from becoming net buyers. The shallower local food and labor markets are, the more prices can be expected to be positively correlated with movements in shadow prices. Lack of a landless class, high homogeneity in factor endowments, and high levels of synchronicity in labor needs across households frequently leave little room for local labor markets. Behavior toward risk affects the band width of price certainty equivalents, but once a household's shadow price falls within the band, risk plays no significant additional role in decision making. Restrictions on purchases and sales (generically speaking, quotas) affect farm household decisions, possibly paralleling agricultural work with varying degrees of centralized direction such as is thought to have characterized at least some portions of lower Mesopotamia in the fourth to second millennia B.C.E.[6]

The difficulty of acquiring, processing, storing, and transmitting information is another root cause of imperfect or missing markets, particularly markets for various risks and various rental markets. Information costs can be important components of transactions costs. Moral hazard and, possibly to a lesser extent in small, agrarian communities in antiquity, adverse selection situtions, which

[6] See, for example, the discussion of apparently different levels of decision-making authority in a rural town in lower Mesopotamia during the Early Dynasties of Ur in Wright (1969, Chapter VI, esp. 106–116), from which it would seem that many farm households had constraints placed on their choices by people with various kinds of authority.

are informational asymmetries about characteristics of individuals rather than of their actions, can restrict the scope of a number of important markets. Limitations on information, and the adaptation of institutions to those circumstances, will be a recurrent theme throughout the rest of this chapter.

Transaction Costs. Transaction costs are like taxes in that they impose a difference between what, to an outsider, it appears that someone pays for a good and what they actually pay or what someone appears to receive for a good and what they actually get, creating a price band within which some households do not find it profitable to participate in a market.[7] Transaction costs can be quite household-specific since some of them may derive from a household's characteristics, its location, and its activities. One consequence of transaction costs is that a given price movement may present an incentive to one household to either buy or sell but may not offer an incentive to another household. Consequently, overall market responses to price changes can appear sluggish or even perverse at times. Price elasticities characterizing aggregate market responses will depend on how many households enter or leave a market and how their production changes when they enter or leave a market. To provide an idea of the magnitude of this entry-exit phenomenon, Key et al. (2000, 246) found that 60% of the price response in a 20th century C.E. Mexican corn market came from producers who entered the market when the price increased, only 40% coming from producers already participating in the market. When households don't participate in markets, their production decisions become non-separable from their consumption decisions. When a household leaves a market and becomes autarkic in that good, its price responses are perfectly inelastic until a price movement is great enough to induce them back into the market.

Transaction costs can be proportional to the quantity of a good transacted or fixed—invariant to the magnitude of the transaction. Proportional transaction costs (PTCs) include per-unit costs of accessing a market created by transportation costs and imperfect information. Fixed transaction costs (FTCs) can include a search for a market or for the buyer or seller offering the most favorable price; negotiation and bargaining, which may be important when information about prices is spotty; screening of buyers and sellers for reliability and product quality; and supervision and enforcement of transactions and other agreements, particularly important in the use of hired labor.

The following adaptation of an agricultural household model to incorporate transaction costs shows how these costs affect market participation and market behavior once participation has been chosen. Accordingly, market participation is a choice variable in the model, just as the quantity of goods to consume or labor to apply to agricultural operations are choice variables. The household maximizes its utility by choosing quantities of an array of consumption goods c_i: max $u(\mathbf{c})$, subject to (1) a cash constraint, $\sum_{i=1}^{N} p_i^m m_i + T = 0$, where T is exogenous income, p_i^m is the market price of good I, and m_i is the quantity of good i the household decides to market, with $m_i > 0$ implying sales and $m_i < 0$ purchases; (2) a resource balance for each good i, $q_i - x_i + A_i - m_i - c_i = 0$, $i = 1, \ldots, N$, where the q_i are the household's output of the good, the x_i are the amount of the good used as an input to another production process, the A_i are endowments (stocks, hold-overs) of the good, and the m_i and c_i are sales or purchases and consumption as noted above; (3) the production technology, $G(\mathbf{q}, \mathbf{x}) = 0$; and (4) non-negativity constraints $c_i, q_i, x_i \geq 0$.

In this problem setting, proportional transaction costs raise the effective price paid by a buyer above what the seller receives and lowers the effective price received by a seller. The cash constraint becomes $\sum_{i=1}^{N}[(p_i^m - t_{pi}^s(z_i^s))\delta_i^s + (p_i^m + t_{pi}^b(z_i^b))m_i] + T = 0$, where $\delta_i^s = 1$ if $m_i > 0$, zero otherwise, and $\delta_i^b = 1$ if $m_i < 0$, and zero otherwise. The effective price received by a seller is lower than the market price p_i^m by the unobservable amount t_{pi}^b. The PTCs are expressed as functions of observable exogenous characteristics z_i^s and z_i^b that affect costs when selling and buying respectively. Fixed transaction costs also are generally unobservable although their causes may be observable. When both PTCs and FTCs exist, the cash constraint becomes $\sum_{i=1}^{N} [(p_i^m - t_{pi}^s(z_i^s))\delta_i^s + (p_i^m + t_{pi}^b(z_i^b))m_i - t_{fi}^s(z_i^s)\delta_i^s - t_{fi}^b(z_i^b)\delta_i^b] + T = 0$, where the z_i^j are determinants of the fixed costs. The household pays the fixed cost t_{fi}^s if and only if it sells good i and pays t_{fi}^s if and only if it buys it. This latest cash constraint then replaces the first cash constraint shown above in the household's utility maximization problem.

The Lagrangean used to derive the supply and demand functions for a household facing both PTCs and FTCs is $\mathcal{L} = u(c) + \sum_{i=1}^{N} \mu_i(q_i - x_i + A_i - m_i - c_i) + \varphi G(q, x) + \lambda\{\sum_{i=1}^{N} [(p_i^m - t_{pi}^s)\delta_i^s + (p_i^m + t_{pi}^b)\delta_i^b]m_i - t_{fi}^s\delta_i^s - t_{fi}^b\delta_i^b + T\}$, where μ_i, φ, and λ are the Lagrange multipliers associated with the resource-balance, technology, and cash constraints. The FTCs create discontinuities in the Lagrangean, and the optimal solution cannot be obtained by simply solving for the first-order conditions as we have done so many times before. The solution has to proceed in two steps, first solving for the optimal solution conditional on a market participation regime and then choosing the particular participation regime that yields the highest utility. Then the optimal supplies and demands are found by solving the first-order conditions. For the consumption goods, the first-order conditions are $\Delta\mathcal{L}/\Delta c_i = \Delta u/\Delta c_i - \mu_i = 0$, with the $c_i > 0$; for the outputs, $\Delta\mathcal{L}/\Delta q_i = \mu_i + \varphi\Delta G/\Delta q_i = 0$, with the $q_i > 0$; for input use, $\Delta\mathcal{L}/\Delta x_i = -\mu_i + \varphi\Delta G/\Delta x_i = 0$;[8] and for traded goods $\Delta\mathcal{L}/\Delta m_i = -\mu_i + \lambda[(p_i^m - t_{pi}^s)\delta_i^s + (p_i^m +$

[7] The following discussion and model are from Key et al. (2000).

[8] For those puzzling over the apparent negative sign of φ in this first-order condition, it is an artifact of the implicit production function specification, with $G = f(x) - q$, which reverses the sign on output q without implying negativity of the marginal value of production.

$t_i^b)\delta_i^b] = 0$, $m_i \neq 0$. Notice that the optimality conditions don't include fixed transactions costs, since they are invariant to the levels of the m_i chosen.

Now, define decision prices for the household as a seller, a buyer and under self-sufficiency as $p_i = (1) p_i^m - t^s$ when $m_i > 0$ and the household sells, or (2) $p_i^m + t_{pi}^b$ when $m_i < 0$ and the household buys, or (3) $\tilde{p}_i = \mu_i/\lambda$ when $m_i = 0$ and the household is autarkic or self-sufficient in good i. In this last case, when the good isn't traded, the decision price is the unobserved internal shadow price μ_i/λ, which is the ratio of the marginal valuation of additional consumption of good i to the marginal valuation of increasing the cash constraint. Using these decision prices, the first-order conditions above have the same structure as first-order conditions that would emerge from separable producer and consumer decision problems, which says that the solution can be written as that of a separable model, although the endogeneity of the decision price clearly makes the model non-separable. In this case, maximizing profit subject to the technology constraint yields systems of output supply functions q(p) and input demand functions x(p), while maximizing utility subject to the single income constraint $y = \sum_{i=1}^{N} p_i c_i = \sum_{i=1}^{N} [p_i(q_i - x_i + A_i) - t_{fi}^s \delta_i^s - t_{fi}^b \delta_i^b] + T$, where y is measured at decision prices, which leads to a system of demand functions for the consumption goods c(p,y).

Now the conditions that determine the market participation of a household facing PTCs and FTCs can be established. To simplify the exposition, let there be a choice of participation regime for only one crop that the household produces and consumes. Market participation is determined by comparing the utility from selling, buying or remaining outside the market. Using an indirect utility function V(p, y) for the comparison, where p is the decision price, which takes one of the three forms specified above, the utility levels to be compared are $V^s = V(p^m - t_p^s, y^*(p^m - t_p^s) - t_f^s)$ if the household sells, $V^b = V(p^m + t_p^b, y^*(p^m + t_p^b) - t_f^b)$ if the household buys, and $V^a = V(\tilde{p}, y^*(\tilde{p}))$ if the household does not participate in the market (is autarkic). In these indirect utility functions, $y^*(p) = \sum_{i=1}^{N} p_i(q_i - x_i + A_i) + T$. Figure 2.1 shows these three indirect utilities as functions of the market price. The vertical line at V_a shows the utility, which is independent of market prices, that an autarkic household can obtain. First consider a household facing proportional, but not fixed, transaction costs. The utility expressions above show that the household is indifferent between selling and being autarkic if $p^m - t_p^s = \tilde{p}$, at point C. From the first-order conditions reported above, utility is increasing in the decision price for selling households and decreasing in it for buying households. Starting from the autarky point C_o, a household facing no FTCs will be better off selling at market prices above $\tilde{p} + t_p^s$, reaching utility V_0^s in Figure 2.1 along line C_oD_o. The household also will be indifferent between buying and remaining autarkic if $p^m + t_p^b = \tilde{p}$ and will be better off buying at any market price below $\tilde{p} - t_p^b$, reaching

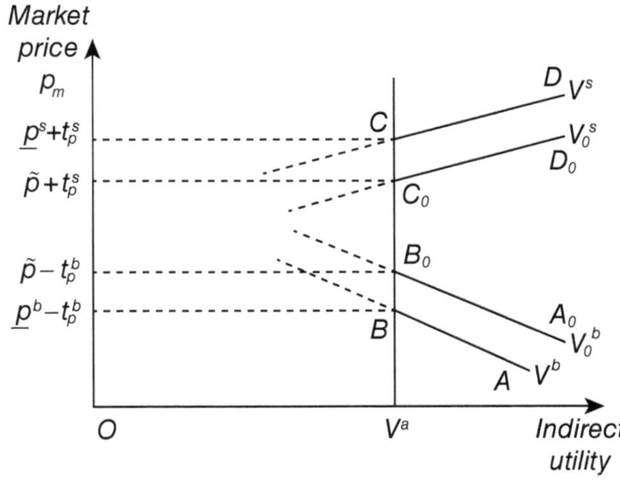

Figure 2.1. Household indirect utility under fixed and proportional transaction costs (Reproduced from Key, Sadoulet, and de Janvry. 2000, figure 1, p. 249, by permission of Wiley.).

utility V_0^b, represented by line B_oA_o. If there are no PTCs, $B_o = C_o$.

The expression for the full-income constraint, y, in the as-if-separable utility maximization two paragraphs above shows that an increase in FTCs directly lowers household income and consequently lowers utility at any given market price. This shifts the indirect utility curves to the left in Figure 2.1. Households facing a market price of p^m and both PTCs and FTCs can reach utility V^s as sellers and V^b as buyers. There is some market price above $\tilde{p} + t_p^s$ such that utility from selling just equals utility from self-sufficiency, point C in Figure 2.1. The corresponding decision price at which the household enters the market as a seller is $\underline{p}^s = p^m - t_p^s$, the decision price, defined by $V(\underline{p}^s, y^*(\underline{p}^s) - t_f^s) = V(\tilde{p}, y^*(\tilde{p}))$. In Figure 2.1, if the household faces a market price above $\underline{p}^s + t_p^s$, it's better off selling (line CD) whereas for market prices below $\underline{p}^s + t_p^s$, it's better off not selling. Analogously, there is a buying decision threshold $\underline{p}^b$ that solves $V(\underline{p}^b, y^*(\underline{p}^b) - t_f^b) = V(\bar{p}, y^*(\tilde{p}))$, below which utility from buying is greater than V^a. The household will buy the good if the market price is below $\underline{p}^b - t_p^b$, line BA in Figure 2.1. The optimal market participation for a household facing both PTCs and FTCs is to follow path ABCD, buying when market prices are below $\underline{p}^b - t_p^b$, being self-sufficient when market prices are $\underline{p}^b - t_p^b < p^m < \underline{p}^s + t_p^s$, and selling when market prices are above $\underline{p}^s - t_p^s$.

Figures 2.2 and 2.3 show the household's supply of the home-produced good as a function of the market price under PTC and FTC. Curve SS is the supply curve without any transaction costs, $q(p^m)$. With transaction costs, the supply curve has three parts: $q^s = q(p^m - t_p^s)$ for selling households, $q^b = q(p^m + t_p^b)$ for buying households, and $q^a = q(\tilde{p})$ for autarkic households. Fixed transactions do not affect the supply curve, since they are independent of quantity transacted. PTCs shift the supply curve upward for sellers and downward for buyers. Combining the market

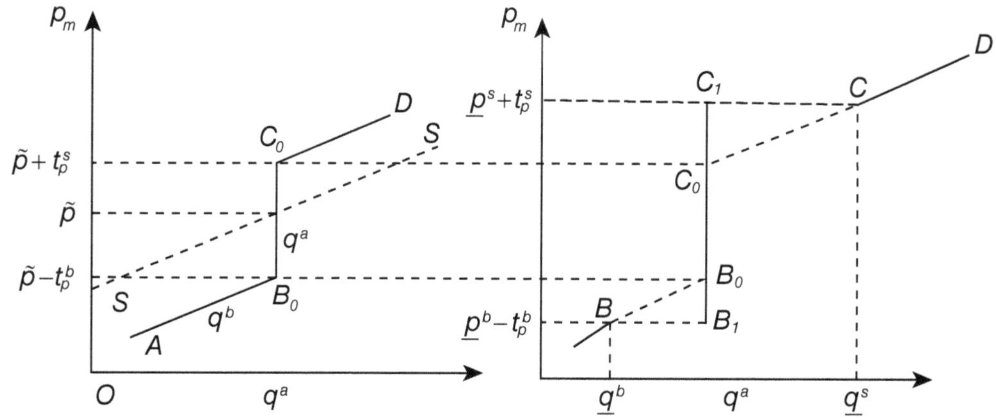

Figure 2.2. Household supply under proportional and proportional and fixed transaction costs (Reproduced from Key, Sadoulet, and de Janvry. 2000, figure 2, p. 250, by permission of Wiley.).

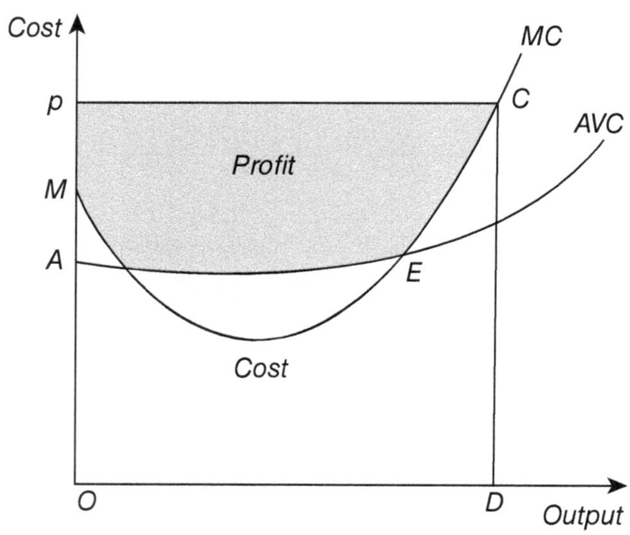

Figure 2.3. Producer surplus (Adapted from Newbery and Stiglitz, 1981, figure 5.2, p. 62, by permission of David M.G. Newbery and Joseph E. Stiglitz).

participation decision with the supply curve under each regime gives an overall supply curve with three distinct regions: (1) follows the buyer's supply curve q^b for $p^m < \tilde{p} - t_p^b$, (2) follows the seller's supply curve q^s for $p^m > \tilde{p} + t_p^s$, and (3) between these two thresholds, the autarkic supply. The entire curve is represented by line segments AB_0C_0D in Figure 2.2.

With FTCs, a household's entry into the market as a seller is delayed until the market price reaches the higher level $\underline{p}^s + t_p^s$, but once in the market, supply is not affected by FTCs because only marginal returns to production affect supply decisions. In Figure 2.3, the seller's supply curve is CD. Entry into the market as a buyer is also delayed until the market price is sufficiently low, at $\tilde{p} - t_p^b$, but the buyer's supply curve BA is independent of FTCs. The household remains autarkic between these two thresholds. The broken line ABB_1C_1CD represents the household's overall supply response. Supplies $\underline{q}^s$ and $\underline{q}^b$ are production levels at which the household enters the market as a seller (m > 0) or a buyer (m < 0), when decision prices are at threshold levels $\underline{p}^s$ and $\underline{p}^b$. The supply curves are now $\underline{q}^s \equiv q(\underline{p}^s)$ and $\underline{q}^b \equiv q(\underline{p}^b)$. The selling decision price threshold $\underline{p}^s$ implicitly defined by the indirect utility function above is an increasing function of FTCs but is not a function of PTCs because the utility that sellers reach doesn't depend on the market price and PTCs independently, but only on the net of the two, the resulting decision price. The household switches from autarky to selling when the decision price it will receive is high enough to compensate for the FTCs. Therefore the selling production threshold $\underline{q}^s$ is also a function of FTCs but not of PTCs. Similarly, $\underline{p}^b$ decreases in FTCs, and the buying threshold $\underline{q}^b$ decreases in FTCs but is not affected by PTCs. The other variables that enter the definition of the production threshold are the determinants of utility levels—T and A—whose impacts cannot be signed unambiguously.

To summarize, a household's relationship with markets results from comparison of its desired production level and two production thresholds. The market participation and corresponding functional relations for output and supply under PTCs and FTCs are:

- If $q(p^m - t_p^s,) > \underline{q}^s(t_f^s, T, A)$, the household sells and its supply function is $q^s = q(p^m - t_p^s,)$.
- If $q(p^m - t_p^s,) \leq \underline{q}^s(t_f^s, T, A)$ and if $(p^m + t_p^b) \geq \underline{q}^b(t_f^b, T, A)$, the household is autarkic and its supply function is $q^a = q(\tilde{p})$.
- If $(p^m + t_p^b) < \underline{q}^b(t_f^s, T, A)$, then the household is a buyer with the supply function $q^b = q(p^m + t_p^b)$.

So while market participation depends on both PTCs and FTCs, supply decisions depend only on PTC.

Other Routes to Non-Separability. Consider several other examples Bardhan and Udry (1999, 11–14) report of situations that affect whether or not a farm household's production and consumptions are separable. With a perfect labor market and no other markets missing, a farm family would pick a labor supply that maximized the farm's profits, F(L, E^A) – (w/p)L, where F is the production function, L is labor, E^A is its fixed endowment of land, w is the wage rate and p is the price of the farm's product. There are no household characteristics in the production function, so the separation property holds. Now, suppose there is involuntary employment in the rural labor market, possibly a binding constraint on off-farm labor supply. Then the household's problem is to: $Max_{\{c,\lambda,L^h,L^f\geq 0\}} u(c, \lambda)$ subject to the three constraints $pc = F(L^f + L^h, E^A) - wL^h + wL^m$, $\lambda + L^f + L^m = E^L$, and $L^m \leq M$, where c is a consumption good, λ is leisure, L^f is family labor, L^h is hired labor, L^m is family labor supplied to the labor market, and M is the constraint on off-farm labor supply. If the third constraint doesn't bind, i.e., the family can indeed supply all the off-farm labor it wants, the first constraint becomes $pc + w\lambda = F(L, E^A) - wL + wE^L$, where L is the total amount of labor used on-farm. The household maximizes its profit and separation occurs again. But if the first constraint does bind (e.g., if M is small and the family would like to supply a large amount of labor off-farm), $L^m = M$ and $L^h = 0$, and the household's problem becomes to $Max_{(c,\lambda\geq 0)} u(c, \lambda)$, subject to $c = F(E^L - M - \lambda, E^A) + wM$. The first-order condition for the maximization is $u_\lambda / u_c = F_L$(F_L representing the marginal product of labor), and the household's production clearly depends on its endowments (E^L) and its preferences (embedded in λ). Consequently, separation doesn't occur.

Next suppose that the labor market works well but that production is risky and the household is quite risk-averse, but there is no insurance market. The household's problem is to $Max_{\{L\geq 0\}} Eu(c)$, subject to $c = \theta E^A f(L/E^A) - wL + wE^L$, where E is the expectations operator (meaning that the household is maximizing the expected utility of its consumption), and θ is a random variable representing the riskiness of production, with a mean (expected value) of 1. Then the first-order condition for the household's optimal allocation of labor is $Eu'(\theta f' - w) = 0$. Since it is optimal for the wage rate to equal the marginal product of labor ($f' = w$), and this first-order condition implies that $f' < w$, the absence of the insurance market has created a compensating imperfection in the labor market, and separation again fails to occur.[9]

2.2.3 Consequences of Non-Separable Production and Consumption Decisions

For all their reputed ability to transmit undesirable signals, markets offer households institutional means for adjusting to supply and demand shocks. The absence of some markets forces farm households to shift more of the burden of adjustment onto internal markets ("markets") for goods they produce but don't trade. In some instances these internal adjustments can result in very weak, or even apparently irrational, external responses.

The Household Model.[10] The household produces two crops, a cash crop, q_c, and a food crop, q_f, with two inputs, labor, q_L, and another input such as fertilizer, q_x. Production technology is represented by an implicit production function, $G(\mathbf{q}, \mathbf{z}) = 0$, in which $\mathbf{q}$ is a vector of outputs (with positive values; q_c, q_f 0 and inputs (with negative values; $q_L, q_x < 0$), and $\mathbf{z}$ is a vector of structural characteristics of the farm household. The household consumes food, c_f, a manufactured good, c_m, and leisure, c_L, which is the complement in total time of its labor supply. The time endowment is T_L; initial endowments of other commodities i are T_i, and the household has an initial cash endowment of S. The cash crop is only sold on the market, other inputs and manufactured goods are provided only through the market, and the household has no price influence in any market. Food and labor are both provided by the household and are eventually traded in markets. When markets exist there is perfect substitutability between domestic and market supply, and prices are exogenous. Market failures are considered for food and labor. In these cases, the household faces the constraint of balancing supply ($q_i + T_i$) of and demand (c_i) for these nontradable commodities.

The household maximizes a utility function subject to a cash income constraint and the equilibrium condition for tradables and nontradables. Its problem is $Max_{\{c,q\}} U(\mathbf{c}, \mathbf{z})$ subject to $\sum_i p_i c_i \leq \sum_i p_i(q_i + T_i) + S_i$, the cash income constraint; $G(\mathbf{q}, \mathbf{z}) = 0$, the production technology; $p_i = \bar{p}_i$, the exogeneity of the market price for tradable goods; and $q_i + T_i \geq c_i$, the equilibrium condition for nontradables. The Lagrangean is $\mathcal{L} = U(\mathbf{c}, \mathbf{z}) + \lambda[\sum_i \bar{p}_i(q_i + T_i - c_i) + S] + \phi G(q, z) + \sum_i \mu_i(q_i + T_i - c_i)$. From the first-order conditions for the maximization of this Lagrangean, the household's behavior can be decomposed into production and consumption decisions. As producers, the household chooses levels of inputs and outputs that are equivalent to maximizing a profit function defined over all tradable and nontradable goods, which leads to a system of input demand and output supply functions, $q_i = q_i(\mathbf{p},\mathbf{z})$, and to a maximum profit equal to $\pi = \sum_i p_i q_i$. As a consumer, the household chooses levels of consumption that maximize its utility under the full income constraint, leading to consumption represented by $c_i = c_i(\mathbf{p},Y)$, where $\sum_i p_i c_i = Y = \pi + \sum_i p_i T_i + S$. If all markets exist and there is no nontradable good, all prices are exogenous to the household, and decisions can be made sequentially, as consumption decisions depend on the outcome of production decisions but not conversely, which is the standard case of separability of a household model. If some commodity market or the labor market doesn't exist, these two sets of decisions are linked through the endogenous price p_i that satisfies the equilibrium condition between supply and demand emerging from the first-order conditions, $c_i + T_i = c_i$. There are no explicit transactions between the producer and consumer sides of the household, and the endogenous shadow prices can't be observed, but

[9] The first-order condition can be rewritten as (with some manipulations) $f'Eu'(\theta - 1) = Eu'(w - f')$, but $E\theta = 1$, so $f'\text{cov}(u', \theta) = (w - f')Eu'$, where "cov" is the covariance between the marginal utility of consumption and the random variable, which is negative (think of that fact this way: when $\theta > 1$, there has been a good season and consumption will increase, but marginal utility, u', declines as consumption increases). So $\text{cov}(u', \theta) < 0$, $f' > 0$, and $Eu' > 0$, so $f'\text{cov}(u', \theta)/Eu' = w - f' < 0$, which is the result in the text.

[10] The model below is from Janvry, Fafchamps, and Sadoulet (1991, 1403–1408).

nontradables prices play a role similar to tradables' prices in household decisions. When they apply, these shadow prices are equal to the marginal utility of consumption of food and leisure and to the marginal product of labor. As such, they indicate the price the household would be willing to pay to have the associated constraint relaxed by one unit. They serve as indicators of the internal perception of the severity of the constraint imposed on the household. The external view of farm household behavior is based on its supply and demand responses on markets that do exist.

Supply of and Demand for Marketed Commodities when a Market Is Missing. The full supply elasticity of good j in response to a change in the price of good i when some market is missing can be derived by specifying the responses of the supply function that emerged from the first-order conditions, $q_i = q_i(\mathbf{p},\mathbf{z})$, yielding $\phi_{ji}^{mm} = \phi_{ji}^* + \phi_{ja}^*\varepsilon_{ai}$, where ϕ_{ji}^* is the cross-price elasticity of supply of product j with respect to the price of good (or input) i when all markets exist, $\phi_{ja}^* > 0$ is the corresponding all-markets cross-elasticity of supply with respect to the good whose market will be missing, and ε_{ai} is the elasticity of the shadow price of good a with respect to a change in the price of good i. Similarly derived from the consumption functions emerging from the first-order conditions, $c_i = c_i(\mathbf{p},Y)$, the full, missing-market consumption elasticity of good j with respect to a change in the price of good i is $\theta_{ji}^{mm} = \theta_{ji}^* + \theta_{ja}^*\varepsilon_{ai}$, in which $\theta_{ji}^* = \theta_{ji} + \eta_j(s_{\pi Y}s_{j\pi} + s_{jY})$. In this latter expression, θ_{ji} is the usual cross-price elasticity of consumption from consumer theory; η_j is the income elasticity of consumption for good j, $s_{\pi Y} = \pi/Y$, the share of farm profits in full income; $s_{i\pi} = p_i q_i/\pi$, the ratio of the revenue from good j to total household profits; and $s_{jY} = p_j T_j/Y$, the share of the household's initial endowment of good j in full income. And correspondingly for θ_{ja}^*. ε_{ai} is the same shadow price elasticity that appears in the full supply elasticity formulation.

The Effect of Market Price Changes on Prices in Missing Markets (Shadow Prices). Suppose that one market, that for food or for labor, is missing. By specifying the responses of the supply-equilibrium condition from the first-order conditions, and substituting in it the quantities of supply and consumption that emerge from the first-order conditions, the elasticity of an internal price, p_a, to an external price, p_j, can be derived: $\varepsilon_{aj} = -[\varphi_{aj} + \theta_{aj}r_a + \eta_a r_a(s_{\pi Y}s_{j\pi} + s_{jY})]/[\varphi_{aa} - \theta_{aa}r_a - \eta_a r_a(s_{\pi Y}s_{a\pi} + s_{aY})]$, where the terms are defined as follows: $\varphi_{aa} > 0$ and $\varphi_{aj} < 0$ are the own- and cross-price elasticities of supply from the household's output supply functions; $\theta_{aa} < 0$ and $\theta_{aj} \geq 0$ or ≤ 0 are the own- and cross-price elasticities of consumption from the consumption functions; $\eta_a > 0$ is the elasticity of demand for good a with respect to full income Y; r_a is the ratio of the consumption of good a to the quantity of good a produced by the household, which is 1 if good a is food and is a negative number if good a is labor; $s_{i\pi} = p_i q_i/\pi$, the ratio of the revenue from good i to profits; and $s_{iY} = p_i T_i/Y$, the share of the household's initial endowment of good i in full income. The numerator of this elasticity shows the direct disequilibrium created on the missing market for good a by a change in price p_j. The first term, φ_{aj}, is the supply change while the other two terms show changes in demand coming from the cross-price effect, θ_{aj}, and the income effect, η_a. The change in income contains two terms, the profit effect and the value of the initial endowment. The denominator shows the disequilibrium created by the change in the endogenous price p_a. The overall expression shows that the endogenous price p_a will change in response to the exogenous price p_j in order for these two disequilibria to compensate each other and for the missing market to be equilibrated within the household.

When the missing market is that for the food crop (price p_a above) and the exogenous price change occurs in the market for the cash crop (price p_j above), the elasticity expression for the shadow price above reduces to $\varepsilon_{aj} = -[\varphi_{aj} - \eta_a v_{jY})]/[\varphi_{aa} - (\theta_{aa} + \eta_a v_{aY})]$, where v_{jY} and v_{aY} are shares of the values of goods a (the food crop) and j (the cash crop) in full income. In the denominator, the term in parenthesis represents the elasticity of demand for food, which is negative if the direct substitution effect, the absolute value of θ_{aa}, is greater than the indirect full income effect deriving from the price effect. Production and consumption effects operate in the same direction, and the denominator is positive. The numerator is unambiguously negative (the preceding negative sign turns it positive), so $\varepsilon_{aj} > 0$, and an increase in the price of the cash crop raises the shadow price of food, which heightens the farm household's perception of food scarcity.

Using the first elasticity expression above, an increase in the price of the manufactured good also will cause the shadow price of the food crop to rise. If the labor market exists and the market wage increases, the effects in the numerator of the first elasticity expression are more complicated than in the cases of price increases for the cash crop or the manufactured good. On the household's production side, an increase in the market wage causes a downward shift in production of the food crop, as the labor input now costs more. Two effects occur in consumption, a substitution from leisure, which the wage increase makes more expensive, into food and an income effect which is positive if the total value of labor use on the farm is smaller than full income. Thus both production and consumption responses to an increase in the market wage put upward pressure on the shadow price of the food crop. The potential exception is the case of a very large farm with large employment, for which the increase in labor cost could reduce income considerably (notice that the income effect in the numerator, $\eta_a v_a$, works in the opposite direction to the own-price consumption effect, θ_{aa}). An increase in the price of a purchased production input such as fertilizer can have an ambiguous effect on the shadow price of food. The two terms in the numerator have opposite signs, since the supply of the food crop will respond negatively to an increase in the fertilizer price (or any input price) while the negative income effect will depress the household's food demand. If the supply effect is small, the income effect would probably dominate and the shadow price of food would decrease, but with a low income elasticity of demand for food, demand would not fall by much while production becomes more costly, the shadow price of food rising in consequence.

Looking back to the full supply elasticity formulation, ϕ_{ji}^{mm}, consider an own-price supply response of the cash crop (in which case good j is the same as good i) with a missing food-crop market. The first term will then be a complete-markets own-supply response, $\phi_{ji}^{*} > 0$, where i = j. The first component of the second term, ϕ_{ja}^{*}, is negative. The indirect effect of the price of the cash crop on the price of the food crop was shown above to be positive, so the complete effect of the second term is of opposite sign to the direct, full-markets effect, dampening the household's market response to an increase in the cash crop's price. In contrast, if the price of the manufactured good or the market wage rate increased (or the price of the food crop if the labor market were missing instead of the food crop market), the indirect effect from the change in the shadow price would reinforce the direct negative effect, and the household's supply response is heightened by the missing market.

2.3 Agricultural Production and Supply

Production, the subject of the first sub-section, deals with the best way to produce a good or service. Supply, the subject of the second sub-section, addresses how much of a good or service to produce, given that producers have figured out the best way to produce it. The third sub-section returns to an important characteristic of much agricultural production, the fact that people need to both eat agricultural products and hold some of them back to produce more things to eat in subsequent seasons. While this issue is a production topic, it is addressed at the end of the section to avoid interrupting the continuity between production and supply in the first two sections.

2.3.1 Characterizing Agricultural Production

Introductions to the economic theory of production typically use a very simplified view of a generic production process: the amount of output produced in some specified time period is just a function of the amounts of various inputs applied in the process. To add just the barest flesh to those bones, the inputs were referred to as capital (capital services, actually) and labor. The production had a single stage, and the timing of the applications of the inputs was not of importance. Production also took place at a single location, with any physical movement of inputs of no consequence: think of a potter sitting at a wheel (which of course is a simplification of that process and ignores the acquisition of the clay and firewood). The length of time elapsing between the application of the inputs and the appearance of the output is not of particular importance or interest and so is not modeled. No other external events influenced the output independently of the inputs, and, implicitly, the operator of the production process applied all the inputs himself or herself and had complete control over the choice of levels of those inputs. And the output itself was not produced simultaneously and jointly with the production of any other good. While that abstraction might not be a bad representation of some small-scale manufacturing activities in antiquity, agricultural production is more complicated than that.

Circumstances of Production: Uncertainty and Space. The first major incremental intricacy of agricultural production is the lag between applications of inputs and the appearance of the output.[11] Additionally, there is frequently a complex series of sequential input decisions spread out over the time between the first application of inputs and the output. During the interval(s) between applications of inputs and the appearance of the output, there is limited observability of the progress of the output, due to the biological processes set into motion by the production process. External factors such as weather and pests impose uncertainty in the relationship between inputs and outputs. Frequently, the operator of the production process uses labor other than his or her own during at least some segments of the crop season, which introduces moral hazard[12] into the application of some inputs, when monitoring of the people applying the inputs is costly and imperfect and the relationship between whatever inputs those people do apply and the final output is affected by external events such as weather and pests. The moral hazard problem of using hired labor may be lower at harvest, when monitoring is relatively easy, than in earlier operations such as seeding and weeding. Nonetheless, family labor is superior to hired labor for many functions, and the two types of labor are generally not perfect substitutes. And the production takes place over expanses of land, which requires most inputs to make costly trips over a field.

Both quantities of inputs and the timing of their application are decision variables in agricultural production. The timing of the application of inputs is a crucial production decision because of weather. Some input responses depend on the weather during the crop season. The date chosen for harvest may not be the date that would yield the maximum output because of labor and equipment scheduling problems, uncertainty about the crop's maturity, and uncertainties about weather. Labor and equipment available may not be sufficient to harvest all plots at the same time, if they all mature at the same time. Consequently the shadow prices of inputs may vary considerably over the production season.

None of the foregoing is particularly new to students of ancient agriculture, but enumerating these distinct characteristics of agriculture may be helpful in providing background for models of agricultural production choices in subsequent sections.

---

11 The following characterization of agricultural production is adapted from Just (2001, 632–636).

12 Moral hazard introduces uncertainty because of the unobservability of actions taken by an agent at the direction of a principal. See Jones (2014, Chapter 7, section 4.1).

Formalizing the Logical Structure of Production. These intricacies of agricultural production can be codified by expanding the functional representation of the production technology. The simple representation of a production function used to introduce production theory is Q = F(K, L), where K represents capital or equipment inputs and L represents labor inputs; or generalizing slightly, $q = f(x_1, x_2, \dots x_n)$, where the x_i represent any number of inputs that might be used in the production of output q. You can read "Q = F(K, L)" as "output is a function of capital and labor," which translating slightly means that the output (production) of product Q is a function of capital services and labor applied.

The following functional specifications add some of the intricacy described above and are offered as examples of how to think economically about agricultural production (Just 2001, 637–640, 646). The first specification characterizes production as a sequence of input applications: $q = f(f_1(\mathbf{x}^1, t_1), \dots, f_m(\mathbf{x}^m, t_m))$, where the bolded $\mathbf{x}^i$ is a vector of variable inputs (i.e., it represents inputs such as labor, equipment services, seed, fertilizer, and so on; the notation for a vector is bold font) applied at time t_i and $\mathbf{x}^m$ is the harvest inputs applied at the end of the crop season. The quantities of the $\mathbf{x}^i$ and the timing of their application are decision variables. Because of the lags between input applications and the harvest, each $\mathbf{x}^i$ is relevant to the final output, which is characterized by the relationship $\Delta f/\Delta \boldsymbol{x}^i = (\Delta f/\Delta f_i)(\Delta f_i/\Delta x^i) \neq 0$, where the $\Delta \bullet_i / \Delta \bullet_j$ notation means a change in variable i caused by a small change in variable j. Thus in this case, working from right to left, a change in the vector of inputs $\mathbf{x}^i$ causes a change in the sub-product f_i, which in turn causes a change in the final harvested product, f (using the function f to represent the output q). The long delays between the applications of inputs to observations of productivity tend to confound the observed effects of inputs applied in multiple stages. Consequently, the farmer cannot easily infer which stages' operations are efficient and which are inefficient. Observing the effects of inputs on neighboring farms may not transfer readily to one's own farm because of differing soil and micro-climatic features.

The following specification more specifically represents the intraseasonal unobservability of productivity: $q = f^*(f_1(\mathbf{x}^1, q_0), \dots, f_m(\mathbf{x}^m, q_{m-1}))$, where q_0 represents the initial conditions. In this specification, the intermediate production of each stage, q_i, provides an output with which the variable inputs work in the immediately succeeding period. The intermediate outputs are largely unobservable, unlike the case in most manufacturing processes. Efficient management involves maximizing each intermediate inputs, ensuring that $q_i \leq f_i(\mathbf{x}^i, q_{i-1})$.

If the shadow prices of farm-controlled inputs vary widely from stage to stage, the previous specification of production may not fully capture the decision making required. To emphasize the difference between stocks and flows, particularly important with items of capital equipment, but not entirely irrelevant with labor as well, let $\mathbf{x}^i$ represent a vector of purchased inputs used in stage t_i, $\mathbf{z}^i$ represent a vector of farmer-controlled inputs such as family labor and capital services used in stage t_i, and $\mathbf{k}$ be a vector of maximum availability of services from the fixed stock of farmer-controlled resources in each stage. The production technology is represented then by $q = f^o(\mathbf{x}, q_0 | \mathbf{k}) = \max_{\{x^i, k^i\}}\{ f^*(f_1(\mathbf{x}^1, q_0, \mathbf{z}^1), \dots, f_m(\mathbf{x}^m, q_{m-1}, \mathbf{z}^m)) | \sum_i \mathbf{x}^i = \mathbf{x}; \mathbf{z}^i \leq \mathbf{k}\}$, where the notation f^o indicates the maximized value and the symbol $|\bullet$ means "given that the following condition holds." What does this mean? The distinction between the actual use of the farmer-controlled resources in the vector $\mathbf{z}^i$ and maximum available use denoted by $\mathbf{k}$ allows for the shadow prices of these inputs to vary across production stages (think of the rush of initial sowing, possible replanting, and harvesting, interspersed with down periods of, say, nothing more to do than maintain or repair equipment and feed animals, or periodically to weed), while indicating that no more than k^i of an input z^i is available to be deployed (where the absence of bold font indicates a specific input in the vector of inputs).

Additionally, one could specifically include the weather events in the formulation: $q = \{f^*(f_1(\mathbf{x}^1, q_0, \mathbf{z}^1, \varepsilon^1), \dots\}$. Farms typically product multiple outputs over the same span of time, although with differences in timing of peak input applications, which can allow more efficient use of farm resources. A multiple-product production process could be specified by $q^j = \{f^*(f_{1j}(x^{1j}, q_0^j, z^{1j}), \dots\}$, subject to $\sum_j z^{ij} \leq k$, where the i superscripts represent production stages and the j superscripts indicate different products.

2.3.2 Agricultural Supply

Supply and production refer to the same units of a good but address them from different perspectives. Production theory investigates the most economical way of producing a particular quantity of a good, while supply theory studies how much of the good a producer ought to make. While production decisions, such as how much of different factors of production (inputs) to use (i.e., factor proportions) to make a particular quantity of a product, involve economic calculations, production theory brings us, as students of the subject, in touch with the physical production technology—the specification and parameter values of the production function. While this information is tucked inside the formulations used to study supply decisions, much of it can remain tucked away as inside-the-box details while supply theory focuses on the profitability of producing particular quantities of the good in question.

In the analysis of supply, it is useful to keep in mind the difference between short-run and long-run supply responses. A short-run period is defined by certain factors of production being fixed in supply. In the long run, the quantities of all factors can be varied, and we can suppose that the factors that were fixed in the short run have been adjusted to their optimal levels. Will that long-run date and its full, optimal adjustment of factors ever be reached?

Possibly not; something else could change between the date we might define to be the short run and the date at which the long-run adjustment to conditions expected at the earlier date could be completed. Is it a useful concept? Definitely: immediate responses to changes in conditions are smaller than the full responses when farmers have had time to create the necessary adjustments. Just because the new conditions don't hold forever (remember, the initial conditions didn't either) doesn't mean that farmers won't begin to make longer-run adjustments in the initially fixed factors immediately.

Short- and Long-Run Agricultural Supply and Magnitudes of their Elasticities. To emphasize the profit-making aspect of supply decisions, the profit function is used to derive supply response.[13] Start with a restricted (i.e., short-run) profit function of an individual producer: $\pi(\boldsymbol{p}, \boldsymbol{w}, \boldsymbol{k}, T) = \max_{\{y,v\}}(\boldsymbol{pq} - \boldsymbol{wv} : \boldsymbol{q}, \boldsymbol{x} \in T)$, where **q** is a vector of Q outputs (i.e., there are Q different outputs; Q could be 4 or 12 or whatever); **x** is a vector of J inputs decomposed into variable, **v**, and fixed, **k**, components, **x** = (**v**, **k**), with dimensions (J_v, J_k), $J_v + J_k = J$; T is the available technology set; and **p** is a vector of output prices and **w** a vector of input prices, the latter of which can be decomposed to conform to the decomposition of **x**. The "**q**, **x** ∈ T" part just means that the inputs are in the technology that's available to the farmer for making outputs **q** and that the outputs **q** are attainable with the inputs **x** using that technology. Notice that the profit function is a maximized function, which means that the farmer has adjusted all the factor input ratios and the product mix that can be adjusted in the effort to get the greatest value from the year's crops. The factor demand and product supply functions are q_i(**p**, **w**, **k**, T) = $\Delta\pi/\Delta\boldsymbol{p}$ and v_j(**p**, **w**, **k**, T) = $-\Delta\pi/\Delta w_j$. To assess how the supply function responds to price changes, we need to see how $\Delta\pi/\Delta\boldsymbol{p}$ responds to a change in product price: $\Delta q_i/\Delta p_i = \Delta^2\pi/\Delta p^2 \geq 0$, which means that as product price increases, the quantity of the product supplied will either increase or not fall, which of course gives us the familiar, upward-sloping supply curve, with a vertical slope in the limit, which would mean that the quantity supplied stays the same regardless of price (i.e., completely inelastic supply).

The strength of response of **y** and **v** to changes in prices depends on the decomposition of **x**. In the unrestricted, or long-run case, all of the inputs are variable (J_v = J). The unrestricted factor demand and product supply functions are **q***(**p**, **w**, T) and **k***(**p**, **w**, T)—the level of the fixed inputs is not in these functions, since they will vary freely. The relationship between the restricted and unrestricted supplies is given by an identity, q(**p**, **w**, **k***, T) ≡ q*(**p**, **w**, T). Consequently, the responses of the short- and long-run supply functions to a change in product price are related to each other by $\Delta q_i^*/\Delta p_i \equiv \Delta q_i/\Delta p_i + \sum_{(\Delta q_i} /\Delta k_j^*)(\Delta k_j^*/\Delta p_i)$. Thus the long-run response is the sum of the short-run response and an indirect price effect that acts on investment in the factors that are fixed in the short-run. In terms of elasticities, the relationship between short- and long-run supply elasticities is $\varepsilon_{ii}^{LR} = \varepsilon_{ii}^{SR} + \sum_i \beta_{ik}^*\varepsilon_{ki}$, where ε_{ii}^{LR} and ε_{ii}^{SR} are long-run and short-run elasticities.; $\beta_{ik}^* = (\Delta q_i/\Delta k_j^*)(k_j^*/q_i)$ is the production elasticity of fixed factor k_j in the production of the ith product; and $\varepsilon_{ki} = (\Delta k_j^*/\Delta p_i)(p_i/k_j^*)$ is the demand elasticity of fixed factor k_j with respect to output price p_i.

A relationship between supply elasticity and scale elasticity gives a single expression that is useful for evaluating the magnitude of the supply elasticity for a single-product production function. Begin with a production function that is homogeneous of degree $\mu < 1$ in the variable inputs;[14] the degree of homogeneity in the variable inputs is less than 1 because of the contribution of the fixed factor(s). A cost function for such a production function could be written as $c = \varphi(w, q)q^{1/\mu}$, with marginal cost $\Delta c/\Delta q = q^{(1/\mu)-1}\phi(w, k)/\mu$. Under competitive conditions, the marginal cost of production will equal the price that can be gotten for the product, or $\Delta c/\Delta q = p$. From these last three relationships, the supply elasticity can be derived as $\varepsilon = (\Delta q/\Delta p)(p/q) = \mu/1 - \mu$, which highlights the sensitivity of the magnitude of the elasticity of supply to the degree of homogeneity of the variable factors in the production function. For example, if $\mu = 0.9$, i.e., most of the contribution to production comes from the variable factors, $\varepsilon = 9$, a very considerable responsiveness to price. If $\mu = 0.1$, representing a case in which most of the contribution to output comes from the factors fixed in quantity in the short run, $\varepsilon = 0.11$, a very low degree of responsiveness. To develop a different view of this relationship which yields an expression for supply elasticity in terms of factor shares (i.e., the percentage contributions of each input to the output), consider a production function q = f(v,k), and let α_j represent the output elasticity of variable input v_j: $\beta_j = (\Delta q/\Delta v_j)(v_j/q)$. From profit maximization conditions, $\beta_j = w_j v_j/pq \equiv s_j$, where s_j is the share of factor j in total output. Because the production function is homogeneous in variable inputs v, the degree of homogeneity, which was defined by the symbol μ above, is $\sum_j \beta_j$ and thence $\varepsilon = \sum_j s_j/1 - \sum_j s_j$, where j = 1, . . . , J_v, defined above is the number of variable factors (i.e., the dimension of the vector of variable factors). The numbers that come out of this definition depend on the classification of inputs to v and k, but it is useful for giving order-of-magnitude estimates of supply elasticity. For example, if land, equipment and even labor are fixed in the short run, and they account for around 80% to 90% of total output, the supply elasticity of that product would be between 0.11 and 0.25.

[13] The following discussion is adapted from Mundlak (1996; 2001, 49–50).

[14] The degree of homogeneity of a function is a simple concept: if you increase each argument of the function—in the case of a production function, each of the inputs—by the same percent, the value of the function—the output of a production function—will increase by that percent times the degree of homogeneity. Jones (2014, Chapter 1, section 5) discusses constant-returns-to-scale production functions, i.e., those possessing homogeneity of degree 1. If all inputs are increased by the same percent, output will increase by that same percent.

The division between variable and fixed inputs is, to some extent, arbitrary, and assumes a zero supply elasticity for the fixed inputs and infinite elasticities for the variable inputs, neither of which, strictly speaking, is likely to be the case. For a production function homogeneous of degree $\mu \leq 1$ in its variable inputs, the supply elasticity is $\varepsilon = \mu[(1-\mu) + \sum_j (\alpha_j/\xi_j)]^{-1}$, in which $\xi_j \neq 0$ is the supply elasticity of factor j and α_j is the cost share of input j. This generalizes the expression for the supply elasticity in the previous paragraph. To see how to use the supply elasticity expression above in cases in which some of the inputs are fixed, i.e., the case of $\xi = 0$, consider a two-input production function, $f(x_1, x_2)$ with one input variable and the other fixed. Let $x_1 = v$ be the variable input and $x_2 = k$ the fixed input. Then inverting the usual procedure for seeing how variations in the quantity of an input applied change output, consider how the requirements of these two inputs change as output is increased: $(\Delta x_1/\Delta q)(q/x_1) = 1/\beta_1$, the inverse of the output elasticity β defined several paragraphs above, $(\Delta x_2/\Delta q)(q/x_2) = 0$ since x_2 is fixed. The degree of homogeneity of the variable factors, μ, defined above, is equal to β_1, and $1-\mu$ is β_2, which is equal to 0. Adding the factor shares over the variable inputs only, $\alpha_1 = 1$ since input x_1 is the only variable factor. Then $\varepsilon = \beta_1[(1-\beta_1) + \alpha_1/\xi_1 + \alpha_2/\xi_2]^{-1} = \beta_1[(1-\beta_1) + \alpha_1/\xi_1 + 0/\infty]^{-1} = \beta_1[(1-\beta_1) + 1/\xi_1]^{-1}$.

For a constant-returns-to-scale production function ($\mu = 1$), this simplifies to $\varepsilon = (\sum_{\alpha_j}/\xi_j)^{-1}$. This simplified expression offers insight into the inverse relationship between the length of run (i.e., just how long a "short-run" period under discussion actually is) and the magnitude of the supply elasticity. The shorter the run, the more restrictions there are on factor adjustments and the smaller the supply elasticity will be. Restrictions on overall factor supplies, such as farm land, do not apply to the allocation of a factor to alternative crops, so the more specific the crop (or output, in general) under discussion, the larger the supply elasticity will be, and vice versa for more aggregated groups of outputs.

A farm gets from a short run to a long run by investing in factors that are fixed in the short run. To illustrate the economics of this, begin with a simple, general production function, $q_t = f(v_t, k_t, T_t)$, where each of these variables is subscripted with a t to indicate that it can take different values at different dates. The income flow at date t is $R_t = f(v_t, k_t, T_t) - c(I_t) - w_t v_t - \psi_t I_t$, where ψ_t and w_t are real prices (in terms of output, i.e., ψ_t/p_t and w_t/p_t) of an investment good I and the variable input v. The $c(T_t)$ term at the end of the revenue expression is the real adjustment cost reflecting the fact that the marginal cost of investment increases with the rate of investment, so that if a farmer were to act too quickly to bring some equipment or land stock up to their desired long-run levels the cost would be excessively high. The farmer's optimization problem is to maximize the farm's expected value at the present date by adjusting the time paths of v_t and k_t over all time periods j in the planning horizon, which for simplicity is assumed to go on forever. This maximized value is $\{E_0[\sum_{j=0}^{\infty} \beta^j [f_j(v_j, k_j, T_j) - w_j v_j - \psi_j I_j - c(I_j)]]\}$, subject to $I_j = k_{j+1} - (1-\delta)k_j$, and an initial value k_0 (ignoring terminal conditions), where $\beta = (1+r)^{-1}$ is the discount factor, r is the interest rate, k_j is the capital stock at the beginning of a period, δ is the depreciation rate, and E_0 is the expectation over future prices and technology.

The first-order condition for optimal use of the variable inputs is $E[\Delta f(\cdot)/\Delta v_j - w_j] = 0$, which indicates that in equating the marginal productivity of the variable inputs to their prices at each date to determine the optimal level of variable input use, the level of variable input use at any particular time has no effect on revenue in subsequent periods. This independence of variable input usage at different dates permits solution of the overall optimization problem in steps. First the time path of the optimal levels of the variable inputs can be determined as a function of prices and the levels of fixed inputs at dates j, k_j, for all the periods in the planning horizon. This solution can be substituted then into the production function to yield a function $f(k_j, \mathbf{s}_j)$, where $\mathbf{s}_j$ is a vector of exogenous variables $(w_j, \psi_j, r, \delta, c, T_j)$. Then a second-stage problem solves $\max_{\{k_{j+1}\}}\{E_0[\sum_{j=0}^{\infty} \beta^j [f_j(k_j, s_j) - \psi_j I_j - c(I_j)]]\}$, subject to $I_j = k_{j+1} - (1-\delta)k_j$. Define the rate of capital appreciation as $\hat{\psi} = \dot{\psi}/\psi$, where $\dot{\psi} \equiv \Delta\psi/\Delta t$, and the rental cost of capital as $\tilde{\psi}_j \equiv \psi_j[r + \delta - (1-\delta)\hat{\psi}_j]$, or "the rental rate" at date j (the $\hat{\bullet}$ notation for c is analogous to that for ψ). This rental cost is the product of the price of the capital good, ψ, and the annual charges—the discount and depreciation rates, adjusted for capital gains, $\hat{\psi}$. Similarly, $\tilde{c}_j \equiv c_I(j)[r + \delta - (1-\delta)\hat{c}_j]$ gives the change in adjustment cost due to changes of the timing of a unit of investment on the optimal path from one year to the next (the notation $c_I(j)$ indicates that $\Delta c/\Delta I$ is a function of dated variables).

The first-order condition for the optimal amount of capital equipment at each date is $E_0\{\beta f_k(j+1) - [\tilde{c}_I(j) + \tilde{\psi}_j]\} = 0$, where $f(j) \equiv f(k_j, s_j)$ and similarly for the other functions which are arguments of dated variables. With static expectations, which could characterize much of antiquity, $E(\hat{\psi}) = E(\hat{c}) = 0$, and the last expression becomes $E\{\beta f_k(j+1) - (r+\delta)[c_I(j) + \psi_j]\} = 0$. The addition of an adjustment cost affects the rental rate, so it affects the optimal level of capital equipment as well as the pace of investment. The solution to the optimization problem can be expressed in terms of the shadow price of capital defined as the present value of the marginal product of capital, net of adjustment costs, in present and future production: $S_t \equiv \sum_{j=0}^{\infty} [(1-\delta)\beta]^j f_k(t+j)$. This system can be solved to yield $E_t\{S_t - [\psi_t + c_I(t)]\} = 0$, which says that investment is carried out to the point where the shadow price of capital generated by the investment equals the cost of investment including the adjustment cost. So, where the optimal levels of capital equipment in the short-run case were found to be $\mathbf{k}^*(\mathbf{p}, \mathbf{w}, T)$, the full-adjustment (long-run) optimal levels of capital equipment are given by $k^*[E(\psi, \hat{\psi}, \delta, r, c, \mathbf{w}, \mathbf{p}, T)]$.

Having worked fairly abstractly through the additional economic forces operating to move a farm from a short run to a long run, application of this model of investment to a Cobb-Douglas production function may illustrate more graphically how the investment affects output by changing the level of the fixed (capital) inputs. Consider a simple Cobb-Douglas production function with just two inputs, a variable input v and a capital input that is fixed in the short run: $q = Av^ak^b$. Recalling the structure of the first-order condition from the long-run model just above, the optimal level of the variable input will be $v = (a/w)q$. Substituting this for v in the production function and simplifying yields $q = (Aa^a)^{1/(1-a)}w^{-a/(1-a)}k^{b/(1-a)}$. This is the short-run supply function of the farm output, conditional on the level of the fixed input, k. If the wage increases relative to the product price (remember that the real wage w is defined as w/p), supply decreases since the exponent on w is negative. However, an increase in p is symmetrically a decrease in w, so supply increases in the product price.

Continuing on the develop the long-run supply function, the marginal product of capital is $\Delta q/\Delta k|_w = (b/1-a)(Aa^a)^{1/(1-a)}w^{-a/(1-a)}k^{(a+b-1)/(1-a)}$, which, when equated to the rental price of capital, yields the long-run optimal level of capital, k*. Ignoring the adjustment cost in the first-order condition for the optimal choice of the next period's level of capital stock, that condition simplifies to $E_0\{\beta f_k(j+1) - \tilde{\psi}_j\} = 0$, which says that the expected rental cost of capital equipment equals the next period's expected marginal product of that equipment. Using the first-order condition for the variable input found just above and using the relationship between the equation of the marginal product of capital and its expected rental cost, the long-run values of the capital equipment level and output can be found: $k^* = (b/\tilde{\psi}_j)q^*$ and $q^* = (Aa^ab^b)^\varepsilon w^{-a\varepsilon}\tilde{\psi}_j^{-b\varepsilon}$, where the asterisks indicate long-run optimal values and $\varepsilon = 1/(1\text{-}a\text{-}b)$; 1-a-b represents the share of fixed factors such as management and land.

It is clear from these expressions that prices affect desired capital equipment levels directly through the rental rate on capital and indirectly through their effect on desired output levels. A change in the wage rate has only an indirect effect, with an elasticity of desired capital with respect to the real wage of $-a\varepsilon$. The elasticity of desired capital with respect to the direct effect of the rental cost of capital is -1, while the elasticity with respect to the indirect effect through the desired output level is $-b\varepsilon$, for a total effect of $-(1\text{-}a)\varepsilon$ for the total effect of the rental cost on desired equipment level. The direct, indirect, and total elasticities of desired equipment level with respect to the price of the product are 1, $(a+b)\varepsilon$, and ε. The indirect effect of the product price on the desired equipment level is larger than the direct effect. To offer a rough guide to magnitudes, empirical estimates of a from modern agriculture are in the range of 0.1 for machinery only and around 0.3 for a broader measure of capital that includes structures. The magnitudes of these elasticities of demand for capital equipment can vary widely depending on the magnitudes of a and b. For instance, if the output elasticity of the variable input a is 0.6 while that of the equipment and structures is 0.3, ε would take a value of 10, and the elasticity of demand for capital with respect to the product price would also be 10, but with the same value of a, if the output elasticity of the variable input were only 0.2, the responsiveness of capital demand to a product price increase would drop to only 2.5.

Effects of Uncertainty. I will develop the effects of uncertainty on agricultural supply beginning with the simple exposition of riskless supply. Next, uncertainty will be added, but with risk-neutral farmers, then the assumption of risk neutrality will be relaxed to admit the far more likely case of risk aversion.[15]

Agricultural Supply without Risk. The supply curve is based on profit maximization, with profits defined as $\pi = pf(\mathbf{x}) - \sum_i w_i x_i$, in which the profit-maximizing values of the inputs x_i are the solutions to the first-order conditions $p\Delta f/\Delta x_i = w_i$, or the value of marginal product equals the cost of the input. The simple specification of input costs can be replaced with a cost function, $c(q,\mathbf{w})$ as the minimum cost needed to produce an output of q at input prices w: $c(q,\mathbf{w}) = \min \sum_i w_i x_i$ subject to $f(\mathbf{x}) \geq q$. In a competitive industry, farmers will maximize profits, $\pi = pq - c(q,\mathbf{w})$ by choosing output q such that marginal cost equals price, or $\Delta c(q,\mathbf{w})/\Delta q = p$. In this case, each farmer's supply curve can be added horizontally to obtain the industry supply curve. Figure 2.3 showed the riskless average variable and marginal cost curves AVC and MC. The supply curve is the marginal cost curve at each point where it is above the average variable cost curve. Total industry costs are the area under the supply curve and industry profits are the area between the price and the supply curve. The supply curve follows the average variable cost curve from point B to point C and the marginal cost from C to D and beyond. In the absence of risk, the supply curve can be graphed as a function of price, independent of demand.

Risky Agricultural Supply with Risk-Neutral Farmers. When production risk is introduced, average supply is a function of a certainty-equivalent price which depends on demand as well as supply conditions. From a farmer's point of view, agricultural risks can be divided into production risks and price risks. Production risks affect output and arise from weather variations, pests and disease, and other natural incidents such as fire. Price risks affect output and input prices. For the entire market, variations in output produce variations in prices, with a negative relationship. The farmer's profit is random, where the tilde over a variable indicates a random variable: $\tilde{\pi} = \tilde{p}\tilde{q} - wx$. A farmer who maximizes $E\tilde{\pi}$ is said to be risk-neutral. Although a farmer may be risk neutral, his or her maximization problem is not max $Ep \cdot Eq - wx = \bar{p}\bar{q} - wx$, where a bar over a variable indicates an expected value. Unless the price and output are uncorrelated, expected revenues are not simply the product of expected price and expected output but are $E\tilde{\pi} = \bar{p}\bar{q} + \mathrm{Cov}(p,q) - wx$, where

[15] This treatment is adapted from Newbery and Stigliz (1981, Chapters 5 and 6).

Cov(p,q) is the covariance between price and output.[16] If a negative correlation existed between a farmer's output and the price received at harvest (i.e., larger harvest means lower price) and the farmer omitted that effect in estimating profit, he would over-estimate the profitability to increasing his output.

Focusing on production risk, risky production can be specified as q = f(**x**, $\tilde{\theta}$), where $\tilde{\theta}$ describes the state of nature—weather, incidence of pests, and so on. More operationally, production risk has been specified multiplicatively and additively, with the former making more economic sense: $q = \tilde{\theta}f(x)$, $E\tilde{\theta} = 1$, $\text{Var}\,\tilde{\theta} = \sigma^2$. The interpretation of multiplicative risk would be, for example, that if rain just before harvest ruins half of the crop of a 2-hectare farm, it would ruin half of the harvest on a 3- or 4-hectare farm too, whereas an additive formulation would specify 1 hectare of ruined crop on a 2-hectare farm, on a 3-hectare farm, and so on.

Turning from production risk to price risk now, the foregoing concepts provide the tools with which to understand the action certainty equivalent price, which is the price, if it prevailed on the market and there were no risk, which would yield the same supply response as the random price $\tilde{p}$ does. Consider a stochastic price with two sources of variability, supply risk, $\tilde{\theta}$, and all other risk uncorrelated with supply risk, $\tilde{\nu}$: $\tilde{p} = \bar{p} + \beta(\tilde{\theta} - \bar{\theta}) + \tilde{\nu}$, $E\tilde{\nu} = 0$, $E\tilde{\nu}\tilde{\theta} = 0$. This price formulation corresponds to a linear demand function with multiplicative risk and an independent additive demand risk $\tilde{\nu}$, p = a - b$\bar{Q}$, where $\bar{Q}$ is expected industry output, with $\beta = -b\bar{Q}$, where −b is the slope of the inverse demand function, and demand has entered the random price. Risk neutral farmers maximize expected profit as $E\tilde{\pi} = E[\bar{p} + \beta(\tilde{\theta} - 1) + \tilde{\nu}]\tilde{\theta} f(x) - wx$, $E\tilde{\theta} = 1$, or $E\tilde{\pi} = \hat{p} - wx$, where $\hat{p}$ is the certainty equivalent price: $\hat{p} = \bar{p} + \beta\sigma^2 = \bar{p} + Cov(p,q)/\bar{q}$. Then $\hat{p} \gtrless \bar{p}$ as $\beta \gtrless 0$. Since $\beta < 0$ is far more likely to characterize the relationship between $\tilde{p}$ and $\tilde{q}$, the certainty equivalent price is likely to be below the expected price.

To treat this response of supply to uncertain price, trace through a representative farmer's actions. The farmer chooses an expected supply of $\bar{q}$ (which aggregates to total supply $\bar{Q}$), that yields a marginal cost equal to the certainty equivalent price, MC = $\hat{p}$. However, the price when market supply is $\bar{Q}$ is p($\bar{Q}$) = (1+m)MC, where m = $\hat{p}/p(\bar{Q}) > 0$, and there is a mark-up over marginal cost, as shown in Figure 2.4. The average variable and marginal cost curves are the same as in Figure 2.4, but rather than the segment of the marginal cost curve above the average variable cost curve being the supply curve, there is a long-run pseudo-supply curve above the riskless supply curve by a factor of 1 + m, represented by SS. The short-run supply curve is vertical and will fluctuate around $\bar{Q}$, leading to various market-clearing prices along the demand curve.

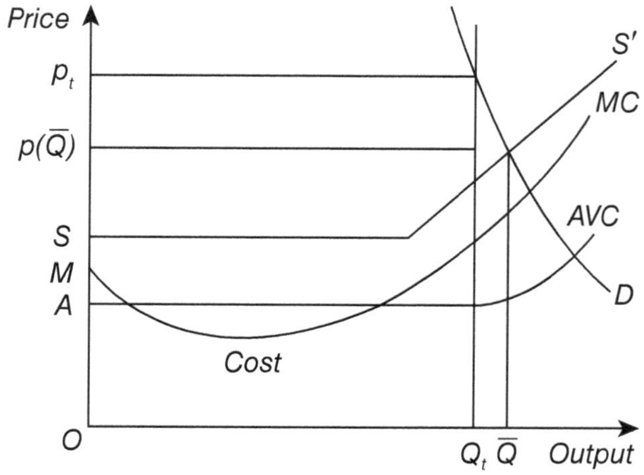

Figure 2.4. Demand and supply with supply risk (Reproduced from Newbery and Stiglitz, 1981, figure 5.3, p. 67, by permission of David M.G. Newbery and Joseph E. Stiglitz).

Costs are still the area under the non-random MC curve while revenue will be random, profits being the difference between random revenue and non-random cost rather than the area between the price and the long-run pseudo-revenue curve.

Risky Agricultural Supply with Risk-Averse Farmers. Supply behavior of risk-averse farmers involves attitudes toward risk as well as the physical facts of risk dealt with above. Risk aversion is an attitude toward the expected utility of an outcome, not simply toward the expected value of the outcome itself. An individual maximizes EU($\tilde{y}$), the expected utility of the stochastic (random) outcome $\tilde{y}$. Figure 2.5 depicts utility as a concave function of a random income $\tilde{y}$, which means that continuing increases in income produce smaller and smaller increases in utility. Suppose E($\tilde{y}$) = $\bar{y}$, with utility of that expected income identified by tracing to the horizontal axis from that value on the utility function. Now consider a variation of $\pm\delta$ around $\bar{y}$, with each displacement having a $\frac{1}{2}$ probability. Denote the expected utility of this random income as EU($\tilde{y}$) = $\frac{1}{2}$ [U($\bar{y} + \delta$) +U($\bar{y} - \delta$)]. The utility of each of these two displacements from the expected (mean) value is shown on the horizontal axis, and its expected value is half-way between them, and is below the utility of the certain value of expected income $\bar{y}$. So with the expected utility of the risky income $\bar{y}$ below the utility of the certain income of the same magnitude as the expected value of the risky income, how much income would the person possessing this utility function be willing to give up and still prefer the certain income to the risky income? In other words, what certain income is equivalent in utility terms to the risky income? That income, called the certainty-equivalent income, is $\hat{y}$, the income associated with the expected utility of risky income $\bar{y}$: EU($\tilde{y}$) = U($\hat{y}$). The difference between the expected income and its certainty equivalent is sometimes referred to as the risk premium, or the cost of this amount of risk.

As can be seen, risk aversion derives from the curvature of the utility function as y increases. The risk premium is

[16] The covariance is defined as Cov(x,y) = E[(x − E[x])(y − E[y])], which can be simplified to E(xy) − E(x) · E(y), and is typically calculated as Cov(x,y) = $[\sum_i^n (x_i - \bar{x})(y_i - \bar{y})]/n$.

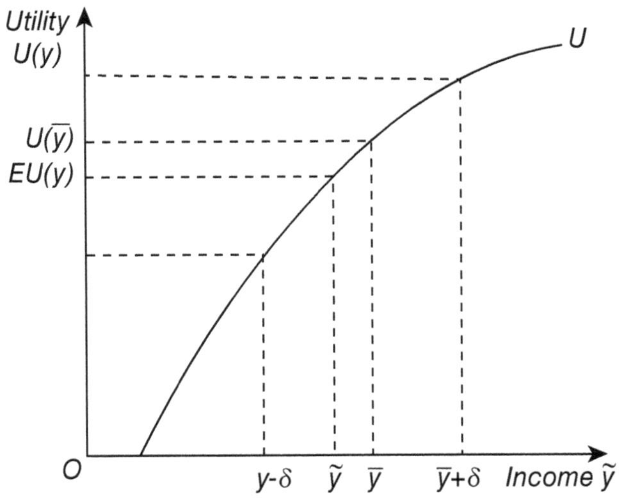

Figure 2.5. The value of risky income (Reproduced from Newbery and Stiglitz, 1981 figure 6.1, p. 71, by permission of David M.G. Newbery and Joseph E. Stiglitz).

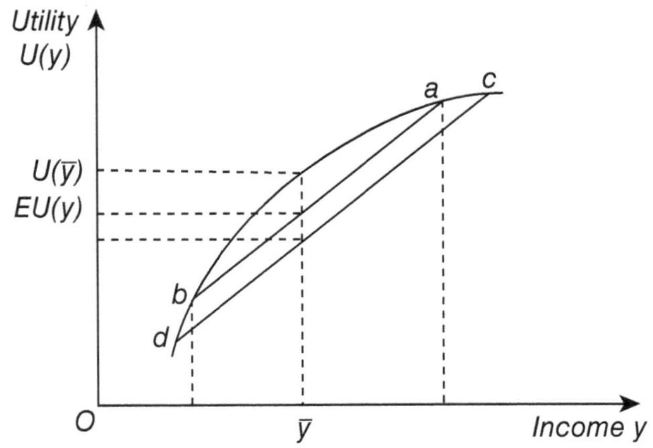

Figure 2.6. A mean-preserving spread with a concave utility function (Reproduced from Newbery and Stiglitz, figure 6.5, p. 80, by permission of David M.G. Newbery and Joseph E. Stiglitz).

one measure of risk aversion, but it depends on specifying a particular expected income. Several other more general measures are commonly used. The coefficient of absolute risk aversion (CARA), $A(y) = -u_{yy}/u_y > 0$ is the ratio of the curvature of the utility function to its slope.[17] With constant risk aversion, people with higher income will find their risk aversion a smaller proportion of their expected income. The coefficient of relative risk aversion (CRRA) is a dimensionless elasticity related to CARA, $R(y) = yA(y) = -yu_{yy}/u_y > 0$. If A(y) is restated as 1/(a+by), the general form of the utility function generating the measure is $u(y) = (y - a/b)^{1-1/a}/(1 - 1/a)$. If b = 0 in this utility function, the function exhibits constant absolute risk aversion, since A(y) = 1/a, which is a constant; if a = 0, the function exhibits constant relative risk aversion, as yA(y) = 1/b, which is also a constant. Constant relative risk aversion implies decreasing absolute risk aversion, but the reverse is not always the case, as, for example, the case of u(y) = log(y) implies A(y) = 1/y and R(y) = 1. An example of a utility function with increasing absolute risk aversion is $u(y) = y - by^2$, with a(y) = 2b/(1 − 2by). In general, a utility function with greater curvature exhibits greater risk aversion. An expected utility function exhibiting CRRA is $u(y) = y^{1-R(y)}/1\text{-}R(y)$, which has a constant intertemporal elasticity of substitution of 1/R(y).

Equipped with a definition for risk aversion, and with some manipulations of the equality between the expected utility of income and the utility of expected income, a measure of the risk premium can be derived as $\rho \approx \frac{1}{2}$ A Var($\tilde{y}$), where A is the coefficient of absolute risk aversion derived just above. So the risk premium associated with a risky income increases roughly proportionally to the income's variance.

Now, we need some ways to measure changes in risk. Some simple measures are a change in the variance of a distribution or a change in its range (from lowest possible value to highest). However, the variance of a distribution could be reduced with the mean remaining the same and expected utility could still be reduced, so neither of these measures is foolproof. The mean-preserving spread, is a concept widely used for studying the effects of changes in risk (see Jones 2014, Chapter 7, section 1). Figure 2.6 illustrates its operation. Begin with the chord closer to the utility function, with end points labeled a and b, which represent a pair of percentage points of the distribution of income (e.g., on either side of a and b, only $2\frac{1}{2}$ % of the random draws on income will occur). The mean of the distribution is $\bar{y}$. The utility of expected income is $u(\bar{y})$ and the expected utility of that income is $Eu(\bar{y}) < u(\bar{y})$. Now, let the percentage points widen, so that the 5% of the possible realizations of random income are now higher and lower than they were before, with the mean remaining unchanged at $\bar{y}$. Utility of expected income remains unchanged at $u(\bar{y})$, but $Eu(\bar{y})$ falls, which is intuitively reasonable.

Equipped now with the concepts of expected utility of income versus utility of expected income, risk aversion, and measures of changes in risk, the issue of how risk affects agricultural supply can be addressed. First, because of the intervening chances between the applications of inputs to production and the quantity of output at the end of the season, it has been common to examine the impact of risk on inputs as indicators of intended output rather than directly on outputs. To examine the impact of increased risk on a farmer's effort, consider a farmer producing a single crop with only labor, x. The revenue is $\tilde{y} = \tilde{p}\tilde{\theta} f(x)$, and the farmer maximizes $Eu[\tilde{p}\tilde{\theta} f(x)] - wx$. The first-order condition for optimal effort is $Eu_{\tilde{y}}\tilde{p}\tilde{\theta}\Delta f/\Delta x = w$, which can be solved for the optimal level of effort x*. Note that the expectation includes only the revenue, as the costs are not subject to uncertainty (in this specification, although they could be; nevertheless price and output uncertainty are far more important empirically than is input cost uncertainty). Now consider a mean-preserving spread of $\tilde{p}\tilde{\theta}$ that leaves $E\tilde{p}\tilde{\theta}$ unchanged. To simplify the notation, redefine $\tilde{p}\tilde{\theta}$ as $\tilde{r}$ and re-write the first-order condition above as $Eu_{\tilde{y}}\tilde{r}\Delta f/\Delta x = w$. Thinking back to the shape of the concave utility function, we need to determine if this first-order condition is concave (shaped

[17] $u_y = \Delta u/\Delta y$ and $u_{yy} = \Delta^2 u/\Delta y^2$.

like the utility function) or convex (bent in the opposite direction) to determine whether effort will increase or decrease with an increase in risk. First, as $\tilde{r}$ increases, $\Delta u_{\tilde{y}}\tilde{r}/\tilde{r} = u_{\tilde{y}} + u_{\tilde{y}\tilde{y}}y = u_{\tilde{y}}(1 - R(y))$, which is negative for values of $R > 1$, giving a negative slope of expected utility as $\tilde{r}$ increases. Next, change $\tilde{r}$ again to see whether the shape of the curve is concave or convex: $\tilde{r}\Delta^2 u_{\tilde{y}}\tilde{r}/\Delta\tilde{r}^2 = u_{\tilde{y}\tilde{y}}y(1 - R(y)) - u_{\tilde{y}}yR_{\tilde{y}} \lesseqgtr 0$, where $R_{\tilde{y}} = \Delta R/\Delta y$. If the sign of this expression is negative, the function is concave; if positive, it is convex. If $R_{\tilde{y}} = 0$ (constant relative risk aversion), the farmer increases or decreases effort as $R \lesseqgtr 1$. Very risk-averse people, worried about worst possible outcomes, increase their effort when risk increases, to avoid a catastrophe. Less risk-averse people will view the return to farming as having fallen and accordingly reduce their efforts. A more likely case is that risk aversion is greater at lower incomes, $R_{\tilde{y}} < 0$, and it becomes more important to avoid low outcomes, and hence an increase in risk is more likely to increase output. So altogether, whether farm effort increases or decreases as risk increases depends critically on the degree of risk aversion of the farmers making those decisions, which will depend in turn on their income levels.

Responses to Risk. There are two types of response to risk beyond altering one's level of effort, sharing it with or transferring it to someone else and reducing it.[18] Risk can be transferred to someone who is more able (say, because of wealth) or more willing (because of attitude toward risk or possessing a covariance with the risk) to bear it. In sharing risk with others, the risk facing each person is reduced, as is the total.

It was noted above that a person's risk premium is proportional to the size of his or her risk aversion. A person with lesser risk aversion faces a lower cost of bearing risk than someone with greater risk aversion. There is an opportunity for a profitable exchange here, just as there is between a shoemaker and a carpenter in trading tables for shoes. The source of this difference in risk aversion may be in wealth or income, particularly with decreasing absolute risk aversion. Thus, landlords are likely to be less risk averse than are tenants and landless agricultural laborers. Alternatively, preferences toward risk may simply differ, some people being born gamblers and others quite cautious. Another reason for differences individuals require in compensation for bearing risk may be quite project-specific: their income may be negatively correlated with the risk of the project another person faces. To see how this works, consider a person with risky income $\tilde{y}$ thinking of accepting a small risky project with outcome $\tilde{v}$. Equating his or her expected utility with and without this project, and including the price needed to equate the two prospects, we can back out the price required to bring about indifference between the alternatives: $EU(\tilde{y}) = EU(\tilde{y} + \tilde{v} + p_v)$, where p_v is the price the person would be willing to pay for the additional project. After some manipulations, it turns out that $p_v \approx \bar{v} - \frac{1}{2}A[\mathrm{Var}(\tilde{v}) + 2\mathrm{Cov}(\tilde{v}, \tilde{y})]$, where the bars over v and y indicate expected values and A is the coefficient of absolute risk aversion defined above. The larger the negative covariance between the new project and the person's other income, the greater the price he will be willing to pay for the new project, because it in effect provides insurance. Who would be characterized by such a negative covariance with farm income? When agricultural prices are high, presumably because yields are down (and prices are not completely stabilized by trade), people who use agricultural products as inputs to their production processes pay high prices for their inputs, and their profits are lower; when agricultural prices are low, their profits are high. So their incomes are negatively correlated with farm incomes. Thus people using agricultural products as intermediate inputs to their own production processes are likely candidates to share agricultural risks with farmers. These occupations would include processors (e.g., millers in situations in which farmers did not mill their own products), producers (think of industrial occupations that make cloth out of flax, for example), and marketers.

As to spreading risk actually reducing it, recall that the size of an individual's risk premium, ρ, is proportional to the variance of the income risk: $\rho = \frac{1}{2}A\,\mathrm{Var}(\tilde{y})$. Consequently, in dividing the risk between two individuals, the variance is divided by 2^2, and the size of the risk premium for each individual is divided by four.[19] The total risk premium is halved. As the number of people, n, sharing a risky endeavor increases, the aggregate risk premium goes to zero as $1/n$ becomes very small.

Risk-spreading and -sharing are limited by moral hazard and adverse selection. As for the moral hazard (in which being insured affects the behavior of the person buying the insurance), supposing a tenant's landlord is providing the insurance, the landlord would like assure himself or herself that the tenant is acting to contain the risk of the farming activity while the landlord is providing some insurance against bad outcomes. In the adverse selection, potential insurers may not know who are better and worse risks, although low mobility in small agrarian communities may largely reduce this problem, as reputations are well known.

How could risk-spreading have been accomplished? Presently, futures markets, in which farmers can sell their outputs forward (i.e., sell them before they're produced, to people willing to take the risk) are the prime vehicle for risk sharing. However, with the general absence of futures markets in antiquity (as far as I'm aware), people would have been left with working for fixed wages, in which the employer bears the risk (assuming the employer pays his workers) of productivity fluctuations, and renting land on share contracts, which is dealt with at greater length below. Those two options would not have been mutually exclusive. On very large estates owned by a single individual or family, which engaged in cultivation, processing,

[18] This discussion is based on Newbery and Stiglitz (Chapter 12).

[19] Divide $\tilde{y}$ into two income streams and find the variance of the sum: $\mathrm{Var}(\tilde{y}) = \mathrm{Var}(\tilde{y}/2 + \tilde{y}/2) = E(\tilde{y}/2 + \tilde{y}/2)^2 = E[\frac{1}{4}(\tilde{y} - \bar{y})^2]$ for each component of the divided income stream, which $= \frac{1}{4}E(\tilde{y} - \bar{y})^2 = \frac{1}{4}\mathrm{Var}(\tilde{y})$.

and marketing of various agricultural products, negative covariance across the different stages of production would have provided some self-insurance which could have been shared with workers and tenants, assuming employment options existed for them in the locale.

Farmers would have had a number of options for directly reducing risks that remained after they had transferred some to others as described above. Crop diversification and choice of technique would have been the two principal means. Appealing to portfolio theory, a farmer could have planted a combination of crops (see Jones 2014, Chapter 7, section 3). With an example of two crops, the expected return per unit of land from two such crops would be $\bar{r} = s_1\bar{r}_1 + (1 - s_1)\bar{r}_2$, and the variance of this return would be $E(\tilde{r} - \bar{r})^2 = s_1^2 E(\tilde{r} - \bar{r})^2 + (1 - s_1^2)E(\tilde{r} - \bar{r})^2 + 2s_1^2(1 - s_1^2)\text{Cov}(\tilde{r}_1, \tilde{r}_2)$. If the two crops have the same distribution of returns but their returns are uncorrelated (i.e., their covariance is zero), the variance reduces to $s_1^2 E(\tilde{r} - \bar{r})^2 + (1 - s_1^2)E(\tilde{r} - \bar{r})^2$, which can be minimized by allocating half of the land to each crop, which yields an overall variance equal to half the variance of each of the crops individually. However, more generally, with a non-zero covariance, particularly with a negative covariance between the two crops, a farmer would have been willing to trade off some of the crop with the higher expected return to get some of the insurance provided by the covariance with the crop with the lower expected return. The extent to which this would be done would have depended on a farmer's preferences for expected return and risk, as shown in Figure 2.7. Curve TT is the transformation curve of the portfolio's (the portfolio of the farmer's two crops) expected return for different proportions of the land allocated to the two crops. The curve is the parabola of a quadratic equation (the formula for the variance is a quadratic); it will have a straight-edged cone shape as the covariance between the two crops' expected returns approaches -1, will approach a straight vertical line as the covariance approaches $+1$, and will have a modest bulge to the left with a zero covariance (see Jones 2014, 232–233, Figures 7.21 and 7.22). Curves I_1 and I_2 in Figure 2.7 are a farmer's indifference curves between expected return and the standard deviation (the square root of the variance) of expected return. The most preferred choice of crop combination will be determined by a tangency between the transformation curve and an indifference curve. A farmer with indifference curve I_1 has a greater preference for return relative to risk than does a farmer with indifference curve I_2. Accordingly, the farmer with the greater taste for risk (with indifference curve I_2) will choose a higher proportion of the riskier crop.

Similar reasoning would apply to the choice or use of scattered parcels. Of course, parcels would not be as easily adjusted as acreage under various crops, as many farmers might inherit whatever set of scattered land parcels they may have, with only occasional opportunity to adjust them through sale and purchase. Nevertheless, the application of various inputs to different parcels, in anticipation of the return per unit of input on different parcels, would take the form of the portfolio adjustment described above for

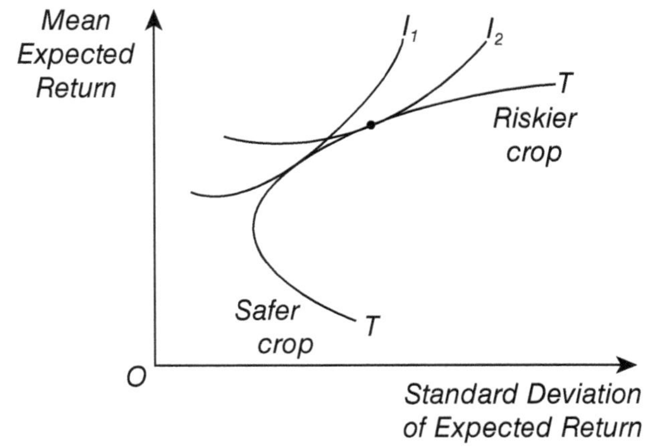

Figure 2.7. Portfolio analysis of alternative agricultural projects or crop choices.

crops. For both crop choices and use of parcels, portfolio optimization, once accomplished—howsoever informally, of course—probably would not change a lot over the years, unless the productivity of crops or land changed noticeably.

It may also be possible to choose farming techniques so as to reduce risk. The types of non-labor inputs, principally capital equipment (however primitive), might be subjects of choice, as possibly such choices of depth of plowing, the timing of various operations, fallowing rotation, manuring, irrigation if any, and many other options. When most seed was saved out of the previous harvest, seed type would not be an important element of most farmers' choices for reducing—or taking on more—risk. Practices such as intercropping might qualify. Some of these choices might not be subject to marginal adjustments to reach optimal quantities, but rather adjustable only discretely, with alternative choices either falling short of delivering sufficient risk adjustment to justify them or offering more compensation than would be strictly necessary.

An Alternative Approach to Risk: Safety First Rather than Expected Profit Maximixation. Rather than maximizing income or profit, some poor farm households may implement a type of safety-first principle, in which the object is to minimize the likelihood of some catastrophe occurring (Moscardi and Janvry 1977; Qazi Shahabuddin, Mestelman, and Feeny 1986). The problem can be formulated as Max y^e subject to $\Pr(y^e \leq d) \leq \alpha$, in which the agent maximizes expected income subject to the probability of expected income falling below the disaster level d is less than some chance α. The first-order condition for choice of agricultural inputs with this model has the form $w_i = p^e_Q(\Delta Q^e/\Delta X_i) + [(d - y^e)/\sigma_{y^e}](\Delta\sigma_{y^e}/\Delta X_i)$, in which w_i is the price of input i, p^e_Q is the expected price of the crop, Q^e is the expected output of the crop, X_i is the amount of the input applied (notice that it is not an expected value, since the farmer has direct control over it, if not over its productivity), and $\sigma^2_{y^e}$ is the variance of the farm's expected income. The risk coefficient, $\Psi = (d - y^e)/\sigma_{y^e}$ gives the impact of the risk on the decision maker, in which the relative magnitude of d and y^e determine whether the household is able to trade expected return for reduced risk (d > y^e) or is forced to gamble (d > y^e). In the gamble, if the disaster level of income is larger than the income the household can expect to make from its farming operations, the household has to take on risk to maximize its chances of survival by devoting greater resources to riskier but higher-expected-profit crops.

An alternative expression of the first-order condition on input choice highlights the reliability of a particular input: $w_i = p_Q(\Delta Q^e/\Delta X_i)[1 - k(s)c_{y^e}]$, where c_{y^e} is the coefficient of variation of the crop (its standard deviation—the square root of the variance—divided by its mean) and k(s) is the marginal rate of substitution between expected net income and risk, a measure of risk aversion, which is a function of household characteristics s.

Marketed Surplus. In subsistence and semi-subsistence agriculture, the quantity of agricultural output that reaches markets is better conceptualized as marketed surplus rather than a supply function although the latter is quite appropriate to use for predominantly cash crops grown on semi-subsistence farms. As the term itself suggests, marketed surplus is simply the difference between a farm's production and its consumption. Nevertheless, within this conceptual simplicity a number of different formulations of the problem can be modeled, differences revolving largely around timing of different activities and responses.

First, price can affect marketed surplus, but the price at harvest time will not affect production, which was determined within the usual parameters of uncertainty at planting time. Anticipated price at the time of planting will have influenced production, but not the price at harvest. The price at harvest time will, however, affect consumption. Second, the timing of the release of output by a farm need not be limited strictly to the period immediately post-harvest, which implies that household inventories are involved in the problem, which now becomes intertemporal. Third, how the households involved are modeled also makes a difference to results of analysis. Specifying household production introduces a profit effect of a price change in addition to an income effect and can change the sign of the response of marketed surplus to a price change, eliciting a positive own-price consumption response and a negative marketed surplus response.

The Basics of Marketed Surplus Response. For the first model, consider marketed surplus in a small village community, which is largely closed to inflows and outflows of agricultural products. Farmers allocate the total production of the crop under consideration, Q, among consumption, net payments to non-farmers in the village, N, and marketed surplus, yielding the accounting identity $Q \equiv C + N + M$.[20] Since production Q doesn't depend on the current (harvest-period) price, it can be considered exogenous in the short-run, as are the payments to non-farmers, and the farmers' immediate decision is to allocate Q – N between consumption and sales. Since Q – N is fixed (exogenous), a choice of either C or M determines both, so marketed surplus really involves only one decision. Focusing on the consumption decision, which has considerable theory to support its analysis, the farmers' consumption of the crop will depend on its relative price, p, and their net income, Y^f, which includes the income from sales of the crop. Accordingly, $C = C(p, Y^f)$. Since marketed surplus M is determined as a residual and can be specified as $M = K - C(p, Y^f) = M(p, Y^f, K)$, where $K = Q - N$. The non-farmers' demand for the crop, D^n, is a function of the crop's price and their income, Y^n: $D^n = D(p, Y^n)$. Since part of non-cultivators' demand for the crop will come out of the payments of crop made to them by farmers, marketed surplus will be $M = D^n - N$.

Gross farm income depends on the value of the crop and other income farmers may receive, Y^{fo}, which is considered exogenous to the current problem, so $Y^f = pK + Y^{fo}$, which indicates that the portion of the crop farmers consume, evaluated at the sale price of the marketed surplus, is included in their income. Income of the non-farmers in the community will likely depend on the level and possibly the composition of the farmers' income, and non-farm income can be specified as $Y^n = y(Y^f, Y^{fo}, p, Q, N, Y^{fol})$, where Y^{fol} is the percent of Y^{fo} derived from animal husbandry activities, to represent how the composition of farm income may affect non-farm income, although the diversification of crops certainly could affect non-farm income as well.

From these model components, the short-run price elasticity of marketed surplus is $(\Delta M/\Delta p)(p/M) = \eta_{Mp} = \varepsilon_{Mp} + \varepsilon_{MY}$, where the ε_{Mi} are the pure price and income elasticities of marketed surplus. An equivalent elasticity can be expressed as comprised of farmers' price and income elasticities of demand for this crop: $\eta_{fp} = -b(\varepsilon_{cp} + s_K\varepsilon_{cy})$, in which b = C/M, or the ratio of consumption to marketed surplus, and $s_K = pK/Y^f$, the share of net crop income (net of payments to non-farmers, N) in total farm income.

The value of ε_{cp} has been estimated as negative, as is intuitive, and in the range of -2 to -3 in the Ghanian grain case studied by Haessel, as is the estimated value of ε_{MY}, which has values from around -0.9 to -1.1. The estimated values of ε_{cy} and ε_{Mp} are both positive, the former taking values in the range of 0.6 to 0.9 and the later values from around 3.0 to nearly 3.5. The overall estimate of η_{fp} ranges from 2.75 to 3.3. So with this model specification, a higher own-price that a household can get for a crop will reduce its consumption of the crop. The income effect of the price change increases consumption (note that this is not an ordinary income effect since the higher price of a consumption good would reduce a household's effective income) and decreases marketed surplus. The net effect of a higher price in this case, however, is strongly positive. Thus, while output elasticities are often small, marketed surplus elasticities can be quite large (Haessel 1975, 114).

Marketed Surplus Explicitly Modeling Farm Household Production. To incorporate household production, simplify the structure of the transactions slightly, specifying

[20] The model is from Haessel (1975, 111–112).

marketed surplus of good i as $M_i = Q_i(\mathbf{p}, \mathbf{z}, \mathbf{k}) - C_i(\mathbf{p}, \eta, A, p_L T(\mathbf{m}), +\pi(\mathbf{p}, \mathbf{z}, \mathbf{k}))$.[21] In this formulation, Q_i is household output of good i (which could be labor as well as a crop), C_i is the household's consumption of that good, **p** is a vector of prices, **z** is a vector of farm characteristics including fixed inputs, **k** is a vector of technology parameters, η is household characteristics affecting tastes, A is exogenous income, p_L is the price of labor, **m** is a vector of household characteristics determining total household time T, and π is farm profits. The household's full income is $A + p_L T + \pi$, which is a function of prices, production technology including fixed inputs, and household characteristics determining total time availability.

The elasticity of marketed surplus with respect to the price of any good j is $(\Delta M_i/\Delta p_j)(p_j/|M_i|) = (\Delta Q_i/\Delta p_j)(p_j/Q_i)(Q_i/|M_i|) - (\Delta C_i/\Delta p_j)(p_j/C_i)(C_i/|M_i|)$, which is the weighted difference of elasticities of output and quantity consumed. The weights are the ratios, respectively of output and quantity consumed to the absolute value of marketed surplus, since marketed surplus could be negative. Simplifying, the expression is $\eta = s_{QM}\varepsilon_{Qpj} - s_{CM}\varepsilon_{Cpj}$, where the s_{jM} are ratios of output and consumption to marketed surplus. The total price elasticity of consumption can be written as $\varepsilon_{Cp_j} = \varepsilon_{Cp_j}|_{\Delta u=0} - s_{Cy}\varepsilon_{Cy} + \varepsilon_{Cy}s_{\pi y}\varepsilon_{\pi p_j}$, which adds a profit effect into the effect of income on consumption, which is the major contribution of explicit consideration of household production in estimates of marketed surplus response to price.

Strauss provides estimates of the supply effect which are quite small—generally around 0.1 or smaller—for a range of farm products, for Sierra Leone households. However, the marketed surplus elasticities are considerably higher and typically are highest for poorer households. For example, the output elasticity of rice is 0.11 while its marketed surplus elasticity is 0.89 for the poorest households and 0.71 on average. For root crops and other cereals, the output elasticity is 0.10, while the marketed surplus elasticity for the poorest households is 3.1, and 0.46 on average. Some cross-price elasticities of marketed surplus are relatively large and negative, in the range of -0.2 to -0.4, because of strong profit effects on consumption. In fact, holding profits constant in many instances would yield a positive marketed surplus elasticity whereas letting them vary as a product price increases yields a negative surplus elasticity (Strauss 1984, 326–329).

Marketed Surplus Coming out of Stocks instead of Current Production. The two previous models have taken output, consumption and sales as occurring at the same time, which may not be the case within a given crop cycle. In the model presented next, the output from which marketed surplus is drawn exists as currently held inventories, hold-over from a recent harvest, or both.[22] Stocks on hand and expected future output may influence short-run marketing decisions, but principally through wealth effects on consumption. Semi-subsistence households have two principal motivations for holding inventories of staple foods: to minimize reliance on local markets to satisfy their basic food needs by holding stocks as a contingency against unanticipated supply disruptions, and as a possible source of profit from seasonal price movements.

The household produces a single storable food commodity, X_1, that it either consumes or trades for a composite commodity, X_2, and derives its utility from consuming these two goods and leisure, X_L: $U_t = U(X_{1t}, X_{2t}, X_{Lt})$. It maximizes its expected discounted stream of current and future utilities through the end of the current crop cycle, each of which is comprised of T+1 periods (0, . . . , T), extending from harvest to harvest. Cycles overlap in the sense that period T of one cycle coincides with period 0 of the next. At the beginning of each cycle, Q_0 of the crop is harvested. In each period, the household sells or buys a quantity M of the crop at price p_1 (> 0 for sales and < 0 for purchases), consumes X_{1t} of the commodity it produces, and purchases X_{2t} of the composite good at price p_{2t}. The portion of marketable surplus not sold or consumed in a given period is stored, and the disappearance of the crop in period t is governed by the stock identity, $I_t - I_{t+1} + Q_t = X_{1t} + M_t$, where I_t and I_{t+1} are carry-in and carry-out inventory levels and Q_t is the household's output of the crop in period t. Production of the crop is a function of one variable input, labor, and one fixed input, land: $Q_T = Q(L_0, \ldots, L_{T-1}; A_0)$, indicating that the crop appears only at the end of the cycle, in period T, i.e., $Q_t = 0$ for all periods $t = 1, \ldots T-1$, while labor inputs are applied throughout the crop season and the land input is chosen at the beginning of the season. Total labor in each period, L_t, includes both family and hired labor.

The 1-period cost of carrying inventories from period t to t+1 is $C(I_{t+1}, X_{1t}) = a_0 + \frac{1}{2} f^{-1} \bullet (I_{t+1} - g_0 - gX_{1t})^2$, where a_0, f, g_0, and g are positive parameters, with f and g representing the strength of the arbitrage and food security motives for holding inventories. This expression says that inventory costs have two offsetting components, the physical cost of holding stocks, which increases in the amount held till the end of the period, and a convenience yield expressed as a linear function of consumption. The latter effect is the value to the household of being able to meets its demand for this commodity out of its own stocks.

The household's sources of cash income are sales of its agricultural crop, off-farm labor earnings at wage p_{Lt}, and exogenous non-wage income, Y_t. The household can borrow an amount B at the 1-period interest rate r. Its expenditures are on commodity purchases, storage, production, and loan repayments. Each period it faces the budget constraint $p_{1t}M_t + p_{Lt}(F_t - L_t) + Y_t + B_t = p_{2t}X_{2t} + C(\bullet,\bullet) + (1+r)B_{t-1}$, where F_t is family labor. If $F_t - L_t > 0$, the household is a net supplier of labor to the labor market. For simplicity, the model assumes that markets exist for all the commodities and labor, that the household cannot

[21] This model is from Strauss (1984, 321–322).

[22] The model is from Renkow (1990, 665–668).

influence any prices, and that hired and family labor are perfect substitutes. A time constraint completes the model. In each period, the total time available to the household, T^* is allocated between leisure, X_{Lt} and labor, F_t: $T^* = X_{Lt} + F_t$.

The household maximizes its utility subject to the constraints of the inventory identity, the production function, the inventory cost relationship, and its budget and time constraints. Solving the inventory identity for M_t and the time constraint for F_t. Then substituting those solutions and the production function into the budget constraint yields the Lagrangean $\mathcal{L} = E_t \sum_{s=t}^{T} b^{s-t}\{U(X_{1s}, X_{2s}, X_{Ls}) + \lambda_s[p_{Ls}(T^* - X_{Ls} - L_s) + p_{1s}(Q_s + I_s - I_{s-1} - X_{1s}) + B_s + Y_s - p_{2s}X_{2s} - C(I_{s+1}, X_{1s}) - (1-r)B_{s-1}]\}$, where the control variables for the maximization are X_{1t}, X_{2t}, X_{Lt}, I_{t+1}, B_t, and L_t., E_t is the expectation operator conditional on information available at time t (which is the current and past values of the control variables and prices), and $b = (1+r)^{-1}$ is the discount factor.

The fact that the output from which marketed surplus is drawn exists as inventories or new production, both of which are predetermined (remember that some of the most important production decisions, such as cropped acreage, were made at the beginning of the season) affects the response of marketed surplus to its own price. The response of marketed surplus in the inventory identity above to changes in its own price is $\Delta M_t/\Delta p_{1t} = -\Delta X_{1t}/\Delta p_{1t} - \Delta I_{t+1}/\Delta p_{1t}$. Rearranging the first-order conditions for optimal choices of amount to borrow and end-of-period inventory level and substituting the inventory cost expression shown earlier yields $I_{t+1} = g_0 + f(bE_tp_{1t+1} - p_{1t}) + gX_{1t}$, which gives the optimal end-of-period inventory holding as a function of expected price appreciation (the second term) and the value of supporting current consumption (the third term). Expanding upon the inventory response term in the expression for the own-price response of marketed surplus yields $\Delta I_{t+1}/\Delta p_{1t} = (\Delta I_{t+1}/\Delta E_t p_{1t+1})(\Delta E_t p_{1t+1}/\Delta p_{1t}) + (\Delta I_{t+1}/\Delta p_{1t})(\Delta X_{1t}/\Delta p_{1t}) = -f(1 - b\Delta E_t p_{1t+1}/\Delta p_{1t}) + g\Delta X_{1t}/\Delta p_{1t}$. Substituting this back into the initial expression for the own-price response of marketed surplus yields $\Delta M_t/\Delta p_{1t} = -(1+g)\Delta X_{1t}/\Delta p_{1t} + f(1 - b\Delta E_t p_{1t+1}/\Delta p_{1t})$, which decomposes that response into releases from foregone consumption and inventories, although the release from inventories is dampened by retentions in anticipation of a higher price the next period. If the effect on the expected future price of a price increase this period is positive, its magnitude will generally be less than 1, and the discount factor b will further reduce this effect, so on balance the releases from inventories in response to an own-price increase will produce a positive marketed surplus response. However, the overall sign of $\Delta M_t/\Delta p_{1t}$ will still depend on the price responsiveness of consumption: normally an increase in a product's price will reduce consumption of it, but the household experiences a profit effect as well as a higher consumption cost when the price of its crop increases.

To decompose the consumption effect into a pure price response and a wealth effect, one of the first-order conditions from the maximization of the Lagrangean implies that the demand function for the good the household produces and sells can be expressed as $X_{1t} = X(p_{1t}, p_{2t}, p_{1t+1}, W_t)$, where W_t is the household's wealth in period t, $W_t = Y_t + [p_{1t}(I_t + Q_t) + b^{T-t}E_t(p_{1t}Q_t - \sum_s p_{Ls}L_s)] + p_{Lt}T^* = Y_t + \Pi_t + p_{Lt}T^*$, in which profits, Π_t, include expected net revenue over the planning horizon. Using this specification of current-period wealth, the effect of a change in p_{1t} on current consumption is $\Delta X_{1t}/\Delta p_{1t} = \Delta X_{1t}/\Delta p_{1t}|_{\Delta\Pi=0} + (\Delta X_{1t}/\Delta\Pi_t)(\Delta\Pi_t/\Delta p_t) = \Delta X_{1t}/\Delta p_{1t}|_{\Delta U=0} - X_{1t}\Delta X_{1t}/\Delta W_t + [I_t + Q_t + \hat{Q}_t\Delta\hat{p}_{1T}/\Delta p_{1t} + \hat{p}_{1T}(\Delta\hat{Q}_{1T}/\Delta\hat{p}_{1T})(\Delta\hat{p}_{1T}/\Delta p_{1t}]\Delta X_{1t}/\Delta W_t$, in which the $\hat{\bullet}_T$ notation indicates an expected present value of a variable at time T. The first term in the last equality is the usual price effect on consumption, which is negative. The second term is the usual income effect of a change in price, which for a price increase also has a negative effect on consumption. The third term, in brackets, is the profit effect which is a function of stocks on hand, $I_t + Q_t$, expected future profits based on the price change, and the household's mechanism for forming price expectations.

Using household data from western India, Renkow finds that profit effects are large enough to turn ordinarily negative demand elasticities for foodgrains positive (Renkow 1990, 670–674). Statistically significant evidence of arbitrage motives in inventory demand (parameter f in the inventory cost relationship above) is present only for the largest farms; significant current food security motives (parameter g in the inventory cost formulation) for holding inventories appear for large and medium-sized farms but only weakly for the smallest. Marketed surplus was negative for all three sizes of farm during the lean season (the two quarters preceding harvest), meaning that they are net buyers, and the estimated response of these purchases to price increases indicates that a price increase leads to more market purchases. During the harvest season (the two quarters during and succeeding harvest), marketed surplus of all three farm sizes is positive and the marketed surplus response to price increases is uniformly negative, in the range of -1, indicating that these households respond to price increases for their products by increasing consumption, presumably by virtue of strong profit effects.

2.3.3 Production when Output is Both a Consumption Good and a Capital Good

For most field crops, a substantial fraction of production in ancient times had to be withheld from consumption to provide seed for the next season's crop. For many crops, 25 percent would have represented the typical hold-back ratio. What was consumed this year couldn't be used to grow next year's crop, and if people were still hungry this year, their most immediate mechanism for alleviating that hunger would have been to take a chance on tightening their belts next year. Purchase from outside the community, of course, may have been an option, but not necessarily always. The possibility of famine presents another type of constraint on outside purchases in instances of local productivity shocks. Abstracting from possibilities of outside supplementation, farming communities faced an inter-temporal trade-off between food, and possibly survival, this year and food and possibly survival next year. This interposes a capital-good aspect to what otherwise is commonly thought of as a consumption problem. With most field crops, the time from seed to edible crop is ordinarily a year, and although several years might be required to return to a long-term seed stock level after a sharply bad season, the return to the long-term allocation of a crop between consumption and seed need not take a decade. The case with animals is similar in movements but different in response time. An animal slaughtered for food this year can't breed next year to produce meat for the table in subsequent years, but animals take several years to reach breeding maturity, and changes in slaughter ages induced by either a good or bad disturbance to the local economy can create fluctuations in herd size for years. Nonetheless, for both field crops and animal husbandry, rational responses to market disturbances can produce consumption and supply responses that appear to be perverse or irrational yet are neither.

In both cases—field crops and animals—the nature of the disturbance to ordinary expectations is important. A disturbance, or shock, is a displacement of the outcome of a random (stochastic) variable from its normal, or expected value. Such a disturbance can be short-lived or transitory, lasting only a single season, or it can be more lasting, even permanent. Disturbances can act directly upon productivity, such as weather events or pest infestations or disease, or they can act on demand or on other aspects of production costs. The duration of a disturbance can affect the responses to it—assuming, of course, that the farmers correctly anticipate the duration, which need not always be the case. Mistaking a permanent disturbance for a transient one can be disastrous, as an improper response may be impossible to correct. The source of the disturbance—demand, productivity, cost—will determine the direction of effect on outcomes and may affect the duration of the disturbance. Most disturbances surely were within the experience of farmers of the time and they had reasonably accurate expectations of source and duration, hence the utility of assuming rational expectations in the models presented below. By rational expectations is meant simply that people understand the processes at work well enough to forecast their consequences fairly well (see Jones 2014, Chapter 7, section 5 on rational expectations).

The models presented below of farmers' responses to disturbances in seed crops and animal husbandry are, frankly, complicated, as are most inter-temporal models. I have endeavored to simplify where possible, explain, and suggest just accepting some intermediate steps where necessary to get to a result.

Crops with Seeds Held Back. Many crops are capital goods as well as consumption goods.[23] An inter-temporal trade-off is required by the fact that a sizeable fraction of a crop is needed for seed, and these inter-temporal choices affect supply decisions. This produces unusual market dynamics. Seed crop capital is an important part of total production. Adjustment of seed stock inventory affects supply decisions in ways that can confuse demand and supply responses in many situations. For example, when demand increases, short-term consumption can fall, and when quantity supplied decreases, consumption can increase.

Begin the model with the production function, $Q_{t+1} = (1+g)S_t$, $g > 0$, where Q_t is the total crop output, g is the net reproductive rate (which subsumes other inputs in the model), and S_t is the size of the seed crop. A magnitude of g in the range of 5 to 6 probably would not be out of line with ancient seed productivity.[24] Total output is allocated between consumption and the seed crop inventory: $Q_t = C_t + S_t$, where C_t is consumption. Consumption contains no inter-temporal elements. Market demand is $C_t = C(p_t)$, where p_t is the price of the crop. Supply is determined by farmers' decisions to either sell their crops for immediate consumption or hold some over the season for seed. The return from selling is the current price p_t (ignoring labor inputs). Withholding a unit of stock and replanting it produces 1+g units of crop the following season, which can be sold for the expected price p_{t+1}. Let the direct marginal cost of planting and storage be k(S), $\Delta k/\Delta S \geq 0$, and r be the interest rate. The marginal return to replanting is $Gp_{t+1} - k(s)$, which is the inter-temporal arbitrage relationship, where $G = (1+g)/(1+r)$. If $G > 1$, the crop is renewed; if $G < 1$, renewal is not economic and cultivation ceases. The inter-temporal arbitrage relationship is one restriction on the paths of stocks and supply prices. Combining the demand function, the production function and the production-consumption-storage identity, the stock-flow dynamics imply another restriction, $S_{t+1} - S_t = gS_t - C(p_{t+1})$: the change in seed stocks between time periods is equal to the reproductive rate of the seed stock stored in the previous period minus the consumption demand expected next period.

If supply and demand are unchanging over time, the long-run equilibrium values of p, C, Q and S are determined by the production-consumption-storage identity, the arbitrage relationship and the stock-flow relationship governing the growth of seed stock, with $p_t = p_{t-1} = \ldots = \mathbf{p}$ and $S_t = S_{t-1} = \ldots = \mathbf{S}$. Using the steady-state price and seed stock, the inter-temporal arbitrage relationship can be written as $\mathbf{p} = k(\mathbf{S})/G\text{-}1$, which says that the long-run supply price is the marginal planting and carrying cost of inventory grossed up by the inverse of the net internal rate of return from growing the crop. Renewal implies that this rate of

[23] This model is from Rosen (1999).

[24] Baer (1963, 12, n. 79), estimates roughly 10% of barley and emmer crops withheld for seed ca. 2000 B.C.E.

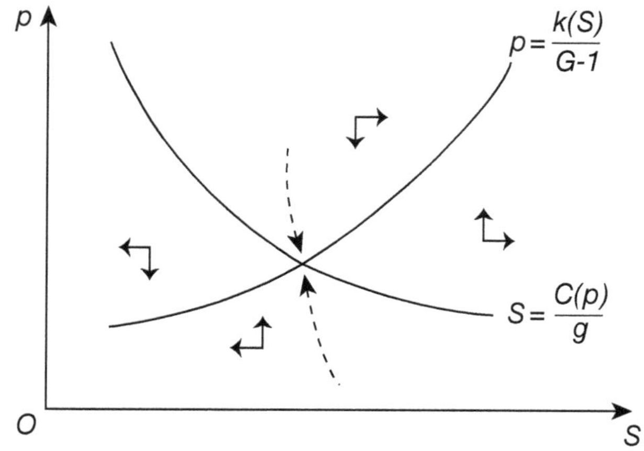

Figure 2.8. Dynamics of seed crop (S) and potato price (p) (Reproduced from Rosen 1999, figure 1, p. S298, by permission of the University of Chicago Press.).

return, $G-1 = (g-r)/(1+r)$, is positive. When marginal cost is increasing in S, this relationship defines an upward sloping curve in the **p-S** plane in Figure 2.8.[25]

At these steady-state values, the stock-flow relationship describes the seed inventory required to sustain long-run consumption as $\mathbf{S} = C(\mathbf{p})/g$. Using the long-run supply-price relationship, the inter-temporal arbitrage relationship can be re-written as a price-change relationship relating period-to-period price changes in terms of deviations from steady-state values: $p_{t+1} - p_t = (1\text{-}G)(p_{t+1} - \underline{p}) - [k(\mathbf{S}) - k(S_t)]$. The first term of this expression is the intertemporal aribitrage relationship between the productivity of seed stock and the interest rate; the second term is the difference in the storage cost of the stock that has varied from the steady-state stock, which dampens returns of price to its steady-state level as long as $\Delta k/\Delta S_t > 0$. Since $1\text{-}G < 0$, the price change $p_{t+1} - p_t < 0$ for all values of p and S above the curve defined by $\mathbf{p} = k(\mathbf{S})/(g\text{-}1)$ in Figure 2.8 and > 0 for all values of p and S below it. Similarly with the steady-state seed inventory relationship, which can be re-written as $S_{t+1} - S_t = g(S_t - \mathbf{S}) - [C(p_{t+1}) - C(\mathbf{p})]$, in which the first term represents the natural increment of the differential seed stock from the production function, the second term being the difference in consumption associated with the price at the date in the period immediately following the initial jump from the steady-state (long-term) price and the steady-state price. From this relationship seed inventory is growing for any values of p and S to the right of the curve defined by $\mathbf{S} = C(\mathbf{p})/g$ and falling for values to the left of that curve. Trajectories follow the arrows that converge on the intersection of the **p** and **S** curves in Figure 2.8. In Figure 2.8, transitory (1-period) shocks have spill-over effects on future periods. For example, if a 1-year crop failure reduces the initial seed stock below its steady-state level, price jumps initially and thereafter declines to its long-run value as seed inventories grow back to their normal level. After a shock hits, larger seed inventories are needed to sustain long-run customary consumption. The high initial price discourages current consumption and encourages accumulation of seed inventory, but prices fall thereafter as production and inventory return to their steady-state levels. The recovery is drawn out in time. The speed of adjustment will vary according to the magnitudes of g and r.

Permanent shocks to demand or supply shift both steady-state curves in Figure 2.7, as shown in Figure 2.8. For example, an unanticipated but thereafter permanent increase in demand shifts the **S** curve in Figure 2.8 upward and to the right. If the seed stock is too small when the shock occurs, the price initially rises to discourage consumption and encourage holding more crop for seed. The high price gradually falls thereafter to the higher steady-state value as consumption increases. The quantity supplied to the consumption market can decrease initially in response to a permanent increase in demand, which is intuitive once the capital aspect of the crop is recognized. As an example of an unanticipated but permanent supply shock, suppose productivity g falls and remains smaller forever because of, say, the arrival of a new plant disease. Depending on initial conditions, demand elasticities and other parameters, a permanent negative supply shock can cause price to fall initially. A decrease in g reduces the return to cultivation in the long-run marginal cost relationship and raises the minimum long-run supply price $k(\mathbf{S})/(G\text{-}1)$. The $\underline{p}$ curve shifts up, shown in Figure 2.9. Sustaining any given level of consumption in the long run requires larger seed stock inventories: $C(\mathbf{p})/g$ increases, and the **S** curve shifts to the right. Both forces guarantee a higher market price in the long run, but the effect on seed inventory could go in either direction. If, when a shock hits, the initial stock is less than the new steady-state stock, the productivity decline causes the price to rise to limit consumption and encourage accumulation. But if the initial stock exceeds the long-run target, the price initially falls to induce capital consumption. Whether target inventories rise or fall depends on the elasticity of demand for the crop. Variation of g in the long-run marginal cost and seed inventory relationships yield the following relationships of g to long-run price and seed stocks: $\Delta \log \mathbf{p}/\Delta g = -\{[1-(r/g)]+\varepsilon\}/\varepsilon(g-r)[1-(\eta/\varepsilon)] < 0$ and $\Delta \log \mathbf{S}/\Delta g = -\{\eta + [1-(r/g)]\}/(g-r)[1-(\eta/\varepsilon)]$, in which η is the elasticity of demand and ε is the elasticity of long-run supply. The first of these expressions shows that long-run price always increases in g. The sign of the seed stock response is ambiguous however. It is positive or negative according to whether the absolute value of the demand elasticity is greater or smaller than $1 - (r/g)$. If demand is sufficiently elastic, **S** falls when seed productivity g falls, and steady-state consumption decreases so much that steady-state inventories decrease despite the fact that more seed crop is required. In this case, the adverse shock could cause

[25] Figure 2.8 is a phase diagram, which is more intricate than a diagram of ordinary algebraic relations such as a supply-demand graph. The curves in a phase diagram are the combinations of values of variables for which a differential or difference equation yield a zero value for the equation. In other words, the relationship represented by the equation is at rest, or in equilibrium, at any point along the line. The diagram is used to consider how displacements from equilibrium will behave, whether they move back toward equilibrium or unstably away from it. From the expression behind each line in a phase diagram, it can be determined whether a displacement of the value of a variable above or below the line will move back toward the line or away from it.

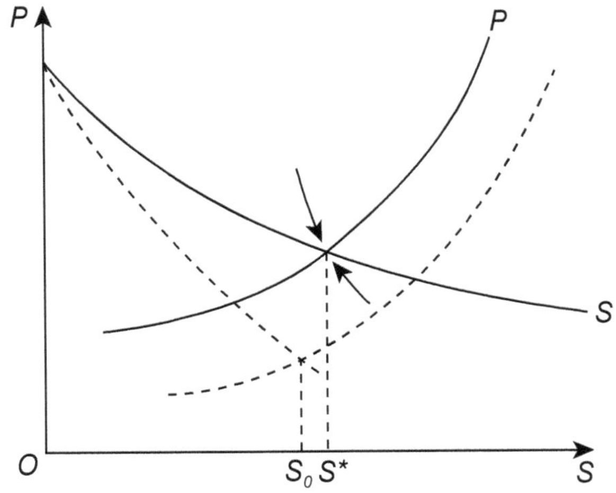

Figure 2.9. Effect of a permanent productivity shock (Reproduced from Rosen 1999, figure 3, page S301, by permission of the University of Chicago Press.).

price to fall and consumption to increase initially, in which case dumping inventory on the market smoothes the necessary price and consumption adjustments instead of worsening them. If demand is sufficiently inelastic, steady-state seed inventories increase when g falls. Since consumption doesn't fall as much, the smaller productivity of seed requires a larger seed stock to sustain it. In this case, the inter-temporal stock adjustments exacerbate the price and consumption movements.

If the crop can be fed to animals as well as eaten by people, the elasticity of derived demand for the crop fed to the animals tends to be larger than the demand elasticity for human consumption since farmers have additional possibilities for inter-temporal adjustments of animal stocks. When feed is expensive, breeding stock is sold off or consumed. The crop is released for human consumption although substitution is limited because animals eat lower-quality varieties of a crop. Animal stocks are replaced later. Fewer females are slaughtered and more are bred when feed becomes more plentiful and cheaper.

Animals. In executing inventory decisions about breeding stocks of animals, low fertility rates of cows and substantial lags and future feedback between fertility and consumption decisions cause the demographic structure of herds to respond cyclically to exogenous shocks in demand and production costs.[26] Cattle, as well as sheep and goats among the principal domesticated animal species, are both consumption and capital goods. In the United States presently, the reproductive stock accounts for about 40 percent of the total stock of cattle.

An increase in the demand for beef reduces current supply if younger animals are held back to achieve greater slaughter weight or if more females are withheld for reproduction to increase herd size. The model presented below shows how reproductive inventory decisions at the breeding margin combine with production lags to produce cycles in animal stocks.

A cow has at most one calf after a 9-month gestation period, and at the present time the effective reproductive life of a cow is 8 to 10 years, the fertility rate of beef cattle is in the range of 0.80 to 0.95, and the natural death rate is around 10 percent. Gestation and birth delays embody "time to build"[27] features in the age structure of stocks and cause cyclical feedbacks between current consumption and future reproductive decisions. Exogenous shocks have persistent effects by changing the slaughter and breeding stock decisions. Those decisions alter the age distribution of the herd and cause cyclical echo responses as the age distribution converges to its stable equilibrium structure.

The model assumes a 1-year gestation-birth delay and a fixed 2-year maturation lag for both breeding and consumption. With exogenously fixed lags, the critical economic decision is whether to breed or consume a mature female. Some heifers are always slaughtered at maturity; males are strictly inframarginal and can be treated as females marked for slaughter. There are no imports or exports of live animals in the model. Adult stocks are held for breeding or are slaughtered. After a 1-year lag, each animal reserved for breeding gives birth to $g < 1$ calves. At birth, all surviving calves enter a pipeline and remain there for 2 years before joining the adult stock at maturity. Beef quality is invariant to age and breeding history. Mature cows are consumed on equal terms with mature steers and heifers; all adults are treated with an exponential death rate δ. There are only three capital goods in the model: adults, yearlings, and calves. The total number of mature animals is allocated between consumption and breeding stock: $k_t = x_t + c_t$, where k_t is the total number of mature animals in period t, x_t is the breeding stock in that period, and c_t is the number consumed. The gx_{t-1} calves born at time t enter the pipeline. The gx_{t-2} calves born 1 year earlier remain there as yearlings. The head count, y_t, of all stocks is the sum of adults, yearlings, and calves: $y_t = x_t + gx_{t-1} + gx_{t-2}$, in which x_t is the current breeding stock, gx_{t-1} is last year's breeding stock, and gx_{t-2} is the breeding stock 2 years ago. All stocks in the pipeline in Figure 2.11 move up one place each year. A total of c_t adults is sent to slaughter (all steers and a positive fraction of heifers), and δk die of natural causes. The gx_{t-3} yearlings in the pipeline at time t-1 enter the adult herd in period t, so the breeding stock evolves according to $x_t = (1 - \delta)x_{t-1} + gx_{t-3} - c_t$, where gx_{t-3} is last year's yearlings. The three variables x_{t-1}, x_{t-2}, and x_{t-3} represent the state of the population because the current stocks of calves, yearlings and adults are easily calculated from them. Figure 2.11 shows these population relationships graphically.

Farmers choose between breeding and slaughtering adults. Profits are equated at both margins. With constant returns

[26] This model is from Rosen, Murphy, and Scheinkman (1994).

[27] A reference to a business cycle model by Kidland and Prescott (1982), in which the production of capital goods requires multiple time periods, resulting in fluctuations in some variables over time but not in others.

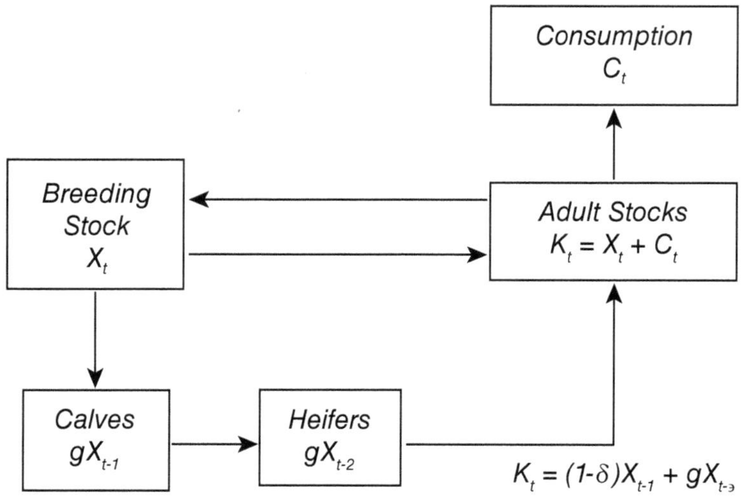

Figure 2.10. Population life cycle and dynamics (Reproduced from Rosen, Murphy, and Scheinkman, 1994, figure 2, page 471, by permission of the University of Chicago Press.).

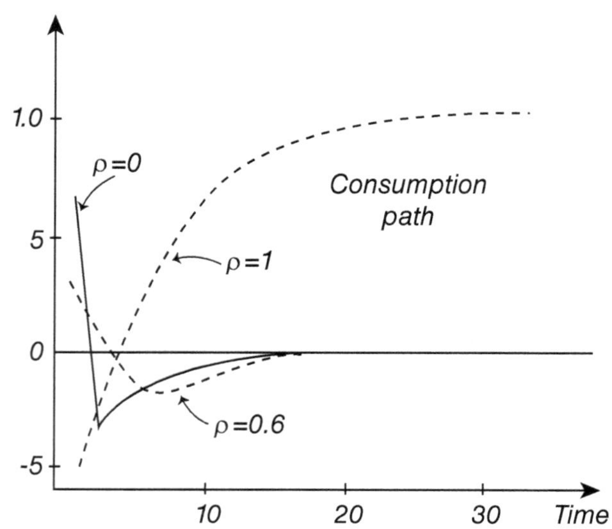

Figure 2.11. Distributed lags of breeding stock (Reproduced from Rosen, Murphy, and Scheinkman, 1994, figure 3b, p. 477, by permission of the University of Chicago Press.).

to scale, the typical farmer's calculation is independent of herd size, and profits are equated on the average as well as on the margin: $q_t = p_t - m_t$ is the net return from selling an animal at time t for consumption, where p_t is the price of the animal on the hoof and m_t is the feeding cost of preparing the animal for slaughter. The return from breeding an adult animal is the opportunity to sell it and its progeny later, minus holding costs and foregone interest. A cow survives with probability 1-δ and is worth $E_t(1-\delta)q_{t+1}$ next year, where E_t is the expectation given information available in period t. The cow's g progeny sit in the pipeline for 2 years and have values $E_t g q_{t+3}$ when they are potentially sold three years from now. The gross return from breeding is $E_t[\beta(1-\delta)q_{t+1} + \beta^3 g q_{t+3}]$, where $\beta = 1/(1+i)$ and i is the interest rate. The net return subtracts holding costs. The discounted holding costs are $z_t = h_t + \beta g \gamma_0 h_{t+1} + \beta^2 g \gamma_1 h_{t+2}$, where h_t is the unit holding cost of an adult, assuming proportional adult equivalent holding costs of $\gamma_0 h_t$ and $\gamma_1 h_t$ for calves and yearlings. In this expression h_t is the holding cost for the breeding cow this year, h_{t+1} is the holding cost for the cow's calf next year, and h_{t+2} is the holding cost for the cow's calf when it's a yearling a year later. With strictly positive supply, market equilibrium requires equal value to both slaughter and breeding: $q_t = E_t[\beta(1-\delta)q_{t+1} + g\beta^3 q_{t+3} - z_t]$, in which the first two terms within the brackets are the gross return from breeding—the first of which is the cow's value next year and the second is its progeny's value when it matures 2 years later—and the z_t term is the holding cost of the cow and its progeny. This expression results from maximizing the discounted expected value of beef production in a competitive market.

Demand and boundary conditions complete the model. Since population dynamics are linear, demand is specified as approximately linear also: $c_t = \alpha_0 - \alpha p_t + d_t = \alpha_0 - \alpha q_t - \alpha m_t + d_t$, where $p - m = q$ (the net return from selling an animal) and d_t is a demand shifter. The six previous relationships can be reduced to two linear third-order difference equations in x_t and q_t: $x_t = (1-\delta)x_{t+1} - g x_{t-3} = -\alpha_0 + \alpha q_t + \alpha m_t - d_t$, which is a rearrangement of the breeding-stock evolution relationship, substituting the demand equation for c_t; and $E_t[q_t - \beta(1-\delta)q_{t+1} - \beta^3 g q_{t+3} + h_t + \beta g \gamma_0 h_{t+1} + \beta^2 g \gamma_1 h_{t+2}] = 0$, in which q_t is the net return from selling the animal this year, the β and β^3 terms are the net returns from holding the animal for breeding over the next two years instead of selling it, and the three h_t terms are the holding costs that have to be subtracted from the returns from breeding. In these two difference equations, if feeding costs (m), holding costs (h) and exogenous influences on demand (d) remain unchanged and the breeding stock (x) and the net return (q) settle down to their steady-state values, two necessary renewal conditions emerge from those relationships, that births exceed deaths, $g - \delta > 0$, and that the gross return from reproduction exceed the return to slaughter at the steady-state price, $\beta^3 g + \beta(1-\delta) - 1 > 0$; if the latter condition isn't satisfied, holding costs wouldn't be covered and the farmer rationally would drive the herd to extinction.

Characteristics of the solution to these two equilibrium relationships are shown graphically as responses to

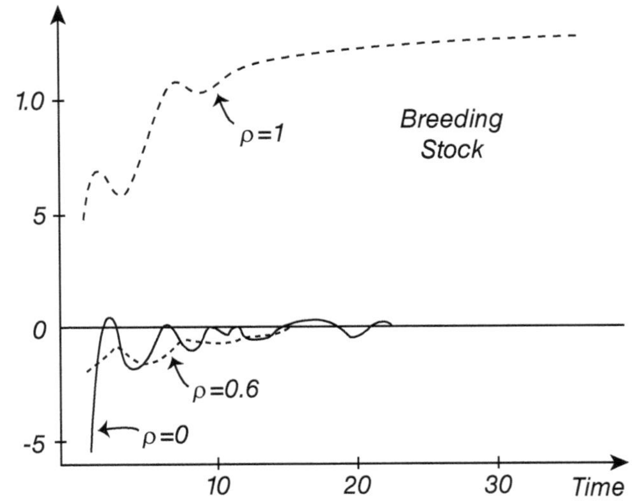

Figure 2.12. Comparison of breeding stock and total stock, $\rho = 0$ (Reproduced from Rosen, Murphy, and Scheinkman, 1994, figure 4a, p. 478, by permission of the University of Chicago Press.).

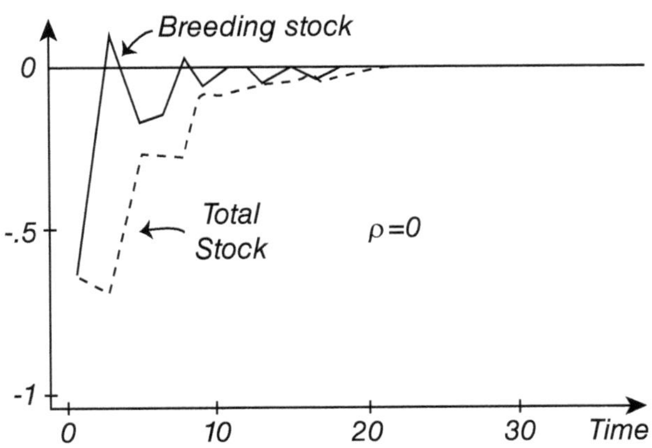

Figure 2.13. Distributed lags of consumption (Reproduced from Rosen, Murphy, and Scheinkman, 1994, figure 3a, p. 477, by permission of the University of Chicago Press.).

alternative types of shocks. The results are cycles of breeding stock size, total stock size, and consumption. These cycles arise from demographic echo effects because the current age distribution constrains future reproductive capacity. Demand and supply shocks cause farmers to change their breeding stock inventories, and those decisions percolate through all future birth cohorts of cattle. These effects generally oscillate for breeding stock but not for consumption or prices in this model, although allowing for inelastic supplies of other productive inputs will yield oscillatory behavior in consumption and prices as well. Figures 2.12 through 2.15 show the responses of stock and consumption to positive, persistent and transitory demand shocks. While the meanings of "persistent" and "transitory" as applied to shocks to an economic system are reasonably intuitive—a persistent shock lasts longer than a transitory one—the terms can be given some more precision by defining the structure of shocks. Suppose the structure of the equilibrium breeding stock relationship has the form $x_t = x^* + u_t^x$, in which x^* is the "normal" value and u_t^x is the deviation from the normal value in period t, or the shock to breeding stock x in period t which causes its

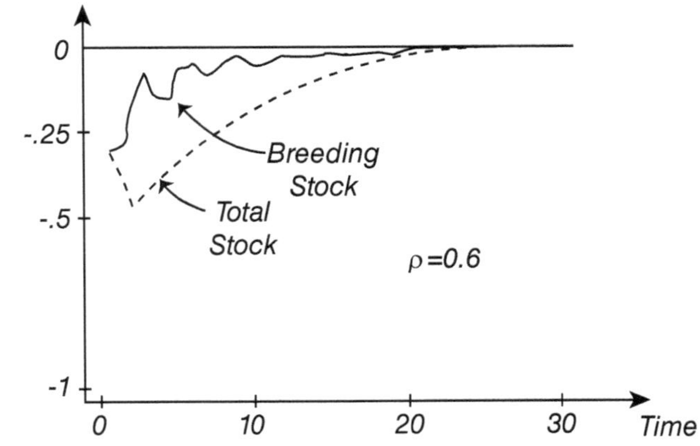

Figure 2.14. Comparison of breeding stock and total stock, $\rho = 0.6$ (Reproduced from Rosen, Murphy, and Scheinkman, 1994, figure 4b, p. 478, by permission of the University of Chicago Press.).

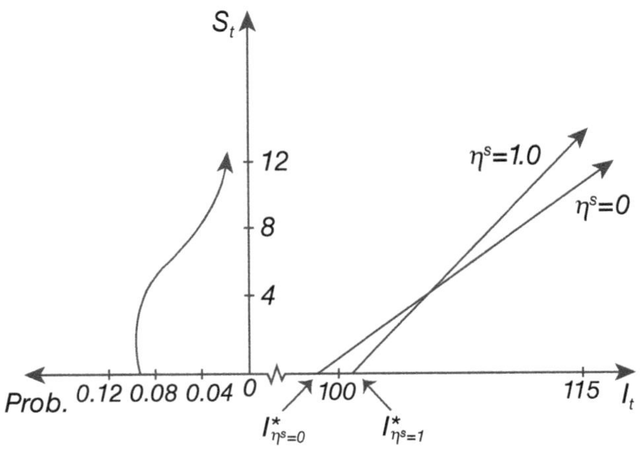

Figure 2.15. Storage rules and distribution (Reproduced from Wright and Williams, 1982, figure 1, p. 600, by permission of Oxford University Press.).

value in that period to move away from what it normally would be. The issue in persistence versus transitoriness is how well the magnitude of a shock in one period predicts the magnitude of a similar shock in following periods, or the serial correlation of the shocks, which is measured by $\rho_x (0 < \rho_x < 1)$ and enters the shock with the structure $u_t^x = \rho_x u_{t-1}^x + \varepsilon_t^x$ in which ε_t^x is pure noise with mean value of zero. The closer ρ_x is to 1, the more persistent is the effect of ε_t^x, whereas a shock term with $\rho_x = 0$ would be a purely transitory shock consisting of only random, non-recurring noise. Shocks are permanent in an economic sense when ρ_x is larger than the overall response speed of the economic system.

With a transitory demand shock, $\rho_x = 0$, adult stocks are sold off and consumption is increased in the period the shock occurs. In Figure 2.11, consumption is reduced later so that stocks can be built back up to sustain normal demand. The initial sell-off of adults disturbs the age distribution of young animals in the pipeline and causes the oscillatory response of the stocks in Figure 2.13. Farmers sell more when demand is high because they anticipate that demand is likely to fall back to normal soon. The dynamics of response are quite different when shocks are permanent, $\rho_x = 1$. Consumption initially falls when demand increases, because farmers know that the increased demand is likely to be sustained for a long time. An above-average number of females must be bred initially to reach the larger herd size necessary to satisfy the higher future demand. Consumption turns positive when stocks get large enough and converges smoothly to its new steady state. Breeding stocks initially increase and then grow cyclically to their new steady state because of the initial disturbance to the age distribution. The responses in Figures 2.12 and 2.13 represent a backward-bending supply response to transitory shocks and the normal rising response to persistent shocks. Figure 2.14 reproduces the response of breeding stock from Figure 2.13, but with the addition of the response of total stock, while Figure 2.14 shows the response of breeding and total stocks to an intermediate degree of permanence of the shock, using a value of $\rho_x = 0.6$.

Further insight can be obtained into the cyclicality of the responses by more detailed analysis of the expectations and error structures.[28] The farmer's expectation at date t of the net price τ quarters in the future is $E_t q_{t+\tau} = \beta^{\tau} q_t + \sum_{t=1}^{\tau} E_t h_{t+\tau-i} \beta^i$, which is a linear function of the current price and expected future costs. For supply to the market, of the number of animals slaughtered, the farmer's expectation is $E_t s_{t+\tau} = \alpha + E_t d_{t+\tau} - \gamma(E_t m_{t+\tau} + E_t q_{T+\tau})$. Substituting the expectation of net price q into the expectation for supply to the market s, and that result into the intertemporal constraint, $x_t = E_t \sum_{\tau}^{\infty} [F(q_{t+\tau} + m_{t+\tau}, d_{t+\tau})]/(1+g)^{\tau}$, where F(•) is the demand function for beef, yields an expression for net price (q) as a function of supply to the market (s) and expectations of future shocks (d). Comparable expressions for s and herd size x can be derived similarly. Values of all three in period t can be expressed as a deviation from the normal value, e.g., $q_t = q^* + u_t^q$.

These deviations can be expressed as shocks, $Q_t = q_t - q^*$., from which three equivalent expressions can be derived, each of which illuminates a different aspect of the dynamics of animal herds. First, some further manipulation yields an expression for Q_t in terms of shocks, the natural reproductive rate, and the interest rate as $Q_t = (1+g-\beta)[-X_t + \sum_{\tau}^{\infty} E_t v_{t+\tau}/(1+g)^{\tau+1}]/\gamma$, where $E_t v_{t+\omega} = u_{t+\tau}^{E_t d} - \gamma u_{t+\tau}^{E_t m} - \gamma\beta u_{t+\tau}^{E_t h}/(1+g-\beta)$, where the notation $u_{t+\tau}^{E_t d}$ is the expectaton at time t of a demand shock τ periods in the future. For supply to the market, similar manipulation yields $S_t = (1+g-\beta)[X_t - \sum_{\tau}^{\infty} E_t v_{t+\varsigma}/(1+g)^{\tau+1}] + u_t^d - \gamma u_t^m$, in which the last two terms are actual disturbances rather than expectations. An expression comparable to that for S_t can be derived for X_{t+1}: $Xt+1 = \beta Xt + (1 + g - \beta) \cdot \sum_{t}^{\infty} E_t v_{t+\tau}/(1+g)^{\tau+1} + u_t^y - \gamma u_t^m$. These three ugly expressions have simple structures: $Q_t = \theta[\varphi_1 \Sigma$ (Expected d-, m-, and h- shocks) $- X_t]$, $S_t = \theta[X_t - \varphi_2 \Sigma$ (Expected d-, m-, and h-shocks)] + actual d- and m-shocks, and $X_{t+1} = \beta X_t + \theta\varphi_2 \Sigma$ (Expected d-, m-, and h-shocks) actual y- and m-shocks. Thus each can be expressed as a sum of appropriately weighted values of X_t, expected shocks, and in some cases, actual shocks.

Second, some manipulations are made with the demand and supply shocks of the expressions for Q_t, S_t, and X_{t+1} which highlight the degree of permanence or transitoriness of the shocks, measured by ρ_j: ρ_j closer to 1 implies more permanence, ρ_j closer to 0, more transitoriness. Substituting the expression for the shock term introduced above into these expressions yields, for net price, $Q_t = (1+g-\beta)\gamma^{-1}[-X_t + u_t^d/(1+g-\rho_d) - \gamma u_t^m/(1+g-\rho_m] - \beta u_t^h/(1+g-\rho_h)$, in which $1+g-\beta > 0$ because g > r. For supply to the market (or number slaughtered or consumption), $S_t = (1+g-\beta)X_t + u_t^d(\beta-\rho_d)/(1+g-\rho_d) - \gamma u_t^m(\beta-\rho_m)/(1+g-\rho_m) + u_t^h\beta\gamma(1+g-\rho_h)$. For next period's herd size, $X_{t+1} = \beta X_t - u_t^d(\beta-\rho_d)/(1+g-\rho_d) + u_t^m\gamma(\beta-\rho_m)/(1+g-\rho_m) - u_t^h\beta\gamma/(1+g-\rho_h)$. From these three complicated-looking expressions (which actually have simple structures when you examine them closely), regardless of the degree of persistence of the disturbances, net price (Q_t) varies positively with the disturbance to the current level of demand (u_t^d) and negatively with the disturbances to the current costs (u_t^m and u_t^h) and with current stocks (X_t). The expression for current supply to the market, S_t, shows that when the shocks are not highly persistent, $\rho_i < \beta$, current supply increases with shocks to current demand and holding cost (h) and decreases with shocks to current marketing cost (m). On the other hand, if the shocks are sufficiently long-lasting, $\rho_i > \beta$, current supply will fall when current demand increases (positive shock to demand) and when current marketing costs increase. These details account for the observation above in Figures 2.11 and 2.12 that supply responds normally to transitory shocks and in a seemingly irrational manner to permanent shocks.

Third, proceeding with further ugly expressions, the reduced-form solutions for price, sales and stock just expressed as functions of current-period stock X_t and properties of current disturbances to cost and demand, can be expressed alternatively in terms of the history of the disturbances ε_τ^j. These expressions use a notation from time-series econometrics called the lag operator, L, which simply means that the variable or expression immediately following it is lagged by the number of periods indicated. For example $LX_t = X_{t-1}$ for all $t > 1$, and $L^k X_t = X_{t-k}$. Since X_t is in the reduced-form expressions for S_t and Q_t above, it is expressed in lag form first so that X_t can be substituted out of the other two reduced forms. Thus $X_t = \frac{L}{1-\beta L}\{-[(\beta-\rho_d)/(1+g-\rho_d)] \cdot (\varepsilon_t^d/1-\rho_d L) + [\gamma(\beta-\rho_m)/(1+g-\rho_m)] \cdot (\varepsilon_t^m/1-\rho_m L) - [\beta\gamma/(1+g-\rho_h)] \cdot (\varepsilon_t^h/1-\rho_h L)\}$, where the ε^i are shocks to variable i. Substituting this expression into the expressions for Q_t and S_t yields $S_t = \frac{1-(1+g)L}{1-\beta L}\{[(\beta-\rho_d)/(1+g-\rho_d)] \cdot (\varepsilon_t^d/1-\rho_d L) - [(\beta-\rho_m)/(1+g-\rho_m)] \cdot (\gamma\varepsilon_t^m/1-\rho_m L) + [\beta\gamma/(1+g-\rho_h)] \cdot (\varepsilon_t^h/1-\rho_h L)\}$ and $Q_t = \frac{1+g-\beta}{1-\beta L}[(\varepsilon_t^d/\gamma)/(1+g-\rho_d) - \varepsilon_t^m/(1+g-\rho_m)] - \beta\varepsilon_t^h[1-(1+$

[28] The expressions presented below are from Rosen (1987). The basic model is quite similar to that in the subsequent article by Rosen, Murphy and Scheinkman (1994), presented above, so only some alternative expressions of results are reported here.

$g)L]/[(1+g-\rho_h)(1-\rho_h L)(1-\beta L)]$. These expressions show that demand and cost shocks have current and future impacts, even if the shock is transient and the relevant $\rho = 0$, because any disturbance necessarily affects the current stock, x_t, and this impact interacts with the population dynamics and the economic decisions in the management of the herd inventory to distribute the effects over time. The direction of response of stock x_t to a positive demand shock (ε_t^d) depends on the sign of $\beta - \rho_d$, as shown in Figure 2.13. The distributed lag responses to positive holding cost shocks ε_t^h and feeding cost shocks ε_t^m reverse the signs of the responses to the demand shocks.

2.4 Farm Operation

The subject of this section is how the major factors of production are coordinated to ensure the successful functioning of a farm. While much of the scholarly literature on ancient agriculture addresses in considerable depth issues of crops grown, equipment used, and choices of technique (fallowing, depth of plowing, and so on), the subject of what is called "farm operation" here has been addressed in somewhat lesser depth than the technical topics have, under the titles of personnel management, agricultural organization, agrarian systems, coping strategies, and surely others I have not discovered (White, 1970, Chapters XI-XII; Osborne, 1987, 34–40); Isager and Skydsgaard, 1991 Chapter 6). The Roman writers on farming discussed aspects of these subjects (White, 1970, Chapters XI–XII).

Many people were involved in agricultural production decisions, from owners down to the most menial laborer, and as Wright inferred from his analysis of the archaeological and textual remains of the early Mesopotamian settlement at present-day Sakheri Sughir near Ur, different types of decision were made by many different people with different extents of authority and responsibility (Wright, 1969). Clearly such a hierarchical set of authorities didn't just emerge but resulted from a series of choices. To give an explicit example to flesh out the abstraction, Jameson's quite detailed, but ultimately speculative, work on farm labor in Classical and Hellenistic Greece reports the widespread existence of large (10–18 hectares; the Roman latifundia were considerably larger, reaching 200–400 ha. and larger) agricultural holdings in a number of regions of Greece—Laconia, Messenia, and several of the islands, among others—holdings too large to be operated with the technology of the time by its owner's family alone, not to mention the Spartan system of supporting its soldiers Jameson (1992).[29] Jameson calls the farming operations of the helots in Sparta effectively sharecropping since they were required to deliver half the output to the Spartiate family assigned the land they operated, but beyond that label, the operation of all these estates is fully characterized as operated by slaves or serfs. Who told them what to do, and who checked on them to make sure they did what they were told? Getting closer to the operational level of decision-making, Osborne summarizes some contractual terms of a number of agricultural leases from Classical and Hellenistic Greece and reports in detail the many specifics in a surviving lease for operation of a piece of land sacred to Zeus on Amorgos (Osborne 1987, 36–37, Table 2, 42–43).

Despite his strong inclination to see most agricultural labor in Classical and Hellenistic Attica conducted by slaves, Jameson (1992, 145) is willing to imagine that some poorer Athenian smallholders probably hired themselves out as seasonal labor despite the stigma since they were hard-pressed to make ends meet with their own land alone. However, Jameson is inclined to see their livelihood as urban, which would make high transportation costs for regular cultivation, although seasonal agricultural employment could be handled by temporary relocation.[30] Osborne notes the ability, and willingness, of wealthy landowners to purchase scattered plots far enough apart to be beyond economical travel distances, but does not address how those plots, sometimes quite small, were cultivated (Osborne 1987, 38). Put together, this seems like an opportunity for leasing agricultural land as well as a diversification opportunity, as Osborne notes for the scattered holdings.

Dropping back in time several centuries, Tandy and Neale (1996, 39–42), in their introduction to Tandy's translation of Hesiod's *Works and Days*, devote detailed discussion to debt, which caused Hesiod's brother Perses to lose his farm. The emphasis is implicitly on consumption debt, not production loans, and from lenders outside the farm community rather than from local lenders who would be well-placed to assess a borrower's creditworthiness. How an outsider would make effective a claim on land for debt is unclear, even if the claim was only on the output of the land rather than on the asset itself. Would a tenancy contract be in order? How would supervision be conducted?

Altogether, how does rural labor get productively employed, how does land get fully utilized, how does everyone involved defend their interests to the best of their abilities, and how are the proceeds split up between the participants? These topics are treated in this section under the concept of contracts despite the fact that the term "contract" implies an element of choice and slave labor formed part of the agricultural labor force in a number of places at various times. The use of slave labor imposes many of the same costs as the contractual employment of free labor, if not more, or the leasing out of land, so the analogy is not entirely misplaced. The use of markets and exchange to execute a farm's operations entails contracting for diverse services to be supplied over a crop season.

29 On the Roman latifundia sizes, see White (1970, 387–388).

30 Without wishing to enter into the Attic agricultural slavery debate, if lower-income Attic farmers had been forced off their small holdings by competition from slaves on larger holdings and into the city where they formed the urban poor with farming skills, why did not the agricultural wage fall to a level which would have made paying good drachmas for slave assets uneconomical?

Before proceeding into the issue of contract choice, the first sub-section below discusses consequences for farm operation of some very broad environmental characteristics of a region, basically associated with its population density. The second sub-section introduces the concept of contract choice in farming. The third sub-section focuses on share contracting for farm tenancy, which is a useful device for integrating the treatment of owner operation and fixed rental as well. The final sub-section deals with the linkage of transactions for other services and goods with transactions for land, a common feature of agriculture with imperfect or missing markets.

2.4.1 What Kind of Area Are We Talking About?

Most, although not all, of the territories that are the subject of this chapter, were dry, sometimes with rainy winters but still essentially moisture-constrained overall. The Black Sea region was not, nor northern parts of Italy, and parts of the Balkans, but even those areas do not compare with South and Southeast Asia and the greater part of Sub-Saharan Africa which have greatly influenced the development economics literature. That basic physical environmental constraint considered, however, the degree of scarcity of land is a major conditioning factor in the operation of a number of markets involved in non-modern agriculture. This characteristic, essentially population density, is as much a chronological characteristic as it is a region-specific one. During the Classical and Hellenistic Periods, most regions of Greece were relatively heavily populated, making prime agricultural land quite valuable. During the Neolithic and for several centuries following the Mycenaean collapse, populations probably had trouble filling up the available land. In Mesopotamia and Egypt, access to river water made land quite valuable, but elsewhere in the ancient Near East, in regions far from the major rivers, land-to-population ratios probably were high enough to weaken or preclude land markets. Italy and the North African Mediterranean rim were not notably high land-labor ratio regions, at least during Roman times. Consequently there is substantive motivation to discuss the higher population density condition before turning to characteristics of lower population density.[31]

High-population-density areas will experience high yield-risk covariance. That is, a lot of farms will be in close proximity to one another and will experience very much the same variations in yield. This feature seriously hinders local farm income insurance, outright crop insurance being out of the question. Major elevation differences within small areas, as characterizes much of the central Peloponnese, may interrupt this characteristic of high-density farming, although the effective insurance provided by separated parcels may be dampened by differences in crops grown at the different elevations. Self-insurance by holding reserves of various sorts, from food stocks to precious metals and other durables that could be sold is an alternative. Nonetheless, when most farms in a small area suffer the same bad crop season, selling assets locally may be of limited utility since most neighbors would be selling at the same time, and getting access to outside regions unaffected by the reverse involves both information and transportation costs. Similarly with recourse to local credit markets, and of course the same applies to land and animal sales under these conditions—few would have the money to buy the assets, and flooding the market would depress their prices anyway.

Land markets will generally exist, but sales will be constrained by the common need to pay cash (or its equivalent in kind in a non-monetized situation). Land will be one of the few forms, or possibly the only form, of acceptable collateral for either production or consumption loans in a traditional, agrarian community. Land purchases using mortgages would not be profitable. Unmortgaged land has collateral value which elevates the land's value above the present discounted value of its agricultural output. The owner of mortgaged land could not use it for collateral, consequently can't capture the credit advantage of land ownership, and thus wouldn't be able to repay the mortgage out of the land's production income. In good years, few land owners would want to sell, and in bad years, few people would have savings to buy. Distress sales would be at low prices, or transfers of pledged land at prices as of the time of the loan, would be largely to moneylenders. Consequently there would be a tendency for land to accumulate in the hands of people already possessing greater endowments.[32]

The operation of large estates as single operations suffers from scale diseconomies deriving from the use of hired (or slave or serf) workers. Rentals are generally more efficient than managing a large holding because of the supervision and coordination costs required on the large holding unless they are offset by scale economies in processing output combined with coordination problems between harvest and processing—which are difficult to find for the ancient world's crops.[33] An exception is tree crops, with long-duration growing stocks and high maintenance requirements, which agrees with the reports of Roman olive plantations. Thus, if rental markets are available, there is likely to be a tendency for large ownership holdings to be farmed as smaller-scale operational holdings. If land

[31] The following discussion, with allowance to references on ancient situations already cited, owes much to Binswanger and Rosenzweig, (1986, 503–539) and Binswanger and McIntire (1987, 73–99).

[32] Muhs (2016, 90–91, 140, 171–172, 210) traces the progress of documentation of land titles over the long span of Egyptian history. Written documentation, sometime of labor obligations associated with a plot of land, permitted greater security of title and gradually allowed land prices to increase accordingly.

[33] Bagnall (1993, 150–153) discusses large estates comprised of multiple holdings of absentee urban land owners in 4th Century C.E. Egypt. Individual units were managed by an on-site overseer, and some of them appear to have had extensive facilities such as would be expected on a plantation—mills, water storage facilities, storehouses, wine and olive presses, and living facilities—but evidently an unknown proportion of the land on these units was cultivated by lessees, while the overseer-managed farming was supplemented by part-time workers. These arrangements may have gotten around some of the diseconomies of scale in coordination not compensated by economies in processing.

rental markets exist and the large holdings are farmed as smaller operational units, the landowners are likely to be the providers of credit to the tenants, since the land owner, at least a locally resident one, is likely to have better information on a tenant than other potential lenders do.

The output per unit of land on large operations will, other things being equal, be lower than those on smaller holdings because of the larger operation's higher labor costs (which itself is an indication of non-separablity in the household model). Capital-labor ratios will be higher on larger operations because of higher labor costs. Credit costs will be lower on larger ownership holdings, because of the reduced credit risk associated with the larger collateral, leading to both higher capital-labor ratios on larger ownership holdings and, ceteris paribus, higher output per unit of land. Thus, differences in output per hectare on small and large operational units depends on both the ownership status of the operational unit and the importance of credit for purchased inputs.

Lightly populated areas typically do not show the sharp inequalities in land tenure that the higher-density areas do. Labor markets may not exist at all, nor credit markets or even output markets. Land itself may effectively have a zero price. During peak-demand seasons, there is unlikely to be local non-household labor to draw upon, although temporary, seasonal migration by outsiders may be coordinated with these peaks. Climatic conditions being the same, lightly populated areas experience greater farm income risk because of the information costs deriving from spatial isolation. Animal husbandry is frequently a risk management strategy as it typically has lower production risks than crops. A minor drought that eliminates a crop harvest may leave some vegetative growth that animals can eat, and in a major drought it may be possible to move the animals to areas not affected by the drought. Transhumance is a common form of animal husbandry, with full-time herders contracted for the job, since the skills of sedentary farmers differ from those involved in managing animals and knowing locations and times available for grazing. Given the moral hazard and potential theft problems involved with such contracts, cultivator-herder relationships will tend to be long-term.

Because of the isolation and high transport costs, most trade of these low-density communities is likely to be of items of low weight and volume. Farms are generally self-sufficient in food, but holding of stocks for use or sale during bad years is only marginally economic, if at all. Limited labor supplies during harvest season make it difficult to accumulate stocks beyond a household's anticipated consumption. Storage losses and limited durability of grains make stocks costly, and in very dry regions with attendant high variances in rainfall, weather uncertainties combine to give storage negative expected returns. Given the greater distances between communities, social institutions such as extended families can't perform well as insurance substitutes, leaving capital accumulation as the principal insurance substitute. Livestock is typically the principal form of wealth holding.

Again, with the exception of the negative correlation between rainfall and its variance, the same region could slip between these situations of land scarcity and land abundance, with concomitant changes in many of their institutions. With this background, the following sub-section introduces the basic concepts in contract choice that will be developed further in the sub-section on share tenancy.

2.4.2 Contract Choice: Who Decides What, Who Does What, and Who Gets What?

Leaving plantations aside for the moment, the three principal options for the operation of a farm are owner operation, fixed rental, and share rental. Owner operation could be conducted with family labor alone, with hired labor alone, or with a combination of the two. If a land owner uses only family labor, the extent of the land the household can farm effectively is limited. If the household owns more land than it can cultivate with its own labor, it has the choice of hiring labor or renting out some of its land. Using hired labor, the owner must incur the costs of supervising the non-family labor, whether that labor is free labor contracted for the season, free casual labor hired for peak periods, or resident slave or serf labor. If the household rents out some of its land, it must supervise the rentals.

Fixed rentals specify an amount of rent to be paid, typically at harvest time, although the rent could be in kind or in cash. A land owner might not want to offer a fixed rental to a potential tenant without sufficient wealth to pay the rent in the event of a particularly bad harvest, although given the flexibility of contracts, some allowance could be specified in advance for payment in such a circumstance. With payment of a fixed rent in either cash or kind, the contracting parties face the risk of a variance between the expected and actual value of rent in terms of food at harvest time. With a fixed cash rent, in a low-harvest year, the landlord would get lesser purchasing power over food than anticipated at the time of contracting—if he even gets the rent—whereas with a fixed in-kind rent, he would get a bonus. While it would appear that a fixed rent contract places all the risk of farm income on the renter, the chance of the renter defaulting leaves the landlord at some risk. For this reason, there is a tendency for landlords to agree to fixed rent contracts only with tenants with sufficient wealth to cover the rent in the event of complete crop failure. Recent literature on farm tenancy leaves open the possibility of a fixed renter leaving the area and setting up in another place where his or her reputation does not follow, but the mobility of small cultivators in antiquity, together with the likelihood of acquiring anonymity in another location in a relatively small overall population, combine to make this largely a non-issue at most times and places in antiquity.

Share rental, or sharecropping as it is also called, has acquired an undeservedly negative reputation, between the opinions of famous economists over the past two centuries and more and the experience with the institution in the Black Belt of the Post-Bellum American South. The institution contains a number of economic subtleties which economists have only recently begun to understand fully (we think), but its durability over three or four millennia and in many settings lend a reasonable inference of its utility and even efficiency.[34] More space will be devoted to the economics of share rental in the following sub-section, but here the basic outlines of the institution will be delineated. As the term indicates, the renter and the land owner agree in advance to split the output in some proportion. Typically, the share rental contract may include provisions to split the non-labor expenses in proportions that may differ from the output share. In this sense, share renting shares the risk of farming between landlord and tenant in a proportion related to the output share (net of the input shares). With that obvious observation, it should be added that the presence of risk is insufficient to account for the existence, or choice, of share rental contracts. This will be explained at greater length in the sub-section on share tenancy.

Some of the major facts of sharecropping also are less than obviously correct. There is a belief that shares in share contracts are always the same in a given region, for one reason, to avoid the possibility of renters conspiring to shift output to renters contracting to keep larger shares of the harvest. Evidence exists from recent times that belies this belief, and there is no reason to believe that this variance is a new phenomenon (Reid 1976). There is a parallel belief that output shares in share contracts tend to be constant for long periods of time in a region; again, evidence from recent share contracts is at variance with this belief, although there might be a tendency for relative constancy in many regions. Evidence exists of tenants renting different plots from the same landlord, one on a fixed-rent contract, the other on a share contract.

Notions of landlords being uniformly wealthier than tenants, and tenants uniformly poor, are too simplistic. The real world of farming is far more complex than any intelligible theory can be, and ample evidence from around the world—again, in recent times—indicates that land owners who cultivate their own holding may rent in additional land on either shares or fixed rent. In many parts of the world, a high proportion of renters also are land owners. Some landlords are widows with small children and no nearby family to supply labor; the condition of widows surely varied over time and region in antiquity, making this last scenario more or less likely accordingly. Share tenants are often landowners themselves.

In either type of rental contract, both landlord and tenant must find the contract terms satisfactory or the contract will not be offered or accepted. This puts constraints on both tenant and landlord and connects the land market to the labor market. Several points can be noted about the two rental contract types. Although share rentals cannot be explained by their risk-sharing properties alone, they do share risk. Consequently, the landlord receives a risk premium in addition to the contribution of the land to the output in his or her output share. Accordingly, a fixed rent would be smaller than the landlord's share of a share rental on the same plot of land, farmed identically because the

[34] Postgate (1992, 185) reports share rental contracts, with shares usually $\frac{1}{3}$ to the landlord and $\frac{2}{3}$ to the tenant, during the Old Babylonian Period. §46 of Hammurabi's Code makes a casual reference to rents paid in shares, suggesting the commonness of that contract type (Meek (1969, 168). Eyre (2010, 293–294) reports the common use of share contracts between both institutional and private landlords and tenants as early as the Middle Kingdom (2040 B.C.E. – 1674 B.C.E.), with tenant shares between $\frac{1}{2}$ and $\frac{2}{3}$. Janssen's (1986) review of Stuchevsky (1982) presents at least dual, if not conflicting, evidence on share leasing by state-owned temples in 20th Dynasty Egypt. Private cultivators of temple land turned over $\frac{1}{3}$ of their harvest to temple administrators from the threshing floors; whether that amount is called a tax or a land rent, as long as it constitutes approximately the full payment for the use of the land, it corresponds structurally to a landlord's share in a sharecropping contract (Janssen 1986, 353). Nevertheless, elsewhere in theWilbour Papyrus, leases are fixed, at $1\frac{1}{2}$ sacks of grain per aroura leased (Janssen 1986, 363). Gardiner (1941, particularly 28–29 and 51) refers to taxes taking the form of parts of agricultural outputs of land owned, such as the concept applies, by temples or held and operated on behalf of Pharaoh, but these payments have the structure of land rents paid by farm operators of one sort or another possibly supervisors of large-scale operations of one sort or another. Katary (1989, 193–194) takes up the issue of a share of a harvest as land rent versus some other sortof obligation. Possibly the most complete set of land leases from Egypt documenting share tenure arrangements are the seven leases in Hughes (1952, 10, 18, 29, 45, 52, 68–69, 71, 73). These leases specify shares, which depend on which party supplied which inputs (oxen, seed, additional labor); limited-duration leases; sometimes specific crops; penalties for abuse of land in two cases and a penalty for the landlord in event of termination of the lease during the crop year; and one apparent instance of a tenant working off a debt, which is the only hint of landlord-provided loans. Eyre (1997, 381–382) reports later Egyptian evidence for sharecropping, from the 25th and 26th Dynasties (early 8th through late 6th centuries B.C.E.), with tenant shares around $\frac{2}{3}$, although provisions for landlord provision of seed and equipment could reduce that effectively to around $\frac{1}{3}$; leases typically were short-term, generally one year. Share leases were quite common during the Graeco-Roman period in Egypt. Gurney (1954, 84–85) interprets Hittite land tenure as taking the form of payent in service convertible into a form of ground rent, on both privately held and extensive temple lands, but does not report payment terms, if indeed anything is known of them. Ventris and Chadwick (1973, Chapter 8 and 443–456) cite a number of tenancies around Mycenaean Pylos, as well as around Knossos on Crete, with apparent payments in both output (as would be expected in a non-monetized economy), possibly on shares (445), and possibly services of some sort, but the evidence from the tablets is very sparse. Alison Burford (1993, 177–181) notes the prevalence of share tenancy in Greece from the Archaic through the Hellenistic Periods. Léopold Migeotte, (2009, 78–79) reports that 5th century Attic farm owners of hoplite rank could rent additional land "if they needed to," although the types of rental contracts used are not noted. Robin Osborne, (1988, 279–323) leaves an impression of the extensiveness of land rentals, both institutional-to-private and private-to-private (293-294); although no distinction is made between type of rental, the quotation of rents in drachmas implies fixed rentals. Osborne notes that land leasing regulations on Salamis go back to the early 6th century, with a continuous tradition of leasing thereafter (311). Using boundary-stone inscriptions to a great extent, Osborne reports a number of lease claues. An interesting incentive clause appears in Attic and Delian leases: a defaulting renter would be required to pay the difference between his contracted rent and the subsequently contracted rent, post-default, on the reasoning that the difference represented the degradation to the land imposed by his mismanagement (294, 299); unless the penalty were the present discounted value of the difference, the penalty would be mild. While institutional-private leases tended to be longer, private-private leases in Attica generally were short-term, often a single year (314). From owners' perspectives on Salamis and Lesbos and in Attica, leasing distant plots avoided (prohibitively) costly supervision (314), while from lessees' perspectives, acquiring enough land to fully employ a family's labor resources was a common motivation (322). Guardians' leasing out of land owned by minor orphans was common (305–306).

fixed-rent tenant is receiving a risk premium for absorbing all of the risk. In parallel fashion, the larger is the tenant's share of output, the larger the proportion of the risk that he or she assumes.

2.4.3 The Theory of Share Tenancy

The purview of the theory of share tenancy extends well beyond sharecropping. In a more restricted interpretation, it deals with the choice of tenancy of a farm or a plot of farmland, i.e., whether the owner of the farm finds it preferable to operate the farm himself or herself or to lease it out for either a share of the output or a fixed rent. Since the prospective tenant has a decision to make as well—whether the share or the fixed-rent contract is preferable, or whether working as a hired laborer is preferable to either of the routes to farm operation—there is an implicit connection to the labor market or at least to other employment or occupational opportunities. Looking inside the contracts takes us beyond the simple (or not so simple) choice of contract into specific operational details of managing a farm, from specification of crops to choice of technique to various maintenance and investment activities—essentially, how to run a farm. Additionally, focusing exclusively on the contract choice may give the student of the farming in question a partial and unbalanced view of the choices being made by both land owner and tenant. The choice of tenure type may be only one of several choices made simultaneously and endogenously by both landlord and tenant, and ignoring one or more of these major choices may yield a distorted understanding of why a particular tenure choice was made. Specifically, in backward (a shorthand for high information costs and weak market organization—otherwise these agrarian communities may possess considerable sophistication in solving the problems they face with the means available), agrarian communities it may be to the advantage of both contracting parties to link several non-land transactions to the land transaction. Where credit markets are weak or non-existent, loans may be tied to a farm rental contract. In the complete absence of formal insurance markets, contract terms may provide for some protection against vagaries of nature. Similarly with substitutes for markets for consumption goods and for farm outputs. Altogether, the theory of share tenancy addresses considerably more than sharecropping.

What has emerged from the research on farm tenancy is not a single explanation, not even a single general explanation that is so broad as to be meaningless and boring. Instead, a number of possible explanations has emerged, which is not a bad thing, because share tenancy has occurred in so many places and at so many different times that a single explanation for it is unreasonable to expect (Reid 1987, esp. 565). The corollary to this wide appearance of share tenancy is that at all times and places, people have settled upon contractual structures for operating their agriculture. The more broadly considered theory of farm tenancy (I am consciously substituting "farm" for "share" now) offers a vehicle for understanding farm management quite generally, with the caveat that an explanation for choices in one region at one broad time period need not apply to another region at the same time or the same region at a different time, because conditions can differ or change. Thinking of tenure choice theory as a theory of managerial structure, it becomes obvious that no single management structure fits all products and all technological regimes at all times.

It is useful at this point to define a distinction between the terms "management structure" and "management practices." So far I have discussed only management structure—how the management of a farm firm is organized to assign rights to make certain kinds of decisions. This does not in itself address the management practices that the managers make—e.g., what crops to plant; when to sow, weed, and harvest; whether to interplant or not; whether to acquire through purchase or rental noncontiguous plots; and so on. These decisions are not the subject of tenancy theory. Many of these practice questions need to be hammered into suitable form to be addressed theoretically; otherwise, thinking about them remains at the level of, "Yes, farmers do that," and "They could do the other thing too," and "Yes, that would work, too, wouldn't it?" At the end of the day, we wouldn't know what the trade-offs between these alternative actions are and what the best combination of them is. That said, some of these decisions, such as what to plant, to the extent they are influenced by risk management behavior, can be put into a portfolio diversification framework, introduced in this chapter in section 2.3.2.

The following sub-section provides some background on the literature of farm tenancy theory. It is an effort to avoid belaboring a very dense literature and give the reader a sense of what is being omitted by the focus on the principal-agent approach, and even within that approach, in the subsequent sub-section. A substantial proportion of recent sharecropping models has used the principal-agent model as a vehicle because that approach deals with the phenomena of interest. I have chosen to concentrate on that approach because the other approaches to explaining tenure choice do not seem to fit the mobility conditions, in particular, of antiquity.[35] They are well suited to circumstances of other times and places but not to the subject times and locations of this handbook. After introducing the basic model of tenancy contracting, the next sub-section addresses how and why input costs are shared under share tenancy contracts. The final sub-

[35] For example, the agricultural ladder mechanism (or hypothesis), whereby younger, less experienced, and lower-wealth farmers contract with more experienced and wealthier farmers on shares to learn about farming from their landlords, then graduate to fixed renting and finally to ownership and owner-operation, seems suited to societies in which younger people break away from their families at relatively early ages, but not of signal relevance to societies based on extended families and often remaining in the same area for centuries. There are varieties of this view of sharecropping as joint management and joint provision of inputs, but they all reduce to situations of relatively inexperienced farmers operating on their own, separately from their families.

section introduces interlinked transactions as providing a comprehensive view of farm management choices.

Background of the Current Understanding. Share tenancy, or sharecropping, has a bad reputation, much but not all of it deriving from its history in the post-Civil War American South although it was practiced widely in the Post-Bellum northern states as well (Reid 1973; Ransom and Sutch 1977; Jones 1982). Beyond its social disapproval, generations of leading economists, before and after the American Civil War, proclaimed it inefficient, without asking why it had remained so for so long. And to date, contemporary analysis has yet to explain the small number of share allocations. It is useful to review this literature before embarking on the contemporary analyses of farm tenure contracts.

The Intellectual Baggage. The economics of share tenancy has a lengthy intellectual history. Adam Smith was kindly critical of it, and Alfred Marshall offered a trenchant if misleading analysis of it which some recent scholars have endeavored to rehabilitate with reference to the famous "footnote 2," which presaged much recent work, re-started by D. Gale Johnson (Smith 1937 [1776], Book 3, Chapter 2, 366–367; Marshall 1964 [1920], Book 6, Chapter 10, 535–536, fn. 2, p. 536; Johnson 1950). John Stuart Mill (2004 [1865], Book II, Chapter VIII, 296–311) actually found favor with the system, but with the duo of Smith and Marshall ostensibly critical of the institution, regardless of what they actually said, sharecropping has had a difficult, uphill struggle to gain respectability among economists in the late 20th century (if not necessarily with the share tenants and their landlords themselves). Smith briefly discussed the French metayers as a successor institution to slavery, noting that they did not get the entirety of their production, although he noted that they did have an interest in the magnitude of the total output since they got a constant share of it. Smith was particularly dubious that incentives to maintain the land existed in the arrangement however. Marshall had familiarized himself with the French arrangements as well as with the late 19th century American arrangements, although he over-emphasized its prevalence in the South. Having recently developed the graphical approach to marginal analysis (the supply-demand diagrams used throughout this book), he trenchantly likened the share of the output a share tenant paid to a landlord as a tax, reaching the conclusion that the effect of this tax was to give the tenant only a fraction of the value of his marginal product, and implying that share tenants would stint on their labor and over-use land. Ignoring Marshall's footnote 2 on the second page of his treatment of sharecropping, which suggested some means of avoiding this under-application of labor, in lines of analysis picked up by economists during the last quarter of the 20th century, the crispness of the conclusion of the inefficiency of sharecropping let the conclusion stick and go by-and-large accepted for decades by economists who didn't know anything about either farming or sharecroppers. Johnson, a farmer himself as well as a Chicago economist, developed Marshall's inefficiency analysis formally to show exactly what the problems with the analysis were. As a farmer, he knew the conclusion was wrong, and as an economist he sensed that such a gross inefficiency should not persist over centuries and millennia. He raised the same contract additions that Marshall packed into his footnote 2 as potential remedies for the incentive structure characterized by Marshall's tax analysis—short leases and specification of the tenant's duties so that he doesn't stint on labor.[36]

The first 175 years of economic thinking about sharecropping were easy to summarize and characterize. The heyday of sharecropping theory in the 20th century extended from about 1968 through about 1995; a few more applications dribble into the literature, but no path-breaking analyses. A good part of the literature has been quite practically motivated, with development policies in many Third World countries, encouraged by international development agencies, emphasizing land reforms, tenancy reforms, and reforms in labor and credit markets moving well ahead of any understanding of what their results were likely to be. The resulting literature is extensive, dense, tedious, technical, and confusing to an outsider dipping into a random part of it. I do not recommend it to archaeologists, philologists, and ancient historians interested in farming and tenancy, although with the traditional warning of caveat emptor, I will provide references to several survey articles, all of which were published by 1993. The remainder of this sub-section gives a brief, non-technical tour of what was learned during this period of intense research.[37]

The Major Ideas of the Recent Literature. Throughout the research of this period, the Marshallian inefficiency thesis formed a backdrop to the structure of models and a touchstone of analytical outcomes—would the resulting choices tenants and landlords make be efficient or inefficient? The question of efficiency or inefficiency is addressed by whether, first, the marginal products of labor on sharecropped and fixed-rental land would be equal or not—they must be equal for efficiency—and second, whether tenants' and landlords' marginal rates of substitution between riskless and risky income were the same—they should be. Of course, the marginal product condition for land is paralleled in all the other factors of production; if marginal products of labor aren't equalized between types of tenancy, none of the other factors will have their marginal products equalized either.

At the root of efficiency or inefficiency are incentive structures. In the Marshallian analysis, the inefficiency of the theoretical result (taking care to distinguish the result of the model of sharecropping from the result of sharecropping itself) derives from the incentive structure

[36] Foxhall (1990, 101) characterizes short leases (5 years, with little or no record of non-renewal) during the Imperial period in Roman Italy as means of intimidation of tenants by landlords, without recognizing the incentives of either party to a share tenancy contract.

[37] The reviews are, in chronological order of their publication: Newbery and Stiglitz, (1979), Quibria and Rashid (1986), Otsuka and Hayami (1988), Singh (1989), and Otsuka, Chuma, and Hayami (1992).

of the contract. As far as the Marshallian analysis went, the share tenant equalized the product of his output share and his marginal product of labor to the wage he could earn in an alternative activity: $\alpha MP_L = w$, or $MP_L = w/\alpha$, where $0 < \alpha < 1$ on a share contract. This leaves the marginal product of labor on a sharecropped farm higher than the alternative wage, be that on a fixed-rent contract or working as an agricultural laborer or working in town. The application of more labor would drive its marginal product down to the market wage rate. How does a landlord give that incentive to a tenant? He can lease him a certain amount of land and tell him how much labor to use; knowing the relationship between the land-labor ratio and marginal product (an experienced farmer will have a good idea how much labor a piece of land he's owned for a long time needs in order to produce its long-term best output), he can specify the amount of labor the tenant should apply. Combined with a short lease (a year or a crop season), which allows the landlord to not renew the lease if the tenant doesn't perform according to the terms of the contract, these contract terms should give the proper incentive to the tenant to apply labor to the landlord's farm. And from a modeling perspective, the Marshallian inefficiency result derives from the absence of the landlord's optimization behavior in the model; the landlord could adjust the share and a fixed payment so as to reach the same level of utility he could expect from a fixed rent contract.

Introducing the concept of contract terms, it is useful at this point to offer a modest formalization of them which unifies share tenancy, fixed rental, and wage labor. A tenant's (or worker's) income under one of these contracts would be $y = \alpha Q - \beta - \gamma \mathbf{px}$, where α is the share of the crop going to the tenant ($1-\alpha$ goes to the landlord), β is a fixed payment from the tenant to the landlord, γ is the tenant's shares of costs for the vector of purchased inputs **x** at prices **p**. A pure share rental is characterized by $0 < \alpha < 1$ and $\beta = 0$; $0 < \gamma < 1$ is also likely. A pure fixed rental is characterized by $\beta > 0$, $\alpha = 1$ and $\gamma = 0$. Working as an agricultural laborer is characterized by $\alpha = 0$ and $\beta < 0$.

However, the story of creating efficient tenancy contracts doesn't end here. Agriculture is a risky activity and it is spread out over space. When a particularly small yield is harvested, it may be difficult for the landlord to tell, after the fact, how much of the low yield is attributable to the tenant's lack of diligence and how much to the vagaries of nature. The tenant knows pretty well what the allocation of responsibility is, but the landlord will (or may—the subject warrants further consideration, which I'll give soon) have difficulty determining it. If the landlord could monitor the tenant's activities sufficiently, he (or she) could be sure the tenant satisfied the terms of the lease, but the landlord has his or her own activities to attend to, be it operating a farm of his or her own or conducting some other business. The spatial distribution of the land, particularly if the landlord has several tenants, adds to the costs of monitoring. There is an asymmetry of information between tenant and landlord—the tenant has information that the landlord doesn't about activities and conditions that affect the landlord's income from the farming operation. Another way of saying this is that some of the tenant's actions are unobservable by the landlord, or at least are only partially observable with the application of economical monitoring.

So, while we can envision a set of contract terms that would deliver efficient utilization of the landlord's and the tenant's resources, those contract terms might not be enforceable because they can't be observed well by the landlord. Observability has been an important assumption in many share tenancy models: if a tenant's labor input is considered observable, it is modeled as a contract term under the control of the landlord; if it is considered unobservable, it is not made a contract term and is a variable under the control of the tenant in his or her utility maximization, while the landlord must add a constraint to his or her utility maximization problem to account for the tenant's labor reaction to the remaining contract term, the output share. However, the literature has stressed the difference between simple labor hours, which may be relatively easily observable, and effort, which is an intuitive but observationally more elusive concept. Labor inputs might be a regular 60 hours a week; effort is more akin getting out of bed at 2 o'clock in the morning during a rainstorm to channel some water flow away from a vulnerable fence or wall, or planning for coordination of production activities several months in advance. Observability is not a logically demonstrable condition; it may occur in some circumstances and not in others. In a small, low-mobility, agrarian community, a landlord might know pretty well whether a tenant has been satisfying the effort terms of a contract by making some simple observations and a little inference. The landlord's knowledge might derive from the facts that, say, he's farmed in the area for 40 years, has several other tenancies in the area with which to compare results, and has a sufficient idea of what the weather did, to factor all the information together and figure out whether the tenant in question had done what the terms of the contract specified, the resultant harvest would have been considerably better, regardless of the weather. An absentee landlord without a resident supervisor cannot observe a tenant's behavior at all.[38] Nonobservability, or limited observability, of an agent's actions creates a moral hazard situation. A share tenant who was also a land owner would impose an additional moral hazard problem since he could devote greater effort per hectare on his own land than on the share-rented land and might even divert share-purchased inputs from a landlord's plot to his own.

This incentive problem with labor or effort supply does not occur under a fixed rental, since the tenant gets the entire fruit of his or her labor—but at the cost of bearing all of the risk of the venture. Under share contracts, the labor incentive problem decreases as the tenant's output share

[38] Baer (1963, 16) notes a Theban functionary of the 21st Dynasty informally renewing a Nubian's lease via a letter, which was to serve as the informal contract, specifying that a local official was to be entrusted with supervision of the tenant. Katary (1989, 189-190), citing Menu (1970), suggests the existence of farm supervisors on large temple farming operations.

approaches 1, but as the share approaches 1, the share tenant bears more and more risk. So there is a trade-off in contract terms between addressing the incentive problem for the landlord and solving a risk-sharing problem for the tenant that exists because of the absence of an insurance market. Marshall worried about a share tenant's disinclination to invest in land maintenance, and writers have noted that a share tenant's incentive to actually mine the land increases as his output share increases. Thus, between alternative contract types there is a tradeoff between optimal incentives and risk sharing, but on the route from share renting toward fixed renting, there is a another tradeoff between different types of incentives, the labor incentive getting better the closer to a fixed rental the share term is, the land incentive getting worse.

However, if these tradeoffs become too frustrating or otherwise unsatisfactory, the landlord always has the option of cultivating the farm or plot under consideration with his or her own resources, either family labor or hired labor, but the use of hired labor just shifts the labor incentive problem, as labor hired at a fixed wage has no incentive at all to work—unless we envision a 1950s epic movie with overseers with whips in their hands walking around the fields, but even then the landlord has to pay the overseers—and trust them to do their jobs. This incentive problem either does not exist or is considerably less extensive with the use of family labor. Thinking back to section 2.2.2 on transaction costs, this is a case of a labor market imperfection in which the cost to a farmer of using labor from the market is higher than the cost of using family labor, and in fact is even higher than the market wage paid to the labor since the use of the non-family labor imposes monitoring costs on the family labor.

While share tenancy shares risk between landlord and tenant, risk alone is insufficient to explain the existence of share contracts or the choice of a share contract, because the tenant could achieve the same risk with a combination of a fixed-rent contract and labor at a fixed wage, a result from portfolio theory of combining a risky asset (the fixed-rent contract) with a risk-free asset (the fixed wage). This result having been laboriously discovered several times, it was soon observed that the fixed wage was largely a figment of imagination in the real world of agrarian communities. The correlation between wages and agricultural yields is high, because the income going to the labor market that determines the wage comes largely from agriculture. Additionally, contracts on a fixed wage throughout a crop year, while observed at times and places, are not all that common. A contract for a fixed annual wage would have to average the marginal product of labor during periods of both peak and slack demand. The wage would be below the value of marginal product during peak demand periods and above it during slack periods. The wage in the casual (non-contract) labor market would reflect these seasonal shifts in demand, but work being contracted by the day, the wage can be matched to the marginal product. So, once it was noticed that the labor market at many places and times doesn't offer the opportunity to diversify risk that would make sharecropping redundant for risk spreading, the risk-spreading role of sharecropping was back in play. However, the root cause underpinning the existence of sharecropping was not risk itself, but the non-existence or imperfections of other markets, beyond just the labor market, and the attendant asymmetry of information.

The preceding ideas have been studied in a variety of types of model. As would be expected for problems involving uncertainty and moral hazard, principal-agent models have been used extensively. Nevertheless, a number of models have either addressed the moral hazard problems indirectly or have addressed aspects of tenancy not involving moral hazard. In a number of cases, one tenancy type is assumed and questions are posed about the extent of its usage in a region. Some models abstract from all sources of risk and assume tenant behavior is perfectly observable in order to examine the effect of imperfections in some other market, a legitimate simplification, but one that risks missing effects of interactions between the markets remaining in the model and some that are omitted; picked up out of context by an unwitting reader, such treatments could cause confusion.

What Hasn't Been Accomplished in the Recent Literature. One of the more salient facts of share renting around the world is and always has been the roundness of the shares assigned to the two parties: $\frac{1}{2}$ and $\frac{1}{2}$, $\frac{1}{3}$ and $\frac{2}{3}$ being very common pairs of shares. Most of the modeling of sharecropping choices makes the tenant's share of output an endogenous variable, without restricting its values to particular discrete numbers, which would be difficult mathematically. While the models generally are not solvable for absolute levels of each of the endogenous variables, the lack of restriction on the value the share can take probably affects the behavior of the other endogenous variables, at least quantitatively if not qualitatively. Some models have been developed to account for shares varying over some restricted range, such as between $\frac{2}{3}$ and $\frac{1}{2}$, but they have not been particularly convincing otherwise as models of farm behavior. This is a widely acknowledged gap in the understanding of share contracts.

All models of tenure choice limit the number of alternative market participation alternatives for prospective tenants. For example, some models of tenancy choice specify a labor market in which a tenant could participate in lieu of or in addition to taking a tenancy contract; some do not. Most do not simultaneously model the choices of input sharing agreements; studies of these contract terms generally specify a share contract and work from that basis to understand the rationale for cost shares differing from output shares. There are a plethora of transaction opportunities between tenant and landlord in other market areas—output markets and credit markets being the two most prominent. The basic tenancy contract models are difficult enough to solve with intelligible analytical solutions without these additional complications. As desirable as it would be to have a model that incorporated all the options that tenants and landlords face, it would be too complicated to solve.

The Principal-Agent Approach: Information, Risk, and Incentives. Consequences of the unenforceability of a tenant's effort have been studied in various ways, some explicitly using a principal-agent approach, others as noted above relying on modeling the costly use of time in monitoring and supervision. Considering the near-consensus that tenant effort should be modeled as unobservable by the landlord, actual implementations of principal-agent models in the literature have not been all that common. A number of non-principal-agent models assume one type of tenancy, or do not distinguish between types of rentals, and assume away risk to focus on the effect of variables such as tenant wealth or family size or separate tenant ownership of land or interlinking of transactions. The principal-agent approach might restrict tenancy options, but it will incorporate uncertainty, unobservability of at least some tenant actions, and the landlord-principal's understanding of the tenant-agent's reaction to the contract terms.

First consider an early and very simple model, which considers only share tenancy. A tenant's effective labor supply is eL, where e is the level of effort.[39] Output per acre is a function of effective labor supply per acre, $z = eL/T = ex$, so that output on a tenancy is $q = \theta Tf(z) = Tf(ex)$, where T is the plot size and x is the labor-land ratio. The income of a share renter is $y_t = \theta\alpha f(ex)/x$. The tenant's utility is $u = Eu(y_t) - v(e)$ since output and hence income is uncertain while effort is not. In the contract, the landlord specifies the tenant's output share, α, and the labor-land ratio on the plot, $x = L/T$, although the actual effort cannot be controlled. The sharecropper chooses e to maximize u and will only accept a contract that guarantees a base level of utility, $u(\alpha, x) = \max_{\{e\}} u \geq \bar{u}$. Competition between landlords will eliminate the less appealing contracts and leave the inequality utility constraint as an equality, which will define a relationship between x and α and since $e = e(\alpha, x)$, a relationship between e and α. A risk-neutral landlord will choose α to maximize rent per acre, $y_r = (1-\alpha)\theta f(ex)$ subject to the tenant's utility constraint, which has the effect of combining the reservation utility constraint with the tenant's incentive compatibility constraint by re-stating maximized utility as a function of the contract terms. The first-order condition from this maximization yields $\alpha/1-\alpha = s_L/(1-s_L) + s_L\epsilon_\alpha^e$, where s_L is the imputed share of effective labor in the value of output and ϵ_α^e is the elasticity of effort with respect to the tenant's share of output. When the elasticity of substitution between effective labor and land is unity, the second term goes to zero and the tenant's share is the same as the imputed share of labor, $\alpha = s_L$, but with an elasticity of substitution less than 1, a tenant gets a higher output share but less land, reducing his effort and the optimal crop share α is less than the imputed share of labor s_L.

While this is a crisp and interesting result, care needs to be taken with it. First, there is the mechanism between the output share in a share tenancy contract and the functional share to a factor of production. Although the model does not specify the risk aversion of the tenant, a payment for the insurance against production risk associated with θ would tend to push the output share α below the functional share, i.e., what the tenant's labor actually produces, independently of the elasticity of substitution in production. Second, a problem with all models that solve for an optimal value of the output share, output shares in the real world appear to take a small number of easily calculable values, such as $\frac{1}{2}$ or $\frac{2}{3}$. These values are below labor's share in most contemporary agriculture, so it is possible that the mechanism that is generating the actual crop shares differs from what is being modeled in tenancy models. *Caveat emptor*, the authors of these models would agree.

At the opposite end of the spectrum of simplicity is a more recent principal-agent model of tenancy. Consider a situation with a competitive casual labor market but no land market, landless workers (tillers) who may take either permanent labor or a tenancy, and landlords with fixed amounts of land who can cultivate some of their land and rent out the rest.[40] Both a landlord's and a tiller's cultivation requires hiring casual labor for peak season work which can be easily monitored, but both the cultivating landlord and tillers engage in intricate work which is not easily monitored or supervised. Considering only one season, i.e., not the possibility of a continuing tenancy, the landlord's production function is $q_\ell = \theta f(e_\ell, M_\ell, H\text{-}N_t h)$, where θ is again the random variable representing the state of nature, $E\theta = 1$, e_ℓ is the landlord's own effort, M_ℓ is the man-days of casual labor he or she hires, H is the amount of land the landlord owns, and N_t is the number of tenants to whom the landlord rents a plot of size h. Each tenant's production function is $q_t = \theta f(e_t, M_t, h)$, in which e_t and M_t are the tenant's effort throughout the season and casual employment during the peak season. The landlord cannot observe e_t. A casual laborer's income is $y_c = wm$, where w is the real wage rate and m is the days worked. A tenant's income is $y_t = \alpha(q_t - wM_t) + \beta = \alpha\pi_t + \beta$, where α is the tenant's share of the net output and β is the fixed payment which allows for a fixed-rent contract if $\beta < 0$ and $\alpha = 1$, or a permanent labor contract if $\beta > 0$ and $\alpha = 0$. A landlord's income is $y_\ell = N_t[(1-\alpha)\pi_t - \beta] + q_\ell - wM_\ell$. A tenant's utility depends on his income and effort, $u_t = u(y_t, e_t)$, in which, again using subscripted letters to represent characteristics of the utility function that otherwise would rely on the clumsier $\Delta x/\Delta y$ notation, $u_y > 0$, $u_e < 0$, and u_{yy}, u_{ee}, and $u_{ye} \leq 0$. The first two conditions say that utility increases with income but decreases with effort, $u_{yy} \leq 0$ implies either risk aversion (< 0) or neutrality ($= 0$), u_{ee} and $u_{ye} \leq 0$ indicate that the marginal disutility of effort increases with more effort, and with more income. Tenants maximize their expected utility, $Eu(y_t, e_t)$. The casual laborer's utility function is the same as the tenant's, and his utility maximization problem is $\max_{\{m\}} u(y_c, m) = V$. The first-order condition for the casual laborer's utility maximization is $u_y w + u_m = 0$, and since both m and the casual laborer's income depend only on the competitively

[39] This model is from Newbery and Stiglitz (1979, 318–321, 339).

[40] This model comes from Otsuka et al. (1992, 1977–1985).

determined wage w, maximized utility V is also determined by w. A tiller will not accept a tenancy or a permanent labor contract unless it provides him with at least his reservation utility, so $Eu(y_t, e_t) \geq V$ must hold, although the condition $u_{ye} \leq 0$ allows this constraint to hold with equality, so $Eu = V$ will ensure that there is no excess supply of tillers in equilibrium. The landlord's utility function is $u(y_\ell, e_\ell)$ and has the same properties as that of the tiller.

A contract must be based on variables that both the landlord and the tiller can observe or ex post conflict will arise. Thus, it is assumed that net output π_t is observable to both parties. A fixed payment at harvest time is enforceable, so there will be no defaults of either a fixed rent payment by a renter or a wage payment by a landlord, which is a concern in a one-period model. Since effort is unobservable and hence unenforceable, α, β and h are the only contract parameters for either a tenancy or a permanent labor position. The landlord is unable to identify e_t from observations of q_t, M_t and h in the presence of the randomness of production represented by θ. This leaves e_t a choice variable of the tenant, and the first-order condition for a tenant's utility maximization is $Eu_y\theta\alpha f_e + Eu_e \leq 0$. This FOC suggests that the tiller has no incentive to work under the fixed wage contract, in which $\alpha = 0$, and that resource allocation under a share contract, with $0 < \alpha < 1$, will be inefficient because the expected marginal product of effort, f_e, is not equated to the marginal rate of substitution between effort and expected output, $-Eu_e/Eu_y\theta$. Under uncertainty, risk aversion on the part of the tiller, and endogeneity of the contractual parameters, this first-order condition implies a reaction function for the tiller's effort, $e_t = e_t(\alpha, \beta, M_t, h)$, in which the incentives to supply effort are affected by α, β, M_t, and h. The landlord's optimization problem under these conditions is to maximize his or her utility by choosing the contract terms α and θ and making the production choices of land per tiller h, the number of tillers N_t, the person-days of casual labor on both his own farm and on each tenant farm M_t and M_ℓ, and his own effort, e_ℓ, subject to the tenant's reservation utility constraint and the tenant's reaction function. The landlord can affect the tiller's effort, as either tenant or wage worker, by choice of output share, fixed rent, plot size and hired labor on the tenant farm, each of those choices taking into account the tenant's reactions to each.[41]

Several first-order conditions from the landlord's maximization are easily extracted, but others involving the arguments in the tenant's reaction function are too complex to be understandable. Nonetheless, some results of interest do appear in the conditions that are readily interpretable. The one of most interest is that in deciding whether to add another tenant, the landlord's utility gain from adding another contract cannot be smaller than the utility he foregoes by not cultivating that land himself: $Eu_y[(1-\alpha)\pi_t - \beta] - Eu_y\theta f_{H*}h \leq 0$, where f_{H*} is the marginal productivity of the landlord's production to land he retains for his own cultivation. Considering the questions regarding the relative productivity of land under owner cultivation or fixed rent and share-rents, this is an interesting result. For the landlord's income from this land rented on shares to equal what it could have given him had he worked it himself (under his own direction), the tenant's incentives cannot be so distorted as to yield less than the owner himself could have gotten operating it himself.

Sharing Input Costs under Sharecropping. Imperfect information is the basis for cost sharing in sharecropping.[42] A landlord could simply specify the amounts of purchased inputs to be used, but between the time the contract is agreed upon and the inputs are to be used, conditions could have changed. Leaving input decisions, including amounts and timing, to the tenant puts those decisions in the hands of the person better placed to be aware of conditions on the farm. Cost sharing is a mechanism that encourages the tenant to adjust the inputs to changes in circumstances, again assuming that the tenant has superior information. These factors involve asymmetry of information regarding the productivity of purchased, monitorable inputs. Productivity can vary both temporally and spatially over the farm, and is affected by weather, soil, the characteristics of the tenant and any workers he or she hires, and the equipment they use. Consequently the contract terms will depend on both institutional features and characteristics of the technology.

Cost shares may differ from output shares, and cost shares for different inputs may vary, depending on the effect of the use of a particular input on the tenant's effort. For example, if one input is complementary to effort, a landlord might try to increase the tenant's effort by lowering the tenant's cost share for that input below the tenant's output share.

A tenant determines labor effort, e, under the share contract and also determines the application of a purchased input, x. The tenant's income is $y = \alpha\theta f(e, x) - \beta - \gamma p_x x$, where θ is the uncertainty factor with $E(\theta) = 1$, and p_x is the price of the purchased input (relative to the output price, which is assumed to equal 1). Abstracting from the continuous character of farming operations over a crop season, the tenant makes decisions about effort and the purchased input before observing the realization of θ. The absence of any non-farm income in the expression for the tenant's income means that labor market opportunities have been assumed away to simplify. The tenant's problem is to maximize utility: $\max_{\{e,x\}} EU[y(e,x), e]$, in which $EU_y > 0$ and $EU_e < 0$. The first-order condition for effort arising from the maximization is, using subscript notation instead of the clumsier $\Delta x/\Delta y$ notation, $f_e = -(1/\alpha\rho) \cdot (EU_e/EU_y)$, in which $\rho = EU_y\theta/EU_e$ is the risk aversion factor restricted to $0 < \rho < 1$.[43] For a risk-neutral tenant,

[41] More detail on the tenant's reaction functions as constraints in the landlord's utility maximization problem when tenant effort is unobservable is reported in Otsuka and Murukami (1987).

[42] The model presented below is from Braverman and Stiglitz (1986, 642–652).

[43] The risk aversion coefficient $\rho > 0$ because $\mathrm{cov}(U_y\theta, \theta) < 0$, since the larger the value θ takes, the larger is the output θf and accordingly the larger is the tenant's income. Then since $U_{yy} < 0$, the marginal utility of income decreases as output increases.

ρ would take a value of 1. The FOC for application of the purchased input is $f_x = \gamma p_x/\alpha\rho$. The ratio of the cost and output shares, $\delta = \gamma/\alpha$, will be used in the remainder of the presentation to simplify the focus on the relative shares. Rewriting the tenant's income and the FOC for the purchased input accordingly yields $y = \alpha(\theta f - \delta p_x x) - \beta$ and $f_x = \delta p_x/\rho$. Taken together, $\delta p_x/\rho$ serves as an internal, as opposed to market, price of the input; i.e., if the tenant were risk neutral and the cost and output shares were the same, the purchased input's effective price on the farm would be simply p_x. The two FOCs can be solved to yield functional expressions for effort and purchased input application and mean output in terms of these re-defined contract shares: $e = e(\alpha, \delta, \beta)$, $x = x(\alpha, \delta, \beta)$, and $q(\alpha, \delta, \beta) = f[e(\alpha, \delta, \beta), x(\alpha, \delta, \beta)]$. Although the landlord cannot control the tenant's effort, he or she will recognize that effort can be affected through changing the terms of the contract. How that is accomplished in addressed next.

The landlord's problem is to find the contract composed of terms α, δ, and β that maximizes his or her expected utility while yielding the tenant his reservation (indirect) utility. Assuming a risk-neutral landlord for simplicity, since $E\theta = 1$, the landlord's maximization problem can be written as $\max_{\{\alpha,\delta\}} \pi = (1-\alpha)f(e, x) - (1-\alpha\delta)p_x x + \beta$ subject to $EU(\alpha, \delta, \beta) = \bar{U}$.[44] If the landlord and tenant had identical information, the landlord could do exactly as well (no better and no worse) by specifying input levels as by sharing input costs. For any contract that specifies a particular level of purchased input application, there is a corresponding cost-sharing contract that leaves its application to the tenant's discretion, as long as the purchased input application is observable and effort and purchased input application, as well as both landlord's and tenant's income, are identical whatever the value of θ (i.e., whatever the state of nature turns out to be). This equivalence corresponds to the equivalence noted previously regarding share contracts with a combination of fixed rental and wage labor—as long as cost sharing is part of the tenancy contract, some of the assumptions, such as the invariance of effort and purchased input applications to the state of nature or the observability of the tenant's behavior to the landlord, must not hold. This means that cost-sharing terms in a share rental contract must be attributable to some form(s) of asymmetric information between landlord and tenant.

Cost sharing provides flexibility of incentives under risk and asymmetric information. Instead of specifying the state of nature to affect the productivity of all inputs identically, let it affect the productivity of the purchased input only, $q = \theta f(e, \varphi x)$, where φ is observable to the tenant but not to the landlord and is observable prior to the application of the purchased input. In a world of perfect information and markets, the productivity of the purchased input would equal its price, $\varphi f_x = p_x$. With missing markets inducing sharecropping and cost sharing by a risk-averse tenant, the previous productivity-market price relationship becomes $\alpha\varphi\theta\rho f_x/\gamma = p_x$, or $\varphi\theta\rho f_x/\delta = p_x$. Since $f_{xx} < 0$, when the input-specific state of nature φ takes a larger value, making the purchased input more productive, the tenant will apply more of input x. Cost sharing induces the tenant to apply more of a purchased input at times when and places where it is more productive. Since those inputs are only partially purchased by the landlord, the tenant will accept more risk in doing so, but will accept the extra risk only if the expected increase in his share of the output more than offsets the increase in the risk he bears. If the purchased input were a sufficiently strong substitute for effort actually to reduce the tenant's effort, cost-sharing would not be a desirable contract term from the landlord's viewpoint.

The equivalence between the contract specifying input levels and the one specifying cost shares under perfect information and full markets allows the relationship between the output share and the cost share, $\alpha(\delta)$—which says that the output share is a function of the cost share, and in its inverse form says that the cost share is an inverse function of the output share—to be established. Substituting this relationship into the last version of the landlord's maximization problem yields $\max_{\{\delta\}} \pi(\delta) = (1-\alpha)q(\alpha, \delta) - (1-\alpha\delta)p_x(\alpha, \delta)$, subject to maintaining the tenant's utility at $\bar{U}$, in which α is shorthand for the functional notation $\alpha(\delta)$.[45] The cost-sharing rules can be derived from the first-order condition of the landlord's maximization problem: $\pi_\delta = 0 = (\delta p_x x - q)\alpha_\delta|_{\bar{U}} + \alpha p_x x$ (the direct effect) $+[(1-\alpha)q_x - (1-\alpha\delta)p_x]x_\delta|_{\bar{U}}$ (the indirect effect on the purchased input) $+(1-\alpha)q_e e_\delta|_{\bar{U}}$ (the indirect effect on effort). In this expression the effect of the cost-share ratio on the application of the purchased input, with tenant's utility held constant is $x_\delta|_{\bar{U}} = x_\delta + x_\alpha \alpha_\delta|_{\bar{U}}$; the tenant's-utility-constant effect of the cost-share ratio on effort has the same structure; and the tenant's-utility-constant effect of the cost-share ratio on the output share is $\alpha_\delta|_{\bar{U}} = -U_\delta/U_\alpha = \alpha s_x/(\rho - \delta s_x)$, where $s_x = p_x x/f$ is the share of the purchased input cost in the expected value of output (recall that the price of the output was normalized to 1). When the output and cost shares are the same, $\delta = 1$, this first-order condition simplifies to $\pi_\delta = \alpha q s_x(\rho - 1)/(\rho - s_x) + (1-\alpha)p_x(\rho^{-1} - 1)x_\delta|_{\bar{U}} + (1-\alpha)q_e e_\delta|_{\bar{U}}$, which need not be zero. Several conclusions can be seen from this last expression. First, if there are no incentive effects, $e_\delta = 0$, and tenants are risk neutral, $\rho = 1$, then $\pi_\delta = 0$, and it is indeed optimal for output and cost shares to be equal. Second, if there are no risk effects, i.e., $\rho = 1$, $\delta = 1$ will not maximize the landlord's expected profit—$\pi_\delta \neq 0$ at this level of δ. The first two terms in the FOC go to zero, leaving only the indirect effect on effort through a change in the sharing ratio to affect the landlord's expected profit. So the

[44] The fixed payment β is not one of the control instruments the landlord uses in this case since the tenancy contract has already been determined to be on shares and for simplicity, no other fixed payment goes in either direction. The term is left in the landlord's income expression for completeness.

[45] This derivation is for the case of no side-payments, $\beta = 0$, which makes the results more easily interpretable than is the case with full optimization of all three contract terms.

landlord's expected profit will be improved by changing δ, i.e., raising or lowering the cost share γ relative to the output share α, depending on the sign of e_δ. However, the response of e_δ is difficult to sign. If the purchased input has no effect at all on the productivity of effort, $e_\delta > 0$ from a pure substitution effect: with a higher price of the purchased input, the tenant will substitute effort for it. As the productivity effect of the purchased input on effort becomes stronger, assuming that it is positive, at some some level of positive cross-effect, e_δ will turn negative; since a positive productivity effect will elicit more effort, if the direct marginal productivity of effort does not fall much as more effort is applied, the overall sign of e_δ will be negative. In general $e_\delta < 0$ is the more general presumption: a higher δ increases the effective price of the purchased input to the tenant, who decreases its application, reducing in turn the productivity of effort, which in its turn elicits a reduction in effort. So the presumption is that $\delta = 1$ is too high to maximize landlord profit, so some subsidization of the purchased input will be an improvement—adjusting α as necessary to maintain the reservation level of utility for the tenant. Third, if there is no effect of δ on effort, then $\delta = 1$ is too high since the first two terms in the FOC are negative, and as just explained, a reduction in δ when $\pi_\delta < 0$ will raise the value of π_δ to zero. Examination of the FOC of the landlord's more general maximization problem including choice of the fixed payment β shows that $\pi_\delta = 0$ can be attained only when $\gamma < \alpha$.

Putting the Land Market into Perspective: Interlinked Contract Terms. The necessary incompleteness of tenancy contracts leaves a landlord unable to specify many actions he might like a tenant to take. However, the frequently modest formation of markets combined with the personal situation of many tenants leaves landlords with additional options. For instance, a landless tenant is likely to be able to offer only his or her own future income stream as collateral for either consumption or production loans, and that is likely to be unacceptable to most potential lenders. A landlord, on the other hand, is well placed to know the creditworthiness of a tenant and, renting on a crop share, has easy access to recovery of a loan in the event of a default. Under certain conditions, cross effects between a tenant's consumption and production decisions through the leisure-effort trade-off will let a lending landlord affect a tenant's production decisions via loan terms when they would be unenforceable directly through the tenancy terms. Such interlinking of transactions can make both landlord and tenant better off.

2.4.4 Interlinked Transactions in Agrarian Economies: Land, Insurance, Labor, Credit

With multiple sources of risk, the tenancy contract itself is a joint land-market / insurance market transaction, as the previous sub-section identified.[46] Insurance markets have been particularly difficult to establish for agriculture. In non-modern agrarian communities, the areal extent of markets for difficult-to-trade items would have been limited by both transportation and information costs. While grains and wines could be traded hundreds, if not thousands, of miles, services such as insurance would have found it difficult to transmit the necessary information over sufficiently large areas to make a market feasible. Insuring against a house fire or a farm accident would have been one matter—generally not everybody's house catches on fire at the same time, leaving those unaffected able to help the person whose house did burn down build a new one. Similarly with the personal accident (assuming a war clause would exist in such an insurance contract). Those events are sufficiently random that a relatively small area will have a sufficiently large number of agents that the incidents will strike small proportions of them at any one time. The problem with agricultural crop insurance is that, to a great extent, what hits one hits all at the same time. Of course, there are microclimatic events in particularly hilly or mountainous terrain or areas of localized hailstorms that could provide the idiosyncracy required to make some risks insurable, but a common theme of agricultural risks is their pervasiveness in an area where they strike. Crop insurance would have been very close to contemporary catastrophe insurance, such as hurricane insurance in the states along the Atlantic and Gulf Coasts of the United States and earthquake insurance in California. There are perennial difficulties maintaining those markets—insurance companies providing such coverage frequently go out of business after such events because they can't hold sufficient capital to cover the insured losses, and many of the surviving firms threaten to exit the market because they can't make sufficient rates of return to attract adequate capital to meet the next possible event. This leaves various forms of self-insurance for ancient agrarian communities, from extended marriage circles ("social storage") to holding reserves of one sort or another, to joining land owners and farm workers together to share risks.[47] Share tenancy does not, of course, substitute for catastrophe insurance but it provides a buffer that offers both landlord and tenant partial insurance for an expected range of events.

Where the tenant's family has resources that cannot be marketed easily, the tenancy contract helps employ those resources in the absence of direct markets for them. Typically hard-to-market family resources include managerial human capital, draft animal power, and family

[46] The characterization of these interlinkages during the Republican and Imperial periods in Italy and in the Roman Imperial period in Greece as evidence of a "multi-stranded dependency relationship" by Foxhall, (1990, 99) does not address the issue as the consequences of missing markets, and of individual incentives in general, on both landlord and tenant. De Neeve (1984, 123) notes that, "It is extremely significant that precisely this combination of landownership and money-lending occurs relatively often in the ancient sources." Baer, (1963, 10) discusses an 11th Dynasty Egyptian account entry as a possible loan, which might have been a tied contract.

[47] Christakis (2014) finds no archaeological evidence for social / communal storage – nothing between storage at the centralized / governmental level and the household level on Bronze Age Crete.

labor, particularly labor of women and children.[48] Markets for draft animal services typically are weak to non-existent. Rental markets for draft animals without their driver generally have been non-existent because of the moral hazard associated with an owner's inability to determine how the renter has treated the animals. If the animals die, it is generally impossible to determine the extent to which responsibility lay with the renter versus natural causes: a renter could mistreat the animals and an owner could rent out a bullock that was about to drop anyway. Even when a draft team rental would come with the team's own driver, the demand for such services is seasonally quite intense, and many potential renters of such services would be leery of being unable to obtain the required services at the right time. Between these two types of contingency, rental markets for draft animal services have rarely been strong, if they have existed at all. When competition for share rentals exists, families with access to greater resources of all these types can get selected into tenancy while less well-endowed families are relegated to contract labor Pant (1983). While these intra-family resource allocation improvements made possible with tenancy contracts generally do not involve separate agreements, they may provide informal screening mechanisms for the allocation of tenancies.

To show how interlinking works and why it is beneficial to both parties, the analysis of one model is presented in some detail below.[49] The landlord generally benefits by non-coercively getting the tenant to do something he otherwise would not have been inclined to do without the side-benefit provided by the tied transaction, and the tenant generally sees his or her utility increased by a voluntary action that would otherwise be more costly. To simplify the analysis, the model assumes that a pure sharecropping agreement exists. It implicitly assumes that tenants have no off-farm employment opportunities and that share tenants are not also land owners themselves.

The Tenant's Side of the Problem. The tenant receives share α of output q, which itself is a function of the tenant's effort, e; risky environmental factors θ; and the choice of technique Ω, for which an increase represents an increase in risk: $q = q(e, \theta, \Omega)$. To simplify this expression, it can be re-written as $q = gf(e)$ in which g is a positive random variable with a probability density function $h = h(g, \Omega)$, with Eg designated by $\bar{g}$. The tenant's utility is a function of his income, $y = \alpha q$; his effort e; his production technique Ω; of other variables that may be under his control, z; and a set of variables under the landlord's control, q: $u = u(y, e, \Omega, z, q)$. Several special cases of this general utility specification are investigated. In the case of a landlord selling consumption goods to a tenant (the proverbial company store), if z is the tenant's consumption of some commodity he buys from the landlord, q will be the price the landlord charges, and c is the tenant's consumption of other goods, his utility function can be re-written as $U = U(c, e, \Omega, z) = U(y\text{-}zq, e, \Omega, z)$. In the case of the landlord offering a consumption loan to the tenant, suppose the tenant has an initial level of wealth w_0, the landlord charges interest rate r, and the tenant borrows amount b, and the tenant's consumption in the ith period is c_i (to study the credit market, at least two periods must be modeled, the period when the loan is borrowed and the period when it is repaid). Then the tenant's utility function would be written $U = U(c_0, c_1, e, \Omega) = U(w_0 + b, y - (1+r)b, e, \Omega)$. The tenant chooses e, z, and Ω to maximize expected utility, taking into account the production relationships implied by the production function: $\max_{\{e,z,\Omega\}} Eu(y, e, \Omega, z, q) \equiv V(\alpha, q)$, where V represents the maximized value of the tenant's utility as a function of the landlord's control variables. The tenant's level of effort $e = e(\alpha, q)$; level of consumption of the good or service provided by the additional transaction with the landlord, $z = z(\alpha, q)$; and production technique, $\Omega = \Omega(\alpha, q)$ can be derived from the first-order conditions of this maximization as functions of the instruments at the disposal of the landlord, the output share on the tenancy contract and the terms on which the tied good or service is provided.

The Landlord's Side of the Problem. The landlord is assumed to be risk-neutral. His or her expected income Y has two parts, the share of the crops from the sharecroppers, $(1-\alpha)f(e)\bar{g}$, and the return from the interlinked activity, $\pi(z, q)$, which may be negative. If it is optimal for the landlord to subsidize some aspect of a tenant's operation or consumption, his full expected income is $Y = (1-\alpha)f(e)\bar{g} + \pi(z, q)$.

In the first of the examples above where the landlord sold a consumption good to tenants at a price q, the landlord's income from the interlinked transaction is $\pi(z, q) = (q - q_0)z(q)$, where q_0 is the cost to the landlord of the consumption good and z(q) is the tenant's demand for the good as a function of the price the landlord charges. In the lending case, the tenant borrows at interest rate r and the landlord's return from the lending is the difference between that rate and the rate he could get elsewhere for his capital, times the amount borrowed. The landlord chooses α and q to maximize his expected utility subject to meeting the tenant's reservation utility constraint: $\max_{\{\alpha,q\}} Y$ subject to $V(\alpha, Q) \geq \bar{U}$, where the V function, being a maximized utility, incorporates the tenant's reaction to the various contract and transaction terms. The first-order condition for the landlord's problem can be written as $\Delta Y/\Delta q = (1-\alpha)[\bar{g}f' \Delta e/\Delta q + f(\Delta\bar{g}/\Delta q)(\Delta\Omega/\Delta q)] + \pi_q + \pi_z \Delta z/\Delta q - \lambda\Delta V/\Delta q$, where λ is the Lagrange multiplier on the constraint. In this expression, the landlord recognizes that changing q has an indirect effect on his income through its effect on a tenant's level of effort and choice of technique—the terms in brackets—as well as the direct effects in the π_z and π_q terms. The indirect terms provide the fundamental motivation for interlinkage of these transactions with the tenancy contract. The following analysis analyzes how outstanding loans affect tenant effort and choice of technique, then uses those results to study the optimal choices of the landlord.

[48] Bagnall, (1993, 152) notes the common occurrence of land leases on large estates in 4th Century C.E. Egypt which mixed labor and land agreements in the same contract.

[49] The model presented below is from Braverman and Stiglitz (1982).

Interlinking the Credit Market: The Tenant's Perspective on a Consumption Loan. To analyze how the fact that a tenant must repay the amount $(1 + r)b$ affects his labor supply, the choice of technique is assumed to remain constant. Using B to represent $(1 + r)b$, the tenant's consumption in the period of repayment, assuming separability between consumption and effort at any one date and consumption and effort at any other date,[50] is $c = \alpha y - B$, and the tenant chooses effort to maximize utility: max $EU(c, e) = \max\{e\} EU[\alpha g f(e) - B, e)$. The first-order condition for this maximization is $\alpha f' EU_c g + EU_e = 0$. Further manipulation of this first-order condition shows that $\Delta e/\Delta B \gtrless 0$ as $-E(U_{cc}\alpha g f' + U_{ec}) \gtrless 0$. Since $U_{cc} < 0$ unambiguously, if increased consumption increases the marginal disutility of effort or leaves it unchanged, i.e., if $U_{ec} \leq 0$, increased borrowing will increase a tenant's effort and increase the return to the landlord.

Now consider two institutional arrangements to deal with default, bankruptcy and bonded labor. A bonded labor clause in a loan agreement would stipulate that if the tenant fails to repay the loan, he must provide labor services to the landlord, presumably an undesirable outcome from the tenant's perspective. He would try to avoid decisions that would increase the probability of his output falling below a level that would let him repay the loan and thus put him into bonded labor service. The tenant's effort increases with increasing loan amount if the agreement includes a bonded labor clause. If a bankruptcy clause is agreed to instead, it can decrease the tenant's effort. In fact, a bankruptcy clause can alter the shape of a tenant's utility function from concave (upward but decreasingly so) to convex (upward and increasingly so) over some regions of the level of consumption, effectively converting him from a risk averter to a risk seeker. An increase in borrowing makes bankruptcy more likely, which reduces the marginal return to effort, an effect which is counterbalanced by the same combination of second-order effects in consumption that determined the sign of $\Delta e/\Delta B$ in the case above of neither bankruptcy nor bonded labor clause. Only if these second-order consumption effects increasing effort outweigh the direct dampening effect that an increased probability of bankruptcy has on effort will effort increase with increased borrowing under a bankruptcy clause.[51]

Now turn to the effect of borrowing on choice of technique, with effort fixed. An increase in Ω represents a choice of a riskier project, which is represented by a mean-preserving spread of the probability distribution of returns relative to a less risky project, i.e., a shifting of probabilities from the central part of the distribution, representing the higher-probability outcomes, to both tails, meaning that both much better and much worse outcomes are more likely than with the less risky project although the expected value remains the same. Increased borrowing will either increase or decrease risk taking (it will have no effect only if the utility function is quadratic, which is an empirical matter on which evidence is scanty). Precisely, $\Delta\Omega/\Delta B \gtrless 0$ as $U_{ccc} \lesseqgtr 0$. $U_c > 0$ is marginal utility; $U_{cc} \leq 0$ describes how marginal utility changes as consumption (or income) increases, and it is ordinarily negative, although it is zero for a risk-neutral individual; U_{ccc} characterizes an individual's differential reaction to upside and downside risk. Nonnegativity of U_{ccc} is called prudence or downside risk aversion; such a person would not accept a gamble that promised a lower expected value but with a higher probability of a very high gain. Thus, if a tenant is prudent in this sense, greater borrowing would disincline him to choose a technique with a higher expected output but that also has a higher risk of a bad outcome. This can also reduce the landlord's income if the tenant wants to use a less risky technique than the landlord would prefer. Thus, with a bankruptcy clause, increased borrowing will reduce a tenant's risk taking. A bankruptcy clause could actually increase it, as a tenant might choose techniques with higher expected returns and higher risk, a choice which would increase the landlord's return. Altogether, the tenant's behavior is affected by the total of his rent payment and his loan commitment, and it is useful to the landlord to know the total magnitude, which provides the motivation for interlinking the land and the credit transactions.

Interlinking the Credit Market: The Landlord's Perspective on a Consumption Loan. The landlord could experience either a positive or a negative externality from a consumption loan transaction tied to a share tenancy contract. In the former case, in which increased borrowing increases the landlord's returns, there will be an incentive to subsidize the loans and to encourage the tenant to go into debt to him so he will work harder to repay the loan. In the latter case, the landlord would like to restrict the tenant's borrowing although he would not want to eliminate it completely. Since the restriction reduces the tenant's expected utility, in a competitive environment, the landlord will have to provide the tenant with some compensation in another contract term. Formally, the landlord specifies the loan function r(b) since the interest rate will generally be a function of the size of the loan. While the tenant chooses the size of the loan, b, the equivalence of a large number of loan functions for all practical purposes allows treatment of both variables, r and b, as under the landlord's control. With ρ representing the landlord's cost of capital, his problem is $\max_{\{r,b\}} Y \equiv (1 - \alpha)f(e)g + [1 + r - (1 + \rho)]b$, subject to the tenant's reservation utility restriction, $EU(w_0 + b, \alpha f(e)g - (1+r)b, e) \geq \bar{U}$. Again assuming that U is separable in c_0 and c_1, from the first-order conditions, the relationship

[50] Separability means that a change in either consumption or effort in one of the periods does not affect the marginal utility of consumption or disutility of effort at the other date.

[51] This is a case of model specification affecting the results of the model. Without a labor market, Braverman and Stiglitz's result that an increase in the interest rate (or the amount borrowed) will increase a tenant's effort is contradicted by a model otherwise entirely similar in structure but which has a labor market. Subramanian (1995. 333) introduces an off-farm labor market and finds that a tenant faced with an increase in the interest rate charged or in the amount borrowed will leave cultivation labor unchanged if his utility function exhibits constant absolute risk aversion, or with decreasing absolute risk aversion (possibly less likely in circumstances likely to have been typical of antiquity) would withdraw labor from cultivation.

between the ratio of the tenant's marginal utilities of consumption in the two periods and the landlord's cost of capital is $EU_c(c_1, e)/u'(c_0) = [(1 - \alpha)f'(e)g \cdot (\Delta e/\Delta B) + 1]/(1 + \rho)$. This expression is to be compared with the same relationship between marginal utilities and the cost of capital in the circumstance that gave the tenant and landlord equal access to the capital market, $EU_c(c_1, e)/u'(c_0) = 1/(1 + \rho)$, which is a reminder that consumption (and expected consumption) should be adjusted so that the intertemporal ratio of their marginal utilities equals the intertemporal rate of transformation, which is one plus the interest rate. The former expression will be greater or smaller than the unrestricted-access case according to whether $\Delta e/\Delta B \gtrless 0$. Thus the optimal contract the landlord will offer will induce tenants to borrow more than they would have in an unlinked market to which they had equal access as the landlord if the borrowing increases their effort, and vice versa.

If the landlord cannot restrict the level of borrowing as assumed in the previous case but can charge an interest rate different from ρ and can alter the tenant's crop share α, the previous relationship becomes much more complicated: $EU_c g/EU_c = \{1 - [(1 - \alpha)/\alpha]s_e\epsilon_\alpha^e - (r - \rho)\epsilon_\alpha^b/f\} \div \{1 + [(1 - \alpha)/\alpha](s_e/s_b)\epsilon_B^e\epsilon_r^B + (r - \rho) \cdot (\Delta b/\Delta r)/b\}$, in which s_e is the share of effort in output, $f'e/f$, and s_b is the ratio of the interest payment on the loan to the output. Whether the landlord sets $r \gtreqless \rho$ depends on the tenant's risk aversion and the elasticities of effort with respect to the tenant's output share and total indebtedness B.

Production Loans. Extending the loans from pure consumption loans to production loans is straightforward. Let output be a function of the amount borrowed as well as effort: $q = gf(e, b)$. Substituting this into the previous landlord maximization problem, the previous (simpler) first-order condition becomes $EU_c/EU_c\alpha gf_b = [(1 - \alpha)f_e \cdot (\Delta e/\Delta B) + 1]/\{(1 - \alpha)[f_e(\Delta e/\Delta b) + f_b] + (1 + \rho)\}$, which has the form of $X/[Y + (1 + \rho)]$, analogous in structure to the previous result in its relationship between the marginal rate of substitution and the marginal rate of transformation. The left-hand side of this relationship derives from the tenant's optimization and the right-hand side from the landlord's. The landlord takes into account the facts that (1) he appropriates a fraction of the return from the increased output, $(1 - \alpha)f_b$; (2) the increased input level affects the tenant's effort, $\Delta e/\Delta B$; and (3) the increase in the tenant's borrowing increases his utility, letting the landlord change some other contract term in his own favor while still being able to attract other tenants. However, the effect of an increase in other inputs is ambiguous. If effort and other inputs are complements, $f_{eb} > 0$, as might be expected reasonably, the increased borrowing to finance additional inputs increases the marginal return to effort, and effort will increase. However, the increased output would have an income effect as well which would be expected to decrease the level of effort. Without subsidization of the interest rate, the tenant would have set $EU_c/EU_c\alpha gf_b = 1/(1 + \rho)$, so whether the landlord prefers to subsidize or restrict borrowing depends on whether $EU_c/EU_c\alpha gf_b \gtrless (f_e\Delta e/\Delta B)/[(f_e\Delta e/\Delta B) + f_b]$. Either sign is possible, depending on the degree of complementarity, f_{eb}, and the specific characteristics of the utility function. Production loans have the effect of changing the relative prices of inputs, allowing the landlord to induce the tenant to apply more of inputs which the tenant otherwise would be inclined to use more sparingly.

Interlinking Tenancy and Product Markets. The landlord may serve as an intermediary between the tenant and both input and product markets. Requiring tenants to market their output through him is one way for the landlord to monitor tenants' chiseling on reported output, one source of moral hazard in a share contract. If no restrictions exist on output shares, the landlord would pay the tenant what he could receive himself for the output. If shares are restricted by either social norms or laws, the landlord can extract surplus from a tenant by paying him a lower price than the landlord himself receives for the output. Formally, if the landlord buys the output from the tenant at a price p_T which differs from the price the landlord receives for it, p_L, the tenant's income is $y = \alpha p_T f(e, x) - \gamma x$, where γ again represents the tenant's share of input costs. The tenant's maximization problem is $\max_{\{e,x\}} U[y(e, x), e]$. The first-order conditions yield $f_x = \gamma/\alpha p_T$ and $f_x = -[U_2(y, e)/U_1(y, e)]\alpha p_T$, which indicate that the tenant's decisions are fully determined by the contract terms γ and αp_T. Substituting $\hat{\alpha}$ for αp_T, the tenant's effort and input supply decisions can be expressed as $e = e(\hat{\alpha}, \gamma)$ and $x = x(\hat{\alpha}, \gamma)$. The landlord who faces the output price p_L maximizes his income subject to the tenant's utility constraint: $max_{\{\alpha,\gamma,p_T\}}(1 - \alpha)p_L f[e(\hat{\alpha}, \gamma), x(\hat{\alpha}, \gamma)] - (1 - \gamma)\ x(\hat{\alpha}, \gamma)$ subject to $U[y(\hat{\alpha}, \gamma,\ p_Y), e(\hat{\alpha}, \gamma)] = \bar{V}$. Through several substitutions, particularly inverting the tenant's utility constraint in the landlord's maximization problem, the landlord's problem can be expressed as $max_{\{\hat{\alpha},\gamma\}}\ p_L f(\hat{\alpha}, \gamma) - x(\hat{\alpha}, \gamma) - \phi(\bar{V}, \hat{\alpha}, \gamma) = \pi(\hat{\alpha}, \gamma)$, which indicates that the landlord cares only about $\hat{\alpha}$, not α and p_T separately.

It may also be in the landlord's interest to link the credit market with his marketing activity. The landlord pays a single price for the output he buys from his tenants and sets this price so the marginal cost of buying an additional unit equals the marginal revenue he can get from re-selling it. Since the price the landlord pays is less than the marginal cost, from his perspective, the tenants have insufficient incentive to produce more at the price he offers, so it may be worth his while to subsidize credit to boost their output. Thus a landlord's ability to alter product market prices does not give him any additional instrument for exploiting his tenants.

Interlinking consumption good markets, a landlord may wish to alter the relative prices of consumption goods that his tenants face, encouraging the consumption of those that increase effort and discouraging those which are complementary to leisure, such as alcohol.

2.5 Agricultural Commodity Storage

Storage of agricultural commodities is a costly productive activity that transforms a commodity from one period to the next. It may be operated by a public agency with the purpose of stabilizing prices. Given the relationships between availability and price on the one hand and between price and consumption on the other, using commodity storage to alter prices is roughly equivalent to altering what the availability of food would otherwise be. Storage also may be supplied competitively by private agents with the goal of making a profit, as with any other activity.

A Commodity Storage Model. There are interactions between production, consumption, price expectations, and storage, with each affecting the other three.[52] These relationships will be introduced as follows. First, the costs of the storage activity are presented, and storage at the level of the individual storer is related to aggregate market storage. Next, the inter-temporal arbitrage relationship between prices at different dates and storage costs is shown. To this point in the explanation, the difference in relationships between prices and storage costs at the levels of an individual storer and the total market do not look greatly different, but when the endogeneity between prices and quantities is introduced to the model, it is important to pay attention to the distinctions between actions at the individual level and consequences at the aggregate market level. The profit maximization behavior belongs to the individual storage supplier, although assuming agents in this market are identical, the aggregation of their decisions to market totals is a matter of simple addition.

The total cost for an individual storage agent i to store an amount of commodity s_{it} from period t to period t+1, as of period t+1, is $K_i(s_t) = ks_{it} + ap_ts_{it} + r(p_ts_{it} + ks_{it})$, where $k \geq 0$ is the net unit cost of storage services, a $(0 \leq a \leq 1)$ is a spoilage or loss rate, p_t is the price in period t, and r is the real interest rate. The profit that a profit maximizing storage agent i expects at time t to earn in period t+1 is $E_t(\pi_{it+1}) = E_t(p_{t+1})(1\text{-}a)s_{it}(1+r)^{-1} - p_ts_{it} - ks_{it}$. The first-order condition for maximizing this expected profit is $\Delta E_t(\pi_{it+1})/\Delta s_{it} = (1\text{-}a)E_t(p_{t+1})(1+r)^{-1} - p_t - k = 0$, in which the storage agent adjusts the amount stored to make the discounted expected price equal the sum of the loss-weighted current price and the unit storage cost.

With N identical storage agents, total storage from period t to period t+1 is $\sum_i^N s_{it} = S_t$. Storage may, of course, be zero, but it cannot be negative, an important source of asymmetry in the economics of commodity storage. If storage is positive, its magnitude equates the current period's price with the price expected in the next period, less the marginal cost of storage services, losses, and interest on the capital invested: $(1 - r)^{-1}aEp_{t+1} - (p_t + k) = 0$ if storage is positive $(S_t > 0)$, or $0 \leq$ if $S_t = 0$. Accordingly, the basic inter-temporal arbitrage condition is that if $S_t > 0$, $E_a(p_{t+1}) = (p_t + k)(1 + r)/(1\text{-}a)$, or the expected price in period t+1 is the price in period t, plus storage costs and interest charges, with allowance for loss, which is the market equivalent of the individual storage agent's first-order condition for profit maximization. However, this relationship that holds between adjacent periods does not extend beyond the next period, because conditions may dictate zero storage in the intervening time period.

The demand for the commodity can be specified as an inverse consumption demand, $p_t = p(Q_t)$. The total quantity consumed in the market is $Q_t = X_t + (1\text{-}a)S_{t-1} - S_t = I_t - S_t$, in which X_t is total production in period t, S_t is the total amount stored from period t to period t+1 after loss of aS_{t-1}, and I_t is the total amount of the commodity on hand at time t. Using a multiplicative disturbance to production, the supply function is $X_t = \hat{X}(p_t^r)(1 + v_t)$, in which v_t is a random production disturbance which is serially uncorrelated (i.e., there is no relationship over time between magnitudes of event v_t). The price p_t^r is the action certainty equivalent price at time t-1, when the planned production $\hat{x}(p_t^r)$ must be decided upon, a specification which gives perfectly inelastic short-run supply. Production, like storage, is a competitive, expected-profit-maximizing activity. The profit that storage provider i expects at time t is $E(\pi_{it}) = E[p(q_t)x_{it}] - C(\hat{x}_{it}) = E(r_{it}) - C(\hat{x}_{it})$, in which E denotes the expectation operation (conditional expectations given information available at time $t - 1$), C is total cost, x_{it} is an individual producer's output in period t, and r_{it} is revenue in period t. While provider i's revenue depends on provider i's output, the price depends on total consumption. The producer recognizes that the production disturbance affects all producers identically, and hence affects the market for the commodity as it affects his own output. Then the producer's first-order condition for maximizing profit is $\Delta E(\pi_{it})/\Delta\hat{x}_{it} = \Delta E(r_{it})/\Delta\hat{x}_{it} - \Delta C(\hat{x}_{it})/\Delta\hat{x}_{it}$. The producer's action certainty-equivalent price, p_t^r, is the marginal expected return per unit of planned production: $p_t^r = \Delta E(r_{it})/\Delta\hat{x}_{it} = \Delta E\{p[\hat{X}(p_t^r)(1 - v_t) + (1 - a)S_{t-1} - S_t]\}/\Delta\hat{x}_{it}$, in which $\hat{x}_{it}(p_t^r)(1 - v_t)$ is planned production as a function of action certainty equivalent price p_t^r and the entire expression inside the p[•] function is consumption, or the sum of current production and draw-down from last period's storage less the set-aside for this period's storage.

The price private storage suppliers receive depends on the size of the harvest, which depends in turn on the amount planted. The amount stored influences what producers expect to receive at the end of the crop season, so the amount planted is a function of current storage. The price of what is put into storage depends on the amount currently in storage because what isn't stored out of the total amount available is consumed, and price is determined by consumption. Simultaneous solutions must be found for current-period storage, S_t, and planned production in the following period, $\hat{X}_{t+1}$. The arbitrage conditions for private storage can be expanded accordingly as $(1 - a)E_t(p_{t+1}\{\hat{x}_{t+1}[p_{t+1}^r(S_t)](1 + v_{t+1}) + (1 - a)S_t - S_{t+1}\}(1 + r)^{-1}) - p_t(I_t - S_t) - k = 0$ if $S_t >$

[52] The exposition of the model is adapted from Wright and Williams (1982a; 1982b) and Williams and Wright (1991, Chapters 2 and 4).

0 (or < 0 if $S_t = 0$). The thicket of functional notation in this expression calls for some explanation. Starting with some simplification, the basic expectation is $E_t(p_{t+1})$, the expected value of next period's price, p_{t+1}. Next period's price p_{t+1} is a function of next period's aggregate consumption, Q_{t+1}, which from the crop disposition identity will be next period's production plus the difference between carry-in and carry-out storage next period, $X_{t+1} + (1\text{-a})S_t - S_{t+1}$. The expression uses the functional notations of each of those terms to indicate the dependencies of the various terms on other influences. Thus, next period's planned production, which in functional notation is $\hat{x}_{t+1}$, is a function of the action certainty equivalent price, p^r_{t+1}, which is the producer's marginal expected return per unit of planned production. That certainty equivalent price is in turn a function of current storage S_t. The term $p_t(I_t - S_t)$ is simply the current period's known price as a function of current consumption, $Q_t = I_t - S_t$, or total availability I_t less what is stored. So in simplified form we can recover the original arbitrage equation $(1\text{-a})E_{t+1}[P_{t+1}(Q_{t+1})]/(1+r) = p_t(Q_t) + k$. Returning to the functional-thicket expression that occasioned this excursion, it implicitly contains the relationship between equilibrium storage in period t and exogenous and pre-determined variables. Since planned production in period t+1 is a function of storage in period t and the parameters, a functional form for storage can be expressed as $S_t = f(I_t)$, $0 \leq \Delta f/\Delta I_t \leq 1$. There is an associated planned production rule which can be reduced to $\hat{x}_{t+1} = g(I_t)$. Next period's planned production $\hat{x}_{t+1}$ is in an equilibrium with this period's storage S_t because S_t refers to the carry-out from period t and the carry-in to period t+1. Producers and storage agents commit to the levels of both of these variables in period t. These two variables are determined simultaneously.

So, with these relationships between the current outcome of last period's production decisions, current consumption which determines the current price, the current period's storage decision and the current period's commitment to next period's production, is there a simple rule to guide storage choices that would be optimal in the sense of maximizing profits in each period according to the first-order conditions of producers and storage agents? The simple answer is "no." Given current inventory and other inter-temporal conditions, the current period's optimal storage is the solution to a stochastic dynamic programming problem for which an analytical (i.e., a single equation) solution is intractable. However, the problem can be solved numerically, and sensitivities of optimal storage choices to various parameters, and the effect of storage on other market variables can be studied accordingly.

The rule for optimal storage is really nothing more complicated than what proportion of the amount of a commodity available should be stored. That said, the rule will depend on the characteristics (price elasticities) of supply and consumption demand, the loss rate, the cost of storage services, and the interest rate. Two diagrams of simulation results from Wright and Williams (1982) are adapted here to show the magnitudes of several aspects of storage. Figure 2.15 shows two storage rules for a particular combination of parameter values, one with no supply response (supply elasticity $\eta^s = 0$), the other with highly responsive supply ($\eta^s = 1$).[53] The total amount of the commodity available is graphed on the horizontal axis and the amount stored on the vertical axis. Also along the vertical axis, but measured in the negative direction, is the probability distribution of the amount stored in the inelastic supply response case (production being stochastic—recall the v_t disturbance term in the supply function—the simulation is executed many times with different realizations of the disturbance term, the only source of uncertainty in the model). Several important properties of the storage rule emerge immediately. First, the range of total availability generated by the model extends from around 90 to around 115. No storage at all emerges until availability reaches close to the 100 level. I* in the graph is the critical level of total availability, below which no storage occurs. That is, below some critical level of availability, no production is allocated to storage; it is all consumed. Second, the total amount of storage at the upper end of amounts stored reaches around 11 percent of total availability, but with a probability of occurrence less than 1 percent. The most likely amounts stored are a little less than 2 percent of availability. No storage at all is nearly as likely as the most likely percent of availability stored. Profit-maximizing storage is never large enough to ensure there will not be a shortage. Third, in both cases of the storage rule, when storage does begin, the percent of incremental crop available that is stored is quite high—this is called the marginal propensity to store. Fourth, the considerable difference in price responsiveness of supply between the cases of $\eta^s = 0$ and $\eta^s = 1$, doesn't make a lot of difference in the amounts stored. In fact, as availability is greater, the marginal propensity to store with the more elastic supply is somewhat smaller. Fifth, the availability at which storage begins changes as the supply response changes, reflecting the relationship between current and expected net-period price governed by the inter-temporal arbitrage condition: when the current price rises sufficiently that it is higher than the discounted expected future price net of storage costs, no storage occurs. Elastic supply response pushes this critical current-price point down, so that storage doesn't begin until availability is somewhat higher than it would be under an inelastic supply response. With these general observations, I proceed to some sensitivities that are not apparent from the graphical presentation.

A lower variance of the supply function, a higher interest rate, and a higher loss rate all push the critical availability level I* to the right, which means that storage doesn't begin until total availability is greater, as well as that non-zero storage is more frequent. The marginal propensity to store (the slope of the storage rule line) increases as the variance of the supply disturbance term v_t, σ_v, increases, but not greatly: as σ_v triples in magnitude, the critical availability level falls by about $2\frac{1}{2}$ percent

[53] Readers interested in the full array of parameter values that produced the simulation results can consult Wright and Williams (1984).

and the marginal propensity to store increases by about 9 percent. However, the difference between degrees of supply responsiveness of $\eta^s = 0$ and $\eta^s = 1$ can make as much as a 50 percent difference in marginal propensity to store, and the difference in supply responsiveness removes most of the impact of σ_v Wright and Williams (1982, 600, Table 1).

To examine the effect of storage on market demand for the commodity, the current price can be expressed as a function of the amount in storage, using the consumption demand function, the reduced-form storage function, and the consumption-storage identity $p_t = p[f^{-1}(S_t) - S_t] = \varphi(S_t)$.[54] This relationship is a function of the costs of other inputs into the storage process, including losses, direct storage service costs, and the cost of capital (which has not been explicitly modeled). Figure 2.16 shows the demand for the commodity (on the horizontal axis) as a function of its current-period price (on the vertical axis. Also measured on the vertical axis are the probability distributions of current-period price, with and without the option of storage, with distance along the horizontal axis measuring the probability of each current-period price occurring. The numerical values on this graph come from the $\eta^s = 0$ simulations underlying Figure 2.15. The horizontal addition of storage demand to consumption demand, which enters at p_t^*, yields market demand. As mentioned above, at current-period prices above some critical level, denoted by p_t^*, no storage occurs. As is quite apparent from Figure 2.16, the existence of storage possibilities tightens up the distribution of current-period price, although the degree of concentration is probably less than the graphic presentation suggests, the peak probability increasing from a little less than 3 percent to a little less than 6 percent, although the lower end of the tail (the probability of prices below p_t^*) is tightened much more than the upper end. In fact, the minimum price in the distribution is nearly doubled by the option of storage. Thinking of the relationship between price and availability, this indicates that storage is more effective in helping suppliers eliminate periods of low farming profitability during good years than it is in helping consumers eat more during lean years.

The asymmetric change in the distribution of current-period prices caused by the introduction of storage when supply is not responsive occurs despite a symmetric distribution of the supply disturbance v_t: the change in distribution is not a mean-preserving spread. Storage lowers the mean current-period price by about 2 percent and as noted above, changes the distribution mostly by shifting the probability mass from the lower end of the tail toward the mean. In the $\eta^s = 0$ case storage doesn't affect average consumption, although storage does lower the likelihood of higher-than-average consumption by more than it reduces that of lower-than-average consumption.

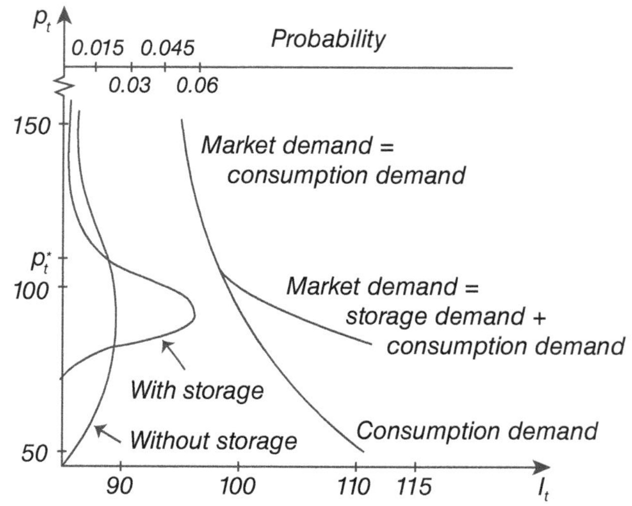

Figure 2.16. Demand curves and price distributions (Reproduced from Wright and Williams, 1982, figure 2, p. 602, by permission of Oxford University Press.).

With price-responsive supply, the $\eta^s = 1$ case, the existence of storage affects current-period price by two routes. First, whatever the current output, the demand to put some of the commodity into storage increases price by adding to consumption demand. Second, for any current production, any carryover from the previous year depresses realized price in the current year. The relative strength of these two effects on incentives to produce varies from period to period, as p_t and $\hat{x}(p_t^r)$ are sometimes lower than they would be without storage but more often higher. Without storage, planned production would not change over time because the disturbances to production are serially uncorrelated. When storage is introduced, planned production obtains a probability distribution, and that distribution has a long right tail, meaning that lower-than-average planned production is more likely than higher-than-average. Rather than thinking of storage as a mechanism for stabilizing production, it is more correct to view it as a means of dispersing the effects of production disturbances (i.e., weather and pests) throughout an economy. Storage is a substitute for production: when price is low, it is cheaper to put the commodity into the consumption stream later by releasing it from storage than it is to plan additional production for the next year. The higher the supply elasticity, the greater the variability of these two methods of accommodating consumption, but their combined operation produces more stable consumption. The option of storage has a very small impact on production, which could be negative or positive depending on the magnitude of the consumption demand elasticity.

The contribution of responsive production, the difference between the $\eta^s = 0$ and $\eta^s = 1$ cases, to the consequences of storage is asymmetric. Planned production reaches its maximum whenever storage is zero, so responsive production is not good insurance against a run of bad harvests, as it provides at most a maximum increase in expected availability of a little over 2 percent. Production responses help protect farm incomes (price)

[54] The f^{-1} notation means the inverse of the function designated by f, so where storage was a function f of availability I in the original function, the inverse function calculates availability from information on storage, and the entire new price function is a function of availability minus storage, or consumption.

in good years, as the minimum planned production when storage exists as an option is about 9 percent below its mean level. Reductions in planned production moderate build-ups of storage in a series of good years. Supply responsiveness enhances the decrease in the price dispersion that the introduction of storage causes, but it exacerbates the skewness in the price dispersion. Given the existence of storage, responsive supply substantially reduces the variability of consumption relative to the case of unresponsive supply. Probability mass is transferred from both tails of the distribution toward the center, reducing the coefficient of variation of the distribution by nearly 25 percent, with virtually no change in the mean, although the resulting distribution is highly skewed. Maximum consumption is reduced by $12\frac{1}{2}$ percent even though maximum planned production is increased. With unresponsive supply, very high consumption levels follow a consecutive run of good years, but with responsive supply, planned production is reduced after a good year and storage is increased, yielding the net effect of lower consumption in both the current year and the next relative to the situation with fixed long-run supply. On the downside, following a series of bad years, this compensation doesn't occur because when total availability falls below the level at which any storage occurs, further reductions in production don't increase the action certainty equivalent price. Consequently minimum consumption is raised by responsive supply by less than 1 percent even though maximum consumption is sharply reduced.

Both the slope and curvature of consumption demand affect storage behavior. The flatter the slope, the lower is average storage and the less frequently storage occurs. Greater curvature of the demand curve implies greater risk aversion, which is reflected in somewhat higher storage and a smaller variance of consumption when curvature is greater. However, the dispersion of current-period price is greater when the curvature of consumption demand is greater, whether storage is possible or not, although the magnitude of the effect is not great.

Who benefits more from storage, producers or consumers, a subject that is called "distributional implications" (income distribution, that is)? To address this question, Wright and Williamson calculate the present value of producer rents at the time of harvest (selling price minus production cost), to which they give the shorthand term "land value," and the present value of consumer surplus (the area below the demand curve but above the current-period price). Effects of changes in parameter values from their values in the base-case simulation cause changes in these two measures, an increase in land values benefiting producers and an increase in consumer surplus benefiting consumers. Three parameters are particularly important in affecting the distributional consequences of storage, η^s, η^d, and the degree of curvature of the demand function (c). The direction of effect, i.e., whether land value or consumer surplus increases or decreases, hinges largely on the magnitude of c, the degree of curvature in the demand curve, reflecting consumers' degree of risk aversion. With risk neutrality and unresponsive supply, storage favors producers, at high risk aversion it greatly favors consumers, and at intermediate values of risk aversion there are only minor distributional effects. For example, with high consumer risk aversion, a condition that might characterize much of aniquity's agrarian population, the introduction of storage increases the present value of consumer surplus relative to its magnitude without storage by nearly 40 percent while it reduces the present value of land rents by one-third. With risk-neutral consumers, the direction of those two effects is reversed but the magnitude is much smaller, consumer surplus 7 percent lower and land rents 12 percent higher. When $\eta^s = 1$, storage always increases the expected welfare of consumers, but the magnitudes of the changes are much smaller than with unresponsive supply. For example, the high-risk-aversion case that increased consumer surplus by nearly 40 percent increases it by a little less than 12 percent with responsive supply while the reduction in land rents is dampened from a one-third decline to a fall of a little less than 6 percent.

In sum, commodity storage is much more effective in eliminating low prices and excessive consumption than in preventing the appearance of high prices and low levels of consumption. This asymmetry results from the non-negativity constraint on storage: physical storage can never be negative—the physical, as opposed to asset, character of commodity stockpiles means that it is impossible to borrow from the future. Although individual storage agents may borrow current stocks from one another (although the current model, in eliminating any differences among storage agents, precludes this possibility from emerging), stocks at any one time cannot be augmented from production that hasn't occurred yet.

How Much Stocks Do (Did) People Hold? As the reader will have observed from Figures 2.15 and 2.16, the Wright and Williamson model gives storage amounts between 2 and 6% of total availability, depending on crop supply elasticity (and on values of a number of other parameters as well). Newbery and Stiglitz's commodity storage model yields average magnitudes of around 5% of total availability for a configuration of parameter values representative of tropical commodities (less perishable typically) with a normal distribution of yields, 9% for a crop with a more diffuse distribution of yields, and a "very small" average stock percentage for parameter values characteristic of contemporary U.S. grains (Newbery and Stiglitz 1981, 426; Newbery and Stiglitz 1982, 413).

Table 2.1 reports estimates of end-of-year stocks of major grains for various groups of countries. As percentages, they run in the teens to low 20s, with one 33% stock for wheat in the United States resulting from a sharp decrease in exports in 2009/10, which was not on track for repetition in 2010/1, and a 34% stock in major importing countries that same year, resulting from a bumper crop which apparently dampened U.S. exports that same year.

Table 2.1. Holdings of Grain Stocks, Crop Years 2008–09 and 2009–10: End-of-Year Stocks as Percent of Supply (Production plus Imports), by Major Region.

Region	Wheat	Rice	Corn
World	12–23	17–18	16–17
United States	22–33	12–14	11–12
Major Exporters	13	18–21	17–18
Major Importers	29–34	19–21	8–11

Source: U.S.D.A, F.A.S. (2010).

Otherwise, between 1950 and 2010, U.S. end-of-year wheat stocks ranged from a high of 121% in 1955 to a low of 15% in 2007, for an average of 53%, with a coefficient of variation of 0.57. Between 1960 and 2010, comparable world wheat stocks ranged between a high of 37% in 1968 and 1986 and a low of 20% in 2007, with a mean of 29% and coefficient of variation of 0.04 (U.S.D.A., E.R.S. 2010). In the early and mid-1990s, a number of African countries held end-of-year grains stocks amounting to 6 to −32% of total availability, with an unweighted average of −8% Trueblood (2010).

Against this background, archaeologists have found quite a few structures that have been interpreted as centralized facilities for holding grain stocks, as well many as rooms in private houses and outbuildings that have been interpreted similarly, not to mention innumerable large pithoi which indisputably were used for storage of both grains and oils, as well as other perishable commodities. Nonetheless, these facilities would have been built for the maximum maximorum of harvests, and ordinarily would not be filled at the end of the year, and possibly not at most harvests.

The written record has reported occasional instances of very large end-of-year grains stocks, such as the estimate of a 14- to 16-month supply in Thessaly in the 2nd century B.C.E. (Garnsey, Gallant, and Rathbone 1984; the quantity estimate appears on 44).[55] Considering the productivity of much ancient agriculture, in terms of the non-farm population that could be supported by one farm worker's annual output, this report surely has survived at least in part for its quality as an outlier. Gallant's contention that "ancient peasants" (in Greece) strove to maintain 10 to 16 months' supply of food in their private storerooms seems high, considering the storage technology Gallant (1991, 97–98). As Gallant himself has documented, grain storage in antiquity was notoriously subject to loss from moisture and pests, suggesting losses might have been as high as 50 to 80% Gallant (1991, 97).[56] With losses such as these, most farmers with harvests substantially beyond their own anticipated consumption over the coming year could have done well to sell their outputs immediately to avoid losses. The receipts from the sales could be more easily converted back into food later, if need arose, than could spoiled food. Erdkamp (2005, 143-167) reports limited scope for storage of grains by low-income Roman farmers, but somewhat greater scope for larger estates.

Several adjustments to the implicit comparison above might be suggested. First, agricultural subsidies and other support policies may boost the contemporary grain stocks reported in Table 2.1. Second, recourse to food following a poor harvest in antiquity may have been more limited than it has been even in contemporary developing countries, so even with anticipated storage losses, precautionary motives for storage could have been relatively stronger than at present. Third, a lot less food may have been carried across crop years in antiquity than some scholars presently believe.

Third is the issue of "who provided the storage?" The issue of the practicality of ancient farmers taking their harvests in to centralized storage facilities has been addressed already. A local alternative is local communal storage, which is not particularly common at present. The moral hazard problems of being able to retrieve what one put into storage, debiting losses during storage have placed most storage with individual producers in contemporary agrarian communities in developing countries.[57] The administration of commercial storage facilities in the contemporary industrial countries has ironed out such problems.

2.6 The Theory of Famines

A.K. Sen's entitlement theory of famines is an economic substitute for a rather unsubtle approach Sen identified as the food availability approach, which explains famines by simply saying that there's not enough food around and nobody was able to rush in relief supplies. Although awareness of Sen's approach has reached some parts of the ancient history / archaeology community,[58] his two expositions of his alternative model are not highly accessible, written primarily in a set-theoretic language, with one algebraic treatment of Malthus's model of the effect of the English Poor Laws and on price of grain Sen (1981a; 1981b).[59] The distinction of Sen's model is that it focuses on food availability to individuals rather than the gross amount of food available in a region. His central point is that starvation, on scales sufficient to be called famines,

[55] Gallant (1991, 97) makes the calculation relative to Thessaly's total food requirements.

[56] Nonetheless, Gallant's pessimism about ancient storage losses is not shared by Forbes and Foxhall (1995, 73–74).

[57] Jones, K. Wardle, Halstead, and D. Wardle, (1986, 98,) appear to favor an interpretation of communal storage at this Late Bronze Age site in Macedonia by virtue of its capacity. They also accept the belief that societies' agricultural surpluses were stored at the Minoan and Mycenaean palaces (p. 96).

[58] Garnsey (1988, 33) notes that Sen's model cannot be illustrated and tested with detailed case studies from antiquity but that it does make possible a more intelligent use of such information as the sources provide, although his reports of food crises in Roman Italy focus on periods of food-price spikes (Garnsey 1988, 205, 222, 227). Gallant (1991, 6) notes the model's prediction of selective starvation, and (139, and n. 19) its prediction that turning to wage work may not be a successful strategy for replenishing one's entitlement when a broadly defined group's entitlements are substantially diminished, more in keeping with Sen's entitlement approach.

[59] Sen (1981a; 1981b, Chapter 5 and Appendix A) present the model, and (1981b Appendix B) applies the model to Malthus's analysis of the English Poor Laws and their effect on grain prices.

can occur in the midst of plenty without any malicious intent on anyone's part. From that starting point, Sen's model provides mechanisms by which food can become unavailable to definable (even predictable) segments of a population.

Sen's famine model begins with the concept that the individual gains access to food through what can be called a set of endowments and social/legal rights that combine to generate what Sen calls an entitlement—the society's legally sanctioned rights to food, and if there's anything left over, to other consumption items as well. The endowments Sen calls an ownership vector—the things an individual owns, including his or her human capital skills, be they only so humble as those of a simple laborer. Some of these assets can be eaten directly, some can be exchanged at given ratios (prices) for food, and others can be transformed into food, either directly through farming or indirectly through producing something else that can be exchanged for food. Each of those assets has a price relative to food. Beyond the assets an individual owns, the society in which the individual lives may have legally authorized certain rights, direct or indirect, to food in the event that the individual becomes unemployed, along the lines of what would be called social welfare benefits today; additionally a society's mores may include help from extended family and various associations. There exists an amount of food the individual must consume to avoid starvation. Ordinarily, that is during ordinary times, an individual will acquire a sufficient amount of food, and typically with some to spare, without exhausting his or her ownership vector. If something happens to the ownership vector such that it, together with any other entitlements, will not acquire for the individual the minimum amount of food required for survival, the individual starves.

Starvation is produced by collapse of an individual's endowment vector. That can happen directly, through the destruction of some of the individual's assets, or indirectly, through changes in the prices of those assets in terms of food. People's vulnerability to endowment-vector collapse may be best characterized by their occupations since occupation identifies the most significant asset in the ownership vector—human capital. Sen made some distinctions along the lines of what, having progressed this far in this chapter, readers might be inclined to call contract type, particularly small landowners and sharecroppers. The small landowners possess assets that can be transformed into food, and sharecroppers have legal title to a substantial proportion of the crop they have produced. In fact, both of these occupational / contract groups may be vulnerable to severe local crop failure since it takes longer to grow most crops than it does to starve to death, although these groups may be more likely than most to have stored food reserves which could provide some buffer as part of their endowment vectors. And as selling assets is one of the strategies of converting one's ownership vector into food, small landowners and share tenants would be putting their assets into the same glutted market with landless individuals. Of course, that assumes that whatever external event affects some individuals' ownership vectors will affect those of these farmers, and as Sen's examples from India and Bangladesh make clear, that need not be the case. Some farmers or other primary producers such as fishermen, could be affected by some event which left many other farmers unaffected. But the destruction of farm output directly reduces farmers' ownership vectors, and since food is their primary asset, they have not only lost an edible asset but find themselves without an exchange mechanism for obtaining food. In the world of demand theory, their demand for food has dropped dramatically, even though they are hungry to the point of starvation. They possess no means of demonstrating their need for food, which if they could, would push up the price of food and bring it rushing to them.

An additional point Sen makes is that once one major asset loses value and an individual tries to sell off other assets—cows, land, his or her own labor skills—many other individuals are likely to be trying to sell the same assets, driving their prices down and leaving the selling individuals short of attaining a sufficient food entitlement. The ability to sell labor skills may also be hindered by the demand for those skills falling at the same time many others are entering the market offering the same skills, the leftward-shifting demand curve and the rightward-shifting supply curve literally dropping the bottom out of the market for that occupation's labor. Secondary effects may be felt by occupations only indirectly linked to the occupations hit directly by whatever event has set off the chain of endowment destruction, to the extent their incomes depend on spending by people whose endowment vectors have collapsed.

Sen's approach to famines also distinguishes between starvation deaths and the many other deaths that typically accompany famines, from epidemics induced partly by starvation, but also from other famine characteristics such as population movements and the breakdown of sanitation facilities.

2.7 Open Access and Common Property Resources

Open access and common property are not synonymous (see Jones 2014, Chapter 13, section 2). Over-use and degradation of the resource will occur with open access. In contrast, common property management of a natural resource that possesses many characteristics of a public good involves a well-defined group with rights to use the resource and clearly specified and well-understood rules governing use by members of that group.[60]

An open access resource is a depletable (you can use it all up), fugitive (to own it, you must capture it) resource characterized by rivalry in exploitation (first come first served and what someone else captures, you can't have). It is subject to use by anyone who has the capability

[60] I have relied on Stevenson (1991, Chapters 1–3).

and inclination to harvest or otherwise exploit it. The exploitation results in symmetric or (more commonly) asymmetric negative externalities.[61] An example of a symmetric negative externality would be overgrazing in open access pasture; an asymmetric externality would be represented by a charcoaler, say, who burns wood near the pasture and makes the other agents' sheep sick. There are no enforceable property rights over the resource. Limiting the number of entrants who can exploit the resource is insufficient to reach optimal use. Each individual's use must also be limited.

The concept of overgrazing can be given some more precise definition with a simple model. Suppose each of h herdsmen has a herd of n cattle when the grazing area is optimally stocked: N = nh. The net value of each animal is equal to 1 at this point. Let a be the percent decrease in net value of each head of cattle as the result of adding a cow beyond the optimum number, and suppose for simplicity that it stays constant, which will give a conservative estimate in the calculations that follow. The next step is to derive a condition that will indicate when overgrazing has occurred. If extra cattle are added beyond the grazing optimum, with a constant, the value of each additional head will be $1 - ax$. The total number of cattle will be $N + x$, and the total value of the herd will be $(N+x)(1\text{-}ax)$. Overgrazing occurs if the addition of an extra head decreases the total value of the herd in the last expression. Also, this occurs when x increases from $x = 0$ to $x = 1$, so the value of the herd must be lower when $x = 1$ than when $x = 0$: $(N+1)(1-a) > N$. This can be re-written as $a > 1/N+1$, which is a definitional constraint on the value of a, which can be called the overgrazing constraint. To interpret this last inequality, substitute the approximately equal condition $a > 1/N$; if this condition holds true, $a > 1/N+1$ does also. The simpler version says that if the percentage drop in the value of each head of cattle exceeds the percent of the total herd value that that cow represents (1/N), then overgrazing has occurred. When this condition is reached, the addition of an animal adds less to the total herd value than the sum of the losses in value incurred by all the other animals in the herd.

Open access to a resource will result in underinvestment in common improvements. No one can be assured of reaping the benefits of the resource before others do (first come, first served). Additionally, competition for current use causes users to ignore user cost, the present value of future extraction benefits, or increased future extraction costs caused by current use; in other words, if current users were to hold back some, what they left this period could be even more valuable next period—if it were still there.

Common property management is a resource management institution in which a well-delineated group of competing users participate in extraction or use of a jointly held, fugitive resource according to explicitly or implicitly understood rules about who may take how much of the resource. This form of resource management involves a set of property rights designed to eliminate open access exploitation. The number of users is limited, each user understands how much of the resource he or she can extract, and decisions about the resource allocations are made by a group process among the users. Common property management has seven characteristics. (1) The resource has well-defined bounds. (2) There is a clearly identified group of rights-holders who are distinct from people excluded from use. (3) Multiple included users extract the resource. (4) Explicit or implicit, well-understood rules exist among users regarding their rights and duties regarding the resource. (5) Users share joint, non-exclusive rights to in-situ (a woodlot or a pasture) or fugitive (game in a forest) resources prior to use or capture. (6) Authorized users compete for the resource and impose negative externalities on one another, although they may also cooperate. (7) The rights-holders may or may not coincide with the group of users; i.e., rights-holders can rent out their use rights. Rights to use the resource do not necessarily imply rights to equal amounts of it.

Common property resources are similar to public goods (club goods, actually) in that they are both held or owned by a group. However, a public good is a type of good or service while common property refers to a type of management. A public good could be managed with a common property arrangement. For example, land is an excludable good, but it can be managed by common property arrangements (see Jones Chapter 6, section 2 on excludability and non-excludability). With public goods there is difficulty in excluding users, and those goods are usually supplied under open-access conditions—think of a bridge that gets crowded at certain times of day. Public goods are typically manufactured (or more generally, made by people), and supplied in discretionary amounts. Common property resources, in contrast, generally are natural resources whose growth or harvest rate must be managed to obtain optimal use.

In Classical Athens, public entities such as demes owned land which they would rent out to individuals for their private use for specific periods of time, sometimes for specific uses such as grazing (Burford Cooper 1977–78, 171–173). The arrangements Burford Cooper describes may have included some common property management schemes but others are clearly rentals for excludable use. The Laureion silver mines were a slightly different case, as the resources discovered late in the 6th century B.C.E. were mostly if not entirely under private land and hence potentially excludable. However, the Athenian state claimed the mineral rights and leased out extraction to private mining operations, overseen and regulated by the board of *poletai* (sellers) (Bitros et al. 2021, 22–23).

[61] With a symmetric externality, each individual imposes an externality on all others exploiting the resource, but each of those others also impose negative externalities on all the others; think of contemporary automotive traffic congestion. With an asymmetric externality, the actions of one agent enter the utility or production functions of other agents, but they do not pose any reciprocal externality on the first agent (see Jones 2014 Chapter 6, section 2).

2.8 Cases from Antiquity: Farming - Between the Plow and the Agreements

Much is known about the physical conditions of ancient agriculture, but far less about the contractual and otherwise legal conditions under which it was conducted. The contemporary agricultural household model (AHM) and models of contemporary agricultural contracts under conditions of missing and imperfect markets offer at least a few observable pole stars to seek in the literature on ancient agriculture which might influence further thinking, research, and interpretation of existing evidence.

Pointers from the Agricultural Household Model. One of the contributions of the AHM is to demonstrate the effects of various types of quotas – restrictions on outputs or inputs. Labor was diverted compulsorily from privately cultivated farms to royal farms throughout the Eastern Mediterranean realms during the Bronze Age. Corvée labor duties were the norm in Bronze Age Mesopotamia, Egypt, and palatial-period Mycenaean Greece (Zaccagnini 1984, 702, 708, 714–715, 720 for Nuzi; Liverani 1975, 155 for 2nd millennium Syria; Moreno-Garcia 2001, 419 on 13th Dynasty Egypt; 2008, 123; and 2014a, 41, 61 on agricultural production constraints in Egypt; Uchitel 2005, 484–485 for Mycenaean Pylos and 15th century Middle Hittite land tenure). These levies were time-sensitive constraints on the otherwise optimal programming of households' annual agricultural production schedules.

Corvée labor requirements ("chores") could be predictable or otherwise. Predictable ones would have altered what would otherwise have been optimal cultivation plans of small farmers into second-best programs. Taking labor out of such second-best programs for unplanned corvée work likely would have cut into second-best anticipated output. Payment of taxes in money, which gradually worked its way into the Egyptian rural economy, would have reduced these non-optimalities by substituting cash, which could be saved, for time, which couldn't.

Agricultural and non-agricultural labor markets existed, at least around the margins of the royal redistribution system in Egypt and elsewhere (Moreno-Garcia 2014b, 30 for seasonal or permanent "salaried" employment – "emploi ≪salarié≫" in Egypt; Zaccagnini 1984, 710 on seasonal harvest labor at Nuzi; Liverani 1975, 150 on seasonal labor paid by the day at Alalakh). Were they accompanied by at least fixed transaction costs such as paying a facilitator? The most likely variable transaction cost in labor markets would have been transportation costs if workers moved considerable distances.

Some other markets existed, at least in barter terms, early on. Others may not have, forcing existing markets to compensate with their own prices, which thereby became skewed. Moreno-Garcia (2014b, 28) reports the existence of markets around the edges of the royal redistribution system in Egypt and reports on temples using royal donations of precious metals to engage in market transactions (2001, 435). Zaccagnini (1999, 36) judges from the small size of plots around Nuzi that most farm families must have derived off-farm income.

Pointers from Land / Farm Tenure and Agricultural Contracting Models. Most research on ancient land tenure has focused on who owned land parcels and who worked them, but on what terms remains largely hidden. In the case of the Pylos land tenure tablets, assessing the meaning of the adjectives describing the type of land is very complicated although analysis by many scholars over several decades has reached as much of a conclusion as seems possible that some of the land was privately owned by the damos, a collective governing body separate from the wanax (king), and rented out to various tenants, small and large, under tax obligations which gave rise to the tablets keeping track of them. Tenancy of some of the lands entailed responsibility for some additional obligations, possibly military (Lupack 2008, Chapter 4, esp. 60, 63, 67, 72).

Halstead (1999, 323) identified share leases in grain production and wool clipping on Mycenaean Crete, and a side agreement that landlords furnish fodder for oxen to ensure they maintain their strength. Foxhall (1990) has noted many terms and conditions in Roman and Greek farm leases, making comparisons with contemporary, Third-World farm tenure conditions. What she calls alternative rationalities to profit maximization on the parts of these ancient tenants and landowners are what I have called alternative objective functions, such as risk minimization or minimizing the likelihood of dipping below a target output.

The fact that some poor farmers entered servitude or even slavery through defaults on loans may suggest the existence of loans tied to farm leases and without bankruptcy clauses to protect them. Liverani (1982, 157) notes the delivery of a son to the Ugaritic royal workshops as the cost of a loan default in 2nd millennium Syria, and Moreno-Garcia (2001, 420) reports a loss of property through insolvency in the Egyptian 4th Dynasty. Zaccagnini (1999, 38, 45) analyzes a land sale system at Nuzi that apparently derived from debts; absentee landlords held such plots all over the country that continued to be worked by former owners, now become tenants. It is not known if the defaulted loans were consumption or production loans, but apparently they were not tied to leases since owners defaulted and lost their land rather than their leases. Lending landlords would have had incentive to bear with their short-changing tenants for lack of practical alternatives unless contract conditions put the tenants into some kind of bondage, which might not have been much different from the prior crop-sharing agreements.

Moving into the Hellenistic and Roman period in Palestine, Kloppenborg (2008, 34) identifies three types of leases – 1) fixed quantity of output, 2) fixed cash amount – used primarily for houses, movables, and traction animals, and 3) crop share, with the lessee's share ranging from one-third to one-half. Land given to veterans may have been farmed directly by them, but they could have leased it to local farmers if they had neither the inclination nor the competence to till it themselves (2008, 42). Altogether, Kloppenborg (2008, 46) thinks, "We should therefore picture a situation in which smallholders supplemented their own incomes by assuming tenancies on Apollonios's (an official of Ptolemy Philadelphos II) estates in Palestine," a circumstance found in recent and contemporary farming in both industrialized and developing countries. These rented plots could have supplied ecological niches that reduced overall risk of a smallholder's portfolio.

Storing Agricultural Products. Storage of agricultural products in antiquity must have been nearly ubiquitous. Just about everybody farmed, and once the harvest was in, the farmer had to do something with the crop until it was either eaten or sold. Smallholders commonly had to have recourse to the market toward the end of the year, as they would not have harvested a year's supply. Garnsey (1988, 53–55) believes in widespread holding of stocks by peasant farmers, but with scant, hard evidence. Erdkamkp (2005, 156) thinks that the extent of storage during this period in the Roman Empire is easy to exaggerate. The debate over storage and field scattering in Medieval Europe among Fenoaltea (1976), McCloskey and Nash (1984), and Komlos and Landes (1991) turns ultimately more on absence of data on storage than on theory. Data on storage are no better for antiquity.

Erdkamp's examination of agricultural storage (2005, 143–170) is the most thorough that I have found. His conclusion is that smallholders generally held only inter-annual stocks from their harvests and commonly ran out before the subsequent harvest. Interest rates were unlikely to influence their holdings since capital markets were not sufficiently developed to deal with the small amounts of sales they were likely to choose as alternative to storage. Wealthy, commercial farmers clearly held stocks in storage despite the interest cost and the price risks. They possessed the resources to build and maintain storage infrastructure and sufficient cash reserves to wait until prices rose to sell (Erdkamp 2005, 158). What does not seem to appear in the literature is that when smallholders sold some crop immediately after harvest – at low, immediately post-harvest prices – to pay off debts and commercial farmers posted some sales, some other, unidentified agents must have been willing to store those crops for subsequent sale into retail markets. Things we don't know are the volumes of individual holders' stocks and total, market stocks or their inter-annual time paths. It appears that holding stocks in storage for two or even three years was physically possible, despite some deterioration (Erdkamp 2005, 158–159).

Erdkamp (2005, 156) is not sanguine regarding the usefulness of archaeological evidence in understanding agricultural storage: "In general, archaeology is of limited use, since it is often impossible to determine the purpose of containers and their economic use." Christakis (2008) defies that limitation with a detailed study of contexts, containers, and characteristics of pithoi, the principal container for larger scale, longer term storage of agricultural products on Neopalatial Crete, principally Late Minoan I (LM I). He studies 430 Neopalatial buildings that could be defined as residences of simple and wealthy households, 120 of which provide evidence ("testimonies") of storage activities (2008, 55). Christakis begins with a quantitative summary of the storage capacity of the principal palaces before proceeding to what are more likely to be private operations. The palatial storage capacities vary greatly, but as they were governmental stores collecting output of palatial properties, at least partly to provide for palatial personnel as well as special events, I do not dwell on them here. What appear to have been private – but sometimes possibly combination public (governmental / palatial)-private operations seem more interesting. Without completely enumerating Christakis' sites, they range from possibly government-sponsored storage facilities at Hagia Triada to what appear to be simple pantries of part-time farm households. In a subsequent study, Christakis (2014) sees no clear evidence for any "communal" storage – storage between centralized and household, which makes its own kind of sense – different households could be unable to retrieve their own contributions to such storage plans, and crop contributions could vary significantly in important characteristics.

While Christakis notes each type of ceramic container, its size and likely use, he focuses on pithoi, which he categorizes into high or low capacity, transportability, stability, and accessibility to contents (2008, 64). He explains how these characteristics are likely to identify planned length of storage and, depending on the architectural context, the likely owner of the stored material. One of the most interesting contexts is the Villa Reale at Hagia Triada, where numerous Linear A tablets were found. The North Magazines of the Villa Reale contained the main storage repository. The magazines were filled with pithoi of high-capacity, low transportability, high stability, and low accessibility – container characteristics associated with longer-term storage. I would not be surprised if the Linear A tablets found throughout the Villa Reale identified the private owners of staple crops stored in its magazines rather than inflows and outflows such as the later Linear B tablets at Knossos and Pylos recorded. In the Southwest Quarter at Hagia Triada small and medium-sized pithoi were found, with high accessibility and transportability, suggesting shorter-term storage and more frequent movement of the commodities. Christakis calculates that 41% of the ground floor of the Villa Reale was devoted to storage, with a capacity of 30 thousand to 33 thousand liters of product. Compared to his estimate of the capacity of the Knossos palace magazines – 300,376 liters, with possibly an overflow capacity at the Northeast House of another 24,800 to 32,000 liters (Christakis 2008, 120) - the capacity at Hagia Triada was small, but compared to some larger, private houses such as House 1 at Chania-Kastelli with an estimate of 1,900 to 2,100 liters (Christakis

2008, 57), the Casa Est at Hagia Triada, which could have been an annex of the Villa Reale, with a capacity of 3,120 to 3,620 liters, and Mansion A at Tylissos, whose capacity Christikis estimates at 9,900 to 11,880 liters (Christakis 2008, 60), the Villa Reale appears to have contained a set of centralized storage facilities for south central Crete during the Neopalatial period. Christakis' site reports allow distinction between major storage sites, farm household storage facilities, and household pantries, although the reader is left to make those distinctions.

So what can we make of these capacity calculations, container descriptions, and pithos calculations? First, the North Magazines of the Villa Reale at Hagia Triada, with the fallen Linear A tablets, look to me like longer-term storage of dry and liquid agricultural products by larger-scale producers. Why would they store their harvests if there were not markets that looked at least somewhat like those Erdkamp describes for two millennia later in the Roman Empire? The Southwest Quarter at Hagia Triada looks like a shorter-term storage facility, with its smaller containers and more of them with pouring spouts, possibly a way-station from the North Magazines to retail markets. The single-household cases look like stashing the season's output for consumption until it runs out and pantries where a few weeks' purchases (with what? Whatever the household might have made with its non-agricultural time) were kept. From this LM I Cretan archaeological evidence, it seems clear that organizations from palaces through wealthy households through smallholding households were storing agricultural staples, with possibly different motivations between the palaces and the various wealths of households. I suspect we can never hope to recover data that would inform parameter values of contemporary models of agricultural storage, but it seems clear that the ancients were engaging in storage, some of them as simple households trying to get through the coming year, but others gauging how seasonal price fluctuations might make the timing of their releases more profitable.

2.9 Using this Chapter's Information: Archaeological Applications

I think the models and other information in the previous sections of this chapter will find clear applications by ancient historians and philologists. As a number of my archaeologist friends have said, however, "I think I have a better understanding of agriculture as an economic endeavor now, but how can I apply this information to my material that comes out of the ground?"

This section addresses that important question, although I deliberately choose the verb *address* rather than *answer*. My "answers" may have the solidity more of ruminations than instructions. Furthermore, when I find specific points at which models from this chapter can be applied to interpretation of archaeological finds, I will not often pursue the application very deeply, as that would be a research task on its own. I begin with my impressions of the array of products of what I will call agricultural archaeology, particularly as I have found it practiced in study of the time periods and regions targeted by this text. Additionally, I will avoid making many references to specific works to avoid the appearance of picking on innocent victims. Accordingly, some archaeologists may disagree with some of my classifications and interpretations of this research; fair enough.

2.9.1 Animal Bones

First, there are species identifications and counts of animal bones. Sometimes these counts remain at the status of inventories. Some years ago, Sebastian Payne (1973) offered several models of kill-off patterns of sheep and goats, depending on farmers' strategies of producing different products or mixes of products from their herds. The models were age distributions of bones—the percent of individual animals of particular age groups in a herd. It is not clear how the age-distribution models were derived, but that is not a point at issue at the moment. Taking Payne's model to the field, the distribution of bones of individual animals identified from excavated remains would be determined and compared with the distributions associated with the product strategies identified in the models. Payne applied his model to Late Hellenistic-to-Roman and Medieval periods at Aşvan Kale in east-central Turkey. The animal models of section 2.3.3 suggest that additional care be taken in interpreting such distributions of animal bones, since kill-off patterns can represent short-term adjustments to either short- or long-term desired changes in herd sizes. Beyond this observation, I leave it to the archaeologists to determine how to make the adjustments.

2.9.2 Agricultural Implements

Second, there are identifications of the remains of agricultural implements, ranging from chipped stone tools to metal components of more advanced equipment. Indeed, a good bit of the study of ancient agriculture involves the identification of the physical characteristics, and the likely operation—rather like a user's manual—of farm equipment. This work primarily involves itemization of finds, sometimes concluding with an assessment of the level of technology at the site relative to those of other sites considered relevant comparisons, either chronologically or spatially. These are technology studies rather than studies of the economics of ancient agriculture, akin to the types of clothes people wore only typically more intricate. Economically speaking, these remains of equipment represent ancient investments. The more complicated of them, typically those involving metal parts, surely represent the consequences of trade (farm exports), whether the metals were crafted into implement components locally from imported metal ingots or were imported already manufactured. At any given time and general technology regime, more intricate equipment should be found at sites with greater access to water transportation for export.

2.9.3 Agricultural Plant Remains

Third, more recent excavations in particular, record finds of grains and seeds, frequently charred in storage facilities. Within this category of study, I include analyses of pollen remains from bogs or lake sediments. These remains provide answers to the questions, "What did they grow around this site?" and "When did they start growing this crop?" The distribution of species sometimes is used to estimate combinations of crops that may have been chosen as parts of risk management strategies, a subject dealt with in section 2.3.2. Ancient historians and philologists, with additional epigraphic evidence at their disposal, evidence typically not from an excavation recording agricultural plant remains, have pushed the analysis of risk management strategies somewhat further, introducing the scattering of plots. Generally it is a luxury to know whether such distributed plots were owned by the farmer operating them or were rented, and pushing the luxury even further, if rented, whether for a fixed rent or a share of the crop. Risk management strategies can contain a number of instruments: crop diversification, inter-cropping, field scattering, tenure terms on rented-in and rented-out land (and possibly structures and equipment), other transactions linked to a tenure contract, informal insurance arrangements among relatives and neighbors, storage, accumulation of salable assets (self-insurance), and trade outside the immediate area. Not all of these instruments need be effective for some events. As was noted in at several places section 2.4, some events have catastrophic qualities, in that they affect most or all farmers in an area, rendering the local insurance, salable assets and trade less effective, or even possibly totally ineffective. How can this knowledge of a broader array of risk management tools be applied to materials coming out of the ground? Again, I am speculating, but comparison of risk management devices employed at one site with evidence of such strategies at other sites, both nearby and in regions with different geographical and locational characteristics might yield interesting variations which could imply the application of unobservable strategies at a number of the sites.

2.9.4 Storage

Fourth, storage of agricultural products, in either fixed structures or movable devices such as pithoi, has been a perennial topic in agricultural, and even in a number of non-agricultural, excavations. In fact, charred remains of stored grains in town settings have been an important source of information on ancient crops, possibly as critical to current knowledge as finds excavated at rural farmstead sites. The quantities of agricultural products stored, storage losses, length of effective nutritional life of stored grains, and the private or centralized (government) character of storage have been treated extensively in the archaeological and ancient historical literature on the Aegean and Ancient Near Eastern regions. Views have differed widely on losses and consequently on the supply of stored products (measured in terms of months of consumption), but many of the opinions emerging from the literature have suggested far larger proportions of crop outputs stored than contemporary models of section 6 would suggest. With Pharaonic Egypt's more centralized government, the case has been made for more extensive, and centralized (definitely government) storage facilities, but a good proportion of the collection of agricultural grain output was as tax, which to be converted into non-fattening items for the Pharaonic government and its employees would have had to be sold fairly quickly. Accordingly, Egyptian agricultural storage structures were surely part treasury facility and part crop carry-over facility. Returning to the Aegean and ANE storage facilities, views on the uses of storage jars might be revisited to either consider what was being stored and potential purposes—e.g., future consumption versus immediate trade, or for storage of items other than agricultural products. Interpretations of fixed facilities as agricultural storage devices might be examined more closely. Surely, further post-excavation or non-excavation research is needed on storage losses and storability of specific crops in various regions, but a wider view of storage volumes in conjunction with the productivity of ancient agriculture might be taken: considering widely held beliefs regarding the life-on-the-edge quality of much of ancient agriculture, some of it coming from examination of human remains, how could some of these ancient farm communities have produced sufficient volumes to store fifty percent or double the coming season's consumption requirements of their crops? What adjustments are required to make these beliefs consistent? Why would such productivity levels in a non-exporting community not have led to population increases that eliminated the putative surplus? This consideration leads to possible interpretation of what would otherwise appear to be excessive crop storage capacity as evidence of collection points for exports rather than for domestic hoarding.

Another topic in storage regards the degree of centralization or decentralization of agricultural crop storage. Linear B tablets in particular have given some scholars the impression of an impressive degree of mobility of harvested crops, moving them from the threshing floors of individual farms to a central, government-operated facility, from which the farmers' outputs would be doled back out to them. Some structures at Knossos and Malia on Crete have occasionally received similar interpretations without epigraphic evidence. There are at least three issues here. First, but not necessarily in any order of relative importance, would have been the ability of the government to monitor and enforce accounting and transfer of crop outputs across widely dispersed farm sites. Even the Pharaonic Egyptian governments, with their well established bureaucracies, were unable to accomplish that task (Eyre 1997, 371–372). While a problem applied to agriculture, this is really an information collection and enforcement problem, which is more general than agriculture. Second, obtaining the cooperation of farmers to surrender their crops to a centralized facility rather than letting them store their own output individually, under their own control, would have been a considerable task in its own right. Evasion surely would have been a problem. Again, evasion is an asymmetric information problem with broader application than to agriculture.[62] Third, the sheer transportation costs, in both directions—from the farmsteads to the central facility, then back again at whatever rate the government dispensed their "rations" to the farmers who produced them would have consumed a considerable proportion of the output. Section 2.5 alluded very briefly to the moral hazard problems of any joint, as opposed to individual, storage. The transportation problems involved are an empirical matter of ancient land transportation costs rather than a theoretical issue. Altogether, appearances of transfers of crop output to central storage facilities in Mycenaean Linear B tablets probably refers to tax collection, comparable to the Egyptian case, than to any large-scale confiscation and redistributive rationing system.

2.9.5 Ancient Fields and Carrying Capacities

Neither of these types of analysis particularly involve reasoning about resource allocation in ancient agriculture. Studies sometimes identify ancient fields, either from air photos identifying field boundaries or direct field observation of ancient furrows or other remaining evidence of previously cultivated land. Estimates of ancient populations or maximum possible populations are made sometimes using contemporary estimates of food intake or direct estimates of ancient production levels, sometimes from remains of storage capacity. Such estimates tend to be rather mechanical, depending on a series of ratios multiplied together, with either no allowance for local behavioral differentials from some norm or such behavior already embedded but not characterized explicitly.

2.9.6 Other Applications

Knowledge of ancient societies grows accretively, and excavations over a number of years have added information beyond that from any individual site, as information from individual sites enhance existing knowledge of other sites. Suppose it is either known or suspected that a region opened to trade in agricultural products—became an exporter—over some period of time. What actions on individual farms might have been involved? First, the increased profitability of agricultural production in the region would have called forth increased production. There would have been both short-run and long-run adjustments to the new situation, with investments in structures and equipment taking the farms from the pre-trade long run to the post-trade long run. The increase in output achieved at the very opening of trade would have been smaller than the increase when the full adjustment had been achieved. This is the subject of section 2.3.2 on short- and long-run supply elasticities and the role of investment in moving from one to the other. Evidence would include expansion of farmstead structures over the period beyond replacement of worn-out or abandoned units. Movement from the pre-trade farm organization to the post-trade organization might not have proceeded smoothly, particularly because of incomplete markets and intermittently varying transaction costs. During some periods, an individual farm might have abstained from the emerging export market simply because its costs did not justify participation; such periods might have existed for a long enough period to be identified archaeologically, with lesser investment in facilities than neighboring farmsteads. Other farms down the valley or across a ridge might not have experienced such periods of optimal autarky, their remains showing earlier expansion. This is the subject of section 2 on the farm household model.

Thus far I have had in mind situations in which written evidence is not generated in the excavation of an agricultural site. Henry Wright's work on the rural town in the hinterland of Early Dynastic Ur exemplifies the type of agricultural site, most likely in the Ancient Near East or Egypt, which yields production artifacts—structures and equipment—output remains—both plant and animal—and written records, one type of text indicating share rentals (Wright, 1969, 109). Egypt has produced some relatively late (Saite Period) written records on farm (or at least land; it is not clear whether an entire farm is under contract or just a plot or so) tenancy, although whether production equipment was found with the records is seldom clear. It would certainly be too much to ask to find, say, an Egyptian or Mesopotamian farm house with either a papyrus or clay tablet detailing the contractual conditions between the owner of the land and the last occupant of the house on it, but on approaching the excavation of a farmstead, it could pay some presently unknown return to keep in mind the question whether the last operator or occupant was an owner or a tenant, and if a tenant, what kind. Evidence distinguishing the contract types may be either completely ephemeral or too slight to make it through the centuries in the soil.

Beyond this relatively concrete example of a possible situation in the field, having a clearer sense of agricultural operations as social systems devoted to resource allocation may give archaeologists an extra eye with which to question the possible interpretations of their finds as they come out of the dirt. Despite current apparent isolation of such a rural site, the social system of which it was a part, rather than involving only people on that single operation, may have involved people in the neighborhood, through local contracts and informal insurance systems, and possibly people at quite a distance, through trade.

---

[62] Wright (1969, 120–121), dealing with ambiguous texts from a rural area in the hinterland of Third Dynasty Ur, assumes that while a centralized storehouse entry of grain was recorded, landholders' output was stored in their residences.

References

Baer, Klaus. 1963. "An Eleventh Dynasty Farmer's Letters to His Family," *Journal of the American Oriental Society* 83: 1–19.

Bagnall. Roger S. 1993. *Egypt in Late Antiquity*. Princeton: Princeton University Press.

Bardhan, Pranab K. 1980. "Interlocking Factor Markets and Agrarian Development: A Review of Issues," *Oxford Economic Papers* N.S. 32: 82–98.

Bardhan Pranab, and Christopher Udry. 1999. *Development Microeconomics*. Oxford: Oxford University Press.

Binswanger, Hans P., and Mark R. Rosenzweig. 1986. "Behavioural and Material Determinants of Production Relations in Agriculture," *Journal of Development Studies* 23: 503–539.

Binswanger, Hans P., and John McIntire. 1987. "Behavioral and Material Determinants of Production Relations in Land-Abundant Tropical Agriculture," *Economic Development and Cultural Change* 36: 73–99.

Bitros, George C., Emmanouil M. L. Economou, and Nicholas C. Kyriazis. 2021. *Democracy and Money: Lessons for Today from Athens in Classical Times*. London: Routledge.

Braverman, Avishay, and Joseph E. Stiglitz. 1982. "Sharecropping and the Interlinking of Agrarian Markets," *American Economic Review* 72: 695–715.

Burford, Alison. 1993. *Land and Labor in the Greek World*. Baltimore: Johns Hopkins University Press.

Burford Cooper, Alison. 1977–78. "The Family Farm in Greece," *The Classical Journal* 73: 171–173.

Christakis, Kostandinos S. 2008. *The Politics of Storage; Storage and Socipolitical Complexity in Neopalatial Crete*. Philadelphia: INSTAAP Academic Press.

Christakis, Kostis S. 2014. "Communal Storage in Bronze Age Crete: Re-Assessing Testimonies," *ΚρητικάΧρονικά* ΛΔ': 201–218.

de Janvry, Alain, Marcel Fafchamps, and Elisabeth Sadoulet. 1991. "Peasant Household Behaviour with Missing Markets: Some Paradoxes Explained," *Economic Journal* 101: 1403–1408.

De Neeve, P.W. 1984. *Colonus: Private Farm-Tenancy in Roman Italy during the Republic and the Early Principate*. Amsterdam: J.C. Gieben.

Erdkamp, Paul. 2005. *The Grain Market in the Roman Empire; A Social, Political and Economi Study*. Cambridge: Cambridge University Press.

Eyre, Christopher J. 1997. "Peasants and 'Modern' Leasing Strategies in Ancient Egypt," *Journal of the Economic and Social History of the Orient* 40: 367–390.

Eyre, Christopher. 2010. "The Economy: Pharaonic," in *A Companion to Ancient Egypt*, Vol. 1, edited by Alan B. Lloyd, 291–308. Oxford: Blackwell.

Fenoaltea, Stefano. 1976. "Risks, Transaction Costs and the Organization of Medieval Agriculture," *Explorations in Economic History* 13: 129–152.

Forbes, Hamish, and Lin Foxhall. 1995. "Ethnoarchaeology and Storage in the Ancient Mediterranean: Beyond Risk and Survival," in *Food in Antiquity*, edited by John Wilkins, David Harvey, and Mike Dobson, 69–86. Exeter: University of Exeter Press.

Foxhall, Lin. 1990. "The Dependent Tenant: Land Leasing and Labour in Italy and Greece," *Journal of Roman Studies* 80: 97–114.

Gallant, Thomas. 1991. *Risk and Survival in Ancient Greece*. Stanford: Stanford University Press.

Gardiner, Alan H. 1941. "Ramesside Texts Relating to the Taxation and Transport of Corn," *Journal of Egyptian Archaeology* 27: 19–73.

Garnsey, Peter, Tom Gallant, and Dominic Rathbone. 1984. "Thessaly and the Grain Supply of Rome during the Second Century B.C.," *Journal of Roman Studies* 74: 30–44.

Garnsey, Peter. 1988. *Famine and Food Supply in the Graeco-Roman World; Responses to Risk and Crises*. Cambridge: Cambridge University Press.

Gurney, O. R. 1954. *The Hittites, 2nd Ed*. London: Penguin.

Haessel, Walter. 1975. "The Price and Income Elasticities of Home Consumption and Marketed Surplus of Foodgrains," *American Journal of Agricultural Economics* 57: 111–115.

Halstead, Paul. 1999. "Surplus and Sharecropper: The Grain Production Strategies of Mycenaean Palaces," in *Meletemata: Studies Presented to Malcolm Wiener as He Enters his 65th Year*, Aegaeum 20, edited by Philip P. Betancourt, Vassos Karageorghis, Robert Laffineur, and Wolf-Dieter Niemeier, 319–326. Liège and Austin: Histoire de l'art et archeology de la Grèce antique, University de Liege, and Program in Aegean Scripts and Prehistory, University of Texas at Austin.

Hughes, George Robert. 195. *Saite Demotic Land Leases*, Studies in Ancient Oriental Civilization No. 28. Chicago: University of Chicago Press.

Isager, Signe, and Jens Erik Skydsgaard. 1991. *Ancient Greek Agriculture; An Introduction*. London: Routledge.

Jameson, Michael H. 1992. "Agricultural Labor in Ancient Greece," in *Agriculture in Ancient Greece; Proceedings of the Seventh International Symposium at the Swedish Institute at Athens, 16–17 May, 1990*, Skrifter Utgivna av Svenska Institutet I Athen 4°, XLII, edited by Berit Wells, 135–146. Stockholm: Paul Astroms Forlag.

Janssen, Jac. J. 1975. *Commodity Prices from the Ramessid Period; An Economic Study of the Village of Necropolis Workmen at Thebes*. Leiden: E. J. Brill.

Janssen, Jac. J. 1986. "Agrarian Administration in Egypt during the Twentieth Dynasty," [Review of I.A. Stuchevsky (1982)], *Bibliotheca Orientalia* 43: 352–366.

Johnson, D. Gale. 1950. "Resource Allocation under Share Contracts," *Journal of Political Economy* 58: 111–123.

Jones, Donald W. 1982. "Location and Land Tenure," *Annals of the Association of American Geographers* 72: 314–331.

Jones, Glynis, Kenneth Wardle, Paul Halstead, and Diana Wardle. 1986. "Crop Storage at Assiros," *Scientific American* 254.3: 96–103.

Just, Richard C., 2001. "The Agricultural Producer: Theory and Statistical Measurement," in *Handbook of Agricultural Economics, Vol. 1*, edited by Bruce Gardner and Gordon Rausser, 629–741. New York: Elsevier.

Katary, Sally L. D. 1989. *Land Tenure in the Ramesside Period*. London: Kegan Paul.

Key, Nigel, Elisabeth Sadoulet, and Alain de Janvry. 2000. "Transactions Costs and Agricultural Household Supply Responses," *American Journal of Agricultural Economics* 82: 245–259.

Kidland, Finn E., and Edward C. Prescott. 1982. "Time to Build and Aggregate Fluctuations," *Econometrica* 50: 1345–1370.

Kloppenborg, John S. 2008. "The Growth and Impact of Agricultural Tenancy in Jewish Palestine (III BCE-I CE)," *Journal of the Economic and Social History of the Orient* 51:31–66.

Komlos, John, and Richard Landes. 1991. "Anachronistic Economics. Grain Storage in Medieval England," *Economic History Review* 44:36–45.

Liverani, Mario. 1975. "Communautés de village et Palais royal dans la Syrie du II[é]me millénaire," *Journal of the Economic and Social History of the Orient* 18: 146–164.

Lupack, Susan. 2008. *The Role of the Religious Sector in the Economy of Late Bronze Age Mycenaean Greece*. Oxford: Archaeopress.

Marshall, Alfred. 1964 [1920]. *Principles of Economics*, 8th Ed. London: Macmillan.

McCloskey, Donald N., and John Nash. 1984. "Corn at Interest. The Extent and Cost of Grain Storage in Medieval England," *American Economic Review* 74: 174–187.

Meek, Theophile J., translator. 1969. "The Code of Hammurabi," in *Ancient Near Eastern Texts Relating to the Old Testament, Third Edition with Supplement*, edited by James B. Pritchard, 163–180. Princeton: Princeton University Press.

Menu, Bernadette. 1970. *Le régime juridique des terres et du personnel attaché à la terre dans le Papyrus Wilbour*. Lille: Université de Lille, Faculté des lettres et des sciences humaines.

Migeotte, Léopold. 2009. *The Economy of the Greek Cities; From the Archaic Period to the Early Roman Period*, trans. by Janet Lloyd. Berkeley: University of California Press.

Mill, John Stuart. 2004 [1865]. *Principles of Political Economy*. Amherst, N.Y.: Prometheus Books.

Moreno-Garcia, Juan Carlos. 2001. "L'organisation sociale de l'agriculture dans l'Egypte pharaonique pendant l'ancien empire (2650-2150 avant j.-c.)," *Journal of the Economic and Social History of the Orient* 44: 411–450.

Moreno García, Juan Carlos. 2008. "La dépendance rurale en Égypte ancienne." *Journal of the Economic and Social History of the Orient* 51: 99–150.

Moreno-Garcia, Juan Carlos. 2014a. "Penser l'économie pharaonique," *Annales. Histoire, Sciences Sociales* 69: 7–38.

Moreno-Garcia, Juan Carlos. 2014b. "L'organisation sociale de l'agriculture pharaonique: Quelques cas d'étude," *Annales. Histoire, Sciences Sociales* 69: 39–74.

Moscardi, Edgardo, and Alain de Janvry.1977. "Attitudes Toward Risk among Peasants: An Econometric Approach," *American Journal of Agricultural Economics* 59: 710–716.

Muhs, Brian. 2016. *The Ancient Egyptian Economy, 3000–30 BCE*. Cambridge: Cambridge University Press.

Mundlak, Yair. 1996. "On the Aggregate Agricultural Supply," in *The Economics of Agriculture, Papers in Honor of D. Gale Johnson, Vol. 2*, edited by John M. Antle and Daniel A. Sumner, 101–120. Chicago: University of Chicago Press.

Mundlak, Yair. 2001. Production and Supply," in *Handbook of Agricultural Economics, Vol. 1A*, edited by Bruce Gardner and Gordon Rausser, 3–80. New York: Elsevier.

Newbery, David M. G., and Joseph E. Stiglitz. 1979. "Sharecropping, Risk Sharing and the Importance of Imperfect Information," in *Risk, Uncertainty and Agricultural Development, edited by* James A. Roumasset, Jean-Marc Boussard, and Inderjit Singh, 311–339. College, Laguna, Philippines: Southeast Asian Regional Center for Graduate Study and Research in Agriculture and New York: Agricultural Development Council.

Newbery, David M. G., and Joseph E. Stigliz. 1981. *The Theory of Commodity Price Stabilization; A Study in the Economics of Risk*. Oxford: Clarendon Press.

Osborne, Robin. 1987. *Classical Landscape with Figures; The Ancient Greek City and its Countryside*. Dobbs Ferry, N.Y.: Sheridan House.

Osborne, Robin. 1988. "Social and Economic Implications of the Leasing of Land and Property in Classical and Hellenistic Greece," *Chiron* 18: 279–323.

Otsuka, Keijiro, and Yujiro Hayami. 1988. "Theories of Share Tenancy: A Critical Survey," *Economic Development and Cultural Change* 37: 31–68.

Otsuka, Keijiro, and Naoki Murukami. 1987. "Resource Allocation and Efficiency of Sharecropping under Uncertainty," *Asian Economic Journal* 1: 131–134.

Otsuka, Keijiro, Hiroyuki Chuma, and Yujiro Hayami 1992. "Land and Labor Contracts in Agrarian Economies: Theories and Facts," *Journal of Economic Literature* 30: 1965–2018.

Pant, Chandrashekar. 1983. "Tenancy and Family Resources; A Model and Some Empirical Analysis," *Journal of Development Economics* 12: 27–39.

Payne, Sebastian. 1973. "Kill-off Patterns in Sheep and Goats: The Mandibles from Aşvan Kale," *Anatolian Studies* 40: 281–303.

Postgate, J.N. 1992. *Early Mesopotamia; Society and Economy at the Dawn of History*. London: Routledge.

Quibria, M. G., and Salim Rashid. 1986. "Sharecropping in Dual Agrarian Economies: A Synthesis," *Oxford Economic Papers* NS 38: 94–111.

Ransom, Roger L., and Richard Sutch. 1977. *One Kind of Freedom: The Economic Consequences of Emancipation*. Cambridge: Cambridge University Press.

Reid, Joseph D., Jr. 1973. "Sharecropping as an Understandable Market Response - The Postbellum South," *Journal of Economic History* 33: 106–130.

Reid, Joseph D., Jr. 1976. "Antebellum Southern Rental Contracts," *Explorations in Economic History* 13: 69–83.

Reid, Joseph D. Jr. 1987. "The Theory of Sharecropping: Occam's Razor and Economic Analysis," *History of Political Economy* 19: 551–569.

Renkow, Mitch. 1990. "Household Inventories and Marketed Surplus in Semisubsistence Agriculture," *American Journal of Agricultural Economics* 72: 664–675.

Rosen, Sherwin. 1987. "Dynamic Animal Economics," *American Journal of Agricultural Economics* 69: 547–557.

Rosen, Sherwin. 1999. "Potato Paradoxes," *Journal of Political Economy* 107: S294–S313.

Rosen, Sherwin, Kevin M. Murphy, and José A. Scheinkman. 1994. "Cattle Cycles," *Journal of Political Economy* 102: 468–492.

Sen, Amartya. 1981a. "Ingredients of Famine Analysis: Availability and Entitlements," *Quarterly Journal of Economics* 96: 433–464.

Sen, Amartya. 1981b. *Poverty and Famines: An Essay on Entitlement and Deprivation*. Oxford: Clarendon Press.

Shahabuddin, Qazi, Stuart Mestelman, and David Feeny. 1986. "Peasant Behaviour Towards Risk and Socio-Economic and Structural Characteristics of Farm Households in Bangladesh," *Oxford Economic Papers* NS 38: 122–133.

Singh, Nirvikar. 1989. "Theories of Sharecropping," in *The Economic Theory of Agrarian Institutions*, edited by Pranab Bardhan, 33–72. Oxford: Clarendon Press.

Slotsky, Alice Louise. 1997. *The Bourse of Babylon; Market Quotations in the Astronomical Diaries of Babylonia*. Bethesda, Md.: CDL Press.

Smith, Adam. 1937 [1776]. *An Inquiry into the Nature and Causes of the Wealth of Nations*, edited by Edwin Cannan. New York: Modern Library.

Stevenson, Glenn G. 1991. *Common Property Economics: A General Theory and Land Use Applications*. Cambridge: Cambridge University Press.

Stiglitz, Joseph E. 1986. "Cost-Sharing Arrangements under Sharecropping: Moral Hazard, Incentive Flexibility, and Risk," *American Journal of Agricultural Economics* 68: 642–652.

Strauss, John. 1984. "Marketed Surpluses of Agricultural Households in Sierra Leone," *American Journal of Agricultural Economics* 66: 321–331.

Stuchevskij I.A. 1982. *Zemledelcy gosudarstvennogo hozyajstva drevnego Egipta jepohi Ramessidov.*/ Stuchevsky IA. *Farmers of the state economy of Ancient Egypt of the era of the Ramessides*. Moscow: Academy of Sciences SSSR Institute of Oriental Studies.

Subramanian, Shankar. 1995. "Wage Labor, Sharecropping and Credit Transactions," *Oxford Economic Papers* N.S. 47: 329–356.

Tandy, David W. and Walter C. Neale. 1996. *Hesiod's Works and Days; A Translation and Commentary for the Social Sciences*. Berkeley: University of California Press.

Temin, Peter. 2002. "Price Behavior in Ancient Babylon," *Explorations in Eonomic History* 39: 46–60.

Trueblood, Michael A. 2010. "Can Regional Policy Initiatives Help Achieve Food Security in Southern Africa?" Food Security Assessment/GFA-9, Economic Research Service/USDA, November 1997, 30–35, Table B-1—Cereal Balance Information, Southern African Countries, 1993–1995, 31, http://www.

ers.usda.gov/publications/gfa9/gfa9c.pdf, accessed November 2010.

Uchitel, Alexander. 2005. "Land-Tenure in Mycenaean Greece and the Hittite Empire: Linear B Land-Surveys from Pylos and Middle Hittite Land-Donations," *JESHO* 48: 473–486.

United States Department of Agriculture (U.S.D.A.), Economic Research Service (E.R.S.), *Wheat Yearbook.* 2010. Wheat Data: Yearbook Table Table 4, World and U.S. Wheat Production, Exports, and Ending Stocks, http://www.ers.usda.gov/Data/Wheat/YBtable04.asp, accessed November 2010.

United States Department of Agriculture (U.S.D.A.), Foreign Agricultural Service (F.A.S.). 2010. "World Agricultural Supply and Demand Estimates," WASDE – 488, Approved by the World Agricultural Outlook Board November 9, 2010, http://www.usda.gov/oce/commodity/wasde/latest.pdf, accessed December 2010.

Ventris Michael, and John Chadwick. 1973. *Documents in Mycenaean Greek, 2nd Ed.* Cambridge: Cambridge University Press.

White, K.D. 1970. *Roman Farming.* London: Thames & Hudson.

Wlliams, Jeffrey C., and Brian D. Wright. 1991. *Storage and Commodity Markets.* Cambridge: Cambridge University Press.

Wright, Brian D., and Jeffrey C. Williams. 1982a. "The Economic Role of Commodity Storage," *Economic Journal* 92: 596–614.

Wright, Brian D., and Jeffrey C. Williams. 1982b. "The Welfare Effects of the Introduction of Storage," *Quarterly Journal of Economics* 99: 169–192.

Wright, Henry T. 1969. *The Administration of Rural Production in an Early Mesopotamian Town*, Museum of Anthropology, University of Michigan, Anthropological Paper No 38. Ann Arbor: University of Michigan.

Zaccagnini, Carlo. 1984. "Proprieta fondiaria e dipendenza rurale nella Mesopotamia settentrionale (XV–XIV secolo a.C.)," *Studi Storici* 25: 697–723.

Zaccagnini, Carlo. 1999. "Economic aspects of land ownership and land use in northern Mesopotamia and Syria from the late 3rd millennium to the Neo-Assyrian period, in *Urbanization and Land Ownership in the Ancient Near East*, Peabody Museum Bulletin # 7, edited by Baruch A. Levine and Michael Hudson, 331–352. Cambridge, Mass.: Harvard University Press.

3

The Economics of International Trade

3.1 Problems and Models in International Trade

The economic theory of international trade strives to understand why countries export and import the goods and services they do. If all trade were of the sort in which countries exported goods only they could produce or extract and imported similarly unique goods from other countries, there would be little for economics to explain. When different countries are capable of producing essentially the same goods, yet some of them choose to import part of their consumption of some of those goods and produce other goods in volumes that exceed domestic consumption, selling abroad what is not consumed locally, there are some resource allocation choices to be explained. Even countries with unique resources, or at least resources that are not present in every country, are apt to import quantities of some goods they also produce domestically. Bronze Age Cyprus, with its famous copper deposits, is an example, importing olive oil from foreign lands to supplement its own oil production.

Trade theory offers considerably more information than an explanation of trade patterns. Concomitant with the explanations of trade patterns are predictions of a number of consequences of trade. Trade models are general equilibrium models, and commodity prices, factor prices, and the welfare of various members of society are determined along with trade patterns. These models run counter to the models of trade occasionally encountered in discussions of ancient economic activity, to the effect that people exchanged their surpluses: no surplus, no trade. The models of international trade theory nowhere rely on the concept of a surplus. This part of trade theory generally abstracts from the use of money, and the problems associated with different moneys circulating among countries; it is called the "real" theory of trade, sometimes the "pure" theory. Most of this chapter will deal with topics in the real theory of trade although I will introduce some topics in international monetary economics toward the end. This is appropriate to the generally limited flexibility of money in the economies of this period as I currently understand them.

The first model of production and trade focuses on production to the exclusion of consumption and emphasizes technological differences in production as the motivation for trade. Known as the Ricardian model, it is used in contemporary analysis to study the short run—that period of time in which factors like capital and land are fixed in quantity and quality—and characteristically focuses on labor productivity differentials among countries as the basis for trade. The Ricardian model was the first to use the concept of comparative advantage, rather than absolute advantage, as the criterion governing the profitability of trade. The specific factors model introduces a separate factor specific to each industry in a country in addition to the labor that Ricardian model supposes is mobile between industries. This model represents an extension of the Ricardian model. The Heckscher-Ohlin model, which forms the basis of most contemporary real trade theory, entertains long-run adjustments and offers an explanation for a country's comparative advantage in its factor endowments relative to those of other countries—i.e., the proportions in which it possesses land, labor, and possibly capital. Pursuing the short-run/long-run distinction between the Ricardian and Heckscher-Ohlin models a bit further, it takes less time to install new machines embodying a different technology, à la the Ricardian model, than it does to noticeably alter the ratio of land to people, along the lines of the Heckscher-Ohlin model's structure, although this view emphasizes chronological time rather than the concept of factor adjustments in the pure theory of the length of "run." Following these two major expository sections, we will touch more briefly on some other explanations for trade that may be useful in accounting for ancient trade patterns.

Trade models invariably begin with the simplest case possible: two countries and two goods. More complicated models involving production as well as exchange keep the 2-country, 2-good structure but add only two factors of production. Factors of production are presumed to be immobile between countries but perfectly mobile within countries (the specific factors model is a partial exception); only goods move between countries. These models also generally abstract from transportation costs—i.e., they assume them away. Of course, the world contains more than two countries, more than two goods are produced and traded, and transportation costs can be quite high. Such simple models have been retained for two primary reasons: they give penetrating insights into the causes and consequences of trade, and those insights carry over in large part, although not totally, to the cases of multiple goods and factors; the multiple-country case has not been much studied other than to see if 2×2 results carry over. Explicit treatment of transportation costs has been specified in several manners, and while some interesting results have emerged, the fundamental results of the simpler models have not been much altered. In fact, well-specified transportation looks a lot like a third good. I briefly discuss these extensions of the basic models in sub-sections 3.4.7 and 3.4.9. Trade in intermediate goods (goods that are used as inputs rather than for final consumption) and international investment are departures from the strict immobility of factors of production, although if we consider only the so-called "original" factors—labor and land, possibly capital—trade in intermediate goods is still goods trade rather than factor mobility.

While the basic models of real trade take completely free trade as their expository starting points, government interference with trade in one form or another long has been the norm. Section 3.6 introduces the analysis of various types of commercial policies, of which tariffs are particularly prominent. The customs union is one type of bargain that countries can reach over commercial policy; I introduce it to provide a benchmark against which to think about the consequences of ancient trade agreements.

The multinational firm may sound like an especially recent phenomenon, but the resident Assyrian traders in Hattuša in the 19th century B.C.E. fit the bill, and the literature has held up several Phoenician endeavors as candidates for multinational enterprise status as well.[1]

The last section turns to monetary topics. Without a monetary or capital account, the balance of payments is trivially balanced continually. The value of one country's money in terms of another's is called the foreign exchange rate. There is much more to the topic when fiat currencies are issued in different countries, but there are some useful lessons even for bullion moneys; when one considers the claims made for grain commodity money in Egypt, there clearly is scope for investigation of the relationship with the moneys of trading partners.

3.2 Gains from Trade

In the general equilibrium exchange model, as the name implies, we abstract from production. The demonstration of the gains from trade begins with two countries initially in states of autarky. It will be convention to discuss one country as if it were the reader's country by calling it the "home country." The other country in 2-country trade models is called, naturally enough, the "foreign country." Frequently, trade theory investigates how just one country responds to some change, either because the change affects just one country or because one of the two countries is assumed to be so small relative to the other that it cannot affect world prices of traded goods. In our simple exchange model, the home country, in autarky, faces constant costs of producing each of two goods, food and manufactures, represented by the relative price line p_A in Figure 3.1. In this simplest model we do not deal with how the goods are actually produced. The combination of food and manufactures the country "chooses" depends on the preferences of its residents, represented by the community indifference curve, u_A, for the level of welfare reached by

[1] The aptness of the analogy in the latter case may be questioned (Jones 1993).

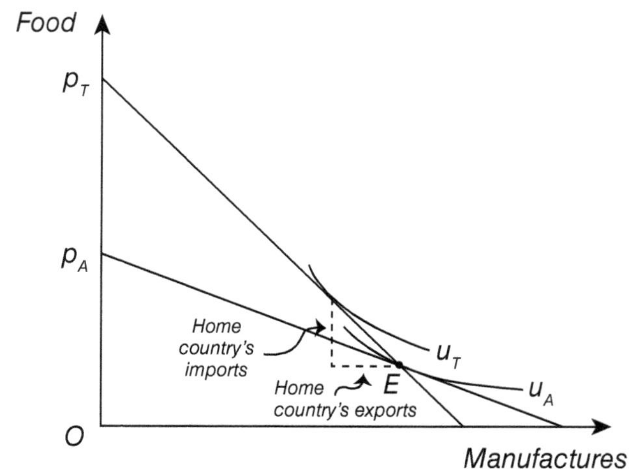

Figure 3.1. Gains from trade: home country.

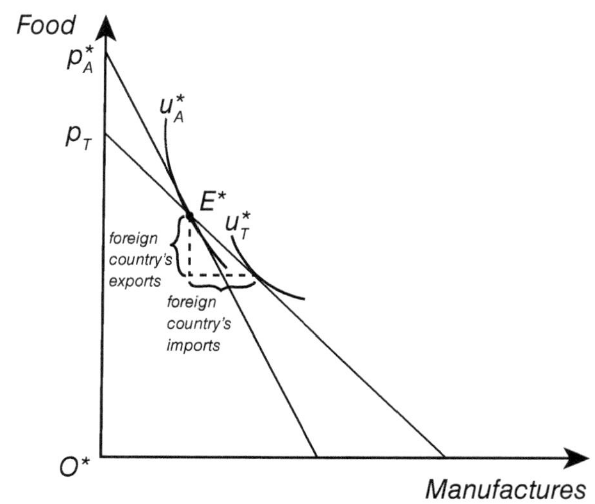

Figure 3.2. Gains from trade: foreign country.

the home country in autarky.[2] We can call the point of tangency, E, the endowment point.

The foreign country's opportunities for consuming food and manufactures in autarky are represented in Figure 3.2 by the relative price line p_A^*. (A notational convention is to use asterisks to denote variables pertaining to the foreign country.) Given the preferences in the foreign country, its endowment point is E*, at the tangency of utility level u_A^*.

Trade opens between the two countries and results in the "world" price, p_T, in both Figures 3.1 and 3.2. Line p_T goes through each country's endowment point since each country must find its original endowment attainable at the new set of prices. From the perspective of the home country, trade increases the price of manufactures and

[2] Community indifference curves contain more assumptions within their construction than do individual indifference curves, particularly homogeneity of preferences of all residents, as well as some specific properties about how the level of individual well-being increases as consumption levels rise. The use of community indifference curves makes it difficult to study how trade may affect different categories of residents (such as capital-owners versus pure labor-suppliers). Alternative methods have been devised to represent well-being that involve less restrictive assumptions, but working with them is somewhat more difficult and at times less intuitive. For present purposes, the imprecisions introduced by the use of community indifference curves will not be important.

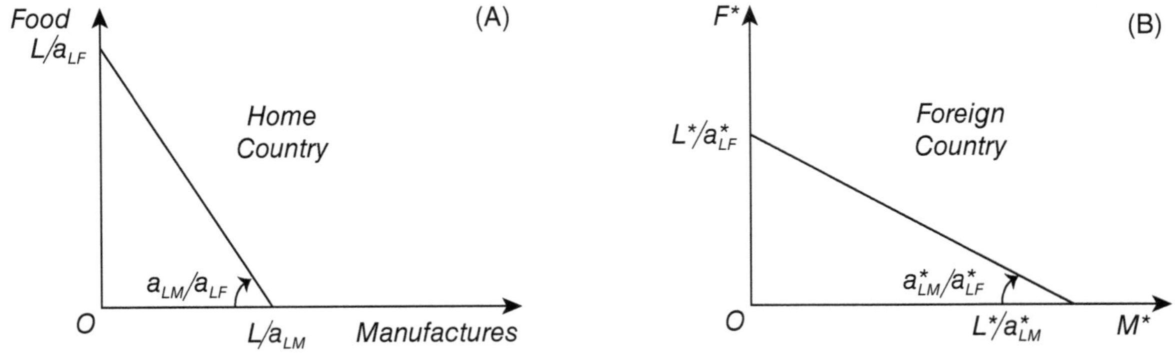

Figure 3.3. (A) Ricardian model: home country's technology. (B) Ricardian model: foreign country's technology.

reduces the price of food. Trade has just the opposite effect on relative prices in the foreign country. The home country is able to reach the higher indifference level u_T by virtue of the opportunity to consume at the new price ratio. It now consumes more food and fewer manufactures than it did in autarky. Correspondingly in the foreign country, consumption shifts toward the good that has become cheaper with trade—manufactures—and the country is able to reach the higher level of community indifference, u_T^*. Since we have excluded production from this model, the fixed endowment of each country now differs from the consumption bundle. The home country exports manufactures and imports food equal in value to its exports. The home country's manufactures exports in Figure 3.1 are equal to the foreign country's manufactures imports in Figure 3.2, and home's food imports equal foreign's food exports. The value of exports equals the value of imports. Trade is balanced, and both countries gain from the opening of trade, although there is no guarantee that one of them does not gain more than the other: the welfare gain is in terms of utility, not in terms of the value or volume of trade, which is of course the same for the two countries.

3.3 Theories of Trade 1. Differential Technology: The Ricardian Model

While the exchange model is indeed a *model* of trade, we have not called it a *theory* of trade because it makes no serious attempt to explain why the intercountry differences that make trade beneficial exist in the first place. Henceforth, the trade models I present account in one fashion or another for those differences. The Ricardian model of trade emerged from early 19th century efforts to provide intellectual support for liberal policies toward international commerce. Its principal goal was to demonstrate the gains from trade, with the particular pattern of trade that emerged (from the model) of secondary importance. Accordingly the production model underlying the trade is quite simple, and it took several further generations to incorporate the influence of demand satisfactorily. Despite the model's simplicity and its reliance on a labor theory of value, it still finds uses today in exploring the role of differential labor productivity in accounting for trade patterns.

3.3.1 Production in the Ricardian Model

As I treat each of the models of trade, I will use the two-country scenario: either the "world" of the model consists of only two countries, or I model one country in detail and consider "the rest of the world" (typically identified as ROW) as if it were a single country. Each country in the Ricardian model produces two goods with a single input, labor, which is perfectly mobile between industries. The production technology has constant costs, or is characterized by what are called "fixed coefficients": i.e., a constant amount of labor is required to produce each unit of a particular product. The production function for, say, manufactured goods in the home country is $M = L_M/a_{LM}$, where $1/a_{LM}$ is the labor per unit of manufactured output,[3] L_M is labor used in manufacturing (call the other good food and subscript it "F"), and M is the quantity of manufactured goods produced in the home country. In the foreign country, I write the manufactures production function $M^* = L_M^*/a_{LM}^*$, in which the asterisk indicates the foreign country. Similarly for the food production functions: $F = L_F/a_{LF}$ and $F^* = L_F^*/a_{LF}^*$. In general, a_{Li} and a_{Li}^* are not necessarily equal; in fact, if both countries' pairs of coefficients are equal, no trade will occur.[4]

Competition within each country will ensure that the wage in each industry, prior to trade, will equal the value of its marginal (and in the fixed-coefficients case, average) product: $w = p_i/a_{Li}$ and $w^* = p_i^*/a_{Li}^*$ for each industry i. The same competition also will lead to full employment of the labor force: $L = a_{LM}M + a_{LF}F$ in the home country and $L^* = a_{LM}^*M + a_{LF}^*F$ in the foreign country. In fact, with fixed coefficients, a country's production is limited only by the size of its labor force. Figure 3.3 shows the production possibilities curves for the home country (panel A) and the foreign country (panel B), which are derived from the full-employment condition and production coefficients.

The slope of each straight-line production possibilities frontier (ppf) is the ratio of the labor coefficient in manufacturing to that in food production; or expressed alternatively, the ratio of labor per unit of food to labor per unit of the manufactured good. From the cost conditions,

[3] Equivalently, a_{LM} is the manufactured output per unit of labor time.
[4] As we'll see a little further on, the condition is even weaker: if the ratios of the coefficients are the same across countries, no trade will occur.

Table 3.1. Ricardo's Comparative Cost Example.

	Cloth	Wine
	Labor Costs	
England	100 workers	120 workers
Portugal	90 workers	80 workers
	Production in Autarky	
England	100 workers → 1 unit	120 workers → 1 unit
Portugal	90 workers → 1 unit	80 workers → 1 unit
World total	2 units	2 units
	Production with Trade	
England	220 workers → 220/100 units	
Portugal		170 workers → 170/80 units
World	2.2 units	2.125 units

we also have the relationship $a_{LM}/a_{LF} = p_M/p_F$, so the slope of the ppf is also equal to the relative commodity price. In autarky, the country's production and consumption patterns will be determined by the tangency of a community indifference curve to the ppf (Figure 3.3 doesn't show this).

3.3.2 The Comparative Advantage Concept

The heart of the concept of comparative advantage is that a country need not be more efficient at the production of a good than its trading partner is in order to be able to trade (export) that good. This may sound counterintuitive at first, but it simply points to the ratio of goods that each partner can produce as the source of advantage in trade: when the goods are finally produced, regardless of the cost of either in terms of labor (the only factor in the Ricardian model), countries are faced with how much of one good they have to sacrifice to produce one unit of the other. We'll show Ricardo's original numerical example of England and Portugal producing cloth and wine and work through the arithmetic of production to show that specializing in the good in which one has a comparative advantage and trading is superior to producing and consuming in autarky, even for a country that is more productive at both goods.

Both countries produce one unit of cloth and one unit of wine, England requiring 100 workers to produce its cloth and 120 to produce its wine, Portugal requiring only 90 to produce its cloth and 80 to produce its wine. The cloth and wine in the two countries are of the same quality. Portugal is more efficient in producing both cloth and wine: it has an *absolute* advantage in both goods. However, the relative cost of producing cloth is lower in England than in Portugal (100/120 = 0.833 in England and 90/80 = 1.125 in Portugal). This is equivalent to comparing the labor costs of each good across countries: the cost ratio of producing cloth is 90/100 = 0.900 (Portugal to England) and that of wine is 80/120 = 0.667, which also shows Portugal with a lower *relative* cost (relative to England) of wine. The top panel of Table 1 shows these base labor cost figures. In the cost-coefficient terminology of sub-section 3.1, with Portugal the home country, $a_{LC} = 90$, $a_{LW} = 80$, $a^*_{LC} = 100$, and $a^*_{lw} = 120$. Thus, before trade, $a_{LC}/a_{LW} = p_C/p_W (\equiv p)$ and $a^*_{LC}/a^*_{LW} (= p^*_C/p^*_W \equiv p^*)$, where $p > p^*$, which indicates that England has the comparative advantage in cloth and Portugal in wine. Of course, when trade opens, $p = p^* = p^T$, ignoring transportation costs, or assuming that they are small enough to ignore for the purposes of initial analysis).

The second panel of Table 1 shows the total production of wine and cloth each country can produce if they don't trade, and the corresponding world total. Each country produces one unit of each good, yielding two units of each good in the whole world. In the third panel, England has specialized in the production of cloth and Portugal in wine: i.e., each country has devoted all its labor to the production of the good in which it has the comparative cost advantage. They have to trade to consume some of both goods. By specializing in cloth production, England is able to "convert" the single unit of wine it would have produced into another 1.2 units of cloth, for a total of 2.2 units of cloth. Portugal has "converted" its cloth into wine by reallocating its cloth labor into wine, yielding an additional 1.125 units of wine. The specialization permitted by trade has permitted the world to produce 10% more cloth than its individual countries would have been able to produce in autarky and $6\frac{1}{4}$ % more wine.

3.3.3 Patterns of Trade

Let's return to each country's production and consumption in autarky before we open trade between them. Figures 3.4A and B introduce community indifference curves to the production possibility. Both countries are constrained to consume at their production points, E and E* in the absence of trade. Introduce trade, and the good in which each country has a comparative advantage becomes more expensive. The relative price of food and manufactures becomes the same in both countries with trade. At the new terms of trade, drawn as the dashed line through points E and E*, both countries can reach higher community indifference curves, which is what we saw with the exchange model in Section 3.2. However, in the Ricardian model, production can respond as well as consumption to the price movements following the opening of trade.

To study the production responses, we can think of each country's national income as the value of its output. Returning to the "food and manufactures" example, we have Y = pF + M, where $p \equiv p_F/p_M$ for the home country. Remember that the home country's production

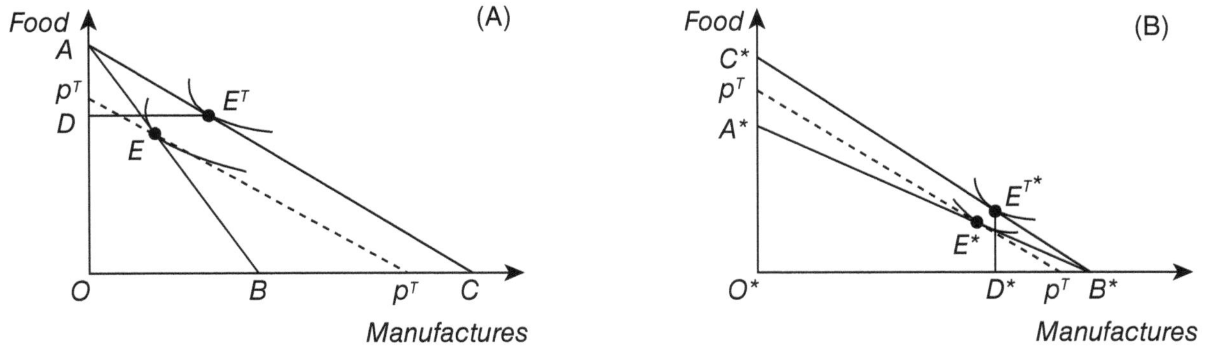

Figure 3.4. (A) Ricardian model: home country's pattern of trade. (B) Ricardian model: foreign country's pattern of trade.

possibilities are expressed by $L = a_{LF}F + a_{LM}M$, which relates the amount of labor available, L, to the quantities of food and manufactures the country can produce. How would each country respond to gain the most from the changed relative prices? We can formulate this problem as one of each country maximizing its national income subject to the factor and technological limitations contained in its production possibilities frontier. For the home country in Figure 3.4A, the part of the new terms-of-trade line to the left of its endowment point E is below its production possibilities frontier; producing at any point on p^Tp^T to the left of E would leave some labor unemployed and fail to give the greatest possible national income. To the right of E, the home country's production would have to stay on the ppf, which would involve producing more of the good that has become cheaper, which would reduce its national income rather than increase it. Thus, maximizing national income would involve moving the production point from E upward along the ppf as far as the availability of resources allows—all the way to the intercept with the vertical axis at A. So the home country completely specializes in the production of food. The world terms of trade is represented by line AC, parallel to p^Tp^T. This line identifies the terms on which the country can consume, and it can be called the consumption possibilities frontier (cpf). The home country can reach community indifference level $E^T > E$ on the cpf. The triangle E^TDA is the trade triangle, representing balanced trade with the foreign country: AD exports of food for DE^T imports of manufactures.

For the foreign country, maximization of the value of output entails sliding down its ppf toward specialization in manufactures at B*, with consumption at E^{T*} on its cpf, which is, of course, the same cpf facing the home country. Its trade triangle, $B^*D^*E^{T*}$, indicates D*B* of manufactures exports in return for D^*E^{T*} food imports, which must be equivalent to the quantity of food the home country is willing to export for this particular quantity of manufactures. The implicit "if" in this equality points to the fact that the terms of trade I have identified as p^Tp^T are arbitrary so far: I have not deduced it from the preference patterns of the two countries and the relative supplies of the two goods in the world's production possibilities, to which I now turn.

We can construct the world production possibilities frontier by adding the ppfs of the two countries, as in Figure 3.5.

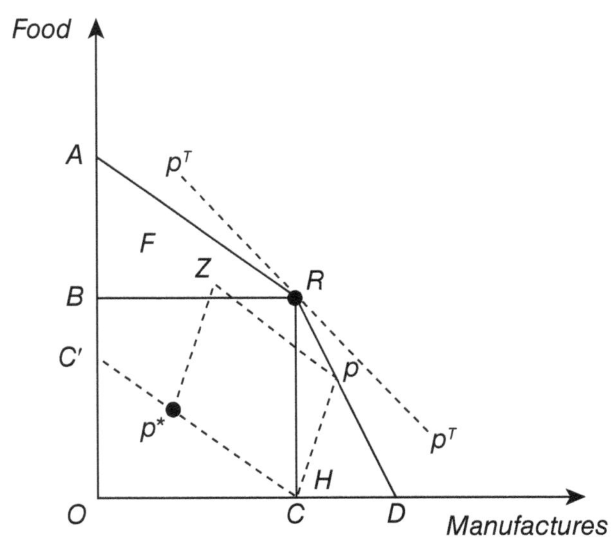

Figure 3.5. Ricardian model: world production possibilities frontier.

First, draw the foreign country's ppf as line OCC'. Next, draw the home country's ppf as triangle CDR, using the foreign country's manufactures specialization point as origin. Now, slide the home country's ppf triangle up the face of the foreign country's ppf, line CC', to get world production possibilities OAD. Triangle ABR is the foreign country's portion of the world's production possibilities, and triangle CRD is the home country's. Now, suppose that neither country specialized: say, the home country produced at point P* and the home country produced at point P. Adding points P and P* yields point Z, which is inside the world ppf. The only combination of production points that will put the two countries on the world production possibilities frontier is complete specialization by both, which will put them at point R (called "Ricardo's point"). Now, let's find the world community indifference curve that touches R. Since R is a kink, no tangency of a world community indifference curve can be tangent to the world ppf at R. However, we can be assured that the slope of the terms of trade line, p^Tp^T, must be between the slopes of the two countries' faces of the world ppf, lines AR and RD. While this analysis narrows down the range of possible world prices, it leaves open some range of indeterminacy. To complete the elimination of this indeterminacy, I turn to the construction of offer curves for the Ricardian model.

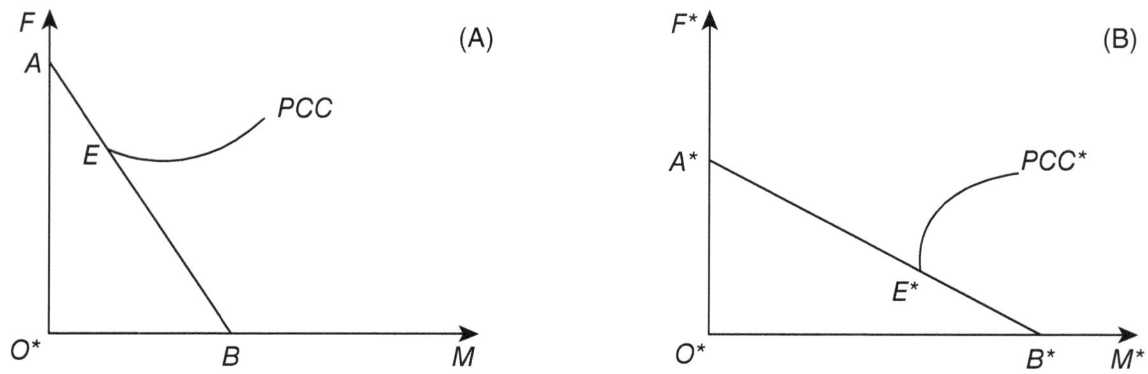

Figure 3.6. (A) Ricardian model: home country's price-consumption curve. (B) Ricardian model: foreign country's price-consumption curve.

The Ricardian offer curve, which shows quantities of exports offered for different quantities of imports, is derived from price-consumption curves which are derived in production space rather than export-import space. However, the conversion of the price-consumption curves in production space to offer curves in export-import space yields offer curves that look exactly like the price-consumption curves. I'll show the determination of the equilibrium terms of trade with price-consumption curves and conduct further analysis with offer curves. The Ricardian price-consumption curve is constructed in analogous fashion to the offer curve of the exchange model. Consider figure 3.6A, which shows the home country's production possibilities frontier, the slope of which (a_{LM}/a_{LF}) is greater (steeper) than what the world terms of trade must turn out to be (i.e., we don't know yet exactly what p^T is, but we already *do* know that it has to be smaller than a_{LM}/a_{LF}). Rotate alternative terms-of-trade lines around point A (the home country's specialization point) in Figure 3.6A, beginning with the autarkic terms of trade $p^T = a_{LM}/a_{LF}$, and observe the point of tangency with the country's community indifference curve at each relative price. Thus, when $p^T = a_{LM}/a_{LF}$, the home country consumes at E; when p^T is a little smaller (geometrically speaking, flatter), the consumption point is somewhere out on line PCC. We can continue until p^T is horizontal. For a country whose autarkic price ratio is greater than what the equilibrium terms of trade must be (the foreign country in our example), we start from the opposite specialization point, point B* in Figure 3.6B. Rotate the alternative terms-of-trade lines around point B* and derive the price-consumption line PPC* from the autarkic consumption point E*.

Now we make a box diagram in Figure 3.7, out of the ppfs of the home and foreign countries (triangles OLN and O*MN, respectively), putting the origin of the foreign country's ppf at the lower left and the origin of the home country's ppf at the upper right, so that the home country's ppf is measured downward. The two countries' price-consumption curves emerge from the respective autarky production-consumption points. The line connecting point N (the manufactures and food specialization points for the two countries) and the intersection of the price-consumption points is the equilibrium terms of trade,

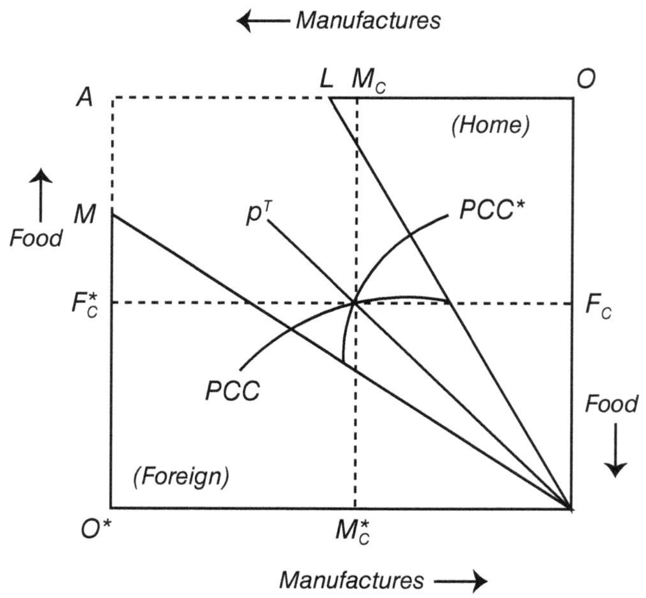

Figure 3.7. Ricardian model: offer curves and trade equilibrium.

p^T. Both countries specialize—Home in food, Foreign in manufactures. The home country consumes OM_c manufactures and OF_c food and exports F_cN food to pay for its manufactures. The foreign country consumes $O^*M_c^*$ manufactures and $O^*F_c^*$ food and exports M_c^*N.

Next, suppose that the countries have greater disparity in size than I have drawn so far. Figure 3.8 keeps the home country the same size as before but considers two smaller sizes for the foreign country. First, suppose that the production possibility frontier represented by O*MN represents the foreign country. The intersection of its PPC* with PPC of the home country leads to terms of trade p^T, which is much closer to a_{LM}/a_{LF} than was the case in Figure 3.8; as is intuitively sensible, when trade opens, the post-trade prices will be much closer to those in the larger country prior to trade than to those in the smaller. Nonetheless, both countries still specialize since the intersection occurs on the PCC segments rather than on the straight segments. Second, suppose that the foreign country is even smaller: represented now by O**M′N. Its PCC** intersects the straight segment of the home country's price-consumption line, which tells us that the

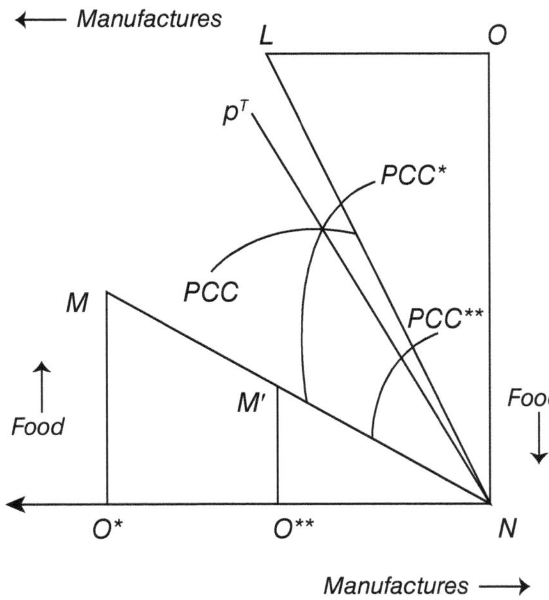

Figure 3.8. Ricardian model: large disparity in country sizes.

foreign country will specialize in manufactures but the home country will not specialize. The foreign country's demand for food is too small to permit the home country to specialize in food production without driving the relative price of food below what it would have been in autarky, which would of course make trade unbeneficial. Along the same lines, the foreign country is not large enough to satisfy the home country's demand for manufactured goods with its exports alone.

If we displace the pre-trade production-consumption points to the origin of an offer curve diagram, we would measure exports and imports on the axes of the Ricardian offer curve diagram, as Figure 3.9 shows. The slope of the straight segment of the home country's offer curve is a_{LM}/a_{LF}, and the corresponding slope of the foreign country's straight-line segment is a^*_{LM}/a^*_{LF} and the equilibrium terms of trade, p^T, lies between them. The offer curves are labeled H and H*. The Ricardian offer curves contain both supply and demand adjustments.

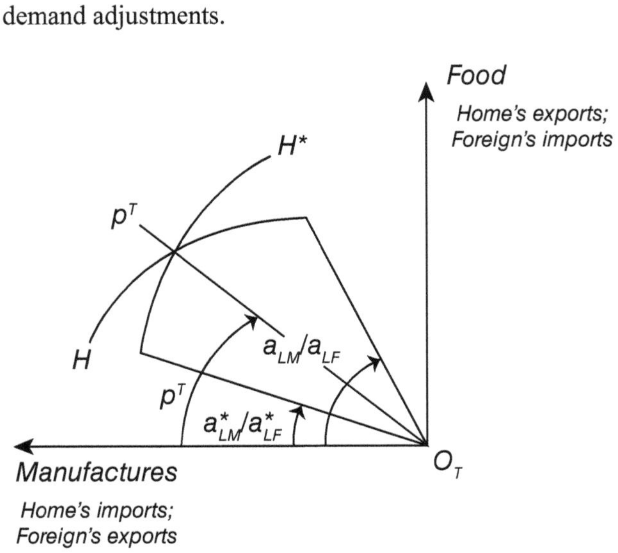

Figure 3.9. Ricardian model: measuring exports and imports only.

3.3.4 Effect of Trade on Factor Prices

Trade does not generally equalize factor prices (i.e., wage rates) in the Ricardian model. Recall the competitive profit conditions introduced above for each industry: in the home country, $a_{LM}w = p_M$ and $a_{LF}w = p_F$. There are two equivalent ways of interpreting these conditions: (1) the quantity of labor per unit of output of each good, times the wage rate, will equal the price of that product since there are no other inputs; (2) taking the labor coefficients over to the right-hand sides of these expressions we have the familiar relationship that the marginal physical product of labor ($1/a_{Li}$, which is equal to average product because of the fixed-coefficients) times the price of the product equals the wage payment to the factor. In each country, these conditions will hold in autarky.

Now, open trade and let both countries specialize. In the home country, $a_{LW}w = p_F$, and in the foreign country, $a^*_{LM}w = p_F$ (I omit the asterisk on post-trade p_F because that price will be common to both countries—measured, of course, in terms of manufactures). The ratio of wage rates in the home and foreign countries, or the factoral terms of trade, is $w/w^* = [1/a_{LF}/1/a^*_{LM}] \cdot p_F/p_M$.

The price ratio p_F/p_M is the home country's commodity terms of trade (the price of the good in which it possesses a comparative advantage, relative to the price of the other good); an improvement in a country's commodity terms of trade will raise the wage rate at home relative to that abroad by a factor proportional to the ratio of home to foreign marginal products (or labor productivities, since marginal product equals average product in this model).

But this relationship only holds for commodity terms of trade that lead to complete specialization by both countries. When one or both countries incompletely specialize, the ratio of wage rates in, say food production, in the two countries would be $w/w^* = [(1/a_{LF})/(1/a^*_{LF})] \cdot p_F/p^*_F$, but trade equalizes p_F and p^*_F so the ratio of wage rates will equal the ratio of the two countries' labor productivities in the good they both produce. Figure 3.10 shows these relationships graphically. If the foreign country possesses absolute advantages in both goods, the ratio of the home wage to the foreign wage, w/w*, must fall below one. Although comparative advantage permits the less efficient country as well as the more efficient to trade profitably, a uniformly higher efficiency of a country will permit (require, via competitive forces) it to pay higher wages.

3.3.5 Theories of Trade 2. The Specific Factors Model

The specific-factors model of trade extends the Ricardo model to the analysis of more than a single factor of production and diminishing, instead of constant, marginal returns in production. In a two-country, two-good setting, each country has three factors of production, one specific to each industry and a third mobile between industries. The two immobile factors are the "specific" factors. The model

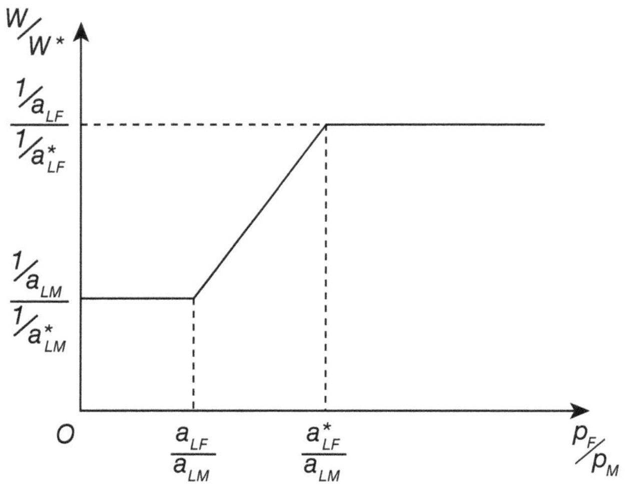

Figure 3.10. Ricardian model: effect of trade on wages.

is on a continuum of generality between the Ricardo model and the Heckscher-Ohlin model and is useful for helping think about the effects of trade over a time period before all the adjustments to changed economic circumstances can be made. We can think of the specific factors as requiring more time to become intersectorally mobile than does labor. The specific factors model lets us ask questions that the Ricardian model does not and offers some different answers to questions that the Ricardian model does let us ask.

3.3.6 Dutch Disease

This syndrome is named after the stagnation of a number of the Netherlands' traditional manufactured export industries following natural gas discoveries in the late 1960s. The specific factors model is well suited to analyze this problem in changing comparative advantage. Consider a small country that has an established export industry selling at prices determined in the world market. A new export industry arises, possibly because of the discovery of a new resource that could be mined and exported or because of a technological change that increases productivity in another long established industry. The established export industry uses labor and another factor that, at least in the short- to intermediate-run, cannot leave the industry. The boom in the new industry raises the VMP of intersectorally mobile labor, which puts a squeeze on the profits of the traditional export industry, which cannot raise its price. The traditional industry must cut back its employment drastically to raise the VMP of its labor to the new wage rate, and the lower production volume sharply reduces the return to the factor specific to that industry.

The technology and other circumstances in the traditional industry need have nothing out of the ordinary happen to them. The events causing the profit squeeze are strictly outside the control of agents in that industry, although the reverse could serve as inducement to technological innovation if the anticipated returns were large enough to justify the investment. Bitros et al. (2021, 145 and n. 7) characterize the Athenian reception of tribute during the period of the Athenian League as leading to the earliest recorded case of Dutch disease. The tribute funds were funneled into nontradable construction projects, driving up wages there. Wages elsewhere would have risen in competition. The increase in wages in exportable activities, which had world prices, would have reduced Athenian manufacturing competitiveness in those industries.

3.4 Theories of Trade 3. Factor Endowments: The Heckscher-Ohlin Model

The Heckscher-Ohlin (H-O) model is the basic model in the contemporary study of international trade. In its standard expositional format, it relies on two factors of production in each country, where the Ricardian model relied on only labor. The production technology the H-O model uses also is more general than the fixed-coefficients technology posited in the Ricardian model: each of two industries has a production function that exhibits diminishing marginal productivity to both of the two factors of production. Generalizing beyond the specific factors model, the basic expositional format of the H-O model permits full mobility of both factors between industries.[5]

Another advance of the H-O model over previous trade models is that it actually proposes a cause of comparative advantage rather than simply presenting a country's comparative advantage as a fait accompli, as the Ricardian model does with technical efficiency. The source of comparative advantage proposed by the H-O model is the pattern of factor endowments of a country: a country with a high proportion of a particular factor will be able in autarky to produce the good that uses that factor intensively more cheaply than it can produce the other good. When trade opens, each country has a comparative advantage in the good which is relatively cheaper in autarky, the cause of which cost pattern can be traced back to the countries' relative factor endowments.

The H-O model can make some powerful predictions about the responses of economies to changes in various circumstances, but it does this at the cost of a number of assumptions. The failure of the world economy to look just like the simplest version of the H-O world economy can be traced readily to the violation of a number of these assumptions, but the tendency of actual economic patterns to move in response to various stimuli in the directions predicted by the H-O model substantiates the usefulness of the model for thinking about trade. One of the strongest predictions of the H-O model is that, under a particular set of conditions, trade alone will equalize factor prices (actually factor rentals) in the trading countries: trade will substitute fully for factor movements such as migration of labor. The failure of standards of living to be identical

[5] I use the term "basic expositional format" because the H-O model is capable of incorporating many special conditions that complicate analysis and thus are omitted from the initial exposition. I discuss some of those conditions in subsequent sub-sections.

among countries of the world points us toward specific assumptions of the model that are violated in the real world.

What are these assumptions of the H-O model? First, production technologies are identical in the different countries. This may seem at first like such a violation of simple observational power as to render a model relying on it not worth the trouble of serious study. Look at it another way though: if production technology in different countries were strikingly different, you wouldn't need an economist to help you explain trading patterns. Much of the contemporary world's trade is between partners with quite similar economies and technological bases. In the ancient world, while different crops were grown in different climatic regions and different countries were famous for certain manufactured products, to a great extent, the technological know-how of different countries had a great amount of overlap. The great Near Eastern empires exchanged craftsmen, which surely transferred a good deal of technology. It's also true that new technologies such as those involved in iron manufacture diffused unevenly in the early years of the Early Iron Age (Snodgrass 1980; Waldbaum 1980), which is a departure from the strict H-O assumption, but one that lets the H-O model offer interesting predictions.

Second, the production technologies exhibit constant returns to scale, an assumption that can be relaxed readily. Third, no externalities or other distortions such as those associated with monopoly or government intervention in the economy, which implies, among other things, free and unrestricted trade. The latter assumption may give scholars of the ancient world further pause, but the H-O model has proven a splendid vehicle for understanding the consequences of many forms of government intervention, both domestic and international, and resultant economic distortions. Fourth, factors are completely immobile internationally but perfectly mobile domestically. Again, the real world is well known for international migration and other international factor movements as well as slowness of intersectoral movements of factors within countries. Again, consider the H-O world as a benchmark. Fifth, factors are homogeneous—i.e., labor and capital are the same throughout a country and in different countries. If they were assumed to be substantially different, we should simply call them different factors, so this really isn't much of an issue.

Before settling in to studied objection to these assumptions—as well as a few more that are added here and there—let's see what is produced with them and how their systematic relaxation produces further understanding. We introduce the basic model of production in a country in the first sub-section, then proceed in the following four sub-sections to present the most important basic results (predictions) of the H-O model. In the remaining four sub-sections of this section, I introduce some of the complications I've held constant in the introductory exposition: the existence of nontraded goods and goods that are used strictly as producer (or "intermediate") goods, the existence of many goods and factors, natural resources as factors of production, and transportation costs. Section 3.6 deals with government-introduced distortions such as tariffs and other trade restrictions as well as more strictly domestic interventions that affect the trading economy.

3.4.1 The 2-Good, 2-Factor Model

The production component of the Heckscher-Ohlin model is the key element of its structure, although demand can play a deciding role in certain instances. I will focus on the production model here, and for that of a single country; the interaction of this country with another will remain implicit in this sub-section and become explicit in the following. Each of two industries produces a good with two factors of production, which I'll call labor and capital, and both industries' production functions have constant returns to scale. That is, increasing the quantities of *both* factors by the same percent leads to an identical percent increase in output. The general form of these production functions is $X_i = F_i(K_i, L_i)$, where X_i is the output of industry i (i = 1, 2 for the two industries, which I'll identify just by number). F_i stands for the functional relationship between capital (K_i) and labor (L_i) on the one hand and output (X_i) on the other. For instance, F_i could stand for a Cobb-Douglas production function, or a CES (constant elasticity of substitution) production function, or any one of a number of others; for present purposes we don't need to commit ourselves to one or another of them. The following exposition is adapted from Kemp (1969, Chapter 1).

Production is constrained by the factor supplies available in the economy: $L_1 + L_2 = L$ and $K_1 + K_2 = K$. L and K are the total labor supply and capital stock, and the fact that they add up to the allocations of labor and capital to the two industries gives us the full-employment condition for equilibrium.

Let's introduce some abbreviations we'll use in the rest of this exposition. First, $k_i \equiv K_i/L_i$, or the capital-labor ratio in industry i. This is the measure of factor intensity we'll use. If $k_1 > k_2$, we say that the first industry is the relatively capital-intensive industry. Figure 3.11 shows

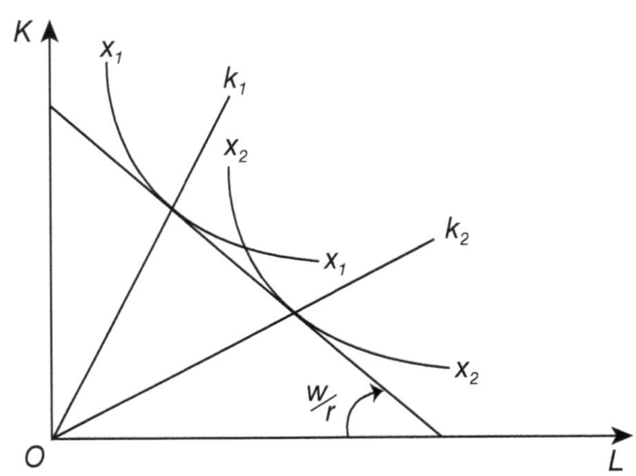

Figure 3.11. Heckscher-Ohlin model: different factor intensities across industries.

different capital intensities in two industries at a given wage-rental ratio. Using the k_i, we can write the full-employment condition for capital as $k_1L_1 + k_2L_2 = K$. Second, $\omega \equiv w/r$, or the wage-rental ratio. Profit maximization in each industry, plus interindustry mobility of both factors will ensure that the wage-rental ratio is the same in both industries, hence I don't subscript this term by industry. Third, $p \equiv p_2/p_1$, which is simply the relative price of good 2 in terms of good 1. (I could have defined p oppositely; nothing substantive would be altered, but I would have to draw parts of a number of our diagrams going in the opposite directions.)

Because production is characterized by constant returns to scale, we can write the production function in terms of the capital-labor ratio: $X_i = L_if_i(k_i)$, which simply says that the output of industry i is a function f_i (not F_i) of the capital-labor *ratio*, times the quantity of labor used in the industry. The functional notation, f_i, is used in several further abbreviations. First, the marginal product of capital is denoted $f_i' > 0$; this denotes the incremental change in output per increment in the capital-labor ratio, which is positive. Second, diminishing marginal productivity is denoted by $f_i'' < 0$, which simply says that although an increment in the capital-labor ratio will give additional output, each subsequent increment will give a smaller increase in output than the previous increment did.

Proceeding with the "working parts" of the model, cost-minimizing (or profit-maximizing) behavior on the parts of producers leads the rental rate of capital to equal the value of marginal product of capital and the wage rate to equal the value of marginal product of labor: $r = p_iMPP_{Ki}$ and $w = p_iMPP_{Li}$. The same producer behavior makes the capital-labor ratio that producers choose, given the technology contained in an industry's production function, a function of the wage-rental ratio. This relationship is denoted by the expression $k_i(\omega)$. Specifically, the capital-labor ratio in each industry increases as the wage-rental ratio increases: $\Delta k_i/\Delta\omega > 0$. The intuitive explanation of the direction of this relationship is that producers substitute capital for labor when labor gets relatively more expensive.

Figure 3.12 shows the relationship between capital intensity and the wage-rental ratio for two industries. R_1 is the locus of capital-labor ratios employed in industry 1 as the wage-rental ratio increases; similarly for R_2.[6] The economy-wide capital-labor ratio is indicated by k on the horizontal axis. Draw a line upward at k to intersect with R_1 and R_2, then draw lines parallel to the horizontal axis back to values of ω on the wage-rental ratio axis. The minimum and maximum values of the wage-rental ratio compatible with the production technologies and overall factor supplies in this economy are $\underline{\omega}$ and $\bar{\omega}$. if both industries are to produce something, the wage-rental ratio in this economy must be between $\underline{\omega}$ and $\bar{\omega}$. At $\underline{\omega}$, the country's entire capital stock is absorbed into the lower capital-intensity industry at a

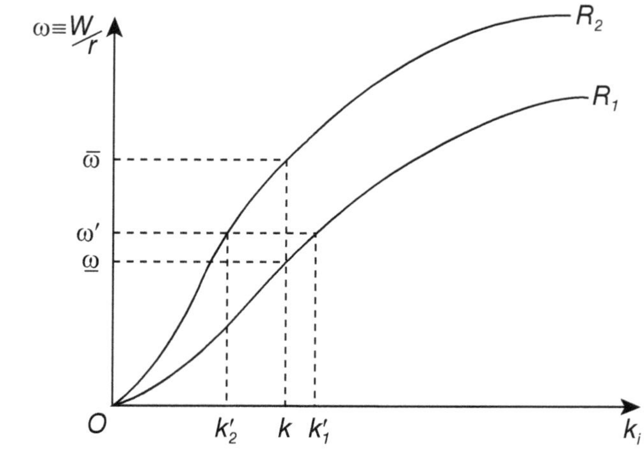

Figure 3.12. Heckscher-Ohlin model: relationship between capital intensity and wage-rental ratio.

value of $k_1 = k$. At a wage-rental ratio as high as , the entire capital stock is absorbed into the higher capital-intensity industry. At these limits of the wage-rental ratio, the economy specializes: i.e., it produces only one good—the other industry shuts down. At the wage-rental ratio ω', industry 2 would produce at capital-labor ratio k_2' and industry 1 at k_1'. These two k_i being on opposite sides of the overall, economy-wide value of k, we can find some weights (the corresponding L_i) that will permit the two industries' employment of capital add up to the total capital stock in the economy.

The commodity price ratio, p, is a function of the factor price ratio, ω. To see how this is so, define p as the ratio of the average cost of producing good 2 divided by the average cost of producing good 1. The total cost of producing good 1 is $wL_1 + rK_1$, and the total cost of producing good 2 is $wL_2 + rK_2$. The total output of good 1 can be written as L_1f_1, and the total output of good 2 as L_2f_2. Then the average cost of good 1 is $(wL_1 + rK_1)/ L_1f_1$, and the average cost of good 2 is $wL_2 + rK_2/L_2f_2$. Divide the average cost of good 2 by the average cost of good 1, and we have p. These expressions for average cost can be rewritten in terms of the wage-rental and capital-labor ratios: $[\omega + k_i(\omega)]/f_i$. Using the ratio of these expressions, the elasticity of p with respect to ω, or the $\%\Delta p/\%\Delta\omega$, is the difference between labor's cost share in industry 1 and industry 2:[7] $\omega/(\omega + k_2) - \omega/(\omega + k_1)$, where each of the $\omega/(\omega + k_i)$ terms is the cost share of labor in industry i. If we denote $\%\Delta p/\%\Delta\omega$ as $\varepsilon_{p\omega}$, $\varepsilon_{p\omega} > 0$ if $k_1 > k_2$ and $\varepsilon_{p\omega} < 0$ if $k_2 > k_1$. That is, at a constant capital-labor ratio, the relative price of good 2 increases when the wage-rental ratio increases if good 2 is labor-intensive relative to good 1; and vice versa. Think about it for a minute and this'll make perfect sense: a unit of good 2 requires more labor than a unit of good 1; an increase in the relative cost of labor will increase the cost of good 2 by more than it increases the cost of good 1.

[6] If industry 2 were the relatively capital-intensive industry, line R_2 would be below line R_1.

[7] Don't worry about how to get to the last expression of this relationship; pay attention instead to how the simplified expression can tell us about the responsiveness of output price to changes (or differences) in the ratio of input prices. If you want the derivation, see Kemp (1969, 8).

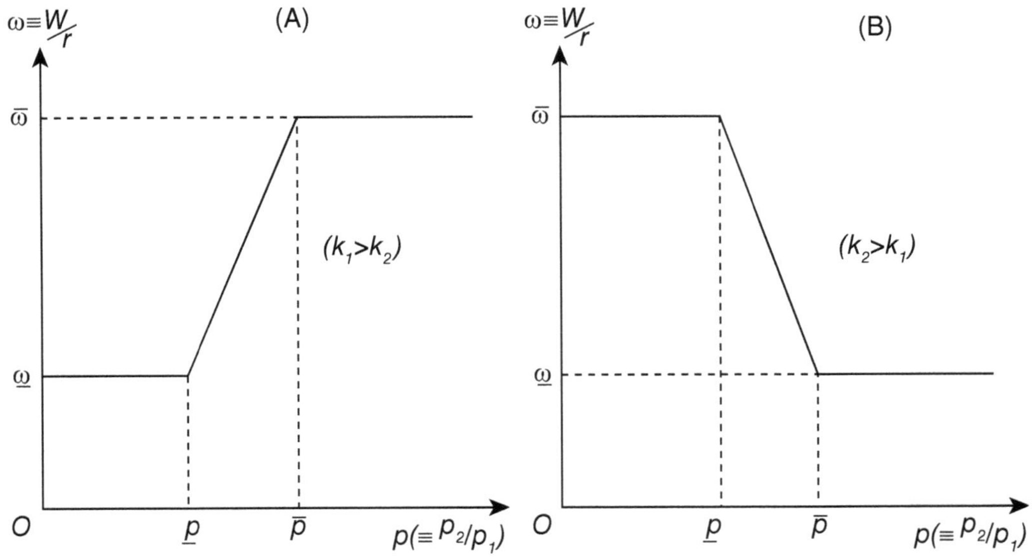

Figure 3.13. (A) Heckscher-Ohlin model: relationship between product prices and factor prices, $k_1 > k_2$. (B) Heckscher-Ohlin model: relationship between product prices and factor prices, $k_2 > k_1$.

This relationship is depicted in Figures 3.13A and B. When industry 1 is the capital-intensive industry, the relationship between p and ω is positive. The lowest relative commodity price, $\underline{p}$, is that price associated with the lowest wage-rental ratio; at $\underline{\omega}$ lower than this, industry 2 shuts down because it can't produce at costs lower than the price it can receive. At relative prices higher than $\bar{p}$, industry 1 shuts down for the same reason. Panel B shows the corresponding relationship when the second industry is capital intensive.

We can connect the ω-k_i and ω-p relationships in a back-to-back diagram to show the full relationship from commodity prices through factor prices to production conditions. Figure 3.14A shows the case for $k_1 > k_2$ and 3.14B that for $k_2 > k_1$. Let's presume that this country is a small one—i.e., that it takes levels of and changes in commodity prices as given. In Figure 3.14A, suppose that the relative price of good 2 rises from p′ to p″; the wage-rental ratio increases, inducing producers of good 2 to raise the capital intensity of their operations from k_2' to k_2'' and producers of good 1 to raise theirs from k_1' to k_1''. From the greater increase in capital intensity in industry 1 than in industry 2, we can tell that the output of industry 2 has expanded (which we should expect from the increase in the relative price of good 2) while that of industry 1 has contracted. Also, the percent change in the commodity price ratio is much smaller than the percent change in the factor price ratio, as you can see by comparing the relative distances between p′ and p″ on the left side of the horizontal axis and between ω' and ω'' on the vertical axis. We will see these relationships again in separate sub-sections below.

So far I've discussed commodity prices as if they were exogenous, but in a general equilibrium model, as trade models are, they are endogenous, in each country in autarky as well as in the integrated, trading world. Considering our model economy here in autarky, we could form a demand function for each good in terms of relative prices, $D_i = D_i(p)$.[8] The supply function for each good is given by the corresponding production function, and equilibrium price is determined by equalization of supply and demand for one product or the other (with only two goods, when the market for one good is in supply-demand equilibrium, so is the other one: Walras' law). If preferences are sufficiently biased toward one or the other good, the equilibrium price could lodge against one of the specialization points and only one good would be produced and consumed in autarky. Some demand functions would rule out zero consumption of one good.

3.4.2 Causes of Comparative Advantage

The heart of the Heckscher-Ohlin insight into trade is codified in what has become known as the Heckscher-Ohlin theorem. Given the assumptions of identical technologies, constant returns to scale, homogeneous factors of production, the relative unimportance of transportation costs, and absence of distortions, a country will export the commodity whose production uses intensively its relatively abundant factor.[9]

Recognizing the relationship between factor endowment ratio and shape of the ppf, consider Figure 3.15, which shows the home country to have a comparative advantage in the production of good 1. If good 1 is the relatively capital-intensive good, the home country possesses a relatively abundant endowment of capital and the foreign country has a relatively abundant endowment of labor. Note that the causality runs from relative factor endowment to relative

[8] I could make demand for each good a function of income as well, and separate demand functions for different categories of factor owner. For the present purpose of simply showing the role of demand in determining relative commodity price, price suffices.

[9] Factor abundance can be measured in physical terms, as ratios of capital to labor in each country, or in value terms, as autarky wage-rental ratios. The robustness of some of the H-O results depends on which measure of factor abundance one uses, but for present purposes it's sufficient to work with only the physical measure.

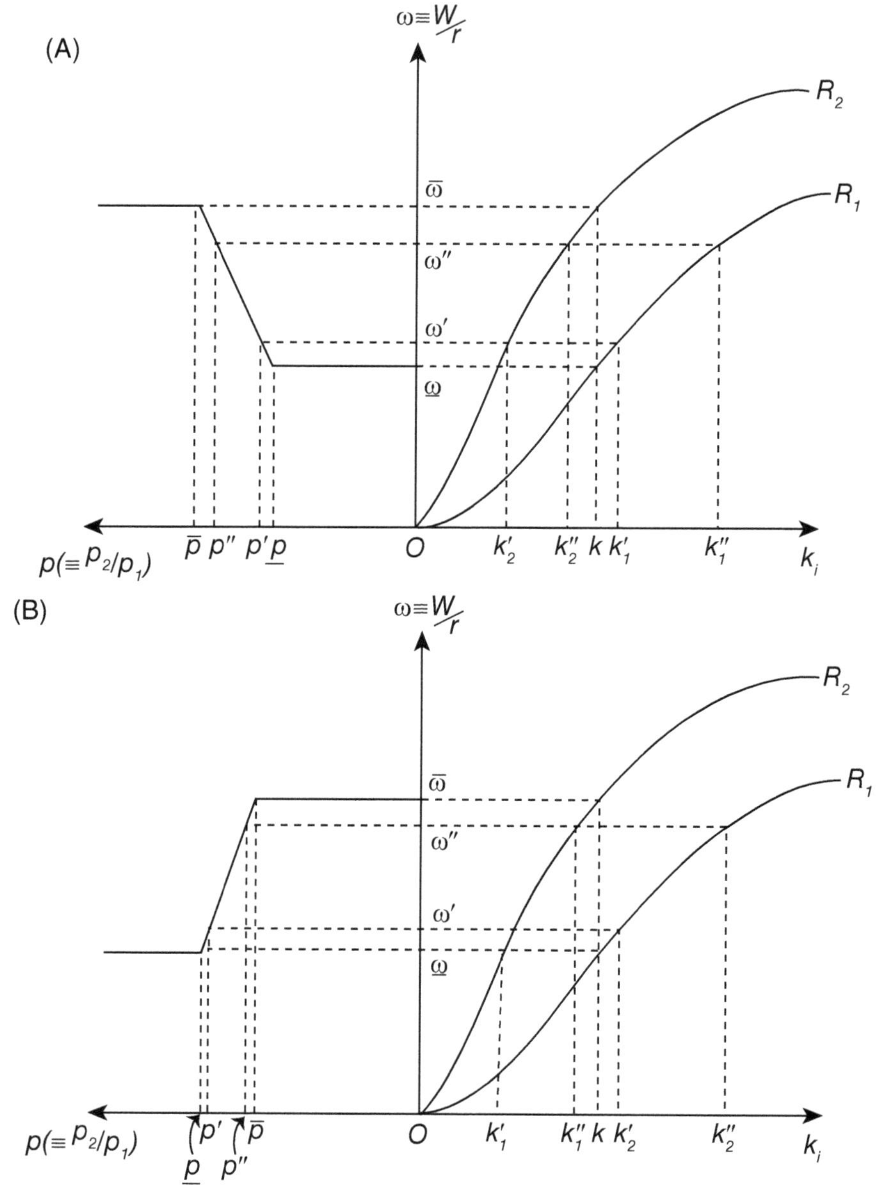

Figure 3.14. (A) Heckscher-Ohlin model: relationship between factor intensities, factor prices, and product prices, $k_1 > k_2$. (B) Heckscher-Ohlin model: relationship between factor intensities, factor prices, and product prices, $k_2 > k_1$. Adapted from Kemp 1969, 8, figure 1.2(a), by permission of Pearson.

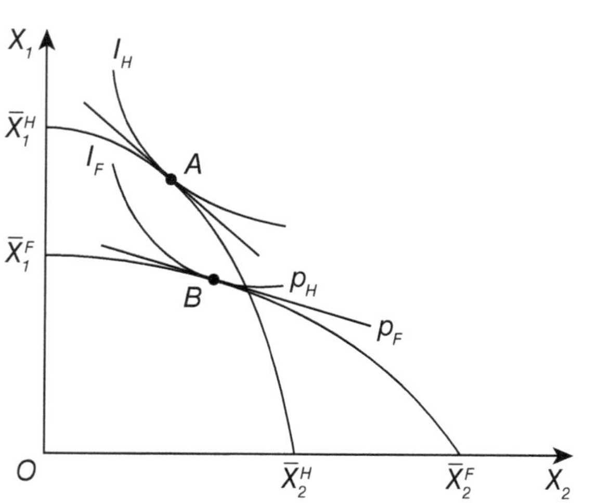

Figure 3.15. Heckscher-Ohlin model: production possibility frontier for home and foreign countries.

shape of the production possibility frontier. Both countries in Figure 3.15 have the same community indifference system (the shape of I_H is the same as that of I_F). In autarky, the home country will produce and consume at A, determining its autarky relative price, p_H. The foreign country produces and consumes at B and faces an autarkic equilibrium commodity price of p_F, in which the relative price of good 2 is cheaper than in the home country. Accordingly, the home country consumes a higher ratio of good 1 to good 2 than does the foreign country.

Trade opens, and residents of the home country will find it cheaper to buy some of their units of good 2 from the foreign country, while some foreign residents will find it cheaper to buy some good 1 from the home country. They drive up the relative prices of each country's good that was cheaper in autarky, until the relative commodity price is the same in both countries: the equilibrium terms of trade, p^T. Each country can reach a higher level of community

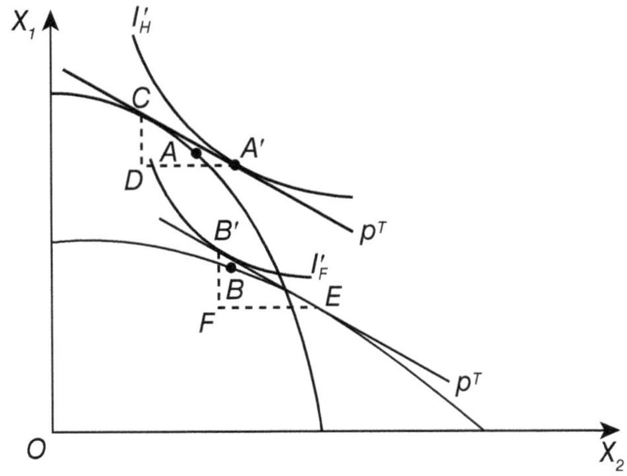

Figure 3.16. Heckscher-Ohlin model: pattern of trade.

indifference in the trade equilibrium, as denoted by the move from A to A′ by the home country and from B to B′ in the foreign country in Figure 3.16. The home country exports CD of good 1 and imports DA′ of good 2, while the foreign country imports B′F of good 1 and exports FE of good 2 in return. For trade equilibrium, these trade triangles must be equal in size as well as the relative commodity price being equalized in the two countries. Figure 3.16 is drawn with the trade triangles equal-sized, although use of offer curves would ensure that trade was equalized at the equilibrium terms of trade.

We can decompose the gains from trade into those coming from changes in production and those attributable to the ability to consume at different relative prices. Figure 3.17 shows the production possibility frontier of the home country. Its production and consumption levels in autarky are at point A, with relative prices p^A and community indifference level I. The opening of trade presents the country with terms of trade p^T, which gives it a higher relative price of good 1. Accordingly, it shifts its production pattern to point T, which involves a higher proportion of good 1 production than did point A. If the country were constrained to produce at the autarky combination of goods

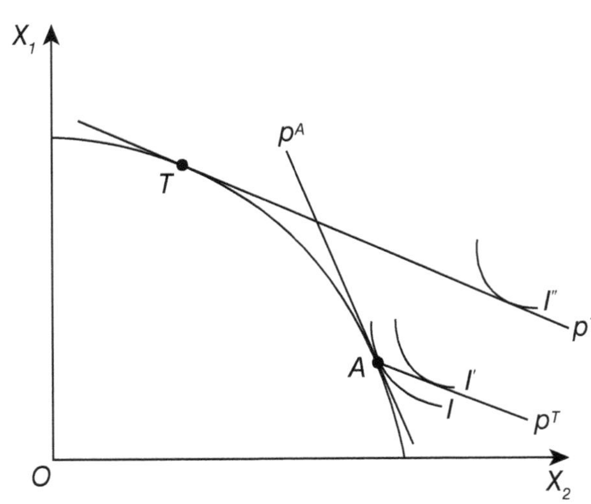

Figure 3.17. Heckscher-Ohlin model: home country's gains from trade.

1 and 2, but still could consume at the international prices, we could draw a price line parallel to p^T, coming out of point A; the country could reach community indifference level I′. The move from I to I′ is the pure consumption gain from trade. If the country can consume at international prices and also change its production to point T, it can reach indifference level I″, the move from I′ to I″ being the pure production gain.

3.4.3 Factor Price Equalization

Another salient feature of the H-O model of trade is that under a certain set of conditions, trade in goods alone—i.e., with international immobility of factors—will equalize relative factor prices in the trading countries. To the list of assumptions we've piled up so far, add the conditions for factor price equalization that factor endowments must not be "too different" and non-specialization occurs in both countries. We'll define "not too different" shortly. Figure 3.14 has already shown that there is a unique factor-price ratio for each commodity-price ratio, as long as both goods are produced.

Figures 3.18 and 3.19 offer two perspectives on the range of differences in factor endowments compatible with

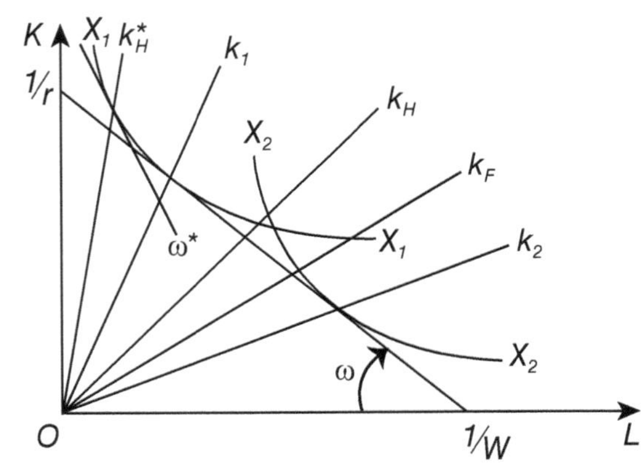

Figure 3.18. Heckscher-Ohlin model: scope for factor-price equalization viewed from isoquants and factor intensities.

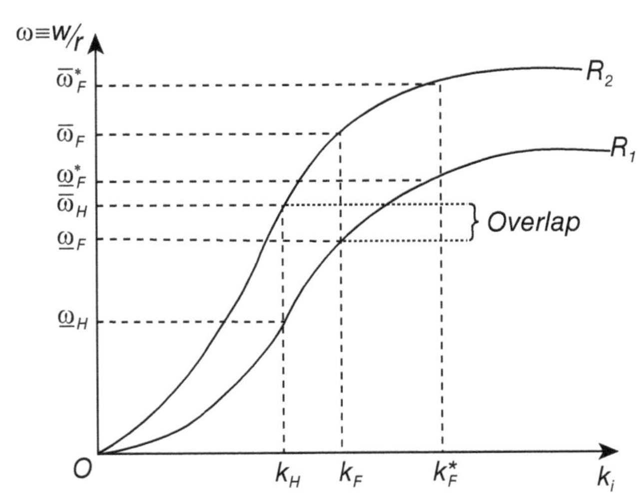

Figure 3.19. Heckscher-Ohlin model: scope for factor-price equalization viewed from the factor-price / factor-intensity relationship.

factor-price equalization. Figure 3.18 shows what are called "unit-value" isoquants for the two industries.[10] Since both countries have identical technologies and trade has equalized commodity prices, the unit-value isoquants are identical for the two countries. The isocost line 1/r-1/w is a relative factor-price line with slope ω compatible with a commodity price ratio equal to unity, and X_1X_1 and X_2X_2 are the unit isoquants for industries 1 and 2. Cost minimization requires tangency of each isoquant with the isocost line, and those tangencies define the cost-minimizing factor intensities in the two industries. Constant returns to scale in production ensures that expanding the outputs of each industry at the same factor price ratio will yield a series of tangencies along the lines labeled k_i for the two industries. As long as both countries' endowment ratios are between the two industry factor-intensity ratios, both countries can produce some of each good at this factor price ratio. The area between the two industry factor-intensity ratios, $k_1 0 k_2$ is called the "cone of diversification." As long as both countries' factor endowments are within the cone of diversification, factor price equalization is possible. Should one of the countries' endowments lie outside this cone, such as the alternative endowment ratio for the home country, k_H^*, factor price equalization is not possible; the home country would produce at factor-price ratio $\omega^* > \omega$.

Figure 3.19 uses the ω-k_i diagram to demonstrate the same point differently. R_1 is the relatively capital-intensive industry. The home country has the factor endowment ratio k_H on the horizontal axis while the foreign country has endowment ratio k_F. The range of wage-rental ratios compatible with the technologies represented by R_1 and R_2 and endowment ratio k_H extends from a minimum of $\underline{\omega_H}$ to $\bar{\omega}_H$; for the foreign country, with its endowment ratio k_F and the same technologies, the possible factor price ratios range from a low of $\underline{\omega_F}$ to a high of $\bar{\omega}_F$. These endowments produce an overlap of possible wage-rental ratios between $\bar{\omega}_H$ and $\underline{\omega_F}$, and factor-price equalization is possible. However, if the foreign country has a sufficiently higher endowment ratio, k_F^*, the lowest possible wage-rental ratio in the foreign country, $\underline{\omega_F^*}$, is higher than the highest possible one in the home country, $\bar{\omega}_H$. Trade may drive factor price ratios to those upper and lower specialization points, but equalization of commodity prices cannot equalize factor prices.

An implication of the factor-price equalization theorem is that small increases in factor supplies, within the cone of diversification, will not affect factor prices. Thus, population growth in a small, trading country will not depress wages. Neither will immigration—or emigration—within limits.

3.4.4 Effects of Factor Endowments on Production

While this relationship and the next one, that between commodity prices and factor prices, are not restricted to the Heckscher-Ohlin trade model, they form two of the most important allocative mechanisms that the H-O model relies on. The general-equilibrium relationship between changes in factor endowments and changes in outputs, known as the Rybczynski theorem (Rybczynski 1955), offers what may appear initially to be a counterintuitive result. With constant relative commodity prices and non-specialization (i.e., the country continues to produce some of both goods), an increase in the supply of one factor leads to an increase in the output of the good using that factor intensively and a reduction in the output of the other good. The percent increase in the output of the expanding industry is larger than the percent increase in the expanding factor.

To understand how this mechanism works, remember that the supplies of both factors are fixed (the expanding factor simply has a new fixed size). With unchanged commodity prices, there is no basis for changing factor intensities. Suppose that the labor supply has increased. The X_2 industry takes up a unit of the new labor, but it needs some extra capital to go with it (nonzero quantities of both factors are required for nonzero production). The extra capital has to come from somewhere, and the X_1 industry is the only place where some is to be had. But in releasing the capital required to go with the new labor in X_2, it has to release some labor too. At fixed factor intensities in both industries, the only way to absorb all the new labor and get the capital required to go with it, is for the labor-intensive industry to expand, which requires the capital-intensive industry to contract. If the country experiencing the growth in factor supply is a large country—i.e., it influences world prices—the relative price of the expanding industry's output will fall, dampening the contraction in the other industry.

The Rybczynski theorem can inform how we view relatively well known episodes, either from archaeological or ancient historical evidence. Consider the issue of Athenian grain supply in the Classical period (and by extension, beginning as early as the Archaic period). Garnsey (1985, 74–75) has concluded that "... a serious disequilibrium between Athens' food needs and its capacity to meet them from Attica and nearby dependencies did not develop until well into the post-Persian war period in consequence of population growth ..." The application of the Rybczynski theorem can both account for Garnsey's claim and identify some of its concomitant implications. The Rybczynski theorem would say that under given "international" prices (which probably was the case for Athens in the 5th and 4th centuries; probably earlier and later too, but that's another matter), an increase in a factor of production (labor—i.e., population) will increase absolutely (i.e., not just relatively) the production of the output that uses that input intensively (i.e., has a higher labor/land ratio) and decrease absolutely the output of the other industry (simplifying the model to a two-output problem; complicating the model to include a larger number of outputs and inputs leaves the essence of the Rybczynski result intact). So a population increase in Attica reduced the output of grain and increased the output of, likely, olive oil. This offers a mechanism by which Garnsey's contention

[10] Unit-value isoquants are characterized by the relationship $p_1X_1 = p_2X_2$, or $X_1/X_2 = p_2/p_1 \equiv p = 1$.

of a population increase leaving Attica in a food-importing position could have occurred. As for other implications, this tells us that the labor/land ratio would have been lower in grain production than in olive oil production. This may be something that research could check out. If it turns out to be the reverse of the case, then we should reconsider at least one of Garnsey's contentions.

This same principle applies to the entire period of Greek colonization, from the 8th century through the 6th or 5th. One of the traditional explanations—not necessarily mutually exclusive of other causes—has been population growth: growing populations caused some kind(s) of problem that made it more comfortable for some people to leave. Was the "problem" one of depressed earnings with more people on roughly the same amount of land (or on a smaller increase in cultivated land)? If the home cities were engaged in trade during the time, the population growth in some of the cities shouldn't have depressed wages but rather should have rearranged people into different productive activities. So, if we believe in trade—at least later if not necessarily earlier—we're hard pressed to be able to believe that colonization occurred because of earnings-depressing effects of population growth. Maybe because of some other consequence of population growth, but not earnings reductions. If we want to continue believing in population-induced earnings reductions leading to the colonizations, we have to give up the trade. It's possible that these societies had difficulties in reallocating their productive resources—mostly labor and land—to different activities, and it was easier to just send people off and leave some local resources (mostly land?) unemployed than it would have been to shift people from certain groups of activities to some others.

3.4.5 Effects of Commodity Prices on Factor Prices

Known as the Stolper-Samuelson theorem (Stolper and Samuelson 1941), this relationship is the dual, or price, version of the Rybczynski theorem. Again, with constant returns to scale in production and nonspecialization, an increase in the relative price of a good will raise the real return to the factor used intensively in its production and decrease the real return to the other factor. For instance, if our commodity price ratio p increased, representing an increase in the relative price of good 2, the real wage, measured in terms of either good, would rise and the real capital rental rate, also measured in terms of either good would fall.

In seeing how this mechanism works, remember again that total factor supplies in the economy are fixed. When the relative price of good 2 increases, profit-maximizing producers of good 2 are led to produce more of it until they have driven their production costs up to the higher price. Expanding production requires proportionally more labor than capital, so they bid labor away from industry 1, which must contract. Industry 1's contraction releases more labor than capital, so the demand for capital falls. The wage-rental ratio is bid up in both industries, which induces producers in both industries to use more capital-intensive techniques, which reduces the marginal physical product of capital and increases that of labor—in both industries. Remember the relationship between the wage rate and the marginal physical product of labor: $w = pMPP_L$, or $w/p = MPP_L$. Since we know that the marginal physical product of labor rises in both industries, the wage rate has to rise by more than the commodity price rose to keep the equation in balance. If we separate the relative price p into p_1 and p_2, in industry 2, since MPP_{L2} increased, and that was precipitated by the increase in p_2, the wage rate has to rise by more than the commodity price of that good increased. Thus the real wage rises in terms of its purchasing power over good 2, which itself has risen. In the other industry, we have the same increase in the wage rate by virtue of inter-industry factor mobility, and we know that p_1 remained unchanged by our assumption, so the real wage definitely rises in terms of good 1. This relationship also is known as the magnification effect.

This particular mechanism operates directly on the income distribution between owners of capital and labor in an economy. Thinking of the introduction of trade from a condition of autarky, it tells us that both factors (factor owners) do not benefit from the opening of trade. The relatively abundant factor benefits by more than the total benefits from trade, while the relatively scarce factor, whose price was higher in autarky than it will be after trade is opened, loses. The gainers could, in principle, compensate the losers and still be better off than they were in autarky, but whether that happens is generally outside the scope of trade theory to predict. This mechanism also points to particular groups in society who would be opposed to the opening of trade, or to reductions in tariffs when trade already exists.

3.4.6 Many Goods and Factors

The four major theorems of Heckscher-Ohlin trade theory were developed originally for the simplified case of two goods and two factors. Even economists recognize that the observational world is more complicated than this. This sub-section presents the modification of the basic H-O model to accommodate two important complications that raise the numbers of goods, factors, or both above the mathematically handy number of two. "Two" is such a handy number because it permits unambiguous identification of relative capital intensity between industries and goods, changes in relative factor and commodity prices, and changes in outputs and employment. The sacrifices in realism have been deemed worth the benefits from the insights into how the economic mechanisms described so far in this section operate. The research on "higher dimensional" issues in trade theory investigates the extent to which these mechanisms carry over to the cases of commodities and factors arbitrarily greater than two. The factor-price equalization and Stolper-Samuelson theorems survive well in higher dimensions, although commonly as tendencies or correlations rather than exact relationships. The consequences for the Heckscher-Ohlin and Rybczynski theorems are somewhat more complicated but still are amenable to correlation relationships. The discussion in the remainder of this sub-section is based on the expositions of Jones and Scheinkman (1973) and Ethier (1984).

Multidimensionality has been divided into three types of case: 1) the number of goods equals the number of factors, but their numbers exceed 2; 2) goods outnumber factors, with factors numbering at least 2; and 3) factors outnumber goods, with at least two goods. The case of equal numbers of goods and factors is in many ways the easiest because the number of unknowns to be determined (factor prices) is equal to the number of equations available with which to solve for them (commodity prices broken down into their cost components, expressed as cost functions (see Jones 2014, Chapter 2). The case of more factors than goods is the most problematic, in the sense that there are more variables than there are equations, which means that not enough information on cost relationships is available to solve for all the factor prices; typically supplemental information on endowments, or on the amount produced of some commodity is required to solve for factor prices. In the case of more goods than factors, there is more information available to solve for factor prices than is necessary, but it is more difficult to determine precise output levels associated with any set of prices. All this is, in one sense, just mathematical detail, but it addresses the critical matter of whether the logic implied by the basic version of the H-O model is sufficiently robust to be extended to more realistic cases, and what modifications are required for specific types of extension.

The distinction between goods and factors can become blurred, particularly when we refer to inputs into one production process that are actually goods produced in other production processes. Add to that complication the fact that trade theory addresses the issue of how trade in goods alone can substitute for international movement of factors; if many of the goods that are being traded are in reality factors of production rather than final-consumption goods, we have the makings of some real confusion.[11] It will be useful to return to thinking of factors as the two or three primary inputs—labor, land, and capital, with capital being "more" primary in shorter time periods. The critical issue actually is the relative numbers of international markets and factors, with international markets including both commodity and produced-and-traded factor markets (Ethier 1984, 178–180). The case of goods equaling or exceeding factors in number probably is the more relevant case, so I do not discuss the frequently more problematic case of factors exceeding goods.

I turn to the fate of the four basic trade theorems in the case of the number of goods greater than or equal to the number of factors. The factor-price equalization theorem carries over readily to dimensions higher than two. To consider how the Stolper-Samuelson theorem fares in higher dimensions, it's useful to break it into its two parts—the direction of response of relative factor-price changes to relative commodity-price changes, according to relative factor intensities; and the differential movement of factor prices in real terms. The first part of the relationship survives as a tendency for changes in relative commodity prices to be followed by increases in the returns to factors employed most intensively in the production of the goods whose prices increase relatively most and employed least intensively by those goods whose relative prices have fallen the most. As for the pattern of changes in real factor rewards, a rise in the price of any good generally raises the returns of some factor in terms of every other good and lowers it in terms of no good. In this sense, every good is a "friend" to some factor and an "enemy" to some other factor. These results are valid if the number of goods exceeds the number of factors.

To examine the Rybczynski theorem's higher-dimensional validity we can separate it into two parts also: the direction of output changes following endowment changes and the magnitudes of the output changes relative to the endowment changes. The following results are valid for the number of goods equal to or greater than the number of factors. On the magnitude, at unchanged factor prices, an increase in any factor endowment will cause the output of *some* good to rise relative to all other factors and to fall relative to no factor, and it will cause the output of some other good to fall absolutely. The H-O model cannot predict precisely *which* goods will have their outputs increase, only that it must happen for some good. To each good there corresponds a factor such that an increase in its endowment at unchanged commodity prices will permit (but not require) an increase in its output by enough that the total value of all other goods falls. Analogously, another factor corresponding to each good will permit (again, not require) a reduction in the good's output when the factor's endowment increases. For each factor, there is some good whose output will be reduced when the endowment of the factor is increased. On the direction issue, endowment changes tend to increase the outputs of those goods using relatively intensively those factors whose endowments have increased the most. This correlation is analogous to the one that appears in the higher-dimensional Stolper-Samuelson relationship. To each factor corresponds a good whose output will rise by a greater proportion than an increase in the factor.

Finally, the Heckscher-Ohlin theorem, which predicts the pattern of trade on the basis of relative factor endowments, extends to higher dimensionality in the form of a series of correlations. First, countries tend to have a comparative advantage in producing goods that use intensively their relatively abundant factors. Second, countries tend to export, indirectly through their commodities, their relatively abundant factors; and third,

[11] Trade theory does deal with the issue of international capital movements as well as with migration, but as separate matters from the movement of commodities. If factors themselves moved around the world so as to equalize their returns in all locations, trade in commodities would be unnecessary.

countries tend to export goods that make relatively intensive use of their relatively abundant factors. Fourth, a country tends to import those goods that make relatively intensive use of their relatively scarce factors. These results are valid when the number of goods equals or exceeds the number of factors.

The detail just presented may seem unpurposively overwhelming for students interested primarily in applying ideas of trade theory, not in the arcane spinning of models. On the contrary, I believe that this information is exactly what such students need to feel safe in using "Heckscher-Ohlin intuition" in the much richer context of ancient trade, which cannot be expected to always squeeze satisfactorily into the 2 × 2 format of the basic model. It is this sort of information that leaves me feeling comfortable with the application of the Rybczynski theorem to the case of Classical Attic population growth and food supply.

Having considered the effects of increasing the numbers of goods and factors of production, you may wonder about how increasing the number of countries would affect the results. As long as production is characterized by constant returns to scale, adding more countries to the analysis would make no difference: we could just make the "foreign country" (or "the rest of the world") larger, and it would be harder for the home country to affect world prices, but as long as it's a "small country," making it smaller wouldn't affect its inability to influence world prices. However, with increasing returns to scale, chopping up the world into smaller countries within which factors are free to congregate for productive purposes, the lower is total output. In antiquity, increasing returns to scale probably would not have been important enough to worry us a whole lot.

3.4.7 Nontraded and Intermediate Goods

Having just completed a quick tour of very general results of how the major trade theorems generalize beyond the 2 × 2 format, I turn in this sub-section to two higher-dimensional cases of particular interest. Not all goods enter into international trade, for one reason or another: their transport costs may be inordinately high, as in the case of housing and many personal services; governments may prohibit export of items considered of strategic significance—e.g., some types of military equipment; some goods may be subject to prohibitive tariffs, effectively making them nontradable. Objects of tourism – religious sites and healing/medical sites – in antiquity are also nontradable goods. Other goods are used partially or wholly as inputs into the production of final consumer goods, whereas the models developed so far deal with final consumption goods that enter individual utility functions (or community indifference systems). This type of intermediate good in fact may form a larger proportion of traded goods than do final consumption goods. The importance on intermediate goods in an economy was first brought to attention by Wassily Leontief in a series of works (1936; 1953; 1986) – in fact, most of his professional life's work, for which he received the Nobel Prize in Economics in 1973 – which developed and implemented input-output economics, the basis of commercial, economic impact models worldwide today. This sub-section examines the extent to which the results of the 2 × 2, "final goods" model are modified by the incorporation of these two types of goods, relying on expositions by Batra (1973, Chapters 7, 8, and 12), Hazari and Suh (1978), Hazari et al. (1981, Chapters 2 and 5), and Woodland (1982, Chapters 5 and 8). The initial analysis of the nontraded good case was Komiya (1967).

I begin with nontraded goods. There are several alternative ways to model nontraded goods. I pick one that gives a 3 × 2 production structure with two tradable goods produced by a small country which faces world prices for the tradable goods. Designate the quantities produced of the two tradable goods X_1 and X_2 and that of the nontradable X_n. All three goods are produced with labor and capital. Let $p \equiv p_2/p_1$ be the international terms of trade and $p_n \equiv p_n/p_1$ is the price of the nontradable relative to good 1. The capital-labor ratios in the three industries are k_1, k_2, and k_n. We'll look at one cases of relative factor intensities: $k_1 > k_n > k_2$, i.e., when the capital intensity of nontradables is between the capital intensities of the two traded goods, which ensures that all three goods get produced; an extreme capital intensity for the nontraded good can result in production of only the nontraded good. The production functions in intensity notation are $X_i = L_i f_i(k_i)$, where i = 1, 2, and n; remember that the notation f_i' means $\Delta f_i/\Delta k_i$, or the marginal product of capital in the ith industry.[12] The rental rate on capital is then $r = p_i f_i'$ and the wage rate is $w = p_i(f_i - p_i f_i')$. By virtue of intersectoral mobility, the wage-rental ratios are equalized across all three industries, which gives us the relationships $p = f_1'/f_2'$ and $p_n = f_1'/f_n'$. The wage-rental ratio is $\omega = (f_i/f_i') - k_i$. Recall that the capital intensities are functions of the wage-rental ratio—$k_i = k_i(\omega)$; then $\Delta k_i/\Delta\omega = -(f_i')^2/f_i f_i'' > 0$, where f_i'' describes the degree to which the marginal product of capital diminishes with increasing doses of capital, and is negative: $\Delta[\Delta f_i/\Delta k_i]/\Delta k_i < 0$. Then the elasticities of the two relative commodity prices with respect to the capital-labor ratio are $\varepsilon_{p_2\omega} = (k_1 - k_2)/(\omega + k_2)(\omega + k_1)$ and $\varepsilon_{p_0\omega} = (k_1 - k_n)/(\omega + k_n)(\omega + k_1)$. Then the relationship between the relative price of the nontradable good and the international terms of trade can be written as the elasticity $\varepsilon_{p_n p_2} = [(k_1 - k_n)(\omega + k_2)]/[(k_1 - k_2)(\omega + k_n)]$, which is positive or negative depending on the relationship between factor intensities in the three industries. The relative price of the nontradable increases as the international terms of trade increase (the elasticity is positive) if industry 1 is either the most or least capital intensive; and vice versa if the capital intensity of the nontradable is intermediate between the capital intensities of the two tradable goods.

[12] Recall that "Δ" means "change in." Below, a "Δ of a Δ" means "a change in a change." That is, "If a change in k causes a change in f, will further change in k cause a larger or smaller change in f?"

The full-employment conditions are $L_1 + L_2 + L_n = \bar{L}$ and $K_1 + K_2 + K_n = k_1L_1 + k_2L_2 + k_nL_n = \bar{K}$. The community indifference function contains the consumption levels of all three goods: $U = U(C_1, C_2, C_n)$, where the C_i are the consumptions of the two tradable goods and the nontradable, and the equilibrium consumption levels are defined by equalization of ratios of marginal utilities to relative prices—$[\Delta U/\Delta C_2]/[\Delta U/\Delta C_1] = p_2$ and $[\Delta U/\Delta C_n]/[\Delta U/\Delta C_1] = p_n$. The relationship between production and consumption levels are completed by the specification of imports and exports: $C_1 = X_1 + M_1$ and $C_2 = X_2 - E_2$, which specifies that the country has a comparative advantage in good 2 and imports good 1. Trade balance is specified by requiring the value of exports to equal the value of imports: $pE_2 = M_1$. This is the same model developed in sub-section 3.4.1, except that our economy now produces three goods instead of 2. These relationships can be drawn out in a diagram comparable to Figure 3.14A and B, except that we will need a third quadrant to show the relationship between the relative price of the nontradable and the terms of trade. I do this in Figure 3.20, which I have adapted from Hazari et al. (1981, 32, figure 2.4A), where $\omega \equiv w/r$ is the wage-rental ratio, and $p \equiv p^2/p^1$ and $p_n \equiv p^n/p^1$ are the relative prices of good 2 and the nontradable good in terms of good 1. The diagram allows us to quickly and intuitively see the relationships between goods prices, factor prices, and factor intensities.

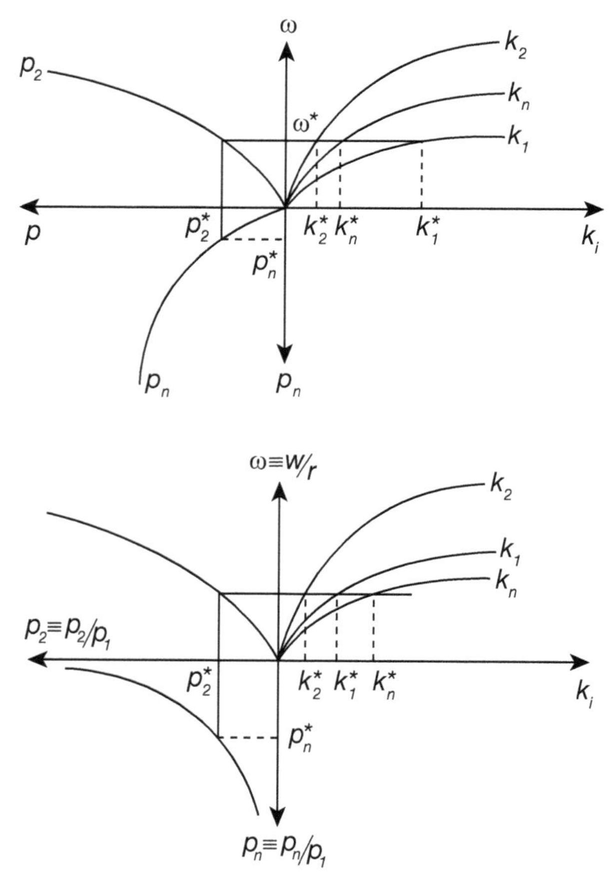

Figure 3.20. Heckscher-Ohlin model: production and trade with a non-traded good, medium capital intensity in the non-traded good (Adapted from Hazari, Sgro and Suh, 1981, figure 2.4A, p. 32.)

The relative price of the nontradable good is a function of the terms of trade. The two relative prices are related to one another by the factor intensities, so the equilibrium relative price of the nontraded good is determined once the k_i are determined since this is a 3-good-2-factor model (Komiya 1967; Samuelson 1953). An implication of this relationship is that, with identical production functions across countries, the relative price of the nontradable good is equalized across countries even though it does not enter trade. This shows what income effects can do in models of trade even when all goods are normal in consumption.

Now let's consider how the model with a nontradable good responds in terms of the usual trade theorems. The H-O and factor price equalization theorems operate just as they did with only tradable goods. You can see from Figure 3.20 that a higher economy-wide capital-labor endowment ratio will make the relative price of good 1 cheaper in autarky than it will be once trade opens (we don't draw all these lines; you learned how to do it with Figures 3.14A and B, so go ahead and try working it out if you don't believe it). As long as the two trading countries are within the same cone of diversification, their relative factor prices will be equalized. The Stolper-Samuelson theorem also comes through intact, as you can see by changing the terms of trade on the home country (moving p_2 up or down). Within the Stolper-Samuelson relationship, the relative price of the nontradable good will change when the terms of trade change, but the real factor rewards will change as in the 2-good case in terms of all three goods.

The Rybczynski effect doesn't show up on a diagram like Figure 3.18A. An increase in the endowment of either factor generally will raise the national income of a country (it always will for a small country), and this income increase will always increase the consumption of the nontradable good, regardless of relative factor intensities and the directions of change of the two tradable goods (as long as it isn't an inferior good—one whose demand falls as income rises). Once some of both factors are reallocated from the two tradable goods to the nontradable to permit its expansion, the usual Rybczynski relationship operates between the two tradables, only with an exacerbated effect because of the reallocation of some factors to the nontradable.

The relationship between the prices of tradable goods and their outputs may not be as regular with the presence of a nontradable good as without. When the relative price of one of the traded goods (i.e., the terms of trade) changes, the changes in outputs of the traded goods are influenced by income and substitution effects in demand for all three goods, in addition to the substitution effects in production. The net result isn't predictable without information on these other details. Consequently the offer curve for a country with a nontradable good may not always be negatively sloped.

Let's turn now to intermediate goods—goods that may or may not enter into final consumption. There are two different types of intermediate input, and trade involving them can behave differently. The type of intermediate input called "inter-industry flows" can be used both as a final consumption good and an input. An example of this type of intermediate good might be olive oil: some of it could be used for final consumption, say for cooking or lighting, while other portions of it might be used as an "industrial" lubricant for construction pulleys. Shelmerdine (1985, 27–28, 30, 152–153) notes that Pylian perfumers imported henna from Cyprus and, judging from the quantities of final perfume produced, exported some. The "pure intermediate" good is not used as a final consumption good at all; examples would be copper ingots and raw glass lumps such as have been found on the Ulu Burun wreck, off the southwestern Anatolian coast. I'll offer models of each so you can see the structure of these problems, but I'll treat the pure intermediate case in greater detail.

In the inter-industry-flows case, intermediate goods serve the dual roles of inputs and final consumption goods. Let's take the case in which there are two goods and two primary factors—the usual labor and capital—and some of each good is used as an input into the other good. The production functions look like $X_1 = F_1(K_1, L_1, X_{21})$ and $X_2 = F_2(K_2, L_2, X_{12})$, where X_{ij} is the amount of good i used as in input in good j. This input-output structure introduces the distinction between gross and net outputs and factor intensities. The net output, x_i, is the amount of good i available for final consumption, while the gross output is the total amount produced, X_j: $X_1 = x_1 + X_{12}$ and $X_2 = x_2 + X_{21}$. The net, or apparent, capital-labor ratio in each industry is $K_j/L_j \equiv k_j$, but the gross ratio is the ratio of the total capital used directly and indirectly to the comparable quantity of labor. Here's how the total requirements of primary factors are calculated: Let a_{ij} be the direct input requirements of input i into product j. For example, $a_{K1} = K_1/(x_1 + X_{12})$ and $a_{21} = X_{21}/(x_1 + X_{12})$. Through some substitutions, the sum of the direct and indirect requirements of, say, labor, in good 1 would be $(a_{L1} + a_{L2}a_{21})/(1 - a_{12}a_{21})$, in which the term $a_{L2}a_{21}$ is the amount of labor per unit of good 2 times the amount of good 2 per unit of good 1, which is added to the amount of labor directly used in good 1, a_{L1}.[13] The denominator deflates for the portion of good 1 which is produced indirectly by itself through its contribution to good 2, which in turn enters good 1. The gross capital-labor ratio in good 1 would be $(a_{K1} + a_{K2}a_{21})/(a_{L1} + a_{L2}a_{21})$, the denominators of the two total-requirements calculations canceling. In the inter-industry-flows model, the gross and net relative factor intensities are the same; i.e., if good 1 is the relatively capital-intensive good in net terms, it also will be relatively capital-intensive in gross terms. This need not be the case in the pure intermediate good case.

None of the four theorems requires any material modification because of this type of intermediate good, although the Rybczynski theorem has exacerbated effects relative to the pure final-good case. This stronger expansionary-and-contractionary pattern emerges because the increase in the expanding industry requires additional units of output from the contracting industry to be withdrawn from final consumption. Net and gross production possibilities curves must be distinguished as well, with the net curve everywhere inside the gross curve. It is possible for the gains from trade to be greater in the presence of such an imported intermediate good than in the pure final goods case, but only in the cases of production close to one end of the production possibilities curve. Nonetheless, the possibility remains that a country could benefit even more from trade in a good used partially as an input than from one used strictly for final consumption.[14]

Turn now to the pure intermediate good. The fact that net and gross relative factor intensities may differ means that the theorems that depend on relative factor intensities may have to be modified. In fact, both the Stolper-Samuelson and Rybczynski theorems are true only if factor intensities are defined in the gross sense. As a variant on the Stolper-Samuelson relationship, an increase in the price of an intermediate good will raise the price of the primary factor used intensively in the industry that doesn't use the intermediate good intensively, relative to the price of the other primary factor. The Heckscher-Ohlin and factor-price equalization theorems are unaffected by the pure intermediate good.

The net capital-labor ratio in an industry is simply K_j/L_j, while the gross, or total-requirements definition is $K_j + (M_j/M)K_M$, where K_M is capital employed directly in intermediate-good production, M_j is the amount of the intermediate good used in production of good j, and M is the total output of the intermediate good. A similar definition is required for the gross input of labor, with which to form the gross capital-labor ratio.

Let's set up an entire model with a pure intermediate good.[15] Consider a small country once again, so we face given relative prices denoted by the subscripts: $p_2 \equiv p^2/p^1$ and $p_3 \equiv p^3/p^1$. Suppose our home country produces two final goods, one of which uses only domestic, primary inputs, the other using two primary inputs and an imported, pure intermediate good. Let good 1 be the importable good and good 2 be the exportable good. Good 1 uses

[13] These a_{ij} are Leontief fixed input-output coefficients, chosen to avoid problems with the diagram introduced by factor substitutability.

[14] For details, on both the net and gross transformation frontiers and on the possibility of "extra" gains from trade, see Batra (1973, 163–165, 169–171, and Figures 7.1 and 7.2).

[15] This particular version of the pure intermediate good is from Hazari and Suh (1978). It is only one of a number that could be constructed. If we had all three goods produced domestically, we would need to make one of them nontradable or our model would be left to solve for two factor prices, w and r, with three cost functions, one for each of the final goods and the intermediate, all of which prices would be determined in world markets. Batra (1973, Chapter 8) alternatively specifies a nontraded, domestically produced, pure intermediate used in both final goods and a similar structure of production with trade in the intermediate but one of the final goods nontradable. The Hazari and Suh (1978) specification, as well as that of Hazari et al. (1981), sidesteps that problem by effectively letting the foreign country deal with the relation between the price of the intermediate good used by the home country and the payments to the primary factors used in producing it.

the imported intermediate: $X_1 = F_1(K_1, L_1, M_{31}) = L_1 f_1(k_1, m_{31})$, where M_{31} is good 3, which is strictly imported (hence its designation by M) and is used in good 1 (hence the 1 in the subscript 31). Good 2's production function is $X_2 = F_2(K_2, L_2) = L_2 f_2(k_2)$. Both of the capital intensities are in net terms. The unit requirement of the intermediate in good 1 is a_{M1}, which tells us that $a_{M1}X_1 = M_{31} = M_3$: the intermediate requirement per unit of good 1, times the quantity of good 1 produced equals the total quantity of good 3 (the imported intermediate) used in producing good 1, which itself equals the total import of good 3 since it's a pure intermediate.

The country's community indifference system contains the two final goods as its arguments: $U = U(D_1, D_2)$. Since good 1 is the importable good, the total consumption of good 1, D_1 can be comprised of local production, X_1, and imports, M_1: $D_1 = X_1 + M_1$. (Note that M_1 is the imports of good 1 while M_3 is the imports of the intermediate good.) Domestic consumption of good 2 is local production minus exports: $D_2 = X_2 - E_2$ (where E represents exports; there is no E_1, just as there is no M_2). Trade balance requires that the country export enough of good 2 to pay for its direct imports of good 1 and its imports of the intermediate good that help produce its domestic units of good 1: $p_2E_2 = M_1 + p_3M_3$.

The production and trade pattern can be shown with Figure 3.21, adapted from Hazari and Suh (1978), another four-quadrant diagram. Begin in quadrant I with the production possibilities frontier (or transformation curve) between the two final goods, curve TT. The production levels of goods 1 and 2 are on the axes. The slope of the ppf at any point, $-\Delta X_1/\Delta X_2$, is not equal to the terms of trade, p_2/p_1, but rather to the ratio of the price of good 2 to what is called the "value-added price" of good 1, which is less than p_1: $p_2/(1 - a_{M1}p_3)$ because producers of good 1 have to take into account the price of the intermediate good they use. This value-added price is represented by price line AA, tangent to the ppf at point P, the production point for goods 1 and 2 in the home country. In quadrant II, plot the relationship between inputs of the intermediate good and outputs of good 1; line Oa_{M1} represents the fixed input coefficient of the intermediate good. Quadrant III plots the price relationship between the intermediate good and the home country's exportable good, with the level of imports of the intermediate good on the horizontal axis and the output of good 2 measured negatively on the vertical axis. The slope of line Op_3 is p_2/p_3. In quadrant IV a 45° line translates quantities of good 2 on the downward vertical axis into equal quantities of good 2 on the horizontal axis of quadrant I.

The home country faces the slope of line Oa_{M1} in quadrant II by virtue of a given technology and the slope of line Op_3 in quadrant III by virtue of the small-country assumption. The value-added price line AA in quadrant 1 is similarly given by the small-country assumption. The first point identified is the production point P, which identifies OX_2^* of good 2 and OX_1^* of good 1 as domestic production levels. From point P, draw line PQ parallel to the horizontal axis over to line Oa_{M1} in quadrant 2, thence perpendicular downward to the M_3 axis; this identifies the quantity of good 3 required to produce X_1^* of good 1. Continue that line from the M_3 axis to point R on line Op_3, thence parallel to the horizontal axis to point E_3^* on the vertical X_2 axis; OE_3^* is the quantity of good 2 that must be exported to acquire OM_3^* of the intermediate good used in production of OX_1^* of good 1. Extend the line from R to E_3^* over to its intersection at point D with the 45° line connecting production levels of good 2. The projection of point D on the horizontal X_2 axis at X_2' identifies the amount of good 2 left for domestic consumption after paying for imports of good 3: $X_2^* - X_2'$ is the export requirement for good 3. Now, project a line

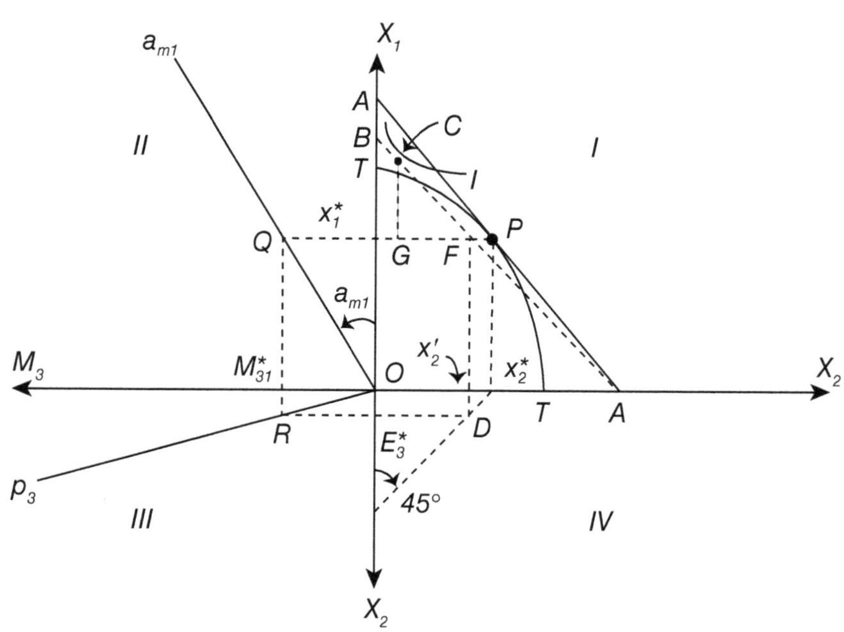

Figure 3.21. Heckscher-Ohlin model: production and trade with an intermediate good (Reproduced from Hazari and Suh, 1978, figure 1, p. 7, by permission of Bharat Hazari.)

from X_2' perpendicular to the horizontal axis intersecting line PX_1^* at point F. If the home country put all its resources into the production of good 2, at the terms of trade p_2, its value of production would be identified by OA; hence the relative price line characterizing the terms of trade extends from point A through the amount of good 2 available for consumption after paying for the intermediate input, which is point F. This gives the terms of trade line AB, which is the relative price facing the home country's consumers (as producers, the home country faced the value-added price line, AA). We've drawn the country's community indifference system as indifference curve I, which is tangent to the terms of trade line AB at point C. Thus the home country consumes X_1^*G of good 2 and $CG + OX_1^*$ of good 1, and exports GF of good 2 to finance imports CG of good 1.

You can use Figure 3.21 to explore how several economic and technological changes will affect this pattern of trade. I'll show which lines in the diagram to change to represent particular events, but I won't clutter the diagram further. If the price of the imported intermediate increases (think of Minoan Crete facing a higher price of copper from Cyprus), the denominator of the value-added relative price shrinks, raising the relative price of good 2 facing producers; the production point shifts down the ppf to the right of point P. At the same time the price line Op_3 in the third quadrant, which represents the price of good 3 relative to that of good 2, rotates counterclockwise around the origin. The production of good 2 will increase, and that of good 1 will fall. The export of good 2 required to purchase the imports of good 3 used in the production of good 1 may rise or fall, depending on the magnitude of the increase in p_3, the slope of the transformation curve in the region of the production change, and the size of the input coefficient a_{M1}. The increased cost of producing good 1 at unchanged relative consumption prices has reduced the real income of the country, and the terms-of-trade line moves leftward parallel to its original slope; the maximum attainable level of community indifference falls, as does consumption of both final goods. An increase in the input requirement of good 3 in producing good 1 largely parallels these changes. The value-added relative price line turns in the same direction, and the terms of trade line remains parallel to its original slope, but line Op_3 remains fixed while line Oa_{M1} in quadrant II rotates counterclockwise, indicating more units of good 3 per unit of good 1. If the price of good 2 rises relative to that of good 1, with the price and input requirements of good 3 fixed, both the value-added relative price line and the terms-of-trade line move clockwise, the former around the transformation curve and the latter rotating from the horizontal intercept of the value-added price line. Imports of good 3 fall, the country consumes more of both goods and exports more good 2 to input more of good 1. The new terms-of-trade line lets the country reach a higher level of community indifference.

Changing models a bit, if the intermediate good were produced locally and used in both final goods, but one of the final goods were nontraded, we can get some interesting output responses as a result of technical improvements in the production of the intermediate.[16] These interactions are worth noting, even if we only informally note the differences in models. Such technical progress has the effect of reducing the capital and labor used in producing the intermediate (which produces a cost effect in final goods production) and raises the supply of the intermediate (which produces a factor supply effect in final goods production). The final change in outputs of final goods depends on the net results of the cost and factor supply effects on the intermediate; they may complement or work against each other. The cost effect depends on the relative shares of the intermediate good in the two final good production functions. If this occurs in a small country—i.e., commodity prices remain constant—the price of the primary factor used intensively in the final goods sector that experiences the larger cost effect will rise. If this industry happens to be the capital-intensive industry, the rental rate will rise relative to the wage rate, inducing a substitution of labor for capital that reduces gross capital intensity in both final goods industries and a reduction in the output of the labor-intensive industry and increase in production in the other. This is the pure cost effect, and it replicates the operation of the Stolper-Samuelson theorem. Turning to the factor supply effect, if we keep constant the output of the intermediate good (analytically, not actually), that industry will release capital and labor in proportion to the capital-labor ratio in that good, k_m. If k_m is between k_1 and k_2, the outputs of both industries will increase; if $k_m > k_1 > k_2$, industry 1 will expand and industry 2 will contract, and vice versa if $k_m < k_1 < k_2$. This is pure Rybczynski effect. Both effects operate simultaneously, and the net result depends on the relative magnitudes of a number of cost parameters. This takes us back to the passing example of Cypriot bronze. Suppose Cyprus smelted its bronze and could make two different final products with it that were sold in international markets, say, tools and weapons. This analysis says that it's not obvious that Cypriot production of both these goods would increase as a result of a technical improvement in the production of raw bronze.

3.4.8 Natural Resources

Natural resources were prominent in the trade of antiquity (they still are). A probably partial listing of categories includes precious metals (gold and silver), base metals (copper, iron, tin),[17] precious and semi-precious stones, construction stone (marble, granite, limestone), timber, fish, and pottery clay. Even these categories probably could be expanded, and certainly the examples of members of the categories could be filled out in detail. To the extent that land is one of the primary factors to which I've occasionally appealed in the trade models so far, I've already considered at least one "natural resource" without special attention to it. The reason for singling out natural resources for

[16] This is the Batra model reported in the previous note.

[17] We probably should call bronze a product, an intermediate good, rather than a "simple" natural resource, since it is the output of the manufactured combination of copper and tin, both previously smelted in other manufacturing processes.

special attention within the structure of the Heckscher-Ohlin trade model is that there are some important economic differences between natural resources and either equipment/capital considered as an original factor and intermediate goods. "Resources," whether renewable like timber or nonrenewable like copper, exist in a finite stock at any given time. The "production" of a resource, or more precisely its extraction, involves the "shaving off" of some of the stock available at the latest point in time. Renewable resources differ from nonrenewables in that they have a natural growth rate if either left alone or tended in some fashion; consequently their harvesting (the renewable equivalent of the extraction of a nonrenewable) can be conducted at a rate consistent with a steady supply of the harvest forever (and a constant size of stock), or a growing or declining (to zero) stock if the harvest falls short of or exceeds the growth rate.

Resources can gain a role in trade in two types of situation: as nontradable factors (land is a prime example, but many of the other resource categories will fit too) and as directly traded goods. I'll define these different situations with production functions. First, let's call the quantity of the resource extracted or harvested in time period t $R_t(S_t)$, which says that the quantity extracted, R_t, depends on ("is a function of") the total stock of the resource at the beginning of the period, S_t. Now, if resources are extracted and used domestically to produce final goods that are traded, production can be described by $X_t = f[K_t, L_t, R_t(S_t)]$, where X_t is the quantity of the final good produced in time period t by applying equipment (capital) and labor to some quantity of the resource. The raw resource is not directly traded, but it goes into the production of a good that is traded. An example would be the production in Cyprus of bronze coal scuttles and axes (from a combination of Cypriot copper and tin or arsenic from somewhere else) that were sold to agents in Sardinia in the 13th century. In the other situation, the resource itself is the object of trade: $R_t = g(K_t, L_t; S_t)$, which says that the producers apply equipment and labor in some production process to the stock of resource to extract a particular quantity of the resource. An example of this situation would be the smelting of copper and subsequent casting into oxhide ingots in Cyprus, with the ingots made available for sale overseas or even the export of raw ore.[18]

Focusing on nonrenewable resources for the moment, a primary difference between trade involving resources in either of these two situations is that the trade might not be able to go on forever because either the resource deposit will be exhausted or because as the stock dwindles its extraction costs rise above the extraction costs of an identical resource elsewhere. Thus, a comparative advantage in, say, gold could be systematically eliminated by exploitation of gold deposits. A country might export gold for several hundred years, then become an importer, because either the continued mining drove up extraction costs as the stock dwindled or people in another country discovered their own deposits that could be extracted more cheaply. If a higher rate of extraction from a stock of given size costs more than a lower rate (e.g., mining 5 tons a year instead of 2 tons from a 200-ton deposit), then a country faced by a lower-cost competitor would still be able to mine economically by reducing its extraction rate. If the extraction cost is invariant to the annual rate of mining,[19] then the older producer will not be able to mine any amount of its resource profitably; any continued extraction would have to be subsidized.[20]

The four theorems of the Heckscher-Ohlin model all transfer satisfactorily to either case of trade involving natural resources (Kemp and Long 1984, 375–395 on theorems). First, the H-O theorem itself remains valid, and countries with a comparative advantage in a particular resource will export that resource. Next, the factor price equalization theorem will hold up, and trade in goods will equalize the ratios (and levels) of prices of nontraded factors among trading countries. If the resource itself is traded, its price will be equalized among countries, trivially, by the trade. Third, the relationship between changes in commodity prices and changes in factor prices specified by the Stolper-Samuelson theorem, applies to the cases of nontraded resources and to other nontraded factors when resources themselves enter trade. Finally, the corresponding quantity relationships between factor endowment changes and production changes of the Rybczynski theorem carry over to cases including resources as either nontraded inputs or as outputs.

Whether processing of a resource, or how much, will be conducted in its home country or at its destination is affected both by comparative and absolute advantage considerations: comparative advantage, to the extent of the effects of the ratios of endowments of inputs required for processing; absolute advantage, to the extent that differential transportation costs counteract comparative cost advantage conferred by endowment proportions. The latter is the subject addressed in Weberian location theory (see Jones 2014, Chapter 11).

Fishing offers an interesting variant on the domestic production ordinarily addressed by trade theory. In fishing, labor and equipment from a country venture into seas that may be effectively a commons—an unowned resource.[21]

[18] A purist could make a case that this sounds like the first situation inasmuch as the copper is smelted and poured, which involve production processes distinct from pure extraction, which would leave raw ore. I concede this point but note that in the case of metals this categorization would leave only the export of ore as an example of this situation. You can think of the export of smelted metals in the form of ingots as either type of situation, according to personal taste or the emphasis of the problem under study. It really doesn't make a lot of difference.

[19] Which does not necessarily imply that the cost of extraction would not increase over time as the stock mined became smaller.

[20] In fact, transportation costs in antiquity probably provided substantial protection of domestic mining, even if gold mined in countries A and B was sold in country C for an identical price (assuming the same fineness of the gold). Nonetheless, gold producers in the higher-cost country would not have experienced the profitability that producers in the lower-cost country did.

[21] Not a common property resource, which is effectively owned and regulated by a group of agents with common interests in the usufruct of the resource. A true commons is likely to be over-used since no agent

In a region of sea equally convenient in location to several countries, comparative advantage in fishing versus other activities would influence the proportions of each country's resources put into fishing, although both countries could still have incentive to overfish. If one of the countries, or both by agreement, were able to lay successful claim to this part of the sea, individual producers (fishermen) from that country still would have incentive to overfish. However, this country would have an incentive to regulate fish catch by its nationals in a way it would not if it could not lay claim to the resource (the area of sea with its renewable fish resources).

3.4.9 Transportation Costs

It doesn't take any particular prescience to recognize that transport costs can eliminate trade entirely. What is more interesting is how the existence of transportation costs affect the mechanics of resource allocation embodied in the four H-O theorems. Transportation costs are important in location theory and in the closely related subject of urban spatial economics (Jones 2014, Chapters 11–12). In neither application is transportation typically modeled as a resource-using activity. Specifying transportation rate schedules as a price per mile, either constant or variable over miles traveled is satisfactory for the essentially partial-equilibrium analyses of locational problems, and even in the general-equilibrium urban models in which the composition of resources used in transportation was not of central interest, we could get by with specifying that "someone" outside the city provided the transportation services and debited real resources as payment. However, in the context of international trade models, the accounting of factor supply allocations, in addition to overall mass-balance accounting, is critical because it influences the directions of production and price changes. Consequently this sub-section will show two methods of studying real transport costs and will discuss in further detail how one of those specifications affects the Heckscher-Ohlin theorems.

The simpler of the specifications, known as the "iceberg" model, introduced by Samuelson (1954, 268 for the model specification), has a portion of a traded good vanish physically for exports and imports. With this specification, the quantity of exports from country A to country B exceeds the quantity of imports to country B from country A, and vice versa. Suppose we call our two goods X and Y, and denote the exported quantities of them with subscripts "e." Without transportation costs, the balanced trade required for equilibrium is $p_x X_e = p_y Y_e$, or $p_x/p_y = Y_e/X_e$, and the same price ratio faces both trading partners. Now put in the iceberg form of transportation costs in which the fractions (less than 1) a_x and a_y of X and Y disappear during transit, supposing that country A exports X and country B exports Y. The price ratios facing the two countries differ. From the perspective of country A, $p_x X = a_y p_y Y$ or $(p_x/p_y)_A = a_y Y/X$, while from the perspective of country B, $p_y Y = a_x p_x X$ or $(p_x/p_y)_B = Y/a_x X$. From these real price ratios, we get the set of equalities and inequalities that $(p_x/p_y)_A = a_y Y/X = (a_y a_x/a_x)(Y/X) = a_x a_y (p_x/p_y)_B < (p_x/p_y)_B$ which gives us the result that the relative price of good X in terms of good Y is higher in country B than in country A. Thus, after trade has driven commodity prices as close together as they will go considering transportation costs, country A faces a lower relative price of good X, which it exports, to good Y, which it imports, than does country B, which exports good Y and imports good X. Each country faces a lower relative price of its export good than does the importing country. Stated yet alternatively, each country faces the f.o.b (free on board or freight on board) price for its export good and the c.i.f. (cost, insurance, freight) price for the good it imports.

Transportation costs give each country a lower relative price of the good it produces that competes with imports (called the "import-competing" good). This is the effect that tariffs are intended to confer on goods subject to foreign competition. Thus transportation costs provide similar protection to domestic production that a tariff wall offers, with the difference that the transportation costs are real while tariffs, being artificial barriers, primarily redistribute real resources between countries and between factor owners within countries, with real income reduced only by some deadweight loss from the distortion of the efficient allocation of resources.

From this equilibrium inequality of commodity prices in different countries after trade, it is obvious that full factor price equalization cannot occur. However, the Heckscher-Ohlin theorem still operates, so countries export the goods that use intensively the factors they possess in relative abundance. For the effect on the Stolper-Samuelson and Rybczynski theorems, I turn to a more sophisticated specification of transportation costs.

The model with transportation costs includes a separate transportation industry whose services must be applied to internationally traded goods but not to domestically retained production (Cassing 1978). It is a 3×2 model (three goods, two factors), just like the problem of a nontraded good in the Heckscher-Ohlin model, which means that the production levels of the goods will be indeterminate without the specification of another relationship besides the cost functions and full-employment conditions. That task was accomplished in the nontraded goods model by the recognition that the supply of the nontraded good must be equated to its domestic demand, and incorporated into the model as a "supply equals demand" condition for the nontraded good. There will be a comparable relationship in the transportation model. First, the production functions for the two final goods and the transportation service all require employment of both capital and labor: $X_0 = f_0(K_0, L_0)$ for transportation services, $X_1 = f_1(K_1, L_1)$ for the home country's exportable good, and $X_2 = f_2(K_2, L_2)$ for its importable. Both the home

owns it and enforces entitlement to the returns to it. All agents using a commons have incentive to equate the full quantity of what they harvest (or otherwise produce) from it to the marginal cost of their variable resources such as labor and shipping equipment.

and foreign countries produce some of both goods, which is why we call the good the home country imports the "importable"—because while the country imports some of it, it also produces some of its consumption of this good; and similarly for the "exportable" good. Capital and labor are allocated among all three industries so as to remain fully employed: $K_0 + K_1 + K_2 = \bar{K}$ and $L_0 + L_1 + L_2 = \bar{L}$.

The specification of transportation is rather spare, but it captures the resource cost and allocation effects of transportation. Only the home country produces transportation services, and only the home country's imports of good 2 incur a transportation charge, an assumption that can be squared with "reality" by assuming that the same vessels that carry good 2 to the home country carry a smaller volume of good 1 back to the foreign country, and the spare capacity on the vessels yields a zero transportation charge for the back-haul carrying good 1 (the demand curve cuts the supply curve at the horizontal axis, yielding a zero price on the return trip; stated alternatively, the marginal cost of an additional unit of export on the backhaul is zero because the ship isn't full).[22] The provision of transportation services is tied to the level of imports of good 2 by the home country, with one unit of transportation being required for each unit of import: $X_0 = C_2 - X_2$, where C_2 is the home country's consumption of good 2 (which is greater than its local production of that good since good 2 is imported). That consumption demand is a function of the local prices of both goods and national income, Y: $C_2 = C_2(p_1, p_2, Y)$. Transportation services are consumed in constant proportion to good 2, so there is no need for a separate consumption relation for it. While the production of shipping services must be equated to the demand for them, $X_0 = C_0$, the derived demand for shipping services is equal to the final demand for good 2: $X_0 = C_2$. Since there are only two final goods, the demand for good 1 is implied by the rest of the relationships in the model.

The home country is a small country relative to the foreign country (which we could call "the rest of the world"), which implies that it faces given prices for the two final goods. For good 1, the home country faces the price p_1, which is equal to the price in the foreign country, p_1^*, by virtue of the zero back-haul rate in our transportation cost structure. However, the home country faces a c.i.f. price for good 2 that exceeds the f.o.b. price of that good in the foreign country by an amount equal to the transportation cost: $p_2 = p_2^* + p_0$. The price of transportation services is not given to the home country but depends on the cost of producing whatever level of transport services is consistent with the consumption of the two final goods. This means that while the home country directly faces a world price for good 1 and a world f.o.b. price of good 2, the c.i.f. price it faces for good 2 depends on the rest of the choices that country makes. In fact, the f.o.b. and c.i.f. prices the home country faces for good 2 need not move in the same direction, which will cause complications in the application of the Stolper-Samuelson theorem to the case of costly transportation in the H-O model.

Before proceeding to the Stolper-Samuelson theorem, note that the Heckscher-Ohlin theorem remains intact in this setting: the relatively capital-abundant country exports the relatively capital-intensive final good regardless of the capital intensity in shipping. Thus we know that the home country is relatively abundant in the factor used intensively in good 1. Second, it is obvious that the factor price equalization theorem loses the force of exact equalization and must settle for a tendency to push factor rewards as close together as the transportation costs on commodities will permit.

The Stolper-Samuelson theorem uses factor intensities in the two final goods alone to predict the sign of the two changes $\hat{w}/\hat{p}_2$ and $\hat{r}/\hat{p}_2$ in which the caret means "percent change in" the variable beneath it—e.g., the percent change in the wage rate in the home country caused by a one-percent change in the f.o.b. price of good 2. Note that we have to work with the f.o.b. price of good 2 in the foreign country because we don't know what the price of transportation services is going to be: we can't manipulate that price exogenously. With the endogenous price of transportation, we must know all three factor intensities in order to know how this commodity price change will affect home country factor prices. We know that shipping cannot use more intensively the good used relatively intensively in good 2 (recall the footnote about the chain of comparative advantage). So, if good 1 is capital-intensive, shipping cannot be more labor intensive than good 2. The ordinary expectation is that an increase in p_2^* would raise the home country's wage rate, but the larger is the proportion of the shipping cost in the c.i.f. price in the home country, the greater is the likelihood that an increase in the f.o.b price overseas will reduce the reward of the home-country factor used intensively in that good. This possibility gives countries good reason to think carefully about whether they want to apply their tariffs on a c.i.f. or f.o.b. basis. When transportation costs are relatively high, a country would be wise to apply its tariffs on a c.i.f. basis; when they are relatively low, that choice is less important.

The Rybczynski effect is complicated by the jointness in consumption between the import good and shipping, and the net output effect of factor endowment changes (growth) depends on the relative factor intensity of shipping as well as those of the two final consumption goods, and on the change in shipping output itself. Suppose that shipping is more capital intensive than good 1—$k_0 > k_1 > k_2$—and that the home country's labor force grows relative

[22] Furthermore, by a chain of comparative advantage, if shipping is capital-intensive relative to both final goods, then only the capital-abundant country will provide shipping. And conversely for relatively labor-intensive shipping: it will be provided only by the relatively labor-abundant country. For an empirical observation, would the skipper of, say, the Ulu Burun ship or the Kyrenia ship have been likely to price the tariffs on merchandise aboard his ship at such a zero marginal cost when he had a less than full cargo? Doubtful, but the theoretical structure of the bi-directional transport rates specified by Cassing captures the real cost structure of transportation that would have operated in antiquity as well as in modernity and, a not inconsiderable point, is easier to work with algebraically than a non-zero backhaul rate that captures no more than the same resource allocations.

to its capital stock. The local output of good 2 will increase, reducing the demand for imports of good 2; the income effect of the additional factor supplies will raise the consumption of both final goods, which tends to dampen the fall in imports. The reduction in imports reduces the output of shipping, which releases relatively more capital per unit of labor than is used in good 1. Consequently the industry producing good 1 has to expand somewhat relative to good 2 to absorb the additional capital. This dampens, but does not reverse, the expansion of labor-intensive good 2 and the contraction of capital-intensive good 1 anticipated from the ordinary operation of the Rybczynski mechanism. The usual Rybczynski effect still emerges when transportation costs are included in the trade problem, but as is intuitive, growth of the factor used intensively in the export industry will increase the volume of trade by less, the higher are transport costs. The magnification of the Rybczynski effect is diminished by transport costs.

You can see that the structure of transportation costs that trade models try to characterize is simpler than those found useful in location theory. In location theory, specific distances are important, and the spatial rate (price) structure (i.e., linear, increasing, or decreasing in distance) frequently is worth describing specifically, because the goal of those models is to distribute activities across a landscape in a continuous fashion. The use of transportation costs in international trade theory is different. The models generally deal with only two countries treated as points (i.e., their internal spatial structures are ignored), and countries don't vary in their distance from one another. The principal perturbation we can give to transportation costs is the technology. Technological changes in the iceberg model are limited to differential changes in the a_j between industries. Technical change in the Cassing model can take a wider variety of forms. "Neutral" technical change would reduce the inputs required to produce a unit of transport services at an unchanged factor intensity. Alternatively, the use of either factor in providing a unit of transport services could be reduced independently of the other, which will produce different interactions with the inputs that can be allocated to the final goods. Although I don't work through a case of technical change in transportation provision here, that is a useful exercise that you may want to try working your way through yourself.

3.5 Theories of Trade 4. Intra-industry Trade in Differentiated Goods

The Heckscher-Ohlin model as developed so far captures a small number of relatively undifferentiated goods—the classic "commodities" such as grain, bulk metals, common qualities of bulk cloth, and so on. The evidence of ancient trade, both from the recoveries of ship wrecks and excavations of sites on land, indicates that there was a good deal of two-way shipment of different kinds of manufactured goods, probably paralleling bulk shipments such as grains and metal ingots. The H-O model as we've developed it so far gives us considerable insights into why these goods moved and what the effects of their movements would have been, but clearly something is lost in the aggregation we've done so far. Recent study of trade in differentiated goods, or intra-industry trade (as contrasted to the inter-industry trade of the standard H-O model) has joined together the analysis of product variety with monopolistic competition models from the theory of industrial organization with the neoclassical production structure of Heckscher-Ohlin trade theory. The result is a series of models with production divided into "commodities" and differentiated goods. Equilibrium is characterized by an output level of the commodity for each country and a number of varieties of differentiated goods, each produced in the same quantity, effectively combining inter-industry trade in the commodities and intra-industry trade in varieties. Still not a digital photograph of trade, but an advance over the aggregated commodity models of pure inter-industry trade.[23]

The distinguishing ingredients of the intra-industry trade model are consumers' valuation of variety as well as quantity of any particular good and increasing returns to scale in the production of the differentiated goods that yield the product variety. The other components are the same as in the standard H-O model: production functions for each industry, which yield the respective cost functions; fixed factor supplies—labor and capital are sufficient; requirements for full employment of both factors, and the specification of demand. But recall that we're dealing now with one industry that is perfectly competitive—the industry that produces a homogeneous commodity (we can call it food) and one that has the industry structure of monopolistic competition, which has different conditions for producers' profit-maximizing equilibrium than the simple "price equals marginal cost" condition of perfect competition. Consequently, the intra-industry model contains a separate equilibrium condition for the representative firm in the monopolistically competitive industry, which says that, by virtue of each firm's profit maximization efforts *and* the unrestricted entry and exit of producers into that industry, the mark-up of price over marginal cost equals the degree of returns to scale. Finally, the model identifies the number of varieties of the differentiated good that will be produced; since it associates each variety with a different firm, and each firm with only one variety, this answer yields the number of firms too, and the output of each firm.[24]

Let's look at the differentiated goods industry somewhat more closely. With a given quantity of resources in the economy, some of which must be devoted to production of the homogeneous good, there is a trade-off between the number of varieties consumers can have and the quantity of each variety. Because of the increasing returns to scale, a greater variety of products comes at the expense of higher unit costs: producing smaller quantities is more

[23] The standard monographic reference is Helpman and Krugman (1985).

[24] The production structure of the differentiated goods industry is specified so that the production function of each variety is identical. This is a substantial simplifier, but little is gained by relaxing it.

expensive than producing larger quantities. Consumers, on the other hand, face decreasing marginal utility in two ways: as the quantity of any good consumed, differentiated or homogeneous, increases and as the number of varieties increases. Between these sets of forces on the production and consumption sides of the problem, there is an optimal number of varieties and output per firm in the differentiated goods industry.

An economy modeled with these components has determinate equilibrium values of the outputs of both industries, the number of varieties and firm size (output per firm) in that industry, the relative product price,[25] and factor prices. If the country were larger, the number of varieties, as well as the output of each variety, could be larger, because of the increasing returns to scale. Now, if we construct another country with a comparable structure of a homogeneous good industry and a differentiated goods industry, and open trade between it and the country we've considered so far, the differentiated goods industry is affected in a way neither homogeneous good industry was affected in the standard H-O model. Each firm in the differentiated goods industry in both countries now faces a larger market than it did before. It can expand its output and lower its price by doing so. But expanding its output requires that it absorb capital and labor from other firms in the differentiated goods industry as well as possibly some from the homogeneous good industry. The upshot is that not all of the individual firms in the differentiated goods industry will survive the opening of trade, even if the aggregate output of the differentiated goods industry increases. (In fact, it is possible for the aggregate output of the differentiated goods industries in both counties to increase after trade, without the output of either homogeneous good industry decreasing—because of the increasing returns to scale.) The total number of varieties available to the two countries together will increase by virtue of the trade, and the output of each variety will increase, but each country will produce fewer varieties, and in larger firms, than it did in autarky.

You can see that the responses of an economy of this description differ from those with the simpler, constant-returns-to-scale (CRS) specification of the standard, H-O economy. This observation naturally leads to the question whether the Heckscher-Ohlin, factor price equalization, Stolper-Samuelson, and Rybczynski theorems still work in this setting. Take the H-O theorem's prediction about a country's trade pattern first. In the CRS specification of the H-O model, three reliable predictors of a country's trade pattern (what it imports and what it exports) are its factor endowments (observed either before or after trade is opened), its autarky factor prices, and its autarky commodity prices. Factor endowments remain a good predictor of intersectoral trade, but neither relative commodity prices nor relative factor prices will be reliable predictors of a country's comparative advantage once trade opens.[26] In the first place, even in autarky those prices will depend on the size of the country, because of the scale economies in production. Second, once trade opens, the change in the market size facing the increasing-returns-to-scale industries may reduce the relative price of exported varieties. Once trade opens, the prices of differentiated goods can be lower in both countries than they were before trade opened. One implication of increasing returns to scale in production is that countries with identical factor endowments will find it possible to trade in differentiated goods, even if they do not trade in homogeneous goods, which are not affected by the size of the market. Trade volumes will be greater when countries are roughly the same size.

Factor price equalization will still occur as long as countries' factor endowments lie within the standard cone of diversification. The Stolper-Samuelson prediction about which factors "win" and which "lose" when a commodity price changes becomes substantially more complicated. With increasing returns to scale, the output levels affect both relative and absolute costs, which in turn means that the effect of a relative commodity price increase on factor prices depends on the feedback of output changes (caused by the initial commodity price change) on sectoral cost configurations. The ordinary Stolper-Samuelson relationship may emerge, but under some circumstances, exactly the opposite relationship may occur: a commodity price increase may reduce the real reward of the factor used intensively in its production. If the interindustry difference in cost shares (of either factor) is greater than the sum of the output effects in both industries, *and* if the average costs in both industries increase with an increase in both factor prices, the usual Stolper-Samuelson relationship will occur. However, if the second condition holds but the scale effects outweigh the inter-industry difference in cost shares, exactly the opposite relationship will occur between commodity prices and factor prices. That is, when one product price increases relatively, the scale effects of increased production in that activity can pull up the real reward of the factor it does not use intensively as well as the one it does use intensively, and if this effect is strong enough it can reverse the ordinary relationship between commodity and factor prices. In the case of the Rybczynski theorem, an increase in any endowment could cause all outputs to increase. However, since the Rybczynski relationship between factor endowments and outputs is the primal version of the Stolper-Samuelson dual (prices versus quantities) relationship, sufficiently strong scale effects can reverse the ordinary endowment-output relationship. For both relationships, the usual response pattern will occur if the degree of increasing returns to scale, the industry in which IRS occurs, or both, is sufficiently small. All this means that more information

[25] Identical production conditions and identical demand—another simplification—for each variety implies an identical price, which represents the price of the output of the differentiated goods industry.

[26] It's possible to adjust actual prices for the effects of the scale of production when increasing returns to scale prevail, and these adjusted prices *will* predict the trade pattern, but the adjustment depends on special conditions in both the consumers' utility functions and in the differentiated goods' production functions. It's not a really practical option for empirical implementation currently.

than just relative factor intensities is needed to predict the commodity price-factor price and endowment-output relationships. These complications are consequences of the increasing returns to scale in the differentiated goods model, not the structure of the equilibrium conditions in monopolistic competition.[27]

In the presence of transportation costs (which, generally, means always), increasing-returns industries will tend to locate where local markets are largest and export from there to other markets, other considerations being equal.

The evidence for intra-industry trade in the ancient Mediterranean is ample. Many of the smaller, less standardized items such as the diptych on the Ulu Burun shipwreck, Mycenaean carved ivory items in Cyprus, the Cypriot bronze wall bracket for a torch found at Tiryns, are items that *could* have been produced at either end of the apparent trading dyads but appear to have been produced relatively systematically at particular sites and exported to the others.

3.6 Commercial Policy

Governments have many instruments with which to affect their foreign trade. They can artificially alter the prices of goods entering or leaving their country with import tariffs, export taxes, and subsidies.[28] Quotas are more direct in restricting the movement of goods, usually imports, but not necessarily. Sub-section 3.6.1 presents the tools for analyzing the effects of these policies. When tariffs are levied on goods that are used as inputs to other goods as well as on final products, the "nominal" tariff rate—the rate the government levies by law—generally departs from the "effective rate of protection" offered to domestic producers who use the imported inputs. The true protective effect of a tariff may be many times greater than what the nominal tariff rate might suggest. Sub-section 3.6.3 deals with the possibility that a country may agree with another country to eliminate tariffs on imports to each other while leaving a common tariff wall around both of them. The structure of economic changes countries can experience upon joining a customs union have parallels in the economic impacts of "joining" an empire, if with a greater degree of free will.

3.6.1 Tariffs, Trade Subsidies, and Quotas

Tariffs (customs duties) are taxes, of one formulation or another, on traded goods. Quotas are limitations on the quantities of imports or exports. Subsidies are payments, generally made directly by an agency of a country's government, to either producers or consumers. All three types of instrument have been used in the official regulation of foreign trade and undoubtedly have a lengthy pedigree. The Roman *portoria* included imperial and local import tariffs, and both import and export tariffs had a prominent role in the finances of the Hellenistic Greek states (Duncan-Jones 1990, 37, 194–195; de Laet 1949). The Roman imports of grain from Egypt for distribution at less than cost to residents of the Eternal City are a rather complicated example of an import subsidy.[29] Accordingly, the additional exports drawn forth by the subsidized imports (which would, of course, be greater in volume than the unsubsidized volume would have been) could have come from parts of the Empire far from Italy. Claims by scholars that some of the ancient Near Eastern kingdoms concentrated all rights to export and import with royal agencies amount to a type of quota system with the government holding all export and import licenses.[30]

This sub-section will explain the operation and consequences of tariffs and related policies affecting international commerce. Since the purposes of most tariffs and other trade interventions differ from those of ordinary domestic taxes, some different concepts, such as that of "protection," will be introduced (see Jones 2014, Chapter 6 on domestic taxes). Most of the effects of quantitative restrictions such as quotas can be analyzed as tax-equivalents, so I will begin with the analysis of tariffs, then proceed to quotas and subsidies, which themselves are more akin to negative taxes.

Tariffs can be levied in two principal forms, ad valorem and specific. An ad valorem tariff is a tax at a specified percent of the price of the imported or exported good. An ad valorem tariff can be levied on either the landed cost (c.i.f. price) of the good at home or on its pre-shipment cost (f.o.b. price) in a port of origin. The relationship between the local price of a tariff-ridden good and the world price, with an ad valorem tariff, is $p = (1+t)p^*$ where p^* is the world price (the price at which the good is imported, ignoring transportation costs, as we will do for most of this section), t is the ad valorem tariff rate expressed as a percentage, and p is the domestic price of the good facing consumers in the country levying the tariff. A specific tariff is levied as a certain amount of tax per unit of the good taxed, such as 1 shekel per oxhide ingot or per ton (or whatever unit of measure) of grain. The domestic price of a good with a specific tariff levied on it would be $p = p^* + t'$, where t' is the specific tariff. An increase in the world price would automatically increase the tariff revenue with an ad valorem tax but not

[27] For the influence of increasing returns to scale on the Stolper-Samuelson and Rybczynski relationships, see Kemp (1969, Chapter 8) and Helpman (1984, 347–348).

[28] Bissi (2009) describes various Greek *poleis*' policies towards international transactions in precious metals, timber and grain.

[29] It's probably useful to consider inter-province trade within the Empire as international trade rather than as intra-country trade in a number of senses, although the Empire does seem to have been a customs union; see section 3.8.4 below.

[30] Opinions on Egypt have varied widely. At the end of more extensive royal control is Helck (1987); if "state control" is extended to temples, Janssen (1975, 163) is willing to sign on; Eyre (2010, 296) occupies some middle ground as does Castle (1992) with considerable detail and nuance; and Kemp (2006, 318) is skeptical. Considering the information available on the Old Assyrian caravan trade, it is difficult to see how a position of official monopoly of foreign trade could be maintained, but Postgate (1992, 220–2221) offers a nuanced explanation of temples commissioning merchants who thereafter would have had extensive freedom of action, which leaves the temples in a quasi-official status.

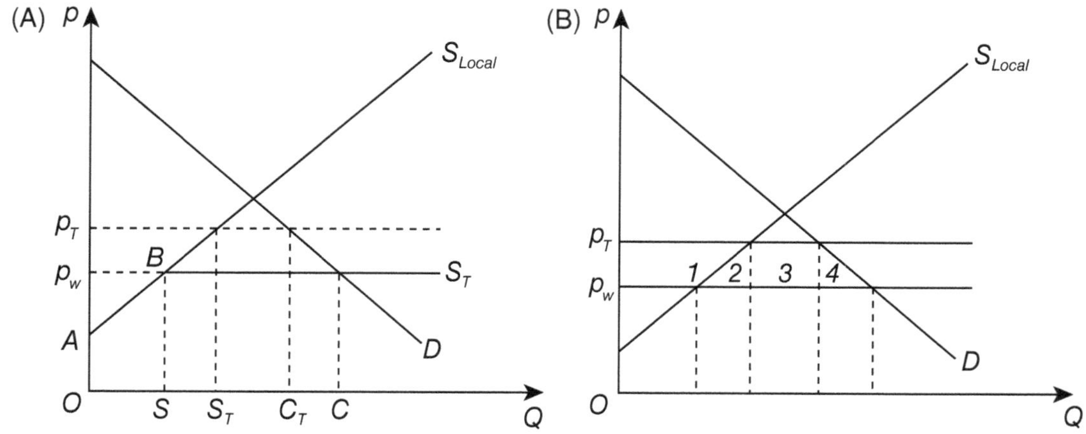

Figure 3.22. (A) Welfare costs of a tariff on a single good: pre-tariff domestic supply curve. (B) Welfare costs of a tariff on a single good: post-tariff production and consumption changes.

with a specific tax. Unless a specific tax is adjusted, the effective tariff rate will fall as commodity prices rise, with the tariff becoming a smaller proportion of the domestic price facing consumers. There are several variants of either type of tariff. A sliding-scale tariff varies with the price of imports. An equalizing tariff adjusts to make the price of imports including the tariff equal some target price, such that a reduction in the pre-tariff price of the good leads to an increase in the tariff. While the import duty may be the most common type of tariff, duties can be, and have been, levied on exports as well.

Tariffs are levied for varied reasons. One, which cannot be dismissed as a major rationale in situations where many taxes are difficult to collect, is revenue, purely and simply. Some of the low duty rates in the Roman Empire may have had such a principal motivation.[31] Revenue may be the principal motivation for export taxes. Otherwise, protection of producers is a primary motivation for import tariffs, despite common proclamations ranging from protection of consumers to the preservation of public morality. Producer protection plans include infant industry and senescent industry protection. Nevertheless, it is not uncommon for commercial policies to be used to accomplish more clearly domestic policy goals such as fostering employment, restricting or redirecting consumption, and modifying the personal distribution of income. Within the protective motivation, the principal mechanism of the tariff is its ability to raise prices, at least domestically. I'll focus continually on this aspect of tariffs, to which I now turn directly.

As taxes, tariffs impose two types of cost—a production cost and a consumption cost. The production cost derives from the fact that the country levying the tariff produces a combination of goods that is worth less at international prices than the country is capable of producing, and the consumption cost derives from the parallel fact that consumers base their decisions on distorted prices, buying fewer imports than they would if they could consume at international prices. If a country is large enough to affect international prices by the imposition of a tariff, it will improve its terms of trade by reducing world demand for the good it imports. Consequently it is possible for a large country to benefit from a tariff despite the distortion costs imposed on its domestic production and consumption decisions; whether it does or not in fact is strictly an empirical question, depending largely on whether it picks a tariff rate in the right range of magnitude.[32] A small country—one not large enough to affect world prices—cannot benefit from the imposition of a tariff; all it accomplishes is a reduction in domestic consumption, which is an unambiguous welfare loss. If other taxes are even more expensive to collect than is a customs duty, such a tariff may still be a second-best optimal policy.

Beginning with the simplest, partial-equilibrium case, Figures 3.22A and B depict the welfare costs of a tariff on a single commodity. Local supply and demand curves for the product govern local production and consumption decisions, but with trade, the country faces a world price for this good, p_w, which, naturally, is lower than the country would face in autarky. With trade, the country's supply curve begins with the local supply curve, where that curve would bring forth supplies at prices below the world price—from its vertical intercept at A to its intersection with the world price line at point B. To the right of B, the country's supply curve is the world price line: altogether the line ABS_T. With free trade, this country will consume OC of this good, OS of which it will produce domestically and CS import. Now let the country impose a tariff of $p_T - p_w$, which raises the domestic price facing both producers and consumers to p_T. Consumers reduce their

[31] Although as Duncan-Jones (1990, 194–195) reports, rates varied widely, and even low rates could be applied multiple times, which sounds much more like revenue motivation by government or public agents than producer protection motivation.

[32] There is a sizeable literature on optimal tariffs, by which is meant the tariff rate that maximizes a nation's welfare. An optimal tariff will be the particular rate that best trades off the domestic production and consumption costs against its terms-of-trade benefits. Optimality in the commercial policy literature generally is defined in terms of the country levying a tariff, excluding the country or countries facing the tariff. Consequently, the optimal tariff is subject to retaliation by other countries, which complicates what would otherwise be a relatively straightforward calculation of costs and benefits.

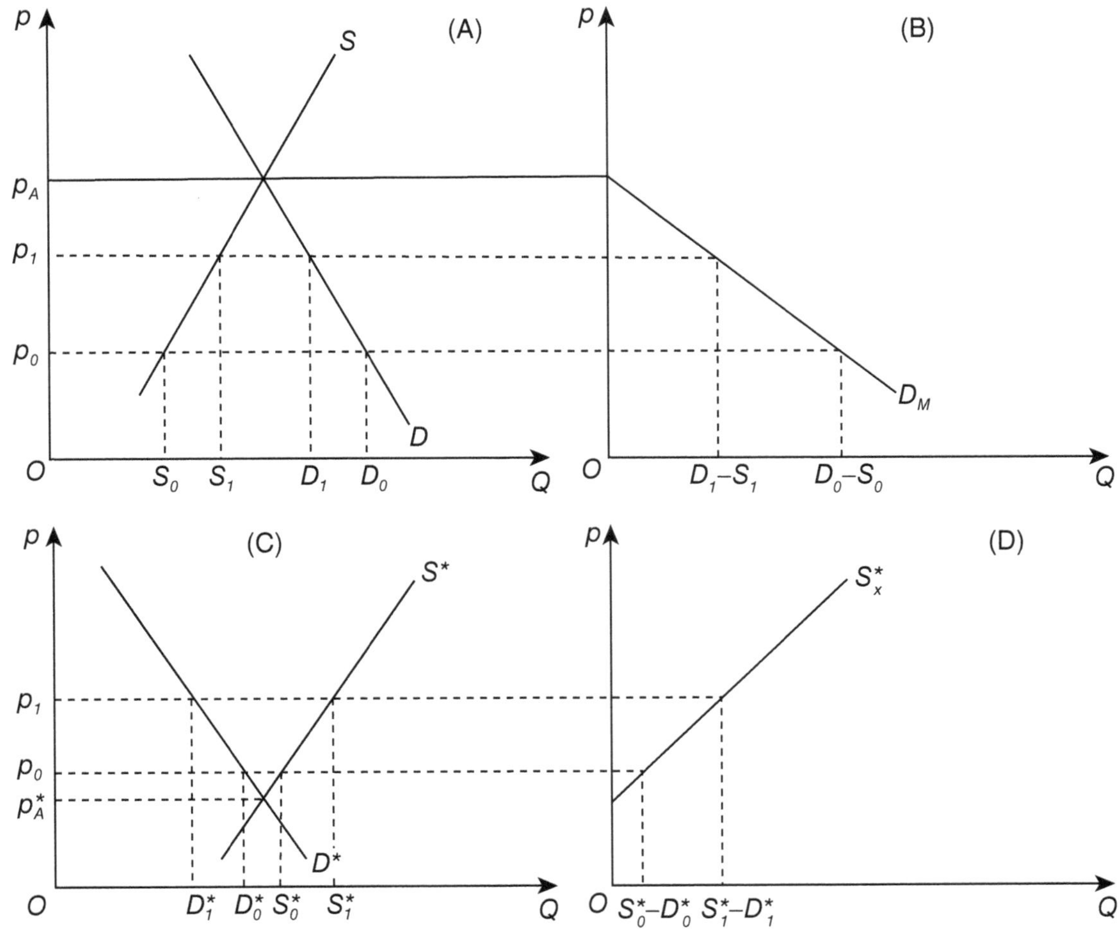

Figure 3.23. (A) Tariff imposed by a large home country: domestic supply curve and demand for home country's imports. (B) Tariff imposed by a large home country: home country's demand for importable good. (C) Tariff imposed by a large home country: foreign country's demand for and supply of its exportable good. (D) Tariff imposed by a large home country: foreign country's export supply curve.

consumption of this good to C_T and domestic producers increase their production to OS_T, reducing imports to S_TC_T. Figure 3.22B identifies the components of the production and consumption changes so we can evaluate them. First, the increase in the domestic price facing consumers causes a reduction in consumer surplus equal to the sum of areas 1, 2, 3, and 4: the entire area under the demand curve and between the original and new prices. This is the consumption loss. It is counteracted partially by benefits to producers in the form of an increase in producer surplus on the units of output it is profitable for local producers to supply under the protected price: area 1, which is the area above the supply curve and under the new price line. The government gets some customs revenue, which is accounted a benefit to this country as a whole: area 3, which is the tariff $(p_T - p_w)$ times the quantity of imports, $C_T - S_T$. The government receipt of customs duties is just a transfer from some residents of the country to others; the government might distribute the revenue to the same people who paid it, in the same proportion as they paid it. (Even if they give it to somebody else, it's still just a transfer, and not a cost from the point of view of the country.) Now let's add up these areas of loss and gain: (1: producers' gain) + (3: government gain) – (1 + 2 + 3 + 4: consumers' loss) = –(2 + 3). Thus, the losses outweigh the gains by areas 2 and 4, both of which are parts of the consumer surplus loss not compensated by other gains. These are deadweight losses of benefits, exactly equivalent to the deadweight losses of taxation (see Jones 2014, Chapter 6). If producers were unable to respond to the higher domestic price (the local supply curve became vertical at B), area 2 would vanish, and if consumers did not respond to the price increase (the demand curve became vertical at C, area 4 would disappear. Area 3—government revenue—would expand to fully offset the consumer surplus loss of areas 2 and 4, while producers would collect pure rents from the domestic price increase.

Next I'll look at how a tariff in one large country can reduce the price of the other large country's export good (a 2-country model), thus improving its own terms of trade. To do this I have to develop the concepts of the import demand and export supply curves. (The import demand curve is different from the demand curve for a country's importable good.) Figures 3.23A-D show the derivation of these two curves from a country's basic supply and demand curves. We begin with the home country's demand for imports in Figures 3.23A and B. Panel A shows the demand curve for the home country's importable good and its domestic supply curve for that product, the intersection of which

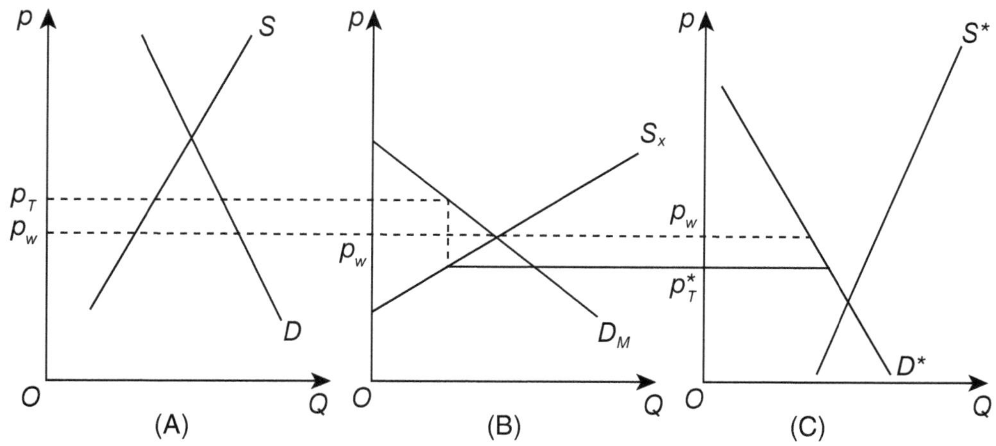

Figure 3.24. (A) Tariff imposed by a large home country: home country's demand and supply curves for its importable good. (B) Tariff imposed by a large home country: determination of world price. (C) Tariff imposed by a large home country: foreign country's demand and supply curves for its exportable good.

yields the autarky price p_A. Prices p_0 and p_1 are two arbitrary price variations designed to show the discrepancy between domestic supply and demand at prices below the autarky price (prices above the autarky price would not sell any imports in the home country). At p_0, domestic producers are willing to supply S_0 of the importable good while consumers are willing to purchases D_0 of it. The difference between D_0 and S_0 is the quantity of imports that the home country demands at price p_0, and is mapped onto panel B at the point $D_0 - C_0$ on import demand curve D_M. At the higher price p_1, local producers supply a larger quantity of this good, S_1, and consumers demand less of it, D_1, which amounts to a smaller quantity of imports, $D_1 - S_1$ in panel B. At the autarky price, p_A, domestic demand equals domestic supply, and the import demand curve reaches its vertical intercept, where import demand is zero. In panels C and D of Figure 3.23, we develop the export supply curve for the foreign country in an analogous manner. At its autarky price, p_A^*, the foreign country's output of its exportable good does not exceed its local demand. At the same prices p_0 and p_1 we used in panels A and B, the foreign country's producers are willing to supply more of this good than its consumers want to purchase, leaving a supply of exports that are mapped onto panel D. The vertical intercept of the export supply curve is the foreign country's autarky price, and the quantities on the export supply curve are excesses of local supply over local demand.

Now let's return to the home and foreign countries' demand and supply curves for this good (Figures 3.24A and C), and their respective import demand and export supply curves in 3.24B. The intersection of the export demand and supply curves in panel B determines the world price, p_w. Tracing the world price onto each country's local demand-and-supply situation, we see that it is below the home country's autarkic supply-demand intersection and above the foreign country's. At p_w, the home country's imports are equal to the excess of its demand over its local supply, and correspondingly for the foreign country's supply. Now, let the home country impose a tariff on this importable commodity, bringing the local price of the good to p_T in panel A. Trace this higher price in the home country across to its import demand curve in panel B. The quantity of imports now demanded by the home country would be supplied by the foreign country at a price below the world price, p_T^*. Trace this point on the export supply curve of panel B over to the home country's demand and supply curves in panel C to see the origin of the reduction in supply price. This reduction of the foreign country's price of its exportable good is the terms-of-trade effect of the home country's tariff.

We now can add this terms-of-trade effect to the production, consumption, and revenue effects of the previous example. Figure 3.25 shows the diagram for the home country in the equivalent of Figure 3.24A, but now reporting the new import price, p_T^*. Areas 1, 2, 3, and 4 remain as before, respectively areas of producer surplus, deadweight consumer loss, government revenue, and more deadweight consumer loss. These changes occur from the world price, p_w. However, imports now arrive in the home country at the lower price, p_T^*, and the tariff is $p_T - p_T^*$, so the government collects duties on areas 3 and 5, area 5 representing the terms of trade effect. So the welfare

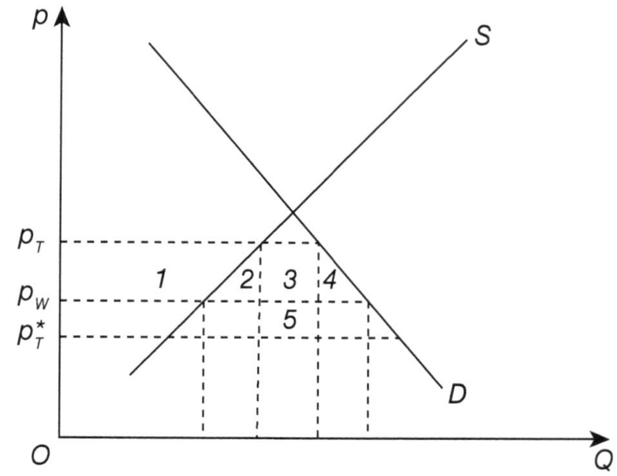

Figure 3.25. Tariff imposed by a large home country: production, consumption, and revenue effects of large country's tariff.

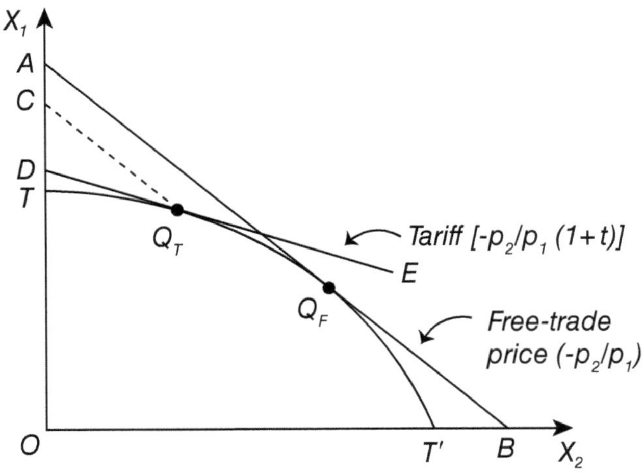

Figure 3.26. General equilibrium production and consumption effects of a tariff.

changes are the producer gain (area 1) plus the government revenue gain (areas 3 + 5) less the consumer surplus loss (areas 1 + 2 + 3 + 4). Netting the transfers, we get the two deadweight loss triangles (areas 2 + 4) plus the terms of trade gain (area 5), and the welfare effect of the tariff on the large country could be positive or negative.

Let's move to a general equilibrium examination of the production and consumption effects of a tariff. Figure 3.26 shows the transformation frontier for a two-good model, TT′, and a world, free-trade relative price line AB. Under free trade, the country would produce at Q_F at relative price p_2/p_1. Good 1 is this country's importable, and it imposes a tariff at rate t on that good, which yields a domestic relative price of $[p_2/p_1(1+t)]$, given by line DE. The tangency of DE with the transformation frontier identifies the output ratio that equalizes producers' domestic rate of transformation (DRT) with the new domestic rate of substitution (DRS). Under the higher relative price of good 1, local producers produce more of it, at Q_T. National income, however, still must be measured at international prices, represented by the dashed line CQ_T, parallel to the world relative price line, AB, and intersecting the new production point on the transformation curve. National income, measured in terms of good 1, falls from OA to OC because of the new production choice.

To isolate the effects of the tariff on consumption, we use a transformation frontier with no substitutability between goods 1 and 2 in production, in Figure 3.27, a device attributable to Caves et al. (1999, 168).[33] The free-trade world price line, AB, touches the transformation frontier TT′ at its corner, point D, and the country produces T′D (= OT) of good 1 and TD (= OT′) of good 2, regardless of prices; the tariff cannot distort production choices. The community indifference curve I_F is tangent to the world price line at point F, leading the country to export X_FD of good 2 in return for TM_F imports of good 1. Now the country applies a tariff on good 1, yielding the domestic price line CD. In the new domestic consumption, the country must stay on its national budget line, which is the value of its production at world prices. However, domestic consumers face different relative prices, so their optimal consumption will be at a tangency of a community indifference curve with the domestic, tariff-ridden prices. If the government returns the full amount of the customs revenue to consumers, this tangency must occur at an intersection of the domestic relative price (budget) line and the world relative price (budget) line. The tariff revenue is distance EC on the vertical axis, measured in terms of good 1. This intersection also guarantees balanced trade. The pure substitution effect of the tariff-induced price rise moves aggregate consumption from point F to point H, where the tariff-ridden relative price line E′E′ is tangent to the community indifference curve I_F. With homothetic demand, the tangencies of this preference system with the relative prices defined by CD (or E′E′) lie on the straight line OZ through point H and the origin of the diagram. Consequently, a community indifference curve must be tangent to a relative price line with the slope of CD exactly where it passes through the world price line AB. This set of intersections and tangency occurs at point E, where community indifference curve I_T is tangent to E′E′. I_T is a lower level of indifference than I_F, and the tariff leaves the country worse off than free trade. In free trade, this country exports X_FD of good 2 in return for imports TM_F of good 1. The pure consumption effects of the tariff reduce the trade volume to X_TD exports of good 2 in exchange for TM_T imports of good 1.

Now we look at a case in which the tariff actually makes the levying country better off than free trade made it. Figure 3.28 uses a convex transformation frontier, TT′. The tangency of TT′ with the world free-trade price line at Q_F denotes the free-trade consumption point, and the tangency of community indifference curve I_F at E is the country's consumption. The country levies a tariff on its importable, good 1, raising its domestic relative price to the slope of line CD. Domestic producers shift their production to Q_T. The tariff consumption point will be at point F (the intersection of a line parallel to CD intersecting at F and the indifference curve tangent there are not shown), which yields a lower level of indifference than free trade. However, suppose that the imposition of the tariff depresses the world relative price of this country's importable (equivalently, increases the country's terms of trade) to line HJ, which passes through the tariff production point, Q_T. This relative price permits the country to reach a level of indifference at which the domestic and external budgets are satisfied at point G, where the country benefits more by the terms-of-trade improvement than it is harmed by the production and consumption distortions.

In this latest evaluation, I've let the terms of trade be affected by the home country's tariff, but without actually showing the determination of the new world prices. For that purpose we use the offer curve. Before using the offer curve apparatus to assess the impact of tariffs on world prices, I have to incorporate the tariff into the offer curve, which I do with Figures 3.29A and B. In panel A we strip away

[33] Also appearing in the excellent first edition of that text: Caves and Jones (1973, 232).

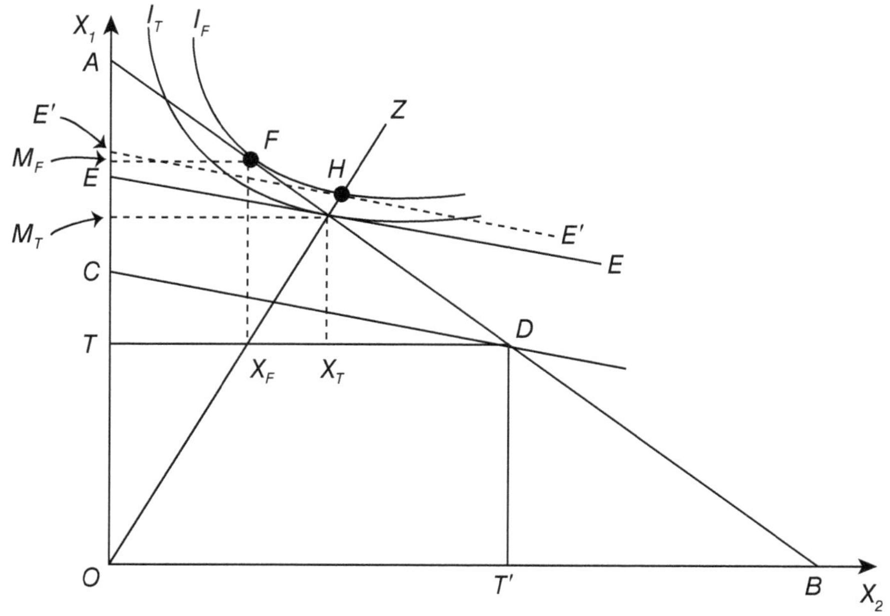

Figure 3.27. General equilibrium effects of a tariff on home country's consumption.

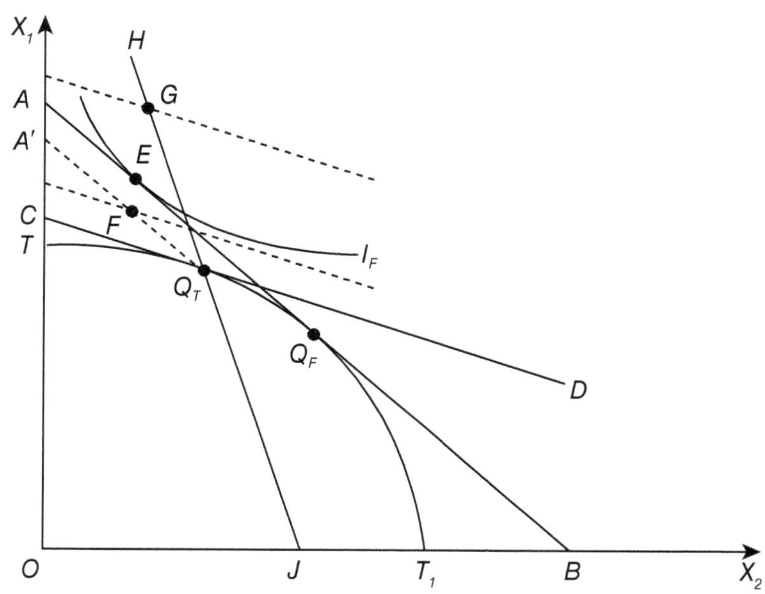

Figure 3.28. Case in which tariff improves the levying country's welfare.

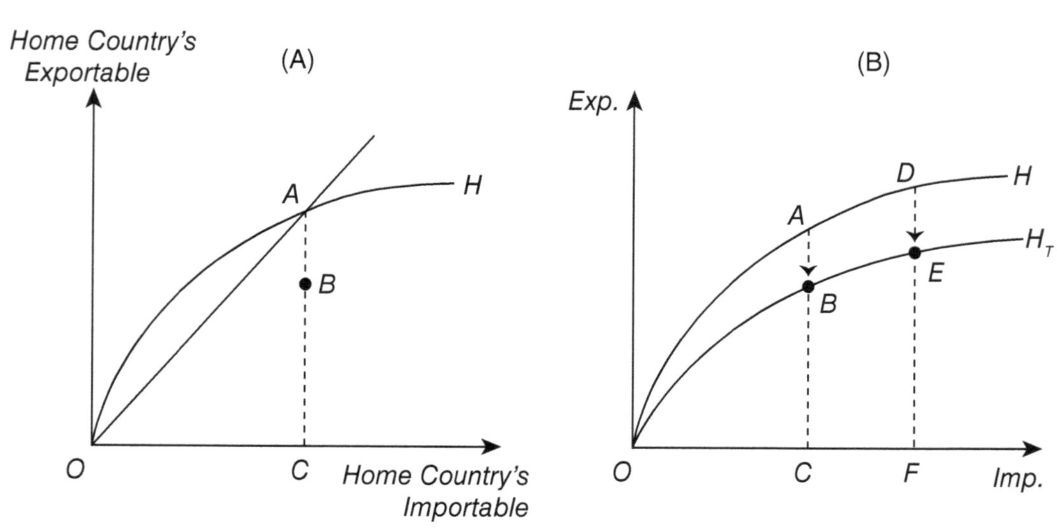

Figure 3.29. (A) Offer curve perspective on the effects of a tariff, pre-tariff base. (B) Offer curve perspective on the effects of a tariff, tariff affects home country's offer curve.

everything except the home country's offer curve and an arbitrary terms-of-trade line which intersects the offer curve at point A. For OA of exportables, the home country would offer OC importables. However, of the OA exportables leaving the home country, the government claims and retains within the country AB as tariff revenue, leaving foreigners receiving only BC. Home country residents still pay OA for their imports of OC, but foreigners receive only BC. Moving to Panel B, we mark out several terms-of-trade intersections with the home country's offer curve (A and D) and take out a constant proportion t for the tariff (AB and DE) at each point along the offer curve. This removal of a constant fraction of the home country's exportable production reduces the free-trade offer curve H to the tariff-ridden offer curve H_T.

You'll have noticed in Figures 3.29A and B that nothing appears to be getting done with the tariff revenue that the government collects, distances AB and DE. We turn to that issue now, in Figure 3.30. Begin with home country offer curve OH and the arbitrary terms of trade Op, cutting OH at point A. Next, have the government take a proportion t of the export good offered for each possible quantity of imports as tariff (the tariff rate t equals the proportion AB/BC), giving the line Op′. At terms of trade Op, the home country offers OE (= AC) of its export good in return for OC of the foreign country's export good. As in Figures 3.29A and B, however, foreigners receive only BC of the home country's exportable, the home country government retaining AB of it as tariff revenue. (Notice that the initial incidence of the tariff is on home country consumers; how much of it they can pass on to foreigners is the subject of the analysis.) Only BC of the exportable actually gets traded. However, the government must decide how it spends its tariff revenue of AB. It can spend it all on the import good (AD), all on its own exportable good (AB), or on any combination in between, along the tariff budget line BD. Suppose the government has the preference system represented by the indifference curve I_G, which is tangent to the budget line at J. Then point A on the free-trade offer curve is translated post-tariff to point J instead of point B, as we did in Figures 3.29A and B. In general, government spending of the tariff on the import good has the effect of pulling offer curve OH_T in Figure 3.29B back closer to the free-trade offer curve OH, but it can never pull it all the way back because even in the limiting case in which the government spends all the tariff revenue on the import, the tariff-ridden offer curve is separated from the free-trade offer curve by distance AD in Figure 3.30.

Now turn to the alternative effects of a tariff on the terms of trade and the protective effect of a tariff. Figure 3.31 shows two elastic, free-trade offer curves, OH for the home country and OF for the foreign country. The equilibrium terms of trade is line Op_F. The home country imposes a tariff that drops its offer curve to OH_T (which includes the spending pattern of the tariff revenue), improving its terms of trade to OP_T, which is a higher relative price of its exportable. The tariff reduces the home country's imports from OM_F to OM_T. Residents of the foreign country face the terms of trade Op_T, but home country residents face a different price, illustrated in Figure 47, which shows the same offer curves as Figure 3.31 but distinguishes between domestic and world post-tariff terms of trade. We denote the post-tariff terms of trade faced by the rest of the world as Op_{Tw}. Despite the fact that foreigners receive only BC of the home country's exports for OC of its own exports, home country residents still have to fork out a total of AC for the OC imports; they just have to give AB of that amount to their government and the remainder to the foreigners. So we draw a straight line from the origin to the position on the home country's free-trade offer curve (OH) directly above the intersection of its tariff-ridden offer curve (OH_T) with the foreign country's offer curve (OF). I denote this domestic price as Op_T^H; notice that the post-tariff domestic price of the importable good—the home country good that is supposed to get protection from the tariff—is higher than it was under free trade. This is good from the perspective of domestic producers of the home country's importable good, but if you'll look closely at how the home and foreign offer curves are shaped between the intersections of Op_F and Op_T^H, you'll begin to recognize that that happy result doesn't have to occur. Next, I'll show how it doesn't.

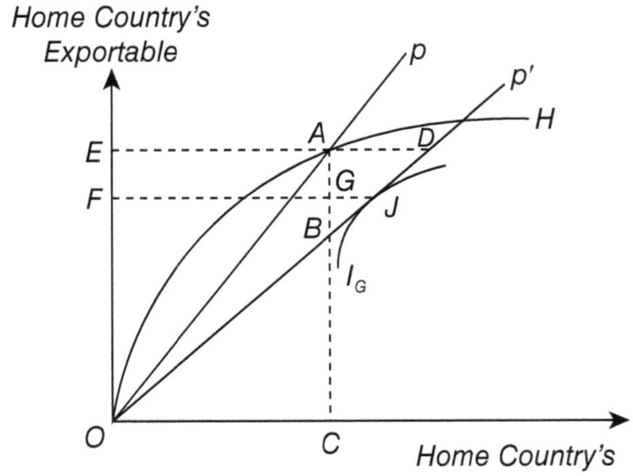

Figure 3.30. Offer curve perspective on the effects of a tariff, government spends tariff revenue.

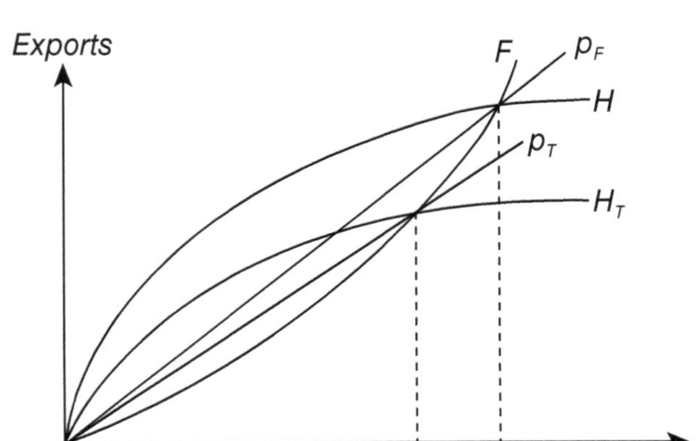

Figure 3.31. Offer curve perspective on the effects of a tariff, effects on home country's terms of trade.

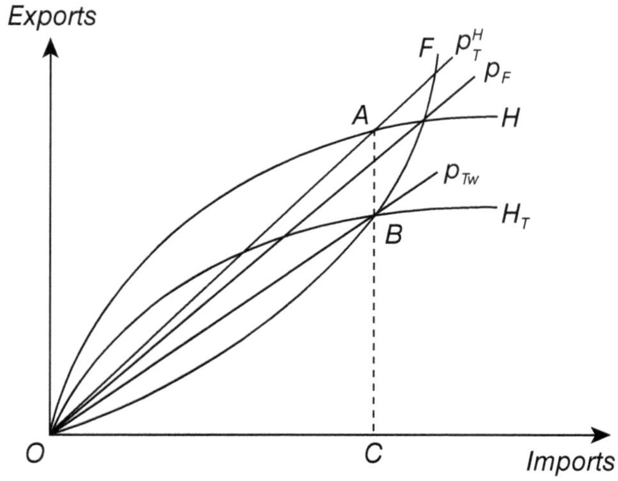

Figure 3.32. Offer curve perspective on the effects of a tariff, home country's tariff with elastic home and inelastic foreign offer curves.

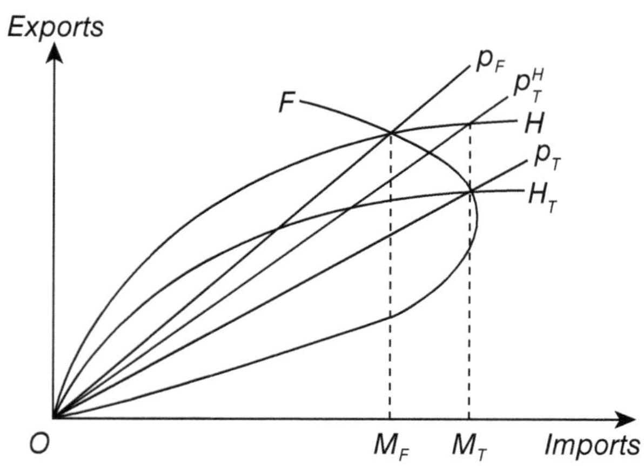

Figure 3.33. Offer curve perspective on the effects of a tariff, home country's tariff with elastic home and inelastic foreign offer curves.

Figure 3.33 depicts an elastic home offer curve and an inelastic foreign offer curve, with a tariff levied by the home country. Op_F is the free-trade terms of trade, and levying the tariff lowers the home offer curve from OH to OH_T, with terms of trade Op_T. Now, trace vertically upward from the intersection of OH_T and OF to OH. Draw a straight line from the origin through this point to find the domestic post-tariff price of the importable. It's lower than it was under free trade, and the home country imports more than it did without the tariff, which has failed to protect the home country's importables industry.

Let's turn to a tax on exports. We'll see that an export tax is equivalent to a duty on imports, a result known as the Lerner symmetry theorem. I can show this with Figure 3.30, which I already used to show how the offer curve will shift when the government spends some of the tariff revenue on both imports and exportables. The government imposes a tax on exports equal to DA/AE, which yields the government revenue of DA in imports. At the domestic price ratio of Op′, consumers and producers exchange OE in exports for AC imports at the world price ratio p, but foreigners have to pay ED of their exports in exchange for OE of the home country's exports, which is the price ratio Op′, with AD of what they pay going to the government as revenue. The price ratio Op′ gives the government BD for its budget line, and with the same preference system as before, the government will consume at J again. The offer curve shifts to the same set of positions with the export tax as it did with the import duty.

We can see this equivalence between an import duty and an export tax by writing out the expressions for domestic and international prices in the two cases. Let's use lower case letters for domestic prices and upper case for world price, or the price received by the foreigners. In the case of the import tariff, $p_m = P_m(1+ t)$: domestic residents pay for their imports 1 + t times what the foreigners receive for them. However, for the home country's own exports, $p_x = P_x$: home country residents receive, and foreigners pay, the same amount for home country exports. Now, form the domestic and foreign relative prices of the home country's import good and its export good by dividing the import prices by the export prices: $p_m/p_x = (1+ t)P_m/P_x$. Now, turn to the case of the export tax. Foreigners pay more for the home country's export good than do home country residents, by the amount of the tax: so, $P_x = p_x(1+ t)$. This time, home country residents pay, and foreigners receive, the same for the home country's importable good (the foreign country's export): $p_m = P_m$. Again, divide the import prices by the export prices: $p_m/(1 + t)p_x = P_m/P_x$; rearrange this to get $p_m/p_x = (1 + t)P_m/P_x$, which is exactly the same thing we got for the import duty. The tariff on the import and the tax on the export produce the same distortion in the relative price of the two goods. The tariff raises the domestic price of imports (and domestically produced importables), and the export tax depresses the price of exportables. Either way, the relative price of importables in terms of exportables rises by the proportion 1 + t. The necessity for balanced trade in equilibrium is the principal mechanism for accomplishing this equivalence. The tariff lowers imports; the trade-balance equilibrium condition reduces exports. Correspondingly, the export tax reduces exports, and balanced trade forces an equivalent reduction in imports.

Let's turn to the subsidization of trade, with the case of a subsidy on imports. With free trade, home country residents and foreigners would exchange AE of importables (foreigners' exports) for OE (= AD) of home country exports in Figure 3.34. Now, let the home country subsidize imports at the rate s = CA/CD. Now, foreigners have to give only EB of their exports (the home country's imports) for CD of the home country's exports, at the price ratio p/(1 − s). The additional quantity of exports, CA, is compliments of the home country government's subsidy. The government still has its preferences regarding its own spending on imports and exportables, even when the spending change is a reduction. Consequently, with a preference pattern represented by the indifference curve I_G, the government will consume at J, and the subsidy on imports swings the home country's offer curve in the opposite direction from its shift in response to a tariff. This

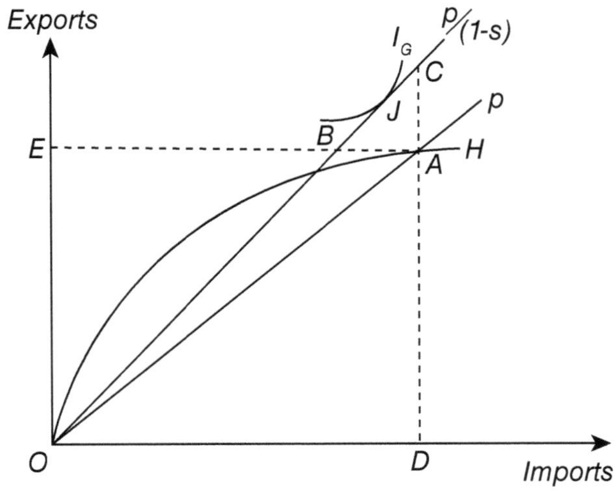

Figure 3.34. Subsidization of imports.

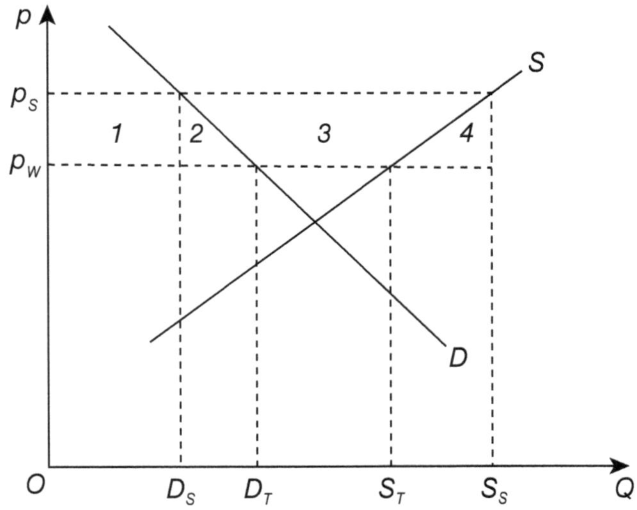

Figure 3.35. Components of effects of an export subsidy.

direction of movement of the offer curve shows clearly the increase in both imports and exports generated by the subsidy on one country's imports.[34]

We'll see the same kind of equivalence between import and export subsidies. In the case of the export subsidy, home country residents pay, and foreigners receive, the same price for the home country's imports: $p_m = P_m$. But home country residents receive more for their exports than foreigners pay for them, by the amount of the subsidy: $P_x = (1 - s)p_x$, where s is the subsidy rate. Form the relative prices and rearrange to get $p_x/p_m = P_x/P_m(1 - s)$. Now consider the subsidy on imports, in which home country consumers pay less for imports than foreigners receive for them: $p_m = P_m(1 - s)$; and they pay and receive the same for exports: $p_x = P_x$. Again form the relative prices and get $p_x/p_m = P_x/P_m(1 - s)$, which is the same price ratio as we got in the case of the export subsidy. So a government could subsidize imports or exports and get the same result. Again, the mechanism is the trade balance equilibrium condition, which requires the subsidizing country to finance its larger quantity of imports with an identical increase in the value of its exports, and it doesn't matter at all whether it interfered directly with imports or with exports.

Trade subsidies have greater scope for welfare consequences of than do trade taxes. Essentially, the effects of an import tariff are limited by the height of the tariff that eliminates trade, called the prohibitive level of the tariff. A higher tariff will have no further consequences since it will not be collected, and the price of domestically produced importables will rise no higher than the prohibitive tariff. Figure 3.35 shows the components of the welfare effects of an export subsidy. Free trade yields the world price of this commodity, p_w, at which price the country is a net exporter: it supplies S_T of the good and demands D_T, for exports $S_T - D_T$. The export subsidy raises the price of exportables, and domestic consumers have to pay this higher price just as foreigners do or all of the local production would be exported. Now the government offers a subsidy equal to $p_s - p_w$, which encourages production of the amount S_S but reduces demand to D_S, increasing exports to $S_S - D_S$. Producers gain producer's surplus in the amount of areas 1, 2, and 3. Consumers lose consumer's surplus of areas 1 and 2. The government pays in subsidy the sum of areas 2, 3, and 4. The net change in welfare is the producer gain (areas 1 + 2 + 3) minus the consumer losses (areas 1 + 2) minus government subsidy payments (areas 2 + 3 + 4), which yields a net loss of areas 2 and 4, both deadweight losses. You can see that the sky is the limit on the expansion of areas 3 and 4, of which area 4 will continue to grow as a net loss as the subsidy is increased. Consumer losses are bounded by the fact that at some price they will cease to demand the good at all (where the demand curve intersects the vertical axis). Area 3 will also grow indefinitely with the rate of subsidy, but it is a transfer rather than a net loss to the entire economy.

The final instrument I'll consider is the import quota. Figure 3.36A shows home and foreign offer curves with free trade imports by the home country of OM. The home country government imposes an import quota of OQ, reducing imports by the amount MQ. The home country's offer curve effectively becomes OBCQ, with BC representing the value of the import permits since home residents are still willing to pay BQ of their exports for OQ imports.

[34] In the application of this analysis of an import subsidy to the Roman grain imports from Egypt (Lo Cascio 2007, 639; Morley 2007, 577; Kehoe 2010, 312), imperial fiscal linkages across provinces create some complications for the assignment of revenue effects to identical locations as production and consumption effects. The Roman government had the capacity to draw on more parts of the Empire than just Rome or even all of Italy for the subsidy—even Egypt, in fact, since it was part of the Empire. Nevertheless, trade-balance effects would still have operated between Egypt as the exporter on the one hand and Italy and other provinces that might have provided part of the subsidy on the other. (For grain exports that may have been tax payments in kind to Rome, adjustment would have operated through income effects at both ends of the transactions, tending to create an additional flow of goods). Collectively, all the provinces contributing to the subsidy would have had to increase their exports by some amount to finance the subsidy, as noted in von Freyberg (1989), despite the fact that the imports were eaten in Rome. Egypt could have spent its export revenues anywhere in the world, India as well as Italy and other parts of the Empire, and the Empire-minus-Egypt could have exported anywhere also to finance the subsidy. This latter aspect of the problem is a complication introduced by the multi-country, real-world example rather than one created by the interprovincial fiscal linkages.

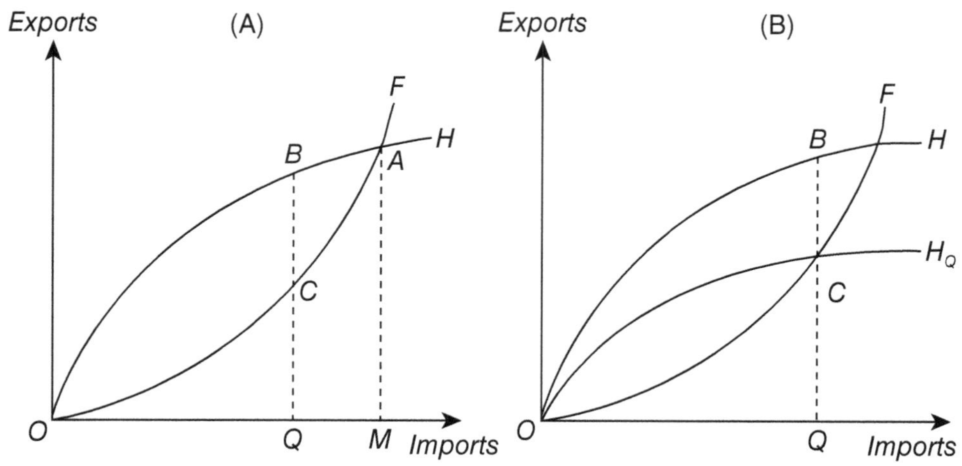

Figure 3.36. (A) Import quota. (B) Tariff equivalent of an import quota.

If the government does the importing itself, the profits amounting to BC will accrue to the treasury. Rather than impose a quota, however, the government could impose a tariff at the rate BC/BQ which shifted the home offer curve downward to intersect the foreign offer curve at the same point, yielding imports OQ in Figure 3.36B. If the home country's government persuaded foreign exporters to voluntarily restrict their exports to OQ, the value of the effective quota allotment would accrue to the foreigners, with no benefits at all to the home country.

3.6.2 Effective Protection

So far in our treatment of tariffs, we have thought implicitly in terms of goods that don't require intermediate goods in their production. The following exposition is adapted from Corden (1971, Chapter 6). Introducing the distinction between final and intermediate goods also introduces the concept of value added by a productive process—the value of the final product over and above the costs of the intermediate goods contained in them, i.e., the costs of labor and capital in production of the final good. It is the value added that is protected by a tariff on the final good, and the smaller is the share of value added in the cost of the final good, the greater the protective effect of a tariff of any given magnitude. What may look like a 10% tariff on the final good may in fact offer effective protection of 40% to the industry providing the value added. The concept of effective rate of protection measures the impact of a tariff structure as a whole on individual industries rather than on goods alone. Industries with higher effective rates of protection will tend to attract resources and expand at the expense of industries with low effective protection.

There are several possible definitions of the term "rate of protection," but the simplest one you should remember is the proportional increase in the domestic price over the foreign supply price that results from the imposition of a tariff. If the terms of trade are affected by the tariff, this amount will be less than the magnitude of the tariff. The magnitude of this effect depends on the elasticities of foreign supply and domestic demand for imports, as well as on the tariff rate. The elasticity of demand for imports is not the same thing as the elasticity of demand of the importable good, but is a combination of the elasticities of the domestic supply and demand for the importable. The elasticity of demand for imports is $\varepsilon_m = (\varepsilon_d + \delta\eta_d)(1 - \delta)$, where ε_d is the domestic demand elasticity for the importable good, η_d is the domestic supply elasticity of that good, and δ is the ratio of domestic production to consumption.

Think of domestic production of importable cloth, produced with the importable intermediate good yarn and a combination of labor and equipment that we call "value added product." A tariff on the final good, cloth, will raise the domestic price of the final good without affecting the price the producers pay for the produced input, yarn. The income per unit of cloth produced available to go to the primary factors (labor and capital) producing the value added increases. Alternatively, consider a tariff on the yarn instead of the cloth. The domestic price of cloth is determined by the world price of cloth and is unaffected by the tariff on yarn, but the price domestic producers must pay for yarn increases, putting a squeeze on the "price" of the value added product. The effective protection of the cloth industry provided by the tariff on yarn is negative!

Suppose a country that exports yarn imposed an export tax on it. The export tax reduces the domestic price of the yarn, indirectly subsidizing the domestic cloth industry by reducing its production cost. Offering a production subsidy to domestic yarn production would have the same effect on effective protection of the cloth industry as levying a tariff on yarn would have. Generally, a production subsidy on an input has the same effect on effective protection as a tariff would. Levying a tariff on an importable input used in an exportable good on which there is no tariff gives negative effective protection to the exportable final good. This example highlights the fact that protection is relative: positive protection for one industry implies negative protection for some other industry.

Effective protection affects only production of the protected industry, not consumption, which still relies only on the nominal tariff. A tariff on cloth, by reducing domestic consumption for it, will reduce the demand for domestically produced yarn as well but does not affect the domestic production of yarn as long as yarn continues to be imported.

It's possible for a tariff or subsidy policy to permit a positive value added in a production process that, in absence of the intervention, would yield a negative value added at world prices. That is, each unit of the output of such a good uses a greater value of resources, valued at world prices, than it's worth when it's finished. The cost of the inputs exceeds the value of the output. If the inputs are imported, the policy has a negative effect on the balance of payments and effectively reduces the wealth and welfare of the country.

There are some useful formulas for the effective rate of protection. First I'll develop the expression for value added, then that for effective protection. Denote the free-trade, world price of a final good as p_j and the corresponding price of an intermediate good used in the production of this final good as p_i. At free-trade world prices, value added per unit of this final good is $v_j = p_j(1 - a_{ij})$, where a_{ij} is the cost share of the intermediate good in a unit of good j; $a_{ij} < 1$. A tariff on the final good, t_j, would raise the domestic price of the final good to $(1 + t_j)p_j$, and a tariff on the intermediate good would raise its domestic price to $(1 + t_i)p_i$. Then value added at post-tariff domestic prices is $v_j^* = p_j[(1 + t_j) - a_{ij}(1 + t_i)]$. The effective rate of protection for the final-goods industry is the difference between post- and pre-tariff value added as a percent of pre-tariff value added: $g_j = (v_j^* - v_j)/v_j = (t_j - a_{ij}t_i)/(1 - a_{ij})$. This expression can be written in several alternative ways that illuminate distinct aspects of effective protection. In the first alternative, we can write it as $g_j = t_j/(1 - a_{ij}) - a_{ij}t_i/(1 - a_{ij})$, in which the first term shows the subsidy effect of the tariff on the final good contributed by the fact that the full amount of the protection falls to only a portion of the cost, and the second term is the tax effect reflecting the proportionate fall in the price of the final good resulting from a tariff on the intermediate good. The second alternative expresses effective protection as the sum of the nominal rate on the final good and the effect of differential tariffs on the final and intermediate goods, which latter term can be either positive or negative: $g_j = t_j + a_{ij}/(1 - a_{ij})(t_j - t_i)$. Finally, we can turn the calculations around and express the nominal tariff on the final good as a weighted sum of the effective rate and the nominal rate on the input: $t_j = (1 - a_{ij})g_j + a_{ij}t_i$. As you can see from these expressions, if the cost share of the input is very high, the effective rate of protection will be extremely sensitive to changes in the nominal tariff rate on the final good.

If the tariffs are levied at the same rate on the input and the final good, the effective rate of protection is the same as the identical nominal tariff rates. If the tariff on the final good is higher than that on the input, the effective rate is greater than either nominal rate. The obverse is also true: if the tariff on the input is greater than that on the final good, the effective rate is lower than the lower of the two tariff rates. If the tariff on the final good is sufficiently smaller than that on the input—specifically, if $t_j < a_{ij}t_i$—the effective rate is negative. If there is no tariff on the final good, the effective rate on that good's industry will be negative: $g_j = -a_{ij}t_i/(1 - a_{ij})$. If there is no tariff on the input, the effective protective rate is simply the subsidy effect in the first alternative expression above: $g_j = t_j/(1 - a_{ij})$.

The sensitivity of effective protection to the three principal parameters—the two tariff rates and the intermediate input's cost share—can be written out formulaically. The response to a change in the tariff on the final good is $\Delta g_j/\Delta t_j = 1/(1 - a_{ij})$, from which you can see that, if a_{ij} is pretty close to 1, even small changes in the tariff on the final good will have a strongly magnified effect on the effective rate of protection. The sensitivity of the effective rate of protection to the tariff rate on the input is not as great, but is of opposite sign to the consequence of a change in the rate on the final good: $\Delta g_j/\Delta t_i = -a_{ij}(1 - a_{ij})$. The effective rate can be quite sensitive to variations in the cost share of the intermediate good, but it can be of either sign, depending on whether the nominal rate on the final good or the input is higher: $\Delta g_j/\Delta a_{ij} = (t_j - t_i)/(1 - a_{ij})^2$. If the tariff on the final good is higher than that on the input, greater effective protection would be afforded to final goods with larger cost shares of intermediate goods, but the reverse is the case where the tariff on the input is higher than that on the final good.

We should distinguish between the rate of protection offered by a tariff and the protective effect of that tariff. The latter refers to the proportional domestic supply increase in response to a tariff, which depends on supply elasticities. The higher the supply elasticity in a particular industry, the greater will be the protective effect of any given rate of protection. On the other hand, if there is a zero supply elasticity—i.e., if the industry cannot respond with greater production to the higher domestic price—there is no supply effect.

In negotiations over tariffs, a country offering to reduce its tariff on imported intermediate goods without reducing the tariffs on final goods using that good is simply offering to get a higher effective rate of protection for its final goods industries. It will get lower domestic production of its intermediate good but more of the final good, with an ambiguous net effect on the total trade volume.

In a complex chain of production using goods produced in earlier stages as inputs in subsequent stages, the nominal tariff rates must rise as we move from the lower-order products to the higher-order ones, just to keep the effective rates of protection constant above the basic stage. Nevertheless, in such an escalating tariff schedule, the effective rates will be higher than the nominal rates.

The concept of effective protection does not extend easily from individual industries to a full, general-equilibrium setting, with the following example taken from Michaely (1972, 126–128). There is no assurance that industries will expand in proportion to their rates of effective protection, or to changes therein. Consider an example of an economy with four industries, A, B, C, and D, with effective protection highest in A and lowest in D. Suppose that A and B have about the same factor intensities, which are much different from those in C and D, and that A is much more highly protected than is B. As A expands, the prices of its intensive factors rise, raising B's costs considerably. But factors used intensively in C may fall in price, reducing C's production cost. So industry C expands and B contracts. In alternative terms, the cross-elasticities of supply across industries are high among industries that use the same factors intensively. In fact, we can't even say that the industry with the highest effective protection will expand. Industry B might be large, have an effective rate of protection close to that of A, and may use in nearly fixed proportion a factor used intensively in A. Expansion of B raises A's costs by more than the difference in effective protection, so A contracts and B expands. This indeterminacy in the relationship between effective protection and industry expansion results from the multi-good characteristics of this case. Even with no intermediate goods, in which case effective rates would be nominal rates, this kind of inclusiveness about the relationship between protection and output expansion will occur.

3.6.3 Customs Unions

The theory of customs unions can be used to think about some of the economic impacts of the territorial expansion of the ancient empires—the Egyptian, Assyrian, Roman, even some of the Athenian leagues—on production in, and trade between, their various regions and lands remaining outside the imperial borders. It is easy to agree that elements of coercion existed in these expansions that is outside the relationships of the typical customs union, but it probably is equally simplistic to view the economic administration of incorporated territories as having been one of mining the local inhabitants for the benefit of the conquering emperor's household. Indeed, the tribute paid by the Phoenician city states to the Assyrian empire in the 8th and 7th centuries have been viewed by some scholars as containing a large measure of benefit taxes paid for Assyrian maintenance of freer and safer trading opportunities under Assyrian tutelage (Aubet 1993, 70–74). So while the coercion involved in imperial expansion does not parallel the generally peaceful negotiations involved in establishing or joining a customs union, the structure of economic consequences of joining a larger administrative unit has common elements. The commercial relations within and between the lands of the Hellenistic empires of the descendants of Alexander's generals—the Ptolemaic and Seleucid in particular—could be interesting to examine as possible instances of customs unions interacting with other countries or even other customs unions. And similarly for trade relations within and between the Roman Empire and the Parthian Empire and its Sassanid successor.

A customs union is one type of geographic discrimination in trade. The loosest form of geographic discrimination is an agreement between two or more countries for partial exemption from tariffs on their imports from one another. A stronger form is the free-trade area, which involves complete elimination of tariffs among members. The customs union is a yet stronger form, involving complete elimination of tariffs between members, the establishment of a uniform tariff on imports from outside the union, and the apportionment of customs revenue among the members in some agreed formula. A common market adds free movement of factors among countries to unrestricted trade in goods. The customs union has been the form of regional economic integration most studied. Because the first-best policy for any group of countries would be complete elimination of their tariffs (with the exception of the optimal tariffs for large countries), the theory of customs unions is another application of second-best theory, combining elements of free trade with other elements of greater protection.

The simplest model of a customs union is more complicated than the usual trade model since it has to include at least three countries: the two that form the customs union and the one that remains outside it, commonly called ROW (the rest of the world). The two countries forming the customs union eliminate all tariffs on imports from each other (and any export taxes or subsidies if those exist) and impose a uniform set of tariffs on imports from the third country. The standard treatment of the problem studies the welfare of just one of the countries forming the customs union, called the home country. Two principal sets of forces result and affect the union countries—trade creation and trade diversion. Additionally, terms of trade may change between the two countries joining the union and between the union and the non-partner country.

When the partner countries eliminate tariffs on imports from each other, both countries shift from consumption of higher-cost domestic goods to consumption of lower-cost imports from the other partner. This is the trade-creation effect of a customs union. There are two aspects of trade creation. First, domestic production of goods identical to those the partner country produces more cheaply is reduced or eliminated and replaced by imports; this is called the production effect. Second, each country's consumers increase their consumption of partner-country substitutes for goods formerly domestically produced, called the consumption effect. Two types of gain are involved: a saving on the real cost of goods previously produced domestically and a gain in consumer's surplus from substitution of lower-cost goods for higher-cost ones.

For the trade diversion of a customs union, eliminating tariffs on the partner country's imports but not on other countries' encourages the shifting of imports from lower-cost foreign producers to higher-cost producers in the customs-union partner. Cost is defined, of course, in terms of prices facing domestic consumers, so what appears to be the lower-cost good coming from the partner may look so only because there is a tariff on the foreign good. As with the trade creation effect, there are two components to trade diversion. First there is (or at least may be) an increase in the cost of identical goods due to the shift from foreign to partner producers. Second, there is the substitution of higher-cost partner goods for non-identical, lower-cost foreign goods, but considering the post-tariff price differences, the goods can satisfy the same final demands. The loss entails the difference in cost between the import sources times the amount of trade so diverted. If the partner's supply curves rise sharply, the home country's losses from trade diversion are greater. The diversion of trade away from the foreign country will reduce its terms of trade with both the customs union members, and the associated gain on any remaining trade with the foreign country will offset to some extent the losses of trade diversion.

One of the lessons of customs union theory is that there are very few highly general predictions about gains and losses—i.e., we have to know many of the specifics of the countries involved; we can't simply make assessments on "easy" indicators such as relative factor intensities alone. Nonetheless, there are some rules of thumb on some indicators such that gains are more or less likely under certain circumstances, "other circumstances being equal," of course, the following summary deriving from Johnson (1962, 57–58) and Michaely (1977, 197–200). The home country is more likely to gain from trade creation of a customs union the higher the initial level of its tariffs, as the trade creation effect will be stronger and the trade diversion effect weaker; there probably will be a stronger consumption effect as well, which is always positive. It is also more likely to gain the more elastic are the domestic demand for goods the partner can supply and the partner's supply of those goods. It's less likely to lose from trade diversion, or likely to lose less, the smaller the initial cost differences between the customs union partner and the other foreign country (or countries) in goods they both produce; and the more elastic is the partner country's supply of these goods and the less elastic is the foreign country's supply of them. A lower degree of substitutability in consumption between different goods coming from the partner and foreign countries also will lessen losses from trade diversion. However, the stronger are substitution effects in consumption in general, the more consumption gains each country will experience from changes in relative prices between formerly domestically produced goods and more cheaply produced goods from the partner. The home country is more likely to gain from terms-of-trade changes vis-à-vis the foreign country the more elastic is the foreign supply of imports and the more inelastic the foreign demand for its own exports. The loss from trade diversion will be smaller the lower is the tariff on foreign products after the formation of the customs union relative to what it was before. A country is more likely to gain from joining a customs union the more it and its partner(s) are similar in the products they produce but different in the pattern of relative production costs. If both union members produce products with high income elasticities of demand, both will gain more as incomes rise. Member countries will gain more the more different they are from the rest of the world, because of smaller trade diversion losses.

3.7 The Multinational Enterprise and Foreign Investment

Contemporary theory about the multinational firm focuses its attention on firms with overseas production facilities—manufacturing plants—leaving the analysis of internationally diversified service firms such as banks and export-import firms to the margins. Some, possibly many, depending on time and place, firms in antiquity owned production facilities in more than one country. A Roman terra sigillata manufacturer, Cnaius Ateius, is thought to have owned workshops in both Italy and Gaul in the Augustan period, and certainly he was not the only multinational at the time, in this industry or others (Greene 1986, 160). On the basis of artifacts found around Ialysos on Rhodes and Knossos on Crete, and on Kos, J. N. Coldstream has suggested Phoenician unguent factories may have operated in those centers in the 9th–8th centuries B.C.E. (Coldstream 1969, 2; 1979, 261–262; 1982, 268–269; 1986, 324).[35] However, such a restriction to production firms in the treatment of multinational enterprise here would omit the equally interesting and important Old Assyrian trading colonies identified in cuneiform tablets at various sites in Anatolia—the kārum Kanesh at Kültepe in central Anatolia being the earliest known, but also at Alishar, Bogazköy—ancient Hattuša—Karahüyük, and Acemhüyuk (Larsen 1987, 2010; Postgate, 1992, 211–216; Veenhof 1995; Kuhrt 1998). Accordingly our treatment will cover economic motivations and constraints facing pure trading firms as well as producers.

We can define a multinational enterprise (MNE) as a firm that controls and manages production facilities (plants) in two or more countries, and still find room for the pure trading firms of the Old Assyrians. Just what constitutes "control" is a matter of judgment, but contemporary theory focuses on ownership of a sufficient proportion of a firm for a "parent" company's views on operation to command attention. If most such firms in antiquity were owned by a single firm (possibly by a single family), ownership shares may not have been a particularly important matter empirically. Having suggested such simplicity in antiquity, Veenhof (1995, 868–869) offers details of the structure of investments in the Assyrian trading operations at kārum Kanesh which indicate the variability of ownership and capital contribution structures.

Multinational operations of a firm are a topic in the organization of industry because the decisions leading to multinationalism are internal to a firm and depend on technical characteristics of production within particular industries. The concept of internalizing transaction costs, from industrial organization theory, offers explanations

[35] Jones (1993) discusses some economic implications of Coldstream's suggestion.

for several types of motivation for overseas investment. Multinationalism is evidence of an industrial structure other than perfect competition, and the models of monopolistic competition-cum-product diversification and oligopoly have proven useful in offering explanations of the industrial pattern of multinationalism (i.e., which industries tend to generate multinationals).

Going multinational involves making a foreign investment, which itself is a special case of international capital flows. In the treatment of trade so far, we've restricted our purview to trade in goods. Creating a multinational production operation is not the only method of trading capital internationally, so we'll look at trade in capital somewhat more broadly than would be necessary only to deal with the creation and growth of multinational enterprises.

3.7.1 The Perspective of the Individual Firm

It's useful to consider the multinational firm as a special case of the multi-plant firm, which for our purposes can be subdivided into three types: the horizontally integrated firm, the vertically integrated firm, and the diversified firm. The separate plants of a horizontally integrated firm produce the same goods in different locations. In a vertically integrated firm, some plants produce outputs that are inputs to other plants the firm operates. The subsidiaries or plants of a diversified firm have no systematic, horizontal or vertical relationship to one another.

For a firm to own and operate horizontally integrated plants outside its home country requires first the existence of locational forces justifying dispersing world production of the product outside the home country. These could be high transportation costs relative to fixed costs in an individual plant. Given such a dispersion, there has to be a transaction-cost advantage to placing these plants under a common administrative control, or they would emerge under separate, domestic ownership. These advantages derive in part from easier logistical coordination but generally more importantly from nonproduction activities that are complementary between different units of the same firm, in the sense that the same activities can benefit more than a single plant. The sources of these activities are nontangible, proprietary assets—special types of knowledge the firm possesses, knowledge that would be virtually impossible to sell and which would be equally difficult to contract to lease to another producer. Some examples of such proprietary assets are the knowledge of how to produce more cheaply, or to make a better product, at a set of prices faced by many other producers as well; or the ability to differentiate one's products stylistically in a way that increases the demand for them above the close substitutes provided by rival producers. Some of these assets may be specific to repeated transactions in a long-term, semi-contractual relationship between a firm and specific clients or customers. A firm can use assets such as these but could not sell or contract upon them. Horizontal integration internalizes the market for proprietary assets.

The motivation for vertical integration of a firm, within even a single country need not involve such proprietary assets. Instead, firms engaged in multi-stage production face the negotiation and monitoring of potentially intricate contracts for delivery of outputs and inputs. In circumstances that make these costs especially high, vertical integration becomes attractive for its cost saving, with its conversion of arms-length, market transactions to internal, administrative allocations. Different stages of production by a vertically integrated firm may be restricted to foreign countries because location-specific resources, such as minerals, are central to certain stages.

A generally diversified multinational firm probably is diversifying its portfolio of earning assets among both different industrial sectors and different countries, with both margins contributing to diversification. Just as some industries prosper when others struggle, the levels of activities in different countries may have little correlation with one another.

An individual firm faces a choice between exporting, licensing a foreign firm to make its products overseas, and making a direct investment in a plant overseas ("foreign direct investment"). The ancient counterpart of contemporary licensing may not have been a sufficiently developed legal concept for us to consider licensing as a viable option in antiquity. A firm facing downward-sloping demands for its product in its home and a foreign market, and whose production costs in either country depend on how much it produces locally, will have an optimal combination of exports from home and local production in supplying an overseas market. Tariffs in the foreign country can shift the optimal combination more toward foreign investment in local production. In general, high tariffs in the countries to which home country firms otherwise would export increase the attractiveness of opening local production facilities, and indeed one of the purposes of tariffs can be to encourage such capital inflows. Additionally, some markets and some products may simply be more difficult to serve from abroad, and a local production presence facilitates both tuning and peddling the product.

Economies of scale in production discourage multiplant operations and hence the formation of multinational firms. High transportation costs erode such single-plant advantages and can encourage overseas production at the expense of local production and exporting.

Although it makes intuitive sense, it can be difficult empirically to establish the case that a firm produces outside its home country to take advantage of lower production costs. When a firm that becomes a MNE possesses proprietary assets that let it transfer cost advantages the home country enjoys to foreign operations, observations may appear to indicate that MNEs are not particularly sensitive to host-country cost conditions.

Empirically, contemporary multinationals have been conservative in their movements and expansions overseas, in the sense that the first moves are to geographical neighbors, and to countries with common language and cultural traditions, all of which reduce transactions costs of conducting business in a foreign environment and communication and coordination costs between the parent and the foreign subsidiary. Frequently, firms have exported to a foreign country prior to making direct investments in it. Subsequent moves may reduce geographical and cultural distance.

A firm faces uncertainties in operations abroad that it may not face at home. In the immediate term, a producer will want to be able to repatriate its foreign earnings. While reinvestment of some retained earnings in an overseas facility may be in the strategic plan, the principal motivation of residents of some home country to invest overseas is to be able to profit at home, so the earnings on the investment must come home.[36] A country that imposes strict controls on capital exports will find difficulty in attracting investments from overseas. In the longer term, the security of ownership of the assets invested overseas will be a concern, although it may be possible to let them run down through lack of maintenance should ownership become jeopardized through, say, nationalization or increased taxation or royalties.

3.7.2 Multinationals from the Perspective of an Entire Economy

At the level of entire countries, we can ask questions about what characteristics of countries will make them senders (owners) or recipients (hosts) of multinational firms, as well as what kinds of activities—i.e., which industries—are most likely to be represented among multinationals. As we've found in our earlier discussion of the different models of trade, different models can give us different answers, which may turn out, on closer inspection, to be alternative insights rather than a multiplicity of answers, most of which have to be "wrong." The specific factors model starts with the circumstance that some types of capital are specific to firms in different industries—in addition to the proprietary, intangible assets to which horizontally integrated firms owe their expansion. The specific factors model predicts an international "cross-hauling" of direct investment, with Country A establishing foreign subsidiaries in some industries in Country B and Country B in turn establishing some foreign subsidiaries in Country A in other industries.

Helpman and Krugman have used their monopolistic-competition modification of the Heckscher-Ohlin model to study the phenomenon of the multinational enterprise by specifying the intermediate production of "proprietary assets," produced only with capital equipment (an unnecessary assumption, strictly speaking, but certainly one that simplifies analysis). Once produced, this proprietary asset can direct the production of final goods at home or abroad. However, in a two-country setting, one of the countries will possess a comparative advantage in the production of the intermediate, proprietary asset and thus will be the only country to send multinationals abroad. This view focuses on the insight that the comparative advantage concept applies to production of such goods as intangible capital that helps firms direct operations from afar, as well as to final consumption goods and tangible and tradable intermediates such as equipment.

The sectors of an economy that attract foreign direct investment will be those in which proprietary assets are common and external contracting is difficult. These characteristics may be related to either technological complexity of production processes or, even more likely, to organizational technology. Either way, perfectly competitive sectors of an economy are unlike to find such proprietary assets worth the cost of developing since the resulting products would be virtually indistinguishable from those of other producers who didn't invest in such assets.

In ancient times, lengthy lags between outlays for inputs and receipts from sales could have required intricate procedures to ensure honesty and sufficient care to keep track of various obligations. Family ties may have supplied an essential component of such intangible assets. The lag between production and revenue could have been a prime motivator for the multinational status of the Old Assyrian trading firms, but whether it would have been a sufficient condition, rather than just a necessary one, needs further consideration. The case of Coldstream's proposed Phoenician unguent factories might have proprietary assets in the recipes, but the recipes themselves could have been susceptible to relatively easy "reverse engineering," and without the more general trading business as a conduit for repatriating earnings in an economy not highly monetized, other conditions for successful multinational activity may not have been satisfied.

A simple, capital-arbitrage view of the multinational enterprise would be supported by the observations that direct investment flowed from capital-rich (high-income) countries to capital-poor (low-income) ones, but this has not been the case in the past half-century. Empirically, high-income countries are net exporters of direct investment, but the net importers have been middle-income rather than low-income countries. The volume of net direct investment outflows from a country drops off rather sharply as per capita income falls. There is considerable two-way flow in direct investment between high-income countries, and generally between countries with similar levels of

[36] If foreign nationals are employed in the operation of the overseas plant, their earnings will stay in the foreign country, mitigated somewhat by the employees' propensity to spend some of their earnings on imports themselves.

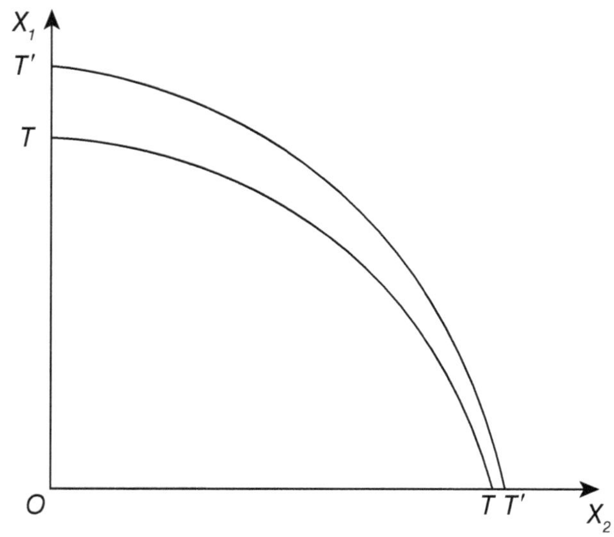

Figure 3.37. Effect of foreign investment on the receiving country's transformation frontier.

labor skills, which also undermines a capital-arbitrage explanation of foreign direct investment.

3.7.3 Foreign Investment and International Capital Flows

Foreign investment (or domestic, for that matter) can be divided into two categories, portfolio and direct. In making a portfolio investment, an investor may either purchase such a small share of a project (or a firm) that having any influence on the operations of the project is out of the question, or simply make a loan to a private party or to a government. (A bond is just a formalized loan.) Direct investments involve the investor in the managerial control and operation of the project. These are the sorts of investments that create multinational firms. It is not entirely out of the question that wealthy individuals or families may have made portfolio investments across what could be called national borders in antiquity, either to individuals or governments (or royal families), despite the absence of what reasonably might be called an international capital market.

Earnings differentials for capital in different countries are the motivation for international capital flows—both loans and direct investments. Our analysis of the Heckscher-Ohlin model showed the restrictiveness of the conditions for trade to equalize factor prices. Direct movements of factors can assist the equalization, or such tendency, of factor prices across countries. In doing so, factor movements may substitute for trade, or it may foster production in recipient countries in such a fashion that the trade in factors is complementary to trade in goods—i.e., actually increases trade. Foreign investment will expand the transformation frontier of the country receiving it, as shown in Figure 3.37 in the shift from transformation frontier TT to T′T′. Industry 1 is the capital-intensive industry in the receiving country.

When we speak of international capital flows, we are excluding the shipment of capital equipment, which we would include under trade in intermediate goods. Capital flows in this sub-section refer to financial capital—loans from people in one country to people in another. When financial capital rather than capital equipment moves internationally, two issues arise particular to that type of capital flow. First, in the case of loans, the recipient must pay the interest and, eventually, the principal; both sets of payments require the borrowing country eventually to produce more than it consumes by the amounts of these two payments. That is, it must run a trade surplus—export more than it imports—at some time in the future. Second, in the case of either a loan or an unrequited transfer of funds, turning the financial capital—either money or other financial instruments—into additional production and consumption in the receiving country, is known as the issue of "transferring" real purchasing power. This is a somewhat more intricate issue, and we devote a separate sub-section to the "transfer problem."

3.7.4 The "Transfer Problem"

The issue of "transfer" arises in all situations in which people in one country try to transfer purchasing power, rather than goods directly, to people in another country, either as a loan or as an unrequited transfer. The classic example, which in fact brought the subject to economists' attention, is the German reparations payments following World War I, which had devasting effects on the German economy. To "effect" the transfer, the sending country has to generate an export surplus equal to the value of the transfer. Stated equivalently, its consumption has to fall below its production by the amount of the transfer.

To work through the mechanics of how this happens, let's suppose Country A makes a gift to Country B—it could be an act of tribute such as occurred not infrequently in the Mediterranean region in antiquity. Each country produces two goods, say manufactures and food; A exports manufactures and B exports food. Country A's income falls immediately by the amount of the transfer, which we'll call T, and Country B's income rises by T. A's demand for imports of B's food falls by the amount mT, where m is A's marginal propensity to import (at unchanged prices, the income elasticity of demand for the food good in Country A). B's demand for A's manufactured exports rises by the amount m*T, where m* is B's marginal propensity to import. Both changes contribute to an increase in the net amount of manufactures A ships to B, and both contribute to a trade surplus of Country A—a surplus of exports over imports. The question remains whether (m + m*)T exceeds, equals, or falls short of the amount to be transferred, T. If m + m* > 1, A's trade surplus will be more than large enough to effect the transfer, and to bring the surplus back into equality with the required transfer, Country A's terms of trade must improve, reducing the quantity of real goods necessary to effect the value of consumption or purchasing power to be transferred. If m + m* < 1, A's terms of trade

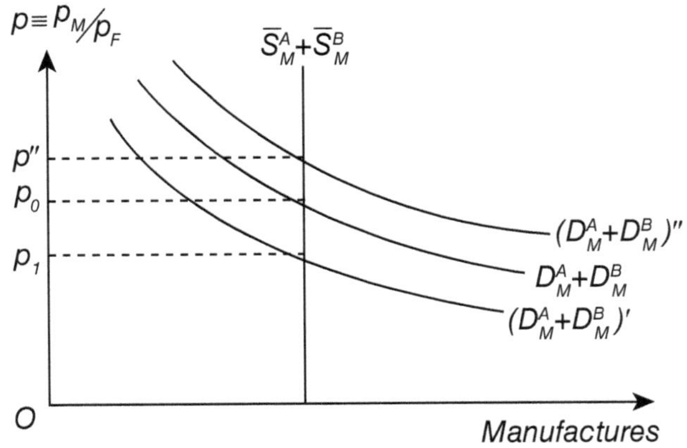

Figure 3.38. The transfer problem.

will deteriorate, and the country will face a secondary burden of effecting the transfer in the form of a further loss of income associated with the reduction in the value of its export good.

We can view the transfer process and any associated change in the terms of trade involved from a different perspective, shown in Figure 3.38. The world supply of manufactures—the sum of both countries' outputs ($\bar{S}^A_M + \bar{S}^B_M$)—is unaffected by the transfer, but Country A's demand for manufactures falls because of the reduction in its income and Country B's rises because of its increase in income. If the increase in the demand for manufactures coming from A exactly offsets the decrease in demand for manufactures coming from B, the total world demand ($D^A_M + D^B_M$) will be unchanged by the transfer and the world price of manufactures—in terms of food—will be unchanged: Country A's terms of trade are unaffected by the transfer, and the world relative price stays at p_0. If the total world demand for manufactures falls because country B's demand for manufactures doesn't rise by as much as Country A's falls ($-\Delta D^A_M + \Delta D^B_M)'$, Country A's terms of trade deteriorate, and there is a secondary burden of the transfer. And vice versa: if B's increase in demand for manufactures exceeds A's reduction, the world demand for manufactures rises, and Country A's terms of trade improve: the sum of the two countries' demand curves shifts to $(D^A_M + D^B_M)''$. Effecting the transfer requires a smaller sacrifice in consumption than the ex ante face value of the transfer would suggest. The same mechanisms operate to transfer a loan of purchasing power as an unrequited transfer such as a gift or tribute.

We can work through these mechanics with an example familiar from the ancient Near East. When Assyria demanded tribute of some of the Phoenician cities during the middle centuries of the 1st millennium B.C.E. (Katzenstein 1973, 162–166), if the tribute took the form of silver rather than consumption or producer goods, the Assyrians had to convert the silver into something directly useful. If the silver took the form of bullion, or even if it took the form of relatively fine coins that were widely acceptable in the countries with which the Assyrians traded, the Assyrians could have spent the silver anywhere, not only in the territory of the Phoenician city paying the tribute. To *effect* the transfer, some consumers outside Assyria would have had to forego consumption in the amount of the transfer (roughly speaking; more on this subsequently) in order to trade goods for the silver. If the tribute commodity had been acceptable only in Phoenicia (more like contemporary fiat currencies rather than a commodity currency in a widely acceptable, precious metal), the Assyrians would not have had to spend the full value of the transfer back in the Phoenician city state, although the Phoenicians still would have had to effect the full amount of the transfer, just not all directly to Assyria. The Assyrians would have spent the tribute in roughly the proportion they would have spent any increment to their national income, part on domestic goods and part on imports from the Phoenician city as well as other trading partners, but again, the additional domestic purchases with the tribute would have squeezed out other purchasers who would have had to seek consumption from overseas, with those funds eventually finding their way back to buy Phoenician goods. The Phoenician income would have been cut back by the amount of the transfer, with the reduction coming partly out of their exportable goods and partly out of nontradables and importables. If the incremental Assyrian demand, out of the transfer, for the Phoenician exportable were smaller than the reduction in Phoenician demand for it, the total demand for that good would have fallen, and the Phoenician terms of trade would have fallen, adding to the real burden of making the transfer. If the reverse had been the case and the Phoenician city's terms of trade had risen as a result of the transfer, the total cost of making the transfer would have been less than its "face value."

Readers may recognize the subject of Hopkins' (1980; 1995/96, reprinted as 2002) precocious article on taxes and trade in the Roman Empire as a case of the transfer problem, although his initial characterization of the subject as taxation stimulating trade may have seemed counter-intuitive. Nonetheless, the mechanisms he discusses are indeed those involved in the transfer problem: converting non-consumable capital imports into consumable items, and the production required to implement that conversion. Hopkins did not address terms-of-trade changes and possible secondary burdens. And Hopkins is correct that capital transfers in kind, such as direct export of a consumable like wheat, avoids the necessity of the sending country increasing production to go along with the capital transfer (1980, 103). Von Freyberg (1989, 180–182) explicitly recognizes the issue as a balance-of-payments and transfer problem and uses a simple, 3-equation, Keynesian international macroeconomic model to demonstrate the balancing of international accounts involved in such capital transfers in his assessment of the effects of these taxes on provincial and Italian production in the Principate.[37]

[37] Von Freyberg's model has three equations: changes in income (production) in Italy and the provinces and the trade balance (181). He appears to solve the system of equations with Cramer's Rule, and in the solution, the change in provincial and Italian income are positively

3.8 Exchange Rates and the Balance of Payments

It's natural to consider the behavior of exchange rates and the balance of payments as elements of a simultaneously determined system, although the behavior of both depend on the institutional arrangements surrounding the international valuation of national currencies. Section 3.8.1 characterizes the relationships between international money valuation arrangements on the one hand and the behavior of exchange rates and trade balances on the other. Section 3.8.2 describes the accounting system for international transactions from which balance of payments concepts emerge. Three different views of the trade balance are shown in Section 3.8.3, emphasizing different aspects of trade imbalances. Section 3.8.4 introduces a model of the relationship between national price levels and the exchange rates between national currencies, known as purchasing power parity. This relationship is central in the explanation of the international distribution of a monetary gold stock, explained in Section 3.8.5, which unites the determination of exchange rates, trade balances, and national price levels under institutional conditions characterizing most of the economies of the ancient Mediterranean region.

3.8.1 Exchange Rates and Exchange Rate Regimes

An exchange rate is the price of one currency in terms of another: dollars per Deutschmark, drachmas per sestertius. Commonly the currencies are those of different countries, issued or minted by different monetary authorities, but if different currencies are issued within a single country the relative prices of those currencies are called domestic exchange rates. If a monetary authority uses a bimetallic currency system, minting, say, silver and gold coins, the exchange rate between the two currencies will depend on the non-coinage values of the metals, with the specific rates of exchange between individual coin denominations depending also on the metallic weights of the denominations. If the monetary authority attempts to declare a particular rate of exchange between the currencies that is different from their relative values in nonmonetary uses, the coins minted in the overvalued metal will be melted down, thus disappearing from circulation in a process known as Gresham's Law ("cheap money drives out dear").

Generally the value of one currency in terms of another depends on the demands for the different moneys—the same demands for money we discussed in Chapter 9: $(M/P)^d = L(p_i, i, Y)$, in which M is the nominal quantity of money, P is the price level, p_i is an array of prices of individual goods, i is "the" interest rate, and Y is income (see Jones 2014, Chapter 9 on the demand for money). The foreign demand for a home country's currency depends on the options for using that currency: buying foreign goods and investing in foreign securities (loaning to foreigners), both of which must be purchased in that country's currency. This source of demand provides the link between a country's exchange rate and its balance of payments.

A monetary authority can fix the domestic value of its currency according to some external standard, possibly a particular precious metal or some other country's currency, or let its value float freely in foreign markets. Countries can reach elaborate international agreements on how they will value their currencies, but such agreements are not necessary to provide for the determination of international values for domestic currencies. If a country fixes the value of its currency relative to the currencies of other countries in what is called a fixed exchange rate regime, it must be prepared to buy and sell its own currency to maintain its market value within close limits around the announced parity rates. For such a regime to operate successfully for any length of time, all the countries whose exchange rates are fixed in terms of other countries' currencies must cooperate to maintain the entire array of relative currency values. Under fixed rate regimes, countries' net exports (frequently called "the" balance of payments) will be positive or negative according to the excess demand for their currencies. If countries do not commit themselves to defending particular exchange rates for their currencies, we have a flexible, or floating, exchange rate system, in which the values of national currencies adjust to eliminate the excess demands for the moneys of different countries. These excess demands for money are equivalent to excess demands for imports, and the equilibration of the market for moneys (equating demands with supplies) will equalize the values of imports and exports for each country, leaving "the" balance of payments (but note that we haven't defined the balance of payments yet; we're still speaking relatively colloquially) balanced, or zero.

This relationship between exchange rate regime and the trade balance introduces the dual relationship between exchange rate determination and balance of payments equilibrium—if the former are fixed, and thus unable to equilibrate markets, the latter must adjust to equilibrate international transactions; if the former are flexible, the latter stays at zero, exactly "balanced," that is. Having defined what foreign exchange rates are and related them to the quantities of international goods movements, we turn to further explanation of the balance of payments.

Virtually all of the monetized or near-monetized economies of the ancient Mediterranean region relied upon precious metal currencies—gold and silver coins, with the odd electrum and bronze tokens for local use, although they do seem to have had an indeterminate expansive capacity through loans. Despite differences in coin weights and fineness, the coins of different countries were tied to a single standard by virtue of their metal content: in international

and negatively, respectively, related to the capital movement (182). It is surprising that von Freyberg's book has received no more attention in the subsequent literature than it has: Andreau's (1992) *Gnomon* review, which was generally favorable, and his more extensive discussion of the work in (1994). In the latter paper, Andreau accepts von Freyberg's application of economic models to an ancient economy as simply applications of logic, while disagreeing on several empirical points. Beyond Andreau's detailed attention, the volume has attracted nothing beyond the occasional citation of its existence.

exchange the coins traded gold against gold or silver against silver in what were effectively fixed exchange rates. The occasional meeting of gold coins with silver introduced media of different value, but generally fixed in relation to one another, mining costs being the ultimate determinant of the exchange ratio. Bonanza discoveries of either metal, which would change the ratio of world stocks could change the relative market value, but otherwise the only force encouraging relative price changes would have been nonmonetary demands for the two metals, which would generally lead to disappearance of the coins of one of the metals. At times and places where gold and silver coins met and found official mint valuations much different from nonmonetary values, either the overvalued coin would disappear from circulation or its monetary authority would reduce its weight. Characterizing these monetary arrangements as cases of flexible exchange rates is not likely to be particularly useful. In flexible exchange rate regimes, the values of currencies—generally fiat currencies with near-costless issue—relative to one another are reassessed continually according to the values of the transactions that can be conducted with them and their relative supplies—generally by the operation of the laws of supply and demand. In a gold coin-silver coin regime, the revaluations ordinarily would be few and far between. Consequently I will have little to say about flexible exchange rates, except for a short comparison of some of their properties with those of fixed rate arrangements, at the very least to see what these ancient economies either missed or avoided through their essentially default choices of exchange rate regimes.

With flexible exchange rate systems of currency valuation, individual countries' price levels are independent of one another, and a monetary authority can control the magnitude of its country's nominal money supply, the value of the currency adjusting rather than the quantity of money. The domestic price level and the exchange rate move together (i.e., the international value of the currency moves in opposite direction to the price level). While mistaken policies of the monetary authority in a flexible rate regime are contained by and large within the country rather than being dissipated abroad, a country on flexible rates correspondingly is insulated from monetary events abroad. With fixed rates, countries are vulnerable to monetary disturbances originating abroad, their price levels uncontrollable by the domestic monetary authority. Real disturbances such as changes in employment also are passed on more easily from country to country under fixed rates, even though at this distance in time it is difficult for us to see and assess periodic changes in unemployment in these ancient economies. On the other hand, fixed rate systems offer considerable stability of "forward exchange"—the value of foreign exchange in the future, which is invaluable to merchants who routinely accept liabilities with future maturities, particularly when overseas transportation is slow. Traders can "cover" future transactions by buying and selling forward exchange to parallel their transactions, reducing or eliminating exchange-rate risk by combining each future purchase of foreign exchange with an offsetting sale, and vice versa. These transactions reduce international trading risk, but they cost real resources that can be used for other purposes under a fixed rate regime. Under fixed rates, the value of foreign exchange tomorrow can be expected with high probability to be what it is today.[38] Additionally, flexible exchange rate systems can impose large changes in real income on people as exchange rates fluctuate to adjust trade volumes. These effects are larger the higher the proportion of tradable goods in an economy; a nearly closed economy—one with a very small share of national income traded or tradable—would find flexible exchange rates beneficial on that score. Both types of exchange rate system confer benefits and impose costs on countries, and it is useful to recognize the array of such benefits and costs that ancient monetary technologies imposed on those economies.

3.8.2 The Balance of Payments Accounts

The balance of payments is a summary, double-entry accounting statement of all the economic transactions between residents of one country and the rest of the world over some given time period, usually one year. Because balance of payments statements use double-entry bookkeeping, the entries are always balanced when taken as a whole: total credits equal total debits. Each transaction—not necessarily sales or receipts—has a corresponding credit and debit entry. Credits arise from exports, and debits from imports. A credit is a transaction that ordinarily, but not necessarily, calls for a payment, sooner or later, by foreigners to residents of the home country. People on either end of a transaction may default, and some gifts may be unilateral but both still need to be accounted for.

Typically a balance of payments account is divided into a current account, unilateral transfers, a capital account, and according to the type of international payments regime, a set of balancing items. The entries in the current account represent transactions involving current-period income: the merchandise and services accounts, the transportation account, tourist expenditures, military and other government expenditures overseas, and current income from capital such as interest, fees, and royalties. Unilateral transfers can be government-to-government transactions such as reparations, tribute or various types of emergency assistance; or private transfers such as earnings remitted by immigrants or emigrants or outright gifts such as envisaged in some interpretations of the gift exchange model. The capital account records increases in assets or reductions in liabilities of home country residents through direct and portfolio foreign investment. We discussed direct foreign investment in section 9, but we have not addressed foreign portfolio investment, the purchase of

[38] The relative values of silver and gold currencies are subject to discoveries of new supplies of either. Harl (1996, 79) cites Heliodorus's report from Hermopolis in Egypt early in the 2nd century C.E. that the price of gold bullion in Alexandria dropped by 25% shortly after royal treasuries plundered during the Second Dacian War added their supplies to the monetary gold stock.

foreign securities or other debts by home country residents. Despite the contemporary importance of foreign portfolio investment, there seems to have been little international trade in debt instruments in antiquity, and that topic is simply omitted in this text. We mention it in the description of balance of payments accounts only for completeness and comparison with contemporary circumstances.

The credit and debit entries for a particular transaction need not both occur in the same component of accounts. For example, a credit in the merchandise account may be balanced by a debit in the capital account. The accounting of entries in the capital account can appear counterintuitive, and the trick to correct accounting of capital transactions is to keep one's eye on what moves. Thus in portfolio transactions, an import of foreign securities is called a capital export because liquid purchasing power is sent from the home country abroad; these capital exports are treated as debits because they involve an import of securities—the debt instrument or international "I.O.U." Securities are treated the same as goods in the merchandise account. If the home country's residents exported securities, these items would be accounted as credits just as would exports of grain, and money flows into the country from both transactions.

A unilateral gift of say, merchandise, is treated as a credit under merchandise exports and gets a fictional debit entry under the category of transactions called "unilateral transfers to foreigners."[39] As a result of such a gift, the home country's current account gets a boost, showing that, at least in this transaction, the country's current income exceeds its current consumption by the amount of this gift. The balancing entry occurs under a part of the overall accounts that receives less attention and that, in fact, obviates the need for a corresponding inflow of goods from foreigners in the capital account.

Government purchases of military supplies overseas are accounted as just as a merchandise import would be. If such purchases were the only change in a country's external accounts, and there were no capital asset other than money, it would have to be accompanied by a money export. This is exactly how millions of Roman denarii arrived in Asia Minor in the 1st and 2nd centuries C.E. (Harl 1996, 133). What happens to the money when it arrives overseas depends on the foreigners' demand for money. If they are able to absorb only some portion of the money inflow into their real balances (i.e., the inflow exceeds their demand for real balances), the remainder will flow back to the originating country to purchase that country's exports, leaving the initial purchase of the foreigners' food for the soldiers accomplished effectively with merchandise exports of the home country, along with some proportion of the original money outflow. We will see the principles governing these flows below.

[39] Bendall (2014) recognizes this distinction regarding a gift of perfume from Pylos to an Anatolian destination.

The balancing items of a balance of payments accounts include short-term official (government) capital movements and shipments of gold and other international reserves of a fractional reserve monetary system. These items gain importance under fiat currency systems and may have seen responses from the expansible, if non-fiat, monetary systems of the ancient Mediterranean. This does not mean that governments did not ship gold overseas in antiquity, but that such transactions would be accounted properly as capital account items rather than balancing items.

To characterize the type of economy found in the Mediterranean region in antiquity, let's consider the structure of an economy whose transactions involve merchandise (ranging from harness trappings to coal scuttles to grain and olive oil), services (ship repairs, medical treatment, and let's throw "tourist" expenditures and transportation charges in this account too, just to simplify), and money. Suppose for the moment that all the money is gold dust, to avoid the complications of different gold currencies or even of unstamped gold dumps which might have to be cut up for some transactions. Both domestically and internationally, people can exchange goods and services either directly for other goods or services or indirectly through exchanges of gold money for the goods and services. So we have only a current account and a capital account, which we can simplify to a money or gold account. For each country, a surplus on one of these accounts implies a deficit on the other. Balance on one account (a "surplus" equal to zero) implies balance on the other. At times and places where no money existed, and by extension, no more complex debt instruments used as a store of value existed to substitute for money, then only a current account would have existed, and trade would have been continually balanced.

3.8.3 Trade and the Balance of Payments

We can divide a country's current income (y) into three components, expenditures on consumption and investment (e), exports (x), and imports (i). The three add up to income: $y = e + x - i$. We can express a trade surplus, t, in three alternative but entirely equivalent ways. First, we can emphasize the difference between current income and current expenditure: $t = y - e$. Second, we can look directly at the difference between exports and imports: $t = x - i$. Finally, looking to the structure of our international accounts and recognizing that a discrepancy between exports and imports implies a corresponding change in gold money in the country, we can view the trade balance as a change in the quantity of money in the country, or a change in the country's money supply: $t = \Delta M$.

These three views represent the three principal theoretical approaches to understanding the behavior of a country's balance of payments, or more precisely, of its current account. The first view is called the expenditure or absorption approach—how much of its current income does a country "absorb" through its current expenditures? The second view focuses on a country's supply of exports and its demand for imports as the relative prices of those goods change. The changes in these two quantities can be related to one another via their respective price elasticities, hence the "elasticities approach" to the balance of payments (again, strictly speaking to the current account balance). The third view emphasizes the fact that the difference between what a country produces and what it spends both domestically and overseas is equivalent to an opposite change in the money balances its residents desire to hold. (Note that if there were no international trade, that is if $x = 0$ and $i = 0$, then $y - e = \Delta M$ and all changes in desired money holdings come out of differences between current income and domestic spending.) In this sense, all balance of payments surpluses and deficits are essentially monetary phenomena. Each view is equally correct. Each can be extended to the case in which capital assets other than money exist, with both domestic and international markets for those assets. The choice of analytical approach one would take depends simply on the aspects of the payments issues in which one is interested. To offer a simple framework for thinking of international flows of goods and money in antiquity, we will concentrate on the monetary approach below.

3.8.4 Purchasing Power Parity

Purchasing power parity (PPP) is a concept for relating the price levels in different countries to one another via the exchange rate between their currencies. Consider the case of two countries. Each country has a demand for real balances of its currency: $M = P\ell(\blacksquare)$ for the home country and $M^* = P^*\ell^*(\blacksquare^*)$, in which the asterisks denote the quantities specific to the foreign country; M is nominal money balances and P is the price level (M/P is real money balances); ℓ and ℓ^* represent the home and foreign demand functions for real money balances, and the $\blacksquare$ and $\blacksquare^*$ represent the arguments in those functions—interest rates, goods prices, income, and possibly other determinants. Purchasing power parity predicts that the exchange rate between the currencies of the two countries is proportional to their domestic price levels (although not necessarily equal to the ratio of those price levels): $E = kP/P^*$, which in turn is equal to the ratio of their nominal money supplies times the inverse of the ratio of their demands for real balances: $E = k(M/M^*)[\ell^*(\blacksquare^*)/\ell(\blacksquare)]$. The value of the k generally is not equal to 1 because the two index numbers for the price levels, P and P^*, will include nontraded or imperfectly traded goods, which would prevent equalization of the prices of identical goods in the two countries, and they may be constructed with different weights. The value of k depends on all the real factors underlying the international division of labor. The forces that influence k in the long term include technological changes, changes in factor supplies, and other forces that alter the productivity of real goods and services. In the short term, the value of k—think of the short-term value of k as $k^\dagger$—can be affected by the failure of prices denominated in local currencies to change quickly in response to economic forces (called "nominal rigidities" in the economic lexicon), but in the long term would return to (or at least towards) the underlying value of k.[40]

The purchasing power parity relationship should not be interpreted as a condition of international equilibrium imposed by arbitrage—the equalization of goods prices internationally by "buying low and selling high," but as a statement about the long-run neutrality of these economies to monetary disturbances. A monetary disturbance (say changes in demands for real balances or changes in nominal money supplies) that is neutral changes no relative prices of goods. Thus PPP predicts that any change in domestic prices must be accompanied by offsetting changes in the exchange rate so as to preserve the relative overall price of domestic goods in terms of foreign goods.

PPP doesn't imply that fluctuations in commodity prices *cause* exchange rate movements or vice versa. The association between exchange rates and price levels expressed in the relationship $E = kP/P^*$ occurs because both endogenous variables—the price level and the exchange rate—are jointly dependent on the money supply as expressed in the other relationship, $E = k(M/M^*)[\ell^*(\blacksquare^*)/\ell(\blacksquare)]$. Any apparent causation is only apparent. There is no route of effect from exchange rates to price levels or from price levels to exchange rates. Additionally, PPP does not require that exchange rates move strictly parallel to the ratios of price levels over time, because the real factors underlying k may change over time and the short-run level of $k^\dagger$ may depart from the underlying long-term value of k. PPP *does* maintain that changes in money supplies affect price levels and exchange rates in parallel fashion, but it does not exclude the possibility of other forces than money supplies acting on price levels and exchange rates.

3.8.5 Exchange Rates, the Balance of Payments, and the International Distribution of Gold Money

The use of precious metal currencies in the countries of the ancient Mediterranean effectively comprises something between a fixed exchange rate system, by virtue of the currencies of different countries having fixed metallic exchange rates in the short run, and a flexible rate system inasmuch as the supplies of these metals could change and alter their relative prices. That is, we should not analyze international economic relationships during the Third Century C.E. inflation in the Roman world (Harl, 1996, Chapter 6) as a case of inflation emanating from Rome in a system of flexible exchange rates simply because the cities of Asia Minor issued drachms while Rome issued denarii (ignoring the gold coinage for the moment) without checking for changes in the gold-silver relative

40 For an example of a nominal rigidity, suppose that the general price level changed, but merchants holding inventories of goods decided it cost more to re-price their inventory than it was worth. The nominal prices of these goods, held by these merchants, stay the same (are rigid) but their real prices—their nominal prices deflated by the new price level—change.

price. Both groups of mints used silver, which had a common international price (in terms of gold; in terms of goods as well, the latter comparison being more difficult to make empirically because of variations in characteristics of goods at different locations), so we are almost comparing silver with silver, except for the gold currency circulating alongside the silver at Rome.[41]

With fixed exchange rates, no country can control its own domestic money supply. It can issue as much as it wants, but the real balances its residents do not demand will simply flow overseas. With a gold coin currency, such additional issues of money would be represented by debasing the coinage or shrinking the size of coins of a constant denomination. The available money in the world flows to the locations where it is demanded, with attendant changes in price levels. We can show the mechanisms underlying these results with a model developed by Niehans (1984, 38–40, 49). In (very rough) keeping with the monetary systems of the ancient Mediterranean, suppose that each of two countries is on a gold specie standard—gold coins circulate as money. Ignore the possibility of adding to the world's gold stock through mining (or of augmenting the monetary gold stock by robbing gold in temples); the world gold stock is fixed at *G*. Also suppose that both countries have defined the gold content of their coins, and that the mints of both are ready to re-coin foreign currency into domestic currency at no charge (a simpler version of letting both coins circulate in both countries at fixed exchange rates determined by their metal contents). Under these conditions, there is a natural level of gold stocks in each country, and it is impossible to depart from these natural levels permanently by any policy or combination of policies.

Let the home and foreign gold prices (the gold contents of the respective coins) be p_G in the home country and p_G^* in the foreign country. Gold arbitrage (the ability to ship gold between countries if its value differs between countries[42]) keeps the exchange rate of these coins equal to the ratio of these two prices (i.e., to the ratio of gold contents of the coins): $E = p_G/p_G^*$. Fixed gold parities for these currencies imply fixed exchange rates.[43] In each country, the gold stock and the commodity price level must be such that the demand for money at predetermined relative commodity prices is satisfied. Using the price of wheat in each country, p_w and p_w^*, as the numeraire: $p_G G = M = p_w \ell(\pi)$ in the home country and $p_G^* G^* = M^* = p_w^* \ell^*(\pi^*)$ in the foreign country, in which π and π^* are the relative commodity prices in the two countries.[44]

Arbitrage in gold and commodities (wheat) results in the equalization of the ratio of gold to wheat prices in the two countries: $p_w/p_w^* = p_G/p_G^*$. It follows from the purchasing power parity relationship that $G/G^* = \ell(\pi)/\ell^*(\pi^*)$, which means that the division of the world gold stock between the two countries is entirely demand determined. It doesn't matter at all where the gold originated. The gold stocks stand in the same ratio as the demands for real money balances. That proportion, along with the total gold stock, then determines the absolute amount of gold and the commodity price level in each country.

Figure 3.39 shows this allocation of gold stocks in a four-quadrant diagram. In the northeast quadrant, the home country's price of wheat is measured on the vertical axis and its gold stock on the horizontal axis. The southwest axis places the foreign country's wheat price on the horizontal axis (measuring to the right from the origin of the graph) and its gold stock on the vertical axis, measured downward. The remaining two quadrants—southeast and northwest—plot the two countries' wheat prices and the distribution between them of fixed world gold stocks, respectively. The lines from the origin in the northeast and southwest quadrants show the demand for gold, derived from the demand for real money balances, as a function of the national price level measured in terms of wheat. The 45° line joining the gold-stock axes in the southeast quadrant lets us allocate the world gold stock between countries; the intercept of this line on each country's gold axis would assign the entire world's gold stock to that country. The line in the northwest quadrant traces out the relative price levels in the two countries, as determined by the relative gold prices, which is equivalent to the exchange rate, E.

The choice of gold prices in the two countries determines the exchange rate, in the northwest quadrant, which determines the ratio but not the levels of commodity prices in the two countries. Now if we go to the rays ℓ and ℓ^* in the northeast and southwest quadrants, we find the quantities of gold demanded in each country at each national price level. For any set of three lines, ℓ, ℓ^*, and p_G/p_G^*, there is only one point on the gold distribution line in the southeast quadrant consistent with points on each line, point A in Figure 3.45; stated alternatively, one and only one rectangle

[41] Comparing silver coinages of some countries with gold coinages of others would take us into a case where using a flexible exchange rate model would be appropriate if the growth of gold and silver supplies occurred through different rates of mining (or expropriation of private and temple hoards, as long as the takings were not restricted to a one-time event); or if the growth in demands for nonmonetary uses of the two metals differed. However, if the stocks of gold and silver were unchanged or grew at the same rate with no difference in nonmonetary demands, a fixed exchange rate model would remain appropriate.

[42] The value of gold can't diverge between countries by more than the "gold points," the cost of shipping gold between them. In antiquity, with uncertain and costly transportation, these gold points could be quite large and consequently the value of gold could differ a fair bit between countries, but the effect on the mechanisms presented here simply would be to alter the value of k in the purchasing power parity formulation. Possibly many private overseas payments would have been made through some kind of clearing arrangements not involving the actual shipment of metal coins. Harris (1998, 174–177) discusses the weights involved in the Roman coinage required to buy just a house—Cicero's house on the Palatine—certainly a very nice house but still just a house: something over $3\frac{1}{2}$ tons.

[43] Harl (1996, 91) notes that in foreign trade, coins were valued by intrinsic worth (metal content) rather than by tariffing, so that debasement did not affect external trade much.

[44] Thus the demands for real money balances are functions of relative commodity prices, rather than incomes and interest rates. With no nonmonetary assets, the interest rate would represent only the time preference of consuming goods, which could affect the demand for money. Income is easy to put back in these money demand functions.

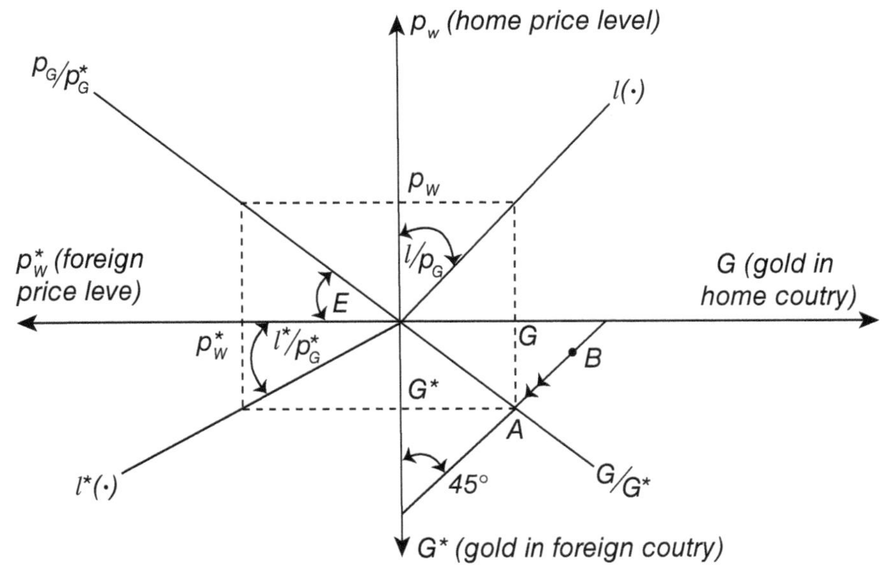

Figure 3.39. Distribution of the world's gold supply (Reproduced from Niehans, 1984, figure 2.6.1, p. 49, by permission of Trudy Niehans.)

can connect points on all four lines. This translates into the following conclusion: given real money demands of the residents of both countries and the gold prices set by the monetary authority in each country, there is one and only one distribution of the fixed world gold stock between the countries.

Suppose the demand for real money balances in the home country increases, with the gold prices and the demand for real balances in the other country unchanged. Line ℓ turns clockwise about the origin in the northeast quadrant, gold moves from the foreign country to the home country, and the price levels denominated in wheat fall in both countries. Alternatively, if the home country raised the price of gold (reduced the gold content of its coins), line p_G/p^*_G in the northwest quadrant turns clockwise about the origin and line P turns counterclockwise about the origin in the northeast quadrant, raising the price level in the home country but leaving the world distribution of gold and the price level in the other country unaffected. The exchange rate rises, requiring more home country coins to purchase a given number of foreign coins.

Suppose the home country forces tribute payments out of the foreign country, shifting the distribution of the world gold stock from A to B in Figure 3.45. With unchanged gold prices and demands for real balances in the two countries, and trade keeping price levels constant at their original levels, home country residents will find themselves with excess cash balances and foreigners with lower balances than they desire. Home country residents will exchange their excess cash balances for goods, the demand for which will spill over their borders to the foreign country, while foreigners spend less than their full incomes in an effort to replenish their cash balances. After a while, the gold supplies return to their original distribution between the two countries, with no lasting effects on the real economy. However, to the extent that the home country spends the tribute payments on investment goods, or inability to maintain durable capital goods in the foreign country leads to accumulation or loss of long-term productive capacity, relative goods prices will change in the two countries and permanent effects of the tribute payments will emerge. Thus, the payment of tribute payment induces a balance of payments surplus in the paying country and a deficit in the receiving country. These payments surpluses and deficits are self-correcting in the sense that they return to zero over time as the excess demand for money in the surplus country and the excess supply of money in the deficit country are reduced to zero over time through the payments imbalances. If the demand for money in the country receiving the tribute increases, the payments imbalances will return to zero before the entire amount of the tribute is returned to the paying country.[45]

Finally, if new gold supplies are discovered, the 45° line in the southeast quadrant shifts out parallel to its original position. Price levels rise proportionally in both countries, the proportion being equal to the percent augmentation in the world gold supply. The gold stocks in each country increase in proportion to their original share of the world gold stock. The exchange rate remains unchanged.

3.9 Cases from Antiquity: Addressing Ancient Trade with International Trade Models

International trade offers a number of cases for the models to add value to historical knowledge. Beginning with the Old Assyrian caravan trade between Assur and Kültepe, we have a combination of trade of cloth and tin for copper based on the Heckscher-Ohlin (H-O) factor proportions model and a case of foreign direct investment (FDI). At the same time, the resource

[45] Harl (1996, 62) notes that the cash that flowed into Italy from the Aegean as plunder during the wars of the 1st century B.C.E. flowed back out largely through trade.

costs of long-distance transportation took donkeys and fodder out of local availability. Back to the metals trade – non-renewable resources – why were the tin and copper not combined in Assur and final products sold to Kültepe and its neighbors? Comparative advantage in metallurgy seems like a reasonable suspect, with another renewable resource – wood for charcoal – more widely available in Anatolia, likely leading to the development of greater technical expertise in Anatolia. And returning to the FDI represented by the extensive tablets, why? Several possibilities appear – higher returns to physical capital in Anatolia with partial repatriation to Assur and opportunities to collect market intelligence and maintain friendly relationships with foreign officials.

Moving ahead some four or five centuries and to the southeast, Elizabeth Barber (1990; 1998, 14–15; 2016, 207) has identified evidence of a lengthy and relatively intense trade in Minoan and Mycenaean textiles with Egypt in multiple tomb paintings – combination of differentiated goods trade and factor proportions. We don't have evidence of the goods that went north – grain seems at least as likely as gold – but Egypt's comparative advantage vis-à-vis at least the Greek mainland if not necessarily some of the bread-basket areas of Crete in grain and the Minoans' and Mycenaeans' in wool surely formed the basis for H-O trade. However, the textiles were highly differentiated goods, not bulk commodities. They would not have been competitively produced but would have yielded some monopolistically competitive returns and would have taken resources from the production of undifferentiated goods which might or might not have entered into international trade.

Next, consider the Ugarit/Levant-Cyprus-Aegean nexus over the 14th to 12th centuries, a case that has generated the the Sherratt-Artzy thesis of an expansion of trade in differentiated goods gradually eroding royal monopolies in bulk commodities with basis in H-O factor proportions and non-renewable resources and contributing to the eventual downfall of the international palatial trade system (Sherratt 1994; 1998; Artzy 2001). Frankly, that thesis hasn't fared well under empirical examination (Birney 2007, Jung 2015), but we do observe the temporal pattern of growth of trade in differentiated final goods – particularly decorated pottery which has survived plus the likelihood of many other items which haven't survived – arising after initial years of mostly trade in bulk commodities such as were found on the Ulu Burun ship and have been documented moving out of Ugarit (Pulak 1988; Routledge & McGeough 2009). Routledge & McGeough, who report Ugaritic royal bulk shipments with no clashes between private and palatial shipping interests (2009, 26). The emergence of the differentiated goods seems well demonstrated – consumer ceramic trade out of Cyprus and probably the Argolid, from the Argolid headed to the Levant and Cyprus (Papademetriou 2015, 436–437; Dabney 2007, 194). A striking example of such goods is referenced in a letter of 257 B.C.E. to Apollonius, the *dioikētēs* of Ptolemy II Philadelphos in Palestine, by Glaukias the supervisor of all of Apollonios's holdings in Palestine: "He gave me a taste of the wine and I could not tell whether it was Chian or local" (Kloppenborg 2008, 46).[46] Cyprus' homogeneous goods would have been olive oil and copper, and possibly some grains and fruits. Could there have been increasing returns in consumer ceramic production? Possibly. The introduction of the wheel, a number of potteries identified by Mountjoy (2018), with specialization in certain shapes and decorations are all possible indicators. And a Ricardian comparative advantage in metallurgy appears to have led to Cypriot final bronze products scattered from the Levant to Sardinia.

Dabney (2016) implicitly uses national income accounts to trace and explain the decline and eventual collapse of the Near Eastern civilizations (including the Mycenaean palatial states) at the end of the Bronze Age. Using the open-economy identities $S = I + NX$ and $S = Y - C - G$, she identifies indicators of potentially excessive C around Mycenae and in 20th Dynasty Egypt, along with interruptions in international trade, reducing saving (S). From the first identity, the reduction in saving reduces investment (I). Relying on the concepts of consumption, debt,trade, and investment, she traces likely microeconomic pathways to slow decline, including lack of saving to invest in labor services to repair damaged palaces at Mycenae, Pylos and Hattusa, and the tailing off of monumental tomb construction in Egypt.

There are some interesting lessons from the Ulu Burun ship. Shipping is a category of intermediate good, as Cassing's (1978) 3×2 model clearly shows. Shipwrecks were a not-unexpected aspect of international trade, just as they are today, so stochasticity was an important factor in decisions to allocate resources to shipping (Jones 2000, 29 n. 108 on 19th century British registry of shipwrecks). Whoever loaded the Ulu Burun ship with its large, valuable cargo did not decide to reduce the risk of losing the entire cargo by splitting it up among ships, possibly in a convoy. We could represent such shipwreck risk by assigning a random risk variable, α, to shipping's production function: $S = \alpha L_S f_S(k_S)$, where L_S is labor in shipping, f_S is the marginal productivity of labor in shipping, and k_S is the capital-labor ratio in shipping.[47] Suppose for simplicity that the other productive activities in the country providing shipping services were not subject to such uncertainty – clearly untrue, but introducing additional α's would not add clarity. Appealing to the mean-preserving spread introduced in Chapter 2, an increase in riskiness can be defined as $\hat{\alpha} = \gamma\alpha + \theta$, where the parameters $\gamma = 1$ and $\theta = 0$ initially shift the variance and mean respectively. The expected value of $\hat{\alpha}$ is $\gamma E[\hat{\alpha}] + \theta$, and its variance is given by $v(\hat{\alpha}) = v(\hat{\alpha})\gamma^2$.

[46] Discussing a shipment of cloth from Mycenae to Thebes, Palaima (1991, 276–277) begins, "Among other problems relating to the identification of *te-qa-de* with Boeotian Thebes in MY X 508, one wonders why a relatively common type of cloth *pu-ka-ta-ri-ja* would be shipped from Mycenae to an obviously rich pastoral district capable of producing its own wool cloth." He proceeds, however, to discuss at length the many ways the Mycenaean cloth shipment could differ from what was produced in Thebes – a prime example of trade in differentiated goods.

[47] The models used in this example are from Batra (1975, 6–7, 65–67).

An increase in the value of γ above its initial value of 1 increases the variance of $\hat{\alpha}$ as well as its expected value, so to keep the original mean of $\hat{\alpha}$, the increase in γ must be accompanied by a decrease in θ by an amount such that $dE[\hat{\alpha}] = 0$, so that $d\theta/d\gamma = -E[\alpha]$. A mean-preserving increase in the distribution of α will, counterintuitively increase the output of shipping and decrease the outputs of the other goods. Risk-averse producers will hire inputs to the point that the expected marginal product of each factor remains above its price. The increase in E[α] raises the expected marginal products of both factors used in shipping. However, for shipping services to rise unambiguously, non-increasing absolute risk aversion (again, see Chapter 2) is required, as an increase in E[α] leads to more optimistic expectations of profits on the part of shippers. As risk aversion declines, shippers lower the spread between the expected values of marginal products of their inputs and their factor prices, leading to a further increase in their offer of shipping services, pulling factors out of other, non-shipping productive activities. So what should we make of this analysis? Piracy as well as shipwrecks could have short-circuited intended shipping ventures, driving increases in mean-preserving spreads and the variance of expected returns. Should more intensive piracy have retarded trade and shipping or should it have had the opposite effect? These considerations would have influenced shipping decisions from the Bronze Age through the Roman period. Whoever loaded the Ulu Burun ship (Pulak 1988) rather than splitting its cargo among multiple ships made a major mistake, but we'll never know the reasoning behind the choices made. Irrational exuberance or rational exuberance? Did additional marines aboard the ship (were they there?) considered sufficient additional resources, but additional ships would have been "excessive"? However shippers thought about putting how many eggs in a single basket, the practice apparently was long-lived, extending from at least the 16th–15th century (Öniz 2019, a recent discovery in the same general area as the 14th–13th century Ulu Burun ship and the 12th–11th century Cape Gelidonya ship (Bass 1967), which deposited at least 73 pillow-type copper ingots and 4 bun ingots onto the seabed) through the 12th or 11th century.

Fast-forward roughly a millennium to the start of the 2nd century CE, which Frier (1979, 223, n. 98 with references) cites as initiating an extended period of agricultural depression in Italy which pauperized tenant farmers on fixed leases. We have little information on the symptoms, but considering the structure of fixed-tenancy farm leases, we can suspect a lengthy and severe reduction in grain (primarily wheat) prices. Rathbone and von Reden (2014) have reported in detail on the paucity and poor quality of Roman grain prices, except for a period in Egypt, so price data are unavailable to help us. This sounds everything like the consequence of the introduction of new trade H-O factor-proportions-based trade partners, along with the Stolper-Samuelson theorem's product prices changing factor prices (tenant incomes), and the prime suspects are the imperial farms along the North African littoral – an area with sharply divergent factor proportions (land quality versus labor) from those of much of central Italy. An alternative, or even a supplementary explanation would be climate change in Italy, which would have accomplished the same effective factor-proportions change via reducing the seed ratio.

3.10 Suggestions for Using the Material of this Chapter

My suggestions for the use of the models of this chapter target archaeologists, ancient historians and philologists alike, although some of the cases may find wider application by one group than others. The first suggested application, in fact, may apply particularly frequently to archaeologists dealing with non-monetized trade. Since the balance of payments is always zero (i.e., trade is balanced, with the value of exports equaling the value of imports) in non-monetized societies, if only imports are found, the exports were ephemeral, and vice versa. In the fortunate case of both imports and exports surviving (at different places, naturally), it may be possible to get an idea—admittedly, on a really lucky day—of the relative valuation the people of the period placed on those goods. Strictly speaking, we would want to observe the full quantity of exports and full quantity of imports, both over the same time period, which admittedly won't be possible. In such a fortuitous case, as a hypothetical benchmark however, that information would yield the valuation of the imports in terms of the exports and vice versa. Since the benchmark availability of remains won't be satisfied, a challenge will be to estimate—or guess—what those relative magnitudes were, and make the corresponding valuation inferences. Where there are simply no possibilities of making an estimate or a reasoned guess of magnitudes, no quantitative inferences on valuation would be possible.

It is not uncommon to read of trade between regions in antiquity as consisting of what each region simply could not produce itself. In periods of very high transport costs, with no access to waterborne transportation, it might well have been the case that the only goods that moved were the products of highly location-specific extractive industries. The specific factors model deals with these cases. More generally, however, countries don't trade simply for what they have none of, but for things that people in another country can produce relatively more cheaply—with the amounts traded governed by comparative advantage and of course transportation costs.

To some extent because of the paucity of evidence, there may also be tendencies to think of trade in what appear to be bulk commodities as trade in undifferentiated goods. As a corollary, there may be temptations to think that because people in one place could grow crop X that they wouldn't want to import any, whereas it is possible that valued differences in, say, agricultural products existed. For instance, one region might have been known for particularly good beans of some variety and even other regions that grew the same species of bean might import some of these beans to satisfy demands of higher income consumers who knew of the "designer" beans from region Y. With products available from manufactured goods ranging from furniture to cloth to ceramics and agricultural goods ranging from consumables such as the beans in the previous example to varieties of flax, wool or cotton among industrial agricultural products, there may be ample scope for the model of intra-industry trade in differentiated goods to offer guidance on the consequences of this kind of trade.

Multinational firms surely existed in the early reaches of antiquity. The Old Assyrian traders whose records have been found in Kanesh in eastern Anatolia formed businesses that were, effectively, multinational firms. We have some idea of their local trading activities within Anatolia; whether they engaged in any production activities in Anatolia is an open question, but Wal-Mart only buys and sells overseas too.

There are many "causes" of trade. The chapter has identified four major models of trade as well as five more idiosyncratic contributors. At any given place and time in antiquity, plausibly elements of all four of the major factors could have been at work, as well as several of the idiosyncratic factors. The job of economists is to figure out how each cause works by itself. The job of ancient historians, philologists, and archaeologists is to determine what all of those causes together generated in the way of trade volumes, as well as income consequences for those involved at each end of the trading. The models introduced here can help assess both causes and consequences of whatever trade is found to have existed. Evidence permitting, the models may even be able to help scholars of antiquity to disentangle some of the contributing causes.

References

Andreau, Jean. 1992. Review of von Freyberg, *Kapitalverkehr und Handel im römischen Kaiserreich (27 v. Chr.-235 n. Chr.)*, *Gnomon* 64: 418–422.

Andreau, Jean. 1994. "L'Italie imperial et les provinces: déséquilibre des échanges et flux monétaires." In *L'Italie d'Auguste à Diocletian*, Collection de L'École Française de Rome 198, 175–203. Rome: École Française de Rome.

Artzy, Michal. 2001. "White Slip Ware for Export? The Economics of Production," in *The White Slip Ware of Late Bronze Age Cyprus*, edited by Vassos Karageorghis, with Ernst Czerny and Ian A. Todd, 107–115. Akademie der Wissenschaften; Denkschriften der Gesamtakacademie, Band XX. Vienna: Verlag der Österreiches Akademie der Wissenschaften Wien.

Aubet, Maria Eugenia. 1993. *The Phoenicians and the West; Politics, Colonies and Trade*. Translated by Mary Turton. Cambridge: Cambridge University Press.

Barber, Elizabeth. 1990. "Reconstructing the Ancient Aegean/Egyptian Textile Trade," in *Textiles in Trade: Proceedings of the Textile Society of America Biennial Symposium, September 14–16, 1990, Washington, DC*. Textile Society of America, 104–111.

Barber, Elizabeth J. W. 1998. "Aegean Ornaments and Designs in Egypt," in *The Aegean and the Orient in the Second Millennium; Proceedings of the 50th Anniversary Symposium Cincinnati, 18–20 April 1997*, edited by Eric H. Cline and Diane Harris-Cline, 13–17. Université de Liège Histoire de l'art et archéologie de la Grèce antique and University of Texas at Austin Program in Aegean Scripts and Prehistory.

Barber, Elizabeth J. W. 2016. "Minoans, Mycenaeans, and Keftiu," in *Woven Threads: Patterned Textiles of the Aegean Bronze Age*, edited by Maria C. Shaw and Anne P. Chapin, 205–237. Oxford: Oxbow Books.

Bass, George F. 1967. *Cape Gelidonya: A Bronze Age Shipwreck*. Philadelphia: American Philosophical Society.

Batra, Raveendra. 1973. *Studies in the Pure Theory of International Trade*. London: Macmillan.

Batra, Raveendra. 1975. *The Pure Theory of International Trade under Uncertainty*. New York: John Wiley and Sons.

Bendall, Lisa M. 2014. "Gifts to the Goddesses: Pylian Perfumed Olive Oil Abroad?" in *KE-RA-ME-JA: Studies Presented to Cynthia W. Shelmerdine*, edited by Dimitri Nakassis, Joann Gulizio and Sarah A. James. Philadelphia: INSTAP Academic Press, 141–162.

Birney, Kathleen. 2007. "Sea Peoples or Syrian Peddlers? The Late Bronze – Iron I Aegean Presence in Syria and Cilicia," Ph.D. Dissertation, Harvard University. Cambridge, Mass.

Bissi, Errietta M.A. 2009. *Governmental Intervention in Foreign Trade in Archaic and Classical Greece*. *Mnemosyne* Supplement 312. Leiden: Brill.

Bitros, George C., Emmanouil M. L. Economou, and Nicholas C. Kyriazis. 2021. *Democracy and Money: Lessons for Today from Athens in Classical Times*. London: Routledge.

Cassing, James H. 1978. "Transport Costs in International Trade Theory: A Comparison with the Analysis of Nontraded Goods." *Quarterly Journal of Economics* 92: 535–550.

Castle, Edward W. 1992. "Shipping and Trade in Ramesside Egypt," *Journal of the Economic and Social History of the Orient* 35: 239–277.

Caves, Richard E., Jeffrey A. Frankel, and Ronald W. Jones. 1999. *World Trade and Payments; An Introduction*, 8th ed. Reading, Mass.: Addison-Wesley.

Caves, Richard E., and Ronald W. Jones. 1973. *World Trade and Payments; An Introduction*. Boston: Little, Brown.

Chacholiades, Miltiades. 1973. *The Pure Theory of International Trade*. Chicago: Aldine.

Cline, Eric. 1999. "Coals to Newcastle, Wallbrackets to Tiryns: Irrationality, Gift Exchange, and Distance Value." In *MELETEMATA: Studies in Aegean Archaeology Presented to Malcolm Wiener as He Enters His Sixty-fifth Year*, Aegaeum 20, Vol. 1, edited by Philip Betancourt, Vassos Karageorghis, Robert Laffineur and Wolf-Dietrich Niemeier, 119–123. Liège and Austin: Université de Liège, Histoire de l'art et archéologie de la Grèce antique and University of Texas at Austin, Program in Aegean Scripts and Prehistory.

Coldstream, J. N. 1969. "The Phoenicians of Ialysos." *Bulletin of the Institute of Classical Studies* 16: 1–8.

Coldstream, J. N. 1979. "Some Cypriote Traits in Cretan Pottery c. 950–700," in *Acts of the International Archaeological Symposium, 'The Relations between Cyprus and Crete, ca. 2000–500 B.C.' 1978*, 257–263. Nicosia: Department of Antiquities, Cyprus.

Coldstream, J. N. 1982. "Greeks and Phoenicians in the Aegean," in *Phönizier im Westen*, Madrider Beiträger 8, edited by H. G. Niemeyer, 268–269. Mainz: Philipp von Zabern.

Coldstream, J. N. 1986. "Kition and Amathus: Some Reflections on their Westward Links during the Early Iron Age," in *Acts of the International Archaeological Symposium, 'Cyprus between the Orient and the Occident' 1985*, 321–329. Nicosia: Department of Antiquities, Cyprus.

Corden, W. M. 1971. *The Theory of Protection*. Oxford: Clarendon.

Corden, W. M. 1974. *Trade Policy and Economic Welfare*. Oxford: Clarendon.

Dabney, Mary K. 2007. "Marketing Mycenaean Pottery in the Levant," in *Krinoi Kai Limenes: Studies in Honor of Joseph and Maria Shaw*, edited by Philip P. Betancourt, Michael C. Nelson and Hector Williams. Philadelphia: INSTAAP Academic Press, 191–197.

Dabney, Mary K. 2016. "Consumerism, Debt, and the End of the Bronze Age Civilisations in the Eastern Mediterranean," in *RA-PI-NE-U; Studies on the Mycenaean World Offered to Robert Laffineur for His 70th Birthday*, Aegis 10, edited by Jan Driessen, 95–107. Louvain: Presses universitaires de Louvain.

Deaton, Angus, and John Muellbauer. 1980. *Economics and Consumer Behavior*. Cambridge: Cambridge University Press.

de Laet, Sigfried J. 1949. *Portorium; étude sur l'organisation douanière chez les romains, surtout à l'époque du haut-empire*. Bruges: De Tempel.

Duncan-Jones, Richard. 1990. *Structure and Scale in the Roman Economy*. Cambridge: Cambridge University Press.

Ethier, Wilfred J. 1984. "Higher Dimensional Issues in Trade Theory," in *Handbook of International Economics*, Vol. 1, edited by Ronald W. Jones and Peter B. Kenen, 131–184. Amsterdam: North-Holland.

Eyre, Christopher. 2010. "The Economy: Pharaonic," in *A Companion to Ancient Egypt*, Vol. 1, edited by Alan Lloyd, 291–308. Malden, Mass.: Wiley-Blackwell.

Freyberg, Hans-Ulrich von. 1989. *Kapitalverkehr und Handel im römischen Kaiserreich (27 v. Chr.-235 n. Chr.)*. Freiburg im Bresgau: Rudolf Haufe Verlag.

Garnsey, Peter. 1985. "Grain for Athens," in *Crux; Essays in Greek History Presented to G.E.M. de Ste. Croix on his 75th Birthday*, edited by P. A. Cartledge, and F. D. Harvey, 62–75. London: Duckworth.

Greene, Kevin. 1986. *The Archaeology of the Roman Empire*. London: Batsford.

Harl, Kenneth W. 1996. *Coinage in the Roman Economy, 300 B.C. to A.D. 700*. Baltimore: Johns Hopkins University Press.

Harris, W. V. 2008. "The Nature of Roman Money," in *The Monetary Systems of the Greeks and Romans,* edited by W. V. Harris, 174–207. Oxford: Oxford University Press.

Hazari, Bharat R., and Dong C. Suh. 1978. "A Geometrical Exposition of Some Theorems in Trade Theory with an Imported Intermediate Good," *Keio Economic Studies* 15: 73–81.

Hazari, Bharat R., Pasquale M. Sgro, and Dong C. Suh. 1981. *Non-traded and Intermediate Goods and the Pure Theory of International Trade*. New York: St. Martin's.

Helck, Wolfgang. 1987. "The Dissolution of the Palace Economy in the Ramesside Period," in *The Function of the Minoan Palaces,* Skrifter Utgivna av Svenska Institutet i Athen 4-, XXXV, edited by Robin Hägg and Nanno Marinatos, 17–19. Göteborg: Paul Åströms Forlag.

Helpman, Elhanan. 1984. "Increasing Returns, Imperfect Markets, and Trade Theory," in *Handbook of International Economics*, Vol. 1, edited by Ronald W. Jones and Peter B. Kenen, 325–365. Amsterdam: North-Holland.

Helpman, Elhanan, and Paul R. Krugman. 1985. *Market Structure and Foreign Trade; Increasing Returns, Imperfect Competition, and the International Economy*. Cambridge, Mass.: MIT Press.

Hopkins, Keith. 1980. "Taxes and Trade in the Roman Empire (200 B.C. – A.D. 400)." *Journal of Roman Studies* 70: 101–125.

Hopkins, Keith. 1995/96. "Rome, Taxes, Rents and Trade." *Kodai: Journal of Ancient History* VI/VII: 41–75. Reprinted in *The Ancient Economy*, edited by Walter Scheidel and Sitta von Reden, 190–230. London: Routledge.

Hopkins, Keith. 2002. "Rome, Taxes, Rent and Trade," in *The Ancient Economy*, edited by Walter Scheidel and Sitta von Reden, 190–230. New York: Routledge.

Janssen, Jac. J. 1975."Prolegomena to the Study of Egypt's Economic History during the New Kingdom," *Studien zur Altägyptischen Kultur* 3: 127–185.

Johnson, Harry G. 1962. "The Economic Theory of Customs Union," in Harry G. Johnson, *Money, Trade and Economic Growth*, 57–58. Cambridge, Mass.: Harvard University Press.

Johnson, Harry G. 1965. "Optimal Trade Intervention in the Presence of Domestic Distortions," in *Trade, Growth, and the Balance of Payments; Essays in Honor of Gottfried Haberler*, by Robert E. Baldwin and 13 others, 3–34. Chicago and Amsterdam: Rand McNally and North-Holland.

Jones, Donald W. 1993. "Phoenician Unguent Factories in Dark Age Greece: Social Approaches to Evaluating the Archaeological Evidence," *Oxford Journal of Archaeology* 12: 293–303.

Jones, Donald W. 2000. *External Relations of Early Iron Age Crete, 100–600 B.C.* Archaeological Institute of America Monographs New Series, Number 4. Philadelphia: The University Museum, The University of Pennsylvania.

Jones, Ronald W., and José A. Scheinkman. 1973. "The Relevance of the Two-Sector Production Model in Trade Theory," *Journal of Political Economy* 85: 909–935.

Jung, Reinhard. 2015. "Imported Mycenaean Pottery in the East: Distribution, Context and Interpretation," in *Policies of Exchange Political Systems and Modes of Interaction in the Aegean and the Near East in the 2nd Millenium B.C.E: Proceedings of the International Symposium at the University of Freiburg Institute for Archaeological Studies, 30th May – 2nd June 2012*, edited by Birgitta Eder and Regine Pruzsinszky, 243–275. Vienna: Austrian Academy of Sciences Press.

Katzenstein, H. Jacob. 1973. *The History of Tyre; From the Beginning of the Second Millenium B.C.E until the Fall of the Neo-Babylonian Empire in 538 B.C.E.* Jerusalem: Schocken Institute for Jewish Research.

Kehoe, Dennis. 2010. "The Economy: Graeco-Roman." In *A Companion to Ancient Egypt*, Vol. 1, edited by Alan Lloyd, 309–325. Malden, Mass.: Wiley-Blackwell.

Kemp, Murray C. 1969. *The Pure Theory of International Trade and Investment*. Englewood Cliffs, N.J.: Prentice-Hall.

Kemp, Murray C., and Ngo Van Long. 1984. "The Role of Natural Resources in Trade Models," in *Handbook of International Economics*, Vol. 1, edited by Ronald W. Jones and Peter B. Kenen, 367–417. Amsterdam: North-Holland.

Kloppenborg, John S. 2008. "The Growth and Impact of Agricultural Tenancy in Jewish Palestine (III B.C.E.-I CE)," *Journal of the Economic and Social History of the Orient* 51: 31–66.

Komiya, Ryutaro. 1967. "Nontraded Goods and the Pure Theory of International Trade," *International Economic Review* 8: 132–152.

Kuhrt, Amélie. 1998. "The Old Assyrian Merchants," in *Trade, Traders and the Ancient City*, edited by Helen Parkins and Christopher Smith, 16–30. London: Routledge.

Larsen, Mogens Trolle. 1987. "Commercial Networks in the Ancient Near East," in *Centre and Periphery in the Ancient World*, edited by Michael Rowlands, Mogens Larsen and Kristian Kristiansen, 47–56. Cambridge: Cambridge University Press.

Larsen, Mogens Trolle. 2010. *Kültepe Tabletlerı VI-a. The Archive of the Šalim-Aššur Family. Volume 1: The First Two Generations*. Ankara: Türk Tarıh Kurumbu Basimevı.

Leontief, Wassily W. 1936. "Quantitative Input and Output Relations in the Economic System of the United States," *Review of Economics and Statistics* 18: 105–125.

Leontief, Wassily W. 1953. *Studies in the Structure of the American Economy*. New York: Oxford University Press.

Leontief, Wassily W. 1986. *Input-Output Economics*, 2nd ed. New York: Oxford University Press.

Lo Cascio, Emilio. 2007. "The Early Roman Empire: The State and the Economy," in *The Cambridge Economic History of the Greco-Roman World*, edited by Walter Scheidel, Ian Morris, and Richard Saller, 619–647. Cambridge: Cambridge University Press.

Markusen, James R., James R. Melvin, William H. Kaempfer, and Keith E. Maskus. 1995. *International Trade; Theory and Evidence*. Boston: McGraw-Hill.

Michaely, Michael. 1972. *Theory of Commercial Policy*. Oxford: Philip Allan.

Morley, Neville. 2007. "The Early Roman Empire: Distribution," in *The Cambridge Economic History of the Greco-Roman World*, edited by Walter Scheidel, Ian Morris, and Richard Saller, 570–591. Cambridge: Cambridge University Press.

Mountjoy, Penelope A. 2018. *Decorated Pottery in Cyprus and Philista in the 12 Century BC: Cypriot IIIC and*

Philistine IIIC. Vienna: Austrian Academy of Sciences Press.

Niehans, Jürg. 1984. *International Monetary Economics*. Baltimore: Johns Hopkins University Press.

Öniz, Hakan. 2019. "A New Bronze Age Shipwreck with Ingots in the West of Antalya—Preliminary Results," *Palestine Exploration Quarterly* 151: 3–14.

Palaima, Thomas G. 1991. "Maritime Matters in the Linear B Texts," in eds., *Thalassa. L'Égée prehistorique et la mer, Aegaeum* 7, edited by R. Laffineur and L. Basch, 273–310, Liège.

Papadimitriou, Nikolas. 2015. "Aegean and Cypriot Ceramic Trade Overseas during the 2ND Millennium B.C.E.," in *There and Back Again – the Crossroads II; Proceedings of an International Conference Held in Prague, September 15–18, 2014*, edited by Jana Mynářová, Pavel Onderka and Peter Pavúk, 423–445. Charles University in Prague, Faculty of Arts.

Postgate, J. N. 1992. *Early Mesopotamia; Society and Economy at the Dawn of History*. London: Routledge.

Pulak, Cemal. 1988. "The Bronze Age Shipwreck at Ulu Burun, Turkey: 1985 Campaign," *American Journal of Archaeology*. 92: 1–37.

Rathbone, Dominic, and Sitta von Reden. 2014. "Mediterranean Grain Prices in Classical Antiquity," in *A History of Market Performance. From Ancient Babylonia to the Modern World*, edited by R.J. Van der Spek, Jan Luiten van Zanden, and Bas van Leeuwen, 149–235. London: Routledge.

Routledge, Brian, and Kevin. McGeough. 2009. "Just What Collapsed? A Network Perspective on 'Palatial' and 'Private' Trade at Ugarit," in *Forces of Transformation. The End of the Bronze Age in the Mediterranean. Proceedings of an International Symposium Held at St. John's College, University of Oxford, 25–6th March 2006*, Themes from the Ancient Near East BANEA Publication Series 1, edited by Ch. Bachhuber and R.G. Roberts, 22–29. Oxford: Oxbow Books.

Rybczynski, T. M. 1955. "Factor Endowment and Relative Commodity Prices," *Economica* 22: 336–341.

Samuelson, Paul A. 1953. "Prices of Factors and Goods in General Equilibrium," *Review of Economic Studies* 21: 1–20.

Samuelson, Paul A. 1954. "The Transfer Problem and Transport Costs, II: Analysis of Effects of Trade Impediments." *Economic Journal* 64: 264–289.

Shelmerdine, Cynthia W. 1985. *The Perfume Industry of Mycenaean Pylos* (*SIMA-PB* 34), Göteborg.

Sherratt, Susan. 1994. "Commerce, Iron and Ideology: Metallurgical innovation in 12th–11th Century Cyprus," *Cyprus in the 11th Century B.C.: Proceedings of the International Symposium Organized by the Archaeological Research Unit of the University of Cyprus and The Anastasios G. Leventis Foundation, Nicosia, 30–31 October, 1993*, edited by Vassos Karageorghis, 59–106. Nicosia: University of Cyprus.

Sherratt, Susan. 1998. "'Sea Peoples' and the Economic Structure of the Late Second Millennium in the Eastern Mediterranean," in *Mediterranean Peoples in Transition; Thirteenth to Early Tenth Centuries B.C.E., in Honor of Professor Trude Dothan*, edited by Seymour Gitin, Amihai Mazar, and Ephraim Stern, 292–313. Jerusalem: Israel Exploration Society.

Snodgrass, Anthony M. 1980. "Iron and Early Metallurgy in the Mediterranean," in *The Coming of the Age of Iron*, edited by Theodore A. Wertime and James Muhly, 335–374. New Haven: Yale University Press.

Stigler, George J., and Gary S. Becker. 1977. "De Gustibus non Est Disputandum." *American Economic Review* 67: 76–90.

Stolper, Wolfgang F., and Paul A. Samuelson. 1941. "Protection and Real Wages," *Review of Economic Studies* 9: 58–73.

Veenhof, K. R. 1995. "Kanesh: An Old Assyrian Colony in Anatolia," in *Civilizations of the Ancient Near East*, Vol. 2, 859–871, edited by Jack Sasson. New York: Scribners.

Waldbaum, Jane C. 1980. "The First Archaeological Appearance of Iron and the Transition to the Iron Age," in *The Coming of the Age of Iron*, edited by Theodore A. Wertime and James Muhly, 69–98. New Haven: Yale University Press.

Woodland, A.D. 1982. *International Trade and Resource Allocation*. Amsterdam: North-Holland.

4

The Economics of Population

4.1 Introduction

This introduction provides some background on the study of population in the discipline of economics, offers justification for inflicting yet an additional piece on population on the scholars of the ancient Mediterranean, and concludes with a reader's guide to what to expect in the ensuing sections.

4.1.1 Background

The economic analysis of population has a long history. David Hume made a number of quite contemporary-sounding observations that stirred the classics community in the 18th century regarding non-sequiturs in the ancient literature involving population (Hume 1970 [1752]).[1] At the end of that century, Thomas Malthus made himself famous and gave the field of economics its reputation as The Dismal Science with a perceptive model of population dynamics that omitted technological change, at least in the first edition. Something over a century followed during which economics relegated population to a supporting role in economic developments akin to the triangle player in an orchestra. The plights and opportunities of the Third World countries after World War II began to bring population closer to an active research subject in economics, to parallel developments of the subject in demography and sociology more broadly, and problems in industrialized countries have come to be recognized as population issues in the second half of the 20th century.

It has been recognized that, to be satisfactorily general, explanations of current population trends must be consistent with explanations of past population trends, specifically the lengthy period of nearly constant, or at least very slowly growing, population until sometime between the late 16th and early 18th centuries, its explosion in Europe during the early decades of the Industrial Revolution, and the subsequent demographic transition which still continues among a number of Third World countries, as well as with current observations. Theories must be able to explain or reproduce both longitudinal (time series) and cross-sectional observations of fertility relationships. In this search for consistent understanding of greatly diverse eras, the economics of population has become largely the economics of fertility, of why people have children. Much progress has been made against a benchmark of mid-20th century understanding, but the field is one of extremely active research. Models have been developed that can explain a large share of the movements in critical fertility and population variables over the past several centuries, but still yield some counterfactual predictions, which means that work remains to be done. Thus this chapter reports on a number of conceptual developments that are widely accepted as successful and others that are works in progress, mainly interesting ideas that may provide suggestions for scholars researching similar topics in antiquity but which should not be taken as any kind of gospel.

4.1.2 Rationale for The Chapter

A number of excellent overviews of the demography of the ancient Mediterranean region have appeared in the past several decades. Parkin's (1992) study of the demography of the Roman Empire appeared nearly three decades ago, followed shortly thereafter by Bagnall and Frier's (1994) study of Roman Egypt. Both contained chapters explaining demographic concepts to students of antiquity. Frier (2000) published an overview of the demography of the Roman Empire iin the *Cambridge Ancient History* series, and Scheidel (2008) published an overview of the demography of both the Greek and Roman worlds in the *Cambridge Economic History of the Greco-Roman World*, in addition to several other works which, while focusing on Roman Egypt, deal with a wide range of demographic topics (Scheidel 1996a; 2001a; 2001b).

Those works provide both conceptual background on demographic concepts and valuable overviews of what is known empirically about many aspects of the populations of, particularly the Greek and Roman worlds; the populations and demographics of Pharaonic Egypt and the Ancient Near East have been studied less extensively. It is difficult to avoid dealing with economic issues involved in having children and in various relationships involving population, and those works do address economic concerns.

The goal of this chapter is to complement these studies and treat in somewhat more depth economic issues they touch upon. The material is largely conceptual, but I have tried to connect the theoretical material to specific problems in antiquity to illustrate the applicability of the economic models in these earlier settings. I have included a brief treatment of demographic theory which is somewhat more detailed than overviews provided by the studies noted above. Presenting the demographic and economic models side by side offers a comparison of the two approaches—sometimes complementary, sometimes alternatives—which is not offered in the previous studies of ancient demography. Going into somewhat more breadth

[1] Discussed at length by Morley (2011, 16–21).

as well as depth than the previous studies have done may offer the student of antiquity deeper understanding of the demographic relationships. While many students of ancient demography have appealed to some economic models, some may benefit from a more formal exposition of those models, as well as others, which details their strengths and limitations.

Finally, demographic projections of population, even for periods as short as ten or fifteen years, are frequently wide of the mark, primarily because, economists tend to believe, they do not rely on behavioral influences on fertility behavior which demographers tend to specify as parametric (Olsen, 1994, 63). While enough degrees of freedom can always be found to make any demographic model fit a previously existing population pretty well, projecting forward requires better understanding of behavior. It may be useful for students of ancient populations to observe more closely behavioral models underpinning population movements.

4.1.3 Guide to the Chapter

The next section introduces a number of demographic concepts, then follows with overviews of demography's major models—the life table and the stable population model in its continuous-time (Lotka equation) and discrete-time (Leslie matrix) versions. Since ancient historians have made considerable use of some of these models in recent years, some of the issues that have been raised in those contributions are discussed, and the concept of natural fertility and the more general issue of fertility control are addressed.

Section 4.3 introduces the economic models of fertility, the Becker-Chicago-Columbia branch of those models and the Easterlin-Pennsylvania branch. The Malthusian model is presented as an aggregate model rather than in a utility-maximizing, individual choice model. Since characteristics of nuptiality form the core of Malthus' preventive checks on population growth, economic insights on whether and, if so, when to marry are offered. As mortality is a major force in demography, some insights on individual behavior involving or affecting mortality are provided. This section closes with a sub-section on issues involved with the economics of the family, including a brief check list of comparanda with ancient families. Section 4.4 brings together the demographic and economic approaches of the previous two sections and examines how they address problems of ancient population changes. This section also addresses methodological issues in using economic models to study population changes.

Sections 4.5 and 4.6 deal with intergenerational issues, at both the individual family level and at the aggregate economy level. Section 4.5 introduces the overlapping generations model, which has become a workhorse in many fields of economics, particularly growth theory. Section 4.6 focuses on intergenerational transfers of resources, at both individual and aggregate levels. Since population growth has been so intertwined with economic growth, section 4.7 deals with models of population growth built into models of economic growth, particularly a class of models in which fertility is endogenous and determined by individual optimizing choices. The final section extracts a rather personal set of major lessons from the previous sections. It is difficult to summarize the material of the previous sections, but reflection on some of the models and findings reported suggest some conclusions, of varying degree of tentativeness, that may help readers find a perspective on what they have read.

4.2 Some Demographic Concepts

Keith Hopkins (1966) introduced demographic models to the study of Roman history, with ramifications for the study of population in all ancient societies and to a lesser extent, for the use of social science models in ancient history and archaeology that are still being realized. Hopkins used the discipline of United Nations model life tables' accounting structure to assess the plausibility of accepting a number of forms of ancient evidence at face value and found the implied age structures implausible. Numerous criticisms of his methods followed quickly, but his use of demographic model life tables was taken up widely by ancient historians of both Greece and Rome in the following several decades, and both the opportunities they offered and their limitations have been explored ever since.

Demographic theory is a sophisticated and thoroughly mathematized accounting system for organizing characteristics of a population. Demographic models assign people with identical or similar characteristics to individual categories and specify rules governing how people change categories over time. The most common categorization of individuals in a population is by age, or by age and sex. A single-period observation of a population assigned to such categories yields an age distribution of the population, e.g., 9 percent of a population between ages 0 and 4, 7 percent between 5 and 9, and so on through the oldest age category. The rules for how the individuals move through various age categories over time specify exits, through death and, in more intricate models, through emigration, and entries, through births in the youngest age group and, again in more intricate models, through immigration. Models that account for a population over its individuals' life spans are the centerpiece of demographic theory, and are called life tables. A cohort life table uses the mortality rates of a single group of people, all born in the same year; naturally, it takes a long time to assemble such information, and purely cohort life tables are rare. Most life tables are period life tables, constructed from people born at different dates and of different ages at the period of observation (sometimes as short as a year when recent censuses are the source of information, but sometimes quite long when constructed from such historical sources as parish records or ancient censuses such as Bagnall and Frier exploited). Life tables can be actual, if they account for an actual population over some particular time period, or model if they refer to a hypothetical population. Model life tables are used for various purposes, from studying how characteristics of a population evolve over time—purely theoretical exercises—to comparing incomplete data on actual populations with known model populations to estimate more characteristic of the actual population than can be observed directly from the available data, the common use of these models in ancient history and archaeology.

There is something of a dichotomy surrounding demography as a field, with a division between what is sometimes called "formal demography," the mathematized, relational accounting system, which offers no behavioral explanations for trends in population characteristics, and population studies, which focuses on causes and correlates of population behavior and is generally less mathematized although some sophisticated statistical analysis is sometimes involved.[2] Extending the dichotomy to a trichotomy, Preston (1993, 594) adds a third category of demographic studies, social demography, which are primarily descriptive although useful studies of population characteristics, such as the incidence of poverty, marital status, living arrangements, and so on. There are few demography departments in universities, with most demographers being housed in sociology departments. Population studies, on the other hand, is populated by sociologists, anthropologists, historians, economists, epidemiologists, geographers, and undoubtedly other less disciplinarily well- defined contributors, as well as people who define themselves as demographers. Possibly because of this diversity of approaches to population studies, there appears to be less of a well-defined body of theory regarding population behaviors than there is regarding the formal demography. The précis below reviews the formal demography, although the discussion of natural fertility veers into behavioral issues. The remainder of the chapter introduces the body of theory that economics has developed to deal with population issues.

4.2.1 Some Common Demographic Measures

Demography uses rates of occurrences and probabilities in its accounting systems. Rates are defined generally as the number of occurrences of a particular type divided by the person-years of exposure to the risk of occurrence of that particular type. Probabilities are the chance that something will occur rather than the rate over time at which it does occur. Using a relative frequency approach, probabilities are calculated as the number of instances in which an event occurs divided by the number of opportunities the event had to occur, for example the probability of divorce, which depends on a person having been in the state of marriage: prob(divorce) = number of divorces divided by number of marriages.

In constructing rates of various types of occurrence as well as probabilities, the concept of a cohort is frequently used. A cohort is all the units of a population that experience a particular type of event during a specific time interval. Probably the most commonly used cohort definition is that of a birth cohort, which is all the people born in a particular period, typically a single year, sometimes a 5-year period when data are scarcer. Sometimes data on actual cohorts can be assembled, but with a longest life span of 75 or 80 years, it takes a long time to compile the data. An alternative concept of a cohort is a synthetic, or period, cohort, as opposed to a real cohort, which uses data from a specific period to construct the accounts, mixing together people of different birth cohorts to construct a single-time depiction of the experience of a population regarding some particular measure, such as mortality or life expectancy. Correspondingly, a life table can be either a cohort (much rarer) or a period life table, as noted above, based on the method of construction of the rates and probabilities used in it.

Returning to the rates used in demography, period rates are defined as Rate [0, T] = the number of occurrences between time 0 and T divided by the person-years lived in the population between time 0 and T.[3] Two of the principal period rates used in demography are the crude birth rate, CBR[0,T] = number of births in the population between times 90 and T divided by the number of person-years lived in the population between times 0 and T; and the crude death rate, CDR[0,T] = the number of deaths in the population between times 0 and T divided by the number of person-years lived in the population between times 0 and T. These two rates are called "crude" because they do not incorporate the influence of age composition. Because they do not incorporate the influence of age composition, crude birth and crude death rates can change, sometimes dramatically, with changes in age composition as a result of, say a war or famine, with unchanged fertility rates and mortality rates that quickly resume their previous regime. Another important rate for the study of ancient populations, the infant mortality rate, IMR, is the number of deaths of individuals under age 1 in a year (or some period) divided by the number of live births in that year.

Several fertility rates are commonly used. The general fertility rate is a first refinement of the crude birth rate that limits the population at risk to women aged 15 to 50: GFR[0,T] = births in period 0 to T divided by person-years lived in the period 0 to T by women aged 15 to 50. This rate can be standardized, typically by age. For

---

[2] Newell (1988, 3–4) offers a formal demographer's characterization of the difference; Riley and McCarthy (2003, 36, 83) report on the recent-to-current division of interests and responsibilities known as formal demography versus population studies, suggesting a closer integration of the two strands in recent years. Examination of recent years' issues of the leading demography journals suggests a balanced presence of articles in the two traditions, although it seems more like cohabitation than a case of out-and-out marriage.

[3] While the concepts described below are nearly universally recognized, I have relied on several textbook expositions in the notation I use below. Newell (1988) is an undergraduate-level text which has been cited as a basic reference in a number of ancient historical studies. Preston, Heuveline, and Guillot (2001) is a more recent, graduate-level treatment.

example, an age-specific fertility rate over the period from 0 to T, typically denoted as ${}_nF_x[0,T]$ = number of births in the age range x to x + n between times 0 and T divided by the number of person-years lived in that age range over the same period. The total fertility rate, TFR[0,T] = $n\sum_{x=\alpha}^{\beta=n} {}_nF_x[0,T]$, in which α and β are the minimum and maximum ages of childbearing, adds the age-specific rates over the childbearing years to yield the average number of children a woman would bear if she survived through the end of her reproductive span and experienced a particular set of age-specific fertility rates at each age. The term n appears in the formula because the woman spends n years in each n-year-wide period. TFR is the most commonly used measure of fertility. It is less demanding of data than the GFR and usually gives much the same results, in terms of degree of fertility and relative ordering of populations in terms of fertility. The gross reproduction rate (GRR), the number of female births to the average woman through her reproductive lifespan, gives a closer measure of whether childbearing women are reproducing themselves; the construction of the GRR is comparable to that of the TFR but uses maternity rates rather than fertility rates. A more realistic account of reproduction also takes account of women's mortality; the net reproduction rate (NRR) multiplies the fertility rate of the GRR by a measure of the mortality rate of women in each birth cohort, and is interpreted as the average number of daughters that members of a birth cohort would bear during their reproductive years if they experienced the observed age-specific maternity and mortality rates throughout their lifetimes. If NRR > 1.0, a cohort of baby girls will leave behind a larger group of daughters than they represented themselves. In general NRR < GRR, the relation between the two measures being approximated by NRR $\cong$ $p(A_M)$GRR, where $p(A_M)$ is the probability of surviving to the mean age of maternity. Since GRR = TFR · S, where S is the proportion of births that are female, NRR = TFR · S · $p(A_M)$. The growth rate of a population, r, is related to the NRR and the mean age of childbearing by r = ln(NRR)/T_G, where T_G is the mean length of a generation.[4] Stated alternatively, the mean length of a (female) generation is the number of years required to multiply the population by the average ratio of daughters to mothers, the NRR. Thus, this generational concept is a relative one; a population with a higher mean age of childbearing will have a longer generational length than one with a lower mean age of childbearing. Substituting the previous expression for the NRR into this relationship demonstrates the separable influences of these components on the growth rate: r = [ln TFR + ln S + ln $p(A_M)$]/T_G.

Using the notation N(t) to define a total population at time t, the crude growth rate is CGR[0,T] = {B[0,T] – D[0,T] + I[0,T] – O[0,T]} / $\sum_0^T N(t)$, in which B[0,T] denotes births between dates 0 and T, D[0,T] represents deaths, and I and O denote inflows and outflows of population through migration; it is equivalent to N(T) – N(0)/ $\sum_0^T N(t)$. An average growth rate over the period 0 to T, which produces a geometric increase in population, can be calculated as the natural logarithm of [N(T)/N(0)]/T = $\bar{r}[0,T]$. Any growth rate r can be associated with a doubling time of the population, which is the length of time required for the population to double, which implies that N(T)/N(0) = 2; therefore ln[N(T)/N(0)] = ln 2 = 0.693, and doubling time is T^D = 0.692/r. For example, doubling time for a population experiencing a 2.5% annual population growth rate (think of East Africa during the 1970s) would be almost 28 years. Doubling time for a population experiencing an average annual growth rate of 0.1 percent per year would be 693 years.

In a population, fertility and mortality rates interact with age composition to generate birth and death rates. With identical fertility rates, a population with larger proportions in the younger reproductive ages will have a higher birth rate than a population with an older age composition. Similarly, with the same mortality rates, a population with a larger proportion in the younger age cohorts will have a lower death rate than a population with an older age composition. The birth rate at date t is $b(t) = \sum_{a=0}^{a=\omega} c(a,t)f(a,t)$, where c(a,t) is the proportion of the population aged a at date t, f(a,t) is the fertility rate of females in that age cohort, and ω is the greatest age attained in the population. The death rate at date t is $d(t) = \sum_{a=0}^{a=\omega} c(a,t)\mu(a,t)$, where μ(a,t) is the age-specific death rate.

4.2.2 An Overview of the Model Life Table

The life table is one way of showing various aspects of the dying out of a birth cohort, either actual or synthetic, using age-specific death rates.[5] The information commonly displayed tabularly can also be summarized mathematically, but the tabular format, shown in Table 1 is more widely accessible and more commonly used to display information. The life table template in Table 4.1 uses 5-year age intervals, except for the 0–1 or infant age and the 1–4 cohort, but unabridged life tables typically use single-year intervals. Separate life tables are constructed for males and females, which has led to occasional problems in calculating the intrinsic growth rates associated with a particular age structure, a subject treated below.

One column of a life table is age, and the remaining columns record age-related mortality functions which can be calculated from one or more of the other columns.[6] Information on any of a number of the columns could serve as the basic building block. For instance, if l_x, the number of survivors of the cohort at age x, is known, ${}_nd_x$ can be

[4] The abbreviation "ln" stands for natural logarithm, or logarithms using the base e, where e $\cong$ 2.71828.

[5] The exposition of the life table again, is found in numerous texts. I have borrowed the format of Preston *et al.* (2001, Table 3.1, 39–40) in the layout and notation of Table 1. Pollard (1973, Chapter 1) offers somewhat more of a treatise approach to life table functions.

[6] Timing is important in the construction of life tables but introduces a degree of intricacy that is better left to interested readers to glean from demography texts rather than from the broad-brush overview intended here.

Table 4.1. The Structure of a Life Table[a].

Exact age	Number left alive at age x	Number dying between ages x and x + n	Probability of dying between ages x and x + n	Probability of surviving from age x to x + n	Person-years lived between ages x and x + n	Person-years lived above age x	Expectation of life at age x
x	l_x	$_nd_x$	$_nq_x$	$_np_x$	$_nL_x$	$T_x = \sum_{a=x}^{\infty} {}_nL_a$	$e_x^0 = T_x / l_x$
0–1[b]							
1–4[a]							
5–9							
. . .							
. . .							
80+							

[a] Notation for the functions in the first row of the table varies according to author. An alternative notation conveying the same meaning would, for example, be d(n, x) for the number of people dying between ages x and x + n, rather than $_nd_x$.

[b] The first age interval includes individuals aged zero to 364 days during the period of observation, while those aged 365 days to four years and 364 days in that period are assigned to the second age interval.

calculated as $l_x - l_{x+n}$, from which $_nq_x$, the age-specific death rate, can be calculated as $_nd_x/l_x$, and the probability of surviving from age x to age x + n as $1 - {}_nq_x$. Person-years lived between ages x and x + n is the sum of the number of person-years lived in that interval by people who survive the interval plus the number of person-years lived by those who don't: $_nL_x = nl_{x+n} + {}_nA_x$.[7] Person-years lived above age x, T_x, is simply the sum of $_nL_x$ from age x through the highest age in the table. Life expectancy at any age x, e_x^0, is the number of person-years lived above age x divided by the number of people living them: T_x/l_x. For example, life expectancy at birth, e_0^0, is T_0/l_0, life expectancy at age 10, denoted, e_{10}^0, is T_{10}/l_{10}, while remaining life expectancy at age 50, e_{50}^0, is T_{50}/l_{50}. Frequently $e_5^0 > e_0^0$ because of high infant mortality rates.

The information in life tables can be presented graphically in various ways. A population age distribution (population pyramid) can be constructed from an appropriate combination of the columns of the table to yield $_nC_x = {}_nN_x/N$, which is the proportion of the population in the age interval x to x + n, examples illustrated in the panels of Figure 4.1. The left panel, Figure 4.1A, shows three age distributions of progressively older populations from left to right. The right panel, Figure 4.1B, shows the population distribution of Europe in 1950 C.E., which clearly shows the loss of life of young adults in World War II as sharp indentations in both males and females aged 25–44 in that year, with a deeper indentation among the males. A similar pattern surely marked the Athenian population by the end of the Peloponnesian War. The age-specific death rate, $_nm_x = {}_nd_x/{}_nL_x$, is shown in Figure 4.2 for several female mortality regimes associated with Levels 2, 3, 6, and 12 of the Coale and Demeny model life tables (Coale and Demeny 1966). Those levels differ by life expectancy at birth and intrinsic growth rate (IGR). Level 2, with a female life expectancy at birth of $22\frac{1}{2}$ and an intrinsic growth rate of −0.05 percent per year, was identified by Bagnall and Frier as closely matching their Egyptian census population.[8] Level 3 has a female life expectancy of 25 and a zero IGR, a growth rate which is not far from the growth rates of many ancient populations. Levels 6 and 12 demonstrate the patterns associated with considerably higher growth rates: IGRs of $1\frac{1}{2}$ percent per year, which is a little faster than that of the United States at present, and $4\frac{1}{2}$ percent per year, which exceeds the population growth rates of East African countries in the 1970s; with associated female life expectancies at birth of $32\frac{1}{2}$ and $47\frac{1}{2}$. Figure 4.2 shows only the beginning of the survivorship curve for Level 3 because the lines become difficult to distinguish over the range of ages from 5 years and on. Survivorship by age, or column l_x in the life table, is a common graphical presentation of life table information, as is depicted in Figure 4.3, again shown for females in West Levels 2, 3, 6, and 12.

Life tables built from a single source of change in the population, such as mortality as an exit process, are called single-decrement life tables. The life table structure can accommodate more than one source of change to a population. A common multiple decrement process is mortality by cause of death, in which deaths by a number of specific causes replace the single-cause $_nd_x$ column. A multiple-cause-of-death life table can be useful for exploring the hypothetical consequences of eliminating or reducing one particular source of death, but in that sort of exercise, care needs to be exercised to allow for increases in the forces of other causes of death that would exert their effects earlier in the absence of a hypothetically removed cause.

[7] The $_nA_x$ term introduces some further intricacies that are not necessary for the current exposition. Interested readers are referred to Preston *et al.* (2001, 42–47) for further precision.

[8] Although Bagnall and Frier (1994) used the 1983 version of the Coale and Demeny life tables (Coale and Demeny, with Vaughan 1983). Graphically, the differences are small.

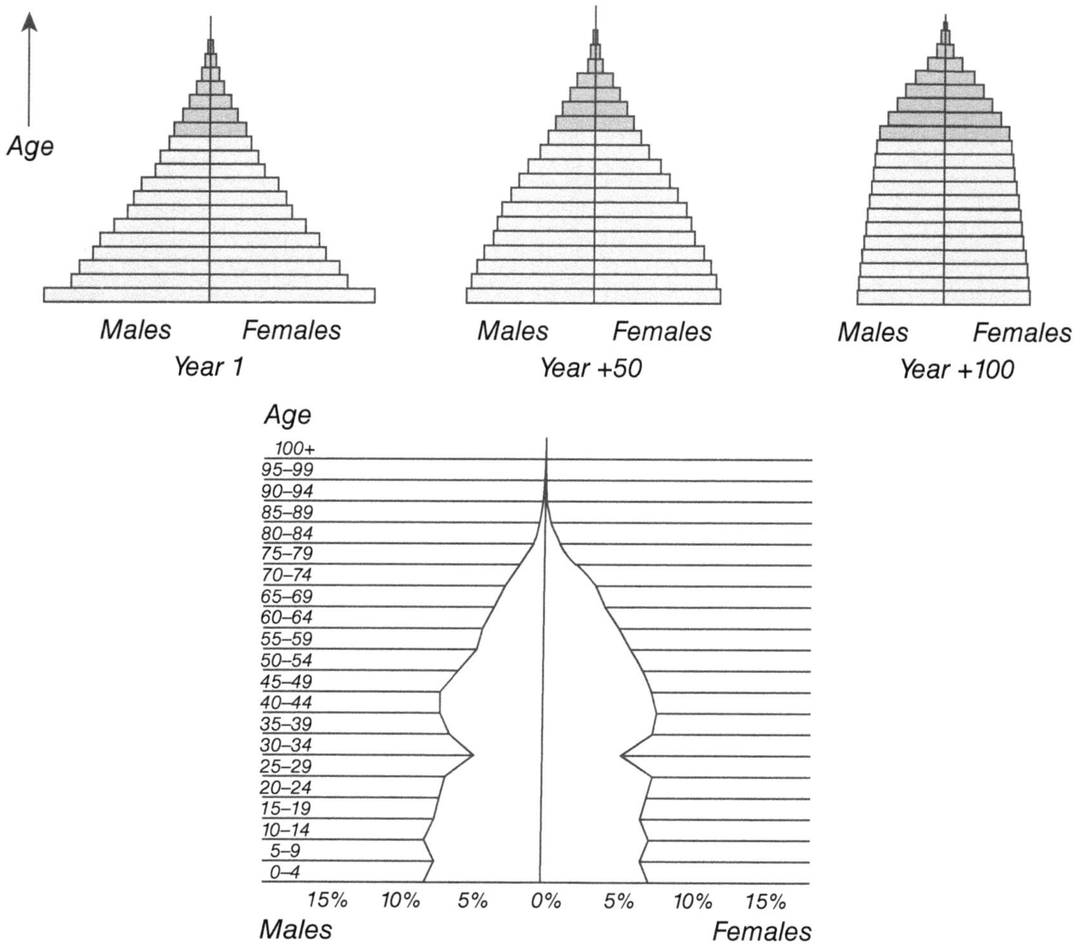

Figure 4.1. (A) Population pyramids of a progressively older population. (B) Population pyramid for Europe in 1950 CE, showing effect of World War 2.

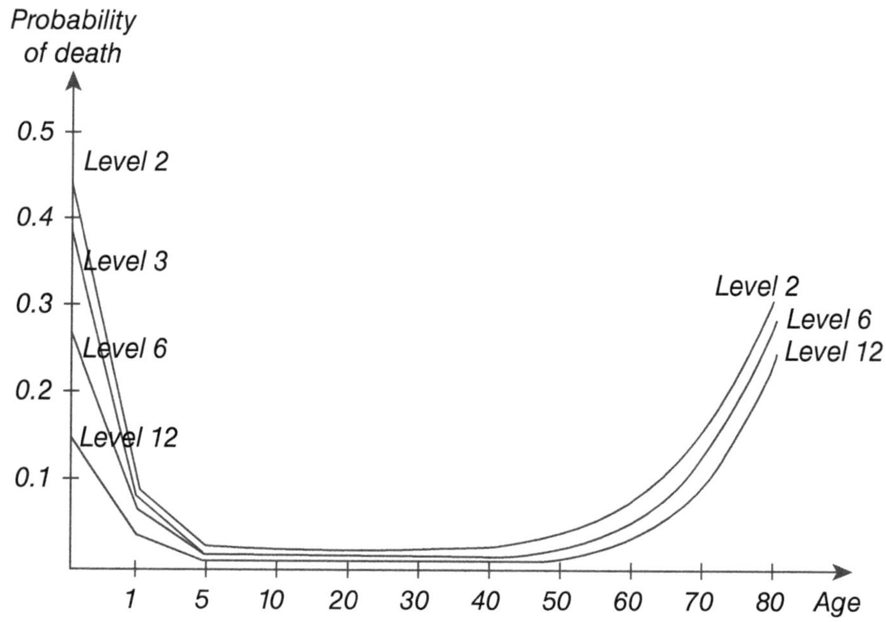

Figure 4.2. Female mortality regimes associated with Levels 2, 3, 6, and 12 of the Coale and Demeny model life tables.

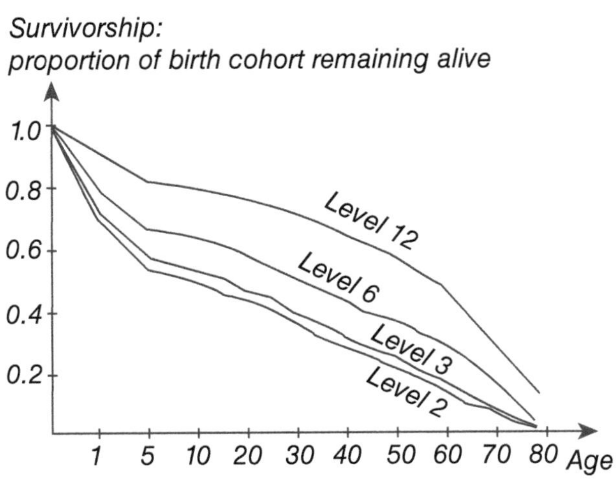

Figure 4.3. Age-specific survivorship for females in West Levels 2, 3, 6, and 12 of the Coale and Demeny model life tables.

4.2.3 Population Theory[9]

The life table forms the basis of three major population models, the stationary population, the stable population, and the non-stable population. A stable population is one in which the age-specific fertility and mortality rates are constant so that the age structure of the population remains constant over time.[10] A stable population may be growing, in which case more births are added at the young end of the age distribution than deaths at the old end, but the proportions of the populations in each age category remain the same. A stationary population is a special case of a stable population in which the number of births equals the number of deaths. A non-stable population is one in which growth rates differ by age, and is a generalization of the stable population.

A life table can be converted to a population model (stationary, stable, or otherwise) with only a modest re-definition of the columns. For example, l_0 becomes the number of births rather than the number of individuals aged zero to one year, and many of the other columns and elements take on alternative meanings. In general, l_x becomes the number of individuals who reach age x in a given calendar year: $l_x = l_0 \cdot {}_xp_0$, where ${}_xp_0$ is the probability of survival from birth to age x.

Before proceeding to a brief overview of the most basic concepts involved in population theory, it may be useful to point out that there are two distinct approaches to the theory, the continuous and the discrete approaches. The continuous approach, formalized by Alfred Lotka in 1907, with an additional solution offered by Sharpe and Lotka in 1911 (Lotka 1907; 1939; 1998; Sharpe and Lotka 1911), treats time and age distributions as continuous, and with a calculus approach, makes extensive use of integrals (which in the treatment below, I have converted to summation signs to lessen any intimidation from mathematical expressions). The discrete approach uses a discrete age scale (i.e., discrete age categories, such as zero to 1 year old, from 1 to 2 years old, from 34 to 35 years old, etc.) and treats time as distinct dates. The relationships which yield cohort population projections are difference equations (a discrete analogue to a differential equation) and are typically represented in a matrix format known as the Leslie matrix, after P. H. Leslie, the third person to publish the approach (Leslie 1945; 1948). The Leslie matrix is likely to be familiar to archaeologists and anthropologists, who have used it for population projection.[11] The two approaches are closely equivalent but offer distinct perspectives on population behavior.[12] Although the Leslie matrix has an appearance of simplicity, the mathematics required to extract information from it on age composition and the intrinsic growth rate is quite advanced. Since the presentation of the continuous approach is more compact and some of the major results are more transparent than with the discrete approach, the précis of population theory below relies more heavily on the continuous approach, the discrete projection approach summarized in a short, third sub-section below which gives only a flavor of the arrangement of relationships from which calculations are made.

Stable, Stationary, and Non-Stable Continuous Population Models. The assumptions for these models do not hold in natural populations, but the models often turn out to provide close approximations to reality. Most low-growth populations have not been genuinely stationary, and growing populations generally do not satisfy the requirements of the theoretical stable population. Fortunately, the departures of both types of population from the simplifying assumptions of these models can be accommodated by the non-stable population model. The stable population and its special cases are hypothetical constructs, not predictions. Demographers are well aware that populations will not maintain the same fertility and mortality rates for something close to a century, but the models provide a valuable analytical framework for investigating the influences of fertility and mortality on population growth, birth and death rates, and age composition.

The Stable Population Model. The life-table relationships of a stable population are constant over time, but the number of births may be increasing (or decreasing) over time. In any period, the number of new entrants to the population via births (assuming zero net immigration in all age groups) exceeds the number of exits from the population via deaths. Births grow at a constant rate such that the number of births

[9] I have relied on a number of treatments of demographic theory to develop this brief exposition of population theory. I have borrowed heavily from Preston *et al.* (2001, Chapters 3, 7, and 8), but have relied additionally on Keyfitz (1968, Chapters 5–7); Coale (1972, Chapters, 1–3); Keyfitz (1975, Chapters 4, 5, and 7); Keyfitz and Caswell (2005, Chapters 5–8); and Schoen (2006, Chapters 1–4).

[10] For simplicity, migration is typically assumed to net to zero, but the model in general can handle any pattern of migration with suitable adjustments.

[11] Chamberlain (2006, 36–38) offers an introduction to the use of the Leslie matrix for population projection.

[12] Keyfitz (1977, 134–138) offers a compact comparison of the Lotka and Leslie approaches.

at any date can be related to the number at some previous date by the relationship $B(t) = B(0) \cdot e^{rt}$, where r is the constant population growth rate. The age composition of this population is determined by its life table and the growth rate. The number of individuals in specific age classes at a given date can be related to the number of births in the current period by the relationship $N(a,t) = B(t) \cdot e^{-ra} \cdot p(a)$, where p(a) is the survival rate for age a. The number of people aged a at date t is smaller than the number of births at date t for two reasons: (1) the growth rate r has increased the number of births above the number of people born a years before, and (2) the force of mortality between this group's birth and the current date. Dividing both sides of this relationship by B(t) yields an expression for the proportion of the total population aged a at date t, $c(a,t) = b(t) \cdot e^{-ra} \cdot p(a)$, which indicates that the population's age composition can be completely characterized by its birth rate b(t), growth rate r, and the survival probability from the life table, p(a). The number of individuals in all age groups grows at the same rate.

Adding the age-specific fertility rate f(a) to this relationship, as N(a,t)f(a), summing the populations in each age group from some date zero when the constancy of fertility and mortality rates began to some date greater than the life of the longest-lived person in the population, and making several substitutions, yields Lotka's characteristic or renewal equation, which is the core of stable population theory. In discrete terms, that relationship is $1 = \sum_0^t e^{-ra} p(a) f(a)$.[13] It can be interpreted as a unit birth in some reference year being the result of a fertility rate f(a) applied to the fraction of survivors to age a p(a) of the e^{-ra} births t years earlier, summed over all ages in the population. The equation can be solved for the growth rate r that will make the right-hand side equal to 1; this growth rate is known as the intrinsic growth rate (IGR) of the population, given its fertility and mortality rates. The value of r that solves this life-table relationship is the growth rate associated with individual the individual pages of the Coale-Demeny life tables, which has on occasion been cited in the ancient historical literature as appearing to fit the data of some ancient population.

The Stationary Population Model. The stationary population model is simply a special case of the stable population model with the crude birth rate equal to the crude death rate. The growth rate of the population is exactly zero: r = 0 in the renewal equation. The model has had special appeal to students of ancient populations simply because so many of those populations were nearly constant in size for extended durations.

Non-Stable Populations. The non-stable population is the most general of these three cases.[14] The stable and stationary populations are simply special cases of it. The constant growth rate r in the renewal equation is replaced by a growth rate specific to age groups and dates; r becomes r(a,t), or to incorporate the influence of non-zero net immigration, r becomes r(a,t) − i(a,t). Growth rates and migration behavior can vary by age. The model is useful for studying the impacts of mortality changes, which typically are age-specific. The age groups affected by a mortality change will start growing (or declining, depending on the direction of the mortality change. The general expression for the age-specific growth rate is $r(a,t) = r_B(t-a) - \sum_0^a \Delta\mu(y,t) + \sum_0^a \Delta i(y,t)$, in which $r_B(t-a)$ is the growth rate of births at date t-minus-a, $\Delta\mu(y,t)$ is the difference in the mortality rate between the cohort aged a at date t and the cohort just incrementally older than a at date t, and i(y,t) is the difference in net immigration at age y between the cohort aged a at date t and the slightly older cohort at the same date. The age-specific mortality changes $\Delta\mu$ cumulate in the age-specific growth rate, causing the age-specific profile of growth rates to rise over time for mortality decreases and conversely for mortality increases: it takes a while for those saved by a mortality reduction to begin to reproduce, and conversely, it takes time for the avoided reproduction of those claimed by a mortality increase to have their impact. This expression also shows that unchanged net migration will have no effect on age-specific growth rates.

Discrete-Time Cohort Component Projection: The Leslie Matrix. The discrete counterpart to the continuous population model is called the cohort component projection method Leslie, 1945; 1948; Pollard 1973, Chapter 4; Keyfitz 1968, Chapters 2–4; 1977, 205–212; Caswell, 2001, Chapters 2–4; Preston *et. al.*, 2001, Chapter 6; Schoen 2006, 12–13). Its most common format is the Leslie matrix. It segments a population into subgroups that different exposures to risks of fertility, mortality, and if included, migration, and computes the changes over time in the numbers in each subgroup. The model, and its Leslie matrix, can be built up with t discrete time periods, t = 0, 1, 2, . . . , and m + 1 age groups, 0, 1, 2, . . . , m, where m is the oldest age in the population. As with the continuous model, it is pretty much standard to work with a female population, although there are methods for calculating an accompanying male population. Thus, $n_{x,t}$ represents the number of females in age group x at time t, and s_x is the proportion of females in age group x at time t surviving to be in age group x + 1 at time t + 1, with x < m, since no one survives past age m: $s_m = 0$. The fertility in each age group of females, the average number of daughters born per female in age group x at time t, is f_x; the daughters born from that fertility survive to be in age group 0 at time t + 1. Then the numbers of individuals of various ages one period ahead can be calculated from these fertility and survival parameters applied to the numbers of those individuals at the present time: $n_{0,t+1} = f_0 n_{0,t} + f_1 n_{1,t} + f_2 n_{2,t} + \ldots + f_m n_{m,t}$, or in more compact summation notation, $n_{0,t+1} = \sum_0^m f_x n_{x,t}$: that is, the number of age zero individuals the next period, born in this period, is the sum of births per female over females of all fertile age groups in this period. While the entire population extends to age

[13] It is more common to encounter the renewal equation in continuous form, which involves the integral rather than the summation notation of the discrete construction: $1 = \int_\alpha^\beta e^{-ra} p(a) f(a) da$, in which α is the lower limit of the reproductive age and β is the upper limit.

[14] This exposition relies heavily on Preston *et al.* (2001, Chapter 8).

m, the highest fertile age will be some age k, such that $f_j = 0$ for all $j > k$ and $f_k \neq 0$. Proceeding with the number of individuals in the next age group, who need not be born in the current period (i.e., they are already alive at time t), $n_{1,t+1} = s_0 n_{0,t}$: that is, the number of females of age 1 at time t + 1 is equal to the number born the previous period times their survival rate. Similarly with the number of individuals in age group 2 in the next period: $n_{2,t+1} = s_1 n_{1,t}$, and so on through the highest age, $n_{m,t+1} = s_{m-1} n_{m-1,t}$, or the number of individuals of the oldest age in period t+1 is the number one year younger at time t times their probability of survival from age m-1 to age m.

This notation can be expressed in a matrix format as the Leslie matrix, shown below:

$$\begin{bmatrix} n_{0,t+1} \\ n_{1,t+1} \\ n_{2,t+1} \\ \vdots \\ \vdots \\ n_{m,t+1} \end{bmatrix} = \begin{bmatrix} f_0 & f_1 & f_2 & \cdots & f_{m-1} & f_m \\ s_0 & 0 & \cdots & \cdots & \cdots & 0 \\ 0 & s_1 & 0 & \cdots & \cdots & 0 \\ \vdots & \vdots & s_2 & \cdots & \cdots & 0 \\ \vdots & \vdots & \vdots & \ddots & \vdots & 0 \\ 0 & 0 & 0 & 0 & s_{m-1} & 0 \end{bmatrix} \cdot \begin{bmatrix} n_{0,t} \\ n_{1,t} \\ n_{2,t} \\ \vdots \\ \vdots \\ n_{m,t} \end{bmatrix}$$

Both rows and columns represent age groups, which can be in individual- or multi-year intervals. The first row in the matrix is the age-specific fertility rate of each group. Each succeeding row contains only the age-specific survival rate to the next period of individuals in each age group, forming what is called the sub-diagonal of survival rates. There is no necessity for a row below the one with the survival rate for age group m_{i1}, s_{m-1}, because $s_m = 0$. A bit of terminology: the column of age-specific population segments at time t + 1 on the left-hand side of the equals sign and the column of the corresponding age-specific population segments at time t, to the right of the Leslie matrix, are both called vectors: they are effectively one-column matrices.[15]

The matrix equation can be represented more compactly by $\mathbf{n_{t+1}} = \mathbf{An_t}$, which implies $\mathbf{n_t} = \mathbf{A^t n_0}$, in which the bold font indicates a vector for lower-case symbols and a matrix for upper-case symbols. The last expression says that the population at any given time t can be related to the population at any previous time, designated zero, by multiplying the vector of age-specific populations at the earlier time by the Leslie matrix to the power t, the number of time intervals in between.

Matrices are deceptively simple looking arrays of numbers or symbols, but square matrices, ones with the same number of rows and columns as the Leslie matrix has, possess a number of substantially deeper, and informative, properties, expressed in the form of eigenstructures known as eigenvalues and eigenvectors. A square matrix will have as many eigenvalues, not all of which need be distinct, as it has columns (vectors) and a number of eigenvectors at least as great as the number of distinct eigenvalues. The largest eigenvalue associated with a Leslie matrix is the population's growth rate, corresponding to r in the continuous population model. Some elements of an eigenvector represent the ultimate contribution of the corresponding age (or other) category of the population to a particular age category of the ultimate stable population. Other elements give contributions to future births.[16]

Population projection using the Leslie matrix has been used fairly widely in anthropological studies of historical populations and in projections from skeletal remains in archaeological studies as well as in contemporary demographic analysis.

Comparative Statics and Other Results of Stable Populations. Comparative statics of a population model changes some parameter and observes the difference in equilibrium properties. The first sub-section below summarizes the comparative statics of the two most important parameters of the stable population model, the fertility and mortality rates. The following sub-sections address two aspects of the model's behavior (and populations' behaviors as well), the lingering growth effect after population growth has ceased, and the tendency of a population to "forget" transient events.

Changes in Fertility and Mortality Rate. In a closed population, changes in fertility and mortality have different effects. A change in fertility changes the population's growth rate in the same direction as the fertility change, but not the probability of survival to any particular age. Higher fertility increases the size of more recently born cohorts relative to older ones, making the population younger. A change in mortality changes the probability of survival to various ages, a decrease in mortality making the population older because people live longer. However, a decrease in mortality increases the number of women of childbearing age, which raises the population growth rate, tending to make the population younger. The life-cycle or aging effect and the growth rate effect of mortality changes offset each other. In high-mortality populations, the growth rate effect dominates, and a population becomes younger with a decrease in mortality (Lee 1994, 10–12). Lee calculates a one-year increase in life expectancy to increase the growth rate of a population with a 20-year e_0 life expectancy by 0.16 percent (Lee 1994, 13, Figure 2-2). In an ancient population with a growth rate around 0.1 percent, such a mortality decrease would effectively double the growth rate.

[15] Specifically, they are called column vectors; a one-row matrix, which would run across rather than down, is called a row vector. The distinction is required for matrix arithmetic operations.

[16] But this dominant eigenvalue is not identical in value to the intrinsic growth rate r, a number such as 0.01, in the Lotka model; a dominant eigenvalue in the Leslie model less than 1 indicates a contracting population while a growing population is associated with a dominant eigenvalue greater than 1. Accordingly, the dominant eigenvalue of the Leslie matrix will be 1 + r: Chu (1998, 22–23). Schoen (2006, appendix A) offers a demographic interpretation of eigenvectors.

Population Momentum. If a population's fertility schedule were to be instantaneously changed to the replacement level, NRR = 1.0, and maintained at that level until a new stable equilibrium is reached, the size of the population would continue to grow for some time as young people born before the fertility revolution move through their life cycles and bear children at the new rate.[17] The ratio of the size of the population just before the fertility revolution to its size when it reaches its new stable equilibrium is the measure of what is called the population's momentum. If a population were stationary when the fertility revolution occurred (that is, there would be effectively no revolution), the measure of momentum is 1.0. For a population that was growing prior to the revolution, the measure is greater than 1, and for a population that was not replacing itself, the measure is less than 1. The measurement is derived from the renewal equation and is $M = \sum_0^\beta \frac{c(a)}{c_s(a)} \cdot w(a)$, in which c(a) is the pre-fertility revolution age structure (the proportion of the population in age group a), $c_s(a)$ is the age structure in the new equilibrium, and w(a) is an intricate distribution of the expected number of births to individuals aged a and above through the rest of their reproductive spans in the new fertility regime, divided by the mean age at birth in that new regime. The summation is from age 0 through the end of the reproductive span, β. The distribution w(a) takes its highest values for the ages from zero (newborns) until the earliest age of fertility, during which the future number of expected births is greatest, and declines steadily until age β is reached. The ratio $c(a)/c_s(a)$ is highest at young age groups in a rapidly growing population, and is lower in slowly growing or declining populations. A rapidly growing population characterized by $c(a)/c_{s/}(a) > 1$ for relatively large, younger age groups, and relatively high w(a) for those ages, will have values of $M > 1$, as high as 1.5 for populations in contemporary Africa and South Asia. M can take values as low as 1.006 to 1.05 in some European countries still growing modestly, to values ranging from 0.88 to 0.95 in industrialized countries with birth rates currently below replacement.

Since the survival schedule is in the renewal equation, which forms the basis for this measurement of population momentum, it is natural to believe that mortality changes would have a parallel effect, and there in fact is (Guillot 2006, 283–294). The momentum effect of mortality change is not a boost to future population because of more favorable mortality regimes in the future but rather a measure of the effect of a previous mortality change, once the improvement (or worsening) has ceased, on future population size. Just as the population momentum measure M captures the effect on population size of large, younger cohorts moving through their reproductive years at a lower fertility schedule until the population reaches a new stable equilibrium, the mortality momentum captures the effect of larger cohorts who benefited from the mortality reduction moving through their reproductive years until the population reaches a new stable equilibrium. In populations with fertility levels that yield slow growth or even decline, one-time improvements in mortality schedules can be a considerable source of population growth to a new, stable size. In some slowly growing populations, the momentum of mortality may account for a large proportion of a population momentum greater than unity. In general, it is possible for a population with all cohort fertility rates below replacement level to grow if improvements in mortality more than compensate for the decreasing initial sizes of successive birth cohorts.

Ergodicity.[18] Most simply stated, ergodicity is the property that the asymptotic state of a system—that is, its configuration in the long run when it has had time to reach a stable equilibrium (assuming one exists)—is independent of its initial conditions. Specifically, the age structure of populations may differ at some initial date, but if they experience the same fertility and mortality regimes for long enough, their age structures will become the same eventually. There are weak and strong versions of ergodicity, the strong version assuming that age-specific fertility and mortality rates are constant, the weak version that they may change, with the result that two populations with different initial age structures will approach the same age structure if both experience the same fertility and mortality regimes that may change over time. Eventually such initially differing populations will have the same crude birth and death rates if they have the same fertility and mortality rates.

Ergodic results are useful because, when they exist, they imply that population patterns might reveal something about processes rather than initial conditions. If a model can be shown to not be ergodic, its results can be used to explain differences in processes in situations where the patterns are the same and would thus suggest that the processes are different without further analysis.

Strong and weak ergodicity have been proven for the Lotka and Leslie versions of the population model,[19] with several implications of interest. First, how will populations subjected to major disruptions such as infectious epidemics or natural disasters recover? Will they eventually return to their previous age distribution? If their fertility and mortality regimes return to their previous structure, they will. Second, nonsustained migration will have only a transient effect on a population's age distribution if the migrants do not affect the prevailing fertility and mortality patterns. Third, the length of time required for two different populations' (either in different locations and unrelated or the same population tracked over time) age structures to converge depends on how different the initial conditions

[17] Adapted from Preston *et al.* (2001, 161–170).

[18] I have drawn on Pollard (1973, 44–46, 51–55); Keyfitz (1968, 88–94); Caswell (2001, 18); Preston *et. al.* (2000, 145–146); and Schoen (2006, 28).

[19] In the continuous model, the age distribution and birth, death, and growth rates of a stable population depend only on the fertility and mortality functions. In the discrete model, a mathematical characteristic generally found in the Leslie matrix yields what is called a primitive matrix, which in turn results in only the first eigenvector remaining non-zero (or of trivial magnitude) when the A matrix is exponentiated by a sufficiently large value of t.

are. Preston *et. al.* (2001, 146) suggest 70 years as a rule of thumb, although extreme differences could require over a century to work themselves out.

4.2.4 Demographic Models and the Study of Ancient Populations

Model life tables, primarily those of Coale and Demeny (also sometimes called the Princeton Regional Life Tables) (Coale and Demeny 1966; Coale and Demeny, with Vaughan1983), have been applied to various ancient Greek and Roman populations to test the verity of ancient evidence and to estimate total populations of several poleis in Greece and population age structures in both regions. Hopkins introduced the methodology to assess the plausibility of various sources of ancient evidence that could be used to estimate Roman age distributions and age-specific mortality. The most prominent applications of model life tables to ancient Greek case studies are those of Hansen (Hansen, 1991, pp. 86–94; 2006a; 2006b)[20] and to a lesser extent Osborne (1985), and to ancient Roman populations are those of Frier (1982; 1983), Bagnall and Frier (1984), and Saller (1994, Chapter 3). It is not necessary to go into details of the conclusions from their analyses to consider criticisms to which their studies have been subjected. The primary criticism of the use of contemporary model life tables (principally Coale-Demeny and United Nations model life tables) is that the pattern of age-specific mortality in the model life tables does not or may not represent the patterns in the regions and times to which they have been applied.[21] Probably the most detailed demographic data likely to be retrieved from antiquity are the census data from several centuries in Roman Egypt, investigated exhaustively by Bagnall and Frier. Bagnall and Frier had to extrapolate mortality at early ages from contemporary life tables because of spotty recording of infant and child deaths in the original censuses, and they relied on relative sizes of age groups in the Coale and Demeny model life tables to estimate the sizes, and correspondingly the mortality, of the young cohorts. Parkin noted the heavy urban bias in Bagnall and Frier's census observations (Parkin1995, 2), and Scheidel has considered the urban bias strong enough to render their finding of correspondence to model life tables spurious (Scheidel 2001b, xxvii), while Scheidel and Sallares separately have emphasized the likely departure of small regions' life tables from the model life tables commonly used in the analysis of ancient populations (Scheidel 2002, Chapter 5).They focused in particular on the mortality schedules that would have accompanied the disease regimes of specific, small regions of Egypt (Scheidel) and Italy (Sallares) and questioned the capacity of the Coale-Demeny model life tables to even come close to approximating them. Sallares shows the potential scope of departure of some ancient Italian age-specific mortality rates from those in the Coale-Demeny tables with comparisons of two neighboring communities in Italy and of English mortality rates in a region subject to *P. vivax* malaria and a reminder of the stronger force of mortality in the *P. falciparum* malaria prevalent in the Italian regions (Sallares, 2002, 160–162 Tables 3-5, 163–164 Tables 6-7).

The concerns of Scheidel and Sallares regarding the direct applicability of the Coale and Demeny model life tables to large regions in antiquity (e.g., all of the Roman Empire or even all of Roman Egypt) are reasonable.[22] Those life tables have age-specific mortality schedules derived from the experiences of a number of predominantly European countries in the 19th and 20th centuries, and the entire structure of the life tables derives from those mortality patterns. It is common knowledge that different patterns of age-specific mortality will generate different stable populations with different age compositions. Scheidel and Sallares understand this and, rather than quarrel with the differences between these recent population structures and ancient ones, record pleas for care in using model life tables to formulate estimates of ancient population structures. Their concerns focus on the disease regimes in these ancient societies, which were almost surely quite different from those to which contemporary Western populations have been exposed. These disease regimes will, or could, yield patterns of age-specific mortalities quite different from those in the Coale and Demeny model life tables. One small region—literally a township—Sallares reports from mid-19th century Italy apparently had a negative population growth rate simply because its birth rates could not keep pace with the mortality rates from malaria. Another nearby township had strikingly lower mortality rates and correspondingly higher life expectancies at birth. Without migration into the high-mortality township, its population would have become extinct; the fact that it did not go extinct suggests that either not enough time elapsed to witness its extinction or that it received continuing net inflows of immigrants, who must have been aware of the mortality regime in the destination. The latter case would indicate that a multi-region population model is necessary to understand the age structures of the populations involved, and the same is true of the rural and urban populations in Roman Egypt.[23] For example, urban areas such as Alexandria and Rome might well have had negative intrinsic growth rates considering just their own fertility and mortality schedules, with only net immigration maintaining their populations. This is not news to scholars of the demography of these populations, but reference to a single life table that averages

[20] Akrigg (2011, 37–59) places Hansen's work in helpful context of the history of estimating the Classical Athenian population and in summarizing his application of demographic techniques.

[21] The earliest well-informed scrutiny of the application of model life tables to ancient settings is Parkin (1992, Chapter 3).

[22] Hin (2013, 109–124) offers a sophisticated overview of ancient historians' applications of various model life tables and the limitations on their application due to limited information on ancient, regional mortality regimes.

[23] The standard reference on multiregional life tables is Rogers, (1975, particularly Chapters 3–5). Multiregional demography has remained skewed between the algebra of solving the renewal equation for a single growth rate applicable to all regions and a strong numerical orientation; it has not focused on analysis of consequences of persistent differences in fertility and mortality rates among regions linked by migration. More recent work in multiregional demographic modeling has focused on migration, which while serving as the critical link between regions' populations, is only the connective link; for example, Rogers (1995).

out the different areas' fertility and mortality rates, could one for any place and time but Roman Egypt be constructed, would not be representative of either location. The fact that it might represent the entire population could mask as much information as it reveals.

Complaints about the limited scope of the Coale-Demeny life tables should have been alleviated by now by numerous actual and model life tables constructed for regions with far more extensive disease regimes than those Coale and Demeny relied upon. The later edition of the United Nations life tables for developing countries has long been an obvious option (United Nations 1982). Ancient historians are aware of the model life tables Preston, McDaniel and Grushka (1993) constructed from the records of black American emigrants to Liberia in the first half of the 19th century, which constructs life tables with e_0s (life expectancies at birth) as low as 2 years. Other work has been proceeding on the construction of life tables for high-mortality regions of Africa (INDEPTH Network 2004), and Woods recently has developed high-mortality life tables for regions he calls Southeast Europe and East Asia (Woods, 2007, 379, 380 Tables 2 and 3).Whether these disease regimes sufficiently approximate the disease regimes of ancient Mediterranean regions may be unknowable, despite progress on that latter subject represented in particular by Scheidel's work on Roman Egypt (whose disease regime may have differed from those of the various kingdoms of pharaonic Egypt) and Sallares' on Italy. It is possible, using the logical structure of a model life table, to fill in parts of a specific population's life table for which the population is missing data if sufficient data on age structure or mortality are available for enough other age groups. The difficulty with such indirect infilling is that the mortality regime of the cohorts for which data are missing may be different from that of the corresponding cohorts in a model life table. No external verification other than plausibility or general correspondence to results of other studies is available to determine whether the estimate made with the assistance of the model life table is anywhere close to the actual ancient mortality conditions, a point made in detail by Akrigg regarding Hansen's use of model life tables in his construction of Classical Greek population estimates (Akrigg, 2011, 48–57). Akrigg (2019, Chapters 2–3) since has developed empirical support for Hansen's model life table.[24] Splicing together segments of different life tables, cohorts of which are believed to have experienced similar mortality regimes may not produce new information about an ancient population. If the information that is wanted is the proportion of the population in young age groups, assigning the mortality schedule of young cohorts to the early ages of a life table for an ancient population will indeed produce such a proportion, but that proportion is simply the consequence of the assumption about the mortality schedule of the young end of the age distribution.

[24] Akrigg's (2019) Chapters 6 and 7 are important demonstrations of the economic and social information that can be derived from closely reasoned inferences regarding population size and structure.

There are several ways of conceptualizing the issues involved in these regional differences. First, and possibly most obviously, "What is the 'correct' population to subject to the logical relationships of a static life table and the corresponding dynamic population model?" With several centuries of temporary and permanent circulation of individuals between a countryside and a city, why should individuals' fertility and mortality schedules be assigned to one category or another when both their recorded (such as any "recording" is or was) fertility and mortality depended to a considerable extent on where they were residing on particular dates? In another year, a person who died of tainted water in the city might have been relocated in the countryside and not succumbed to mortality forces for several more years, if not decades. Are the regionally segregated fertility and mortality schedules describing a population or a location? A population or region completely closed to immigration or emigration clearly has a meaningful life table; a sub-group or sub-region inside such a population or region, which is highly open to movements of individuals in both directions across its boundaries can have a life table constructed (in an ideal world or statistical recording) for it, but the interpretation of such a table is not unambiguous. The treatment of geographical boundaries in the identification of populations raises the issue of how to treat non-interbreeding groups. The prevalence of slavery in Italy during the Roman Imperial Period and in various regions of Classical Greece opens the issue of keeping the fertility and mortality schedules of the free and slave populations separate in any estimate of the populations' structures and intrinsic growth rates. This may pose little problem considering the sources—censuses in the historical record and identifiable burials in the archaeological record—but in regions where slaves formed a considerable proportion of the population, any life-table information cobbled together from whatever array of sources would apply to only a part of the population.

Second, a life table prepared for a small region, such as Sallares' example of malaria-infested Grosseto, contrasted with nearby, salubrious Treppio, or even the marshland parishes of southeastern England also reported by Sallares, may measure conditions in a location rather than reliable fertility and mortality statistics of a population. A short-period life table for a small region, such as one prepared from a decennial census, may capture short-term residents and miss longer-term residents temporarily absent, a problem not faced with a long-period life table such as assembled by Bagnall and Frier for Roman Egypt, spread over close to three centuries as their observations are.

4.2.5 Two-Sex Problems and Models

The one-sex population model is not an equilibrium model. It assumes implicitly that the distributions of males who would mate and produce children are compatible in the sense that they would yield the same intrinsic growth rates if modeled separately. An evident weakness of the approach is that female and male single-sex models typically yield different IGRs. Not infrequently, one sex's IGR is greater than one while that of the other is less than one, which implies that eventually one of the sexes will be eliminated.

Distortions of the sex ratio, such as would result from the disproportionate deaths of reproduction-age males in a war, result in a marriage squeeze, in which marriage and reproduction are limited by the availability of the scarcer sex (Schoen 1983; 1988, Chapter 8). As an example, in a growing population (either stable growth or non-stable growth) in which males marry females five years younger than themselves on average, males of a given age will look to a larger cohort of females while the females of that proportionally larger cohort look to a smaller male cohort of marriageable age and encounter a shortage of potential mates, reducing their chances of marriage, and their fertility. A decline in the birth rate would produce the opposite problem, with males caught in the squeeze. Preference patterns for mates can exacerbate a purely numerical squeeze. Whether marriage squeezes in human populations have quantitatively important repercussions on growth rates appears to be an open question, as social changes may operate to accommodate the changed circumstances and attenuate population impacts.

A drastic drop in the numbers of either sex imposes an immediate distortion on a population's sex ratio. An example that cannot have been particularly uncommon is deaths of men in a war. For example, Henry's analysis of the French population in the aftermath of World War I indicated that changes in the average age difference of spouses, marriages to foreigners, and an increase in the number of women never marrying were the primary responses to the vast hole left in males aged 25 to 40 in the 1920s (Henry 1966). The recovery of the Athenian population in the aftermath of the Sicilian disaster during the Peloponnesian Wars may have involved a number of alterations in social customs regarding marriage.[25] The accommodations of the French post-World War I population to the decrease in the numbers of fertile-age males are all accounting changes; incentives to behave differently in such demographically altered circumstances are outside the explanatory scope of demographic theory. Changes in fertility rates would be explained by changing proportions of the population married and changing age of female marriage, but not by predictable changes in decision patterns.

Most demographers have used female population models (sometimes called female-dominant models). Its reproductive range is shorter than the male model, and illegitimate births are more readily attributable to the mother. The difference between results using separate male and female models, however, can yield incompatible results regarding the intrinsic population growth rate. he most widely cited instance of egregious differences in IGRs estimated with female and male models is the instance of Robert Kuczynski's (in)famous estimates for France in 1920–23: the female model yielded a net reproduction rate of 0.977, while the male model's NRR was 1.194. The one-sex female-dominant model predicted a continually decreasing population for France while the male-dominant model predicted a continually increasing population (Kuczynski, 1932, 36–38, cited in, *inter alios*, Pollard, 1973, 82). One implication of this difference in rates of increase for the two sexes is that the relative abundance of males would increase while females would eventually decline to zero. Finding a way to avoid this absurd result while satisfying other conditions of realism has been a long-standing challenge in discovering a satisfactory two-sex demographic model.

Two-sex population models remain a work in progress. Many two-sex models have been proposed but found not fully satisfactory.[26] One common but largely unsuccessful approach has involved various methods of averaging female and male intrinsic growth rates from one-sex models without attempting to model unions or marriages. From a modeling perspective, the two-sex problem is the inability of conventional population models to capture changes in marriage and fertility rates resulting from changes in population composition. A problem hampering the adaptations of the one-sex models to two-sex settings has been the specification of the fertility rate. In the one-sex female dominant models, the female fertility rate is a function of the female's age only; in one-sex male-dominant models, the male fertility rate is correspondingly a function of the male's age only. These fertilities are very much like fecundities. In the two-sex setting, fertility applies to couples, and within any couple depends on the ages of the female and the male. However, since fertility

[25] Parkin (2011, 187) offers a stark clarification of the magnitude of the Athenian population losses: out of 60,000 adult males at the beginning of the war, 20,000 died of the plague in 431 B.C.E. (or through 427) and another 20,000 died in the war, 10,000 in the Sicilian excursion alone. Two interesting problems for applied life table analysis are (1) what proportion of their expected reproductive experience had the 20,000 dead already experienced prior to their deaths, and (2) how many younger Athenian males could have reached reproductive age in the two decades over which the loss of the 20,000 adult men were lost? Pomeroy (1997, 39) reports that after the Sicilian disaster, Athens passed a law allowing a man "to take an additional woman" in order to produce children.

[26] Pollard, (1973, Chapter 7) reports earlier literature on two-sex modeling efforts. Schoen (1988, Chapters 6, 7, and 9) develops two-sex population, marriage, and fertility models. Caswell (2001, Chapter 17) and Iannelli, Martcheva, and Milner (2005) provide the most recent overviews of efforts that I have found. Two models in particular are considered to show promise, but efforts developing them have been intermittent. A model in the continuous (Lotka) framework, the Frederickson-Hoppensteadt model, is summarized by Iannelli (2005 30–34, and studied further in Chapter 3); Frederickson (1971), Hoppensteadt (1975, Part I). In the discrete tradition of the Leslie Matrix is the Birth-Matrix Mating-Rule (BMMR) model of Robert Pollak (1986; 1987; 1990), which has drawn the attention of Caswell (2001, 585–587), and Ianelli *et al.* (2005, 29–30). Chu (1998, Chapter 6, section 2) offers a compact presentation of Pollak's two-sex models, but not with an attempt to extend the theory of the unions between males and females. Bergstrom and Lam (1989) offer a specific marriage model to insert in the general form offered in the Pollak two-sex model but do not try to extend the demographic modeling to calculation of a single, unified intrinsic growth rate; their solution to a disturbance in relative cohort sizes of male and female marriage-partner ages results in a combination of a change in the preferred age difference of marital partners and members of the larger cohort remaining unmarried. The same authors apply the model to Swedish data in Bergstrom and Lam (1994).

is a measure of actual live births, the probability of a single female and a single male entering into marriage (becoming a couple) depends on the numbers of females and males in various age cohorts. Couple fertility rates therefore also depend on probabilities of establishing unions, which depends on the age and sex composition of a population. In equilibrium, male and female intrinsic growth rates must be identical. The marriage module appears to be an especially critical failure component in the two-sex population models that have been tested empirically to date; ones that have been tested have had strikingly poor predictive capacity even one year out (Iannelli *et al.* 2005, 41–42).[27] The additional complexity of two-sex population models, with fertility depending on interactions of individuals in different age cohorts—both individuals forming reproductive unions and other individuals simply posing competition for mates—has posed conceptual intricacies which have not been fully resolved to date. These models remain a research field, if not an especially active one. While the conventional, one-sex population models classify the state of individuals by age alone, the two-sex models classify individuals by both age and sex, which complicates the mathematics considerably.[28]

4.2.6 *Natural Fertility and Fertility*

The first sub-section introduces the concept of natural fertility, and the second addresses the methods of identifying such behavior in a population. The third sub-section discusses methods of controlling fertility and the current state of that subject in the literature on Mediterranean antiquity.

Concept. The concept of natural fertility has had a prominent role in the study of pre-demographic transition populations. The hypothesis appeared in Louis Henry's 1961 article and was quickly taken up by students of pre-industrial and contemporary Third World populations Henry (1961).[29] Stated most simply, the hypothesis identifies a pattern of female age distributions that are (hypothesized to be) the result of no or very minimal efforts at birth control or fertility limitation, or more specifically, family limitation, comprised of parity-based stopping behavior only. Under natural fertility, there is no parity-related stopping behavior in evidence. The hypothesis does not imply that a natural fertility population will approach the human maximum of fertility; in fact a Hutterite population of the early 20th century C.E. in the upper Midwest of the United States and southern Canada, with a total fertility rate above 10, is widely cited as the highest-fertility population ever identified. Nonetheless, the biological maximum is estimated to be somewhere around 15. Both cultural and biological / physiological factors act on the completed fertility rate of a natural fertility population. Cultural practices that affect fertility include breast-feeding, taboos on intercourse during certain times, social rules on eligibility for marriage which affect marriage age, and various practices that would affect birth spacing that are implemented for purposes other than limitation of completed family size, such as ensuring food supplies are adequate and protecting the health of the mother and previous children. The existence of stopping behavior—cessation of fertility after reaching a desired family size—is the only indicator that would separate a natural fertility population from one that practiced fertility limitation according to the Henry hypothesis. Fertility will be terminated only by age-induced sterility in a natural fertility population.

An obvious implication of the natural fertility hypothesis is that a society so characterized does not practice birth control. Its members may not have access to effective birth control knowledge or technologies; they may not want to practice fertility limitation. The subject of contraception in antiquity has been addressed by numerous authors from various perspectives, ranging from recorded medical or scientific knowledge or beliefs of the time to possible or likely practices to inferences of contraceptive behavior from surviving demographic evidence. The subject remains unsettled.

The natural fertility concept focuses on one mechanism of family limitation—parity-specific stopping behavior—which channels thinking toward the use or not of contraceptives. Other methods of family limitation are slipped into the background of natural fertility, leaving fertility and completed family size (allowing for mortality) able to vary considerably among populations classified as living under conditions of natural fertility. Other mechanisms besides stopping behaviors long have known and used to control fertility and limit family sizes. Breastfeeding is one behavior that can modulate birth spacing and thus limit family size, and while length of lactation may have some cultural commonalities within a population, it is, and may have been in various populations of antiquity, under individual control.[30] Similar levels of fertility may be achieved by combinations of quite different

[27] Recent efforts in the economics literature have applied matching models to the marriage market: Dagsvik, Brunborg, and Flaatten (2001) depends on the numbers of men and women in each age group; Choo and Siow (2006) measures couples' gains from marriage and cohabitation relative to remaining single, with the gains shifting between members of a couple as population numbers change; and Siow (2008) reveals considerable flexibility in age preferences for mates as cohort sizes change, mitigating the impact of what otherwise would be a marriage squeeze.

[28] Chu (1998, Chapter 2) offers a generalization of population models' specifications of types of individuals as a generalized branching process, in which individuals may change any of a number of characteristics over time. In both the one- and two-sex models, individuals change only one characteristic, age, over time, but more generally, they could change other characteristics affecting fertility such as location, income, and marital status.

[29] This Anglophone publication followed several previous analyses by Henry: (1953), followed by two mathematical treatments more sophisticated than the first 1961 article: Henry (1957; 1961c), and an empirical counterpart, (1961b); re-stated and modified somewhat: Henry (1979).

[30] Saskia Hin (2011, 110) considers the concept "arbitrary and outdated," for omitting behaviors other than stopping. April Pudsey (2011, 70–72) emphasizes the array of fertility control behaviors beyond natural fertility's stopping behavior and their application in the ancient Mediterranean lands.

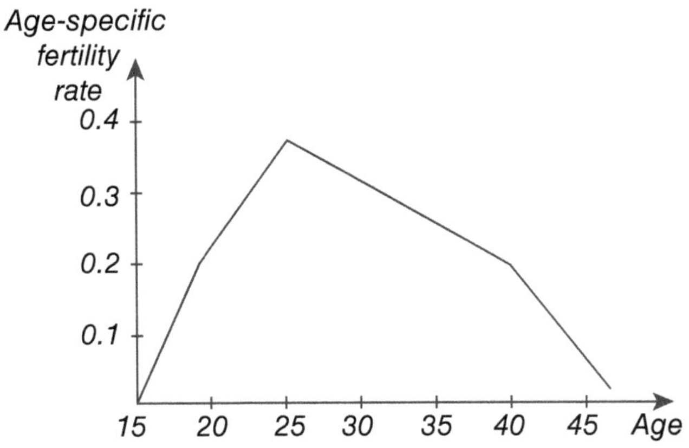

Figure 4.4. Age-specific marital fertility profile.

subcomponents, ranging from age at marriage and duration from marriage to first birth to duration of marriage to birth intervals from various causes Menken (1979, 10).

Measurement. The most widely used, although not the only, statistical test for natural fertility in a population is the Coale-Trussell regression technique (Coale and Trussell 1974; first presented in Coale, 1971, 206).[31] Coale and Trussell suggest that age-specific marital fertility rates, r(a), either follow the age pattern of natural fertility, n(a), characterized by Henry or deviate from it in a regular way according to a schedule v(a). Their model captured variations in the fertility rate between a standard or control population and a population under study with two parameters, M, which reflects the level of natural marital fertility, and m, which specifies the extent of control of marital fertility.[32] Thus, marital fertility either follows a natural fertility or departs from natural fertility in a way that increases with age. Figure 4.4 shows an age-specific marital fertility profile which characterizes both Bangladesh in the mid-1970s and Bagnall and Frier's Egyptian census population.

The ratio of natural fertility, r(a), to a schedule of natural fertility, n(a), is given by $r(a)/n(a) = Me^{m\nu(a)}$, where e is the base of the natural logarithm, M is a scale factor, $\nu(a)$ represents the tendency for older women's fertility to decline with age a by virtue of deliberate control, and m is the extent of the extent of deliberate control. The schedules n(a) and $\nu(a)$ are taken from data external to the population under study. The relationship in rearranged to form an expression suitable for regression analysis: $\ln [r(a)/n(a)] = \ln M + m\nu(a)$. If $m = 0$, $e^{m\nu(a)} = 1$, and the model yields natural fertility $\ln r(a) = n(a) + M$. Coale and Trussell suggest that m = 0.0 represents pure natural fertility, m = 0.2 "very moderate control of fertility," and m = 0.4 "quite moderate control of fertility"; m = 0.2 to 0.4 "seems a sensible choice for a Latin American population in which no major decline of fertility has occurred" (Coale and Trussell 1974, 195, 200; 1978, 203–204).

If the rate of decline of fertility with age is slower than the standard, estimated m will be negative. If it is faster, the interpretation is that women are practicing parity-dependent fertility control by older women who have achieved their desired family size. The extent of stopping behavior is indicated by m, but it is not possible to infer the proportion of women who control their fertility, or the effectiveness of contraceptive efforts, from the value of m. The interpretation of M is less obvious. It can be regarded as indicating the level of natural fertility in a population, influenced by such factors as the duration of breast-feeding and coital frequency, but this interpretation is untenable if there is a significant amount of birth spacing. M has been interpreted as reflecting spacing behavior, but it cannot reveal whether such behavior represented deliberate efforts to control fertility or was the byproduct of behavior such as breastfeeding (Wilson, Oeppen, and Pardoe1988; Okun, 1994).

The full Coale-Trussell marital fertility model includes a module to account for nuptiality, the proportion of the population at each age ever married. The full model is $f(a) = G(a) \cdot r(a)$, where G(a) is the nuptiality schedule and r(a) is the age-specific marital fertility schedule already described (Coale, 1971, 206, 209, 214; Coale and Trussell, 1974, 186–187).[33] The nuptiality model is specified as $G(a) = C \cdot G_s(x) \cdot [(a - a_0)/k]$, where C is a factor reflecting the ultimate proportion of the population ever married, $G_s(x)$ is the proportion of the population ever married x years after first marriages begin, a_0 is the age at which first marriages begin, and k is a scale factor relating the number of years of nuptiality in the population under study relative to that in the reference population (19th century Sweden).[34] Substituting the marital fertility model into the age-specific fertility model yields $f(a) = G(a) \cdot n(a)e^{m \cdot \nu(a)}$, where G(a) is the proportion ever married by age a. Mortality (widowhood) is not accounted, but has an effect similar to the effect of $\nu(a)$ depressing marital fertility. Illegitimate and premarital births have effects equivalent to a slightly lower earliest age at first marriage, a_0, while illegitimate births at older ages are equivalent to a very modest increase in marital fertility (Coale and Trussell 1974, 190). The marital fertility model is commonly estimated without the addition of the nuptiality model.[35]

---

[31] Wood (1994, 39–46) offers a more accessible treatment of the Coale-Trussell model.

[32] Actually, the interpretation of the M parameter is not entirely clear. Trussell, (1979, 46–48) concludes that the M parameter is composed of several factors, one of which is the underlying level of natural fertility, but that the parameter also contains information on the extent and particular type of fertility control, which involves some interaction with the m parameter. The difficulty in the interpretation of this parameter derives from the construction of the Coale-Trussell model as essentially an engineering model to represent behavior.

[33] On the calculation of the G(a) function and estimation of the k and C parameters, Coale and McNeil, (1972).

[34] If k = 1, first marriages occur at the same pace as in 19th century Sweden; if k = 0.5, they occur at twice the pace, which is defined by the proportions of people married in various age cohorts. Coale (1971, 206) describes the role of k as relating the number of years between first marriage and the age of modal marriage in a population under study and the reference population.

[35] Coale and Trussell (1978) report regression procedures for the marital fertility model alone.

Coale and Trussell's suggestion that a value of $m < 0.2$ could be interpreted as indicating the absence of control is an overstatement. It is more accurate to express the interpretation as $m > 0.2$ indicating positive evidence of significant control and $m < 0.2$ as being inconclusive. The value of m is not very sensitive to increases in the proportion of women practicing parity-dependent control behavior. Simulations by Okun indicate that a value of m as low as 0.255 was consistent with 81 percent of women practicing stopping behavior using methods with 60 percent effectiveness. With less effective methods, 80 percent of women could be practicing stopping behavior and yield an estimate of m below 0.2. Withdrawal is about 90 percent effective, and a value of m of 0.2 would be consistent with 32 percent of women (or rather their husbands) practicing control. Additionally, $m = 0.2$ is consistent with anywhere from 25 to 65 percent of women practicing stopping behavior, depending on the effectiveness of contraceptive measures ranging from 100 percent to 60 percent (Okun, 1994, 201 Table 1, 202 Figure 2).[36] Estimating levels of natural fertility with a simulation model, Leridon calculates mean number of children per mother to be able to range from 12.8 under conditions of low incidence of sterility, early marriage and no breast-feeding to 4.7 with late marriage, medium incidence of sterility, and a long breast-feeding period—all with no contraception.[37]

Alternatives. Scheidel's wholesale condemnation of Riddle's two monographs risks rejecting acceptable findings Riddle reports, particularly within the scope of what he calls Riddle's assumptions A and B—that efficient contraceptive agents exist in nature and that they were known and could be properly administered (Scheidel, 2001a, 38–39, n. 160, 39–40). Hines' early analysis indicated that some of the Egyptian, Greek, and Roman prescriptions could have been chemically effective, and a number of subsequent reviewers have largely accepted his assessments.[38] Scheidel's construction of assumption B which he assigns to Riddle links two assumptions together rather than letting them be assessed independently. Clearly some people knew of these prescriptions if male doctors, whose duties included a far wider range of illnesses and treatments than contraception, found out about them. Midwives, not an especially literate group, are a logical suspect, as well as old crones who knew of "potions," knowledge which could put them at risk of being considered witches; the former was unlikely to have had the means to publicize her knowledge, and the latter would have had definite incentive to keep it quiet.[39] Proper administration is another matter, and undoubtedly would have varied substantially across users (assuming, of course, for the moment that there were any users). Beyond his errors in assessing demographic impacts, which are clear, a strategic error Riddle makes with his material is overstatement or over-estimation. The standard against which to evaluate his case for the existence and use of contraceptives in antiquity is not their widespread adoption (by say, 60 percent of the population) and efficacy (say, 90 percent or greater), but occasional use by a far more limited proportion of women and efficacy something like 30 to 50 percent when used.[40]

Eyben (1980) considers methods beyond contraception, but believes that contraception itself was considered primarily women's business whereas the sources record the actions of men. McLaren (1990, 26) also considers that among the ancient Greeks, "limitation of births was primarily a woman's business," while most of the texts were written by men who didn't know what the women were doing. McLaren considers the extant reports of contraceptive methods "demonstrates the serious intent with which women's control of procreation was pondered and pursued," regardless of the effectiveness of many of them (1990, 28). For Rome, McLaren cites Tertulian's report of pessaries (58), and that douches, with vinegar and brine solutions, were employed by Romans. Hines, (1936, 96) believes that douching was unknown to the Greeks and Romans. McLaren (1990, 29–31) cites Papyrus Ebers as containing potentially effective methods and cites pessaries, potions, douches, poultices, and fumigation as Greek and Roman contraceptive methods (1990, 47, Table 1.1).

36 Guinnane, Okun, and Trussell, (1994) report the limited ability of both the Coal and Trussell m&M measures and the other measures commonly used to assess fertility during the Demographic Transition, the index of marital fertility, I_g, to detect the beginnings of a population's fertility transition, or what amounts to the same thing, to low levels of fertility control. The index of marital fertility is $I_g = B_m / \sum_{a=15-19}^{a=45-49} m_a h_a$, where B_m is the number of births to married women of all ages, m_a is the number of married women of age a, h_a is the Hutterite fertility rate for married women aged a, with the summation taken over 5-year age groups from 15 to 19 through 45 to 49. I_g is sensitive to behavioral changes that are unrelated to Henry's concept of deliberate control, and an increase in breast-feeding or birth spacing could mask increases in parity-dependent fertility control (pp. 5–7). In fact, Coale and Trussell, (1978, 205) note that their estimates of m for the 13 populations in Henry's 1961 article range from −0.15 to 0.39, from which they reason that a departure of m from zero as far as 0.39 does not necessarily indicate that fertility is being controlled, a conclusion apparently based on acceptance of Henry's identification of his populations as practicing natural fertility. They also note that inferences of control or no control from single-period observations are difficult to make and offer a hypothetical example of a population observed at various dates with estimates of m rising monotonically from −0.08 to 1.0, in which an estimate of $m = 0.2$ would indicate control, if at a relatively low level.

37 Leridon (1977, 117–119, Table 7.2) is devoted to a discussion of influences on and measurement of natural fertility.

38 Hines (1936, 66) on the Ebers Papyrus (c. 1550 B.C.E.), the prescriptions of which he considers effective; Hines (1936, Chapter 4) on various Greek and Roman treatments of varying possible effectiveness.

39 Hines (1936, 100) on the contrary beliefs that the contraceptive knowledge of antiquity was confined largely to the medical encyclopedists, and that the average citizen was probably quite ignorant of the subject. I would concede the ignorance of Hines' "average citizen" but not that of the specialists—the midwives and the old crone herbalists. Fontanille (1977, 7–8) emphasizes the dependence of ancient male physicians on the specialized gynecological knowledge of midwives. Scheidel (2001a, 42–43, n. 169) ridicules Riddle's version of subsequent preservation of contraceptive knowledge by midwives without dealing directly with the thesis.

40 Hines (1936) believes that some use of contraceptives was "doubtless made" by the Greeks and Romans, but not on a scale comparable to modern usage. David and Sanderson (1986, 359) report simulations based on survey data from the 1890s which demonstrate the incremental effectiveness of male and female contraceptive practices. With a monthly coital frequency of 4, in a regime of irregular coitus interruptus practiced by the husband (roughly half the time), supplementation of independent, regular douching with inferior solutions practiced by the wife would reduce the number of expected births from age 30 through the end of the wife's fertile years by some 35 percent. The technique and materials used may not be that different from those available in antiquity, and the example is cited simply for the potential magnitude of effect, not to contend that contraceptive behavior was widely practiced during centuries of high mortality rates. Michael (1973, S141–A142, Table 1) calculates a reduction in monthly probability of conception of 20% using no contraception to a 1.4% probability using withdrawal; of course, overall effectiveness will depend on coital frequency and the proportion of instances in which the technique is practiced. Becker (1991, 141–142, and nn. 6 and 7), calculates that the practice of withdrawal in half of coitions would be expected to reduce lifetime fertility by nearly 25%, although the magnitude of this effect depends on the ratio of the average time required to produce a conception resulting in a live birth to the average period of sterility during and after the production of a live birth. Sheps and Menken, with assistance of Radick (1973, 300–305) report differences

In difficult times, some farm spouses' circumstances may have prompted them to decide to try to avoid further children while still engaging in coitus. To maintain some rudimentary knowledge of these prescriptions through the ages, which it appears did happen, some low level of continuing use of them would have been requisite. Of course, to chemical contraceptives possibly used in family limitation efforts, the possibilities of coitus interruptus, anal intercourse, continence, and in the extreme, abstinence, should be added.[41] Additionally, while the Henry model incorporates the effects of local breastfeeding practices within his concept of natural fertility, it is not inconceivable that ancient families used breastfeeding as an instrument for modulating their fertility on an individual-family basis rather than as only the implementation of a community-wide practice.[42] The aggregate demographic impact could be quite small, undetectable in ancient and even in more recent evidence as noted above in the assessment of the Coale-Trussell m&M and I_g tests, but in populations with close matches between crude birth and crude death rates, a factor that could provide the margin between +0.001 and −0.001 growth rates (these numbers being arbitrary rather than the results of any calculations). Scheidel rests his high degree of certainty regarding the natural fertility of the Roman Egyptian population on Bagnall and Frier's estimated value of the Coale-Trussell m of 0.3 (Bagnall and Frier 1994, 141), which as noted above, is well within the range of possibly large proportions of women practicing stopping behavior with relatively high efficiency. It is not clear that the Bagnall and Frier estimate will support as heavy a weight as Scheidel places on it.[43]

While Henry's model of natural fertility appeared toward the earliest part of the period of intensive family planning efforts in the Third World sponsored by industrialized countries' development agencies, the use of the concept reached a peak in the study in the 1970s of the demographic transition that accompanied the Industrial Revolution in northern Europe and North America. Is it cynical to see at least a loose relationship between the two phenomena? According to one of the prominent students of pre-industrial German fertility, John Knodel, "Whether pre-industrial families practiced birth control is important to know. If they did, the potential impact of introducing modern family planning techniques to contemporary LDCs would seem to be quite limited. If, in contrast, the very idea of family limitation was foreign, both then and now, then the potential of programs designed to spread awareness and increase the availability of means to limit family sizes would be inherently greater" (Knodel 1978, 482). Carlsson published two studies of pre-industrial fertility in Sweden that pointed to substantial regional variations in fertility and to fluctuations in marital fertility that appeared beyond the capacity of nuptiality to explain. He noted in both publications that these findings suggested that family limitation was practiced well before the demographic transition (Carlsson 1970).[44] In the earlier publication, he framed the issue as one of adjustment of a population with existing knowledge to differing circumstances versus innovation, the taking in of new information; he favored adjustment. His articles were more disapproved than disproved.[45] Lee also inferred some fertility control in pre-industrial England, over several studies, from findings of variations in nuptiality, as a Malthusian preventive check, which were inadequate to account for variations in fertility Lee (1975; 1978, 187, 194, 203; 1980, 540).[46] Pericles, in the funeral oration Thucydides reported he delivered for the soldiers fallen in the first year of the Peloponnesian War, exhorted the women of Athens to produce more children, a thought which surely would not have occurred to him had it not been common knowledge that the Athenian women of the time were controlling their fertility (Pomeroy 1997, 39; Thuc. 2. 44. 3).[47]

There is an important difference between married couples' behaviors that limit fertility and external influences—what could be called institutional factors or the behavior of people prior to or outside marriage—that affect fertility. The former behaviors deliberately target fertility, whether they affect it or not; the latter incidentally affect fertility.[48] Specifically, married couples can practice a

in consequences of contraception and induced abortion as methods of fertility control. To achieve the same reduction in fertility with the two methods, the use of contraceptives is associated with a reduction in the number of conceptions while the induced abortions actually increase the number of conceptions. To the extent that induced abortion was or may have been used more frequently as a fertility control measure in antiquity, health dangers of additional conceptions should be added to those of the abortions themselves.

[41] Julian Simon (2000, 33) expresses the point crisply: "The first increments to knowledge were probably fire, tools of stone, and the information that the absence of sexual intercourse and the practice of coitus interruptus prevent births." While this is a trenchantly expressed opinion, it needs to be placed in the context of the grossly inaccurate beliefs in antiquity about human reproduction, at least by the male medical and philosophical writers, as summarized for the Classical-period Greeks by McLaren (1990, Chapter 1).

[42] Olsen, (1983, 32) detects the use of breastfeeding among Malaysian village women in the 1970s as an instrument for modulating fertility.

[43] Scheidel (2001a, 44) qualifies the strength of his natural fertility case on the basis of early modern Chinese family limitation, but focuses on post-natal control (infanticide). His primary concern appears to be to discredit theories linking contraception alone to population decline in antiquity.

[44] Similar conclusions were reached by Gaunt (1973, 47–57, who found evidence of both extended birth intervals and stopping behavior in a family reconstruction study of a rural population from 1745 to 1820.

[45] According to Dudley Kirk (1996, 378), Carlsson (1966. 165) said of his paper on innovation or adjustment that, "Birth control behaviour is contagious and the fertility behaviour of a population is not the simple aggregate of isolated individual decisions, but the end product of complex social interactions." Nowhere in that article does Carlsson make such a statement, and the overall thrust of his paper is that demographic transition in Sweden appeared to be largely a process of adjustment of behavior to changing conditions.

[46] Tilley (1978, 43–44) accepts Lee's doubts regarding the existence of natural fertility in pre-industrial England. About the same time, Grigg (1981, 40–42, 100) expressed belief in a growing consensus that pre-demographic transition families were controlling their family sizes through active choices, that is, beyond the more remote instruments, if they can be so thought of, such as celibacy and later marriage age, i.e., through contraceptive practices, among them coitus interruptus and extended duration of lactation.

[47] Whether Pericles actually brought up this subject in his oration is immaterial: if he didn't, the thought occurred to his contemporary, Thucydides, and seemed like a good one.

[48] This simple dichotomous taxonomy suffers from the plague afflicting most taxonomic exercises, that it omits some category that may cross the lines established by the taxonomy. In this case, I have omitted social or cultural influences that may affect sexual and reproductive behavior

variety of contraceptive behaviors, abortive behaviors, or both to limit fertility, and they can deliberately space births, either to control completed family size or for other reasons. Of course, the spacing of births may be accomplished by the same behaviors that are otherwise called contraceptive actions. The demographic results depend on the effectiveness of the practices (as well as their possible impacts on subsequent reproductive health), the extent of these practices across a population, and of course, desired completed family size. Age at first marriage and the percent of a population never married both affect a population's fertility, and both could be said to be the consequences of individual choices—a person may decide to defer marriage for a variety of reasons or to never marry for any of an equally broad array of reasons—but the motivations for determining a marriage age or choosing celibacy generally would not include limiting the number of children one brings into the world.[49] The causes of variations in first marriage age or the proportion of people never marrying can be chalked up to "institutional factors" or "social norms" or "external economic considerations," most of which amount to giving different names to forces that students of the subject largely agree upon, and I will not dwell upon them further here other than to say that they are qualitatively different from choice behaviors of spouses within a marriage.[50] Beyond this point, contrary to comments made occasionally in the literature, societies would not create such institutional channels in order to ensure its reproductive survival: marital reproductive decisions are made at the husband-wife level and upon the motivations and options they see for themselves. The ancient Egyptian farmer and his wife would not have formed their fertility decisions on a calculation of what their actions would do for the propagation of their society, even if they could have conceived such a notion.[51] The critical point of the distinction between internal and external influences on marital fertility is that first-marriage age and the proportion of a population remaining celibate, although they affect a population's fertility, are not individually or socially created mechanisms for modulating fertility. Additionally, while some social conventions or norms, commonly called "social constraints," such as women's and men's ages at first marriage or periods of sexual abstinence after a birth have effects on a population's fertility, there is no plausible guiding hand designing these implicit policies so as to modulate fertility.[52]

4.3 The Microeconomics of Fertility

The contemporary economic model of fertility is based on the concept of a demand for children, an application of demand theory, based as always on the price of the good itself (children in this case), the prices of substitutes, and the income of the entity with the demand. The demand for children is supplied through live births, hence the equivalence between the demand for children and the economic theory of fertility. I have avoided the usual adjective "straightforward" to characterize the application, because many aspects of the demand for children are not straightforward, and the application of the concept itself to antiquity may generate at least some discussion, if not controversy.

Two overlapping economic approaches to fertility exist, known as the Chicago-Columbia approach[53] and the Pennsylvania approach. The Chicago-Columbia approach, which could be called the demand-for-children model, is associated primarily with Gary Becker from his years at both Columbia University and the University of Chicago, although the contributors to that analytical approach have been many. It is an application of consumer theory to the demand for children and has stressed constancy of tastes, as is common in microeconomic analyses, since economic theory has long considered taste formation to fall largely outside its purview. Nevertheless, the Chicago model has conceded the possibility of taste changes over time although that has not formed a central part of its explanatory framework. The Pennsylvania model is associated primarily with Richard Easterlin, long of the University of Pennsylvania. The Easterlin model has not achieved the degree of codification that the Chicago-Columbia model has, as it began as a theory to account

within marriage, such as taboos on coitus during certain periods or in situations such as a number of months after a childbirth or for relatively young women who have become grandmothers. This omission does not affect the point being made with the simpler dichotomy.

49 Remarriage is a different case. With a social norm of a 5- to 10-year age difference between husbands and wives, widows and older female divorcees could either choose to remain unmarried, possibly to avoid further childbirth, or simply be unable to find a husband of suitable age because of male mortality rates. Widowers and older male divorcees would not experience identical problems. This complication of forces internal and external to marriages affecting fertility does not materially affect the current argument.

50 This is, of course, one of Malthus' principal preventive checks, and it does have the homeostatic effect of dampening fertility when population density increases beyond some level where income or mortality feedbacks begin to be felt, and vice versa when population density falls—or effective population density, if one allows for technological progress. Consequently, it can affect fertility, and it is a consequence of individual choices, but the choices are not made with the express purpose of limiting family size.

51 A sentiment expressed eloquently by Cowgill (1975, 506): "[A] fundamental weakness of method in many attempts to understand past developments has been a failure to distinguish clearly between 'needs' and 'problems'" of a whole society, viewed as some sort of system transcending any individual persons, and the needs, problems, possibilities, incentives, information, and viewpoints of specific individuals or categories of individuals in different situations. . . . [P]eople who know better when they are thinking about contemporary events, surprisingly often seem to think only in terms of global societal or systemic responses when they are dealing with events that lack good historical records. There is always something wrong if we attempt to understand a change (or for that matter, preservation of the status quo), without being able to suggest plausible (if not strictly testable) answers to the questions, 'People in what situations, if anyone, saw good in this?' and 'People in what situations, if anyone, saw harm in this, and, if they saw harm, why did they fail to prevent it?'" Another Cowgill paper (1975. 129–130), offers a clear distinction between how things individual people want may affect population and negative-feedback models of the general systems variety which never identify individual motivations and behavior.

52 Frier (2001, 153–155) classifies as social constraints on marital fertility institutions as diverse as customary or religious constraints on marital intercourse, seasonal absence of males, and abortion (which is an individual choice which may be facilitated or hindered by social constraints), although he would allow the latter for birth spacing rather than family limitation, which in fact are difficult to separate.

53 Sometimes referred to as the "New Home Economics."

for generation-long cycles in American fertility rates and gradually expanded the scope of its intended application to longer-term fertility changes over the course of the demographic transition in the industrial countries and current demographic transitions in developing countries. It initially relied on systematically changing tastes within a context of labor supply-demand changes. Easterlin's background in economic history, from the economic discipline, and his exposure to sociology and demography have led him to incorporate more mechanisms from those disciplines in his models of fertility, stressing particularly the supply side of fertility, whereas the Chicago-Columbia model has concentrated on the demand side. In an intellectual contest, the Chicago-Columbia model has by far been the dominant choice of explanatory vehicle, as its developers extended far beyond Becker himself, while conceptual development of the Pennsylvania model has not extended beyond Easterlin and a handful of early collaborators. Each model is presented in turn below.

4.3.1 The Issue of Choice

The heart of demand theory is choice, and the concept of choice in the matter of childbearing is the first issue that students of antiquity might question. For fertility to involve choice requires some kind of contraceptive practices, be they no more complicated than coitus interruptus, and the notion that couples in antiquity anywhere in the Mediterranean region practiced fertility controls at a sufficiently large scale and with sufficient intensity to affect aggregate fertility remains controversial. There are a number of routes to the judgments involved in this controversy. First, the records of contraceptive practices contain quite a few recommendations that are no better than amulets or incantations, although a number of methods, from various pessaries to ointments and solutions contain organic chemicals that contemporary scientific analysis indicates could be effective contraceptives. Ancient family planning will be discussed further below, but the existence of means of fertility control is a subject of controversy. Second, there is variable evidence of high infant and child mortality rates, which is largely noncontroversial. Third, as a logical consequence of the high IMRs and CMRs, couples would have had to have high fertility rates to have even one or two surviving children. Fourth, to achieve such fertility rates, given various cultural practices that would have limited fertility anyway, such as extended breastfeeding and taboos on sex at various times, many couples would have had to produce as many live births as possible to have any survivors at all, a notion that fits comfortably with Louis Henry's natural fertility hypothesis, which Bagnall and Frier accepted in their analysis of early C.E. Egyptian census data. Fifth, some scholars may believe that the concept of a couple controlling their fertility would have been either inconceivable or socially unacceptable in most situations found in antiquity—Imperial Roman upper classes being a notable exception.

I will make three points supporting the concept of choice in fertility decisions. First, bearing and raising children are costly activities, and at some point parents face the choice of their own near-term consumption and the costs of an additional child. The recent and contemporary evidence of poor Third World populations reaching unparalleled fertility rates may appear to be a compelling counter to this point, but survival rates in those populations have increased comparably, leaving the possibility of greater economic contributions from larger numbers of children. Second, while social or cultural norms may encourage large families, both the decision to have an additional child and the production process involved in implementing that decision are made in private. Third, the history and prehistory of the populations inhabiting the Mediterranean region in antiquity include extended periods of both population decreases and population increases. Some of the population decreases appear to be the result of major upheavals of one sort or another, such as the general decline in Greece following the collapse, rapid or drawn-out, of the Mycenaean palatial civilization, while other instances appear to be the consequences of disease, such as the Antonine Plague in Italy and Egypt during the Early Imperial period. Attributing the population trends during these periods entirely to choices is surely incorrect. Extended and otherwise unaccounted periods of population decline, such as in Greece from the end of the Peloponnesian Wars through roughly the 6th century C.E., in Roman Italy from around 100 C.E. to around 600 C.E., and in Egypt from around the 2nd century C.E. to around the end of the 6th century need explanation, and voluntary choice of fertility is an hypothesis that surely needs exploration.[54]

4.3.2 Factors Complicating the Basic Theory

Some of what is not straightforward about the demand for children derives from the very structure of the problem and exists even in the theory's application to contemporary

[54] For these three cases of long-term population decline, I have relied on McEvedy and Jones (1978, 111–113 for Greece, 106–107 for Italy, 227 for Egypt). These are not surgically precise numbers; the primary challenge to some of them, specifically the Italian numbers, are Scheidel's (2001, 64–72) loosely anchored speculations. Greece had some emigration via colonization during the early centuries of its period of decline but subsequent immigration from invading Slavs; I do not know the balance of these external movements. Italy also experienced some forced colonizations of native Italians during the early part of this period but also received a considerable number of slaves, also with a net balance that I cannot assess. Egypt experienced no such major migration component to its population during the period of its population decline. These extended periods of population decline, although of small annual percentages, −0.12% per year in Greece on average and −0.14% per year on average in the Italian and Egyptian cases, may give some substance to John Riddle's belief that the use of contraceptives in antiquity had significant demographic consequences, despite criticisms that Riddle was too unacquainted with formal demography to understand that the accounting structure of model life tables to those populations precluded any consequential effects: four hundred to a thousand years of population decline, even if gradual, is difficult to write off as inconsequential, even considering the challenging mortality schedules these populations faced. See Riddle (1992, 4–5, 15) and his reply to critics in Riddle (1997, 17); for critics, Frier, (1994, 328, n. 33); Bagnall and Frier (1994, 150, n. 53; Scheidel (2001, 39–40); Hin (2011, 106–107) explicitly rejects family limitation as a cause for "natural demographic decline" in Roman Italy but otherwise implies that what people could have done they did do, concluding that the Roman population decline was therefore the result of mortality forces rather than fertility choices (116).

industrial societies, and some of the complications arise primarily in applications when infant and child mortality rates are high enough to be an important factor in decisions, such as in many contemporary Third World settings and in antiquity.

The most basic structural feature that sets the demand for children apart from the demands for, say, trousers or apples, is that the price of children is endogenous to the unit making the decision. This means that the typical analytical procedure of maximizing a utility function subject to a budget constraint in which the prices of the goods are given exogenously to the decision maker must be replaced with a different sort of analysis. This will be the subject of the section on the basic model, below.

Most models of the demand for children posit what is called a unitary family decision structure, which means that the parents reach mutually satisfactory decisions. Further analysis of this construct for contemporary industrial societies suggests that the construct may miss some important intra-family bargaining. The application of the construct to antiquity, when at many places and times the status and bargaining power of women was far lower, may be less problematic. It is possible that men may have made decisions about family size with little concern for their wives, although I think this is much more of a concern in the upper-class households for which written records are available than for the far more numerous poorer classes in which wives were necessary helpmeets to their husbands.[55] But at any rate, possible discrepancy between the intra-partner decision structure in the basic models of fertility and those in antiquity is worth keeping in mind.

Possibly the most crucial issue in applying the economic theory of fertility to antiquity is the distinction between births and the desired number of children. Births are what couples produce, but wide agreement has it that the number of surviving children is the ultimate target. People creating and working with the theory are aware of this distinction, particularly in its application to contemporary developing countries, but incorporating this aspect of the decisions into the formal theory has been difficult, as is explained below.

Introducing a difference between live births and surviving children introduces the issues of replacement of children who die during a couple's fertile period and of hoarding, having additional births beyond the number expected to die in infancy or childhood to guard against the possibility of subsequent deaths when the parents are old enough to find replacement difficult.

In high mortality situations, it is possible that the number of children that a couple desires to have exceeds the number they can physically produce. This is the situation commonly associated with the high mortality regimes usually (but not always) found with natural fertility. While this may seem to be a situation in which a model of the demand for children would not be applicable because the number chosen is always the maximum that can be had, it really is nothing more complicated than what is called a "corner solution," a situation common in many microeconomic models, in which the quantity that would chosen of some good exceeds either a budget constraint or a productive capacity. The issue will be addressed in the section on the theory, below.

4.3.3 The Chicago-Columbia Model

The Chicago-Columbia model applies demand theory to children to derive an economic theory of fertility. Attributed to Gary Becker when he was at Columbia University, the model received most of its development while Becker was at the University of Chicago, although both universities, as well as others, were sites of active research with the model. The initial goal of the Chicago model was to understand declining fertility in the face of rising income in industrial countries without appealing to children as inferior goods. The model was applied subsequently to behavior in developing countries and their demographic transitions. The model didn't deal explicitly with the dynamics of transition, but rather simply the effect of rising incomes—especially women's wages and labor force participation—on fertility. More direct treatment of the demographic transition came with the development of economic growth models that had the goal of accounting for pre-modern (pre-Industrial Revolution / ancient) economic growth and the transition to modern economic growth in a single model. The demographic transition is modeled as a shift from high fertility to low fertility but without an explicit treatment of population growth rates.[56]

The Static Model of the Demand for Children. The demand for children is composed for the number of children and what has come to be known as the "quality" of children, which boils down to how much parents want to spend on their children, including discretionary consumption for the child and investment in the child that increases the child's health, future earning power, or both; in other

[55] den Boer, (1973, 44) believes implicitly that farmers of the times would have been very concerned about survival and how it could be affected by an excessive number of children and explicitly that they would have been very concerned about the health of their wives and consequently careful about conception. As to the importance of female labor in agriculture in antiquity, Scheidel (1996b) has gleaned the sparse ancient evidence and relied on comparisons from recent and contemporary peasant agriculture, which reinforce the notion of the importance of a farmer's wife to his own survival.

[56] This is a reasonable place to clarify a misconception regarding the role of economic factors in the demographic transition, and by extension, the scope for economic influences on fertility choices much earlier. Contention that the economic foundations of the demographic transition have been "empirically contradicted" is based on an unwarrantedly narrow conception of "economic." George Alter, 1992, 26) closes a useful interpretive review of research of the 1960s through the 1980s on the European demographic transition with a characterization of the concept of the demand for children, an undeniably economic concept, as a cultural explanation of that phenomenon. Even the acceptability of birth control—which in fact may have been more of a Christian problem than one for the pre-Christian religions of antiquity—depends on economic forces finally becoming sufficiently strong that people become willing to look more closely at their beliefs. I do not wish to reduce all the world to economic forces, but resource allocation decisions are pervasive and may operate through channels that change perceptions before they change actions.

words, investment in human capital for the child. The usual formulation is that the investment in quality is the same across all children.

The signal challenge for the demand-for-children model has been to explain how fertility can decrease with income without children being an inferior good, i.e., a good which consumers would demand less of as their incomes increase, or goods which higher-income consumers would demand less of than lower-income consumers. The maintained hypothesis in addressing this challenge is that children are normal goods. This relationship between income and fertility squares with the demographic transition but does not produce the positive relationship between income and fertility that is the heart of the Malthusian theory, which seems more applicable to pre-transition populations. Thus a fully satisfactory theory of the demand for children needs to be able to explain both positive and negative income-fertility relationships without resorting to the simplistic, and surely incorrect, assumption that children are inferior goods.

The basic model is a static model in which parents make choices for their entire lifetime: the number of children, the expenditure they will make on each child's quality, and their own lifetime consumption stream. The spacing of the children is not addressed, nor when during the parents' fertile period the children will be born. Both of these latter issues, as well as the possibility of differential quality expenditures on children according to each child's inherent endowments (native talents and personal proclivities) have been modeled. The major issues addressed by the static model are the influences on the cost of children and the response of the number of children (fertility) and child quality to changes in income.

Let the parents' utility function be $U = U(n, q, c)$, where n is the number of children, q is the quality of each child, and c is the parents' consumption.[57] The parents choose n, q, and c to maximize this utility function subject to their budget constraint, $I = nq\pi + c\pi_c$, where I is full income, π is the price of the nq combination of a child and its quality, and π_c is the price of parents' consumption. The budget constrain is nonlinear, with the number of children being multiplied by the quality per child, both of which are choice variables. Ignoring the nonlinearity for the moment, the first-order conditions for this maximization are $MU_n = \lambda q\pi = \lambda p_n$, $MU_q = \lambda n\pi = \lambda p_q$, and $MU_c = \lambda\pi_c = \lambda p_c$, where MU indicates marginal utility (e.g., $MU_n \equiv \Delta U/\Delta n$), λ is the marginal utility of income, and the p_i are the marginal costs or shadow prices of n and q. The important point emerging from these first order conditions is that the shadow price of the number of children, p_n, is positively related to the quality level of each child, q, and the shadow price of child quality, p_q, is positively related to the number of children, n. An increase in quality is more expensive if there are more children because the increase applies to more children, and similarly, an increase in the number of children is more expensive if the children are of higher quality because higher-quality children cost more. The prices of child numbers and child quality are determined by the parents rather than being given to a competitive household as in the standard theory of consumer behavior. The parents' demands for the three goods (i.e., the optimal quantities of each) can be written as functions of income I: C(I), N(I), and Q(I).

This specification produces an ambiguity regarding the effect of income on the demand for children. Suppose children are a normal good in the sense that an increase in income, with the price of children fixed, induced a larger demand for children. The income effect on the number of children need not be positive because the increase in income might induce the parents to spend more on quality, raising the price of children. Such a self-induced increase in price might lead parents to have fewer children. Additionally the smaller number of children would make the price of child quality cheaper, generating more expenditure on quality. An increase in income might be spent on quality rather than quantity (number of children). Quality might substitute for quantity as income increases.

Figure 4.5 shows the nonstandard character of this consumer problem using the indifference curves for quality and number of children and the nonlinear budget constraint, assuming that the optimal amount of the budget has already been spent on the consumption good, c. The indifference curves U_0 through U_3 are parallel and indicate the levels of utility that can be reached as income increases. The initial nonlinear budget constraint is the parabola B_0, and the tangency of indifference curve U_0 with B_0 at A represents the parents' choice of number and quality of children. Now let income increase. After additional expenditures

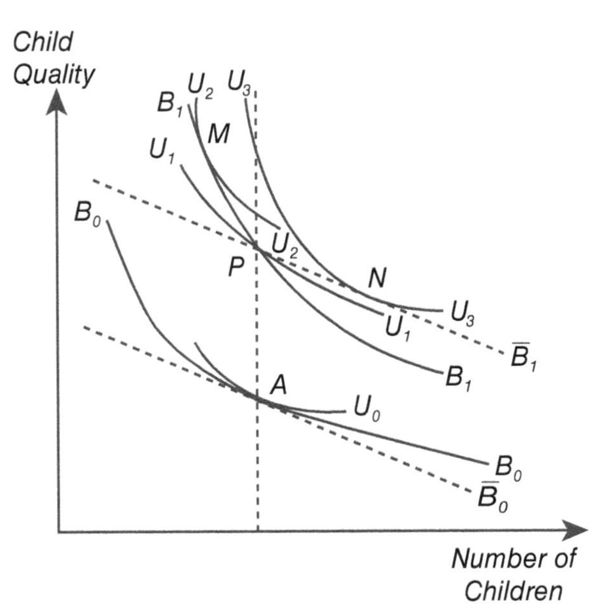

Figure 4.5. The quantity-quality trade-off of children (Reproduced from Assaf Razin and Efraim Sadka, 1995, figure 3, p. 16, by permission of MIT Press.).

[57] The initial analysis is Becker (1960), with further exposition linking it to the household production model by Willis (1973). The analysis of the nonlinear budget presented here is attributable to Becker and Lewis (1973).

on consumption good c, there are resources left over to be allocated to quality and number of children, and the parabolic budget line shifts outward by ΔI to B_1, parallel to B_0, reaching a new optimal choice of child quality and numbers at the tangency of indifference curve U_2 and parabolic budget line B_1 at point M. If the budget had been linear, as dashed budget lines $\bar{B}_0$ and $\bar{B}_1$, the new optimal choice of number and quality would be at point N with indifference level U_3 on budget line $\bar{B}_1$. If the number of children were to remain the same at the higher income, the parents would reach indifference level U_3, which would cut, rather than be tangent to, parabolic budget line B_1 at point P along the dashed vertical line indicating the constant number of children. The fact that the indifference curve is not tangent to the budget line at point P indicates the non-optimality of that choice. The fact that the budget line is steeper than the indifference curve at that point indicates that the tangency will lie above and to the right of point P, at point M, yielding a negative relationship between income and fertility.

There is a way to convert the nonlinear budget constraint to a linear one so that the consumer's optimization problem can be solved using standard techniques.[58] Keeping the same utility specification, rewrite the budget constraint as $c + p_n n + p_q q \leq I + M = R$, in which $p_c = 1$ is the numeraire, the remaining p_i are the shadow prices of child numbers and child quality, and $M = nq\pi$ is a term capturing the interaction of the quantity and quality shadow prices in which π is the joint shadow price. The expanded full income measure, R, is not observed in data, so the true income elasticities of demand for the number and quality of children cannot be computed directly from data, but this expanded specification offers a route to adjust observed elasticities to their true magnitudes.

The maximization of the utility function subject to the new budget constraint is a standard consumer optimization problem, and the demand functions for the three goods can be written as $\bar{C}(p_n, p_q, I + M)$, $\bar{N}(p_n, p_q, I + M)$, and $\bar{Q}(p_n, p_q, I + M)$, remembering that $p_c = 1$ is the numeraire, so that p_n and p_q are expressed in terms of p_c. Now, use numerical subscript notation to designate the effect of each argument on these functions: e.g., $\Delta\bar{N}/\Delta(I + M) \equiv \bar{N}_3$. Normality of each good, i.e., the response of the demand for it to an increase in full income requires that $\bar{C}_3 > 0$, $\bar{N}_3 > 0$, and $\bar{Q}_3 > 0$. Returning to the demand functions for the nonlinear specification, when the linearized specifications are evaluated at $pq = N(I)$, $pn = Q(I)$ (remembering that the shadow price of the number of children is the quality per child and the shadow price of child quality is the number of children), and $M = N(I)Q(I)$, $\bar{C} = C$, $\bar{N} = N$, and $M = N(I)Q(I)$. For example, in the case of the demand for the number of children, $\bar{N}(N(I), Q(I), N(I)Q(I)) = N(I)$, and similarly for child quality and the consumption good.

Varying income I in each of these three equations ($\bar{N} = N$ etc.) and allowing for the own- and cross-price substitution effects of the shadow prices of child numbers and quality on those two goods, expressions for the observed income elasticities of demand for number of children and child quality can be derived. From these expressions, the relationships between the true magnitudes, which remain unobserved, and the observed magnitudes can be studied. For example, the observed income elasticity of demand for the number of children is $(\Delta N/\Delta I)(I/N)$, and similarly for child quality. The observed income elasticity of the demand for child numbers is composed as $\eta_{nI} = k[\bar{\eta}_{nI}(1 - \bar{\varepsilon}_{nq}) + \bar{\eta}_{qI}\bar{\varepsilon}_{nn}]/[(1 - \bar{\varepsilon}_{nq})^2 - \bar{\varepsilon}_{qq}\bar{\varepsilon}_{nn}]\}$, in which $k = I/(I + R) < 1$; $\bar{\eta}_{nI}$ is the unobserved income elasticity of the number of children $\bar{N}$ with respect to expanded income $I + \bar{N}\bar{Q} = R$; $\bar{\varepsilon}_{nn} < 0$ and $\bar{\varepsilon}_{qq} < 0$ are the own-price substitution elasticities of number of children $\bar{N}$ and child quality $\bar{Q}$; and $\bar{\varepsilon}_{nq} > 0$ and $\bar{\varepsilon}_{qn}$ $(\neq \bar{\varepsilon}_{nq}) > 0$ are the respective cross-price substitution elasticities of the two goods. Using the same components, the observed income elasticity of demand for child quality is composed as $\eta_{qI} = k[\bar{\eta}_{qI}(1 - \bar{\varepsilon}_{nq}) + \bar{\eta}_{nI}\bar{\varepsilon}_{qq}]/[(1 - \bar{\varepsilon}_{nq})^2 - \bar{\varepsilon}_{qq}\bar{\varepsilon}_{nn}]\}$, in which all the terms are defined as in the previous expression.

The first thing to note is that when the observed income elasticities are positive, they will generally be smaller than the true elasticities by the factor $k < 1$. Second, the observed income elasticity of demand for the number of children is influenced by the true income elasticity of demand for child quality as well as the true income elasticity of demand for child numbers, and vice versa. Third and most importantly, the observed relationship between income and both number and quality of children can be negative without resorting to the assumption that children are inferior goods.

Several parameter configurations can produce a positive income-fertility relationship. If the substitution elasticity between number and quality of children is equal to one, the observed income elasticity of demand for children reduces to $\eta_{nI} = -(k/\bar{\varepsilon}_{qq})/\bar{\eta}_{qI} > 0$, and fertility increases with income, as will child quality as can be seen by performing the same substitutions in the expression for η_{qI}. This is not a particularly likely configuration of parameter values for most populations during much of antiquity, when investment in child quality—i.e., in children's human capital—was typically quite low except in the numerically insignificant but literarily prominent upper classes. Such a circumstance would be represented, for the vast majority of the population, by high sensitivity to the price of child quality, both own- and cross-price effects, which translates in the concepts of the two elasticity formulations above into a small positive to near zero value for $\bar{\eta}_{qI}$, a large negative value for $\bar{\varepsilon}_{qq}$, and very small positive values for $\bar{\varepsilon}_{nq}$ and $\bar{\varepsilon}_{qn}$.[59] Substituting such values into the expression for η_{nI}

[58] This exposition of converting the nonlinear problem into a standard consumer problem is based on the analysis by Razin and Sadka (1995, 17–21), which in turn is based on the model in Nerlove, Razin, and Sadka (1987, Chapter 5).

[59] Although $\bar{\varepsilon}_{nq}$ and $\bar{\varepsilon}_{qn}$ will generally differ in magnitude, the core of the two elasticities is $\frac{\Delta\bar{N}}{\Delta p_q} + \frac{N\Delta\bar{N}}{\Delta R}$, in the case of $\bar{\varepsilon}_{nq}$ and $\frac{\Delta\bar{Q}}{\Delta p_n} + \frac{Q\Delta\bar{Q}}{\Delta R}$ in the case of $\bar{\varepsilon}_{qn}$, which are equal to each other; the respective elasticities are formed by multiplying these price responses by the ratio of R/p_i. As long as the core price responses are small, both cross-price elasticities will remain small despite their multiplication by different ratios.

yields positive values for that elasticity, which means that increases in income would increase fertility.

What can make the observed relationship between income and fertility negative? If the elasticity of substitution between number and quality of children is less than one, i.e., $\bar{\varepsilon}_{nq} < 1$, there are two configurations of elasticity values that will yield $\eta_{nI} < 0$. A positive denominator for the expression is one case, which will occur when the own-price substitution elasticities, $\bar{\varepsilon}_{nn}$ and $\bar{\varepsilon}_{qq}$ are small in absolute value. In this case, if the income elasticity of demand for quality is considerably higher than that for number of children, the number of children will fall as income increases, i.e., $\eta_{nI} < 0$ and child quality rises, i.e., $\eta_{qI} > 0$. If the denominator is negative, which will happen when the own-price substitution elasticities are relatively high, if the true income elasticity of demand for quality is much lower than that for numbers, i.e., $\bar{\eta}_{qI} \ll \bar{\eta}_{nI}$, then $\eta_{nI} < 0$ and $\bar{\eta}_{qI} > 0$.[60] Accordingly, different elasticity magnitudes, representing different values of human capital investment in children, will yield the income-fertility responses associated with the demographic transition.

Having referred liberally to the costs, or shadow prices, of child quality and child quantity or numbers, it is important to note explicitly what those costs are and are not. There are several ways of approaching this specification. First consider the shadow prices of quality and quantity separately. Both parental time and goods are devoted to both quantity and quality of children. In the price of quantity, the magnitudes of mother's and father's time spent in child raising must be specified, and the productive value of each parent's time applied to the respective time. Wealthier parents would face higher costs. Quantities of resources devoted to child raising similarly must be valued at local resource costs, whether they be purchased on markets or produced at home. The costs of identical resources devoted to child rearing may differ between locations and across time. For the price of quality, the magnitudes of parental time and other resource expenditures required to yield a give quality level (or level of human capital in the child) must be specified and priced as in the case of the shadow price of quantity. The overall cost of a child must be specified for a given quality of child. An increase in expenditures on children does not by itself indicate an increase in the cost of a child since either the cost of a given level of quality may be higher or a choice may have been made to increase quality. An alternative approach to the cost of a child does not distinguish between quality expenditures and basic expenditures associated with raising a child without adding to its human capital. That cost is the present value of expected outlays over the child's time at home plus the imputed values of the parents' time minus the sum of the present value of expected monetary returns from adult children, and the imputed value of children's services to the household while they remain at home. Social pressures could affect the structure of indifference curves relating quantity to quality, but not the cost of raising children. Accordingly, social pressures could affect income elasticities of demand for children but not their price elasticities Becker (1960, 214–215).

An additional constraint useful to consider in the application of the model to antiquity that sprobably would be superfluous in applications to contemporary industrial countries' parents is a physiological constraint on the number of children: $n \leq \bar{n}$, where $\bar{n}$ is the physiological maximum number of children a couple could bear given their cultural constraints. In contemporary industrial societies, this constraint would seldom bind the choices parents make, but in a society with high infant and child mortality it might well bind. In such cases, the number of children ceases to be an effective choice variable, and $n = \bar{n}$. Parents would then adjust the quality of each child to the point where the marginal rate of substitution of q for the consumption good c equaled the shadow price of child quality, $U_q/U_c = p_q = np(t, c)$, where U_q and U_c are the marginal utilities of child quality and the consumption good and p is an increasing function of parental time t and resources c devoted to the acquisition of child quality. Note that the price of quality is multiplied by the number of children.

Return for a moment to the matter of child quality, or investment in children's human capital, in antiquity. This is an important matter, both analytically and substantively: analytically because current models of endogenous fertility and economic growth, to be presented below, rely on growing investment in child quality as the primary mechanism behind the eventual emergence of economic growth in the Industrial Revolution and a key to falling fertility in the demographic transition; substantively because most of us today, dropped down in a 5th century B.C.E. Greek or Roman or Mesopotamian or Egyptian farm, wouldn't have the slightest clue what to do. We can leave the analytical discussion to the exposition of the growth models, but the matter of how ancient children acquired the human capital required to work with the technologies they faced needs consideration. Information is available on apprenticeship, but most people were farmers, for which apprenticeship did not apply. While they were largely outside the literate portions of their societies that left written records of their children's formal schooling, technical skills most probably were learned by helping the father and older male siblings at farming and related tasks or the mother and older female siblings at an array of household tasks. Would midwivery have been learned through apprenticeship of some form or would it have passed down more closely through family lines? This on-the-job-training (OJT) for children would have reduced the parental time cost of child rearing somewhat while it added to the imputed value of children's services noted above, both of which would have lowered the cost of children.[61] Further, to the extent that grandparents, to the

[60] The symbol $\ll$ means "is considerably smaller than."

[61] Nonetheless, it could be easy to overstate the productivity of children in farm activities. Lee and Kramer (2002, 482) estimate that Maya boys at age 8 contribute 20 percent of the labor value of a prime-aged (30-year old) male on remote farms, 35 percent at age 11, and still only 50 percent

extent that they were still alive, were part of extended households and could have taken up a good proportion of time devoted to child care rather than more productive parents, child costs would have been reduced further.[62] Returning to apprenticeship as a form of human capital investment, it is not clear that parents typically paid masters to take on their children, since the masters reaped the value of the apprentices' assistance over the periods of their apprenticeships, but it is worth noting that Bradley reported one apprenticeship contract from 1st century C.E. Egypt in which a mother agreed to pay the required poll tax for her son that would be levied when the boy turned 14 (Bradley, 1991, 108; reprinted from Bradley 1985). Together the wage, or productivity, difference between parental and child labor increases the cost of child rearing and decreases the cost of producing child quality (investing in human capital), the latter inasmuch as a wider differential reduces the foregone earnings of the child during time spent acquiring human capital other than via OJT. Child labor weakens the income effect of the parents' wages relative to the substitution effect, and the optimum number of children with child labor will exceed the optimal without it Hazan and Berdugo (2002). A static model, such as the one presented in this section, is not well suited to illuminating the possibilities of current sacrifices of child labor in return for higher productivity in subsequent periods. Contemporary dynamic, or growth, models of fertility and human capital accumulation implicitly specify children's human capital accumulation as formal schooling or an equivalent activity that requires the child to forego current earnings, which is counter to much of the experience of human capital accumulation undertaken by the great majority of ancient populations.

The robust empirical finding of a negative relationship between income or wages and fertility, which is consequently a critical theoretical issue, remains an active research field. While the quantity-quality trade-off has been a mainstay among the explanations of this negative relationship, it is sensitive to assumptions about the elasticity of substitution between children and parental consumption as well as the sources of family income and who actually cares for children. While economists are understandably unwilling to give up the quantity-quality model, search continues for additional circumstances, such as heterogeneity, at a given point in time, in income or preferences for children or both, which would increase the flexibility of the quantity-quality model to account for the negative income-fertility relationship at a single point in time as well as over time.[63]

Familial Altruism and Dynamics. The basic model of the demand for children treats children as consumption goods or consumer durables—something from which parents derive utility just as they would from articles of clothing or a household appliance in the contemporary industrialized world. Altruism in demand theory is simply that another agent's consumption or wellbeing enters positively in someone's utility function. Altruism has the effect of reducing the consumption of an altruistic agent below what it would have been if the same agent had been purely egoistic. Specifications of altruism can vary widely in economic fertility (demand for children) models. In models of the demand for children, or more generally, models of fertility, introduction of altruism brings with it a time dimension that was not present in the purely static models: altruism of parents toward children or of children toward parents requires that events at different dates be linked in the same model.

Several types of altruistic behavior have been modeled: bequests of parents to children, children's consumption in parental utility functions, children's utility in parental utility functions, parental consumption or utility in children's utility functions—all for a single generation of children or parents. The quantity-quality distinction in the static model contains the motivation for altruistic behavior since investment in child quality implies investing in the future earning power of a child, the motivation for which could be that the parent expects to gain from that higher earning power in old age via old-age support from the child or that the parent wants the child to have the higher utility that derives from higher productivity. These types of behavior can affect fertility by altering consumption and saving decisions of parents.

Dynastic utility is a specification of altruism in which the initial parental generation's preferences toward children's consumption or utility is mirrored in the preferences of each succeeding generation, resulting in an effectively infinite progression of interests in the current parental generation.[64] A particularly literalist interpretation of the dynastic utility specification would surely find quarrels with it—nothing in the way of preferences changes down through many generations—but what it offers is a kind of symmetry between parents and children over time, in which children pass down to their descendants the dynastic utility formulation deals with forecasts of technologies and budget

at age 14. Lee and Kramer further estimate cumulative break-even ages (the ages at which the cumulative value of a child's production equals the cumulative value of its consumption) for males and females to be above the average age of leaving home for both (484). They contrast their findings to the pioneering effort of Cain (1977), who overstated child net productivity by counting only food consumption in costs.

62 While grandparents may be a not atypical resource for child care in contemporary developing countries, and even in the currently industrialized countries within the past several centuries, life expectancies in antiquity well may have made them a scarcer resource, as found by Saller (1987, 33, Table 2).

63 Jones, Schoonbroodt, and Tertilt (2011) presents an encompassing framework for exploring the fertility-income relationship and identifies modeling choices necessary for various models to generate the negative income-fertility relationship. Some models reverse the direction of causality in the relationship between wage income and number of children, which is a major difference from the original Becker model and involves the parental wages being endogenous.

64 The first published use of this specification of utility was Barro (1974), and the first application to endogenous fertility in a context of economic growth was Razin and Ben-Zion (1975).

constraints in the future, so to the extent that components of those aspects of the world change, fertility could change in the future, while preferences involving goodwill toward children and later descendants remain constant.

Accordingly, fertility models that introduce altruism typically go on to consider economic growth with endogenous fertility whether they employ a dynastic or non-dynastic approach to altruism. I reserve presentation of (some of) those complete growth models until a later section, as well as exposition of various specifications of altruism, under the topic of intergenerational transfers. In the remainder of this section, I present the most current version of the dynastic utility formulation, which is of some interest for specifications with far-reaching implications.

The dynastic utility function begins with the adult parent's utility function, $U_i = v(c_i, n_i) + a(n_i)n_iU_{i+1}$, in which U_i is the utility of the adult in period i (the model abstracts from marriage), and v is the standard current period utility function in which c_i is the consumption per adult during adulthood and n_i is the number of children per adult, with the standard properties $v_c > 0$, $v_n > 0$, $v_{cc} < 0$ and $v_{nn} < 0$, i.e., positive and diminishing marginal utility in both adult consumption and children. U_{i+1} is the utility of adult children in period i + 1, and $a(n_i)$ is the altruism function, with the properties $a(n_i) > 0$, indicating that the parents like children; $a(1) < 1$, indicating selfishness of the parents; and $\Delta a/\Delta n_i < 0$, displaying diminishing marginal altruism in number of children (Becker and Barro 1988, 4–6; Barro and Becker, 1989, 481–482; Barro and Sala-i-Martin 2004, 409–410). The altruism function converts utility of children into utility of parents. It is clear from the specification of altruism in the utility function that the discount rate increases with fertility, because the value of the altruism function decreases with a larger number of children. The discount rate, or rate of time preference, is, in effect, endogenous in the model. The utility of each child also depends on its own consumption, the number of its children, and the utility of those children, and so on down through succeeding generations. If the parameters of the utility function remain the same for all the generations, substituting later consumption and fertility into the initial parent's utility function, derives the dynastic utility function as $U_0 = \sum_{i=0}^{\infty} A_i N_i v(c_i n_i)$, in which c_i and n_i are consumption per adult and number of children in generation i, and N_i is the number of descendants in the ith generation. If children are also altruistic to parents, dynastic utility would depend as well on the consumption and fertility of all ancestors as well as those of descendants. The overall budget constraint for an adult in generation i is $w_i + (1 + r_i)k_i = c_i + n_i(\beta_i + k_{i+1})$, in which the adult receives a wage of w_i from supplying one unit of labor, k_i is a parental bequest the adult of period i receives, β_i is the cost of raising a child to adulthood, and k_{i+1} is a bequest the generation-i parent leaves to each child. The relationship of the bequest to adult consumption is the same as that of savings to consumption in models with savings. In conducting the optimization problem, the dynasty head maximizes utility U_0 (beginning in period 0) subject to the budget constraint and the value of the initial assets in that period, k_0, taking as given paths of wages rates and interest rates w_i and r_i, choosing paths for adult consumption c_i, capital stock per adult k_i, and number of descendants in each period N_i. The first-order conditions from the maximization include an arbitrage relationship that shifts consumption between generations and a relationship equating the marginal benefit from creating an additional descendant to its marginal cost. Changes in the level of interest rates or in the degree of altruism mainly affect utility, higher interest rates or a greater degree of altruism motivating a family to have more children. The dynastic family model and its results are treated in greater depth in section 4.5.3.

4.3.4 The Pennsylvania Model

Richard Easterlin's fertility model has had a less stable form than the Chicago model. First conceived to explain long-term movements in fertility in the United States, it has been modified and occasionally expanded to characterize pre-transition demographic behavior as well as low-fertility behavior in industrialized countries.

Although an economic model developed by an economist, Easterlin has made explicit efforts to incorporate traditional concerns of sociologists to which most economists have paid less attention in their analysis of fertility behavior. The Pennsylvania model has also not been subjected to the formal analysis of comparative statics that the Chicago model has gone through. Altogether, the Pennsylvania model has received more attention outside economics than has the Chicago model, probably because of its greater accessibility.

The Original Easterlin Hypothesis. The original Easterlin hypothesis was an informal model of changing birth rates in a society over time, developed explicitly to help understand Kuznets cycles in the post-demographic transition United States, from 1870 through the 1940s.[65] The puzzle demanding explanation was that even after the transition from high to low fertility in the United States, the country's population continued to undergo large cycles in fertility over periods of one to two generations. Easterlin's explanation relied on changing tastes (he called them aspirations) affecting a birth cohort's fertility behavior, leading to changes in birth cohort sizes and consequently in the wages of cohorts according to their relative size. The alternation of conditions between generations led to

[65] Easterlin (1961, 870 on Kuznets cycles, 891 for his exposition of the effect of relative cohort size, 899 on his prediction for an approaching baby bust; 1966a, 1069–1070 for his specification of the three steps in his model: (1) the impact of aggregate demand on labor market conditions, (2) the effect of labor market conditions on the number and spending behavior of households, and (3) the reaction of the latter on the former). The echo effect is a delayed surge of births following several decades after an increase in fertility that produces a larger birth cohort. Another exposition is (1966b, 131–153), which offers greater detail regarding his notion of changing tastes (139–140), which he generously attributes to Brady and Friedman (1947, 140, n. 11); the latter, ironically, was Milton Friedman's wife.

cycles in fertility, birth cohort size, and incomes relative to the previous generation. Following the success of the model in explaining the post-World War II baby boom worldwide and the late 1950s–1960s baby bust, Easterlin and users of the Pennsylvania model predicted another baby boom in the United States in the 1980s and '90s which didn't materialize.[66] This striking predictive failure lost some credibility for the model's robustness, although it has continued to be used to explore cycles in fertility. Macunovich's review of empirical studies of Easterlin cycles worldwide shows considerable support for the hypothesis and its relative wage mechanism.[67] Modeling interactions between cohort sizes and fertility, it has not been possible to derive a model with empirically supported parameter values that yield Easterlin cycles of realistic amplitude and frequency.[68] However, a recent effort using a 4-period OLG model with dynastic altruism has been able to replicate a large proportion of major fertility booms and busts of the 19th and 20th centuries, but based on responses to exogenous productivity shocks rather than a continuing, interaction among endogenous variables (Jones and Schoonbroodt, 2011).

Easterlin's Economic-Sociological Model of Fertility. Easterlin's goal is to develop a single model that is sufficiently general to account for pre-modern (including ancient), transition, and modern fertility behavior. He adds considerable detail on the supply side of fertility that has been prominent in sociological studies of fertility. The Chicago model has dealt with the supply side of fertility in much less detail. The three main components of the Pennsylvania model are supply—both physiological and cultural—demand, and fertility regulation. The model is static, as is the Chicago model, which means that the agents (couples) choose a lifetime's fertility pattern at one time. The model proposes natural fertility as a benchmark, asking the question, "Is desired fertility, F^d, greater than, equal to, or less than natural fertility, F^n?" If $F^d \geq F^n$, couples practice no fertility regulation; if $F^d < F^n$, they do. Easterlin contends that if $F^d \geq F^n$, demand variables are irrelevant to fertility decisions.[69] The actual number of children can exceed the desired number because of the cost of fertility regulation. Easterlin specifies natural fertility as a function of income on the grounds that higher income generally implies better nutrition which in turn enhances fecundity, other factors remaining the same.

Infant mortality plays an important role in this version of the Pennsylvania model. Parents target a desired number of surviving children although live births, regardless of survival, is the immediate decision variable. Easterlin actually uses the desired number of survivors divided by the survival rate as the dependent variable in his demand model, a specification that implicitly assumes either complete inelasticity of the number of survivors with respect to the survival rate or zero cost of infant deaths (DeTray 1973, S78). Empirical analysis has not found the former to be the case, and the latter clearly is not.

In pre-transition populations, income increases fertility via a supply effect—it increases natural fertility) rather than via a demand effect. In transitional situations, families have more children than desired as survival rates increase. Eventually they cut back on births by applying fertility regulation. In modern societies, income can reduce fertility by the same routes as in the Chicago model. The Pennsylvania model also incorporates the quantity-quality demands specified in the Chicago model.

Formally, the Pennsylvania model can be written as a utility maximization subject to a combination of budgetary and demographic constraints.[70] Utility is a function of seven variables, conditioned on "normal" levels of home-produced goods and completed family size, which yields the interdependence of preferences central to the model: $U = U(Z, N, d, a, \ell, \theta, \tau; Z^*, N^*)$, in which Z is commodities produced at home with market goods X and home time t, infant and child deaths d, frequency of coitus a, a vector of practices such as lactation ℓ which affect the number of children born or their survival probabilities, fertility control techniques used θ, and the intensity with which those controls are used τ. The choices of these variables are made conditioned upon the normal levels of Z and N, Z^* and N^* on the right side of the semi-colon.[71] The determination of normal levels (aspirations) Z^* and N^* requires a model in its own right, several of which have been developed by Easterlin co-authors Robert Pollak and Michael Wachter. Some of the models rely on interactions among contemporaries while others depend on behavior of a previous generation, or even a contemporary

[66] Predicting an upturn in fertility between 1970 and 1975: Easterlin (1966a, 149; 1966b, 1091 predicts "beyond 1975"; subsequently 1978, 416–417, in which an upturn in the crude birth rate in the 1980s and 1990s is predicted). One of Easterlin's co-authors produced an econometric prediction of a baby boom in the United States in the 1980s: Wachter (1975).

[67] Macunovich (1998, 92–93), although she considered the jury still out on the existence of self-generating cycles. Pampel and Peters (1995) provide an alternative review of empirical evidence and consider complicating factors such as changing patterns of immigration and female labor force participation.

[68] But not for want of trying: Wachter and Lee (1989, 99–115); Wachter (1991); Chu and Lu (1995). These authors find that models of fertility cycles, involving interactions between cohort sizes and fertility yield unstable equations, implausible cycle lengths, or both.

[69] An alternative way to conceptualize this condition is as a "corner solution," a particular instance of the more general case when a constraint on the magnitude of a choice variable leads an agent to choose its maximum value and be willing to choose a larger value if the constraint were relaxed. It is not an uncommon condition modeled throughout applications of price theory.

[70] The following exposition of the model comes from Easterlin, Pollak, and Wachter (1980, 86–98). Overall, this is the most thorough exposition of the economic reasoning involved in the model. Several other expositions of the model are available in different presentational styles. Easterlin (1978) provides a largely diagrammatic treatment focusing on the effects of the costs of fertility regulation, with presentation of some equations and formulaic definitions. Easterlin and Crimmins (1985, Chapter 2) provide a largely verbal exposition of the framework, and Chapter 3 provides a specification of regression models that are not derived explicitly from a behavioral model via comparative statics analysis; the remainder of the volume is devoted to presentations of empirical analyses of fertility behavior in contemporary developing countries.

[71] Placement on the right side of the semi-colon indicates that the multidimensional relationship between utility U and the variables which jointly determine U, to the left of the semicolon, is shifted by changes in the conditioning variables.

agent's previous behavior (habit formation). The simplest of these is preferences or aspirations determined by a previous generation. The model of preference formation can be held off to the side, with Z* and N* simply being assumed as given by history in the simplest case. Choices are made of the variables to the left of the semicolon in the utility function, together with market goods X which go into the production of home commodities Z, subject to the following constraints: (1) a production function representing home technology, $(Z, X, t) \in T$;[72] (2) a time constraint $\sum_{s=1}^{S} t_{hs} = \bar{t}_h$, with household members identified by h = 1, . . . , H and market and non-market activities denoted by s = 1, . . . , S; (3) a full-income constraint $\sum_{k=1}^{n} p_k x_k + \rho(\theta, \tau) \leq \mu + \sum_{h=1}^{H} \sum_{s \in M} w_h t_{hs}$, where M represents market activities; (4) a birth function $b = B(a, Z, X, \ell, \theta, \tau, \Lambda)$ where Λ represents the family's reproductive life span; (5) a death function $d = D(b, Z, X, \ell)$; (6) and an identity defining completed family size $N = b - d$. The maximizing household takes as given goods prices p_k, wage rates w, nonlabor income μ, the household technology T, the births and deaths functions B and D, the cost function for fertility regulation ρ, the family's reproductive lifespan, and the determinants of the normal aspiration levels of Z* and N*.

The Pennsylvania model has the structure in its utility function and its time and full-income constraints to parallel the analysis that has been conducted with the Chicago-Columbia model. The additional three components of the model address the supply side of fertility, but the birth and death functions have not been explored in more analytical detail than has been presented just above. The model has not been subjected to the extensive comparative statics analysis that the Chicago model has received, nor has it been adapted to analyze specific topics within fertility such as the effect of mortality on fertility behavior.

In the Pennsylvania model, Easterlin has given more attention to high-fertility regimes in which desired fertility equals or exceeds unregulated or natural fertility than have authors using the Chicago-Columbia model. The relationship between live births and both the statistical distribution and realization of infant and child mortality has been a subject of analysis, involving the identification where possible of both replacement and hoarding behavior. Throughout its expositions and empirical applications, the Pennsylvania model has used a particularly simple formulation of the relationship between the desired number of children surviving to adulthood and the number of live births, $B = C/s$, where B is the cumulative number of births, C is the cumulative number of children surviving to adulthood, and s is the probability of survival of a birth to adulthood.[73] This formulation implies a one-for-one replacement of infant and child deaths with an

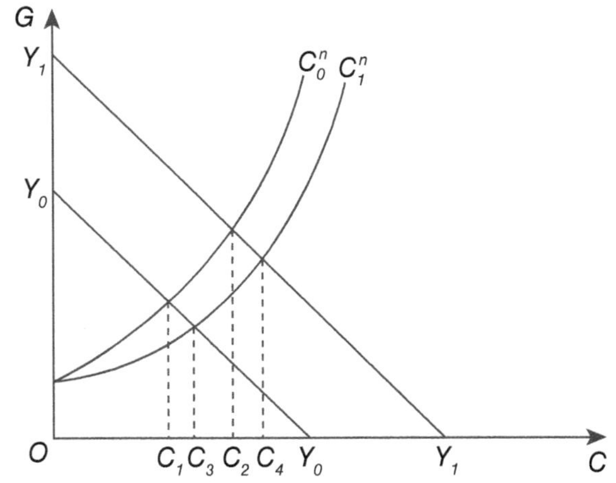

Figure 4.6. The Pennsylvania model of the demand for and supply of children (Reproduced from Easterlin, 2004, 154, figure 8.1, by permission of Richard A. Easterlin.).

additional birth, which does not address the resource costs of having live births or behavioral strategies for addressing expectations of mortality.

The Pennsylvania model has devoted more attention to the supply side of fertility than has the Chicago-Columbia model, but its treatment of supply has been primarily physiological. The Pennsylvania model's treatment of fertility determination under conditions of natural fertility works with a household budget constraint in place of a demand function and a natural fertility function as a supply function, as shown in Figure 4.6. The budget constraint is $Y = p_g Gp + p_c C$, in which Y is income, G_p is goods enjoyed by the parents, p_g is the price of that composite good, C is the number of children, and p_c is the price of children. Natural fertility is a function of overall consumption available to the parents, G_p, $C = f(G_p)$. The model is essentially Malthusian, having an income effect but no price effect. Figure 4.6 depicts the natural fertility function increasing in overall consumption available to parents, with some level of G_p below which fertility is zero. With income level Y_0 and fertility function C_0^n, the number of children a couple has is C_1. With unchanged fertility schedule and expanded income Y_1, the number of children borne increases to C_2. If fertility is more responsive to income, as in fertility schedule C_1^n, the number of children born to a couple increases from C_1 to C_3 at income level Y_0 and from C_2 to C_4 at income level Y_1. The assumption implicit in the increase in income from Y_0 to Y_1 is that no component of that income change alters the price of children by changing any component of child care costs.

4.3.5 The Malthusian Population Model

The Malthus model is roughly an aggregate, implicit version of the Chicago model without a price effect.[74] It is based on diminishing returns to labor applied to a

[72] Which simply says that the ways that market goods X and home time t can be combined to produce commodities Z is governed by some technology called T.

[73] See Easterlin (1978b, 99, Table 2-2) for a summary, but behavioral details of the relationship between the survival probability and the number of live births is little discussed.

[74] Chu (1998, 3) characterizes the Malthus model as a supply-side model, but I disagree. Population growth in the model is driven by income, and the preventive checks are essentially income effects on demand. The supply side of population growth, to the extent it is characterized, is composed of the environmental and physiological effects of the positive checks.

fixed resource and augmented with specifications of how birth and death rates are affected by wages, or whatever the relevant measure of well-being is. It is a long-run, homeostatic model of individual behavior and aggregate market relationships that determines population size and population well-being or the real wage. A homeostatic system is one in which negative feedbacks tend to return the endogenous variables to their equilibrium levels following a displacement caused by a temporary shock.[75]

The "iron law of wages" associated with the Malthusian model (but actually so named by Ricardo) depends on the absence of technical change; adding this feature to the model simply improves it but does not fundamentally change it. The model is demand driven, with supply adjusting to accommodate changes in demand. Supply factors such as the productive capacity of the fixed resource, land, or the weather can change, resulting in a different supply-demand equilibrium, but since the "price variable," the subsistence level of well-being, is fixed, population size adjusts. An equilibrium population is of a size, relative to the fixed resources with which it works, that the returns to labor just meet the minimum standards of living for a society, called a subsistence level of living for lack of more nuanced terms. At this level of living, families just reproduce themselves, so that the population growth rate is zero. Two types of balancing factors operate to keep a population in equilibrium with its fixed resources: preventive checks, which control the birth rate, and positive checks, which affect the death rate. Malthus envisioned societal-level preventive mechanisms such as marriage age conventions and partitive inheritance rules which would move fertility in whichever direction was needed to bring the population back into equilibrium. As positive checks, excess population, that is, population larger than would yield the subsistence level of living, given the fixed land resources and diminishing returns to labor, would depress living standards and nutrition, leaving people more susceptible to diseases and death by starvation during routine harvest fluctuations. Additional effects such as later menarche and earlier menopause would also contribute to moderate population growth.

Figure 4.7 shows the two principal relationships of the Malthusian model, that between the wage rate and the population growth rate and that between the size of the population and the wage rate (the latter being determined by the former in both cases).

The preventive and positive checks can be given graphical representation as well as the major structural forces. Figure 4.8 shows the relation between age at first marriage and the real wage rate, a preventive check, while Figure 4.9 shows the relationship between the crude birth rate and the real wage, a consequence of the age at first marriage. Age at first marriage becomes younger with a higher wage, while as a result of the longer period of wives' exposure to

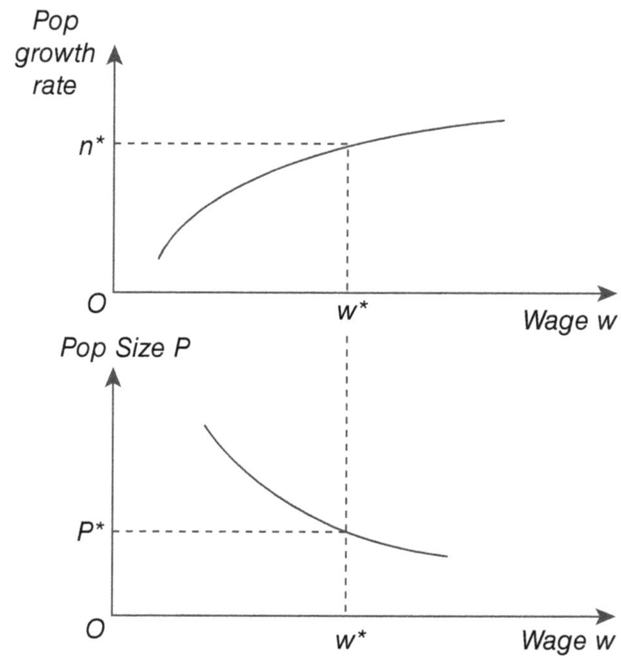

Figure 4.7. Malthusian model's components of economic-demographic equilibrium: population growth rate and size (Adapted from Lee, 1980, figures 9.8, 9.9, and 8.11, pp. 542, 543, and 545, by permission of the National Bureau of Economic Research and Ronald Demos Lee.).

pregnancy, the crude birth rate increase in the real wage. Of course, variation in the marriage age is only one preventive check, and others could be graphed or otherwise modeled. Figure 4.10 introduces a positive check, the relationship between the crude death rate and the wage rate: at lower real wage rates, the crude death rate increases, for a variety of reasons. As with the preventive check graphed in Figure 4.8, the death rate could be a function of other factors as well, such as population size, which with the land area fixed amounts to an increase in population density. Population density could affect mortality by several routes, sanitation and transmissibility of communicable diseases being two leading ones.

Putting together the graphs of the crude birth and death rates in Figure 4.11, in which the gap between the crude birth and crude death rates is the natural rate of population increase, abstracting from migration. In Figure 4.11, wage rate w* would bring the crude birth and death rates into equality, BR = DR on the horizontal axis, yielding a constant population size. An exogenous increase in the demand for labor would increase the real wage to w_1. With the higher wage, the death rate falls to DR_1 measured on the vertical axis, fertility increases to BR_1, and the population would grow by the amount $BR_1 - DR_1$.

The final relationship in the Malthusian model introduces the diminishing returns to labor applied to the fixed land resource, returns to the lower panel of Figure 4.7, which relates the size of the labor force, or population to the wage rate. A larger population drives down the wage. As can be noticed, the model is an aggregate model, with individual choices left implicit.

[75] The following model presentation relies heavily on Lee (1993), and to a lesser extent, (1981, 13–20).

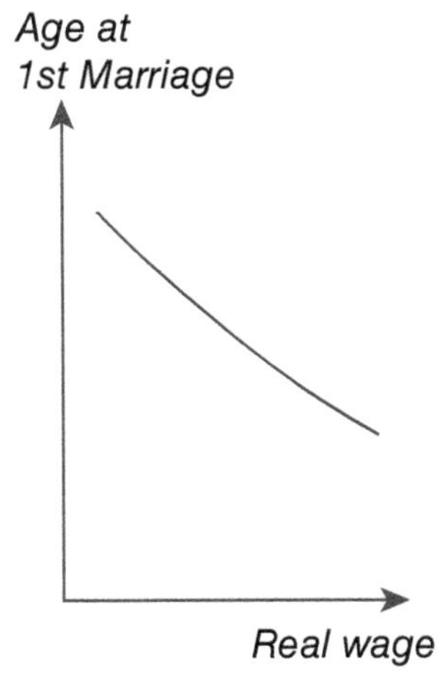

Figure 4.8. Malthusian model's demographic relationships with the real wage: age at first marriage (Adapted from Lee, 1980, figures 9.8, 9.9, and 8.11, pp. 542, 543, and 545, by permission of the National Bureau of Economic Research and Ronald Demos Lee.).

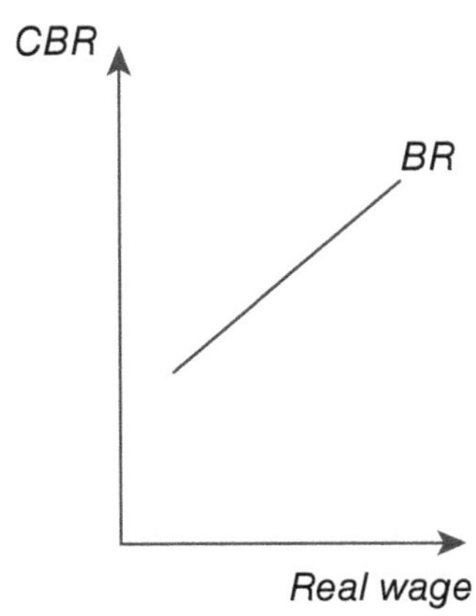

Figure 4.9. Malthusian model's demographic relationships with the real wage: crude birth rate (Adapted from Lee, 1980, figures 9.8, 9.9, and 8.11, pp. 542, 543, and 545, by permission of the National Bureau of Economic Research and Ronald Demos Lee.).

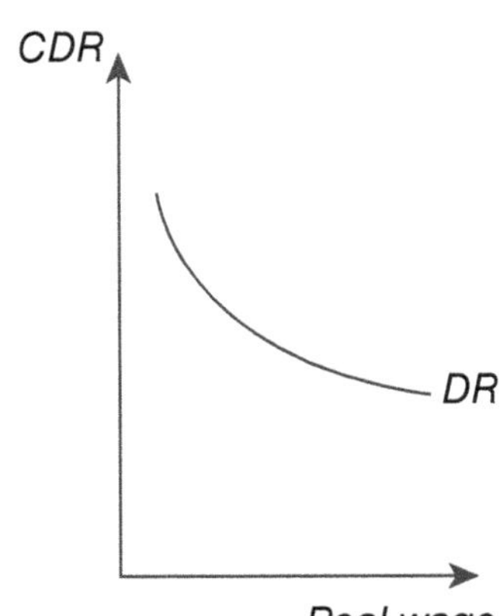

Figure 4.10. Malthusian model's demographic relationships with the real wage: crude death rate (Adapted from Lee, 1980, figures 9.8, 9.9, and 8.11, pp. 542, 543, and 545, by permission of the National Bureau of Economic Research and Ronald Demos Lee.).

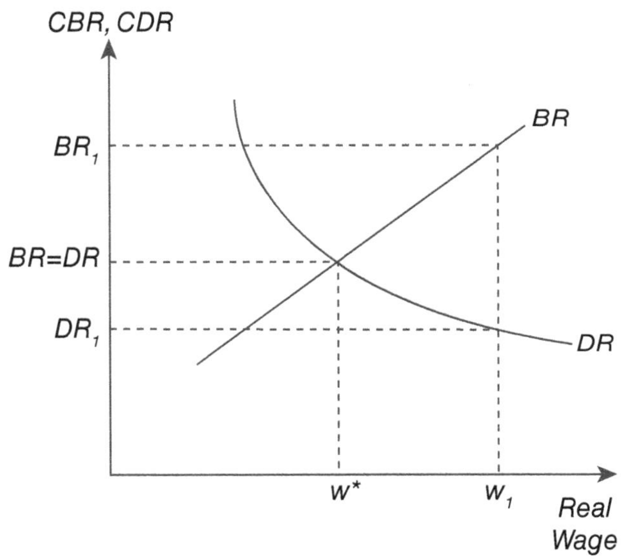

Figure 4.11. Malthusian model's components of economic-demographic equilibrium: crude birth and death rates and the real wage (Adapted from Lee, 1980, figures 9.8, 9.9, and 8.11, pp. 542, 543, and 545, by permission of the National Bureau of Economic Research and Ronald Demos Lee.).

To provide a sense of the flexibility of the model, which some authors have not fully appreciated, several variants are presented below, beginning with a very simplified version which studies the model's dynamics. At the aggregate level, the population growth rate, n, is a function of the population size (relative to other fixed resources, usually thought of as land), P; well-being, either the real wage or some other measure, W; and the mortality rate, d: n = n(P, W, d), where $n_W > 0$,[76] $n_P = 0$ because the effect of population operates through well-being by virtue of the diminishing returns to labor, $W_P < 0$, although many other influences may act upon well-being such as weather or climate, international markets, and technological developments; and $n_d \gtreqless 0$. Figure 4.7 portrays the relationships between well-being and the population growth rate, in the upper panel, and the size of the population and well-being in the bottom panel. The growth rate at time t, n_t, is defined as $\ln P_{t+1} - \ln P_t$, ("ln" stands for the natural logarithm) and the functional relationship between the growth rate and well-being is $n_t = \mu + \alpha \ln W_t + \nu_t$, where ν_t represents disturbances to well-being at time t. The parameter α is a particularly important one; a plausible value for it is 0.02, which implies that a 65 percent increase in well-being (or the real wage) would increase the population growth rate by one percentage point per year. Well-being, or the real wage rate, is related to population by $W_t = \delta P_t^{-\beta} e^{\varepsilon_t}$, or $\ln W_t = \ln \delta - \beta \ln P_t + \varepsilon_t$, where ε_t is a disturbance term affecting population. The parameter β is also particularly important, with a plausible value around 0.5, representing labor's share in output.

Transforming variables W and P to represent deviations of their natural logarithms from the natural logarithms

[76] Again, using the notation that $n_P \equiv \Delta n/\Delta P$, and so on.

of their equilibrium values simplifies subsequent notation. Thus $p_t = \ln P_t - \ln P^*$ and $w_t = \ln W_t - \ln W^*$, where the asterisks indicate equilibrium values, which do not depend on time t. The previous two relationships are now $p_t - p_{t-1} = \alpha w_{t-1} + \nu_{t-1}$ and $w_t = -\beta p_t + \varepsilon_t$. With these latest expressions, population and wages can be represented as the weighed sums of all previous disturbances to carrying capacity, ε_t, and reproduction, ν_t: $p_t = \sum_{i=1} (1-\alpha\beta)^{i-1}(\alpha\varepsilon_{t-1} + \nu_{t-1})$ and $w_t = \sum_{i=0} (1-\alpha\beta)^i[(\varepsilon_{t-1} - \varepsilon_{t-i-1}) - \beta\nu_{t-i-1}]$, where $0 < \alpha\beta < 2$ is necessary to avoid either the explosive amplification of past disturbances on p and w if $\alpha\beta < 2$ and a random walk[77] for p and w, which yields an infinitely increasing variance if $\alpha\beta = 2$. The ε and ν disturbance terms represent historical accidents while the α and β coefficients represent systematic equilibrating tendencies. These moving average representations of population size and the real wage clearly show the interaction of the singular events and the systematic forces.

Using these latest expressions for the deviations of population and wage rate from their equilibrium levels, consider an epidemic or natural disaster that reduces the population in some year t to 10 percent below what its level would otherwise be: $\nu_{t-1} = -0.10$. The wage w_t would be raised by 0.1β, possibly 5%, above its initial value. Homeostasis, represented by the factor $(1-\alpha\beta)^{i-1}$, weights the impact of events i years in the past. If $\alpha = 0.02$ and $\beta = 0.5$, then $\alpha\beta = 0.01$, and $1-\alpha\beta = 0.99$, and the influence of an event a quarter century in the past would be reduced by a factor of $0.99^{25} = 0.78$, and the half-life of an historical accident would by $0.99^t = 0.5$, or t = 70 years. That is, it would take this population 70 years to get back to 5% below its pre-shock size.

Short-run environmental randomness is well represented by the ε and ν shift terms, but longer-run changes would be better presented by changes in the μ and δ terms. The comparative statics of p and w yields $\Delta w/\Delta\varepsilon = 0$ and $\Delta p/\Delta\varepsilon = 1/\beta$. Thus, the wage, whose equilibrium level is invariant at the subsistence level, is unaffected by short-run variations in carrying capacity because population expands and drives the wage back down. Shocks to reproductive behavior, represented by variations in ν, have substantial effects on both the wage and population: $\Delta w/\Delta\nu = -1/\alpha$, and $\Delta p/\Delta\nu = 1/\alpha\beta$. The weaker is homeostasis, that is the smaller is the term $\alpha\beta$, the greater is the effect of a reproductive disturbance on population size. A long-run exogenous change in the population growth rate of 1% per year, $\nu = 0.01$, would change the equilibrium population size by 50 to 100 percent and the wage by about half that amount. A value of $\nu = 0.01$ amounts to an increase in the total fertility rate by 1.6 children or in life expectancy at birth e_0 of 11 years, changes about five times as large as Lee estimated would have been caused in medieval England by a change in temperature of 1° C (Lee 1993, 13–14).

The discussion above has not stressed the stochastic character of both the real wage (the well-being function) and population, which puts a focus on the fact that the equilibrium population sizes and real wages at the center of the model typically were only approached, not reached and maintained. Both were subject to multiple, routine disturbances, small and large, that would have nudged them away from equilibrium levels. Lee estimates the standard deviation of population size from its equilibrium value in medieval England to have been about 7 percent and that with stronger homeostasis it would have been smaller. The real wage would have been within about 20% of its equilibrium (Lee 1987, 452; 1997).

Lee has also emphasized the weakness of these homeostatic forces, that running from well-being to population growth being substantially (the "carrying-capacity" coefficient α in the formulations above) weaker than that running from population size and the wage rate, (the β coefficient). The intuition behind these relative magnitudes is that wages can fluctuate substantially more than can the number of children a woman can, or is likely to, bear. The wage is a short-term, flow variable while the number of children a family produces is a stock variable which depends on the family's expectations over its lifetime: the latter is harder to change and when it does, the family is largely stuck with the consequences.

A slightly more intricate version of the model specifies the relationships between economic variables and birth and death rates rather than go directly to the population growth rate (Lee 1985, 641–643). This version of the model also begins with the demand-for-labor formulation, $w_t = A_t P_t^{-\beta} e_t^{\varepsilon}$, A_t shifts the demand for labor, allowing a trend in labor demand over time, and $-\beta$. The specification of fertility is $b_t = \sigma_0 + \sigma_1 \ln w_t + \sigma_2 d_t + \nu_t$, where $\sigma_1 > 0$ by virtue of the wage's effect on nutrition and, since higher mortality may promote earlier inheritance and family formation or interrupt lactation, $\sigma_2 > 0$ as well. The mortality specification is $d_t = \gamma_0 + \gamma_1 \ln w_t + \nu_t$, in which $\gamma_1 < 0$ represents the positive check. This system is closed with an assumption of zero net migration, yielding the identity that the population growth rate is identically equal to the difference between the crude birth and crude death rates: $n_t \equiv \ln P_t - \ln P_{t-1} \equiv b_t - d_t$. The fertility, mortality, and growth rate relationships can be combined to yield a relationship between the growth rate and the real wage which looks like the specification in the simpler version of the model, but in which the parameters are more complicated combinations of more precise effects: $n_t = \alpha + \delta \ln w_t + \eta_t$, where $\alpha = \sigma_0 - (1-\sigma_2)\gamma_0$, $\delta = \sigma_1 + (1-\sigma_2)\gamma_1$, and $\eta = \nu_t - (1-\sigma_2)\nu_t$. The interactions between

[77] A random walk is a mathematical model of the time trajectory of a variable in which successive steps are random. The size of each step, and whether it is positive or negative relative to the previous value of the variable, are randomly distributed according to some probability distribution. A Markov chain or Markov process, a memoryless specification of such steps in which, conditional on the present value of a variable, its past values and future values are independent of one another, is commonly used to generate a random walk. Variables which have the property of a random walk generate an infinite variance, which causes severe problems in statistical analysis of time series data. Tests are available to determine if a data series is a random walk, and if it is, corrective procedures are available to permit statistical analysis.

the forces acting on fertility and those acting on mortality can be seen clearly. If the demand for labor doesn't change or changes at a constant rate, this system will settle down to an equilibrium configuration of population size, real wage and growth rate in which the population grows at a rate that leaves the real wage unchanged and fertility and mortality are constant at levels consistent with the population growth rate and the real wage. In equilibrium, the solutions for those three variables are $P^* = (A/w^*)1/\beta$, $\ln w^* = (\dot{A}/\beta - \mu)\delta$, and $n^* = \dot{A}/\beta$, where asterisks denote equilibrium values of variables and the dot over A indicates a percent change. If all the disturbances (ε, γ, ν and η) are zero and the rate of change in the demand for labor, $\dot{A}$, is constant, the system will settle down to an equilibrium in which nothing changes but the population size.

Robert Stavins (1988, 100–106) offered another series of variants on the basic model, introducing migration and exogenous technological change. The model begins with the labor demand relationship, $w = \eta P^{-\beta}$, in which η rather than A represents the shifter, and w and P are the real wage and the population size. A second equation captures the relationship between the wage and fertility, allowing for a further effect of mortality on fertility: $f = \mu + \alpha \ln w + \lambda d$, where f is the crude birth rate and d is the crude death rate. The justification for including mortality in the fertility function was noted just above. The model is closed by specifying the population growth rate to be the difference between the crude birth rate and the crude death rate, assuming zero net migration: $\dot{P} \equiv f - d$, where again, the dot over P indicates a percent rate of change. Several variants of the Malthusian model, or hypotheses about how a population behaves, can be created from this model by specifying values of several of the parameters. What Stavins calls the constant equilibrium wage model hypothesizes that the long-term real wage is a function of the labor supply or population but is set by social norms (highlighting the squishiness of the subsistence wage concept), and that fertility behavior adjusts fully to changes in mortality, implying $\lambda = 1$, leaving population growth to be a function of the real wage alone. Alternatively, a constant fertility hypothesis, in which fertility is more or less invariant, being determined by social norms, neither the wage rate nor mortality affects fertility: $\alpha = 0$ and $\lambda = 0$. A reconciliation of these two views, or hypotheses, can be constructed by setting $\lambda = 0$, representing no effect of mortality on fertility and allowing for a wage effect with $\alpha \neq 0$. Migration can be added to the model by adding a relationship between migration and the lagged wage rate, $m_t = \ln \gamma + \rho \ln w_{t-1}$, where m_t is net emigration in period t, meaning $\rho < 0$ is the expected sign of the wage coefficient.[78] Then the net emigration variable must be placed in the population growth rate formulation, making that relationship now $\dot{P} \equiv f - d - m$. Finally, an exogenous technological change can be incorporated into the labor demand equation: $w = \eta P^{-\beta} e^{\delta U}$, where U_t is the percent of the population living in cities above a certain size at time t, not the only possible choice for a driver of technological change, but a reasonable one. If the model were expanded to make urbanization of the population endogenous, this technological change would be endogenized also, although its explanation would remain at the black-box level.

Lee developed an even more intricate application of the Malthus model, giving it an incarnation as a two-sector (agriculture/countryside and industry/cities) model popular in the 1970s and 1980s (Lee 1980). The number of equations proliferates beyond what is fruitful to reproduce here. The signal point is that the same fertility and mortality relationships can be embedded in models with a wide variety of detail on both economic organization and social structures.

In one final note on variants of Malthus' population model, I briefly address a model by James Wood which has been cited in the literature on the demography of the ancient Mediterranean (Wood 1998). Wood finds Malthus' model quite valuable, and in discussing critics of aspects of it, simply notes that Malthus had a more limited view of methods of population regulation that he classified under the preventive check than we and our contemporaries have developed. He also notes that Malthus entertained the concept of technological progress affecting the productivity of a population cultivating a given land area, in contrast to the view encouraged by Ester Boserup (1965; 1981). As to Wood's model, his birth- and death-rate equations have similar forms to those used by Lee and Stavins noted above, but his basic wage equation introduces a concept which I frankly do not understand, "demographic saturation." The wage equation, $w_t = \theta(S_t/N_t)^\kappa$, has a rough similarity to a marginal product equation, with S_t, Wood's demographic saturation taking the place of a fixed input such as capital or land, and increments of labor, N_t, depressing the wage as long as the exponent $\kappa > 0$ (Wood, 1998, 109–110). However, in a subsequent assumption, when the rate of change of S_t is zero, equilibrium $N_t = S_t$, which is not recognizable economically, and the wage equation's similarity to a marginal product equation derived from a production function, which is the standard property of a Malthusian model, disappears. The ratio $S_t/N_t \rightarrow 1$, and the wage takes the value of θ, which had the appearance of a production function shifter in the wage equation but instead is the value the wage takes when population reaches its saturation level, which is defined to occur when the birth and death rates are equal. The birth- and death-rate equations are not solved simultaneously with the wage equation, and the determination of the equilibrium wage

[78] This function has a semi-logarithmic specification, meaning that the dependent variable is not expressed as a natural logarithm while the right-hand-side variables are. A full logarithmic specification, such as the Cobb-Douglas, is an alternative, and at a theoretical rather than an empirical level, there is frequently little or no grounds for choosing one form over the other, beyond the fact that the coefficients of the independent variables in a full logarithmic specification are elasticities—the percent change in the dependent variable per one-percent change in the independent variable. I have retained Stavins' specifications for simplicity. Also notice that the migration relationship involves the values of variables at different dates, migration responding with a lag to the real wage, thus requiring the use to time subscripts absent in the other equations of this version of the model.

and fertility and mortality rates, the explanation of the θ remain opaque.

In antiquity, regions with better agricultural technologies would not generate higher wage levels for their populations but rather increase their populations to levels that drove their real wages back to a common level. It is not inconceivable that different regions would have different subsistence levels for a variety of reasons, although people in each region would have considered them at the minimum acceptable level of living in equilibrium. Explanations for sudden (or even gradual) departure from this equilibrium as technology advanced remain unsatisfactory.

4.3.6 The Economics of Nuptiality

There's really not a field of economics known as the economics of nuptiality, so I've had to pick quite selectively from the extensive field of the economics of marriage to find material that I think will help students of the ancient Mediterranean think about average ages at first marriage and a population's overall propensity to marry or remain single, two of Malthus' primary preventive checks on population growth as well as interesting topics in their own right. Focusing to a great extent as it does on individual choices, economics generally deals with both of these topics from the perspective of the individual whereas for the study of ancient populations, average society-wide tendencies in both of these indicators will be more useful. In fact, both may appear as societal conventions not subject to much leeway in individual choices, but light may be shed on both topics by thinking about age at first marriage and the propensity to marry or remain single from the perspective of individuals. I decline to accept notions that somehow, in some unknown manners, societies collected the wisdom to create institutions, or social conventions, that acted so as to stabilize some aspects of their collectivities, in such opportune manners that they appear to have been in place when they were first needed, possibly well before any crisis appeared for which they were useful to address. That women's age at first marriage in ancient Greece and Rome was quite young is a well-established fact, and I would not contest the notion that women of those times and places would have been unlikely to attempt to deviate from those norms, or even contemplate such actions. Similarly with the much later Medieval, Renaissance, and Early Modern English convention of newlywed couples establishing independent households, which generally required the capital to set themselves up with a house and farm independent of the parents of either spouse: it's a well-established historical finding, and I have no inclination to contest it, although I should justify jumping so far outside the period and region that are the subject of this study. In the spirit of comparisons for the study of any period and place of history, which may become more helpful for periods and places for which direct information is particularly scarce, the English case illuminates possible consequences of short-term income and mortality changes on population growth which may transcend the variance in time and place. If this is too abstract for immediately clear comprehension, don't worry too much; I'll come back to it. To close off a paragraph that may already be too long, I will convey what the economics of marriage has to say about age at first marriage and propensity to marry and strive to apply that thinking to the setting of societies in which the scope for individual decision in either choice was limited.

Background on Marital Production and Consumption. Women and men bring different production possibilities to a marriage. Marriage confers more benefits on both partners when they supply complementary production capabilities; as technological changes convert more of their capabilities into substitutes in production, marriage confers fewer benefits. The ability to produce a child remains a clearly complementary relationship, although greater substitutability may emerge in providing care for the child. In a technological setting in which households must produce much of their consumption items, from clothing to meals to childcare, with little assistance from technologies that increase the efficiency of these household tasks, and most of the raw inputs for household production are produced in the agricultural fields with equipment that doesn't substitute well for raw muscle power,[79] there is a relatively clear division of labor within a family between males and females. Technology can change, however, and those changes can alter the comparative advantages of men and women in household and non-household production. The extent to which such technological changes occurred within the temporal scope of Mediterranean antiquity was probably not great, but the subject is worth keeping an eye on, particularly archaeologically. Nonetheless, since women didn't get highly freed from household work until nearly the end of the second millennium C.E., there may be only the barest changes to detect, but the possibility of eventual change, even if it didn't occur within the periods of interest, highlights the importance of the structure of production within ancient families for various characteristics of families and family formation. Nonetheless, changes in technology can alter the value of intra-family production specializations (Isen and Stevenson 2011, 108–110).

Spouses also are a consumption unit, and complementary and substitute relations exist in consumption as well. Activities in which participation of each spouse enhances the enjoyment of the other are complementary. As technological changes alter the extent of complementary production capabilities between spouses, consumption complementarities become more important in providing benefits from marriage. Consumption complementarities appear to have been rarer than production complementarities in families of the ancient Mediterranean region.

[79] Granted, there are contemporary societies in which women do a good bit, if not most, of the agricultural field work, and they probably pulled their weight if not more in a number of ancient Mediterranean societies, despite upper-class rhetoric about seclusion of women to protect them from various human predators. The lower-income Greek women probably worked in the fields more often than not.

In such a technological setting, women and men accumulated their human capital, even if most of that training was of the on-the-job (OJT) variety and its opportunity cost in terms of lost productivity in alternative activities probably minimal. One of the principal products of marriages in antiquity was children, and children served many productive purposes in addition to any emotional rewards, from low-productivity agricultural labor to child care to savings plans.

One of the principal tenets of contemporary marriage economics is that potential spouses should have their well-being improved by marriage relative to remaining single. When strong sexual division of labor is fostered by both household and market or non-household technology, both women and men are likely to find that their prospects are improved by entering into a marriage, although the exact prospects may depend on the prospective partner. If prospective marriage with available partners would not improve an individual's well-being, that individual would not marry. This analysis considers only the prospective marriage partners as actors in this problem. In antiquity, for various reasons, families—parents—had considerable influence on what would be welfare-enhancing. In fact the unit whose well-being should be enhanced by a marriage might well be the parents of the potential new spouses rather than the prospective marital coupe themselves. The path from the parents being the marital decision unit to the individuals themselves being the decision unit is a long one and outside the scope of the present discussion, although it is not outside the interest of students of antiquity.

Technological changes that increased the productivity of single women relative to single men would encourage women who were their own decision-makers to defer marriage (Lee 1997; 1991, 60). Technological changes that enhanced the productivity of either single men or single women relative to their potential well-being within a marriage, would have encouraged deferral of marriage and lower incidences of marriage, both of which would reduce fertility.

Age at First Marriage. When people have a wide range of options, the greater the opportunity to accumulate human capital useful outside the household, the individuals whose native abilities can absorb those skills will defer marriage and accumulate human capital—get themselves educated or trained. Typically the opportunities those skills open up, to women in particular, reduce both fertility and other benefits to marriage. When technology favors a strong sexual division of labor within households, males require additional time to accumulate physical capital as well as human capital sufficient to support family dependents who would produce only within the household. Under the same circumstances women benefit from embarking on the OJT opportunity of developing their lifetime skills earlier rather than later. The pattern of age at first marriage of men being a decade or older than their wives emerges readily from such a technological setting.

This is pretty much all on the demand side, despite the emphasis on opportunity costs of human capital acquisition. The supply, or cost, side of first marriage ages has been less well developed in contemporary economics, I suspect because such a large proportion of the capital costs of market employment in the societies that are the subject of contemporary economic analysis is fronted by firms, large and small, so that young individuals may take out implicit loans from firms to establish their market productivity. Nonetheless, what could be called set-up costs play an important role in Malthus' homeostatic population theory which had the setting of small, independent agriculturalists and a trivial non-self-employment sector. This is where the English case noted above becomes relevant, at least as an example or a possibility. When mortality was high, young people who were not struck down by whatever mortality spike took off their parents came into their inheritances earlier and were able to either claim an agricultural production unit directly or buy one earlier than they would have been able to do otherwise. When times were good, meaning that parents lived longer, children had to wait longer to marry and begin their own fertility track records. Thus, flush times in which parents lived longer, and because of the flushness of times—higher income, more food, better nutrition, less disease—had more children, put a natural brake on population growth by causing later marriage in the next generation, thus lowering their fertility.

Proportion of a Population Ever Married. Contemporary economics of the family has less to say about proportions of populations that remain single than it does about age at first marriage. That the benefits of remaining single are high relative to the benefits of being married in a population with a high proportion of permanent singles is the economic answer to this question, just as it guided the age-specific probability of marriage in addressing age at first marriage. It offers a relatively content-free framework for thinking about factors that affect both benefits to and costs of being married. For example, people with occupations that require long absences from the home, such as characterized much of Roman soldiery, would reduce the benefits of being married. Lower desired fertility would reduce the benefits of marriage, as would a higher earning capacity of women relative to men.

Of course, age at first marriage can extend to the non-early deaths of adult individuals and back into the issue of proportions of a population choosing marriage and singleness or celibacy (although there are alternatives to celibacy as a single person). Falling back to Medieval English examples again, the removal of individuals from the reproductive pool (or at least lowering their effect on it) by entry into the priesthood or to nunneries would reduce the proportion of a population reproducing, at least at full, society-specific capacity for reproduction. Economic causes of such occupational choices remain a study in themselves, and the choices are likely to be made as much by families (particularly parents) as by individuals themselves, and again, why individuals have such limited scope for making important life decisions is a topic outside the purview of the present analysis.

It is tempting to revert to aggregate models of a systems analysis variety to determine an equilibrium proportion of a population that marries, but that sort of model does not yield insights into how a society arrived at such a mechanism. First, such models are equilibrium models, and variations in the percent of a population marrying may be a disequilibrium phenomenon, even if it lasts for several centuries. Second, they don't specify the behavior of any individuals, so it remains unknown whether people would have behaved in ways such a model would imply they did. Did such shunting of later sons and daughters to such non-reproductive occupations reflect purely ideological choices—to serve a deity—or rather the costliness of search for mates for children who were not scheduled, according to law, for inheritance, combined with weakly developed capital markets that could have helped young people to establish themselves in materially productive occupations? Sex disequilibria and attendant marriage squeezes could affect the proportion of one sex marrying, although fertility has ways of eluding formal marriage structures during periods of severe sex imbalance, as noted in section 4.2.5.

4.3.7 Mortality

Mortality may be considered largely exogenous, but it can be endogenous in important ways. At the aggregate level, individuals may have no direct control over their own mortality but through their fertility and work choices create conditions of crowding and nutrition that affect their mortality schedules. Alternatively, or in addition, individuals may have at least some limited direct influence over their mortality schedules, sometimes through characteristics of their fertility choices, sometimes through activities explicitly intended to safeguard or improve their health.

Mortality schedules also may interact with fertility, with changes in mortality affecting individuals' fertility choices through such behaviors as birth timing and spacing and efforts to replace children who die during parents' fertile periods or engage in what is called hoarding, effectively anticipatory replacement prior to deaths, given parents' expectations of mortality and its timing. These compensating behaviors are symmetric in the sense that they operate in the opposite direction when mortality schedules fall.

The basic Malthusian model contains an overall mortality rate rather than one or more age-specific rates. In the Malthusian model, a reduction in income increases "the" mortality rate, which in turn reduces fertility, so the relation between mortality and fertility is negative. This relationship may apply to a given family over its life cycle, particularly if the income reduction is large and permanent—a couple may revise its desired family size—but it is particularly apt when comparing fertility rates of successive generations who grow up with different income expectations. At the level of the individual family, the relationship between age-specific mortality rates and fertility may be quite different, hence the prevalence of high-fertility families in populations with permanently high—and possibly highly variable—infant and child mortality schedules. How this mechanism operates at the level of the family is through a combination of hoarding and replacement. If the desired number of surviving children is greater than a family is likely to be able physically to produce, hoarding behavior—anticipatory replacement—will operate. If the family is physically capable of bearing the number of surviving children it desires, given the prevailing infant and child mortality rates, it may engage in replacement of realized, rather than anticipated, child deaths.

This section addresses these issues by beginning with a more detailed model of fertility with non-negligible infant and child mortality regimes, which is grounded in individual choice. This model highlights several important relationships between mortality and fertility as well as providing a more realistic view of choices over a family's life cycle. The following sub-section deals with determinants of mortality, over some of which individuals have little or no influence, and others which may influence directly or indirectly by their choices. The final sub-section addresses some consequences of different mortality regimes.

Sequential Decision-Making. The fertility models introduced in sections 4.3.3 and 4.3.4 are static formulations of a full lifetime of decisions made at one abstract point in time. To account for noticeable infant and child mortality schedules, the simple procedure adopted by the Pennsylvania model to form the target utility model was to assume parents produce a number of births equal to the number of desired children divided by the survival rate, a procedure that ignores costs of producing non-surviving children as well as risk aversion in the face of stochastic survival rates.

More realistically, couples make sequential decisions regarding whether to have another child or not—again, supposing they have some sort of control over their fertility. Rather than have the modeler force a lifetime number of (surviving) children on a couple during their honeymoon, the modeler can incorporate many changes over a couple's lifetime: unanticipated changes in income, surprises in fertility, deaths of infants and children. While the changes in income and fertility surprises are interesting theoretically, the most important of these issues is the response to surviving and deceased children over the fertile span of a couple's lifetime. These responses involve spacing, replacement, and hoarding as they are affected by the cumulative status of a couple's family and their expectations for the future. Further, the fertility model so far has abstracted from the discrete character of childbearing decisions: they are integer decisions—one, two, etc.—not continuous.

Some of the models embodying these features of childbearing decisions are dynamic—in the sense that decisions in different time periods are determined jointly—and all are stochastic, in that decisions must be made without any assurance of their outcomes, both of which features add to the models' complexity and accordingly what can be expected of their solutions. Accordingly, models addressing these aspects of family decisions abstract from modeling the quality-quantity trade-off and assume that the allocation of full income between parents' consumption and child-bearing and –rearing are determined optimally but off-stage, as it were, from the child-bearing decisions. The principal new component of these models is one or more exogenous mortality rates. Single-period models address whether a higher infant mortality rate increases fertility and how it affects the number of surviving children. Multi-period models introduce age-specific mortality rates and are able to address how the survival or deaths of previously borne children affect subsequent child-bearing decisions.

The Formal Structure of Sequential Fertility Decisions. The models of sequential fertility decisions involve intricate and tedious calculations to derive responses of fertility to mortality rates and to surviving children. I will not reproduce the derivations of those results here, but will show only the decision structure of one model and report salient results from it.[80]

A couple produces n children, where n is an integer, N of whom survive. Each child's probability of survival is s, 1 > s > 0, giving a mortality rate of 1 – s. The probability that N out of n children survive is the binomial density $b(N, n, s) \equiv \frac{n!s^N(1-s)^{n-N}}{N!(n-x)!}$.[81] Parents' expected utility from the nth birth for a given mortality rate s is $U(n, s) = \sum_{N=0}^{N=n} b(N, n, s)u(N)$, so parents maximize utility by choosing a discrete number of children conditional on the child mortality rate and the number of children they already have. With the discrete representation of births and a single-period representation of the setting of fertility decisions, the marginal utility of a surviving child is $U_N(N) \equiv U(N + 1) - U(N) \geq 0$ for an optimal number of surviving children,[82] which is the difference in utility with N + 1 children and utility with N children, and the change in that marginal utility as an additional child survives is $U_{NN}(N) \equiv U_N(N + 1) - U_N(N) < 0$. Similarly, the marginal utility of an additional birth is $U_n(n,s) \equiv U(N + 1) - U(n,s) \geq 0$, and the change in this marginal utility is $U_{nn}(n,s) \equiv U_n(n + 1,s) - U_n(n,s) < 0$. In both cases, the rates of change rely on change in utility associated with adjacent integer numbers of births or surviving children rather than continuous measures of these variables. In this single-period setting, the number of births is an increasing integer function of the mortality rate, which agrees with the coincidence in antiquity of high infant and child mortality schedules with high fertility.

This single-period model can be expanded to two periods, allowing analysis of how the number of children born in the first period who survive to the second period affects fertility in the second period, as well as how expected child mortality in the second period affects fertility decisions in the first period. The variables n, N, and s from the single-period model are subscripted 1 or 2 to denote the period to which they pertain. Expanding the model to two periods makes it both dynamic, since the fertility decisions in both periods depend on the expected or actual values of variables in both periods, and stochastic, since some decisions must be made before realizations of some stochastic variables are observed. As with many sequential optimization problems, this one is solved backwards in time, the last period's optimization being solved conditional on the previous period's optimization, and so on.[83] In this case, the second period's parental choice after N_1 has been observed is $U^2(N_1, n_2, s_2) \equiv \sum_{N_2=0}^{N_2=n_2} b(N_2, n_2, s_2)u(N_1, N_2)$. The marginal utility of another birth in the second period is $U_n^2(N_1, n_2, s_2) \equiv U^2(N_1, n_2 + 1, s_2) - U^2(N_1, n_2, s_s) \geq 0$. Analysis indicates that the number of births in the second period is an increasing integer function of the mortality rate of second-period children and a decreasing integer function of the number of surviving children from the first period. Turning to the first period's decisions, $U^1(n_1, s_1, s_1) \equiv \sum_{N_1=0}^{N_1=n_1} b(N_1, n_1, s_1)V^2(N_1, s_2)$, where V^2 represents the largest maximized value of U^2. The maximized value of U^1 is represented by $V^1(s_1, s_2) \equiv max_{n_1} U^1(n_1, s_1, s_2) \equiv U^1(n_1(s_1, s_2), s_1, s_2)$, where $n_1(s_1, s_2)$ is the largest optimal value of n_1. This expression says that the couple maximizes its utility by choosing a number of first-period births n_1, conditional on its expectations of infant mortality in both the current and subsequent periods. As with the case of the second period births, the marginal utility of first-period births is $U_n^1(n_1, s_1, s_2) \equiv U^1(n_1 + 1, s_1, s_2) - U^1(n_1, s_1, s_2) \geq 0$. Analysis finds that the number of births in the first period is non-decreasing in the mortality rate of first-period children, but the response of first-period births to a change in the expected second-period child mortality is more complicated. It also will be a non-decreasing integer function of the second-period mortality rate if two conditions are met: (1) a unit decrease in the number of surviving children must not induce more than a unit increase in the optimal number of births in the second period, a condition which has been found to hold in

---

80 The model presented here is from Sah (1991). Wolpin (1997) presents a somewhat more detailed three-period model with two fertile periods; his exposition sheds considerable clarity on the utility comparisons involved in sequential fertility decisions but relies on numerical experiments for analytical results which include counterfactual decreases in fertility to increases in infant and child mortality, the exact sources of which cannot be determined from the publication.

81 The exclamation mark following n, N, and (x-n) is the factorial operator, which multiplies each integer value of the variable from its highest value to one. For instance, if n takes the values 6 through 1, n! = 6 · 5 · 4 · 3 · 2 · 1.

82 The value of this marginal utility can be negative, but that would indicate an excessive number of surviving children according to the parents' preferences.

83 This is an application of dynamic programming, which is a mathematical technique for solving problems in which the optimal value of the endogenous variable in one period depends on its optimal value in the next (or previous) period or periods.

contemporary developing countries, and (2) the decrease in the marginal expected utility of a surviving child from the second period due to one more survivor from the first period isn't significantly smaller than the corresponding decrease due to one more surviving child from the second period. The expected number of total births is non-decreasing in the mortality rate of either first-or second-period children if the two conditions for first-period births to be non-decreasing in mortality are satisfied.

The result in this model that increasing infant and child mortality rates cannot reduce fertility is the sequential model's analog to the invariant number of surviving children in the target utility model, but without the implication of invariance. The discreteness of births and survivals, together with the uncertainty, cause a piecewise linear relationship between births and mortality. For example, at one mortality rate, it may be optimal to have at least, say, n children, but at a slightly higher mortality rate, the expected number of surviving children would drop below n, so it becomes optimal to have n + 1 children, the n + 1st child representing hoarding behavior.

The reader will have noticed a gap between the basic, lifetime fertility decision model of section 4.3.3 and the sequential model of this section: while couples make decisions about desired completed family size in the lifetime model, without any mechanism for in-course corrections as circumstances change, the sequential model focuses only on the next child, without the couple's having formed a target completed family size. Clearly, decisions in the real (observational) world combine the formation of long-term goals with changeable plans. The only model in the literature that has combined these two decisions is that of Wolpin (1984), which is sufficiently intricate that it is solved with dynamic programming using parameter values estimated from a sample of Malaysian families. The extensive comparative statics that have been conducted on the basic, lifetime fertility model have been paralleled only by some parameter variation. The maximization decision of the family in this model is $max_{n_t^i} E_t \sum_{k=0}^{\tau-t} \delta^k U_{t+k}^i(M_{t+k}^i, X_{t+k}^i)$, where $n_t^i = 1$ indicates a birth at time t and $n_t^i = 0$ indicates no birth; E_t is the expectations operator at time t conditional on the information available at that date, δ is the discount factor, superscript i indicates a particular household, M_{t+k} is the stock of children at time t + k, and X_{t+k} is the consumption of a composite good at the same date. The maximization is conducted subject to the budget constraint (ignoring the household superscript i) $Y_t = X_t + b(n_t - d_t) + cn_t$, where Y_t is household income at time t, b is the maintenance cost of a surviving child, $d_t = 1$ is a child death in period t and $d_t = 0$ is a survival, in which d_t has a random component that n_t does not, and c is the fixed cost of bearing a child whether it survives or not. Exogenous determinants of income at time t include factors such as age of the household head, occupation, non-wage resources, health, and so on: $Y_t = H_t\pi_2 + \nu_t$, where H_t is a vector of characteristics, π_2 is their associated coefficients indicating the direction and strength of those characteristics' effects on income, and ν_t is a random component.[84] The stock of children at the time of marriage, $M_0 = 0$, and subsequent values of M_t are defined as $M_t = M_{t-1} + n_t - d_t$, t = 1, . . . T, where T is the last fertile period. It can be seen that an expectation of the lifetime path of income affects decisions in each period, and that the current expected utility is a function of the stock of children in all future periods, which implicitly gives the couple a lifetime fertility plan with a target completed family size at each date. As life unfolds, those plans can be revised. Analytical derivation of comparative statics (i.e., with pencil-and-paper algebra—calculus or calculus of variations actually—that yields mathematical formulas) is out of the question with this model, leaving numerical simulation the technique for studying its properties.

Evidence on Replacement and Hoarding. A number of studies have estimated empirical magnitudes of several facets of infant and child mortality effects on fertility, offering a variety of views and results. Olsen estimated a replacement rate of 0.2 from a 1973 sample of Colombian women—i.e., an infant or child death will be replaced by an additional 0.2 births—averaged, of course, over the sample since one-fifth of a birth is an impossibility for any individual. Using a 1976 sample of Malaysian village women Olsen estimated a direct replacement rate of either 0.17 or 0.21 (he reports both figures) and a replacement effect due to hoarding of 0.14.[85] Using a different sample from the same Malaysian survey data, but fitting a dynamic programming model to the data rather than using a regression approach, Wolpin (1984) estimated a negligible replacement effect of around 0.015. Again using the same 1976 Malaysian survey data, but employing a waiting-time regression model which estimates the effect of the probability of a child death in a family on the duration from age 15 to a woman's first birth, Olsen and Wolpin estimated a replacement fertility response to exogenous mortality of less than one percent, but a response to endogenous mortality six times as large, 0.043 (Olsen and Wolpin 1983). The exogenous mortality reflects inherent endowments of a family, while the endogenous mortality reflects the family's preferences as reflected in their behaviors that affect child health. The great differences in these replacement rates was noted in one publication but otherwise not discussed by either author (Wolpin 1984, 869, n. 37).

A time-series analysis of Swedish mortality-fertility interactions over the period 1750 to 1869 estimated about a 40-percent replacement rate of infant deaths in the first year after a mortality shock. The response during the second year following a shock rose to 122 percent replacement which was fully offset over the subsequent three years by below-average fertility. Replacement was only a matter of the timing of births; it did not raise completed fertility (Eckstein, Schultz, and Wolpin 1985).

[84] For those wondering what happened to π_1, it is a set of coefficients associated with a vector of characteristics affecting child mortality, which I have not reproduced.

[85] Olsen (1980) on the Columbian sample; Olsen (1983) on the Malaysian sample.

Analysis of a 1971 labor force survey in Israel provided detailed estimates of the effects of infant and child mortality on fertility (Ben Porath 1976). With many of the women born outside Israel, there were large differences in completed fertility and replacement responses by origin, illustrating the wide variety of behaviors that can be found in the population of even a small area. Replacement rates varied by the birth order of child deaths, with women born in Asia or Africa replacing nearly 90 percent of deaths at a parity of 2, and nearly 80 percent at parity 3, but falling off to 13 percent at parity 6. Women born in Europe or America and Israel, with substantially lower overall fertility rates, exhibited far lower replacement rates of 30 and 22 percent respectively at parity 2 and negligible rates at higher parities. For women with the same number of births, child mortality shortened birth intervals, with older women exhibiting much stronger responses, probably because of their more limited remaining duration of fertility. While the biological contraceptive mechanism induced by breastfeeding is terminated by a breastfed child's death, the ages of children at death were not specified in the sample, so the proportion of the shortened birth intervals following child deaths attributable to terminated breast feeding cannot be assessed. Nonetheless, the age pattern of shortening responses suggests a behavioral component rather than a purely biological one. The survey data were unable to reveal hoarding behavior, but since hoarding and replacement are substitute strategies for maintaining a desired family size, and the higher-fertility women had higher replacement rates, it would appear that hoarding among these women was minimal, which would be expected in a relatively low-mortality environment.

Determinants of Mortality. This sub-section divides the determinants of—or sources of or causes of or influences on—mortality schedules into exogenous and endogenous categories. The exogenous lie outside the influence of the people subject to the mortality vectors, the endogenous are those that the people who are subject to them can influence, if not necessarily make just the way they would like them. The division is not a clean one. Most of the influences that many scholars would agree to classify as exogenous, if they had to pick one class or the other, they would equally agree pose problems for a population that the individuals can ameliorate to some degree in one fashion or another. Nonetheless, an exogenous-endogenous dichotomy provides a useful set of end points on a continuum of "they were able to do something about it" based on ancient populations' ability to influence sources of mortality or adjust their own activities to ameliorate the problems caused by various sources as well as the utility to contemporary scholars in terms of organizing thinking about problems of mortality in antiquity.

It will prove useful to think in terms of age-specific mortality schedules, in addition to an undifferentiated "mortality," since forces of mortality may operate on different segments of a population's age distribution at different times and in different places. Infant and child mortality are widely recognized as distinct, important concepts even if teasing out what they were from ancient data is difficult; they affect fertility. Youth—late teens to twenties—and prime-age-worker mortality are worth distinguishing where possible, as both affect the value of human capital accumulation and ultimately technological change and economic growth, and the latter affects aggregate productivity of an economy. Old-age mortality may have less direct influence on a population's economy, particularly when the subjects are out of the labor force, but they affect the magnitude of intergenerational resource transfers and hence indirectly economic growth as well as possibly non-growing consumption, and furthermore, a society's treatment of its elderly has been considered an important characteristic of a civilization's humanity, and the condition of that segment of a population surely conditions such treatment.

Exogenous Mortality. Exogenous components of ancient mortality schedules may seem out of place in a treatment of population that emphasizes individual choices, but they form a background against which other choices would have been made as well as being not entirely exogenous at their edges, even if they remained largely or entirely outside the scope of individual choices. Disease, nutrition, and health hazards members of each sex encountered by virtue of sex are called out in this sub-section as major facets of contributor to ancient mortality schedules.

Disease. Infectious diseases such as malaria hit some ancient communities in Greece, Roman Italy, and Egypt quite severely and persistently, while bilharzia or schistomiasis was endemic in parts of Egypt, not to mention various bacteria throughout the Mediterranean region that can produce deadly dysentery (Sallares 2002; Scheidel 2001a). Additionally, ancient populations suffered from non-communicable diseases such as heart disease and rheumatoid afflictions which were essentially untreatable at the time.[86]

Sallares has stressed the density dependence of a number of infectious diseases that appeared at certain dates and times from the Mycenaean period through Late Antiquity, in what he calls an ecological analysis which stresses at least the longer-term endogeneity of some diseases (Sallares 1991, Part II, Chapter 7). With little understanding of most diseases, neither direct treatments nor indirect adjustments such as moving settlements uphill from swampy areas were likely responses to endogenize the incidence of disease influences on mortality schedules. Sallares' emphasis of the density dependence of some diseases depends on transmissibility of communicable diseases from person to person. High population densities, particularly in cities with poor water and sewer systems, offer another route to the endogenization of disease and mortality, although the link remains largely an externality which would require community rather than individual action to make any satisfactory adjustments: an individual in an ancient city

[86] Grmek (1989) discusses many noncommunicable conditions in addition to infectious diseases.

could have full knowledge of the danger of drinking well water but could have no recourse other than drinking wine; it would take the enforced actions of the entire community to upgrade the quality of the well water.

Nutrition. The role of improving nutrition in the Western European Industrial Revolution and its accompanying—or following—demographic transition, in the form of the McKeown thesis, has competed recently and bumptiously with public health and medical technology theories to explain declining infant and child mortality rates, and adult life expectancies. This disagreement about sources of health improvements during the Industrial Revolution, beginning in the late 18th century an underpinning the 19th and 20th century demographic transition, would have little relevance to mortality in antiquity were it not for the timeless role of nutrition in human health, a subject of long standing in the scholarship of the ancient Mediterranean.

Stripped to its bones, the McKeown thesis contested the ability of many public health and medical technology advances to account for lengthened life expectancies in the 19th century, largely because of the timing of the public health and medical advances on the one hand versus that of reductions in the incidences of various diseases on the other, and offered in their place improved nutrition, and its ability to help individuals fight off infections (McKeown and Brown 1955; McKeown 1976).[87] McKeown made his case through a residual argument—after discarding all the temporally inconsistent explanations, only nutrition was left—rather than directly, which offered wide targets for subsequently scholarly criticism, but after nearly a half-century of focused research which his own thesis sparked, a solid core of his thesis appears accepted, and much has been learned about both the causes of health improvements and the roles of nutrition in health as a consequence.[88]

The current status of the debates over the issue of nutritional status in producing health is that more calories, balanced across a variety of nutrients, conditional on the caloric work output demanded of a person, better equips the body to fight off infections. Fogel estimated that in France and England as recently as 1790, the bottom 10 percent of the labor force lacked the energy for any work at all, and the next 10 percent had enough energy for 3 hours of light work per day (0.52 hour of heavy work); in England, the bottom 10 percent had the energy for about 6 hours of light work per day (1.09 hours of heavy work) (Fogel 1994, 373). Stunting is an adaptation to calorific deficiencies of low food supplies which may not impair health, but even when body mass index is maintained at an ideal level, short people are at substantially greater risk of death than tall people; a decrease in fertility may be an additional adaptation (Fogel 1997, 452–466).This is the substance of Malthus' positive check, even though it does not operate through the dramatic route of famines or plagues: in the two centuries between 1550 and 1750, crisis mortality accounted for 6 percent of total English mortality (Fogel 1997, 442).[89] The adaptations of body size, life expectancy, morbidity, and possibly fertility, to short food supplies all give a slipperiness to the concept of a subsistence standard of living, which is a cornerstone of the Malthusian model.

What is exogenous about nutrition as regards mortality? Food intake per capita, in a simple model of production with fixed land supplies, would decline with an increase in population beyond a certain point, although Boserup's concepts of agricultural technology regimes changing in response to increases in labor-land ratios would mitigate such a decrease if not eliminate it. Clearly, over the long term from hunting and gathering to sedentary agriculture and developments within agriculture to accommodate greater food demands from given land areas, people's nutritional status did not consistently decline. Both nutrition and population reflect endogenous adjustments of various components of a society's production systems and demands, but at any given time, particularly over any period for which people planned and acted, technologies of food production surely remained largely unchanged to the eye, and it is reasonable to consider a population's nutritional status as something with the capacity to affect their health and mortality schedules that remained outside their immediate control.

Sex-Specific Hazards. For women, childbearing was the primary exogenous contributor to mortality during the fertile span of the age distribution. There was little or no recourse. I have seen nothing in the literature on antiquity regarding the health hazards of indoor cooking with firewood or other combustibles such as cattle and donkey dung which might have been used in Egypt, but this is a well-known liability for women in the contemporary development literature. Cooking outside can ameliorate the hazards, but by and large, it would have been an exogenous

[87] Sympathetic syntheses of the McKeown thesis which nonetheless summarize the criticisms of the work are in Fogel (1997) and Floud, Fogel, Harris, and Hong (2001, 151–164).

[88] As with all ideas that could challenge contemporary funding programs, McKeown's ideas were attacked with considerable vigor and enthusiasm. Two more recent, thoroughly considered evaluations pick carefully through the research findings on the many issues involved: Robert Woods (2000, 344–359) accepts some of McKeown's interpretations of disease declines, criticizes a number of McKeown's harshest critics as well as McKeown's techniques themselves, and concludes that, "Perhaps it is time to draw a line under the McKeown interpretation and simply acknowledge that its greatest strength has been its ability to stimulate debate." Bernard Harris, (2004, 405) offers a "qualified defense" of McKeown's work, emphasizing the limitation of McKeown's focus on nutrition as diet, which "ignores the extent to which the adequacy of a person's diet may be affected by changes in their epidemiological environment and in the nature and the amount of work they are expected to perform." Harris and other critics would substitute the term "nutritional status" for simple "nutrition" or diet, "which reflects a much better understanding of the synergistic relationship between nutrition and infection on which so many aspects of human health depend" (Harris 2004, 405).

[89] In contrast to the thesis of Massimo Livi-Bacci (1991, 119) providing the capstone of a lengthy argumentation including that humans' resistance to disease appears to increase during episodes of severe nutritional deprivation (43–50), that infants are insulated by breastfeeding to a great degree from nutritional fluctuations facing adults (75–78), and that caloric intake was not particularly inadequate (80–85, and Table 15, 82–83). On the last element, Fogel (1997, 449–452, 451, Table 3) has stressed the difference between average consumptions and the distribution of consumption across various groups. Livi-Bacci's contention contra the nutrition thesis is amplified (Livi-Bacci 2007, 67–69).

contributor to female mortality schedules, possibly at all but the youngest ages.

For men, farm work was the prevalent occupation. Despite the simplicity of farm machinery, to the extent that the equipment could be called machinery, farming is an accident-prone occupation: lacerations, broken bones, amputations, some surely debilitating and life-shortening. Non-agricultural civilian occupations also had their hazards; for instance, Roman court records contain suits from run-away wagons that ran over and injured or killed people, primarily men involved in the transportation industry. Then there was war. Wars were episodic in some nations, alternating between relatively long periods of peace but involving large proportions of the working-age male population when it did break out. The proportion of the working-age males in Italy sucked into the army willingly or otherwise during the wars of imperial expansion was not demographically insignificant. Regardless of the fatality rates of those wars, physical and psychic wounds can shorten the lives of returning soldiers (Costa and Kahn 2010; Costa 2003).

Endogenous Mortality. In a sense, the Malthusian model makes mortality endogenous, as families bear children who survive, resulting in a larger population. With sharp limitations to expansion of the effective land supply (through either changes in cultivation practices to use a given amount of land more times during a given period of time, à la the Boserup model, or expansion to previously completely unused land) and technological changes that are insufficient to raise productivity permanently, food intake falls and the population becomes more susceptible to existing diseases and maladies, reflected in higher morbidity and mortality regimes, i.e., shorter expected lifetimes at birth. The Malthusian model, in its usual expositions (e.g., Schultz 1981, Chapter 2; and Lee 1978; 1980, section 9.4 and Appendix 2; 1997, section 2), is aggregative, not building up from individual choices to aggregate outcomes.

At the level of the individual family, parents may be able to take actions to safeguard or improve their children's health, although medical knowledge in antiquity was far more circumscribed than it has become in the industrialized countries in the past century. Additionally, questions have been raised about the extent to which parents in antiquity cared about their children, especially at particularly young ages[90] and about the interest ancient physicians had in pediatrics.[91] Nonetheless, given the knowledge available, or at least beliefs the ancients entertained regarding infant and child health, it may be a reasonable conjecture that they made special efforts regarding the health of their children.

Rosenzweig and Schultz (1983) have presented a model of the production of child health which, while its comparative statics have not been studied, offers a useful organizing framework for thinking about child health. Each child in a family has a common exogenous family health endowment, μ_i, composed of genetic and environmental attributes affecting his or her health. Each family knows its μ_i, and it differs across families. The health of child j at its birth in family ii, H_{ij0}, is given by a health production function, $H_{ij0} = \Gamma(Z_{ij0}) + \mu_i, +\varepsilon_{ij0}$, in which the Z_{ij0} are prenatal inputs, including birth order, and ε_{ij0} is a stochastic component of health which is observed at the child's birth, where the subscript 0 indicates a newborn. In the next period of the child's life, the health production function is $H_{ij1} = \Gamma(Z_{ij0}, Z_{ij1}, \varepsilon_{ij0}) + \mu_i, +\varepsilon_{ij1}$, in which the Z_{ij1} are the post-natal behaviors, such as breastfeeding, of the parents during the first period and ε_{ij1} is the stochastic component of health during the first period, such as illnesses. The structure of this production function represents child health at any age as a cumulative process involving past as well as current parental inputs and past as well as current stochastic events such as illnesses or injuries. In a dynamic optimizing model in which children's health and some of the inputs Z_{ijk} are arguments in the family's objective function (the function the family maximizes), the demands for prenatal and postnatal inputs will be functions of prices p, income Y and μ_i, while the demand for postnatal inputs will be a function of the realized stochastic health disturbances observed at the child's birth: $Z_{ij0} = \psi(p, Y, \mu_i)$ and $Z_{ij1}, = \psi(p, Y, \varepsilon_{ij0}, \mu_i)$. Parents' consumption choices will reflect their awareness of their children's health endowments, and they will adjust their consumption behavior to perceived exogenous changes in any of their children's health. For example, parents may learn to expect that their children will have higher mortality risks, due, for example, to low birth weight and take certain prenatal actions—surely different in antiquity from what they would be today. Whether parents—or midwives—in antiquity would have made the connection between birth weight and a child's subsequent health is a question that may remain forever open. For postnatal inputs, parents may breastfeed some children perceived to be at particular risk for longer durations. The extent to which parents practice particular behaviors, or purchase goods to treat their children's health, depends on the relative costs of the behaviors and relative prices of any goods, as well as on their income. Additionally, their demands for these behaviors and goods depend on their children's history of stochastic health events.

Consequences of Mortality Schedules. In the long span of history, changes in mortality have had pervasive consequences on societies. For the study of ancient Mediterranean civilizations, it is probably more useful to address a few factors that are affected by mortality schedules with very high infant and child mortality and short life expectancy at birth. High infant mortality rates raise the cost of investment in children, and in societies with

[90] An issue crystallized and laid to rest to the extent possible by Golden (1990; 2011). Golden's (2015) revision of his 1990 book adds temporal nuance to the path of Classical and Hellenistic Athenian childhood. Despite the title, Beaumont (2012) deals with the status of children from the late 7th century B.C.E. through the later 3rd, primarily through the iconography of figured vases and funerary monuments.

[91] Dixon (1992, 15), citing Etiene (1973, 15–61), reports that the ancients had little interest in childhood illness because it was not an area of proper concern for doctors, who were almost exclusively male.

limited scope for women's participation in labor markets, a reduction in the IMR or CMR could raise fertility and the population growth rate temporarily, but this should not be a long-term effect once families adjust to the new regime.

One of the most prominent effects of high mortality regimes is their effect on investment in human capital. Investment in human capital was not a prominent facet of antiquity, but it is probably impossible to determine to what extent the high mortality rates led to society-wide outcomes of unsustained technological advances fostered in turn by lack of systematic training which resulted in turn in limited human capital accumulation. Short and unpredictable (high-variance) life expectancies could make extensive investment in human capital a negative pay-off endeavor. In other words, the mortality schedules of antiquity may have had something to do with the lack of sustained technical progress and the limited scope for human capital accumulation, but our ability to assess that hypothesis is quite constricted. We may never know, and the experiment cannot be re-run under different conditions.

The magnitude of the impact of differential mortality schedules on investment in human capital can be gauged from some calculations provided by David Meltzer on the effect of mortality declines on the rate of return to education and on the variability of those returns (Meltzer 1992). Meltzer estimated the returns to completing the 9th through the 11th grades, using the lifetime earnings schedules of three developing countries (Ethiopia in 1971, Mexico in 1963, and Venezuela in 1975 and 1984) and the United States in 1960, but he applied the mortality schedules of different places and times to those earnings schedules, including seven mortality schedules from medieval England. The rates of return to that human capital investment ranged from 7 to 8 percent to 12 to 13 percent, depending on the earnings and mortality schedules. Reducing the mortality schedule to roughly that of the U.K. in 1985 would increase those rates of return by $1\frac{1}{2}$ to nearly 3 percent, which amounts to increases in the rate of return as low as 11 percent or as high as 41 percent (Meltzer 1992, 11–15, 13 Table 1). Clearly, mortality would have affected the rate of return to human capital investment in antiquity. High mortality schedules on the young end of the age distribution also impose high variability associated with life expectancy. Meltzer calculates break-even ages for investments in completion of the 9th through 11th grades using the same earnings profiles and a zero subjective discount rate. The break-even ages for getting a positive pay-back on the investment range from 26 to 28 years. The medieval mortality schedules indicate that 26 percent of the population for whom the schedules are available (tenants-in-chief) would have failed to live long enough to make a positive return on that investment. Since that comparison combines the variability effect with changes in the mean age at death, Meltzer calculates the variance of the net present value (NPV) of the investment and uses the coefficient of variation (the standard deviation, or square root of the variance, divided by the mean) to compare across mortality schedules while controlling for the effect of the changing mean on the variance. At a zero discount rate, the medieval English tenants-in-chief have a positive NPV of the investment and a coefficient of variation (CV) of 0.96, compared with a CV of 0.19 for the 1985 U.K. mortality schedule. At a 10 percent discount rate, the NPV is still positive, but the CV is 2.54 for the medieval mortality schedule, compared with 0.22 for the 1985 U.K. schedule—a much higher ratio of variability to average outcome with the medieval mortality schedule. At a 20 percent discount rate, the NPV to the education investment is negative (Meltzer 1992, 23–29, 27 Table 5). Decreasing mortality would reduce a risk premium on investments in human capital.

While the effects of changes in fertility are relatively simple to assess since those changes start at age zero and work their way through a birth cohort's life cycle, the effects of changes in mortality depend importantly on the parts of the age distribution affected. Increases in life expectancy at older ages have little effect on productivity but add some burden of dependency on a population. Mortality improvements at the infant and child ages are likely to affect fertility after parents have adjusted their expectations to the change, but the direction of change depends on a number of characteristics of the economic circumstances and opportunities of the population experiencing the change. Little investment in human capital has been made at these ages. Improvements in life expectancy among youth—teens—and among the prime-working-age population—twenties to thirties or forties depending on the population—will affect productivity and may elicit increases in human capital investment.[92] Improvements in mortality schedules—increases in survival rates—would be likely to increase various morbidity rates, as some of the frailer individuals would be the survivors. Morbidity acts much the same as mortality on returns to human capital investments (Meltzer 1992, 29–39).

The degree and permanence of mortality changes in antiquity were much smaller than those experienced in the past century in industrialized and developing countries. It is unlikely that any changes that were experienced were sufficient to have measurable effects on the propensity to make sustained investments in human capital. Such changes would have been essentially random rather than driven by increase in technical knowledge by the populations and would have been transient, without sufficient time in lower-mortality regimes for the infrastructure required for sustained human capital investments to be developed.

92 Meltzer's conclusions on the effects of infant and child mortality reduction on fertility (Chapter 5) should be ignored, since they rely on the results of the 1990 Becker-Murphy-Tamura model, which generates a counterfactual positive relationship between infant and child survival rates and fertility. The BMT model is discussed briefly in Jones (2014, Chapter 7, section 3).

4.3.8 The Family Setting of Fertility Decisions

The family is the institution on which societies rely for the production of their population. The economic theory of fertility abstracts many of the details of the family and to the extent that it does model a particular type of family, that family is the contemporary, independent family. As noted below, progress has been made in modeling the individual differences among families, but the overall family structure remains contemporary. The current structure of families, particularly western industrial-country families, surely differs in many ways from the varieties of family structures and compositions in various parts of the ancient Mediterranean world at various times over several millennia. Rather than try to adapt economic fertility theory to alternative institutional structures of families, which probably would leave it looking much the same anyway, this section offers a very brief overview of certain aspects of economic modeling of the behavior of families. Since the focus of the chapter is on population and population growth, there are many more aspects of the economics of the family than are reported here. Formal presentation of models of intra-family economic behavior is also minimized. Following the overview of the economic offerings is an even briefer overview, considering the size of the literature, on ancient family structure, as relevant to fertility and child rearing.

Intra-Family Economic Behavior. The basic neoclassical model of family demand, known as the unitary or consensus model, relies on several assumptions to simplify the analysis to deal with a single set of preferences, including a single altruistic decision maker. Resources are pooled within the family, and it makes no difference to spending patterns which family member brings in what resources because they are all spent in a single pattern. In a more realistic family, the identity of consumer and the identity of decision-maker become an issue. In families, joint consumption, such as heating in a residence, is important in addition to private consumption, such as individual food consumption. With different preferences of different members, the pooling assumption for resources is unlikely to be adequate when husband and wife each have outside unearned income that they control. Additionally, in a family setting involving love and caring, interdependent preferences become an issue as well, so purely egoistic utility functions must be replaced, as the unitary model is able to do.[93] The economic theory of fertility links fertility rates to the value of women's time and the time price of children, but women's earning power as well as the non-labor resources they command may enhance their decision-making authority within the family and alter consumption patterns as well as fertility, a constellation called empowerment in contemporary social discourse.

[93] Becker (1991, Chapter 8) on altruism treats interdependent preferences.

The alternative approach to intra-familial resource allocation, sometimes called the collective or non-consensus model, uses bargaining models.[94] Models of entry into and behavior within marriage and divorce require a theoretical framework in which agents compare their expected utilities inside and outside marriage. The common preference models can't deal with these decisions. Within a family, control of resources by one spouse or the other has different effects on family behavior, including expenditure patterns and children's health: increases in children's health, nutrition, and survival probabilities are associated with mother's control over family resources; effects of mothers' unearned income on child survival probabilities in Brazilian data is nearly 20 times that of fathers' income (Thomas 1990). Nash bargaining models depend on threat points, utility levels below which a spouse is unwilling to accept, which in turn depend on the availability of unearned income to each partner. Higher levels of unearned income increase threat points, which means intuitively that the more resources a spouse controls, the less disutility he or she is willing to accept from the other's choices. In divorce-threat models, the threat point is the highest utility each spouse can obtain outside the marriage, which depends on income received by each as well as extra-household environmental parameters (EEPs; sometimes called distribution factors, or DFs) such as conditions in the remarriage market and income available to divorced men and women (Manser and Brown 1980; McElroy and Horney 1981; McElroy 1990). In the separate spheres bargaining model the threat point is internal to the marriage, not external as in the divorce-threat bargaining models (Lundberg and Pollak1993). Each spouse provides household public goods, choosing actions that are utility-maximizing, given actions of the other spouse. The alternative to agreement is an inefficient non-cooperative equilibrium within the marriage rather than divorce. This non-cooperative marriage may be better than divorce for both spouses. The separate spheres model is probably more plausible for day-to-day marital bargaining than is the divorce-threat model. Both types of bargaining model generate family demands that depend on who controls income within the marriage.

A very general exposition of a household collective utility formulation is[95] $\mathrm{u}(\mathbf{q}, \mathbf{Q}; \mathbf{z}, \mathbf{d}, \boldsymbol{\theta}) = max_{q^h,q^w}\{\mu(\mathbf{z}, \boldsymbol{\theta})\mathrm{v}^{\mathrm{h}}(\mathbf{q}^{\mathbf{h}},$

[94] Lundberg and Pollak (1996) summarize a number of technical issues in demand theory raised by the multi-person character of families and various bargaining approaches used to resolved them. Vermeulen (2002) offers considerable technical detail on a wide variety of these models and their empirical implementation. Behrman (1997) summarizes the much richer array of analyses of intra-family resource allocation using the unitary or consensus model and the less fully developed literature using the collective, or non-consensus, bargaining models.

[95] Some advance interpretation of notation: (1) bold font indicates a vector, that is, an array of either goods or prices or some characteristics; (2) a prime symbol (it looks like an apostrophe) following some vector variables when they are multiplied by another vector variable is an indication of an operation necessary for multiplication of two vectors; the term "arg max" followed by a subscripted variable means that the expression following in brackets is the largest (maximized) value of the expression that can be obtained by varying the value of the subscripted variable—thus the demand function is maximized by choosing a value

$\mathbf{Q}$; $\mathbf{d}$) + (1 − $\mu(\mathbf{z}, \boldsymbol{\theta})$)$v^w(\mathbf{q^w}, \mathbf{Q}; \mathbf{d})$}, subject to $q^h + q^w = q$ and a household budget constraint $\mathbf{p'q} + \mathbf{P'Q} = x$, in which v^i, i = h, w, represents husband's and wife's utility functions. The $\mu(\mathbf{z}, \boldsymbol{\theta})$ is called the Pareto weight, $0 \leq \mu \leq 1$, which weights the husband's individual preferences according to the values of **z**, a vector of EEPs or distribution factors), and $\boldsymbol{\theta}$, a vector of prices and total expenditure (π, x) in which π is a vector of private- and public-good prices. If $\mu = 1$, only the husband's preferences matter in intra-family allocation decisions; if $\mu = 0$, only the wife's preferences matter; values in between indicate the strength of each spouse in negotiations. **Q** is household public good, **q** is private goods, and **d** is an array of personal factors that condition preference, including such items as age and various other status conditions. Purchase of private goods q_i at price p_i is divided between the spouses (or more generally any two agents comprising the principal decision makers in the household), with $q_i^h + q_i^w = q_i$, i = 1, . . . n private goods. Purchase of the household public good Q_i, i = 1, . . . m public goods, is made at price P_i and are consumed in a nonrival way. The vector of private-good prices is p and that of household public good prices is P. Maximization of the household utility function subject to the budget constraint yields household demand functions for the private goods $\hat{q} = \boldsymbol{\xi}(\mathbf{z}, \mathbf{d}, \boldsymbol{\theta}) = \arg\max_q\{u(\mathbf{q}, \mathbf{Q}; \mathbf{z}, \mathbf{d}, \boldsymbol{\theta})$ subject to $\mathbf{p'q} + \mathbf{P'Q} = x\}$, and similarly for the family's purchase of household public goods.[96] A way to implement collective decisions is via a decentralization procedure that allows husband and wife to divide total expenditure x between them such that $x_h + x_w = x$ and then to allow them to buy their own private goods. A sharing rule, $\rho(\mathbf{z}, \mathbf{d}, \boldsymbol{\theta}) = x_h/x$ is the function that accomplishes this task. Denoting the relationship between the husband's consumption and the prices, family demographics, and total expenditure as $\xi^h(\mathbf{z}, \mathbf{d}, \boldsymbol{\theta})$, by definition the sharing rule is $\rho = \mathbf{p'}\,\boldsymbol{\xi}^h(\mathbf{z}, \mathbf{d}, \boldsymbol{\theta})/x$, from which it can be seen that the sharing rule depends on prices and total expenditure, through the budget constraint and the Pareto weight, the preference shifters d, and the EEPs **z**. The sharing rule is substituted back into the individual spouses' demand functions. The basic preference functions v^i above have been specified as egoistic, that is, neither spouse cares about the utility of the other. This specification can be altered easily as, for example, $U^h = F^h(v^h(\mathbf{q^h}, \mathbf{Q}), v^w(\mathbf{q^w}, \mathbf{Q}))$ and comparably for the wife's utility function including the husband's wellbeing.

It has been found that the use of household averages to investigate such consumption issues as nutrition responses to income increases can mask substantial differences in response by gender (Behrman and Deolalikar 1990). In particular, in developing countries, the response of women's consumption of nutrients to income increases is substantially smaller than men's. Substantial gender differences in consumption may exist within families. Larger negative food price elasticities for female family members mean that a rise in food prices, which typically occurs during the lean period of an agricultural season or during a bad year, falls disproportionately on female household members. However, they also enjoy a disproportionate share of the nutritional increase from falling food prices post-harvest or in years of favorable growing conditions. Nonetheless, this pattern does leave women more vulnerable to malnutrition and starvation during times of greatest food shortage.

While higher earning capacity of women raises the cost of fertility since women bear the majority of time-costs of child care, higher earning capacity of men has been found to increase fertility in a number of countries. In a sample of women from Thailand in the early 1980s, while the women's-wage-fertility relationship was found to be negative, fertility was increased by the presence of higher non-earned income accruing to women, but was unaffected by non-earned income of their husbands. Mothers tend to reap more benefits from their children in the form of old-age support than do fathers (Schultz 1990, 609–617). To the converse, some of the literature on fertility in antiquity suggests that husbands probably or may have had considerably less interest in fertility control than their wives did, despite concerns for dilution of inheritances among people at the upper end of the income distribution.[97] Less speculatively, upper-income Roman women, who presumably controlled ample resources of their own from their families, are known to have been interested in contraceptive techniques.[98]

Families in Antiquity. The literature on families at various places and during various periods in antiquity is extensive, overlapping as it does with those on women, children, and the elderly. In discussing the meaningfulness of signature characteristics of "the Roman family," Rawson noted the dangers of generalizing about family structures that ranged from eastern Anatolia to the British Isles and covered three hundred years, a period over which she considered most family structures would not remain static (Rawson 1986, 6–7, 45 n. 7). Extending the geographic range to include the Ancient Near East and the time range to pick up Neolithic, Early and Middle Bronze Age and Mycenaean Greece and Pharaonic Egypt surely increases the scope for variation. Clearly, the ancient family is a very varied institution. For the present purposes, the discussion here is restricted to characteristics of ancient families which could affect fertility and other population-economy relationships via one route or another.[99, 100]

of the good q_i, or in vector notation indicated by the bold font on $\hat{\mathbf{q}}$, by choosing values for all of the q_i.

[96] This exposition relies on that of Browning, Chiappori, and Lechene (2006).

[97] In contrast to den Boer's belief in footnote 55 above.

[98] Upper-class Roman women are widely cited as being interested in contraception: e.g., Dixon 1992, 122); McLaren (1990, 54).

[99] I have relied on a number of sources for this section, which I will acknowledge at the beginning rather than cite continually: Lacey (1968); Pomeroy (1975; 1994; 1997; 2002); Demand (1994); Patterson (1998); Golden (1990; 2015); Garnsey and Saller (1987, Ch. 7); Rawson (1986; 1991); Dixon (1992); Bradley (1991); Saller (1994); Heubner (2011); from the Bronze Age is Rutter (2003).

[100] The literature on ancient dwellings offers much information, however filtered, regarding family life and possibly about gender, but I have been unable to find help in it for thinking about aspects of family life that would affect fertility and such population-economy relationships

The great majority of the ancient evidence is literary and accordingly deals with the very small proportion of upper-class, literate people in those populations, many of them urban. Care must be taken in extending findings from those parts of ancient societies to the ordinary working people, most of them rural, but even in the cities, most of them quite poor relative to those for whom the direct evidence exists.

What Was a Family? The definition of the family in antiquity varied from situation to situation. Not everyone in a household need have been blood-related, even excluding slaves. Not all family members need have lived in a single household, without accounting uncles, aunts and more distant relatives, as widowed and remarried mothers might change households, leaving children in the household of the deceased father. People thinking of their families might well think of wide circles of kinship rather than the basic conjugal unit.

For the purposes of economic fertility theory, the conjugal family is the primary unit of importance for the context of fertility decisions. However, even within the conjugal unit, decade or longer age differences between husband and wife not infrequently left the wife widowed while still in her fertile years—if she survived childbearing that long herself. In some of the ancient Mediterranean societies, it was the duty of a dead husband's family (or at least the male kin) to see that his widow was remarried. In such a mortality-and-remarriage context, the simplification of the lifetime fertility decision model is clearly not met, but it is not clear that a switch to the sequential decision model captures the decision context. If a widow married a childless man and left her previous children with her deceased husband's family, it is possible that the current number of children would be re-set to zero in the new conjugal unit, particularly if the husband's weight in family decisions, including fertility decisions, was very high relative to the wife's. Women in such circumstances might have a larger number of children over their lifetime than they would have chosen otherwise, or than they and a single husband would have chosen over the fertile years of their marriage. This institutional arrangement was not universal by any means: in Bagnall and Frier's census sample from Roman Egypt, there was a strong tendency for widows not to remarry (Bagnall and Frier 1994, 115).

Women's Status within Families. The status of women within a family could affect fertility by giving a wife greater say over exposure to additional pregnancies. It also could give her greater control over family resources that could be directed toward consumption of children, resulting in higher survival rates which themselves could have a secondary effect on fertility. But what would contribute to higher status besides vague "cultural" proclivities? Within any given society, with its particular status of women, status of individual women probably varied. Variation in the status of individual women may be easier to explain than variation in status across societies, although the latter is probably more important for a society's fertility and population structure. Greater wealth of a bride (or of the bride's father, some of whose wealth accompanied the daughter as dowry) might have enhanced status, but the degree of control she retained, as well as the repatriability of a dowry in the event of divorce or, under certain circumstances, death, would have been an important consideration. Work outside the household may not have been uncommon for lower-income families in both rural and urban settings, but little information is available on those income classes. The larger the earnings of a wife, and the greater the interruption of her earnings by pregnancies and child-rearing, economic fertility theory predicts a smaller number of desired children—abstracting from the issue of births versus completed family size. Such employment is surely not recorded among the upper-income Greek and Roman families who left written evidence. Employment—household spinning and weaving and so on—would have been secluded within the household in Athenian families, and variations in earnings possibilities would have been very low. In lower-income families, for which written evidence is absent, employment outside the household may have been more common, even if the variability among women in earning capacities might have been minimal. Probably more common (or less uncommon) at higher incomes, literacy should have enhanced women's status via its effect on their earning power (Sheridan 1998).

Spartan women of the Classical Period were remarked upon for their ability to own land, which would have given them some kind of asset power in family decision weights. The Spartan birth rate at various times, to the extent it can be discerned, could have been influenced by the distribution of income and wealth within the conjugal unit. A dowry, whether its control remained with the paternal family of a wife or with a wife herself, should have given a wife greater influence over fertility decisions, with greater uxorial influence the greater the wife's control over those assets.

Women in Pharaonic Egypt appear to have enjoyed considerable freedom: each spouse retained control of property they brought into the marriage and could retain or dispose of it as they chose; marital property was divided equally upon divorce, which could be initiated by a woman; men and women inherited equally; and women and men functioned nearly equally under the law—women could enter into contracts as equals, but they evidently were restricted from serving as witnesses in legal transactions, although they could serve on juries. At the lower end of the income distribution, women worked in the fields beside men, although at the upper end, they appear to have been more likely to remain in the home (Trigger, Kemp, O'Connor, and Lloyd 1983, 311–313; Brewer and Teeter, 1999, 96–97). Adding some complexity to what could otherwise seem relatively clear-cut, in an analysis of burials from Deir el Medina, Meskell reports greater

as intergenerational transfers: Wallace-Hadrill (1994, Chapter 5); Nevitt (1995; 1999; 2010); Morris (1999); Ault and Nevett (2005); Trumper (2011).

disparity by sex of wealth in tomb goods in the generally wealthier burials of the Western Necropolis and a generally egalitarian distribution by sex in the apparently lower-income Eastern Necropolis (Meskell 1999, Chapters 4 and 5). However, Meskell (1999, 174) infers that women's well-being and status commonly became more tenuous as they aged,[101] and she finds that funeral items that would have guaranteed afterlife experiences were scarcer for women than for men, a particularly serious consideration in the Pharaonic Egyptian belief system (1999. 210).

In a study of kourotrophic (mother-child or more generally caretaker-child) images from the Bronze Age Mediterranean basin, Budin (2011, 29–34, 327–336) infers a complex set of status relations regarding women. First, outside of Egypt, motherhood appears to have conferred no status, or possibly would have lowered status. But second, to the extent that motherhood and caretaker roles were dissociated, in societies in which women enjoyed higher status, they were less likely to be depicted as caretakers of children, as suggested by their near total absence from Minoan iconography, in a society believed to have bestowed relatively high status on women. While men may have acquired status from having children, they would have gained none from rearing them. The possible trade-off between taking care of children and women's status may find reflections in children's health and survival rates.

Target Family Sizes. Ancient authors do not distinguish clearly among the number of family members at a given observation date, the number of surviving children, and the total number of births to a couple, and many modern authors eschew the distinction as well. Snapshot information on the size of families at various dates and locations in antiquity is not clear evidence of desired completed family size. Nonetheless, some upper-class Roman families during the Imperial period were reputed to have aimed for as few as one survivor to avoid splitting inheritances, but it is doubtful that families at the opposite end of the income distribution were particularly concerned about inheritance. The upper-class Roman families are widely assumed to have practiced family limitation, whether via the use of contraceptives or through other practices such as birth spacing and sending the husband elsewhere for sexual gratification. Whether families at the middle range and lower end of the income distribution adjusted their behavior to balance high infant and child mortality rates with a desired number of survivors is not known although well speculated upon.[102]

In the Archaic Period of Greece, Hesiod's admonition to limit one's offspring to one son is well-known (*Works and Days*, 370; Tandy and Neale 1996, 89). Implicitly his guideline is to shoot for one surviving son, and the poem gives no hint of the number of births required to achieve the single male survivor. Hesiod makes no mention of daughters, but presumably someone had to have some for the son to be of any practical use. Much of the contemporary literature on Greek fertility and family sizes, as well as that dealing with the Ancient Near East, does not distinguish between live births, the number of children living at any one time, and children surviving to adulthood.

The Number of Generations within Households. If parents didn't live long enough to be supported by adult children in antiquity, one major, putative motivation for having children in antiquity—old-age support—would have to be reconsidered. Additionally, the presence of grandparents in a household could reduce the cost of child rearing, to the extent that grandparents' time was less productive than parents'. The ancient literature emphasizes the importance of children's support of aged parents, although that may have tended to be predominantly mothers rather than fathers, as Saller found that the age discrepancy between Roman husbands and wives tended to leave relatively few fathers alive to see their children grown (Saller 1987). Bagnall and Frier report roughly 10 percent of their households contained three-generation families (24 of 233 census returns with household information) (Bagnall and Frier, 1994, 145–146; cf. 7 Table 1.1). Among Clarysse and Thompson's tax-return families in 3rd century B.C.E. Egypt, 31 or 32 households out of 427 had a resident mother of the household head, about a $7\frac{1}{2}$-percent incidence of three-generation households (Clarysse and Thompson 2006, 304–307.[103] Fathers of household heads were not noted. At an early date and further east and north, Galil's collection of lower stratum families from Early Iron Age Assyria reported only 6 3-generation families out of a total of 295 (Galil 2007, 266, 334). While the Hellenistic and Roman Egyptian families included a spectrum of wealth levels, the Assyrian families were definitely at the lower end of the income distribution, including as they did slave families and a number of single mothers receiving state food assistance. The lower incidence of 3-generation families among the stratified lower-income households probably indicates lower life expectancy rather than greater independence of the elderly. For 4th century Greece—Athens or Attica actually—Gallant notes 35 to 40 percent of women mentioned in various orations (which could be a somewhat biased sample) were widows at some point in their lives, and in a sample whose life courses he was able to determine, 65 percent did not remarry. Without trying to quantify percents of households, Gallant believes

[101] On the precariousness of single women's lives, although not in Egypt, Strong (2012, 121–139) offers close readings of both dramatic productions and legal proceedings.

[102] Brunt (1971, 142–143) reasons that "smaller proprietors" would have behaved much as the wealthy Romans did in controlling their (surviving) family size, simply on the grounds that they could not have afforded the additional mouths to feed while they waited for the children's productivity to approach that of adults. Brunt (146–154) accepts a portfolio of regulatory methods including weakly effective contraception, abortion and infanticide.

[103] Clarysse and Thompson use the Cambridge family typology, (Table 7.7, 247), but within that categorization do not attempt in their graphical presentations to distinguish whether extended conjugal families included vertical or lateral extensions, i.e., whether they were multigenerational (vertical) or comprised of siblings' families (lateral). The typology is developed in Laslett, with the assistance of Wall (1972, 28–32, 31, Table 1.1).

that a substantial fraction of Greek households would have had a vertically extended composition at some period in their existence (Gallant 1991, 22–27).

The examples above are snapshots and may not capture temporal changes in households such as recounted by Parkin on the basis of some repeat census observations from 1st and 2nd century C.E. Egypt and characterized analytically by Gallant for Classical Greek households (Parkin 2011, 280–283; Gallant 1991, 27–30).

Divorce and Sequential Marriages. The basic economic fertility model relies on the construct of a husband and wife, at the beginning of their marriage, deciding on the number of (surviving) children they want to have over the course of their fertile years. Nobody really believes this is the way fertility decisions are made, and the (relatively intractable) sequential fertility models, also implicitly assuming the same spouses over the life course, offer a more realistic view of those decisions. In contemporary western societies, divorce has become quite common in recent decades, adding a complication to the setting of those decisions which is likely relevant to ancient families and their fertility decisions as well, as divorce was relatively easy to obtain in Classical Athens, and it was common among upper-class Roman families, although probably somewhat less so among lower-class Roman families, while both societies were anxious to see fertile-age women remarry.[104] Kajanto (1969, 107) believes that divorce was less common among the Roman commoners than among the upper classes. Additionally, Kajanto urges a view of ancient divorce, at least ancient Roman divorce, quite different from the rancorous relationships so frequent between divorcing and divorced spouses in contemporary times, noting continuing, post-divorce expressions of concern and affection between ex-spouses (Kajanto 1969, 108–109).[105] Whether such relationships involved in divorce extended to other societies in the ancient Mediterranean region is an open question, although divorce for abuse, physical, emotional, or both, of either wife or children, is clearly known.[106] With the prime-age mortality schedules of antiquity, widowhood was another force propelling remarriage, but important issues affecting fertility are the same across the two states.

Upon either divorce or death of a spouse, the divorced spouses or the surviving one find themselves with a particular parity and some concept of a completed (surviving) family size. Upon remarriage, second husband and second wife may be of different parities. In both Greek and Roman settings, children tended to remain with the husband's household rather than go with the mother as is common in contemporary western settings. The newly second-marrieds, entering into their second marriage with different parities, may have had different desires for additional children, depending on their first-marriage parities. It is at least a contemporary concept, that couples in a second marriage would have a child to cement the marriage and make it real in some sense, but they may well have different targets for completed family size. Given the differential power between husband and wife, in the typical ancient family, at least in the upper-class ones that have left literary evidence, the husband's target may have had more weight than the wife's. However, overall, the question is whether marriage, or widowhood, and subsequent remarriage would have suppressed or elevated fertility from what it would have been in life-long single marriages. One issue involved in the answer is the length of time women would have stayed unmarried and thus unexposed to conception. Otherwise the impact on fertility is a matter of competing target completed family sizes and budget constraints. Contemporary evidence on the influence of second marriage, or interrupted marital status, on fertility is mixed, partly because controlling for enough circumstances is difficult. A second marriage for a husband has been found to depress fertility in his wife's marriage independently of the wife's marital history, although the number of children the husband had from a previous marriage could not be controlled (Levin and O'Hara 1978, 101). In contemporary societies, this may be attributable to child support payments, but in antiquity such a budget-constraint-effect on a husband with children to support from a previous marriage could have depressed fertility with a subsequent wife. Conflicting contemporary results have been found regarding the effect of first-marriage parity on wives' second-marriage fertility.[107] The interruption of exposure to conception involved with marital disruption resulting from either divorce or widowhood has been found to depress fertility by 0.6 child in a society with between 2 and 3 children the typical family size (Cohen and Sweet 1974). The social and technological settings of these findings are quite different from those in antiquity, but the evidence does suggest several routes by which sequential marriage, for whatever reasons, could affect fertility: time exposed to conception, budget constraints, and intra-familial power distribution.

In ancient populations with growth rates in the neighborhood of 0.1 percent per year, if that, there may seem to be little room for further depression of fertility through the operation of such a social institution such as divorce. Nevertheless, high divorce and widowhood rates have the potential for at least some modest depression of fertility rates.

Effects of Slavery and Prostitution on Fertility. Slavery offered the opportunity for sexual gratification of male slave owners which would have reduced the exposure

[104] For Athens, Pomeroy (1997, 27); for upper-class Romans, Rawson (1986, 32–37) and Dixon (1992, 84); on the Roman commoners, Kajanto (1969); for both upper- and lower-class Romans and Roman-period Greeks, Bradley (1991a, 172–173).

[105] Treggiari (1991, 40–41) concedes that consensual divorce encouraged a couple to remain on good terms but provides examples of emotional distress associated with it.

[106] For example, Alcibiades' wife's suit for divorce because of his dalliance with prostitutes, cited in Pomeroy (1975, 90).

[107] Finding that higher first-marriage parity reduces second-marriage fertility is Wineberg, (1990, 35 Table 3). Finding no effect of parity on having a birth in a second marriage (but not actual fertility) is Griffith, Koo, and Suchindra (1985, 80 Table 1).

of their wives to pregnancy. The substitutability between wives and slaves regarding the sources of desired births within a family was probably low, but is a different matter at the level of the population. If husband and wife achieved desired surviving births while the husband additionally contributed to the fertility of household slaves, the population fertility rate would be in excess of that contributed by conjugal families.[108] Similarly with the availability of prostitutes, who were known or at least reputed, to control their fertility with various methods of contraception, or upon failure of those, abortion.

Postgate notes that in Old Babylonia, a wife who had been unable to bear children could supply her husband with a slave girl by whom he could have children (Postgate 1992, 92, 105). Nonetheless, the wives may have had alternative thoughts on the proclivities of their husbands in some of the more recreational endeavors. An Early Iron Age record from Assyria suggests the possibility of a wife pitching a female slave and her child by the wife's husband out of the household (Galil 2007, 265), while in late 5th century Athens, Alcibiades' wife filed for divorce after he persisted in bringing prostitutes home—an unsuccessful filing, apparently, but Alcibiades appears to have desisted in the practice. The wealth or income status of the Assyrian wife is unknown, but Alcibiades' wife had a 10-talent dowry which would have left with her had the divorce been approved (Pomeroy1970, 90).

4.4 Population Change, Model Life Tables, and Fertility Theory

A number of major population reductions in antiquity are either known or speculated upon—equally sharp increases being largely out of the question since it takes populations a fair span of time to increase. Four well-known instances of population reductions are the depopulation of Greece for several centuries following the decline and disappearance of Mycenaean civilization, the Athenian plague that erupted in 431, the loss of adult males by Athens during the Peloponnesian War, and the Antonine Plague in the 2nd century CE.

The post-Mycenaean, Dark Age population decline appears to have been a sustained affair, possibly with some localized disasters associated with conflicts or natural events.[109] While conflicts may have reduced male members of the population disproportionately to female, at least in the short term, the record of destruction of various cities in the Ancient Near East around the same time or somewhat earlier attests to age-and-sex indiscrimination in slaughters. While the cause or causes of the decline are obscure, infectious epidemic does not seem to have been at the root of the Dark Age population decline.

The Athenian military reverses cost the city state a substantial proportion of one or possibly two generations of its marriage-age males.[110] The epidemic of 431–429 B.C.E. (and recurrent through 427), in contrast, did not discriminate by sex although it might have discriminated to some extent by age, possibly hitting adults more severely than the young, and may have carried off a quarter to thirty percent of the population by the time it abated.[111] The direct war casualties themselves, both battle deaths and deaths from disease, may not have been as important to the future of the Athenian population as the losses from the plague, which affected the female population far more extensively than the military losses: after all, men can father children with more than one woman, but any birth requires exactly one woman. Additionally, the population losses from both sources—plague and war—may have increased the well-being of the primarily wage-earning survivors as the land-labor and capital-labor ratios would have increased, increasing the wage-rental ratio.[112] Nonetheless, the possibility of impoverishment should not be overlooked: even if a higher wage-rental ratio would have increased the incomes of people deriving most of their income from labor relative to those deriving most of their income from capital, including land, absolute productivity might have fallen. Additionally, the loss of overseas income, regardless of who the initial recipients were, would have reduced income. Whether emigration out

108 The contribution, willing or otherwise, of slaves to the fertility of a family contributes some fuzziness to the concept of a conjugal family: should we include the fertility of the slave mother as well as that of the wife, just sweep her under the rug, or go back to the taxonomic exercises? At the aggregate level, most of these effects of slave fertility may be washed out in a single-sex demographic model, since the limiting parameter in population growth is the number of available females, regardless to whom they are available.

109 Dickinson (2006, 67, 70, 77, 93–94, 97–98, 244) summarizes and synthesizes a lengthy literature which is not all of a single mind on the subject but which does agree largely on a sustained and considerable (unquantified, of course) decline in Aegean population during the Late Helladic IIIC and Submycenaean periods. By the Protogeometric period, life in various regions of Greece had become more settled and populations appear to have stabilized: Lemos (2002, 191); on continuing discoveries of Early Iron Age (Protogeometric and Geometric periods) sites, which tends to dampen estimates of Late Bronze Age population decline (2002, 196).

110 Akrigg (2011, 59; 2007, 33; 2019, Chapter 5), whose percent reduction estimate is a wide and broad pair of numbers (one-third and one-half) which, to use his own term describing some of Thucydides' numbers, simply means "a lot"; Parkin, (2011, 187). Akrigg (2007; 2019, Chapters 6–7) does nonetheless sketch out a rough general-equilibrium structure of responses to the plague and the war and war losses, including changes in population density, changes in real well-being of survivors, emigration, and both economic (Malthusian) and social responses in fertility.

111 Thucydides, ii.48–54; Gomme (1933, 6); Sallares (1991, 258–259) on the possible age selectivity of the plague if it was indeed smallpox. Morens and Littman, (1992, 287,) use a simple model of the time pattern of emergent cases of a disease to narrow down the possible diseases causing the Athenian plague, with smallpox and typhus remaining the most likely culprits.

112 How much of the increase in wages reported by Loomis (1998, Ch. 15) during the 4th century is real increase and how much is price-level increase is difficult to assess from his presentation. To my knowledge, the goods price data such as contained in Boeckh (1842; n.d.) have not been mined and paired with wage data in the systematic fashion that has characterized research on Hellenistic and Roman Egypt. Keynes, in work from the early 1920s which remained unpublished for some sixty years, with some very parsimonious use of scattered data, estimated an average annual inflation rate between 590 B.C.E. ("the age of Solon") and 340 B.C.E. ("the end of Demosthenes") of one-third of one percent, but increasing rapidly after 330 B.C.E. as precious metals from Alexander's depredations in Asia flowed in: Moggridge (1982, 227–231). Keynes emphasized the release of temple hoards after the Peloponnesian Wars rather than population losses from the earlier plague or the war itself.

of Athens / Attica would have been positive or negative by the early 4th century is an open question considering the mix of incentives. The net effect of all these changes, and possibly others, on fertility and the subsequent path of the Attic population remains an open question.

The dimensions of the Antonine Plague, of the 160s and 170s C.E., in both Italy and Egypt, are poorly understood, and disagreement remains on the extent and duration of the depopulation in different regions.[113] With virtually no direct population data, some scholars believe it is possible that as much as 30 to 50 percent of the population of some areas perished over periods of two to three years, with follow-on episodes within a decade or so, while others see no fluctuations out of the ordinary range of magnitudes, with excess mortality in the range of 1 to 2 percent. Nonetheless, the period has attracted substantial attention and has been the subject of efforts to obtain indirect indicators of population decline.

It is clear that these three examples are quite different. Their causes differ, their durations differ, and their economic and social consequences may differ as well. Population projection techniques can model population behavior following such declines, making assumptions as necessary regarding the progress of fertility and mortality regimes. Experiments with alternative recovery parameters can help test hypotheses when solid data are sparse or missing. Economic approaches tend to make endogenous predictions regarding some of the parameters that the demographic approach either considers fixed or varies arbitrarily.

4.4.1 Life-Table Approach to Population Catastrophes

Richard Paine has studied a population's recovery from an event such as the 14th century C.E. bubonic plague with the use of a Leslie matrix (Paine 2000). The Leslie matrix of course contains age-specific fertility and mortality schedules, but there are no parameters that specifically characterize the 14th century Black Death, so the analysis is more general than a study of a specific incident. Thus, although Paine names it a Black Death model, the structure of the event could let his analysis represent a variety of causes, from an epidemic to a natural disaster to a war. To simulate the effects of this epidemic, Paine begins with the stable Leslie matrix (i.e., one that meets the very weak conditions for reaching a stable population after the passage of roughly the length of time of the oldest person in the population) and subtracts 30 percent from the survival rate for every age category to represent the population catastrophe. At the same time, Paine reduces the age-specific fertility rates by 30 percent also, but for only the year of the catastrophe or epidemic itself, allowing them to return to their pre-catastrophe levels the following year. He states that more intricate assumptions about fertility have little effect on the model's overall results to justify tinkering with the fertility parameters.[114]

In the first year of the projection, the stable Leslie matrix **S** is multiplied by the stable (pre-disaster) population vector, $\mathbf{v_1}$, yielding a normal year of age-specific deaths and a new vector of the living population who go into the epidemic in the following year, $\mathbf{v_2}$. The following simulation year, the stable age distribution represented by $\mathbf{v_2}$ is multiplied by the Leslie matrix with the catastrophically reduced survival rates, **C**, producing a post-disaster population vector $\mathbf{v_3}$. Over the subsequent 98 projection years, the population vectors $\mathbf{v_3}$ through $\mathbf{v_{101}}$ are multiplied by the same Leslie matrix of fertility and survival rates that generated the original, stable population. The simulation generates an age-at-death curve for the plague year which Paine presents, reproduced here as Figure 4.12. The solid line in Figure 4.12 represents the proportion of the stable (pre-plague) population's deaths in each age group. The proportion of deaths in the stable (pre-disaster) population is very high at infancy, falls dramatically through about age 9, begins to gradually rise from around age 15 to age 23, remains largely flat until the mid-40s, then rises again to the mid-60s, when the smaller numbers in the older age categories cause their proportions dying to fall again. The dashed line in Figure 4.12 is the proportional age-at-death distribution in the plague year. It is nearly a straight, modestly downward sloping line in age, indicating the greater representation of the young (but not the very youngest) ages in the plague deaths. The stable age distribution takes nearly 30 years to generate the same number of deaths in the 5–10 year ages as occurs in the single plague year, and nearly 40 years to produce the number of plague-year deaths in the 10–15 year age interval. The distribution of deaths returns very slowly to the stable distribution, but by the end of the 100-year projection still differ slightly from the stable distribution.

The population's intrinsic growth rate more than doubles immediately after the plague year, not because of any changes in age-specific fertility rates, which simply resume

[113] Duncan-Jones (1996); Scheidel (2002); Greenberg (2003); Bruun (2003; 2007); Frier (2000), who estimates a 10 percent death toll overall and double that percentage in cities and military camps.

[114] Using a 7-age-group Leslie matrix, beginning with a near-stationary population (growth rate 0.26% per year), I find that extending a reduction in fertility for a single year beyond a plague year, but allowing the survival rate to rebound immediately, has a substantial effect on the size of the population after 75 years. Resuming pre-plague fertility in the year following the plague induces an annual growth rate of −0.1% between the plague year and 75 years later; keeping fertility reduced a second year induces an annual growth rate of −0.2% over the same period. Expressed alternatively, the extra year of fertility depression depresses population by 7.4% 75 years later. Cotts Watkins and Menken, (1985, 660) calculate broadly similar results in a simulation of a population subjected to similar changes in single-year mortality rates and two-year fertility rates: although they emphasize that the population regains its size in only 11 years after a year of 110% of the usual mortality rates and two years of 30% lower fertility rates, but after 90 years, the population, otherwise growing at $\frac{1}{2}$ % per year with and without the simulated famine, is still 7 percent smaller than it would have been without the famine. Epidemics have much the structure as famines, especially as regards their gender incidence, if not necessarily their age incidence, except that they tend to linger and recur for a number of years, while famines often are the result of short-term failures in communication or transportation. The longer-term impact of fertility responses to population catastrophes, regardless of their cause or causes, seems to warrant further consideration.

Figure 4.12. Age-at-death proportions produced by the stable model population (dashed line) and by the Black Plague model (solid line) (Reproduced from Paine, 2000, figure 2, p. 185, by permission of Wiley.).

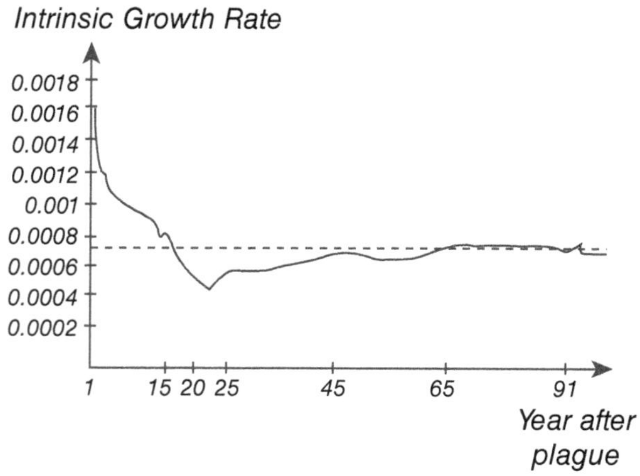

Figure 4.13. Intrinsic growth rate following the Black Plague; dashed line represents IGR of stable population growth model (Reproduced from Paine, 2000, figure 5, p. 189, by permission of Wiley.).

their pre-plague profile, but because of the change in the age distribution of survivors. The growth rate falls back below its long-run stable level after about 15 years, then gradually returns to its stable level after nearly 50 years, after which it continues to vary slightly around the stable level. Figure 4.13 reproduces Paine's graph of the growth rates.

In a subsequent, similar analysis Paine and Glenn Storey apply this model to the Antonine Plague, examining possible effects on the Roman population (Paine and Storey 2006, 69–85). The simulation again uses a 30-percent reduction in survival rates for all ages, depressing fertility in the plague year by the same amount and returning it to its pre-plague level the following year.[115] To replicate the two-strike pattern of that episode, they allow another epidemic to reduce survival rates in the 28th year of the projection, but in that episode, reducing survival probabilities of people under 27, who had not been alive during the first outbreak, by 30 percent but by only 15 percent for people over 27, on the assumption that survivors of the original outbreak had developed some degree of immunity. Paine and Storey present the path of the proportional age-at-death distribution from its pattern in the first year of the plague and at several later dates through the last year of their projections, 91 years after the initial outbreak, a cut-off date chosen to not interfere with another epidemic outbreak in 251 C.E. That time path of distributions is reproduced here as Figure 4.14. They find that by the 91st year, early child and young adult (through age 28) deaths were still substantially above the pre-outbreak distribution. By the 91st year, the simulated population of Rome is still just barely over half its pre-plague size. Paine and Storey add a migration component to the model, which largely restores Rome to its pre-plague population, suggesting that while the native population failed to recover from the plague, immigration from the rest of Italy masked that effect.

Paine and Storey's replication of substantial and long-lasting effects of the Antonine Plague on the population of Rome depend on the magnitude of their reduction in survival rates, as well as the pattern of survival rates they posit for the plague year, but, they imply, to a somewhat lesser extent on post-plague fertility rates. The resulting pattern is interesting and conforms to some scholars' beliefs, but no objective standard for comparison exists to assess whether Rome's population really behaved that way.

What I am calling the life-table approach to studying large population changes, whether with the continuous model or with cohort projections using a Leslie matrix, encounters some difficulties in tracing out likely population responses to war losses, difficulties which go back to the two-sex problem. Wars are likely to generate different losses between males and females. Use of a female projection model by itself will not capture the losses of actual and potential marriage partners; use of a male model by itself will overstate the loss of the population capable of giving birth; and two-sex models have not been developed to the point that they contain marriage models sophisticated sufficiently to deliver reasonable scenarios of marriages in differentially disrupted age distributions. Such modeling may not be entirely out of reach, but it is not available in off-the-shelf editions yet.

4.4.2 Economic Approach to the Same Events

This sub-section offers a highly schematic set of economic reactions to a sharp population decrease, but must distinguish between an epidemic and a natural or man-made catastrophe since the former will leave the capital stock largely intact while the latter generally will not. While the parameters used in the Leslie-matrix projection of population recovery are unaffected by a difference in the source of the perturbation in survival probabilities, at least within that model, the parameters in an economic model are affected.

Consider an epidemic which reduces survival probabilities of all ages by the same percentage. The first effect is to

[115] The parameters of the initial, pre-epidemic stable population are not reported, as Paine does in his 2000 article.

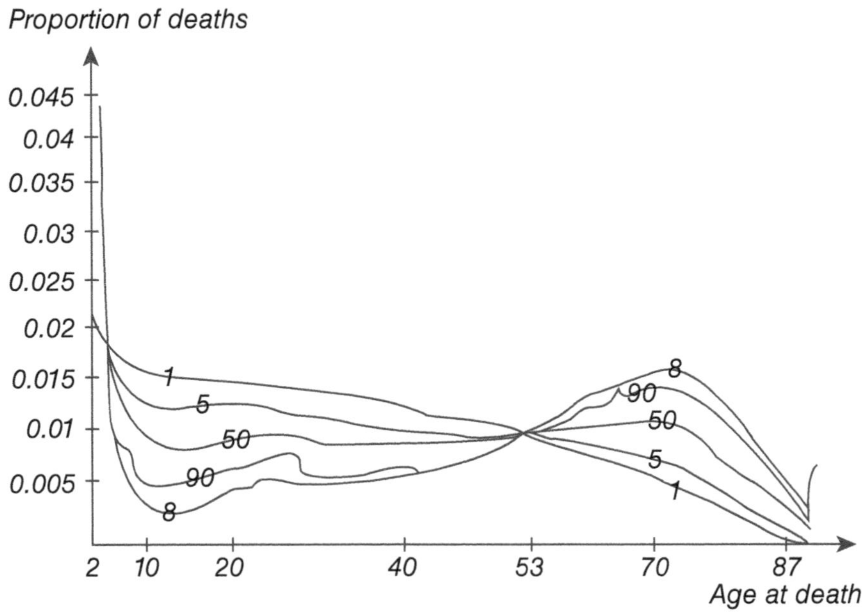

Figure 4.14. Change in mortality profile over course of the plague. The heaviest dark line represents the first plague year. The next heaviest dark line (on the bottom at age-of-death) is the stable population model's mortality profile. The light lines represent the cumulative mortality profiles at 5, 10, 25, 50, and 90 years into the projection. (Reproduced from Paine and Storey, 2006, figure 3.3, p. 76, by permission of the University of Alabama Press.).

reduce the ratio of labor to capital equipment structures and cultivated land. Whether the wage increases relative to the rental rate(s) on capital and land as a consequence of the factor proportions change depends on the territorial scope of the epidemic and the extent to which the affected population is closed to immigration. A change in the wage-rental ratio following the factor proportions change depends on the wage being free to move; if the afflicted population is a relatively small one in a large and largely unaffected area, the wage will not move, or at least not for long; rather some immigration would occur, induced by temporarily higher earning opportunities that would be bid away quickly. The Black Death in 14th century C.E. Europe affected wages relative to rents because the deaths were so extensive. This is the pattern to which Paine and Storey appeal in their simulation of the migration response to an epidemic largely restricted to the Roman metropolis. If the plague extended over all of Italy, it is not clear the migration have occurred, or at least little or no migration that would not have occurred in the absence of the epidemic. However, removal of land from cultivation would move the population back toward the pre-epidemic land-labor and wage-rental ratios. Limits on substitutability in agriculture of other unaffected inputs for labor would encourage disuse of some land.

What could be expected to happen in the way of population recovery? Would individual women's fertility remain the same or change? While the population growth rate skyrocketed immediately after the plague in the population projection model, that occurred with unchanged age-specific fertility rates and only because of a change in the age distribution of the population. It was not caused by individual behavioral changes. In the initial aftermath of an epidemic, many spouses would find themselves widowed, and it would take some time to establish new families, which would parallel Paine's one-year drop in the fertility rate during the year of the epidemic. The impact of a more slowly recovering fertility rate Paine says would make little difference to the century-long recovery path. Nevertheless, if incomes rose among the survivors because of a higher real wage and more income from capital and land (survivors will claim the property of the victims; whether those spoils are relatively evenly divided across the population or concentrated in the hands of some fortunate, or powerful, few would make a considerable difference in resulting income distribution), and a price effect on the demand for children were weak or nonexistent, fertility could be expected to rise in the current fertile cohorts, at least in the younger members. Some replacement births could be expected to occur in addition to long-term increases in desired family size. Additionally, improved nutrition deriving from higher income could reduce mortality and possibly increase fertility through a supply effect as opposed to the demand effect of increased purchasing power.[116] The aggregate outcome of these kinds of temporary and longer-term fertility effects of higher income, the Paine model has not explored. They may or may not have discernible effects on the recovery paths he has identified with the fixed fertility schedule. Alternatively, differential mortality by sex which left more women than men might have given women more control over resources, either by pulling them into the ancient equivalent of the work force or by giving them ownership of assets over which they could direct usage. Either path could have raised the status of women, encouraged them to

[116] Clark and Hamilton (2006) find strong effects of income on fertility in English families from 1200 to 1500, although they hasten to point out that this income effect does not appear to be universal: it has been found in surveys of villages in Austria and southern Germany from the 17th to 19th centuries C.E., but the opposite has emerged for French-Canadian families in the 17th and 18th centuries C.E.

marry later, and reduce (but certainly not eliminate) their reliance on children for old-age support, all factors leading to lower fertility for some period of time.

The other major case involves the destruction of capital equipment and structures along with population, as a consequence of either a natural disaster such as an earthquake or a tsumani or a human event such as destruction in a war. While a population might well be reduced by a quarter or a third or more, the destruction of capital might be even more extensive, in which case the change in factor proportions works against labor, and the wage-rental ratio would fall. In fact, destruction of the productive capital stock of a society with no loss of life would be a limiting case of this type of event, one in which the population reduction was zero but a reduction in the capital-labor ratio reduced incomes sufficiently to reduce fertility. Before proceeding with the possible economic reactions to events of this sort, it is worthwhile to consider what destruction of capital stock in a society with little productive capital equipment and that fairly simple to make. Consider what is known of Mycenaean society and its capital stock: walled acropolises, palaces, some chariots and some bronze weaponry—little or none of it productive, at least directly and possibly not at all. So what if it's destroyed? Agricultural implements would have been difficult for an invader to go around and find and either confiscate or destroy. However, as the example of the Spartan depredations in northern Attica during the Peloponnesian war make clear, destruction of fixed agricultural structures—long-lived trees and vines, terracing, dams, bridges and roads, homes and sturdier agricultural outbuildings, agricultural stockpiles—could severely depress productivity. Whatever happened to the population—substantial or negligible reduction—the fall in income following the event would reduce fertility via the direct income effect. Despite the use of adult children for old-age support, couples would be able to afford to bear and raise fewer children. Families would face a trade-off between rebuilding fixed agricultural capital stocks and having additional children. Although children eventually become productive adults, they have close to two decades of below-adult productivity, and families might be ill-able to afford that period of additional net consumption burden. Thus, the population could well continue to decline for some period after the initial reduction in its numbers and the loss of its capital stock. Rebuilding of the capital stock would be required before the fertility rate began to approach its pre-catastrophe level. The slow, drawn-out end of the Mycenaean palace system might have followed a path roughly along the lines of such a story.

4.4.3 Identifying and Measuring Population Changes and their Consequences

An economic approach to problems involving populations would presume that the basics of individual motivation and behavior would be largely the same across historical and prehistorical situations, even if institutions and technologies differed substantially. Models of institutions and characteristics of technologies can be tailored to individual circumstances, just as they frequently have to be tailored to different circumstances in historical periods. The first sub-section below uses the example of Egyptian population in the 2nd and 3rd centuries C.E. to discuss methodological issues in detecting a poorly documented set of population changes when other non-population data may be available and could be expected to bear certain relationships to population changes. The second sub-section addresses the use of economic models to study population problems in situations where data are actually artefactual remains with different sets of interpretive problems than historical records, however fragmentary.

Measurement in Historical Periods. If high-quality census returns were available for antiquity, there would be no need for indirect methods of estimating whether a population declined or not, such as has been the case with the Antonine Plague. Of course, there aren't any such high-quality census returns for antiquity, and those that do exist have clear limitations, so scholars are left with finding imaginative, indirect means of assessing whether a given population was subject to a serious disruption. Hopes for quantifying the magnitude of such disruptions should be kept to a minimum, but the finding evidence consistent with consequences of such a population disruption may be possible. If price changes are used as an indicator of a population perturbation, it must be kept in mind that small movements in quantities can produce large changes in prices, depending on supply, demand, and institutional conditions.[117] Such strategies run the risk of appearing to be *post hoc ergo propter hoc* arguments, but placed with proper nuance in the historical circumstances may be the best that can be accomplished, given that such methods would be used in conjunction with other indirect indicators. Historical, like contemporary, affairs seldom offer simple and clean, controlled experiments in which the student can observe the effects of only one perturbation, so the student of population would need to maintain awareness of other events which could produce effects that a simple, single-event model would conclude is consistent with a population perturbation. These caveats uttered at the beginning, the remainder of this sub-section concentrates on economic measurements which could be identified as consequences of population changes.

A sharp reduction in population would reduce the labor-land ratio in an economy and increase the wage-rental ratio. Survivors would be better off than they were before. Next, the reduction in population would reduce the demands for many if not all goods. If supply curves for all these goods are upward sloping, their prices relative to labor would fall (remember, not all prices can fall in real terms). However, labor is an input for all goods, and the increased wage

[117] Fogel (1997, 466–467) cites instances from Renaissance England in which a reduction in grain supply of as little as 5%, because of low demand elasticities, could set off a price spiral that cut the consumption of laboring classes by a third, with high inventory demands exacerbating the price rises.

will push up production costs in proportion to labor's cost share in each good's production function. But the cost of land has declined with the reduction in land rentals, an effect probably paralleled in capital goods; these effects would work in the opposite direction. Nevertheless, labor's cost share is considerably greater than land's, and in many production processes was probably in the range of 50 to 75 percent. To take a very simple example, suppose labor's share of a good, say all agricultural goods, was 60 percent, leaving a 40 percent share for land and capital, the wage increased by 30 percent and land and capital rentals fell by 25 percent; without any changes in the cost shares induced by substitutability between labor and inputs whose prices fell, the price of the agricultural goods would rise by 8 percent. Substitutability between inputs would dampen that price increase.

These are real price changes. A monetized economy would also see cash per person increase, which would raise the general price level. However, to the extent that the income elasticity of demand for cash balances was sizeable, say in the neighborhood of unity, the maintenance of additional cash balances could attenuate much of the price-level rise. Continuing with the example of the previous paragraph, the 30 percent increase in the wage and the 8 percent increase in the price of agricultural goods, with a roughly 75 percent budget share going to food, would give a real income increase of 24 percent. A unit income elasticity of demand for money would increase cash holdings per person by 24 percent. If the reduction in population was the same 30 percent by which the wage increased, most of the potential price-level effect of the increase in cash per capita would be absorbed by additional cash holdings.

The economic effects of the Antonine Plague in Egypt, ca. 165–168 C.E., have been studied by several scholars, the most economically focused of those studies being that of Scheidel, who traces the paths of several prices from the beginning of the 2nd century C.E. through the 3rd (Scheidel 2002). Complicating the matter for students of prices during the period is the probable inflation during the period. Scheidel's first subject of study was the wage-rental ratio, which he expects to rise after ca. 165–170 C.E. Using medians of agricultural daily wages and wheat-land rentals over 50- to 100-year periods, he finds the expected increase in the wage rental ratio, inferring a substantial and long-lasting reduction in population, which remained beyond the capacity of measurement. To assess the progress of the real wage, he calculates the progress, again as medians over 50- to 100-year intervals, of the wage relative to various commodity prices—wheat, wine, and oil. Again, the wage rose relative to the prices of these products. Scheidel concludes that the population failed to recover fully from the Antonine plague for up to a century and that "no alternative model can account for the whole range of observed phenomena." The latter contention may be correct, but the assembly and analysis of empirical material in support of it may not be as persuasive as Scheidel contends. Importantly, Scheidel unfortunately dismisses the careful and highly relevant work of Muth (1994) on Egyptian land rentals and wages during this period, which found both declining real land rents and declining real wages from ca. 100 C.E. to 300 C.E., with probably a rising wage-rental ratio since the more reliable estimate of a real wage decline was very modest.

Considering the contrasts in Muth's and Scheidel's methods and, to some extent results, it will be useful to outline what Muth did and compare it with Scheidel's analysis. Muth uses individual, dated wheat prices, land sale prices (which he declines to pursue), wheat-land rentals, and a variety of occupation-specific wage rates, all obtained from A.C. Johnson's (1936) work. He provides scatter plots of the prices against time, which show clear trends, and estimated regressions of price against time. Nominal wheat prices increased about $4\frac{1}{2}$ % per year and nominal land rentals declined about 2% per year. The wage data pose greater challenges since they are for different occupations, which could be expected to earn different wages at any given data and place. Controlling for occupations with dummy variables (variables which take a value of 1 when an observation is of such-and-such an occupation and zero otherwise), nominal wages appear to have increased about 5% per year, but the wide standard error on the constant term does not permit a confident assessment of the trend, since a trend line could have had widely varying intercepts which would move the trend over a wide range. His two alternative regressions use (1) all occupational groups, farm and non-farm, in a single regression and (2) the non-farm occupations only. Both regressions yield highly significant constant terms; the all-occupation trend was around $2\frac{1}{2}$ % per year and that for the non-farm occupations only was around $1\frac{1}{2}$ % per year, with a larger standard error, but one still larger than the estimate of the trend. Muth does not pursue the path of the wage-rental ratio, but the modestly declining wage and the more steeply declining rental trend imply a rising wage-rental ratio even in the presence of both factor prices declining in real terms. The only explanation he finds consistent with the pattern of both real factor prices declining is increasingly heavy output taxation. Increasing taxation of either factor directly would not have produced the decrease in both real prices. This possibility raises the potential for fairly clear-cut instances of population disasters to be combined with other on-going changes which interfere with a clear ability to see the subject of interest, the temporal population movements.

Scheidel's grounds for dismissing Muth's results are found in three footnotes which do not address Muth's findings. First, Scheidel characterizes Muth's objection to the use of median prices for century-long periods as "misguided," contending further that "standard measurements (such as polynomial trend lines) are bound to conceal important discontinuities."[118] Muth does not estimate "polynomial

[118] Scheidel (2002, 104 n. 38), in which he appeals to the use of long-interval median price calculations by Dominic Rathbone (1996, 332 Figure 2). Scheidel calls attention to Rathbone (1997, 239, n. 5), in which Rathbone contends that Muth's use of individually dated prices "ignores the possibility of discrete periods of price-behaviour within those three hundred years," which examination of the data clearly reveals to be absent.

trend lines" but rather linear trends. Examination of the data plots in his graphs of wheat prices, land rents, and wages reveals no discontinuities such as are generated by the use of long-interval median prices. Averaging prices over periods as long as a half- or full century simply loses information. Second, Scheidel contends that Muth's "attempt to relate samples of price and wage data to one another" is "marred by incorrect assumptions" (Scheidel 2002, 106, n. 47, 107–108, n. 54). The "incorrect assumption" appears to be something unspecified about taxes. Muth in fact made no *assumption* about taxes, but rather an inference about taxation—product taxation, not factor (land or labor) taxation. The inference regarding taxation was posterior to the analysis and had no influence on the analysis. Third, while Scheidel contends that Muth "was compelled to admit" that real farm wages did not fall, which is incorrect as is evident in Muth's Table 1, he also contends that "the statistical basis of his finding was weak," which either cuts against Scheidel's first contention or is an unclear referent which at any rate is imprecise if not misleading. Whether Muth's "statistical technique forced him to discard the valuable evidence from the Heroninus archive," as Scheidel further contends is unclear: the price data are dated, and there is nothing in ordinary least squares regressions that would prevent the use of such data if they had been available at the time Muth was working on the problem (Rathbone 1991). Further, since the documents in the archive cover only some 23 years in the third quarter of the 3rd century C.E., it is not clear they would have helped clarify two-century-long price trends (Rathbone1991, 8).

Scheidel indicates that he relies to some unspecified extent on some of Rathbone's 1996 price data, examination of which indicates some potential inconsistencies with Scheidel's other numbers. Rathbone's real rentals in terms of wheat declined from the early 2nd century C.E. through the late 3rd, and the wage in terms of wheat also fell, from the mid-2nd century to the mid-3rd. Putting the two trends together, however, the wage-rental ratio increased by about 40 percent, which is not inconsistent qualitatively with Muth's econometric findings. However, the movements of wheat and wine prices are inconsistent between private and state wheat sales, while the ratio of wages to wine prices fell. The late-3rd century wine and state wheat prices seem especially problematic, being 30 and 37 times their 1st to mid-2nd century prices, which is far out of line with indexes of the other prices and far beyond what ordinary inflation could produce.

Historians, and ancient historians in particular, as well as archaeologists and philologists, have a reputation for being almost obsessively attentive to what their data might mean. Economists like to think that they take equal care in understanding their price data, ensuring that price comparisons are among like goods, or at least understanding the differences in the goods for which prices are being compared. Most prices are, to one extent or another, hedonic prices, or, roughly speaking, prices adjusted for differences in the goods whose prices are to be compared. Bagnall takes Scheidel to task over the latter's failure to adjust land prices for major differences in productivity and between arable and garden land and irrigated and unirrigated land, although he does credit Scheidel for recognizing the difficulty in making meaningful comparisons of land prices. Further, Bagnall points out the complexity of some land rental contracts, citing an example of a contract for rents in both wheat and straw, which Scheidel's source, and Scheidel himself, truncate to rent only on the part of the land planted in wheat, implicitly assigning zero rent to half of the land. Bagnall (2002, 116–119) recalculates the rents on 13 instances, reducing the average rent implied by some 30 percent.

Corresponding care needs to be taken in appeals to price movements at greatly removed dates as corroborating explanations for price movements in antiquity. An obvious comparison for the effect of a major epidemiological disaster is with the Black Death in Western Europe in the 14th and 15th centuries C.E., which Scheidel uses as a comparandum. It may be useful to review Scheidel's appeal to Earl Hamilton's Spanish prices and wages of the 14th and early 15th centuries C.E. as evidence of effects of population reduction on wages and on a possibly lengthy period for price response (Scheidel 2002, 100 n. 22 on wages and 104 n. 38 on prices).[119] Regarding the effect of an epidemic's effect on real wages, Scheidel

Rathbone further contends that "most of his [Muth's] regression equations are extremely poor fits to the data, which focuses on R^2 values (percent of variance explained by the regression) rather than on the statistical significance of the small number of estimated coefficients, which is generally high and which was the point of the econometric analysis, not "explanation" of the full variance of the price series. Nonetheless, the R^2 value for the wheat price trend regression was 0.67, those for the land rentals were 0.24 and 0.25, and that for four occupational groups of farm labor was 0.68. The R^2 values for the all-occupational wage regression and for the non-farm occupations only were considerably lower, at 0.19 and 0.06, presumably the statistics on which Rathbone focused. Despite his criticisms of Muth's methods and results, Rathbone (1997, 186) concedes the fact that averaging prices over intervals as long as a century loses information. This said about the R^2 values in Muth's regressions, they are largely irrelevant since the only independent variable (I hesitate to call it by the usual designation of "explanatory" variable) he uses is the year of the price observation; there's nothing in Muth's regressions that even tries to "explain" the variation in these prices. He wasn't trying to gain understanding of the determinants of these prices, rather only to find out whether they went up or down over time, with some dummy-variables used to account for some obvious differences in the goods or people among the observations. The important statistics to observe are the standard errors on the coefficients of the time trends, which generally indicate high levels of statistical significance—remarkable in itself since the only variables in the regressions are the constant term, the time trend and some dummy variables in the wage regressions. The commonly used t-statistic is simply the ratio of the coefficient to its standard error. Muth reported coefficient values and standard errors.

[119] The original work is Hamilton (1936). Hamilton was a star, young American player in the International Scientific Committee on Price History, which operated actively in the early 1930s but saw its activities interrupted and disrupted by the Great Depression and World War II, with re-direction away from price history thereafter. On the subject of the hedonic character of prices of seemingly well standardized products (but actually not), Hamilton's attention to many dimensions of qualitative details of his commodities is acute, as close reading of this volume (and others of his) reveals. I knew Hamilton when he was an emeritus at the University of Chicago and remember his thoughts on relaxing versus cramming the night before a big exam: "You can't forget what you never knew."

compares the progress of real wages in Navarre, which experienced a severe pestilence (Hamilton's term), with those in Valencia, which S. contends did not experience the plague. Hamilton's wage series for Valencia begins only in 1392 (1348 would have been the first epidemic date, with its recurrences in 1360–62, 1367–69, and 1373–75), so the wage series for Navarre and Valencia cannot be compared for the period in the immediate aftermath of the initial outbreak of the plague (Hamilton 1936, 72 Table 7). Nevertheless, Hamilton reports a nominal (i.e., not "real") salary series for Valencia which begins in 1351 and shows a 9 percent spike between 1351 and 1356, which he attributes to a possible belated adjustment to labor scarcity resulting from the Black Death, although he notes that monetary factors may have been "wholly or partially responsible" (Hamilton 1936, 68 Table 6, 69 Chart 5, 203).[120] Hamilton's data for Navarre are the most complete of his three kingdoms, a money wage series beginning in 1346 and commodity prices in 1351, allowing a real wage series to be constructed from the latter date (Hamilton 1936, 159 Table 23, 180 Table 26). To construct his real wage series for Navarre, Hamilton uses only what he calls "basic food prices," which implies omission of a number of food items from the index used to calculate the real wage index as well as other items ranging from men's shoes to large nails and bricks to earthenware pots and candles, all of which are included in the overall price index.[121] All three of Hamilton's price indexes are arithmetic (unweighted) averages of his prices (actually, price relatives), since he was unable to find data to construct adequate consumption weights (Hamilton 1936, 51).[122] While Hamilton's quinquennial real wage index values using his "basic food" price index rise above a value of 100 in 1352 and continue a nearly unbroken climb for the next 51 years (Hamilton 1936, 186 Table 28), an alternative real wage index using his all-commodity price index as the deflator drops below 100 immediately after 1351, does not reach a value of 100 again for 34 years, and does not remain above 100 for 48 years. It is not unusual for differently constructed price indexes to yield different results since they measure different concepts. What is of some interest in the comparison of these two measures however is the implication that "basic food" prices fell relative to those of other, presumably industrial goods. The continued rise of Hamilton's real wage index for Navarre for the half-century following the first outbreak of plague in that kingdom suggests repeated outbreaks, which are known to have occurred, rather than sluggish adjustment of wages and prices to immediate supply-demand changes and changes in factor proportions. The reduction in the Navarrese real wage index based on all commodities is not easy to understand; with the relatively large number of food products in Hamilton's prices for Navarre, the implicitly equal commodity weights in his price index (possibly differing from their weights in laborers' budgets) should not be a major source of difference between the indexes. The progress of the commodity price indexes for all three kingdoms is choppier—more marked by recessions following advances—than is a typical consumer or producer price index which measures overall price-level change. The real wage indexes are similarly replete with advances and retreats in levels, which appear to indicate the operation of multiple types of event.

Scheidel's second use of Hamilton's data is to support a possibly lengthy period of adjustment of commodity prices to a reduction in population following an epidemic. As noted above, the principal route by which such an effect would occur would be by an increase in the money supply per person, an important implicit assumption being that the money supply stayed constant while population fell. While Valencia maintained a stable currency value during the period Hamilton studied, Navarre "did not enjoy a sound currency," relegating the commodity price increases to which Scheidel refers as taking 30 years to double after the outbreak of the plague to a large measure of price inflation accompanying currency debasement and expansion, although Hamilton did not have any population data to assess a currency-population ratio.[123] Hamilton accompanies his index series with annotations of bad and good crop years, depredations of armies, and political intrigues which prompted currency manipulations affecting price levels, all of which operated simultaneously with epidemic events, which in fact were not a central concern of his narrative. The record of price and wage changes following the 14th century C.E. Black Death is, in fact, more intricate than Scheidel's passing summary of that literature would suggest, with that period's many other intervening events, not least among them the Hundred Years War (or Wars) and various governments' accompanying policy accommodations and adjustments. Thus while Hamilton's real wage series may show some substantial effects of population reductions, they offer no before-and-after comparisons, and his price series contain large components of currency effects rather than being clean evidence of population decrease leaving survivors with more coins. The magnitude of his price and wage movements do not give clear insight into the magnitude of effect of population changes, only the likelihood of some effect, an issue which was not in serious doubt. Some of the other sources Scheidel cites in his comparison of the Antonine plague with the Black Death actually report real wage decreases following 1348 (e.g., Hatcher 1994, 7). It is difficult to slip in and out of these other periods without becoming fairly well immersed in the literature on them and the analyses of the events.

Since the subject of Scheidel's analysis, if not necessarily the direct object of Muth's, is the progress of the Egyptian

[120] Hamilton's price data for Valencia begin only in 1380, and then only sporadically until 1395, so data do not exist to convert the nominal salary series to a real series: 52, Table 4.

[121] Hamilton (1936, 186; Appendix VII, 266–277) reports the products in various subgroup price indexes, but none is identified as a basic food group, and all (even the non-agricultural group) contain food items.

[122] A price relative is the price of a good in one period relative to its price in another period, used as the base period.

[123] Hamilton (1936, 142 on the Navarrese currency, Chapter I on the contrasting monetary experience in Valencia).

population from the mid-2nd century through the late 3rd, his combat with Bagnall and Frier is somewhat more difficult to understand since it does not appear to involve methodological arcanities. Contra Bagnall and Frier's suggestion that Egypt's population might have responded with higher fertility following the plague, Scheidel contends that the claim does not "stand up to close scrutiny of the evidence,"[124] which he reinforces with reference to Paine's simulation work on post-catastrophe population behavior, from which Scheidel reports the finding that the intrinsic growth rate of a population recently subject to a catastrophic population decline will be higher than usual for about 15 years before dropping to something below the long-term trend for the following 30 years (Scheidel 2002, 109 n. 64; Paine 2000).

Economic Inference Regarding Prehistoric Population Change. So far this sub-section has addressed the use of historical data, such as they may be, to either infer suspected but unproven changes in population or assess impacts of more certain population changes. The example of the post-Mycenaean population changes in the first part of this section takes us into the realm of prehistory and archaeology. Skeletal remains from cemeteries have been used to estimate population sizes and growth rates in prehistorical settings as well as in historical periods at sites for which records do not exist. The limitations of such exercises have been clearly noted, and methods are being developed to improve the accuracy of remains-based population estimates. These efforts lie in the intersection of physical anthropology and demography. The only economic effort to elicit insights on population growth from archaeological remains is my own modest work of a decade and more ago, which I believe has been cited once in the subsequent literature on population of prehistoric periods.[125]

I will not reproduce the models of that paper here but simply explain what I was trying to accomplish and emphasize the flexibility of the approach. I developed models to examine the use of two types of artifactual remains—burials and settlements—to estimate population growth during a specific period, the Late Geometric Period in central Greece. The study of burials developed a series of structural models (only implicitly behavioral, but derived from behavioral models) with varying sets of social and economic relationships surrounding burials and found that although observed burials could be expected generally to track population, the alternative hypotheses about the social circumstances of burials would be indistinguishable, regardless of place and time. The settlement model was based on utilities of representative individuals and some models from urban economics. The logic of the model inferred population growth on the basis of the length of time required for villages to get large enough to make some residents better off by establishing a new village. I applied the results of this model to data on settlement growth in Attica, Corinthia, and the Argolid during the last 60 years of the 8th century to make estimates of population growth rates. The period had been suspected of being one of a population growth spurt, and the estimates derived from the burial model were large by standards of antiquity but not implausible for a short period of rapid growth, 0.8%, 0.4%, and 0.3% per year for the three regions—although the model did not try to explain the causes of the growth. I did not actually try to develop a model of the relationship between population and the number of wells because I did not have sufficient information on people's behavior regarding well use and well construction to develop any economic logic.

These models are what could be characterized as "one-off" models. They are not general. They were constructed to apply to specific circumstances and data availability. If circumstances of rural dwelling locations vis-à-vis farms were believed to be similar in a different location at a different time, the model might find application, with or without some modification to accommodate other differences believed to be influential to the relationship between settlements and population. The more general lesson of these efforts is that economic models can be developed to study different circumstances; any lack of sufficient generality to apply to any and all other circumstances is not a shortcoming of a model developed to apply to a specific situation. The general method may even be adapted to assess potential biases in the artefactual remains, as is addressed in an appendix of my paper on the use of settlements and burials (Jones 1999, Appendix 4, 50).

Such a program may sound beyond the acceptable bounds of modernism to some scholars, but in fact it need not be.[126] The terms "modernist" and "primitivist" refer to the behavior, and sometimes the institutions, attributed to individuals and groups in antiquity.[127] A model can

[124] Citing Scheidel (2002, Chapter 2), which deals very interestingly with various aspects of age-, sex-, and location-specific life expectancy, and age distributions at various dates before and after the onset of the Antonine Plague, but not at all with aggregate population trends before and after that event. Scheidel (2002, 162–166, 165 Table 2.5) reports some unexpected age distributions in census samples at various dates before and after the onset of the plague.

[125] Jones (1999), cited by Scheidel (2003, 129).

[126] Concerns and reservations exemplified by, for instance, Morley's (2005) review of *Debating Roman Demography* in regard to the use of contemporary demographic science and models to characterize ancient populations, which borders on questioning the uniformitarian assumption involved in applying those models.

[127] The parallel set of dichotomies is formalism versus substantivism, attributed to Polanyi (1944). The basic work on primitivism is Finley (1973, especially Chapter 1). As a rough try at the difference between the two dichotomies, the modernist/primitivist difference refers to a contemporary student's beliefs about ancient behavior, social organization or both, while the formalist/substantivist distinction refers to that same student's belief in the applicability of twentieth century economic theory to the analysis of ancient behavior, the subtantivist believing in a concept called embeddedness of production and exchange in other institutions, which is held to render economic analysis of the economic behavior of people in antiquity with the intellectual tools of contemporary economics somewhere between the three poles of impossible, irrelevant and incorrect. While different, the two pairs of dichotomies are clearly related, through both their beliefs in the uniqueness of antiquity and their consequent conclusions about the usefulness of contemporary economic theory. As the application of contemporary economic models, adapted to what are believed to be ancient institutional conditions, the modeling program described above might be considered more a case of formalism than of modernism, which could tend to neglect important institutional details.

be developed to characterize any purported behavior: they are simply relatively formally specified hypotheses. As for its modernist cast, this program does, however, proceed somewhat beyond the modernism exemplified by the application of demographic models to ancient populations inasmuch as it models hypotheses about individual behavior rather than remain at the specification of incidences and rates as demographic models do, but this is a matter of technique rather than substance. If we modeled a futures market in, say, 15th century B.C.E. Mycenae, we probably would be creating an anachronism, but if we developed an individual choice model of, say, how a farmer decided on his sowing pattern or a craftsman decided how many implements of particular types to make or a ruler decided on how much crop to exact from his subjects in taxation, we would simply be expressing hypotheses about how we think those individuals solved those problems. At the very least, such use of contemporary modeling techniques can help sharpen questions and dialogue about longstanding issues.

4.5 Modeling Generations

Populations grow over time, as individual families age and produce more children, and as subsequent generations of individuals form families and reproduce. The economic model of fertility presented above represented a single family in a timeless situation. The basic, static model assumed that the family made its entire life-cycle fertility decisions at a single date at the beginning of the family's time together, clearly a simplification of the observational world. Modeling sequential decisions over a couple's reproductive life span has proven too difficult mathematically to solve other than numerically, the numerical solutions offered to date showing how far the modeling has to go. The study of generational behavior—the interactions of individuals of one generation with those of succeeding and occasionally preceding generations—has been underway for some half-century, bringing a new way of studying economic growth, among many other topics. Fertility is a natural application of this generational interaction framework. This section presents a major vehicle for studying intergenerational behavior, the Overlapping Generations Model, and an extension of the static Chicago fertility model to a setting of multiple generations. The first sub-section below introduces the Overlapping Generations Model, and the second sub-section shows its operation in enough detail to gain some comfort with its concepts. The third sub-section presents the Becker and Barro dynastic fertility model, which deals with multiple generations of a single family, using a simple overlapping generations model for its intertemporal framework.

4.5.1 The Overlapping Generations Model

The Overlapping Generations (OLG) model has become one of the prime analytical devices for studying economic growth in the past several decades, largely replacing both the Solow-Swan and the Ramsey growth models, both of which rely on infinitely lived representative agents.[128] In the OLG model, new households arrive over time, introducing a number of new economic interactions not present in the representative agent (RA) class of models. The model can take a wide range of forms, the essential components being the coexistence of agents of different ages who move through their life cycles over time, with the exit of earlier generations and arrival of new generations. For example, the simplest model has two periods, with a young generation and an old generation in the initial period; in the following period, the old generation of the initial period has died, the young generation has become that period's old generation, and another young generation has been born. The two-period model has yielded important insights but is quite restrictive. Its two periods do not capture the typical human life cycle pattern of dependence in youth and old age separated by a productive adulthood. Three-period models have been used extensively to capture these important features, and most of the theoretical insights from the OLG model that appear in models with more than three periods—sometimes continuous models with an essentially infinite number of periods—have emerged in the three-period model. Nonetheless, the simple, two- and three-period models are useful only for abstract analytical investigations. For empirical use, a more realistic number of periods is necessary for quantitative accuracy. A fifty-five period model has been developed to study tax policy, but its analysis required computer simulation. The OLG model permits analysis of intergenerational actions and introduces some conundra of social organization. For example, in the two-period model, exchange between generations is not possible, so markets are unable to smooth consumption; non-market transfer arrangements can be devised (intrafamily or governmental) to permit such an economy to reach efficiency without the use of markets. Rather than representing the observational world, the two-period model highlights a feature introduced by finite lifetimes regardless of the number of periods individuals live. In OLG models with larger numbers of periods, intergenerational exchanges can occur, but the necessity remains for some non-market social arrangement to arise to obligate currently unborn individuals to future transactions as the willingness of younger generations to engage in exchanges with older generations, when the older generation will die without repaying the younger generation, hinges on the future willingness of the currently unborn to engage in similar exchanges with the current young generation when they are old.

The OLG model's social accounting structure incorporates the constraints on a population's age distribution in any period that are implied by its history of fertility and mortality. Measures of life cycle demographic behavior such as age-specific fertility, nuptiality and mortality schedules can be introduced into the OLG accounting

[128] The basic references are Samuelson (1958) and Diamond (1965). Both use discrete-time models. Blanchard, (1985) develops a simplification of the model in continuous time.

structure, and standards results from mathematical demography can be used to relate these life-cycle characteristics to the population growth rate and the age distribution at any date (Willis 1988, 107). There are both life-cycle, or longitudinal, constraints on individuals and cross-sectional constraints at each given date on the economy.

In a simple, 2-period model, the young generation will work and the old generation is retired. While recent versions of the model include the younger generation saving during their working period and spending those savings, plus interest, during their retirement, the initial version of the model assumed that the good produced during the working period could not be carried over to the subsequent period. This evaporating-good assumption sets up the situation in which the young (later) generation supports the early (older) generation during the latter's retirement in a set of transfers that have been likened to a pay-as-you-go social security system. Students of development, growth, and population have seen in this structure a reflection of intra-family / inter-generational income transfers that are common in societies with largely undeveloped capital markets. It is this aspect of the OLG model that will be emphasized here.

One of the lessons of the OLG model is that, with an infinite time horizon and continuing entrants to a population, living generations make implicit contracts with unborn generations which some sort of institutional arrangement, not developed within the model, must enforce.

4.5.2 The Structure of an OLG Model

The model is comprised of a household component, in which decisions are made about consumption and saving, and a production component in which firms produce the composite good that individuals in households consume.[129] Households make decisions on the basis of prices that are determined outside the household by the interaction of all firms and all households. Firms make decisions on the basis of their technology and decisions of households. The optimization behavior of both components can be studied separately, with prices being determined as the outcome of optimal decisions made in both components of the model. The basic model uses two periods and two generations of individuals, an "old" generation and a "young" generation. The first period is denoted period t and the second period as t + 1. The current old generation was born and conducted their working lives in the previous period, denoted period 0; behavior in that period is not modeled, but results in circumstances exogenously affecting both generations in period t, as will become apparent subsequently.

During the first generation, of youth, individuals work, and in the second generation they are retired. The consumption of the older generation can be based on either a transfer of income from the working young generation or the savings of the older generation made when they were young. The latter case is developed here. Individuals are born an experience their working lives during the first period, during which they inelastically supply one unit of labor for which they receive the wage w_t. Lifetime utility of a young individual from the perspective of period t is $u_t^Y = u(c_t^Y) + \frac{1}{1+\rho}u(c_{t+1}^O)$, in which ρ is the pure rate of time preference, a psychological discount factor. This lifetime utility is composed of utility in both periods of life, each period's utility determined by consumption in that period, c_t^Y in period t when young (superscript Y) and c_{t+1}^O in period t + 1 when old (superscript O). The young generation's budget identity shows that they allocate their working-period income between consumption, c_t^Y, and savings, s_t: $c_t^Y + s_t = w_t$. When that generation is old and no longer working, its consumption is determined by its budget in period t + 1, which amounts to its savings in the previous period plus the interest earnings accrued during the subsequent period: $c_{t+1}^O = (1 + r_{t+1})s_t$. Substituting the second period budget constraint into the first period's constraint yields the consolidated lifetime budget constraint: $w_t = c_t^Y + \frac{c_{t+1}^O}{1+r_{t+1}}$. Young agents maximize their lifetime utility subject to this consolidated budget constraint. The first-order conditions for this maximization yield the relationship $\frac{u'(c_{t+1}^O)}{u'(c_t^Y)} = \frac{1+\rho}{1+rt+1}$, where u' is a shorthand symbol for $\Delta u/\Delta c_{period}^{age}$. The relationship says that individuals will shift consumption between working-age youth and retired old age according to the relative strength of their preference for earlier consumption and the interest rate they expect the next period.[130]

These first-order conditions (known as Euler equations for simplicity of reference) and the consolidated budget constraint determine an implicit relationship between endogenous saving during period t, s_t, and the (currently) exogenous period-t wage rate and the future-period interest rate, w_t and r_{t+1}, as saving is determined as a residual after the individual's choice of current and future consumption, c_t^Y and c_{t+1}^O. A number of specifications of the savings function can be constructed, all of which yield the same results; the function employed here is defined as $s_t = s(w_t, r_{t+1})$. Saving is negatively related to the wage rate, a pure income effect, but the effect of the interest rate is composed of offsetting price and income effects and the net direction of its effect is ambiguous (See Jones 2014, Chapter 8, section 6). At the cost of using some complicated looking expressions, it is possible to gain insight into influences on household saving behavior. I will explain the meaning of

[129] For the exposition of this section, I have relied on treatments by Acemoglu (2009, Ch. 9); Barro and Sala-i-Martin (2004, 190–200); Blanchard and Fischer (1989, Chapter 3; de la Croix and Michel (2002, Chapter 1); and Heijdra (2009, Chapter 17).

[130] Of course, an individual in period t generally will not know what the interest rate, or the value of any other variable, will be in the second period, so implicitly I am using a perfect foresight assumption here, which is a very strong assumption. The alternative would be to designate 2nd period variables as expected values, using a superscript e, which would require modeling the formation of expectations, which would not add anything to comprehension of the basic structure of an OLG model. Hence, perfect foresight is assumed here.

these expressions in some detail. The effect of the wage rate on savings is denoted by s_w, which means $\Delta s/\Delta w_t$, and the effect of the interest rate as s_r, representing $\Delta s/\Delta r_{t+1}$. The wage effect is $0 < s_w = \frac{\theta(c_t^Y)/c_t^Y}{\theta(c_{t+1}^O)/s_t+\theta(c_t^Y)/c_t^Y} < 1$, unambiguously positive. θ is the elasticity of marginal utility evaluated at level a of the variable in the utility function: $\theta = -a(u''(a)/u'(a) > 0$, in which u' in the denominator is marginal utility of variable a and $u'' < 0$ is the change in marginal utility as the magnitude of a is increased slightly; its negative sign indicates the curvature of a utility function, as it increases with increases in the level of a but at a decreasing rate. The inverse of θ is the intertemporal elasticity of substitution, $\sigma(a) = 1/\theta(a)$, which tells how sensitively an individual's consumption responds to differences between the rate of time preference ρ and the interest rate r_{t+1}. When σ is high, individuals are quite willing to substitute consumption between periods to take advantage of incentives from a higher future interest rate. A low value of σ means that individuals have strong preferences for similar consumption levels over time. Returning to the expression for the response of savings to changes in the wage rate (income), the elasticities of marginal utilities in both numerator and denominator are positive, so the effect is unambiguously positive, and since the expression is the ratio of the elasticity of utility from consumption during youth to the sum of the elasticities of consumption in both periods, the magnitude of the effect is between zero and one. The effect of the interest rate is $s_r = \frac{1-\theta(c_t^Y)/c_t^Y}{(1+r_{t+1})[\theta(c_{t+1}^O)/s_t+\theta(c_t^Y)/c_t^Y]} \gtrless 0$ since the numerator is a difference that can be positive or negative. If the intertemporal elasticity of substitution $\sigma > 1$ (a "high" value), the substitution effect dominates and saving increases with the interest rate ($\theta = 1/\sigma < 1$ and the numerator is positive). An increase in the interest rate makes the trade-off between consumption in young and old periods of life more favorable for old-age consumption, which tends to increase saving. An intertemporal elasticity of substitution $\sigma < 1$ (a "low" value) lets the income effect dominate, and saving decreases at higher interest rates ($\theta = 1/\sigma > 1$ and the numerator is negative).

In aggregate there are N_t young individuals in the first period of their lives, born in period t, and N_{t-1} old individuals in the second period of their lives, born in period t-1. During any one period there are $N_t + N_{t-1}$ people alive. With an exogenous growth rate of n per period, $N_t = (1 + n)N_{t-1}$. A number of recent models have endogenized population growth. These will be introduced later.

Aggregate production by identical individual firms can be represented by a neoclassical production function, $Y_t = F(K_t, L_t)$, where K_t is total capital stock in period t and L_t is the labor force in the period. In intensive (or per capita or per unit of labor) form, $y_t = f(k_t)$, where $k_t = K_t/L_t$. The optimality conditions for firms yield a wage rate of $w_t = F_L$ or in intensive form, $w_t = f(k_t) - k_t f'(k_y)$, and a rental rate on capital of $F_K = r_t + \delta$, where $0 \leq \delta \leq 1$ is the depreciation rate on capital; in intensive form, that is $r_t + \delta = f'(k_t)$. The current period's capital stock, K_t, is composed of the savings of the current old generation in the previous period and accordingly is a parameter of the model during the periods of active decisions. Thus the current old generation owns the capital stock. It receives the current period's rental rate, $r_t + \delta$. While firms make their wage and rental payment decisions on the basis of current capital stock and labor force, young individuals base their saving decisions in the same period on the next period's capital stock and labor force: $r_{t+1} + \delta = f'(k_{t+1})$.[131]

To determine the market equilibrium, aggregate consumption and the aggregate resource constraint are brought into play. The aggregate resource constraint is $Y_t + (1 - \delta)K_t = C_t + K_{t+1}$, which says that current-period output plus undepreciated capital is allocated between current consumption and the next period's capital stock, the latter via saving. Since the creation of the net period's capital stock is created by investment, this constraint could be written as $Y_t = C_t + I_t$, where gross investment It $\equiv \Delta K_{t+1} + \delta K_t$ and $\Delta K_{t+1} \equiv K_{t+1} - K_t$.

Aggregate consumption, C_t, is the sum of the young and old generations' consumptions: $C_t \equiv N_{t-1}c_t^O + N_t c_t^Y$. Since the old generation owns the capital stock is the rental payments for the capital stock plus the undepreciated part of the capital stock—it is edible: $N_{t-1}c_t^O = (1 - \delta)K_t + (r_t + \delta)K_t = (1+ r_t)K_t$. Total consumption by the young generation is $N_t c_t^Y = w_t N_t - s_t N_t$. Substituting these two definitions of generational aggregate consumption into the aggregate consumption yields $C_t = Y_t + (1 - \delta)K_t - s_t N_t$. Combining this last expression with the initial specification of the aggregate resource constraint shows the relationship between the current period's saving decision and the next period's capital stock: $s_t N_t = K_{t+1}$. Recalling the relationship between the sizes of each generational cohort, the saving function can be written in intensive form as $s(w_t, rt_{+1}) = (1 + n)k_{t+1}$.

There are two types of equilibria in the model, temporary and intertemporal Temporary equilibrium in period t is a competitive equilibrium given expectations of prices which gives equilibrium values of current variables, including prices as a function of variables determined in the past—s_{t-1} and $I_{t-1} = N_{t-1}s_{t-1}$—and expectations about the future. There are three conditions for equilibrium. First, equilibrium in the labor market is determined by adjustment of the wage as a function of the capital-labor ratio, $w_t = \omega(k_t)$, $\omega' > 0$, to equalize firms' demand for labor, L_t, with households' inelastic supply of labor, N_t. Second, equality between realized and distributed capital earnings implies that the rate of return on savings set aside in period $t - 1$ equals the marginal product of capital during period t. Third, equilibrium in the goods market equalizes production by firms and demands by old and young generations. The capital market, which can be eliminated by Walras' Law, is represented by the supply

[131] As a reminder, the expression for the wage rate using the intensive form of the production function, is the average product of capital, $f(k_t)$, minus the marginal product of capital, $f'(k_t)$, times the number of units of capital (per unit of labor), k_t.

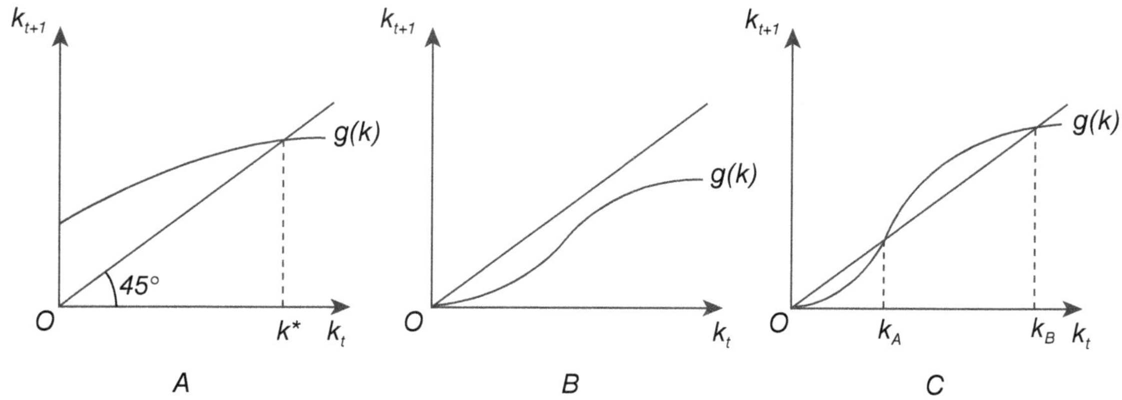

Figure 4.15. (A) Steady-state growth when factors are highly substitutable (Constant-elasticity-of-substitution [CES] production function with $\rho < 0$ (Reproduced from de la Croix and Michel, 2002, figure 1.10, p. 32, by permission of David de la Croix.) (B) Steady-state growth when factors are poorly substitutable (CES production function with $\rho > 0$ there are either no or two non-trivial steady states (Reproduced from de la Croix and Michel, 2002, figure 1.11, p. 33, by permission of David de la Croix.) (C) Two non-trivial steady states; the corner and higher steady states are stable (Reproduced from de la Croix and Michel, 2002, figure 1.11, p. 33, by permission of David de la Croix.).

of capital by households, coming from the utility function of young households and the demand for capital by firms represented by the first-order condition on the production function which equates the rental rate on capital to its marginal product. The temporary equilibrium is defined by the prices—the wage rate w_t and the gross rate of return on capital r_t; the aggregate variables K_t (determined in the previous period), L_t, Y_t, K_t, k_t, I_t; and the individual variables c_t^Y, s_t, c_t^O. Each of these variables can be expressed as a function of k_t, r_{t+1}, or both: $w_t = \omega(k_t)$, $r_t + \delta = f'(k_t)$, $L_t = N_t$, $Y_t = N_t f(k_t)$, $I_t = N_t s_t$, $c_t^Y = w_t - s_t$, $s_t = s(\omega(k_t), r_{t+1})$, and $c_t^O = (1 + r_t)s_{t-1}$.

In intertemporal equilibrium, the values of variables at different dates are in compatible configurations. The link between periods t and t + 1 is given by the rule for capital accumulation and by the formation of expectations. The accumulation rule is that the savings of the current young generation are transformed into the productive capital stock of the next period: $K_{t+1} = I_t = N_t s(\omega(k_t), r_{t+1}^e)$, where the superscript e on the future interest rate indicates an expectation of its value, or in intensive terms $k_{t+1} = \frac{1}{1+n} s(w(k_t), r_{t+1}$. With the simplification of perfect foresight, $r_t + 1 = r_{t+1}^e$. The capital accumulation rule implicitly relates the present capital stock per worker to the future capital stock per worker and can be used to study the evolution of the capital stock over time as well as stability of equilibria. Changes in present and future capital stocks are related as $\frac{\Delta k_{t+1}}{\Delta k_t} = \frac{-s_w k_t f''(k_t)}{1+n-s_r f''(k_{t+1})}$. A steady state equilibrium value of the pair k_t and k_{t+1} is stable only if the value of this change relation is less than 1 in absolute value, which cannot be assured generally. However, with a Cobb-Douglas production technology and a logarithmic utility function, stability is guaranteed with the specific form $k_{t+1} = g(k_t) \equiv \frac{\varepsilon_L}{(1+n)(2+\rho)} k_t^{1-\varepsilon_L}$, in which ε_L is the labor output elasticity in the production function, or labor's share of the product.

Figure 4.15A illustrates the relationship between capital stocks in the two periods, Figures 4.15B and 4.15C show various types of stable and unstable steady state equilibria, and Figure 4.16 shows the effect of a stronger rate of time preference, p, on the steady state equilibrium. The 45-degree line from the origin of Figure 4.15A shows the loci of points along which the capital stock per worker is constant across adjacent periods, while the concave line, $k_{t+1} = g(k_t)$, shows the locus of k_t and k_{t+1} pairs that satisfy the optimality conditions of the various agents in the economy as embodied in the capital accumulation relationship. If some initial period capital stock is k_0 in Figure 4.15A, the dashed lines with arrows between the $k_{t+1} = k_t$ line and the $k_{t+1} = g(k_t)$ line show the approach to the unique, stable, equilibrium at k*. At k*, a line tangent to the $g(k_t)$ line is less than 1 in absolute value (it is flatter than the $k_{t+1} = k_t$ line, which has a slope of 1), so the equilibrium is stable. Because the equilibrium is stable, a departure of k_t from k* will tend to return to k*. The panels of Figure 4.15B show a range of other steady-state equilibria, all with logarithmic utility functions. Panel A shows a constant elasticity of substitution (CES) production function with an

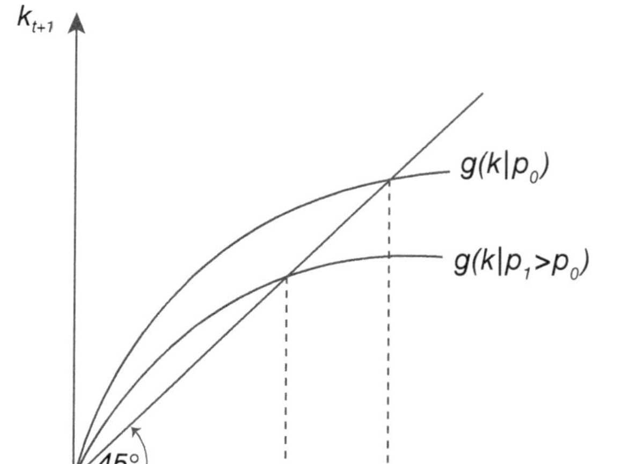

Figure 4.16. Higher rate of time preference ($p_1 > p_0$) yields lower steady-state capital stock (Adapted from de la Croix and Michel, 2002, figure 13.5, p. 151, by permission of David de la Croix.).

elasticity of substitution between capital and labor greater than 1 (the Cobb-Douglas production function in Figure 4.15A has an elasticity of substitution of exactly 1). A stable steady-state equilibrium occurs at k*. Panels B and C illustrate two cases of CES production functions with low substitutability between capital and labor, in which cases there is either no steady state equilibrium or there are two. In Panel C, steady-state equilibrium k_a is unstable (the slope of a tangent to line $g(k_t)$ is greater than 1. An initial capital stock per capita $k_0 < k_a$ will converge to 0, while an initial value of $k_0 = k_a$ will remain there. A positive displacement of k_a, or a value of $k_0 > k_a$ will converge to the stable steady state equilibrium at k_b. The exogenous rate of time preference is an important parameter in the determination of a steady state capital stock. A larger rate of time preference, say 5% per year as contrasted with 2% per year, as might be expected in a population with low income to begin with and high mortality, would rotate the $g(k_t)$ curve clockwise, as in Figure 4.15C, reducing k* and reducing output per capita.

The preceding analysis has dealt with the market solution. There is what is called an optimal golden-age path of capital accumulation, which yields each agent the highest possible utility level and all agents the same utility level. This path maximizes an individual's lifetime utility subject to a steady-state, economy-wide resource constraint derived from the previous aggregate consumption relationship and aggregate resource constraint and substituting to rely on the intensive form of aggregate production, $f(k) - (n + \delta)k = c^Y + c^O/(1 + n)$. In this resource constraint, contrary to the individual utility function in which c^Y and c^O refer to young and old consumption of a single individual, the c^Y and c^O refer to consumption of representative young and old agents at a single point in time. Since the steady state is imposed, and $k_t = k_{t+1} = k$, the time subscripts are omitted. The first-order conditions for the optimal golden-age path are the steady-state resource constraint, $\frac{u'(c^O)}{u'(c^Y)} = \frac{1+\rho}{1+n}$, and $f'(k) = n + \delta$. Comparing the latter two conditions, the population growth rate has replaced the interest rate in the optimality condition for intertemporal consumption allocation and in the rental rate of capital. The market solution will coincide with the golden-age optimal path only if $r = f'(k) - \delta = n$, that is, if the interest rate equals the population growth rate. The first-order conditions for intertemporal consumption allocation and the marginal product of capital are independent: one may hold or not, but the other must still be satisfied; i.e., second-best considerations (see Jones 2014, Chapter 6, section 4) do not imply that departure from the other optimality condition is required. It is possible that a society's institutional arrangements for allocating output among generations inefficiently violates the intertemporal allocation condition, but production efficiency would still require satisfaction of the interest rate-marginal product of capital condition.

Returning to the Cobb-Douglas production function and logarithmic utility function used to examine the stability of the steady-state equilibrium above, this relationship is $r = \frac{(1-\varepsilon_L)(2+\rho)(1+n)}{\varepsilon_L} - \delta$. Olivier Blanchard and Stanley Fischer have substituted representative values into this formula to assess the possibility for economies being efficient or inefficient relative to this golden age standard. With periods lasting 30 years, a labor share (ε_L) of 0.75, $\delta = 5\%$ per year ($1 - 0.95^{30} = 0.785$), 1% per year population growth (implying $n = 1.01^{30} - 1 = 0.348$), and rate of time preference (ρ) of 3% per year ($1.03^{30} - 1 = 1.427$), the (30-year) interest rate calculated with this formulation is 75.4%, which is larger than the 30-year growth rate of 34.8%. The rate of time preference and the capital depreciation rate are the two parameters with the greatest scope for variation among economies in this formulation. Dropping the time preference rate to 1% per year yields a 30-year interest rate of 26.9%, which is less than the 30-year growth rate. With a steady-state interest rate greater than the population growth rate, which is surely to have characterized all of antiquity, there is under-accumulation of capital, and the economies would have been dynamically inefficient. With a population growth rate of 0.1% per year, the steady state 30-year interest rate would be 39.2% compared to the 30-year growth rate of 3.0%. At the same population growth rate, a depreciation rate of 15% per year, probably more consistent with ancient capital equipment than a 5% per year rate, would drop the 30-year interest rate to 5%, still well above the 30-year growth rate at 0.1% per year.

4.6 Intergenerational Transfers

Reallocations of resources across ages and dates occur in many forms and for a variety of reasons. These reallocations can occur via three principal types of mechanism: capital transactions—accumulation or decumulation of real wealth; credit transactions—borrowing and lending; and transfers—gifts as it were, with no contractual obligations involved. Various institutions are used in such reallocations: markets, governments and families. Although only one of three major reallocation mechanisms, this section deals with intergenerational transfers, primarily as a component of the economics of the family that affects fertility behavior, but also, aggregating across all families, as a component of economy-wide capital accumulation.

Intergenerational transfers are a low-profile topic of surprising importance. In a real sense, they are the glue that holds societies together. Humans have periods of dependence both early and late in life, during which they depend wholly or partly on others for their consumption. Intergenerational transfers can occur through a variety of institutions, but primarily families and governments. Transfers include parental support and education of children; children's support and care for parents during the latter's old age, or more generally the support of an older generation in its old age by a younger generation regardless of blood relationship; and bequests. Age and generation-related transfers are closely related to wealth accumulation:

they can be substitutes for wealth and therefore affect life cycle saving, or the desire to leave bequests, on the other hand, can motivate saving and capital formation. The desire to leave bequests makes children more expensive and tends to depress fertility, while children's support of elderly parents encourages higher fertility. The first sub-section below deals with intergenerational transfers as seen by the utility-maximizing family, and the second places these transfers in the context of a society's overall wealth.

The simplest partial equilibrium analysis of intergenerational transfers is conducted with a model of a utility-maximizing household choosing parents' consumption, the number and quality of children, and bequests parents make to children, the last involving some degree of altruism of parents toward their children.[132] People also may be altruistic toward their parents and include parental support transfers in their utility maximizing consumption choices. In general equilibrium analyses, a number of constraints exist that do not affect individual behavior directly but affect aggregate magnitudes of various kinds of transfers.

4.6.1 Utility-Maximizing Intergenerational Transfers at the Individual Level: Partial Equilibrium Analysis

The pension motive for having children invokes intergenerational transfers. Abstracting from any utility from having and interacting with children, parents in this model have children purely so they can be supplied with consumption during the older, non-working period of their lives. The trade-off of interest is between current consumption and future consumption, when children, which reduce current consumption but supply future consumption, are the means of producing retirement consumption. It is most likely true that the concept of retirement is an anachronism in antiquity, but older individuals lost strength, sometimes became disabled, and generally became capable of producing less than they did in their prime working years and looked to adult children to help them survive through their declining years.

In a three-period overlapping generations model consisting of a dependent childhood, a productive parenthood and a dependent grandparenthood, a life cycle gives rise to an optimal stock of children from the parent's point of view and they conduct their fertility behavior accordingly.[133] The only property is land, and rights to it are vested in families. Income is distributed on a share-alike basis, and goods cannot be carried over to periods following the period they were produced.[134] Since goods can't be stored, the only way to consume in retirement is via transfer from the working generation to the retired generation. These transfers are assured by an unwritten but continuing intergenerational contract. The direct decision variable is fertility rather than an intergenerational transfer, since the latter implies the former. The population, P, at any date is composed of children, S, parents, F, and grandparents, G: $P = S + F + G$. Parents make fertility decisions at the beginning of period 2. They look forward to one full period of work and one full period of retirement and dependency. The parents are dead in the third period, but they may have some concern for the state of the world in period 3, so their utility function includes three periods during which their children are alive. Their concern for the future is represented by a utility of consumption of their children in the third period. Parents choose children, S_1, to maximize the utility function $U = u(c_1) + D \cdot u(c_2) + E \cdot u(c_3)$, $u' = \mu > 0$, $u'' < 0$, where D and E are discount factors, the former representing farsightedness and the latter altruism, subject to the constraints of production conditions, the share-alike ethic, the fertility of future generations, and inter-period mortality. Production is characterized by $X = f(F)$, with marginal product equal to average product equal to the wage rate which is equal to output divided by labor inputs: $MP_L = AP_L = w = X/F$. Fertility of future generations is exogenous to the current-period decision makers. Inter-period mortality is defined by p, the probability that a child, S, survives to become a parent, P; q is the probability that a parent survives to grandparenthood, G. For example, $F_2 = pS_1$, and $G_2 = qF_3 = pqS_1$. Thus consumption in period 1 is $c_1 = \bar{X}/P_1 = f(\bar{F}_1)/s1 + \bar{F}_1 + \bar{G}_1$, where the bars over variables denote variables that are exogenous; so in period 1, the number of grandparents has been determined in the past. Similarly consumption in period 2 is $c_2 = X_2/P_2 = f(pS_1)/\bar{S}_2 + pS_1 + q\bar{F}_1$, in which a different set of variables has been determined in the past, and third-period consumption is $c_3 = \bar{X}_3/P_3 = f(p\bar{S}_2)/\bar{S}_3 + p\bar{S}_2 + pqS_1$.

The share-alike ethic compels the first-period product, $\bar{X}_1$, produced by the existing parents, $\bar{F}_1$, to be shared equally with the retired grandparents, $\bar{G}_1$, and however many children, $\bar{S}_1$, the period-one parents choose to have. Consumption in the first period rises as the number of children, S_1, falls: $\Delta c_1/\Delta S_1 = -c_1/P_1 < 0$, and is maximized by having no children. In the second period, per capita consumption increases as more workers are added, as long as the marginal product of labor, $MP_L = w > c = X/P$ (not X/F since the entire population consumes): $\Delta c_2/\Delta S_1 = p(w_2 - c_2)/P_2$. Period 2 consumption is zero of $S_1 = 0$, and it rises to the point where the marginal contribution of an additional worker equals average consumption ($w_2 > c_2$), and falls thereafter. Per capita consumption in the third period falls with larger numbers of children born in the first period: $\Delta c_3/\Delta/S_1 = -pqc_3/P_3$. A given amount of third-period output yields less per-capita consumption with a larger retired generation.

Equilibrium requires that $\Delta U/\Delta S_1 = 0$. Using this condition and the three relationships between first-period fertility and consumption in all three periods, an

---

[132] Models without altruistic behavior do not suppose that parents truly are not altruistic toward their children, but rather are a step toward examining the consequences of altruism by studying behavioral choices in the absence of altruism.

[133] The model is that of Neher (1971).

[134] Hardwiring this income distribution rule eliminates an intergenerational transfer as an independent variable and effectively replaces it with the fertility decision, which determines how many mouths there will be to feed in various time periods, allowing for the generational mortality effects.

equilibrium condition can be derived relating consumption per capita to output per worker. In a steady state with a stable population, $c^* = p/(1 + p + pq) \cdot (X/F)^*$, in which the asterisk denotes a variable's value in the steady state. Steady state consumption per capita, c^*, reaches its maximum when $w = X/F$. From this relationship and another relating the maximized steady-state wage rate to the maximized steady-state consumption per capita, a further relationship can be derived that combines the conditions for economic and demographic equilibrium—at which the parents are satisfied with the number of children they have and the population is stationary): $\hat{w}^* = J \cdot (\hat{X}/F)^*$, in which the "hat" notations indicate an optimal value, and $J = (1/D) \cdot (1 + pD + pqE)/(1 + p + pq)$, in which the discount rates for the second and third periods affect the optimal wage rate in opposite directions: $J_D < 0$ and $J_E > 0$. J is a combination of inter-period survival rates, p and q, and discount factors applied to future utilities, D and E. If $J = 1$, the population will attain the maximum sustainable level of income per capita, which will occur if $D = (1 + pqE)/(1+ pq)$. If parents weight their utilities while working and while retired equally and have an equal regard for their children's utility, $D = E = 1$, and $J = 1$. If parents don't care about their children at all other than by sharing consumption equally with them, $E = 0$, and $J = (1 + p)/(1 + P + pq) < 1$, and overpopulation will exist, in the sense that labor's marginal product is less than its average product, although the degree of overpopulation would depend on characteristics of the production function and the magnitude of intergenerational mortality.

4.6.2 Transfers in the Two-Period OLG Model[135]

Consider an economy in which identical individuals live for two periods. In each period there is an old generation and a young generation in proportions determined by population growth. If the fertility rate is N children per parent (ignoring sex distinctions), the ratio of young to old is F and the population growth rate is $n = N - 1$ per generation. Each individual is endowed with Y_1 units of perishable consumption good when young and Y_2 units when old. For example, endowment $(Y_1, Y_2) = (8, 2)$ corresponds to endowment a in Figure 4.17, in which the horizontal axis measures consumption of young individuals, C_1. The vertical axis measures the consumption of old individuals, C_2. Supposing a case in which the young are less productive than the old, an alternative endowment might be $(Y_1, Y_2) = (3, 12)$, designated by point b in Figure 4.17. Without any transactions, each individual in each generation will consume his endowment in each life period, achieving the level of lifetime utility indicated by the indifference curve passing through his endowment point. Endowment points a and b in Figure 4.17 each provide the same lifetime utility.

Suppose the population doubles each generation. Also suppose that the endowment is point a in Figure 4.17. It would be feasible for each person in every generation to

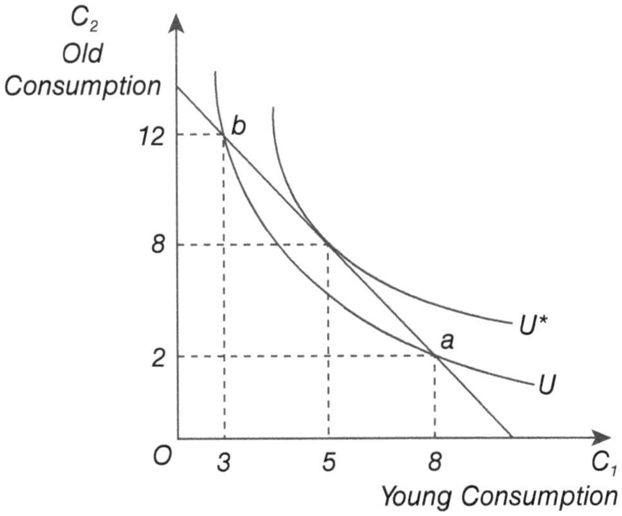

Figure 4.17. Consumption of the old versus consumption of the young (Reproduced from Willis 1982, figure 1, p. 211, by permission of Wiley.).

achieve a life-cycle consumption path anywhere along the straight line passing through points a, g, and b in Figure 4.17. Since this line determines all feasible consumption paths, it can be called the social budget constraint. For example, assume that in each period a levy of 3 units of consumption is applied to each young person and that the proceeds are transferred to the old. Since there are twice as many young as old, each old individual receives a transfer of 6 units. The post-transfer age distribution of consumption is $C_1 = 8 - 3 = 5$ and $C_2 = 2 + (2 \cdot 3) + 8$, which corresponds to point g in Figure 4.17. Given that population growth, endowments, and the levy and transfer program remain the same in the next period, point g also corresponds to the consumption that each young person expects to follow during his life. More rapid population growth poses a smaller burden on a younger generation supporting an older generation at a given level of well-being.

Of all the points along the social budget constraint, the highest attainable level of utility for members of each generation is reached at point g, where U* is tangent to the constraint. In this example, the direction of intergenerational transfers required to reach this maximum level of utility is from the younger to the older generation. If the endowment point were at b instead of a, the direction of transfers required to reach point g would be reversed. A feature of the social budget constraint is that the rate of interest is equal to the population growth rate along the constraint. The interest rate is r, and a young person who foregoes one unit of consumption can increase his old age consumption by 1+r units. Since the social budget constraint indicates the trade-off between current and future consumption, its slope is equal to $1 + r$ in absolute value. Then the social budget constraint in Figure 4.17 can be interpreted as the wealth constraint of an individual born in any period t. Thus, each point on the constraint satisfies the relationship $Y_{1t} = Y_{2t}/1 + r = C_{1t} + C_{2t+1}/1 + r$, which says that the present discounted value of an individual's

[135] This section relies heavily on Willis (1982). For convenience, I have used the numbers in his Figure 1, 211, without change.

life-cycle income and consumption streams are equal when these streams are discounted at the interest rate $r = n$.

If there were a competitive market in which individuals could borrow or lend at the market rate of interest, a typical young individual facing the wealth constraint in Figure 4.17 would maximize lifetime utility, moving from U to U* at point g on the constraint line. If his (her) endowment were at a, a young person would lend 3 units of his endowment at the interest rate of 100 percent; in old age, he (she) would use the principal and interest to increase his consumption by 6 units above his endowment. Alternatively, if his endowment were at b, he would borrow 2 units when young and decrease his old age consumption by 4 units to repay the principal and interest on the loan.

According to ordinary accounting principles, a lender has a positive credit that is offset by the negative credit or liability of the borrower. Later, when the transaction has been completed, the borrower's liability is discharged by the payment of his debt. In this light, both of the cases described above are a puzzle. In the case in which all young people want to lend, they have a positive credit balance. Who are the borrowers on the other side of the transaction to whom the offsetting liability can be assigned. They can't be the current old people, who will be dead in the next period and in no position to repay their debt. The only people who could repay the loan are the young of the next period who are currently unborn. Thus it is the unborn who have an aggregate liability that offsets the aggregate credit of this period. However the unborn young of the next period cannot meet with the young of the current period to sign a loan contract. This barrier to intergenerational trade can be overcome by a pay-as-you-go social security system. The current old contend that they are not welfare recipients, but that they are entitled to these payments in exchange for the levies they paid in the past. Effectively, the current young incurred a liability before they were born that they are morally bound to discharge by paying a levy now. If the young live up to the terms of this social contract, they will simultaneously discharge their liability to the current old and impose a liability on the unborn young of the next period.

In the reverse case, the young would want to be borrowers at the interest rate $r = n$, their aggregate credit balance is negative, and it could be offset by an aggregate positive credit balanced of the unborn young of the next period. In such a case, the old of this period discharge their aggregate liability by making transfers to the young.

Voluntary transactions, institutions, and the like must improve the well-being of all or at least leave some no worse off while benefiting the others. In a case such as the endowment at point a, both young and old can be made better off by a move to point g. In the case of an endowment like point b, transfers from the old to the young would be required to reach point g, and the old would be made worse off by carrying out the transfer, and voluntary private markets would not be able to sustain such loans.

Which situation, point a or point b, is more likely to be the case in non-industrial societies? A key relationship involves the mean age of consumption, a_c, and the mean age of production, a_y, i.e., the mean ages at which individuals consume their lifetime wealth and produce their lifetime wealth. In circumstances in which the productivity of both human and physical capital are low, at any given rate of population growth, the mean age of producing tends to be low, because people can begin to produce when quite young; little formal training is required. People begin producing more than they consume at relatively young ages. If high mortality rates don't reduce a_y by more than a_c, a population's aggregate credit balance, the sum of the individual credit balances of all individuals, is more likely to be positive, and the net direction of intergenerational transfers is more likely to be from the younger generation to the older generation. The value of transfers made from the younger generation to the older reduces the net costs of child rearing from the parents' point of view.

4.6.3 Transfers in an Economy-Wide Reallocation System: General Equilibrium Analysis of Intergenerational Transfers[136]

An accounting framework for flows into and out of the budget of a household or an individual of age x at date t uses a net reallocation system g(x, t), which is composed of schedules of gross flows, $g^{+}(x, t)$ and $g^{-}(x, t)$, into (+) or out of (−) a household or individual budget, at that date. Examples of g(x, t) are labor income or savings, but in general this accounting system handles a flow, or change in a stock, of any resource. This system permits calculation of redistribution over time, or longitudinally, for a cohort born at date t_0, by summing $g(x, t_0 + x)$ for $x = 0$ to ω, which takes an individual from birth to some maximum age ω, as well as across ages at a given date, or cross-sectionally, by summing $g(x, t_0)$ across all ages. The longitudinal, or life-cycle calculation defines the expectation of net receipts beginning at birth and extending over the expected life span of the individual or household: $PV(g,t) = \sum_0^{\omega} \frac{p(x,t+x)g(x,t+x)}{(1+r_t)^t}$, in which p(x, t) is the probability that a person born x years ago is still alive at date t and r_t is the interest rate at date t.The cross-sectional calculation is $Pop(g,t) = \frac{1}{P_t} \sum_0^{\omega} B(t-x)p(x,t)g(x,t)$, in which P_t is total population at date t, and B(t) is the flow of births at date t, such that the calculation B(t − x) is the sum of births over all ages born prior to date t.

A reallocation system is called life-cycle balanced if PV(g,t) = 0 at every date t and is called population balanced if Pop(g,t) = 0 for every date t. Life-cycle balance implies that over a lifetime, a person's consumption and income are equal, while population balance implies that flows add to zero at any given date. A 4-way classification can be made, depending on whether PV(g,t) = 0 or ≠ 0 and whether Pop(g,t) = 0 or ≠ 0. Allocations which obey the longitudinal constraint, i.e., satisfy PV(g,t) = 0, are called

136 The model of this section comes from Lee (2000) and Bommier and Lee (2003).

competitive reallocations because they can be sustained by selfish maximizing behavior over the life cycle subject to the life cycle budget constraint. Allocations that obey the cross-sectional constraint, i.e., satisfy Pop(g,t) = 0, are called conservative reallocations since the age-specific flows neither augment nor deplete the societal stock of goods but rather conserves its level. If the interest rate r equals the population growth rate n, a conservative reallocation is also competitive and vice versa.[137] For transfer systems, Pop(g) must be zero because transfer systems rearrange existing output of a given date among individuals and age groups and are therefore conservative, but in general PV(g) $\neq$ 0 for transfer systems, so they are not competitive. The implicit rate of return on a transfer system involving children supporting aged parents equals the population growth rate, which is usually less than the interest rate, making PV(children supporting aged parents) negative. For all transfers, Pop(transfers) = 0 and PV(transfers) $\neq$ 0. A reallocation system with PV(g) $\neq$ 0 and Pop(g) $\neq$ 0 is a mixture of transfers and credit or capital transactions.

Credit transactions also involve a reallocation of resources among age groups at any date, so Pop(credit) = 0, but PV(credit = 0 also because borrowing and lending takes place at market interest rates. Therefore credit transactions are both competitive and conservative. In capital formation in competitive economies, the result of saving and net investment, PV(investment) = 0 because credit markets are an alternative for savings, so the expected interest rate should equal the rate of return on capital, but in a steady state the capital stock grows at the same rate as population, so Pop(investment) = nK > 0, where K is the average level of capital per person. Consequently investment in real capital is competitive but not conservative.

Average wealth associated with any g is a fundamental part of this accounting system. Wealth of individuals of a given age is the expected present value of future flows of g.[138] For the entire population, the average wealth is the population-weighted average across all ages of these expected present values: $w_g(x,t) = \sum_x^{\omega} \frac{p(u,t+u-x)}{p(x,t)} \frac{g(u,t+u-x)}{(1+r_t)^x}$; cohort or individual wealth at age 0, $w_g(0,t)$ equals PV(g). Aggregate wealth per capita at date t, W(g,t) equals Pop(w_g).

The wealth held in any reallocation system is equal to the size of the per capita flow in the population times the difference between the average age at which people receive inflows or benefits and the average age at which they make payments into the system. In general, $G = g(A_{g^+} - A_{g^-})$, where G is the wealth held in a particular system, g is the average gross reallocation in the population, and A is the average age in the population at which a gross flow takes place: e.g., $A_{g^+} = Pop[xg^+(x)]/Pop(g^+(x)]$. Life-cycle wealth, W(x) = c(A_c − A_y) where A_c is the average age of consumption and A_y is the average age of production, is the amount of wealth or debt accumulated to age x, given the consumption profile c(x) and the labor earnings profile y_ℓ.[139] Averaged across the population, this calculation gives average life-cycle wealth in the population.

A fundamental result is that wealth is the sum of capital and transfers (the aggregate credit balance is zero): W = K + T. Capital is productive and raises output while transfer wealth has no such effect, so the composition of wealth is a matter of considerable concern to a society. Transfer wealth breaks the link between capital accumulation and waiting to consume, so W = K is no longer necessary. In the pre-industrial societies Lee examined, lifetime wealth was uniformly negative, as average ages of consumption are greater than average ages of production: the average person desires to hold negative wealth, or debt, to achieve the desired smoothing of life cycle consumption. The high proportion of young in these societies, despite the putatively young ages of entry to work and productivity differentials between children and adults, outweighs the tendency for elderly to keep working, even at lower productivity, yielding a consistent higher average age of consumption than of production. Thus, resources tend to flow from older ages to younger ages in these societies, in contrast to Caldwell's (1976) influential, but largely unmeasured, thesis to the contrary, which plays a critical role in his theory of demographic transition.[140]

Simple transference to a blanket array of ancient circumstances of Caldwell's assumption of net upward (young to old) income transfers in traditional societies, or Lee's more recent finding of the ubiquity of net downward flows in traditional societies, or of the more circumscribed observations of children's support of aged parents in those societies would not be warranted, although each of the contentions or findings can inform research on ancient cases.[141] It is known that individuals began producing earlier in life in antiquity than they do presently. Current evidence on just how much younger and at what net productivity (debiting supervision of parents and other elders) appears spotty. Similarly with support of aged parents: how long did parents continue to work, and at

---

[137] The coincidence of competitive and conservative reallocations when r = n is not readily apparent from the exposition given above, but derives from an alternative exposition in which $\frac{1}{P_t} \sum B(t-x)$ is constructed from a summation using the growth rate n rather than the birth rate b.

[138] This life-cycle definition of wealth is an expectation, which contrasts with the concepts of assets used by Gale (1973) and Willis (1988).

[139] While this simple but powerful result is derived for the (generally unlikely) case of r = n (the interest rate equals the population growth rate), Bommier and Lee (2003, 143) derive the same result for the more general case of r $\neq$ n.

[140] Even if Caldwell is incorrect empirically in contending that transfers flow from young to old in traditional societies, families in those societies could still use children as a vehicle to provide for old-age support, and consequently it can be economically rational for one or both parents to want higher fertility "as the best deal around," despite the likelihood of very low and even negative rates of return on children as investments: Lee (2000, 46–47).

[141] Parkin (2003, 204) offers a classification of types of support—essentially transfers—to the elderly but in the remainder of Chapter 8 reports that the elderly of ancient Greece and Rome generally received only familial transfers, occasionally bolstered by laws (more in Athens than in the Roman world outside Egypt); the possibility of some tax relief to children in Roman Egypt supporting elderly parents (171–172, 212) stands out as a sole incidence of even an implicit public transfer.

what productivity, and how common were debilitating accidents or diseases that did not kill outright? The current literature on intergenerational transfers offers frameworks for research on these issues in antiquity but no empirical answers.

The intuition of negative wealth yielded by a young age composition begs for further explanation. Of the three components of the wealth identity, $K > 0$ is the only necessary sign; physical capital is necessarily positive. When transfers from parents to children are large ("downward," such that $T < 0$), it is possible that (negative) transfers T are larger in absolute value than (negative wealth), and using those negative values, with $T < W$ meaning that transfers are large negative than wealth, $W - T = K > 0$. Next, how can capital exist at all when life-cycle wealth is negative? First, adults could save enough over their life cycles to support their consumption during older, less productive years, capital (accumulated savings) substituting for transfers. Second, older people could avoid eating their assets and leave them as bequests to children, the $K > 0$ being exactly offset by a larger negative T. Third, older people could make larger transfers to adult children (larger negative T), allowing their children to accumulate capital, yielding the same effect as the second alternative.

Using a similar demographic-economic accounting model, Arthur and McNicoll (1978, 244) developed an expression for expected lifetime welfare based on mortality and consumption profiles and calculated the impact on welfare of a slightly higher population growth rate. In any growth model, as population grows, capital must be increased if a constant capital-labor ratio is to be maintained, an effect referred to as capital widening (as contrasted to capital deepening, which means increasing the capital-labor ratio rather than just extending that ratio to a larger population or workforce). Accordingly, their expression for the welfare impact includes a term accounting for the capital widening effect as well as the intergenerational transfer effect: $\frac{\Delta W}{\Delta g} = \frac{\Delta U/\Delta c(0)}{b(g)}[\bar{c}(A_c - A_y) - kh(g)]$, in which $\Delta U/\Delta c(0)$ is marginal utility at an initial date, b(g) is the population's birth rate as a function of the growth rate, $\bar{c}$ is steady state optimal consumption, k is the capital-labor ratio, and h(g) is the labor force-population ratio. The effect of a higher population growth on lifetime welfare via the capital-widening route is always negative: a higher growth rate depresses lifetime welfare because consumption must be diverted to investment to maintain a constant capital-labor ratio, but the intergenerational transfer effect could work either way. If $A_c > A_y$, it is possible, but not a foregone conclusion, that the welfare effect of higher population growth could be positive. If $A_c < A_y$, the population growth impact on lifetime welfare is unambiguously negative.

4.7 Population Growth and Economic Growth

The relationships between population growth and economic growth, defined as increase in consumption per capita, have attracted considerable attention. Does population growth retard economic growth or propel it or not have much effect one way or the other? Does the size of a population, regardless of its growth rate, affect economic growth? The first sub-section below reports the phenomena contemporary growth models are trying to explain and the strategies employed recently in that effort. The second sub-section describes several well-known authors' ideas about relationships between population and economic growth. The third sub-section summarizes in some detail several recent economic growth models which incorporate endogenous, utility-maximizing fertility choice. Those models differ in several dimensions: motivations for having children, relationships with mortality, substitutability between number and quality of children, and population-technical change relationships. A summary of lessons from these models concludes this sub-section.

4.7.1 Facts to Be Explained and Changing Explanatory Strategies

By the mid-1990s, economic growth models had set themselves the target of replicating the millennia-long period of little to no economic growth and very close to zero population growth, a combination of what was called Malthusian economic growth (or non-growth, or at least only in the aggregate and not in per capita terms), which gave way to modern economic growth (sustained growth), via a demographic transition from high fertility and high mortality to low fertility and low mortality. It's been a challenge. Since the mid-1980s, economic growth theory has searched for mechanisms to replace the exogenous technological change the Solow-Swan growth model relied upon, and various versions of human capital accumulation have been tapped for that role. Romer's AK model, which relied on non-decreasing returns to capital, essentially because of learning effects contained in capital, a long-standing idea, was the first in this series of capital externalities models, all of which were essentially ad hoc in their appeals to mechanisms that might endogenize growth. The growth model that Galor (2005) dubbed the "unified growth model" relies on the devotion of an economy's resources to human capital production and an externality from population size to the rate of technological change, a dressed-up version of the Boserup notion from the 1960s which has the statistical underpinning that a large population will have a larger number of smart people who generate important ideas, essentially increasing the number of monkeys and typewriters to raise the chance of one of them coming up with one of Shakespeare's plays.[142] In these models, a transition from eons of no growth—the Malthusian situation—to exponential growth depends on unexplained jolts to processes that have operated for centuries or crossing of thresholds, neither of which is explained.

[142] Essentially Phelps' (1968) "Mozart effect."

4.7.2 Hypotheses about Population and Technological Change

Before embarking on an overview of contemporary economic models of endogenous population in current economic growth models, I should at least note the work of Ester Boserup (1965; 1981) modifying the Malthusian model. It has sparked research in economics and other fields (Grigg 1974; 1981, Chapter 4; Darity 1980; Pryor and Maurer 1982;[143] Robinson and Schutjer 1984; Lee 1986; 1988; Simon 1977; 1986; Henrich 2004), although space constraints preclude further discussion here. The economic population-and-growth literature studies directions of altruism, children as investments, and endogenous mortality as they affect growth in population and consumption.

4.7.3 Endogenous Fertility in Models of Economic Growth

Endogenous population growth is not a new feature in models of economic growth, but until the microeconomics of individual fertility decisions had been studied fairly extensively, it was modeled at an aggregate level without specification of how individuals would actually behave. Such aggregate modeling is adequate when the individual-level decisions are well understood, but when it is not, we are left with the question, "Would people actually behave that way?" By the late 1980s, microeconomic fertility choices were incorporated into models of economic growth that were exploring mechanisms that could produce continuing economic growth without appealing to exogenous technological change. The early models, such as those of Becker-Barro (1988) (BB), Barro-Becker (1989) (B-B), and Becker, Murphy and Tamura (1990) (BMT), gained early prominence and have been visible to unsuspecting classicists fishing in foreign waters, but had substantive deficiencies upon probing. For example, when the Becker-Barro model is expanded into a growth model, the general equilibrium version, in which the interest rate is endogenous, yields the result that when the infant mortality rate (IMR) falls, fertility rises: the reduction in IMR translates into a reduction in the cost of child rearing, which increases the interest rate, in which case it pays to invest more in the future with a larger family. In a partial equilibrium setting, this doesn't happen, but the general equilibrium case parallels the real world. BMT grafts the BB dynastic utility model onto the Lucas (1992) human-capital-as-ultimate-source-of-growth model, but creates a model in which population and per capita consumption do not grow consistently: the model can produce a steady-state non-growth path, but along this path, fertility is high while mortality is not modeled. Implicitly, population growth would be explosive rather than stagnant. Further, BMT relies on non-decreasing returns to education, which is contrary to empirical findings. BMT ultimately relies on blind chance to move an economy from a millennium-long Malthusian static economic situation to an exponential economic growth path, which means that the model has nothing to tell us about long-term economic growth, and possibly nothing general about short-term growth.

An alternative type of growth model relies on two production sectors making the same composite good with different technologies, one called "Malthusian," which uses land as well as labor and capital, the other called "Solow," which uses labor and capital but not land, a dichotomy reflecting rural versus urban production (Hansen and Prescott 2002). The fixed supply of land, together with the absence of technological change affecting production processes using it, gives rise to decreasing returns to scale, which is why the land-using sector is called "Malthusian." While the original version of this model specified exogenous population growth, a recent extension has incorporated a Barro-Becker utility function that allows endogenous fertility with exogenous mortality to try to replicate a demographic transition as well as an industrial revolution (Bar and Leukhina 2010). In contrast to the popular endogenous growth models, which typically rely on ad hoc mechanisms to obtain continuing growth, this two-sector model relies on exogenous productivity growth. The transfer of activity from one sector to another does not appear to characterize long-term growth (or lack thereof) in antiquity. I only mention this type of model to alert students of antiquity who might encounter it by chance and be tempted to cite conclusions from it as relevant to ancient circumstances.

However, a number of models have been built on the foundation of these earlier models and have more closely addressed the long-term trends of economic growth and fertility, making serious efforts to replicate the demographic transition as well as a shift from the long-term absence of growth of consumption per capita to continuing economic growth.

The Parental Altruism Model. This model uses the Becker and Barro dynastic fertility model as the heart of a growth model. A family's optimal choice is made jointly with decisions about consumption, intergenerational transfers and capital accumulation, in a closed economy in which interest rates and wage rates are determined simultaneously with fertility, consumption, and saving. The model is a 2-period OLG model of childhood and adulthood. As with the Becker and Barro formulation, it abstracts from marriage and birth spacing. Parents' utility depends on their own consumption and on the number of children and the utility of each: $U_i = v(c_i) + a(n_i)n_iU_{i+1}$, in which c_i is the parents' own consumption, $v(c_i)$ is the utility they receive from this consumption, n_i is the number of children they have, $a(n_i)$ is the degree of altruism toward each child, and U_{i+1} is the utility of each of their children. The model relies on a constant-elasticity simplification of the altruism function in which $a(n_i) = \alpha(n_i)^{-\varepsilon}$, with $0 < \alpha < 1$ and $0 < \varepsilon < 1$, the latter restriction guaranteeing that, for given utility

[143] Pryor was the economics graduate student caught behind the Berlin wall in *The Bridge of Spies*, starring Tom Hanks.

per child, parental utility increases with the number of children but at a diminishing rate.[144] Substituting through the various generations of descendant children yields the dynastic utility function, $U_0 = \sum_{i=0}^{\infty} \alpha^i (N_i)^{1-\varepsilon} v(c_i)$, in which $N_i = \prod_{i=0}^{i-1} n_j$ for i = 1,2, . . . is the total number of descendants in generation i and $N_0 = 1$. The consumption portion of utility is simplified with a constant elasticity of v with respect to consumption c, $v(c_i) = (c_i)^{\sigma}$, where $\sigma < 1$.

Each adult has available a single unit of labor and earns wage w_i for time supplied to the market. Parents bequeath nondepreciable capital in amount k_{i+1} to each child, which may be in the form of human capital, at the beginning of the child's adulthood. Capital i earns rent at the rate r_i. The budget constraint of an adult in generation i is $w_i + (1 + r_i)k_i = c_i + n_i(\beta_i + k_{i+1})$, where β_i is real child rearing costs per child. Thus an adult has a full income of w_i, even though some of his or her time is spent in child rearing, to which is added the principal and interest of the inheritance from her own parents, and allocates these resources among consumption, direct child-rearing costs and bequests to each child. The adult maximizes the dynastic utility function subject to the budget constraint, by choosing paths of consumption, capital stock per adult, and number of descendants, taking the paths of wage rates w_i and interest rates r_i as given. For an adult to choose non-zero children, $\sigma + \varepsilon < 1$. The first-order condition from choosing the consumption path is $(c_{i+1}/c_i)^{1-\sigma} = \alpha(1 + r_{i+1})/(n_i)^{\varepsilon}$, which characterizes the arbitrage condition for shifting consumption between generations. This condition contains the standard result from intertemporal consumption optimization that the rate of substitution in utility between consumption in adjoining period depends on the time-preference factor, α in this case, and the interest rate, but adds the modification that an increase in fertility, n_i, lowers altruism per child, $a(n_i)$, thus increasing the discount on future consumption and shifting consumption toward the present, lower altruism amounting to a higher rate of time preference. Thus, higher fertility among generation i is associated with lower consumption in the next generation for given values of the altruism parameter α and the interest rate facing the next generation, r_{i+1}. The first-order condition resulting from choosing the optimal value of fertility n_i is $v(c_i)(1 - \varepsilon - \sigma) = v'(c_i)[\beta_i - 1(1 + r_i) - w_i]$, in which the marginal benefit of an additional child, on the left-hand side of the expression, balances the net lifetime marginal cost of an additional adult in generation i. Using the constant elasticity specification of the consumption sub-utility function v, this condition can be rewritten and solved for consumption in generation i as $c_i = \frac{\sigma}{1-\varepsilon-\sigma}[\beta_{i-1}(1 + r_i) - w_i]$, i = 1,2, . . . , which shows that an increase in the net cost of creating a descendant in generation i, $\beta_{i-1}(1 + r_i) - w_i$, leads to an increase in consumption per adult, ci, for that generation, and that when people are more costly to produce, it is optimal for each of those people to have a higher consumption level.

The endogeneity of the discount rate in the model makes the intergenerational growth rate of consumption independent of the level of interest rates, and for the same reason, the growth rate doesn't depend on the degree of altruism or time preference denoted by α.

The first-order condition for the optimal consumption pattern can be combined with the re-cast first-order condition for optimal fertility just solved for c_i to solve for the optimal fertility rate as $n_i = [\alpha(1 + r_{i+1})]^{1/\varepsilon}[\frac{\beta_{i-1}(1-r_i)-w_i}{\beta_i(1+r_{i+1})-w_{i+1}}]^{(1-\sigma)/\varepsilon}$. This formulation shows that if β_i, r_i and w_i remain the same across generations, the fertility rate n_i would be higher with increases in the interest rate or in the degree of altruism α. Higher interest rates or greater altruism motivate a family to have more descendants, and fertility is the method and rate of investment that creates these descendants.

To find the full equilibrium of this economy, production must be specified. A single composite good is produced with a constant-returns-to-scale production function with labor-augmenting technical progress, $Y_i = F[K_i, (1+g)^i L_i]$, where Y_i is the output of the good, K_i is capital, or goods accumulated—not consumed—prior to the beginning of generation i, L_i is labor, and g is the exogenous rate of technical progress. Output and capital can be expressed as per-effective-worker: $\hat{y}_i \equiv Y_i/[(1 + g)^i L_i]$ and $\hat{k}_i \equiv K_i/[(1 + g)^i L_i]$, so the production function can be expressed in per-effective-worker terms as $\hat{y}_i = f(\hat{k}_i)$. Output from production is paid as rentals to owners of capital, $r_i K_i$, or as wages to workers, $w_i L_i$. Competitive markets and profit maximization guarantee that r_i equals the marginal product of capital and that w_i equals the marginal product of labor: $r_i = f'(\hat{k}_i)$ and $w_i = [f(\hat{k}_i) - \hat{k}f'(\hat{k}_i)](1 + g)^i$.[145]

Raising children involves household production that requires both time and goods inputs, each child requiring $a(1 + g)^i$ units of goods and b units of parents' time, which is valued at w_i, making the child-rearing cost per child $\beta_i = a(1 + g)^i + bw_i$, with $a \geq 0$ and $0 \leq b < 1$. Including the growth rate of labor productivity in the goods portion of the child rearing cost means that those inputs increase as their prospective productivity as adults (the quality of the quantity-quality distinction in the static fertility model), rises. The effective wage rate and the effective child-rearing cost are defined as $\hat{w}_i \equiv w_i/(1+ g)^i$ and $\hat{\beta}_i \equiv \beta_i/(1+ g)^i$. Since each adult devotes bn_i units of time to raising children, the aggregate time allocated to goods production is $L_i = (1- bn_i)N_i$, which requires multiplying y_i and k_i defined above by $(1 - bn_i)$ to change amounts per adult to amounts per worker, which in turn requires revision of the budget constraint in terms of effective units as well. Next, the same re-definitions are applied to the previous expression for c_i derived from the first-order condition for optimal fertility, and the new expression for $\hat{c}_i$ is substituted into the revised budget constraint, yielding the key relation determining the behavior of $\hat{k}_i$ over time. This

[144] This is a coefficient α times fertility n_i, the latter exponentiated to the power $-\varepsilon$, not α as a function of n_i.

[145] The prime notation associated with the function notation f indicates the sensitivity operation, $\Delta f/\Delta k$.

is a critical relationship because $\hat{w}_i$, $\hat{\beta}_i$, and r_i all depend on $\hat{k}_i$ via the marginal productivity relationships from the production function. Finally, the previous expression for fertility is re-defined similarly. In total, three independent relationships are determined, governing the behavior of $\hat{c}_i$, $\hat{k}_i$, and n_i, which in turn determine $\hat{w}_i$, r_i, and $\hat{\beta}_i$. Since in a steady state $\hat{k}_i$ does not change, and from that, n_i, $\hat{c}_i$, r_i, $\hat{w}_i$, and $\hat{\beta}_i$ also remain unchanged, the relationships derived from the re-definitions noted above are simplified. That for fertility is $n = [\frac{\alpha(1+r)}{(1+g)^{1-\sigma}}]^{1/\varepsilon}$, which defines the intertemporal substitution involved in the steady-state relationship between fertility and the interest rate. In this relationship, steady-state fertility n does not depend on child-rearing cost $\hat{\beta}$; child-rearing costs affect the size of a population but not its growth rate. Under conditions regarding a critical value of the interest rate, which implies a relationship between child-rearing costs, altruism, and the growth rate, and the parameters ε (the elasticity of altruism with respect to number of children) and σ (the elasticity of consumption utility with respect to consumption), a unique steady-state value of $\hat{k}$ will exist. Steady state values on fertility and the interest rate are determined by a pair of relationships, one satisfying the intertemporal substitution condition in the steady-state relationship between fertility and the interest rate, the other the combinations of fertility and the interest rate that satisfy the budget constraint. The former relationship, labeled n_1 in Figure 4.18, slopes upward in n-r space, while the latter relationship, labeled n_2 in the same figure, slopes downward if a higher value of $\hat{k}$, and hence a lower r, is associated with a higher n, i.e., if people spend part of an increase in wealth on having more children. However, this relationship is ambiguous because a higher $\hat{k}$ also induces a substitution effect against children through a higher $\hat{w}$ and hence a higher $\hat{\beta}$. Accordingly, the n_2 curve may have positive stretches that yield multiple intersections with the n_1 schedule, as shown in Figure 4.19, although a small enough value of b, the time requirement of child rearing, will keep the slope negative because it limits the effect that a change in the value of time can have on the demand for child.

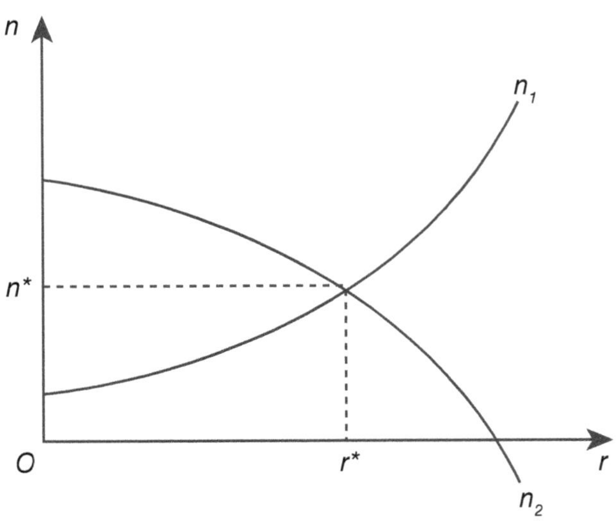

Figure 4.18. Determination of steady-state values of interest rate r and fertility rate n. Curve n_1 shows the combinations of the interest rate, r, and the fertility rate, n, that satisfy the intertemporal-substitution condition. Curve n_2 shows the combinations that satisfy the combination of the intertemporal budget constraint and the determination of consumption. (Reproduced from Barro and Becker 1989, figure 1, p. 489, by permission of Wiley.).

Many economic disturbances are equivalent to changes in initial conditions, represented by k_0, without changes in other parameters: wars, natural disasters or epidemics could alter the existing capital stock or population without affecting the altruism parameters (α and ε), the growth rate g, or child-rearing costs (a and b). If some event sharply reduced population but left the capital stock intact, the new capital-labor ratio $\hat{k}_0$ would exceed the unchanged steady-state value $\hat{k}$. The model's transition from $\hat{k}_0 > \hat{k}$ to $\hat{k}$ would involve temporarily higher consumption per person and fertility if the positive income effect on the demand for children dominated the negative substitution effect deriving from the temporarily high wage rate. A shock that destroyed capital but left population largely intact would lead to a value of $\hat{k}_0 < \hat{k}$, and the economy would experience temporary consumption lower than that in the steady state as well as lower fertility if the income effect from the lower $\hat{k}_0$ dominated the substitution effect of the lower wage.

A change, or difference, in child-rearing costs, $\hat{\beta}$, affects the steady-state $\hat{k}$ and consequently the steady-state interest rate. Higher $\hat{\beta}$ encourages parents to endow each child with more consumption, whereas a higher direct outlay, a, would force a reduction in consumption per person at a given level of $\hat{k}$. Accordingly, parents raise $\hat{k}$. In Figure 4.18, the n_2 curve shifts to the left because $\hat{k}$ is higher (and r is accordingly lower) at a given fertility level. The n_1 curve does not change, so r and n fall. Thus a permanently higher cost of raising children does lead to a lower steady-state population growth rate, but through the indirect channel of a lower interest rate. Differences in child mortality amount

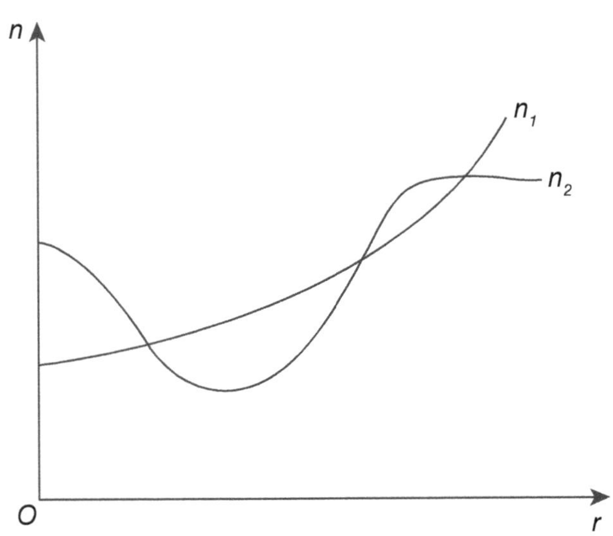

Figure 4.19. Steady-state values of interest rate and fertility rate with multiple steady states. The n_2 curve is modified from Figure 4.18 to allow for multiple intersections with the n_1 curve. (Reproduced from Barro and Becker 1989, figure 2, p. 489, by permission of Wiley.).

to differences in the expected cost of raising a surviving child. A lower child mortality rate would raise the steady-state rate of population growth in this model, which is a problem empirically, since the opposite appears to have been the case, although the Becker and Barro analysis with the dynastic model yields a temporary increase in fertility followed by an eventual reduction.

Jones and Schoonbroodt's (2010) close analysis of the Barro-Becker model indicates that the key problem the B-B model has in replicating a demographic transition, in which fertility responds negatively to an increase in child survival probabilities, is the high degree of intertemporal substitutability in consumption, which has two important implications. First, a high intertemporal elasticity of substitution (IES) implies that family size and child quality are complements in the parents' utility. With a low IES, family size and child quality are substitutes, and increases in productivity growth rates cause population growth rates and fertility to fall substantially. Second, in growth models in general, when the IES is high, reductions in the costs of investment goods are met with large increases in growth rates. The analogue in the Barro-Becker model is the cost of raising surviving children: with a high IES, when infant and child mortality rates fall, the number of surviving children increases substantially and the reduction in fertility is modest. A low IES has the opposite effect: reductions in child mortality rates are met with small increases in fertility and population growth rates and large reductions in birth rates. Jones and Schoonbroodt use the Barro-Becker model but with low IES and generate a sharp reduction in fertility when child mortality falls.

Parents View Children as Investment Goods, with and without Altruism.[146] The model contains three overlapping generations of children, young working parents, and old retired parents. Young parents invest in the number and human capital (quantity and quality) of their children to obtain old-age support, while children are dependent on their parents for support. The model is developed without parental altruism toward children. Young parents form implicit contracts with each child, in which the parent stands to receive an amount of old-age support from each grown child proportional to the stock of human capital the parent had created in the child, $w_{t+1}H_{t+1}$. The compensation rate, w_{t+1}, is determined endogenously. This compensation scheme represents an intergenerational trade in which children compensate parents in strict proportion to the parents' contribution to their incremental productive capacity.

Young parents produce human capital in their children by combining time educating each child, h_t, with their stock of human capital, which is the sum of their native human capital stock $\bar{H}$ and the incremental human capital stock their own parents created in them, H_t: $H_{t+1} = A(\bar{H} + H_t)h_t$, where A is a technology parameter for the conversion of one generation's human capital and time into incremental human capital of the next generation.

Representative agents may not survive through all three stages of the life cycle, so the actual cost to adult children and the expected benefits to surviving old parents are uncertain. The exogenous probabilities of an agent's survival to young and old adulthood are π_1 and π_2, so the expected benefit to a surviving old parent is $\pi_1 n_t w_{t+1} H_{t+1}$, where n_t is the number of children the old parent had as a young parent at date t, and the expected cost to each young adult is $\pi_2 w_t H_t$. If this insurance scheme applied to an extended family whose members agreed to mutually assist one another in the event of random individual deaths prior to the end of old age, these expected costs and benefits could be treated as actuarially fair implicit contracts. In such a circumstance, the budget constraint of a representative young adult at time t is $c_1(t) = (\bar{H} + H_t)(1 - vn_t - h_t n_t) - \pi_2 w_t H_t$, where v ($0 < v < 1$) is the proportion of his or her time a young adult must spend to raise a child, exclusive of time spent in creating human capital for the child. In this formulation, the young adult does not save other than through investment in children's human capital; this specification can be modified to incorporate saving in addition to investment in children. The term $1 - vn_t - h_t n_t$ is the proportion of a young parent's time devoted to work in the labor market or the family farm or family business, i.e., all productive time not spent raising or educating children. The young parent's consumption in period t is also reduced by the requirement to hold back some amount of current consumption to give to his or her aged parent, adjusted by the expectation of that parent's survival to old age. When this young parent is old and retired in the next period, his or her consumption, assuming survival, would be $c_2(t + 1) = \pi_1 n_t w_{t+1} H_{t+1}$. With this extended family insurance scheme, the expected utility of the representative parent is, using an isoelastic[147] utility function $u_t = (\frac{1}{1-\sigma})[c_1(t)^{1-\sigma} - 1] + \delta\pi_2(\frac{1}{1-\sigma})[c_2(t+1)^{1-\sigma} - 1]$, in which σ is the inverse of the intertemporal elasticity of substitution in consumption and δ is a discount factor associated with the rate of time preference ρ such that $\delta = 1/(1 + \rho)$.

The young parent maximizes utility by choosing the optimal values of the number and human capital of their children, $n_t \geq 0$ and $H_{t+1} \geq 0$, taking w_t, w_{t+1} and H_t as given (the compensation rates w_t and w_{t+1} are determined endogenously in a second stage of optimization, and H_t is a fact created in period t − 1). The first-order condition determining the optimal number of children yields the discounted expected rate of return on parental investments in the number of children, $(c_2/c_1)^\sigma \geq \delta(A\pi_1\pi_2 w_{t+1})(\frac{h_t}{v+h_t}) \equiv \delta R_n$, and that for the optimal investment in human capital per child is $(c_2/c_1)^\sigma \geq \delta(A\pi_1\pi_2 w_{t+1}) \equiv \delta R_h$. As long as $w_{t+1} > 0$, the rate of return on investment in children's human capital exceeds that on the number of children. Although equal proportional increases in children's human capital and number of children would yield the same marginal old-age

[146] This model is that of Ehrlich and Lui (1991).

[147] I.e., identical elasticity values at all points along the utility curve.

support benefits, the marginal cost of the number of children includes the cost of both rearing and educating the children while the marginal cost of human capital contains only the educational component. Consequently, the optimal solution requires a corner solution at the lowest possible completed fertility rate, $\pi_1 n$, which must be positive or old age consumption, $c_2(t+1)$, would be zero. Explained alternatively, for parents to obtain a non-zero return on their investment in children's human capital, the number of surviving children must be positive, and since those numbers are discrete, 1 is the smallest possible number of surviving children, and the number of children born must be $n = 1/\pi_1$.

Combining the young-adult and old-adult budget constraints and the first-order condition for investment in children's human capital, the law of motion describing the relationship between the stocks of human capital over time can be derived as $H_{t+1} = a(w_t, w_{t+1})H_t + b(w_{t+1})$, in which a and b are intricate expressions involving survival probabilities, compensation rates, the number of children and the time requirement of raising a child, and the intertemporal elasticity of substitution. The coefficient a is the rate of growth of human capital. The parent chooses w_{t+1} so as to maximize the child's utility, the first-order condition from adjusting w_{t+1} yielding $\Delta u_{t+1}/\Delta w_{t+1} = 0$, which from substitutions $(1 - vn)(1 - \sigma)A = \pi_2 w_{t+1}[A + \sigma(\delta A \pi_1^{1-\sigma} \pi_2 w_{t+1}^{1-\sigma})^{1/\sigma}]$, which provides a unique solution for w_{t+1}, implying that the optimal compensation rate is independent of the level of human capital H_t but generally inversely related to the exogenous determinants of the discounted rate of return on investment in human capital, $\delta A \pi_1 \pi_2$. If the coefficient $a \geq 1$, the economy reaches a steady-state growth equilibrium. If $a < 1$, the economy converges to a non-growing steady-state equilibrium with $H_t = b/(1 - a) > 0$. Thus, the optimal compensation rate derived from the first-order condition for w_{t+1} maximizes the marginal growth rate of human capital, a, and hence the economy's long-run growth rate. Exogenous increases in longevity through increases in either π_1 or π_2, or both, raise the economy's long-run growth rate, as will an increase in the efficiency of investment, A, a reduction in the rate of time preference (an increase in δ), or a reduction in the cost of rearing children, v. The sensitivity of the long-run growth rate to the survival rate of younger people, π_1, exceeds its sensitivity to the survival rate of older people, π_2 for all values of π_1 and π_2. A rise in the expected longevity of either old or young adults raises parents' expected rate of return on investment in human capital of their children relative to their expected marginal rates of substitution in consumption. While the increase in aging represented by π_2 initially increases the cost to the younger generation of maintaining their parents' generation, this effect is offset by an even greater reduction in the compensation rate w. An increase in the younger survival rate lowers the steady-state fertility, $n = 1/\pi_1$, raises R_h, generating an additional incentive to invest in children's human capital.

Adding an altruism component to the parental utility function offers another motivation for having and investing in children, which loosens the implication of the model with fertility based exclusively on material dependency that the representative parent always chooses the lowest possible fertility level. A companionship function for older adults can be specified as $c_3(t+1) = B(\pi_1 n_t)^{\beta} H_{t+1}^{\alpha}$, where $B = 1$ if young adults honor their parents and $B = 0$ if they don't. $R_h > R_n$ still with this formulation. With this component of the demand for children, the model can trace a demographic transition from high to low fertility as mortality rates fall. If an economy with this altruistic component to the demand for children is in a non-growth steady-state equilibrium and experiences a one-time and permanent increase in younger adults' survival probability, π_1, human capital stock H_{t+1} will increase but may converge to a higher non-growing level or continue to grow. Initially following the increase in π_1, fertility n_t may increase or fall, but if human capital continues to grow, fertility must eventually decline toward its minimal level, and the economy reaches a stable, steady-state growth equilibrium. An increase in π_2 has the same qualitative effects, with the exception that fertility must initially increase. An increase in π_1 increases both R_n and R_h but its direct impact on R_n is lower because the higher π_1 reduces the benefits from companionship relative to old-age consumption, c_3/c_2, which is a more important contributor to R_n. Accordingly, an increase in π_1 initiates an unambiguous increase in human capital in the next generation while fertility may rise or fall. An increase in survival probabilities at older ages, π_2 raises R_n and R_h in the same proportion, requiring fertility to rise initially together with human capital. Conversely, large enough reductions in survival probabilities can shift an economy from a growth equilibrium back to a non-growth equilibrium.

Savings can be incorporated into the model as the direct accumulation of physical capital by allowing the representative young parent to save a fraction s_t of income $\bar{H} + H_t$ during the young-adult period of life, which is then used to produce consumption during old age. Excluding bequests of unused accumulated capital by dying old adults requires older adults to consume all the capital during their retired stage of life. The budget constraints of young and old adults are now $c_1(t) = (\bar{H} + H_t)(1 - vn_t - s_t) - (n_t H_{t+1}/A - \pi_2 w_t H_t$ and $c_2(t+1) = \pi_1 w_{t+1} n_t H_{t+1} + D(\bar{H} + H_t)^{1-m}[(\bar{H} + H_t)s_t]^m$, where the efficiency parameter $D > 0$ and the output elasticity m has the range $0 < m < 1$. The last term in the old-age budget constraint represents a constant-returns-to-scale production function of old age consumption using the human and physical capital resources the old adult possesses. Young adults choose an optimal saving rate st along with the optimal number of and human capital investment in children by maximizing their intertemporal utility function above subject to the constraints of the companionship function and the new budgets. The first-order conditions for optimality become, for savings, $(c_2/c_1)^{\sigma} \geq \delta \pi_2 Dm/s_t^{1-m} \equiv \delta R_s$, for number of children, $(c_2/c_1)^{\sigma} \geq \delta A \pi_1 \pi_2 w(1 + \beta N)(\frac{h_t}{v+h_t}) \equiv \delta R_n$, and for investment in children's human capital, $(c_2/c_1)^{\sigma} \geq \delta A \pi_1 \pi_2 w(1 + \alpha N) \equiv \delta R_h$, in which $N = (c_3^{1-\sigma} c_2^{\sigma})/\pi_1 w n_t H_{t+1}$ is the non-pecuniary component of the rate of return on investment in children, which is a decreasing function of the stock of human capital. The rates of return on physical and human capital must be the same, which implies that savings cannot completely displace investment in children's human capital as a means of providing old-age support. This result is guaranteed by the diminishing marginal productivity of accumulated savings in producing old-age consumption and the existence of the altruistic motive for investing in children represented by the companionship function. Developing the corresponding law of motion for human capital accumulation for this specification of the model, in a balanced growth equilibrium, steady-state values of human capital, physical capital and consumption in the two adult phases of life all grow at the same rate. However, the optimal compensation to parents, w, the intergenerational terms of trade, does not maximize the economy's growth rate represented by the a coefficient of the new law of motion for human capital accumulation, because while w maximizes the old-age support adult children provide to their parents, it does not maximize the contributions to old-age consumption provided by savings. Simulations of the model show that the optimal savings rate is inversely related to π_1 and directly related to π_2, and that the optimal w is inversely related to both π_1 and π_2. Saving and investment in children's human capital are substitutes. The growth rate a is an increasing function of young-age survival π_1 and generally but not necessarily an increasing function of older-age survival π_2: while increases in both π_1 and π_2 increase the incentive to invest in human capital, a higher π_2 raises the optimal saving rate, which is a substitute for investment in children's human capital while a higher π_1 reduces it.

Children Are Altruistic Toward Parents.[148] This 3-period OLG model focuses on the impact of infant and child mortality on fertility choices. Agents live for a maximum of three periods—young (y), middle age (m), and old (o). Only in the middle age period do agents have any productive time. Competitive markets exist for land and labor, and there is no technological progress, although adding exogenous growth in labor productivity does not change any substantive results.

People born in period t can reproduce in the succeeding period, t + 1, when they choose the number of children per capita, f_{t+1}. With N^m_{t+1} middle aged people alive, $f_{t+1}N^m_{t+1} = N^y_{t+1}$ children are born in period t + 1. The amount of current consumption required to care for one child is $\theta_t = a + bw_t$, where w_t is the wage rate in period t, which captures the consumption and unit time costs, a and b, of rearing a child. The total resources required for rearing children in any period t is $N^m_t \cdot \theta_t \cdot f_t$.

The mortality rate of young people is given by $m^y_t \in [0, 1)$, which means that the range includes zero but is strictly less than 1; it is the total mortality rate between birth and the attainment of working age. For this version of the model, middle-aged mortality is zero, and the old-age mortality rate is always 1. Thus in a period t + 1, the number of old people is equal to the number of middle aged people in the previous period while the number of middle aged people is equal to $f_t(1 - m^y_t)$ times the number of middle aged people in the previous period. The probability of a young person born in period t surviving to middle age in period t + 1 is $\pi_t = 1 - m^y_t$. Then total population at t + 1 is $N_{t+1} = N^y_{t+1} + N^m_{t+1} + N^o_{t+1}$, and the population growth rate is $1 + g^n_t = \frac{N_{t+1}}{N_t} = f_{t-1}\pi_{t-1} \cdot \frac{1+(1+f_{t+1})f_t\pi_t}{1+(1+f_t)f_{t-1}\pi_{t-1}}$, so along a balanced growth path, $1 + g_n = \pi \cdot f$.

Total consumable output in any period t is $Y_t = F(L_t, K_t)$, where $K_t = K_{t-1} + N^m_{t-1}s_{t-1}$ is the stock of land and capital and $L_t = N^m_t$ is the labor supply form middle aged people. The resources saved and invested to create new capital, s_t, is converted into new capital at a constant 1-to-1 rate; allowing for decreasing returns in investment technology complicates analysis and adds little to insights. The aggregate resource constraint is $Y_t \geq N^o_t \cdot c^o_t + N^m_t \cdot (c^m_t + s_t) + N^y_t \cdot \theta_t$, or total output is at least equal to the sum of elderly consumption, the consumption and saving of the middle aged, and the child care requirements of the young. An additional definition is the capital-labor ratio in production, $k_t = \frac{K_t}{L_t} = \frac{K_t}{N^m_t}$, and an accounting identity specifies the relationship between the current capital stock and the previous generation of savers, $x_t = \frac{K_t}{N^o_t} = \frac{K_{t-1} + N^m_{t-1}s_{t-1}}{N^m_{t-1}} = k_{t-1} + s_{t-1} = \pi_{t-1}f_{t-1}k_t$, which gives the relationship between the capital-labor ratio in production, individual saving, and fertility along a balanced growth path (along which k_t, s_t, f_t, and π_t are constant over time, allowing the time subscript to be dropped from them) that $k^* = s^*/(\pi f^* - 1)$, in which the asterisks denote optimal steady-state levels (mortality is exogenous).

Contrary to the purely altruistic model, children derive utility from their parents' consumption in this model. Assuming that consumption during childhood does not affect lifetime utility, the lifetime utility of a person born in period t−1, and hence a middle-aged worker during period t, is $U_{t-1} = u(c^m_t) + \eta u(c^o_t) + \delta U(c^o_{t+1})$, which says that he or she derives utility from own consumption during period t when middle aged, from parents' consumption during their old age in period t, and own consumption when old in period t + 1, discounted at rate δ; $\eta(0 < \eta < 1)$ represents the weight that children place on parental consumption. Children have no independent budget constraint, but as young working adults (with a single unit of labor time), the budget constraint is $d^i_t + c^m_t + s_t + \theta_t f_t \leq w_t$, where d^i_t is the donation of a middle aged person to his or her parents, and the index i in the superscript indicates the child. When old, the budget constraint is $c^o_t \leq \sum_{i=1}^{n^m_t} d^i_t + R_t x_t$, where $n^m_t = N^m_t / N^o_t = f_{t-1}\pi_{t-1}$ is the number of surviving children per old person, and R_t is the rate of return on capital (or the combination of land and capital otherwise not distinguished) in terms of consumable output net of the undepreciated stock of capital, the old of period t inheriting the full existing stock of capital from their parents who died at the end of the previous period.

---

[148] This model is that of Boldrin and Jones (2002).

Two alternative patterns of adult children's support of parents are explored, what are called cooperative and non-cooperative. In the cooperative solution, the middle-aged children maximize their utilities on the assumption that the parent's consumption, and their utility therefrom, is boosted by equal donations of all siblings. In the non-cooperative solution, each adult child takes the other siblings' contributions as given and maximizes his or her utility by adjusting her own contribution. Whenever the number of surviving children is greater than 1, the cooperative solution yields a higher individual donation and higher consumption for the parents.

The middle-aged individual's planning problem is $max_{s_t, f_t, d_t^i} u(c_t^m) + \delta u(c_{t+1}^o) + \eta u(c_t^o)$, subject to the individual's t− and t + 1-period budget constraints, $c_t^m + \theta_t f_t + d_t^i + s_t \leq w_t$ and $c_{t+1}^o \leq \sum_{i=1}^{n_{t+1}^m} d_t^i + R_{t+1} x_{t+1}$. She adjusts saving, fertility and the intergenerational transfer to her parents to maximize her income in the current and the ensuing period, where her current-period utility includes her valuation of her parents' consumption this period. The first-order conditions are $\Delta u(c_t^m)/\Delta s_t = \delta \Delta u(c_{t+1}^o)/\Delta s_t \cdot \Delta c_{t+1}^o/\Delta s_t$ for savings, $\theta_t \Delta u(c_t^m)/\Delta f_t = \delta \Delta u(c_{t+1}^o)/\Delta s_t \cdot \Delta c_{t+1}^o/\Delta f_t$ for fertility choice, and for the parental donation either $\Delta u(c_t^m)/\Delta d_t^i = \eta n_t^m \Delta u(c_t^o)/\Delta d_t^i$ in the cooperative case or $\Delta u(c_t^m)/\Delta d_t^i = \eta \Delta u(c_t^o)/\Delta d_t^i$ in the non-cooperative case. To the extent that parents are aware of the strategy that children will follow in determining their donations, it is rational for them to take into account the impact that a variation in the amount of savings and the number of children they have may have on the total old-age support they will receive from their children, so $\Delta c_{t+1}^o/\Delta s_t$ and $\Delta c_{t+1}^o/\Delta f_t$ appear in those expressions instead of the competitive rates of return R_{t+1} and $\pi_t d_{t+1}$.

The characteristics of this economy can be considered Malthusian, because there is no technological progress, aggregate production follows constant returns, and children are seen as investment goods by their parents inasmuch as they provide labor to work the land-capital in the future. Along a balanced growth path, per capita income remains constant as the population reproduces at the same rate as the capital stock grows, and there is no technological progress. However, a reduction in mortality always decreases the capital-labor ratio, because the desired k is determined by the condition that the rate of return of return to savings and children are the same and a reduction in mortality increases the rate of return on fertility. Higher fertility in one period yields a larger middle-age group in the following period and a lower capital-labor ratio. The model always yields an inverse relationship between fertility and mortality. When mortality falls, fertility decreases, but the population's growth rate increases, while the capital-labor ratio falls, together with per capita income and consumption, as the wage rate decreases and the rate of return on capital increases. When adult children behave non-cooperatively, the qualitative results are the same, but the quantitative properties differ considerably. With the same parameter values, equilibrium fertility is substantially lower, and the capital-labor ratio is higher than when cooperation prevails. An implication is that when adult children are dispersed and follow different interests, parents' fertility falls.

Parents Are Altruistic Toward Children and Mortality Is Endogenous. In a 3-period OLG model, children's consumption is wrapped with their parents' consumption during the second stage of the parents' life cycle, so there are essentially two periods of consumption choice for people, called periods t and t + 1.[149] Young parents decide on the number of children to have and the quality to devote to them in the form of developing human capital for them. In period t, young adults allocate their current income among their own consumption, raising children, and educating or training them (developing their human capital). The budget constraint for period t is that consumption is what is left over after parents have made their choices about how many children to have and how much to spend on them: $C_{1,t} = (1 - \nu n_t - \theta h_t n_t) w_t(\bar{H} + H_t)$, in which n_t is the number of children they choose (fertility), h_t is human capital investment per child, ν and $\theta (0 < \nu, \theta < 1)$ are the unit costs of rearing and educating a child of simple childrearing as fractions of full income, w_t is the wage or rental price of a unit of human capital and $(\bar{H} + H_t)$ is the quantity of human capital the parents possess, $\bar{H}$ being some innate amount and H_t the amount they received from their parents in the previous period and use in the current period. There is no saving in the model. In old age, the now old parents' budget constraint is composed of the rental income they receive from a fixed asset such as land, which they inherited from their own parents: $C_{2,t+1} = r_{t+1} B_t$, where r_{t+1} is the rate of return they will earn in period t + 1. Altruism is expressed as an explicit consumption which elderly parents consume in period t + 1, called a companionship function and composed of interactions with the number of their surviving children and the quality of those children: $C_{3,t+1} = [Z(\pi_1 n_t)]^\beta [w_{t+1}(\bar{H} + H_{t+1})]^\alpha$, in which $\beta > \alpha = 1$ to ensure that the cost of the number of children is greater than the cost of quality (recall that the cost of quantity is tallied up at the amount of quality decided upon per child), π_1 is the probability of a child surviving to young adulthood, and the subscript t + 1 on w and H indicate that those variables pertain to the adult child's characteristics in period t+1 when the old parents consume the companionship. The children's human capital in period t+1 is produced by the parents' inputs h_t and the parents' own human capital in period t: $H_{t+1} = A(\bar{H} + H_t)h_t$, in which A is a technology parameter. The wages w_t and w_{t+1}, the rate of return on the fixed asset r_{t+1}, and the inheritance B_t are taken as given at the level of the individual, although they are determined endogenously through unspecified

[149] The model is from Ehrlich and Kim (2005). The model differs from that in Ehrlich and Lui (1991) in several important characteristics; the present model 's demand for children is purely altruistic, whereas the 1991 model specified an investment demand for children and included savings but relied on exogenous survival probabilities. Ehrlich and Lui (1997) offers a useful comparison of the Ehrlich-Lui and Ehrlich-Kim models with the dynastic model of BMT (1990).

market processes.[150] Both the wage w_t and the capital rental r_t (and w_{t+1} and r_{t+1}) are determined from a Cobb-Douglas production function: $Y_t = [(\bar{H} + H_t)]^{\gamma} L^{1-\gamma} = w_t(\bar{H} + H_t)N_t + r_t L$. Altruistic expected utility is specified as $U = U_1(C_{1,t}) + \delta\pi_2 U_2(C_{2,t+1}) + U_3(C_3)$, where δ is a discount factor.

A young parent maximizes the utility function above by choosing fertility n_t and human capital investment per child h_t. The first-order conditions for this maximization are not presented here, but from them a formulation for the growth of human capital over time is derived as $H_{t+1} = \frac{(A\nu/\theta-\beta)\bar{H}}{\beta-1} + \{\frac{A\nu}{\theta(\beta-1)}\}H_t$, which forms a system of (human) capital stock growth equivalent to that developed in the exposition of the basic OLG model and shown graphically in Figure 4.15A. The formulation for growth of the population of young workers is $N_{t+1} = \pi_1(C^m_{1,t})n_t N_t$. If the ratio of child rearing costs to the costs of imparting human capital, scaled by the human capital production function's technology parameter, is smaller than the cost share of child quantity in producing old-age companionship (alternatively, altruism strongly favors number rather than quality of children) — $A\nu/\theta < \beta$ — the only stable steady-state level of human capital H_t will be zero and remain there. When this is the case, fertility n_t is reduced by the size of the population of young adults, $\Delta n_t/\Delta N_t < 0$, which ensures a stable, constant population size. The constant population and a high fertility are linked by the number of children born reducing young-adult consumption which reduces survival probability. Should the population grow, the increase in numbers would reduce the wage rate which would in turn depress consumption with the same effect on mortality, so a mechanism exists that keeps population constant. Events that would shift a stagnant, Malthusian steady state to a steady-state growth equilibrium are increases in the technology of producing human capital, A, or the cost of child rearing ν, or an decrease in the unit cost of human capital production θ. Simulations with the model yield initial decreases in population during a demographic transition followed by resumption of continuing population growth.

The survival probabilities in the model are endogenous, with several alternative specifications. The survival probability for children living to young adulthood is $\pi_1 = \pi_1(C^m_{1,t}, D)$ in which $C^m_{1,t}$ is the average consumption level of young parents in the community and D is medical technology. Correspondingly, the probability of a young adult surviving to old age is $\pi_2 = \pi_2(C^m_{1,t}, D)$, in which consumption as a young adult in period t affects old-age mortality. A young adult would take this survival probability as given although it is, in the aggregate, endogenous. The alternative specification allows individuals to recognize that their own consumption affects their own health and survival probabilities: $\pi_1 = \pi_1(C_{1,t})$ and similarly for π_2. When individuals recognize that their own consumption choices affect their health and survival probabilities, results are considerably more intricate, but an increase in fertility reduces the adult parents' consumption which lowers both younger and older survival probabilities, and greater investment in human capital has the same effect. If parents increase their own consumption and increase survival probabilities, the rate of return they expect on investment in children's human capital increases which increases the incentive to make those investments. In the Malthusian equilibrium, these opposing forces on human capital investment just offset each other, but the existence of these forces working in opposite directions offers the mechanism for fertility reduction in a demographic transition, as increasing human capital increases the time cost of raising children.

Population as the Source of Economic Growth. Each growth model hypothesizes a particular source of growth, and some of the hypotheses make more sense than others, but by and large, none is derived from first principles of maximizing economic behavior, which means they are ad hoc. The Solow-Swan neoclassical growth model, from which all the other growth models under study presently derive, made the assumption that technological change was exogenous. At the date of that model's development, that was not a bad assumption, in the sense either of being nonsensical or counterproductive to the analysis of growth, particularly since one of the main goals of the analysis at that date was to model a self-correcting capital accumulation process, which the model accomplished. Nonetheless, the assumption that the ultimate source of economic growth was exogenous to the model kicked the can of understanding the cause(s) of growth down the road. The subsequent adaptations of the Solow-Swan model have proposed a number of can openers although each has brought its own problems.

To get exponential growth of the form $\dot{y} = g$, where $\dot{y}$ is the growth rate of per capita income and $g > 0$ is constant, a model has to include a differential equation that is linear in the sense of $\dot{X} =\_\_X$, where different models fill in the blank with different mechanisms (C. Jones 2003). The four major economic growth models each have offered a different mechanism to obtain this linearity. The Solow-Swan model used exogenous technological change in the form $\dot{A} = gA$. The AK model departs from the Solow-Swan model's neoclassical diminishing returns to capital accumulation, obtaining its linearity in the accumulation of physical or human capita, with the form $\dot{K} = sK^{\phi}$, where s is the saving rate and the assumption that $\phi = 1$ is maintained.[151] Idea-based growth models filled in the blank with resources devoted to research by profit-maximizing entrepreneurs. Thus the Lucas model relied on human capital h in the form $\dot{h} = uh^{\phi}$, where u is the fraction of their time individuals

[150] The amount of the fixed, non-reproducible asset is assumed to be constant in the economy at level L, so the amount inherited per young adult is $B_t = L/(\pi_2 N_t)$, where π_2 is the probability of survival of adults to old age and N_t is the total number of young adults born in period t−1.

[151] The AK model has a pre-neoclassical heritage, as related in Aghion and Howitt, with the collaboration of Bursztyn (2009, 47–52), but its current versions derive from the Solow-Swan model (see Jones 2014, Chapter 14) via Romer (1986).

spend accumulating skills, and another model of Romer's created endogenous technological change with the form $\dot{A} = H_A A^{\phi}$, where A is the stock of ideas and H_A is the resources the economy devotes to research (Romer 1990). In each case, the linearity of these models is unrealistic. The AK model, holding the saving rate constant and doubling the capital stock, net investment doubles, whereas in the neoclassical Solow-Swan model it less than doubles; nonetheless, the AK model eliminates the diminishing returns of the neoclassical model by appealing to an ad hoc mechanism. In the Lucas class of model, holding the fraction of time people spend acquiring skills and doubling the stock of human capital, implies that people with twice the education, however measured, will learn twice as much in a given time, which seems dubious and is the result of an equally ad hoc assumption. In the Romer endogenous-technical-change class of model, doubling the stock of ideas would double the production of new ideas if $\phi = 1$, which violates the commonsense notion of either constant returns, in which case $\phi = 0$, or diminishing returns in which the most obvious ideas are discovered first and the remaining ones are more difficult, in which case $\phi < 0$. The assumption that $\phi \approx 1$ violates commonsensical intuition.

With growth based on endogenous fertility, the differential equation has the form $\dot{N} = (\tilde{n} - d)N^{\phi}$ where N is population, $\tilde{n}$ is the endogenous fertility rate, and d is the exogenous (or endogenous) mortality rate. There is a natural linearity in the fertility relationship between the size of a population N and the number of offspring: double the size of a population, keeping the fertility rate $\tilde{n}$ constant, and the number of offspring doubles. The fertility rate can be endogenized with any of a number of models. Nonetheless, this linear relationship leaves the link between population or the population growth rate and economic growth yet to be specified, but the hypothesis of a causal connection between population and productivity or growth has some history, dating at least from the suggestive writings of Boserup (1965; 1981), endorsed and formalized by Simon (1977, Chapters 6 and 7; 1986), and joined to an aggregative Malthusian model by Lee (1986; 1988). Charles Jones has developed several versions of an endogenous growth model based on a population-technical-change link, which appeals to the effect of population size on the likelihood of bright people appearing and generating useful new ideas (C. Jones 2001; 2003). The population's labor time is allocated between production of goods and production of ideas, or what today would be called R&D, after deduction of time allocated to producing children, which provides the link between idea production and fertility. Idea production is a function of labor and previous ideas, with the possibility of increasing returns in idea production. The Jones models employ the Becker-Barro endogenous fertility model and rely on exogenous funding of idea production. Although he cites previous institutions such as monarchical patronage of inventors as providing such resources to remarkable individuals (C Jones 2001, 5), the practical relevance to economic growth in antiquity of this yet exogenous mechanism for providing what otherwise poses as endogenous growth seems quite limited. Additionally, as one would expect, the magnitude of the critical exogenous parameter, the fraction of an economy's output devoted (by some institution) to R&D, which funds the time devoted to idea production, becomes quite small at dates several thousand years B.C.E., but its parameterization to agree with estimated population figures at those dates produces an unbelievable temporal pattern of magnitude, with a rising trend from 25,000 B.C.E. to twin peaks in 4000 and 1000 B.C.E., and zero thereafter until 600 C.E. (C. Jones 2001, 23, 24 Table 3). Further, while the value of this important parameter varies by two orders of magnitude over twenty-four thousand years and by yet another order of magnitude over an ensuing two thousand years, the absolute value of the parameter varies from three one-hundred-thousandths of one percent to not quite nine thousandths of one percent over a span of nearly twenty-seven thousand years; attributing the emergence of the modern world to these variations in this parameter leaves one wondering about the proverbial importance of being unimportant. The models yield an economic growth rate that relies on the population growth rate, although when the population growth rate goes to zero eventually as the result of a demographic transition, previously exponential economic growth which goes to zero may be replaced by an arithmetic growth rate (C. Jones 2001, 5).

The Kremer (1993) model endogenizes population but only in the aggregate, involving no individual choices regarding fertility. Consequently there is no assurance that people would actually choose to behave in ways consistent with the equilibrium population movements in the model. Otherwise the model relating population size to technology is both ad hoc and mechanical and gives no insights into behavior.

What Does the Current Generation of Endogenous-Fertility Growth Models Tell Us? The endogenous-fertility growth models are a work in progress, and that needs to be kept in mind when reflecting on what they have to teach people interested in antiquity at this point. The first lesson for students of antiquity is that, just as in working with ancient data, in theoretical analysis of possible explanations, both God and the devil are in the details. Whether particular models yield results that are compatible with observational experience or not, even a high degree of abstraction from institutional details requires extensive specification of the few details that remain in a model. It may have seemed cruel to drag readers through the details of the models summarized in the previous sub-sections, but it is useful for potential consumers of their results to gain an appreciation of both the details that are distilled into those results and the process of deriving the results from the initial specifications of behavior and technology.

Methodological lessons aside, a more empirical lesson involves the importance of the intertemporal elasticity of substitution, or how willingly people would have deferred consumption between periods depending on how much more they could get by waiting, which has implications for the substitutability of child quality and child quantity. It is apparently important to think of circumstances in which intertemporal substitutability is relatively low. Another lesson is the importance of infant and child survival probabilities to technologically fairly robust improvement, via the route of human capital investment, whatever the mechanisms for increasing those probabilities. The treatment and condition of children have been topics of considerable research in the past several decades, and despite the slow and erratic progress of technological developments in antiquity, the link between the two topics is worth keeping in mind. A third major lesson is the importance of institutional structures for transferring resources between generations. Caring among generations within a family can affect interest rates; caring, or its observable correlates, can depend on the existence and efficiency of extra-familial mechanisms for shifting consumption between time periods such as a capital market; and geographical mobility that fosters migration can affect the incentives for both fertility and intergenerational transfers. Others may find lessons relevant to their research beyond what is identified here.

Turning to the negative side of lessons, first, the existence of multiple equilibria and the requirement for sharp, and typically large, jumps in particular variables, as contrasted with unique equilibria sensitive to continuous variation in critical variables, is a serious weakness in models of long-term economic growth or stagnation and demographic transition. In effect, a model with this characteristic is not a fully successful model of long-term growth and demographic transition (Boldrin and Jones 2002, 801).[152] Second, trying to find sufficiently parsimonious explanations for economic behavior in circumstances spanning two to twenty millennia is an appealing effort when working with models that possess a claim to some kind of universality, but some of these efforts may simply take on too large a task. The knowledge-production models, such as those of Kremer and Charles Jones, surely rely on a plausible mechanism that is important to technological change but ultimately yield an account that says effectively that the first twenty-five millennia of human experience were not highly differentiated in an economically important feature. Lee with Miller's (2000) effective conclusion that ancient economies failed to grow any more than they did because they lacked patent protection, while potentially satisfying by certain contemporary standards of demonstration, can leave one with lingering appetite for additional insights (Mokyr 2002, 294–297).[153] While they are somewhat less demanding of institutional structure, the models involving parental investment in children's human capital may be too parsimonious to capture important elements of family behavior in antiquity. Growth in children's human capital being the wellspring of economic growth, if per capita economic growth is effectively zero for a thousand years or longer, is one to infer that human capital was not particularly important in antiquity? Additional nuance regarding that subject is probably warranted even in the absence of widespread formal schooling in antiquity.

4.8 Concluding Thoughts

To begin with, I realize that students of the ancient Mediterranean will not possess information that deals directly with many of the topics dealt with here. However, a more thorough awareness of the concepts and issues involved in these topics may be useful in thinking about what evidence is available, as well as about evidence that may be available but hasn't been associated with particular topics to date. Beyond such immediately practical goals, recognition of how economists in particular have gone about studying various issues may offer guidance, insights, and even warnings on fruitful ways to approach various problems involving population.

Several of the major demographic facts to be discovered by research of one sort or another have ranges of magnitude that can be characterized fairly well. First, population growth rates in antiquity simply cannot have crept up to 2 percent per year or more: in most areas, population was nearly stationary for long periods, in the range of 0.05 to 0.2 percent per year when positive, while regionally and temporary restricted population growth spurts surely didn't break the 1 percent per year mark and might not have exceeded $\frac{1}{2}$ percent. Hypotheses that deliver 1970s East African growth rates around $2\frac{1}{2}$ percent per year simply don't warrant consideration. Second, fertility rates probably had more scope for variation than may be considered currently. With near-zero population growth rates in generally disease-prone environments with the most rudimentary medical treatment available, yet with a demand for surviving children to provide middle-to-old-age and disability support for parents, there is more scope for the demand for children to have varied. While the Hutterites checked in with a birth rate of around 10, and the theoretical human maximum is thought to be somewhere around 15, although repeated multiple births and a hardy constitution can push even that limit, in the ancient Mediterranean region anywhere from four to eight live births per mother surviving through her fertile period may

[152] This is not to say that these models are useless; on the contrary, individually and collectively, they have highlighted a number of important relationships, however, models sufficiently general to characterize accurately widely varying regimes of fertility and economic growth have not yet been developed. There are common-sense to ad hoc specifications to generate the growth, from exogenous technological change in early models to constant or increasing returns to scale in human capital accumulation.

[153] My apologies to Mokyr if I have heightened his conclusions somewhat. He is actually of multiple minds regarding the effectiveness of a patent system in promoting technological change but quite decided on the importance of the institutionalization of technological discoveries through such a system and is inclined to downplay the discoveries, likely difficult, made in antiquity by individuals who, if not isolated, generally were not connected by formal networks of knowledge accumulation and dissemination. Mokyr's focus on "Classical Antiquity" in his previous volume (1990, Chapter 2) does not consider the several millennia of slow technological progress in the Ancient Near East and Egypt which contributed greatly to the conditions on which Greeks and Romans built.

be plausible—a range of variation of 100 percent. There's a fair bit to explain here, but with the discrete character of births, that's only a choice of five numbers. Third, relying on these population growth rates and contemporary model life tables, estimates for life expectancy at birth for females are probably in the range of the very late teens to the early twenties. Fourth, research on the age-specificity of disease regimes in the ancient Mediterranean basin suggest that the age distributions of contemporary model life tables, even those for high-mortality regions such as the 18th century C.E. Caribbean and contemporary West Africa, may not offer a faithful portrait of ancient age distributions.

Demographic theory offers a sophisticated intertemporal accounting system which depends for its most powerful results on constant fertility and mortality rates. Thanks to ergodicity, disruptions to a population will not permanently affect its age structure as long as those vital rates remain constant. This is an important "if," one that is addressed by economic fertility theory. Fertile married couples in antiquity clearly did not "max out" their reproductivity, which leaves questions. The natural fertility concept, which several prominent scholars of ancient Mediterranean populations have bought into heavily, is not conceptually crisp—determining whether extended lactation was, say, to better care for a recent birth or to defer another is a matter of giving different names to the same fact—and its statistical measurement with the Coal-Trussell m&M statistics involves far more ambiguity than Classical practitioners have addressed. Parity-specific stopping behavior is simply an alternative to spacing behavior for controlling completed family size and offers additional flexibility to manage child deaths in high infant and child mortality circumstances. Despite extensive and intense rhetoric regarding the unthinkability of contraception or other forms of birth control and the unreliability of contraceptive technology and knowledge, I find it difficult to imagine that human reproductivity was on auto-pilot—or subject to "community control," another very black box—for some two million years prior to about 1875 C.E.[154] I am willing to credit the Chicago-Columbia economic fertility model, or equivalently the Pennsylvania model once a couple's desired completed surviving family size falls below its biologically or culturally determined maximum, with explanatory power over ancient fertility behavior. The Chicago-Columbia model is, to a first order, the Malthusian population model specified at the level of the individual couple, but with a negligible-to-zero price effect of children, so that the positive income effect is the only effective determinant of fertility, at least without throwing additional constraints on the choice problem such as limiting dilution of family assets through partitive inheritance. Literature on even middle-wealth families, not to mention wealthy Roman senatorial families, suggests control of inheritance may have been a consideration in determining desired completed family size even if investment in children was not subject to rising costs of parental time.

Returning to demographic models of populations—the life table and the Lotka-Leslie stable population—and their application to population movements in the wake of major, widespread epidemics and more localized disasters, the recovery pattern of a population predicted by standard projection techniques with unchanged fertility parameters, or with exogenously specified patterns of change in fertility parameters, should be viewed with caution. Estimation of population reductions from changes in real wages, relying on relationships from production theory, is complicated by the need to know about endogenous changes in accompanying productive factors—plainly speaking, on the abandonment of sown acreage by largely agricultural populations. A change in population (labor force) could be inferred from a change in the real wage if cooperating productive factors remained unchanged, but experience indicates that does not happen in the face of epidemic population disasters such as the Black Death in the 14th century C.E. and probably not in suspected earlier ones such as the Antonine Plague of the 2nd century C.E.

The ups and downs of population levels at various locations over various time periods in antiquity pose the contemporary scholar with the following question: were the decreases simply the consequence of mortality overwhelming the best efforts of the populations to maintain themselves as they maximized their reproductive potential, or were the ancient individuals acting out their beliefs regarding their own and their children's prospects and choosing to have fewer children? We can't have it both ways. Either the populations of antiquity were controlling their fertility or they weren't.

While the life expectancies of parents may have limited the proportion of families supporting one or both aged parents—mothers so supported being more likely than fathers because of the typical age discrepancy at first marriage—parental transfers to dependent children as well as adult children's transfers to elderly parents may have comprised a not-insubstantial proportion of societal wealth. Not much quantitative seems to be known about these intergenerational transfers, so the scope for the magnitude of these transfers is probably larger than the variability in population growth rates and life expectancy at birth, if not necessarily greater than the uncertainty about fertility rates. Research on the subject might prove informative. The importance of such intergenerational transfers to ancient families, even at low or even negative rates of return, reflects the lack of development of capital markets as well as probably generalized poverty. Crowding out of productive capital by diversion of wealth to transfers may have had a greater retarding effect on population growth than on per capita consumption growth ("economic growth") via the Malthusian income effect on fertility in the absence of mechanisms fostering the sustained expansion of knowledge. Intergenerational transfers are a

[154] If fertility behavior were simply under community control, fertility theory would collapse to a model of coital behavior.

Table 4.2. The A matrix.

	A Matrix								
	Fertility							n_0	Age group
	0	0.23	0.45	0.645	0.35	0	0	0.133	0–15
	0.75	0	0	0	0	0	0	0.150	16–25
	0	0.85	0	0	0	0	0	0.200	27–35
'Survival probability	0	0	0.9	0	0	0	0	0.180	36–44
	0	0	0	0.9	0	0	0	0.150	45–50
	1	0	0	0	0.875	0	0	0.120	51–65
	0	0	0	0	0	0.75	0.1	0.067	66+

major channel from individual-level population decisions to aggregate-level economic consequences.

The effect of sheer population size on technological change probably had more restricted scope for impact than has sometimes been envisioned. Certainly the Boserup effect of a larger number of people in roughly the same land area causes people to use agricultural technologies with higher labor-land ratios, which has the appearance of a no-brainer when expressed this way. Some scholars call this "agricultural intensification," but frequently with unclear meaning. While there are plausible models of how a larger population can lead to more, and more frequent, inventions that are as likely to become embodied in altered capital equipment as in changed labor practices, the scope for this effect, at least in antiquity, is small: if it hadn't been small, we'd see a completely different economic history during the period, which may have led to a much earlier Industrial Revolution, possibly in a different location.

Growth models with endogenous fertility provide mechanisms by which families make individual decisions that result in economy-wide trade-offs between fertility and capital accumulation—expenses associated with bearing and raising children come partly out of parents' consumption and partly out of their saving, and those decisions can affect the interest rate the entire economy faces. These mechanisms do not imply, however, a long-term trade-off between fertility and economic growth since sustained growth, once the optimal capital-labor ratio has been reached, depends on continuing technological change. If technological change occurs only spottily, some per capita growth may follow these changes temporarily but is dissipated by an increase in fertility.

The text above has not emphasized larger populations as an influence on productivity increases deriving from increased specialization possible in a larger market ("Smithian growth"). While such productivity advances from increased specialization in production activities undoubtedly contributed to some economic growth in antiquity, technical changes in equipment to accommodate continued increases in specialization would have posed a constraint on that source of growth. Without sustained technological change, the scope for continuing productivity improvements from specialization would have a ceiling, possibly a low one. The one thing—actually, it may be many things—that no stripe of growth theory has provided yet is a non-trivial explanation of such a lengthy period of roughly constant income / consumption per person, which, if it could be done, may be equivalent to explaining why the Industrial Revolution occurred when (and where) it did rather than sooner and further southeast. In fact, students of that subject aren't even sure when it started, or at least there is a variety of opinions. But economic growth per se, while possibly related to population, is outside the purview of what economic analysis of population issues has learned to date.

4.9 Cases from Antiquity: Exercising the Leslie Matrix with an Eye to Antiquity

I have reported Paine and Storey's application of a Leslie matrix to the Antonine Plague just above. The technique offers detailed insights into population decimation and recovery and with further research to recover demographic characteristics of ancient populations could become a workhorse in the study of ancient societies. In this section I conduct some comparative statics exercises with a 7-age-group Leslie matrix to demonstrate several characteristics of its results. As there is considerable uncertainty about the structure of life tables for ancient populations, I have not attempted to spuriously fine-tune the demographic characteristics, but instead have applied parameters roughly representative of a contemporary, low-income, developing country with moderately high child mortality. When the population reaches steady growth, the annual growth rate is 0.3% per year, a bit high for most periods in antiquity, but suitable, I believe, for heuristic purposes.

The parameters used in the Leslie matrix are shown in Table 4.2. The top row contains the fertility rates of women in the seven age groups, and the diagonal contains the survival probabilities of women of those ages. The n_0 vector contains the distribution of the population across the age groups. The population is scaled to equal 10,000 women. Beyond a baseline case, I run four experiments, three involving increased mortality and one involving increased fertility.

Table 4.3. Baseline Case. No population shock: population reaches steady growth at 0.285% in year 21.

Age group	Pop_0	Pop_1	Pop_2	Pop_3	Pop_4	Pop_5	Pop_6	Pop_7	Pop_{50}	Pop_{75}	Pop_{77}	Pop_{78}	Pop_{79}	Pop_{80}
1	1330	2931	2531	2194	2131	2430	2464	2300	2661	2858	2874	2882	2891	2899
2	1500	998	2198	1898	1646	1598	1822	1848	1990	2137	2150	2156	2162	2168
3	2000	1275	848	1869	1614	1399	1359	1549	1687	1812	1822	1827	1832	1838
4	1800	1800	1148	763	1682	1452	1259	1223	1514	1626	1635	1640	1644	1649
5	1500	1620	1620	1033	687	1513	1307	1133	1359	1459	1467	1472	1476	1480
6	1200	1313	1418	1418	904	601	1324	1144	1185	1273	1280	1284	1288	1291
7	670	900	984	1063	1063	678	451	993	887	952	957	960	963	966
Total	10,000	10,836	10,747	10,238	9,726	9,671	9,985	10,189	11,283	12,117	12,186	12,221	12,256	12,291
		8.4%	−0.8%	−4.7%	−5.0%	−0.6%	3.2%	2.0%	0.3%	0.3%	0.3%	0.3%	0.3%	0.3%

Table 4.4. Both survival probabilities and fertility fall by 25%. Population shock in year 5, with 1 additional year of reduced fertility: population reaches steady growth at 0.285% in year 19.

Age group	Pop_4	Pop_5	Pop_6	Pop_7	Pop_8	Pop_9	Pop_{10}	Pop_{50}	Pop_{75}	Pop_{76}	Pop_{77}	Pop_{78}	Pop_{79}	Pop_{80}
1	2131	1822	1848	1725	1730	1791	1806	1996	2143	2150	2156	2162	2168	2174
2	1646	1199	1367	1386	1294	1298	1343	1493	1603	1608	1612	1617	1621	1626
3	1614	1049	1019	1162	1178	1100	1103	1265	1359	1363	1366	1370	1374	1378
4	1682	1089	944	917	1046	1060	990	1135	1219	1223	1226	1230	1233	1237
5	687	1135	980	850	825	941	954	1019	1094	1097	1101	1104	1107	1110
6	904	451	993	858	744	722	823	889	955	957	960	963	966	968
7	1063	597	398	785	722	630	605	739	793	795	798	800	802	805
Total	9,726	7,342	7,549	7,682	7,538	7,541	7,624	8,536	9,167	9,193	9,219	9,245	9,272	9,298
	−5.0%	−25.4%	2.8%	1.8%	−1.9%	0.0%	1.1%	0.3%	0.3%	0.3%	0.3%	0.3%	0.3%	0.3%

The Baseline Case

Starting in a period zero, the population is developed for 80 years. Because the parameters are not finely tuned, it takes 21 periods for the population to reach its steady state growth of 0.285% per year, reaching a population of 12,291 in year 80. Table 4.3 reports the population by age group and overall growth rate for selected years.

Plagues

I consider a plague as a shock to the population in Table 4.4. Both fertility and survival probability fall by 25% uniformly across age groups during year 5 but recover fully in year 6. The population returns to its no-shock steady state growth rate of 0.285% per year in year 40. By year 80, the population is still 76% of its 80th–year size in the benchmark – unperturbed – case and $5\frac{1}{2}$% below its immediate, pre-plague size. Total population experiences negative growth in years 8 and 12.

With a second additional year of reduced fertility, population reaches steady growth of 0.3% per year in year 20. Population is 8,537 in year 80. Population in Table 2 is 76% of undisturbed population 75 years after shock. Population in Table 8 is 69% of undisturbed population 75 years after shock.

What happens if the plague lasts longer than a single year? The next experiment keeps the survival rate depressed in year 6 but lets the fertility rate return to its pre-plague level. Population declines another $3\frac{1}{2}$% in year 6 before resuming growth in year 7. Negative overall growth occurs in years 8 through 10 and 14. The population returns to its steady-state growth rate of 0.285% per year in year 38. By year 80, the population is 30% smaller than its undisturbed size and 12% below its immediate, pre-plague size.

Next I consider differential mortality, with the youngest age group's survival probability falling by 15%, the youngest fertile age group's probability falling by 20%, and the three fertile age groups' probabilities falling by 40%. The survival probabilities of the two oldest age groups fall by 25%. The plague-year population decrease is 26%, and the year-80 population is $5\frac{1}{4}$% below the immediate pre-plague population. The directions of change are as expected – when younger age groups' mortality rates are lower than those of older but still fertile age groups, population recovery is more rapid – but small. A more finely grained age distribution could show stronger effects.

A Fifth Century B.C.E. Athenian Baby Boom?

This experiment takes up an interesting speculation by Ben Akrigg (2019, 157): "If [a baby boom – less dramatic than those of post-World War II but akin in causation] did take place in Athens in the 470s, then it may be even more interesting than simply forming part of the explanation for Athens' power and confidence in the *pentecontaetia*. Such booms have 'echoes' in succeeding generations . . . " Akrigg's reasoning lies in a collective Athenian sigh of relief in victorious peace after several decades of war and possible defeat, which parallels his view of the post-World War II baby boom in the United States, which he concedes must have been on a much larger scale than an Athenian post-Persian Wars boom. An economist would characterize such a phenomenon as a change in the demand for children, driven by changes in understood parameters such as the returns from additional children in the 5th century B.C.E.. Population data are insufficient to test such a proposition, but some interesting insights emerge which might eventually find some corroboration . . . or rejection.

Post-Persian wars boom – year 22 boom starts. Year 30, population resumes 1.3% annual growth rate, after varying yearly growth rates.

To introduce a single period of modestly increased fertility, with survival probabilities unchanged from the base case, I chose year 22 as a time when stability of growth had set in. The increases in fertility were from 0.23 to 0.25 in age-group 2, from 0.45 to 0.47 in age-group 3, from 0.645 to 0.65 in age-group 4, and from 0.35 to 0.36 in age-group 6. Year 22's growth rate jumped from 0.26% in the previous year to 1.93%, and continued over 1% per year through year 36. In year 37, it turned negative, to −0.39%, after which it turned positive again and began a march toward its steady-state rate of 0.285% in year 65. By year 72, the population was 13,935, 13% higher than the year-72 population in the base case and 32% higher than the population in the year preceding the fertility increase. A continuation of an elevated fertility would have increased the population increase.

So what does this prove other than the no-brainer that if fertility increases, population will grow more rapidly? Absolutely nothing. What does it demonstrate? That a single period of modestly increased fertility will have effects on the population's growth rate that lasts for decades. This *is* important. We don't know whether such a baby boom, or baby bump, occurred in Athens after the Persian Wars, but if one did, it tells us that families had been controlling their fertility, contrary to the natural fertility hypothesis. This would also be significant. Hin (2013, 195–199) questions the substance of the natural fertility hypothesis, noting a number of alternatives for limiting completed family size.

4.10 Using this Chapter's Information

Material of this chapter may help orient a discussion of the extent to which the fertility decisions upon which population growth in antiquity may have been based on individual choices. Implicit reliance on the natural fertility construct as the default situation in antiquity closes off potential history of people who have been to a great extent excluded from serious scholarly thinking on fertility and population, for example, women, and women of various categorizations such as wives and midwives.

Population disasters are prominent in ancient societies, at least at today's distance from the events, and the use of demographic as well as economic models can be used in thinking about recovery from them.[155] Population booms in antiquity are another matter; combining natural fecundity capacities, mortality regimes, and individual incentives to have children, if such are allowed to ancient couples, may bound possible short-term growth rates to magnitudes well shy of suggestions made in recent decades.

The economic theory of fertility brings together technology and children, in the sense that there can exist a trade-off between the number of children a couple may choose to bear and the difficulty of mastering the technological regime into which those children will have to enter eventually as workers. This brings ancient fertility and ancient technology closer together than they have commonly been associated. What passed as education or training, how did parents provide for it, and how might those decisions have affected the number of births and surviving children they decided, or tired, to have? And since infant and child mortality were so much in the faces of ancient couples, how might they have tried to control these events, and how did their actions contribute to or mitigate mortality profiles?

Whether parents loved children in antiquity as the contemporary model would have them do today and whether children knew their parents well enough to care for them in the latter's old age are topics in the contemporary literature of antiquity. What difference would it make, one way or the other? The overlapping generations models of intergenerational transfers offer a way of thinking transparently, if austerely, about these issues and their consequences for all generations of ancient population.

References

Acemoglu, Daron. 2009. *Introduction to Modern Economic Growth*. Princeton: Princeton University Press.

Aghion, Philippe, and Peter Howitt, with the collaboration of Leonardo Bursztyn. 2009. *The Economics of Growth*. Cambridge, Mass.: MIT Press.

Akrigg, Ben. 2007. "The Nature and Implications of Athens' Changed Social Structure and Economy," in *Debating Athenian Cultural Revolution: Art, Literature, Philosophy, and Politics 430–380 BC*, edited by Robin

155 Beaumont (2003, 109) infers from changes in the iconography of children on figured vases and funerary monuments that the Athenian plague beginning in 430 B.C.E. and the continuing deaths throughout the Peloponnesian Wars raised the status of children.

Osborne, 27–43. Cambridge: Cambridge University Press.

Akrigg, Ben. 2011. "Demography and Classical Athens," in *Demography and the Graeco-Roman World; New Insights and Approaches*, edited by Claire Holleran and April Pudsey, 37–59. Cambridge: Cambridge University Press.

Akrigg, Ben, 2019. *Population and Economy in Classical Athens*. Cambridge: Cambridge University Press.

Alter, George. 1992. "Theories of Fertility Decline: A Nonspecialist's Guide to the Current Debate," in *The European Experience of Declining Fertility, 1850–1970; The Quiet Revolution*, edited by John R. Gillis, Louise A. Tilly, and David Levine, 13–27. Cambridge, Mass.: Blackwell.

Arthur, W. Brian, and Geoffrey McNicoll. 1978. "Samuelson, Population and Intergenerational Transfers," *International Economic Review* 19: 241–246.

Ault, Bradley A., and Lisa C. Nevett, Eds. 2005. *Ancient Greek Houses and Households: Chronological, Regional and Social Diversity*. Philadelphia: University of Pennsylvania Press.

Bagnall, Roger S. 2002. "The Effects of Plague: Model and Evidence," *Journal of Roman Archaeology* 15: 114–120.

Bagnall, Roger S., and Bruce W. Frier. 1994. *The Demography of Roman Egypt*. Cambridge: Cambridge University Press.

Bar, Michael, and Oksana Leukhina. 2010. "Demographic Transition and Industrial Revolution: A Macroeconomic Investigation," *Review of Economic Dynamics* 13: 424–451.

Barro, Robert J. 1974. "Are Government Bonds Net Worth?" *Journal of Political Economy* 82: 1095–1117.

Barro Robert J., and Gary S. Becker. 1989. "Fertility Choice in a Model of Economic Growth," *Econometrica* 57: 481–501.

Barro Robert J., and Xavier Sala-i-Martin. 2004. *Economic Growth*, 2nd Ed. Cambridge, Mass.: MIT Press.

Beaumont, Lesley A. 2003. "Changing Childhoods? The Representation of Children in Attic Figured Vases," in *Griechische Keramik im kulturellen Kontext*, edited by Bernhard Schmaltz and Magdaline Söldner, 108–110. Scriptorium.

Beaumont, Lesley A. 2012. *Childhood in Ancient Athens: Iconography and Social History*. London: Routledge.

Becker, Gary S. 1960. "An Economic Analysis of Fertility," in *Demographic and Economic Change in Developed Countries*, Universities-National Bureau Conference Series 11, 209–231. Princeton: Princeton University Press.

Becker, Gary S. 1991. *A Treatise on the Family*, Enlarged Ed. Cambridge, Mass.: Harvard University Press.

Becker Gary S., and H. Gregg Lewis. 1973. "On the Interaction between the Quantity and Quality of Children," *Journal of Political Economy* 81: S279–S288.

Becker, Gary S., and Robert J. Barro. 1988." A Reformulation of the Economic Theory of Fertility," *Quarterly Journal of Economics* 103: 1–25.

Becker, Gary S., Kevin Murphy, and Robert Tamura. 1990. "Human Capital, Fertility, and Economic Growth," *Journal of Political Economy* 98: S12–S37.

Behrman, Jere R. 1997. "Intra-Household Distribution and the Family," in *Handbook of Population and Family Economics*, Vol. 1A, edited by Mark R. Rosenzweig and Oded Stark, 125–187. Amsterdam: North-Holland.

Behrman, Jere R., and Anil B. Deolalikar. 1990. "The Intrahousehold Demand for Nutrients in Rural South India; Individual Estimates, Fixed Effects, and Permanent Income," *Journal of Human Resources* 25: 665–696.

Ben Porath, Yoram. 1976. "Fertility Response to Child Mortality: Micro Data from Israel," *Journal of Political Economy* 84: S163–S178.

Bergstrom, Theodore, and David Lam. 1989. "The Two-Sex Problem and the Marriage Squeeze in an Equilibrium Model of Marriage Markets," University of Michigan, available at http:/www.escholarship.org/uc/item/ 4r00j58x.

Bergstrom, Theodore, and David Lam. 1994. "The Effects of Cohort Size on Marriage Markets in Twentieth Century Sweden," in *The Family, the Market and the State in Ageing Societies*, edited by John Ermisch and Naohiro Ogawa, 46–63. Oxford: Oxford University Press.

Blanchard, Olivier J. 1985. "Debts, Deficits, and Finite Horizon," *Journal of Political Economy* 93: 223–247.

Blanchard, Olivier Jean, and Stanley Fischer. 1989. *Lectures on Macroeconomics*. Cambridge, Mass.: MIT Press.

Boeckh, August. 1842. *The Public Economy of Athens*, 2nd Ed., Transl. George Cornewell Lewis. London: John W. Parker, 1842 [Nabu Public Domain Reprint, n.d.]

Boldrin, Michele, and Larry E. Jones. 2002. "Mortality, Fertility, and Saving in a Malthusian Economy," *Review of Economic Dynamics* 8: 775–814.

Bommier, Antoine, and Ronald D. Lee. 2003. "Overlapping Generations Models with Realistic Demography," *Journal of Population Economics* 16: 135–160.

Boserup, Ester. 1965. *The Conditions of Agricultural Growth; The Economics of Agrarian Change under Population Pressure*. Chicago: Aldine.

Boserup, Ester. 1981. *Population and Technological Change; A Study of Long-Term Trends*. Chicago: University of Chicago Press.

Bradley, Keith R. 1985. "Child Labor in the Roman World," *Historical Reflections/Reflexions historiques* 12: 311–330.

Bradley, Keith. 1991. "Introduction," in *Discovering the Roman Family: Studies in Social History*, edited by Keith Bradley, 3–12. Oxford: Oxford University Press.

Brady, Dorothy S., and Rose D. Friedman. 1947. "Savings and the Income Distribution," in *Studies in Income and Wealth*, Volume 10, *Conference on Research in Income and Wealth*, 247–265. New York: National Bureau of Economic Research.

Brewer, Douglas J., and Emily Teeter. 1999. *Egypt and the Egyptians*. Cambridge: Cambridge University Press.

Brunt, P. A. 1971. *Italian Manpower, 225 B.C. - A.D. 14*. Oxford: Clarendon Press.

Bruun, Christer. 2003. "The Antonine Plague in Rome and Ostia," *Journal of Roman Archaeology* 16: 426–434.

Bruun, Christer. 2007. "The Antonine Plague and the Third-Century Crisis," in *Crises and the Roman Empire: Proceedings of the Seventh Workshop of the International Network Impact of Empire (Nijmegen, June 20–24, 2006)*, edited by Olivier Hekster, Gerda de Kleijn, and Danielle Slootjes, 201–217. Leiden: Brill.

Budin, Stephanie Lynne. 2011. *Images of Woman and Child from the Bronze Age; Reconsidering Fertility, Maternity, and Gender in the Ancient World*. Cambridge: Cambridge University Press.

Cain, Mead. 1977. "The Economic Activities of Children in a Village in Bangladesh," *Population and Development Review* 3: 201–227.

Caldwell, John C.1976. "Toward a Restatement of Demographic Transition Theory," *Population and Development Review* 2: 321–366.

Carlsson, Gösta. 1966. "The Decline of Fertility: Innovation or Adjustment Process," *Population Studies* 20: 149–164.

Carlsson, Gösta. 1970. "Nineteenth Century Fertility Oscillations," *Population Studies* 24: 413–422.

Caswell, Hal. 2001. *Matrix Population Models: Construction, Analysis, and Interpretation*, 2nd Ed. Sunderland, Mass.: Sinauer.

Chamberlain, Andrew. 2006. *Demography in Archaeology*. Cambridge: Cambridge University Press.

Chiappori, Pierre-André, and Valérie Lechene, 2006. "Collective and Unitary Models: A Clarification," *Review of the Economics of the Household* 4: 5–14.

Choo, Eugene, and Aloysius Siow. 2006. "Estimating a Marriage Matching Model with Spillover Effects," *Demography* 43: 463–490.

Chu, C. Y. Cyrus. 1998. *Population Dynamics; A New Economic Approach*. Oxford: Oxford University Press.

Chu, C. Y. Cyrus, and Huei-Chung Lu. 1995. "Toward a General Analysis of Endogenous Easterlin Cycles," *Journal of Population Economics* 8: 35–57.

Cigno, Alessandro. 1991. *Economics of the Family*. Oxford: Clarendon Press.

Clark, Gregory, and Gillian Hamilton. 2006. "Survival of the Richest: The Malthusian Mechanism in Pre-Industrial England, *Journal of Economic History* 66: 1–30.

Clarysse, Willy and Dorothy J. Thompson. 2006. *Counting the People in Hellenistic Egypt, Vol. 2: Historical Studies*. Cambridge: Cambridge University Press.

Coale, Ansley J. 1971. "Age Patterns of Marriage," *Population Studies* 25: 193–214.

Coale, Ansley J. 1972. *The Growth and Structure of Human Populations; A Mathematical* Investigation. Princeton: Princeton University Press.

Coale, Ansley J., and Paul Demeny. 1966. *Regional Model Life Tables and Stable Populations*. Princeton: Princeton University Press.

Coale, Ansley J., and D. R. McNeil. 1972. "The Distribution by Age of the Frequency of First Marriage in a Female Cohort," *Journal of the American Statistical Association* 67: 743–749.

Coale, Ansley J., and T. James Trussell. 1974. "Model Fertility Schedules: Variations in the Age Structure of Childbearing in Human Populations," *Population Index* 40: 185–258.

Coale, Ansley J., and T. James Trussell. 1978. "Technical Note: Finding the Two Parameters that Specify a Model Schedule of Marital Fertility," *Population Index* 44: 203–213.

Coale, Ansley J., and Paul Demeny, with Barbara Vaughan. 1983. *Regional Model Life Tables and Stable Populations*, 2nd Ed. New York: Academic Press.

Cohen, Sarah Betsy, and James A. Sweet. 1974. "The Impact of Marital Disruption and Remarriage on Fertility," *Journal of Marriage and the Family* 36: 87–96.

Costa, Dora L. 2003. "Understanding Mid-Life and Older Age Mortality Declines: Evidence from Union Army Veterans," *Journal of Econometrics* 112: 175–192.

Costa, Dora L., and Matthew E. Kahn. 2010. "Health, Wartime Stress, and Unit Cohesion: Evidence from Union Army Veterans," *Demography* 47: 45–66.

Cotts Watkins, Susan, and Jane Menken. 1985. "Famines in Historical Perspective," *Population and Development Review* 11: 647–675.

Cowgill, George L. 1975a. "Population Pressure as Non-Explanation," *Memoirs of the Society for American Archaeology* 30: 127–131.

Cowgill, George L. 1975b. "On Causes and Consequences of Ancient and Modern Population Changes," *American Anthropologist* N.S. 77: 505–525.

Dagsvik, John K. Helge Brunborg, and Ane S. Flaatten 2001. "A Behavioral Two-Sex Marriage Model," *Mathematical Population Studies* 9: 97–121.

David, Paul A., and Warren C. Sanderson. 1986. "Rudimentary Contraceptive Methods and the American Transition to Marital Fertility Control, 1855–1915," in *Long-Term Factors in American Economic Growth*, edited by Stanley L. Engerman and Robert E. Gallman, 307–390. Chicago: University of Chicago Press.

de la Croix, David, and Philippe Michel. 2002. *A Theory of Economic Growth; Dynamics and Policy in Overlapping Generations*. Cambridge: Cambridge University Press.

Demand, Nancy. 1994. *Birth, Death, and Motherhood in Classical Greece*. Baltimore: Johns Hopkins University Press.

DeTray, Dennis N. 1973. "Child Quality and the Demand for Children," *Journal of Political Economy* 81: S70–S95.

den Boer, W. 1973. "Demography in Roman History: Facts and Impressions," *Mnemosyne* 4th Ser. 26: 29–46.

Diamond, Peter A. 1965. "National Debt in a Neoclassical Growth Model," *American Economic Review* 55: 1126–1150.

Dickinson, Oliver. 2006. *The Aegean from Bronze Age to Iron Age; Continuity and Change between the Twelfth and Eighth Centuries BC*. London: Routledge.

Dixon, Suzanne. 1992. *The Roman Family*. Baltimore: Johns Hopkins University Press.

Duncan-Jones, R. P. 1996. "The Impact of the Antonine Plague," *Journal of Roman Archaeology* 9: 108–136.

Easterlin, Richard A. 1961. "The American Baby Boom in Historical Perspective," *American Economic Review* 51: 869-911.

Easterlin, Richard A. 1966a. "On the Relation of Economic Factors to Recent and Projected Fertility Changes," *Demography* 3: 131–153.

Easterlin, Richard A. 1966b. "Economic-Demographic Interactions and Long Swings in Economic Growth, *American Economic Review* 56: 1063–1104.

Easterlin, Richard A. 1978a. "What Will 1984 Be Like? Socioeconomic Implications of Recent Twists in Age Structure," *Demography* 15: 397–432.

Easterlin, Richard A. 1978b. "The Economics and Sociology of Fertility: A Synthesis," in *Historical Studies of Changing Fertility*, edited by Charles Tilly, 57–133. Princeton: Princeton University Press.

Easterlin, Richard A. 2004. *The Reluctant Economist*. Cambridge: Cambridge University Press.

Easterlin, Richard A., Robert A. Pollak, and Michael L. Wachter. 1980. "Toward a More General Economic Model of Fertility Determination: Endogenous Preferences and Natural Fertility," in *Population and Economic Change in Developing Countries*, edited by Richard A. Easterlin, 81–149. Chicago: University of Chicago Press.

Easterlin, Richard A., and Eileen M. Crimmins. 1985. *The Fertility Revolution; A Supply-Demand Analysis*. Chicago: University of Chicago Press.

Eckstein, Zvi, T. Paul Schultz, and Kenneth I. Wolpin. 1985. "Short-Run Fluctuations in Fertility and Mortality in Pre-Industrial Sweden," *European Economic Review* 26: 295–317.

Ehrlich, Isaac, and Francis T. Lui. 1991. "Intergenerational Trade, Longevity, and Economic Growth," *Journal of Political Economy* 99: 1029–1059.

Ehrlich, Isaac, and Francis Lui. 1997. "The Problem of Population and Growth: A Review of the Literature from Malthus to Contemporary Models of Endogenous Population and Endogenous Growth," *Journal of Economic Dynamics and Control* 21: 205–242.

Ehrlich, Isaac, and Jinyoung Kim. 2005. "Endogenous Fertility, Mortality and Economic Growth: Can a Malthusian Framework Account for the Conflicting Historical Trends in Population?" *Journal of Asian Economics* 16: 789–806.

Etiene, R. 1973. "La conscience médicale antique et la vie des enfants," *Annales de Demographie Historique* 21, *Enfant et Sociétés* 15–61.

Eyben, Emiel. 1980. "Family Planning in Graeco-Roman Antiquity," *Ancient Society* 11–12: 5–82.

Darity, Jr., William A. 1980, "The Boserup Theory of Agricultural Growth; A Model for Anthropological Economics," *Journal of Development Economics* 7: 137–157.

Finley, Moses I. 1973. *The Ancient Economy*. Cambridge: Cambridge University Press.

Floud, Roderick, Robert W. Fogel, Bernard Harris, and Sok Chul Hong. 2001. *The Changing Body: Health, Nutrition, and Human Development in the Western World since 1700*. Cambridge: Cambridge University Press, 2011.

Fogel, Robert W. 1994. "Economic Growth, Population Theory, and Physiology: The Bearing of Long-Term Processes on the Making of Economic Policy," *American Economic Review* 84: 369–395.

Fogel, Robert William. 1997. "New Findings on Secular Trends in Nutriton and Mortality: Some Implications for Population Theory," in *Handbook of Population and Family Economics*, Vol. 1A, edited by Mark R. Rosenzweig and Oded Stark, 433–481. Amsterdam: North-Holland.

Fontanille, Marie-Thérése. 1977. *Avortement et conception dans la medicine gréco-romaine*. Paris: Laboratoires Searle.

Frederickson, A.G. 1971. "A Mathematical Theory of Age Structure in Sexual Populations: Random Mating and Monogamous Marriage Models," *Mathematical Biosciences* 10: 117–143.

Frier, Bruce W. 1982. "Roman Life Expectancy: Ulpian's Evidence," *Harvard Studies in Classical Philology* 86: 213–251.

Frier, Bruce W. 1983. "Roman Life Expectancy: The Pannonian Evidence," *Phoenix* 37: 328–344.

Frier, Bruce W. 1994. "Natural Fertility and Family Limitation in Roman Marriage," *Classical Philology* 89: 318–333.

Frier, Bruce W. 2000. "Demography," in *The Cambridge Ancient History*, Volume XI, *The High Empire, AD 70–192*, 2nd Ed., edited by Peter Garnsey, Dominic Rathbone, and Alan K. Bowman, 787–816. Cambridge: Cambridge University Press, 2000.

Frier, Bruce W. 2001. "More is Worse," in *Debating Roman Demography*, *Mnemosyne* Supplement 211, edited by Walter Scheidel, 139–159. Leiden: Brill.

Gale, David. 1973. "Pure Exchange Equilibrium of Dynamic Economic Models," *Journal of Economic Theory* 6: 12–36.

Galil, Gershon. 2007. *The Lower Stratum Families in the Neo-Assyrian Period*. Leiden: Brill.

Gallant, Thomas W. 1991. *Risk and Survival in Ancient Greece; Reconstructing the Rural Domestic Economy*. Stanford: Stanford University Press.

Galor, Oded. 2005. "From Stagnation to Growth: Unified Growth Theory," in *Handbook of Economic Growth*, Volume 1A, edited by Philippe Aghion and Steven N. Durlauf, 171–293. Amsterdam: Elsevier.

Galor, Oded, and David N. Weil. 2002. "Population, Technology, and Growth: From Malthusian Stagnation to the Demographic Transition and Beyond," *American Economic Review* 90: 806–828.

Garnsey, Peter, and Richard Saller. 1987. *The Roman Empire: Economy, Society and Culture*. Berkeley: University of California Press.

Gaunt, David. 1973. "Family Planning and the Preindustrial Society: Some Swedish Evidence," in *Aristocrats, Farmers, Proletarians: Essays in Swedish Demographic History*, Studia Historica Upsaliensia XLVII, 28–59. Uppsala: Almqvist and Wicksell.

Golden, Mark. 1990. *Children and Childhood in Classical Athens*. Baltimore: Johns Hopkins University Press.

Golden, Mark. 2011. "Other People's Children," in *A Companion to Families in the Greek and Roman Worlds*, edited by Beryl Rawson, 262–275. Malden, Mass.: Wiley-Blackwell.

Golden, Mark. 2015. *Children and Childhood in Classical Athens*, 2nd Ed. Baltimore: Johns Hopkins University Press.

Gomme, A. W. 1933. *The Population of Athens in the Fifth and Fourth Centuries B.C.* Oxford: Blackwell.

Greenberg, James. 2003. "Plagued by Doubt: Reconsidering the Impact of a Mortality Crisis in the 2nd C. A.D.," *Journal of Roman Archaeology* 16: 413–425.

Greenhalgh, Susan. 1966. "The Social Construction of Population Science: An Intellectual, Institutional, and Political History of Twentieth-Century Demography," *Comparative Studies in Society and History* 38: 26–66.

Griffith, Janet D., Helen P. Koo, and C. M. Suchindran. 1985. "Childbearing and Family in Remarriage," *Demography* 22: 73–88.

Grigg, David B.1981. *Population Growth and Agrarian Change; An Historical Perspective*. Cambridge: Cambridge University Press.

Grmek, Mirko D. 1989. *Diseases in the Ancient Greek World*, transl. by Mireille Muellner and Leonard Muellner. Baltimore: Johns Hopkins University Press.

Guillot, Michel. 2006. "The Momentum of Mortality Change," *Population Studies* 59: 283–294.

Guinnane, Timothy W., Barbara S. Okun, and James Trussell. 1994. "What Do We Know About the Timing of Fertility Transitions in Europe," *Demography* 31: 1–20.

Hamilton, Earl J. 1936. *Money, Prices, and Wages in Valencia, Aragon, and Navarre, 1351–1500*. Cambridge, Mass.: Harvard University Press.

Hansen Gary D., and Edward C. Prescott. 2002. "Malthus to Solow," *American Economic Review* 92: 1205–1217.

Hansen, Mogens Herman. 1991. *The Athenian Democracy in the Age of Demosthenes: Structure, Principles, and Ideology*. Bristol: Bristol Classical Press.

Hansen, Mogens Herman. 2006a. *Studies in the Population of Aigina, Athens and Eretria*, Historisk-filosofiske Meddelelser 94. Copenhagen: The Danish Royal Academy of Sciences and Letters.

Hansen, Mogens Herman. 2006b. *The Shotgun Method; The Demography of the Ancient Greek City-State Culture*. Columbia, Mo.: University of Missouri Press.

Harris, Bernard. 2004. "Public Health, Nutrition, and the Decline of Mortality: The McKeown Thesis Revisited," *Social History of Medicine* 17: 379–407.

Hatcher, John. 1994. "England in the Aftermath of the Black Death," *Past and Present* 144: 3–35.

Hazan, Moshe, and Binyamin Berdugo. 2002. "Child Labour, Fertility, and Economic Growth, *Economic Journal* 112: 810–828.

Heijdra, Ben J. 2009, *Foundations of Modern Macroeconomics*, 2nd Ed. Oxford: Oxford University Press.

Henrich, Joseph. 2004. "Demography and Cultural Evolution: How Adaptive Cultural Processes Can Produce Maladaptive Losses—The Tasmanian Case," *American Antiquity* 69: 197–214.

Henry, Louis. 1953. "Fondements théoriques des measures de la fécondité naturelle," *Revue de l'Institut International Statistique* 21: 135–151.

Henry, Louis. 1957. "Fécondité et famille," *Population* 12: 413–444.

Henry, Louis. 1961a. "Fécondité et famille. Modeles mathématiques (II)," *Population* 16: 27–48.

Henry, Louis. 1961b. "Some Data on Natural Fertility," *Eugenics Quarterly* 8: 81–91.

Henry, Louis. 1961c "La fécondité naturelle. Observation – théorie – resultants," *Population* 16: 625–636.

Henry, Louis. 1966. "Perturbations de la nuptialité résultant de la guerre 1914–1918," *Population* 21: 273–332.

Henry, Louis. 1979. "Concepts actuels et resultants empiriques sur la fécondité naturelle" in *Natural Fertility; Patterns and Determinants of Natural Fertility: Proceedings of a Seminar on Natural Fertility*, edited by Henri Leridon and Jane Menken, 17–28. Liège: Ordina.

Heubner, Sabine R. 2011. "Household Composition in the Ancient Mediterranean – What Do We Really Know?" in *A Companion to Families in the Greek and Roman Worlds*, edited by Beryl Rawson, 73–91. Malden, Mass.: Wiley-Blackwell.

Hin, Saskia. 2011. "Family Matters: Fertility and Its Constraints in Roman Italy," in *Demography and the Greco-Roman World; New Insights and Approaches*, edited by Claire Holleran and April Pudsey, 99–116. Cambridge: Cambridge University Press.

Hin, Saskia. 2013. *The Demography of Roman Italy; Population Dynamics in an Ancient Conquest Society 201 B.C.E.–14 CE*. Cambridge: Cambridge University Press.

Hines, Norman E. 1936. *Medical History of Contraception*. New York: Gamut Press.

Hopkins, Keith. 1966. "On the Probable Age Structure of the Roman Population," *Population Studies* 20: 245–264.

Hoppensteadt, Frank C. 1975. *Mathematical Theories of Populations: Demographics, Genetics, and Epidemics*. Philadelphia: Society for Industrial and Applied Mathematics.

Hume, David. 1752 [1970]. "Of the Populousness of Ancient Nations," in *David Hume; Writings on Economics*, edited by Eugene Rotwein, 108–194. Madison: University of Wisconsin Press.

Iannelli, M., M. Martcheva, and F.A. Milner. 2005. *Gender-Structured Population Modeling; Mathematical Methods, Numerics, and Simulations*. Philadelphia: Society for Industrial and Applied Mathematics.

INDEPTH Network. 2004. *Model Life Tables for Sub-Saharan Africa*. Aldershot, Hants, U.K.: Ashgate.

Isen, Adem, and Betsey Stevenson. 2011. "Women's Education and Family Behavior: Trends in Marriage, Divorce, and Fertility" in *Demography and the Economy*, edited by John B. Shoven, 43–140. Chicago: University of Chicago Press.

Johnson, A.C. 1936. *Roman Egypt, to the Reign of Diocletian*. Baltimore: Johns Hopkins University Press.

Jones, Charles. 2001. "Was an Industrial Revolution Inevitable? Economic Growth Over the Very Long Run," *Advances in Macroeconomics* 1: 1–43.

Jones, Charles I. 2003. "Population and Ideas: A Theory of Endogenous Growth," in *Knowledge, Information, and Expectations in Macroeconomics (in Honor of Edmund S. Phelps)*, edited by Philippe Aghion, Roman Frydman, Joseph Stiglitz, and Michael Woodford, 498–521. Princeton: Princeton University Press.

Jones, Donald W. 1999. "The Conundrum of Greek Population Growth in the 8th Century B.C.: Burials, Settlements, and Wells," *Opuscula Atheniensia* 24: 25–50.

Jones, Larry E., and Alice Schoonbroodt. 2010. "Complements Versus Substitutes and Trends in Fertility Choice in Dynastic Models," *International Economic Review* 5:1671–699.

Jones, Larry E., Alice Schoonbroodt, and Michèle Tertilt. 2011. "Fertility Theories; Can They Explain the Negative Fertility-Income Relationship," in *Demography and the Economy*, edited by John B. Shoven, 43–100. Chicago: University of Chicago Press.

Jones, Larry E., and Alice Schoonbroodt. 2011. "Baby Busts and Baby Booms: The Fertility Response to Shocks in Dynastic Models, ms. June, https:/sites.google.com/site/aliceschoonbroodt/research.

Jütte, Robert. 2008. *Contraception: A History*, translated by Vicky Russell. Malden, Mass.: Polity.

Kajanto, Iiro. 1969. "On Divorce Among the Common People of Rome," *Revue des etudes latines: mélanges Maracel Durry* 47 bis: 99–113.

Keyfitz, Nathan. 1968. *Introduction to the Mathematics of Population*. Reading, Mass.: Addison-Wesley.

Keyfitz, Nathan. 1975. *Applied Mathematical Demography*. New York: Wiley.

Keyfitz, Nathan, and Hal Caswell. 2005. *Applied Mathematical Demography*, 3rd Ed. New York: Springer.

Kirk, Dudley. 1996. "Demographic Transition Theory," *Population Studies* 50: 361–387.

Knodel, John. 1978. "Natural Fertility in Pre-Industrial Germany," *Population Studies* 32: 481–510.

Kremer, Michael. 1993. "Population Growth and Technological Change: One Million BC to 1990," *Quarterly Journal of Economics* 108: 681–716.

Kuczynski, Robert R. 1932. *Fertility and Reproduction*. New York: Falcon.

Lacey, W. K. 1968. *The Family in Classical Greece*. Ithaca: Cornell University Press.

Laslett, Peter ed., with the assistance of Richard Wall. 1972. *Household and Family in Past Time*. Cambridge: Cambridge University Press.

Lee, Ronald D. 1975a. "Natural Fertility, Population Cycles and the Spectral Analysis of Births and Marriages," *Journal of the American Statistical Association* 70: 295–304;

Lee, Ronald D. 1975b. "A Historical Perspective on Economic Aspects of the Population Explosion: The Case of Preindustrial England," in *Population Change in Developing Countries*, edited by Richard A. Easterlin, 517–566. Chicago: University of Chicago Press.

Lee, Ronald D. 1978. "Models of Preindustrial Population Dynamics with Application to England," in *Historical Studies of Changing Fertility*, edited by Charles Tilly, 155–207. Princeton: Princeton University Press.

Lee, Ronald Demos, 1980. "A Historical Perspective on Economic Aspects of the Population Explosion: The Case of Preindustrial England," in *Population and Economic Change in Developing Countries*, edited by Richard A. Easterlin, 517–566. Chicago: University of Chicago Press.

Lee, Ronald D. 1985. Population Homeostasis and English Demographic History," *Journal of Interdisciplinary History* 15: 635–660.

Lee, Ronald Demos. 1986. "Malthus and Boserup: A Dynamic Synthesis," in *The State of Population Theory; Forward from Malthus*, edited by David Coleman and Roger Schofield, 96–130. Oxford: Basil Blackwell.

Lee, Ronald Demos. 1988. "Induced Population Growth and Induced Technological Progress: Their Interaction in the Accelerating Stage," *Mathematical Population Studies* 1: 265–288.

Lee, Ronald D. 1987. "Population Dynamics of Humans and Other Animals," *Demography* 24: 443–465.

Lee, Ronald. 1993. "Accidental and Systematic Change in Population History: Homeostasis in a Stochastic Setting," *Explorations in Economic History* 30: 1–30.

Lee, Ronald D. 1994. "The Formal Demography of Population Aging, Transfers, and the Economic Life Cycle," in *Demography of Aging*, edited by Linda G. Martin and Samuel H. Preston, 8–41. Washington, D.C.: National Academy Press.

Lee, Ronald D. 1997. "Population Dynamics: Equilibrium, Disequilibrium, and Consequences of Fluctuations," in *Handbook of Population and Family Economics, Vol. 1B* , edited by Mark R. Rosenzweig and Oded Stark, 1063–1115. Amsterdam: Elsevier.

Lee, Ronald, with the assistance of Tim Miller. 1990. "Population Policy and Externalities to Childbearing," *Annals of the American Academy of Political and Social Science* 510: 17–32.

Lee, Ronald D., and Karen L. Kramer. 2002. "Children's Economic Roles in the Maya Family Life Cycle: Cain, Caldwell, and Chayanov Revisited," *Population and Development Review* 28: 475–499.

Lemos, Irene S. 2002. *The Protogeometric Aegean; The Archaeology of the Late Eleventh and Tenth Centuries BC*. Oxford: Oxford University Press.

Leridon, Henri. 1977. *Human Fertility; The Basic Components*, transl. by Judith F. Helzner. Chicago: University of Chicago Press.

Leslie, P. H. 1945. "On the Use of Matrices in Certain Population Mathematics," *Biometrika* 33: 183–212.

Leslie, P. H. 1948. "Some Further Notes on the Use of Matrices in Population Mathematics," *Biometrika* 35: 213–245.

Levin, Martin L., and C. Joseph O'Hara. 1978. "The Impact of Marital History of Current Husband on the Fertility of

Remarried White Women in the United States," *Journal of Marriage and the Family* 40: 95–102.

Livi-Bacci, Massimo. 1991. *Population and Nutrition; An Essay on European Demographic History*. Cambridge: Cambridge University Press.

Livi-Bacci, Massimo. 2007. *A Concise History of World Population*. Oxford: Blackwell.

Loomis, William T. 1998. *Wages, Welfare Costs and Inflation in Classical Athens*. Ann Arbor, Mich.: University of Michigan Press.

Lotka, Alfred J. 1907. "Mode of Growth of Material Aggregates," *American Journal of Science* 24: 199–216.

Lotka, Alfred J. 1939. *Théorie analytique des associations biologiques. Part II. Analyse démographique avec application particulière à l'espèce humaine*. Paris: Hermann & Cie, recently available as *Analytical Theory of Biological Populations*, translated by D.P. Smith and H. Rossert. New York, Plenum, 1998.

Lucas, Jr., Robert E. 1988. "On the Mechanics of Economic Development," *Journal of Monetary Economics* 22: 3–42.

Lucas, Jr., Robert E. 1992. "Making a Miracle," *Econometrica* 61: 251–272.

Lundberg, Shelly, and Robert A. Pollak. 1993. "Separate Spheres Bargaining and the Marriage Market," *Journal of Political Economy* 101: 988–1010.

Lundberg, Shelly, and Robert A. Pollak. 1996. "Bargaining and Distribution in Marriage," *Journal of Economic Perspectives* 10 No. 4: 139–158.

Macunovich, Diane J. 1998. "Fertility and the Easterlin Hypothesis: An Assessment of the Literature," *Journal of Population Economics* 11: 53–111.

Manser Marilyn, and Murray Brown. 1980. "Marriage and Household Decision-Making: A Bargaining Analysis," *International Economic Review* 21: 31–44.

McElroy, Marjorie B. 1990. "The Empirical Content of Nash-Bargained Household Behavior," *Journal of Human Resources* 25: 559–583.

McElroy, Marjorie B., and Mary Jean Horney. 1981. "Nash-Bargained Household Decisions: Toward a Generalization of the Theory of Demand," *International Economic Review* 22: 333–349.

McEvedy, Colin, and Richard Jones.1978. *Atlas of World Population History*. Harmondsworth, Middlesex: Penguin.

McKeown, Thomas. 1976. *The Rise of Modern Population*. New York: Academic Press.

McKeown, Thomas, and R.G. Brown. 1955. "Medical Evidence Related to English Population Changes in the Eighteenth Century," *Population Studies* 9: 119–141.

McLaren, Angus. 1990. *A History of Contraception; From Antiquity to the Present Day*. Oxford: Blackwell.

Meltzer, David Owen. 1992. "Mortality Decline; The Demographic Transition, and Economic Growth," Ph.D. Dissertation, Economics, University of Chicago.

Menken, Jane. 1979. "Introduction," in *Natural Fertility; Patterns and Determinants of Natural Fertility: Proceedings of a Seminar on Natural Fertility*, edited by Henri Leridon and Jane Menken, 3–13. Liège: Ordina.

Meskell, Lynn. 1999. *Archaeologies of Social Life: Age, Sex, Class et cetera in Ancient Egypt*. Malden, Mass.: Blackwell.

Michael, Robert T. 1973. "Education and the Derived Demand for Children," *Journal of Political Economy* 81: S141–A142.

Moggridge, Donald, Ed. 1982. *The Collected Writings of John Maynard Keynes, Volume XXVIII. Social, Political and Literary Writings*. London: Macmillan and Cambridge University Press.

Mokyr, Joel. 2002. *The Gift of Athena: Historical Origins of the Knowledge Economy*. Princeton: Princeton University Press.

Morens, David M., and Robert J. Littman. 1992. "Epidemiology of the Plague in Athens," *Transactions of the American Philological Association* 122: 271–304.

Morley, Neville. 2005. Review of *Debating Roman Demography*, *Topoi* 12–13: 429–434.

Morley, Neville. 2011. "Demography and Development in Classical Antiquity," in *Demography and the Graeco-Roman World; New Insights and Approaches*, edited by Claire Holleran and April Pudsey, 14–36. Cambridge: Cambridge University Press, 2011.

Morris, Ian. 1999. "Archaeology and Gender Ideologies in Early Archaic Greece," *Transactions of the American Philological Association* 129: 305–317.

Muth, Richard F. 1994, "Real Land Rentals in Early Roman Egypt," *Explorations in Economic History* 31: 210–224.

Neher, Philip A. 1971. "Peasants, Procreation, and Pensions," *American Economic Review* 61: 380–389.

Nerlove, Marc, Assaf Razin, and Efraim Sadka. 1987. *Household and Economy; Welfare Economics of Endogenous Fertility*. Boston: Academic Press.

Nevitt, Lisa C. 1995. "Gender Relations in the Classical Greek Household: The Archaeological Evidence," *Annual of the British School at Athens* 90: 363–381.

Nevitt, Lisa C. 1999. *House and Society in the Ancient Greek World*. Cambridge: Cambridge University Press.

Nevitt, Lisa C. 2010. *Domestic Space in Classical Antiquity*. Cambridge: Cambridge University Press.

Newell, Colin. 1988. *Methods and Models in Demography*. New York: Guildford.

Okun, Barbara S. 1994. "Evaluating Methods for Detecting Fertility Control: Coale and Trussell's Method and Cohort Parity Analysis," *Population Studies* 48: 193–222.

Olsen, Randall J. 1980. "Estimating the Effect of Child Mortality on the Number of Births," *Demography* 17: 429–443.

Olsen," Randall J. 1983. "Mortality Rates, Mortality Events, and the Number of Births," *American Economic Review Papers and Proceedings* 73: 29–32.

Olsen, Randall J. 1994. "Fertility and the Size of the U.S. Labor Force," *Journal of Economic Literature* 32: 60–100.

Olsen, Randall J., and Kenneth I. Wolpin. 1983. "The Impact of Exogenous Child Mortality on Fertility: A Waiting Time Regression with Dynamic Regressors," *Econometrica* 51: 731–749.

Osborne, Robin. 1985. *Demos; The Discovery of Classical Attika*. Cambridge: Cambridge University Press.

Paine, Richard R. 2000, "If a Population Crashes in Prehistory, and There is No Paleodemographer There to Hear It, Does It Make a Sound?" *American Journal of Physical Anthropology* 112: 181–190.

Paine Richard R., and Glenn R. Storey. 2006. "Epidemics, Age at Death, and Mortality in Ancient Rome," in *Urbanism in the Preindustrial World*, edited by Glenn R. Storey, 69–85. Tuscaloosa, Ala.: University of Alabama Press.

Pampel, Fred C., and H. Elizabeth Peters. 1995. "The Easterlin Effect," *Annual Review of Sociology* 21: 163–194.

Parkin, Tim G. 1992. *Demography and Roman Society*. Baltimore: Johns Hopkins University Press.

Parkin, Tim 1995. Review of Roger S. Bagnall and Bruce W. Frier, *The Demography of Roman Egypt*, in *Bryn Mawr Classical Review*, March 20, 1995.

Parkin, Tim G. 2003. *Old Age in the Roman World; A Cultural and Social History*. Baltimore: Johns Hopkins University Press.

Parkin, Tim. 2011a. "From the Margins to the Centre State; Some Closing Reflections on Ancient Historical Demography," in *Demography and the Graeco-Roman World; New Insights and Approaches*, edited by Claire Holleran and April Pudsey, 181–188. Cambridge: Cambridge University Press.

Parkin, Tim. 2011b. "The Roman Life Course and the Family," in *A Companion to Families in the Greek and Roman Worlds*, edited by Beryl Rawson, 276–290. Malden, Mass.: Wiley-Blackwell.

Patterson, Cynthia B. 1998. *The Family in Greek History*. Cambridge, Mass.: Harvard University Press.

Phelps, Edmund S. 1968. "Population Increase," *Canadian Journal of Economics* 1: 497–505.

Polanyi, Karl. 1944. *The Great Transformation*. New York: Rinehart.

Pollak, Robert A. 1987a. "The Two-Sex Model with Persistent Unions: A Generalization of the Birth Matrix-Mating Rule Model," *Theoretical Population Biology* 32: 176–187.

Pollak, Robert A. 1987b. "A Reformulation of the Two-Sex Problem," *Demography* 23: 247–259.

Pollak, Robert A. 1990. "Two-Sex Demographic Models," *Journal of Political Economy* 98: 399–420.

Pollard, J.H 1973. *Mathematical Models for the Growth of Human Populations*. Cambridge: Cambridge University Press.

Pomeroy, Sarah B. 1975. *Goddesses, Whores, Wives, and Slaves: Women in Classical Antiquity*. New York: Schocken.

Pomeroy, Sarah B. 1997. *Families in Classical and Hellenistic Greece: Representations and Realities*. Oxford: Oxford University Press.

Pomeroy. Sarah B. 1994. *Xenophon Oeconomicus: A Social and Historical Commentary*. Oxford: Clarendon Press.

Pomeroy, Sarah B. 2002. *Spartan Women*. Oxford: Oxford University Press.

Postgate, J. N.1992. *Early Mesopotamia: Society and Economy at the Dawn of History*. London: Routledge.

Preston, Samuel H. 1993. "The Contours of Demography: Estimates and Projections," *Demography* 30: 593–606.

Preston, Samuel H., Antonio McDaniel, and Carlos Grushka. 1993. "New Model Life Tables for High-Mortality Populations," *Historical Methods* 26: 149–159.

Preston, Samuel H., Patrick Heuveline, and Michel Guillot. 2001. *Demography; Measuring and Modeling Population Processes*. Oxford: Blackwell.

Pryor, Frederic L., and Stephen B. Maurer. 1982. "On Induced Economic Change in Precapitalist Societies," *Journal of Development Economics* 10: 325–353.

Pudsey, April. 2011. "Nuptiality and the Demographic Life Cycle," in *Demography and the Greco-Roman World; New Insights and Approaches*, edited by Claire Holleran and April Pudsey, 60–98. Cambridge: Cambridge University Press.

Rathbone, Dominic. 1996. "Monetization, Not Price-Inflation, in Third-Century A.D. Egypt?" in *Coin Finds and Coin Use in the Roman World*, edited by C. E. King and D. G. Wigg, 321–339. Berlin: G. Mann.

Rathbone, Dominic. 1997. "Prices and Price Formation in Roman Egypt," in *Économie antique: prix et formations des prix dans les economies antiques*, edited by Jean Andreau, Pierre Briant, and Raymond Descat, 183–244. Saint-Bertrand-de-Comminges: MuseÏe archeÏologique deÏpartemental.

Rathbone, Dominic W. 1991. *Economic Rationalism and Rural Society in Third-Century A.D. Egypt: The Heroninos Archive and the Appianus Estate*. Cambridge: Cambridge University Press.

Rawson, Beryl. 1986. "The Roman Family," in *The Family in Ancient Rome; New Perspectives*, edited by Beryl Rawson, 1–57. Ithaca: Cornell University Press.

Rawson, Beryl, ed. 1991. *Marriage, Divorce and Children in Ancient Rome*. Oxford: Clarendon Press.

Razin, Assaf, and Uri Ben-Zion. 1975. "An Intergenerational Model of Population Growth," *American Economic Review* 65: 923–933.

Razin, Assaf, and Efraim Sadka 1995. *Population Economics*. Cambridge, Mass.: MIT Press.

Riddle, John M. 1992. *Contraception and Abortion from the Ancient World to the Renaissance*. Cambridge, Mass.: Harvard University Press.

Riddle, John M. 1997. *Eve's Herbs; A History of Contraception and Abortion in the West*. Cambridge, Mass.: Harvard University Press.

Riley Nancy E., and James McCarthy. 2003. *Demography in the Age of the Postmodern*. Cambridge: Cambridge University Press.

Robinson, Warren, and Wayne Schutjer. 1984. "Agricultural Development and Demographic Change: A Generalization of the Boserup Model," *Economic Development and Cultural Change* 32: 355–366.

Rogers, Andrei. 1975. *Introduction to Multiregional Mathematical Demography*. New York: Wiley.

Rogers, Andrei. 1995. *Multiregional Demography: Principles, Methods and Extensions*. Chichester: Wiley.

Romer, Paul. 1986. "Increasing Returns and Long-Run Growth," *Journal of Political Economy* 94: 1002–1037.

Romer, Paul. 1990. "Endogenous Technological Change," *Journal of Political Economy* 98: 71–102.

Rosenzweig Mark R., and T. Paul Schultz. 1983. "Consumer Demand and Household Production: The Relationship Between Fertility and Child Mortality," *American Economic Review Papers and Proceedings* 73: 38–42.

Rutter, Jeremy. 2003. "Children in Aegean Prehistory," in *Coming of Age in Ancient Greece: Images of Childhood from the Classical Past*, edited by Jenifer Neils and John H. Oakley, 31–57. New Haven: Yale University Press.

Sah, Raaj K. 1991. "The Effects of Child Mortality Changes on Fertility Choice and Parental Welfare," *Journal of Political Economy* 99: 582–606.

Sallares, Robert. 1991. *The Ecology of the Ancient Greek World*. Ithaca: Cornell University Press.

Sallares, Robert. 2002. *Malaria and Rome; A History of Malaria in Ancient Italy*. Oxford: Oxford University Press.

Saller, Richard P. 1987. "Men's Age at Marriage and Its Consequences for the Roman Family," *Classical Philology* 82: 21–34.

Saller, Richard P. 1994. *Patriarchy, Property and Death in the Roman Family*. Cambridge: Cambridge University Press.

Samuelson, Paul A. 1958. "An Exact Consumption-Loan Model of Interest with or without the Social Contrivance of Money," *Journal of Political Economy* 66: 467–482.

Scheidel, Walter. 1995a. "The Most Silent Women of Greece and Rome: Rural Labour and Women's Life in the Ancient World (I), *Greece & Rome* Second Ser. 42: 202–217.

Scheidel, Walter. 1996b. "The Most Silent Women of Greece and Rome: Rural Labour and Women's Life in the Ancient World (II), *Greece & Rome* Second Ser. 43: 1–10.

Scheidel, Walter. 1996. *Measuring Sex, Age and Death in the Roman Empire; Explorations in Ancient Demography, Journal of Roman Archaeology* Supplementary Series 21. Ann Arbor, Mich.: Cushing-Malloy.

Scheidel, Walter. 2001a. "Progress and Problems in Roman Demography," in *Debating Roman Demography, Mnemosyne* Supplement 211, edited by Walter Scheidel, 1–81. Leiden: Brill.

Scheidel, Walter. 2001b. *Death on the Nile; Disease and Demography of Roman Egypt, Mnemosyne* Supplement 228. Leiden: Brill, 2001.

Scheidel, Walter. 2002. "A Model of Demographic and Economic Change in Roman Egypt after the Antonine Plague," *Journal of Roman Archaeology* 15: 97–114.

Scheidel, Walter. 2003. "The Greek Population Expansion: Models and Comparisons," *Journal of Hellenic Studies* 123: 120–140.

Scheidel, Walter. 2008. "Demography," in *The Cambridge Economic History of the Greco-Roman World*, edited by Walter Scheidel, Ian Morris, and Richard P. Saller, 38–86. Cambridge: Cambridge University Press, 2008.

Schoen, Robert. 1983. "Measuring the Tightness of a Marriage Squeeze," *Demography* 20: 61–78.

Schoen, Robert. 1988. *Modeling Multigroup Populations*. New York: Plenum.

Schoen, Robert. 2006. *Dynamic Population Models*. New York: Springer.

Schultz, T. Paul. 1990. "Testing the Neoclassical Model of Family Labor Supply and Fertility," *Journal of Human Resources* 25: 599–634.

Sharpe, F. R., and A. J. Lotka. 1911. "A Problem in Age Distribution," *Philosophical Magazine*, Ser. 6, 21: 435–438.

Sheps, Mindel C., and Jane A. Menken, with assistance of Annette P. Radick.1973. *Mathematical Models of Conception and Birth*. Chicago: University of Chicago Press.

Sheridan, Jennifer A. 1998. "Not at a Loss for Words: The Economic Power of Literate Women in Late Antique Egypt," *Transactions of the American Philological Association* 128: 189–203.

Simon, Julian L. 1977. *The Economics of Population Growth*. Princeton: Princeton University Press.

Simon, Julian L. 1986. *Theory of Population and Economic Growth*. Oxford: Basil Blackwell, 1986.

Simon, Julian L. 2003. "What Determined the Onset of Modern Progress in the Standard of Living?" in *Population and Economy; From Hunger to Modern Economic Growth*, edited by T. Bengtsson and O. Saito, 21–48. Oxford: Oxford University Press.

Siow, Aloysius. 2008. "How Does the Marriage Market Clear? An Empirical Framework," *Canadian Journal of Economics* 41: 1121–1155.

Stavins, Robert. 1988. "A Model of English Demographic Change: 1573–1873," *Explorations in Economic History* 25: 98–116.

Strong, Anise K. 2012. "Working Girls: Mother-Daughter Bonds among Ancient Prostitutes," in *Mothering and Motherhood in Ancient Greece and Rome*, edited by Lauren Hackworth Petersen and Patricia Salzman-Mitchel, 121–139. Austin, Tex.: University of Texas Press.

Tandy, David W. and Walter C. Neale. 1996. *Hesiod's Works and Days; A Translation and Commentary for the Social Sciences*. Berkeley: University of California Press.

Thomas, Duncan. 1990. "Intra-Household Resource Allocation: An Inferential Approach," *Journal of Human Resources* 25: 635–664.

Tilley, Charles. 1978. "The Historical Study of Vital Processes," in *Historical Studies of Changing Fertility*, edited by Charles Tilly, 3–56. Princeton: Princeton University Press.

Treggiari, Susan. 1991. "Divorce Roman Style: How Easy and How Frequent Was It?" in *Marriage, Divorce and Children in Ancient Rome*, edited by Beryl Rawson, 31–45. Oxford: Oxford University Press.

Trigger, B. G., B. J. Kemp, D. O'Connor, and A. B. Lloyd. 1983. *Ancient Egypt; A Social History*. Cambridge: Cambridge University Press.

Trumper, Monika. 2011. "Space and Social Relationships in the Greek *Oikos* of the Classical and Hellenistic Periods," in *A Companion to Families in the Greek and Roman Worlds*, edited by Beryl Rawson, 32–52. Malden, Mass.: Wiley-Blackwell.

Trussell, James. 1979. "Natural Fertility: Measurement and Use in Fertility Models," in *Natural Fertility; Patterns and Determinants of Natural Fertility: Proceedings of a Seminar on Natural Fertility* Henri Leridon and Jane Menken, 31–64. Liège: Ordina.

United Nations. 1982. *Model Life Tables for Developing Countries*. Population Study No. 77. New York: United Nations.

Vermeulen, Frederic. 2002. "Collective Household Models: Principles and Main Results," *Journal of Economic Surveys* 16: 533–654.

Wachter, Michael L. 1975. "A Time-Series Fertility Equation: The Potential for a Baby Boom in the 1980's," *International Economic Review* 16: 609–624.

Wachter, Kenneth D. 1991. "Elusive Cycles: Are There Dynamically Possible Lee-Easterlin Models for U.S. Births?" *Population Studies* 45: 109–135.

Wachter, Kenneth D., and Ronald D. Lee. 1989. "U.S. Birth and Limit Cycle Models," *Demography* 26: 99–115.

Wallace-Hadrill, Andrew1994. *Houses and Society in Pompeii and Herculaneum*. Princeton: Princeton University Press.

Willis, Robert J. 1973. "A New Approach to the Economic Theory of Fertility Behavior," *Journal of Political Economy* 81: S14–S64.

Willis, Robert J. 1982. "The Direction of Intergenerational Transfers and Demographic Transition: The Caldwell Hypothesis Reexamined," *Population and Development Review* 8, *Supplement: Income Distribution and the Family*: 207–234.

Willis, Robert J. 1988. "Life Cycles, Institutions, and Population Growth: A Theory of the Equilibrium Rate of Interest in an Overlapping Generations Model," in *Economics of Changing Age Distributions in Developed Countries*, edited by Ronald D. Lee, W. Brian Arthur, and Gerry Rodgers, 106–138. Oxford: Clarendon Press.

Wilson, Chris, Jim Oeppen, and Mike Pardoe. 1988. "What Is Natural Fertility? The Modeling of a Concept," *Population Index* 54: 4–20.

Wineberg, Howard, 1990. "Childbearing after Remarriage," *Journal of Marriage and the Family* 52: 31–38.

Wolpin, Kenneth I. 1984. "An Estimable Dynamic Stochastic Model of Fertility and Child Mortality," *Journal of Political Economy* 92: 852–874.

Wolpin, Kenneth I. 1997. "Determinants and Consequences of the Mortality and Health of Infants and Children," in *Handbook of Population and Family Economics, Vol. 1A*, edited by Mark R. Rosenzweig and Oded Stark, 483–557. Amsterdam: North-Holland.

Wood, James W. 1994. *Dynamics of Human Reproduction; Biology, Biometry, Demography*. New York: Aldine De Gruyter.

Wood, James W. 1998. "A Theory of Preindustrial Population Dynamics: Demography, Economy, and Well-Being in Malthusian Systems," *Current Anthropology* 39: 99–135.

Woods, Robert. 2000. *The Demography of Victorian England and Wales*. Cambridge: Cambridge University Press.

Woods, Robert. 2007. "Ancient and Early Modern Mortality: Experience and Understanding," *Economic History Review* 60: 373–399.

5

The Behavior of Aggregate Economies: Macroeconomics

5.1 Introduction

Macroeconomics is a vast subject. The typical intermediate macroeconomics textbook is around 600 pages. Several are in the range of 800 pages. There are books—textbooks and treatises—on a number of the sections of this chapter that run to 500 to 600 pages. Monographs on the subjects of some of the sub-sections run to 450 pages. In the fifty-some-odd pages of this chapter, excluding the pictures, I cannot hope to reproduce the detail of the textbooks or the full richness of the treatises and monographs. This chapter will not make the reader a functioning macroeconomist. With disclaimers such as these, what excuse is there for writing it?

The goal of this chapter is to introduce the archaeologist, ancient historian, or philologist who has absorbed a fair bit of the material of the preceding chapters to the major concepts of contemporary macroeconomics so she can decide what is useful in interpreting economic data from antiquity. Simply knowing more precisely what some of the terms whose meanings are commonly mangled in everyday, or occasionally scholarly, parlance actually mean can help clarify thoughts. Learning how to state what one means precisely, particularly when working with subject matter primarily outside one's own, can be an immeasurable boon to scholarship and interdisciplinary communication. For example, the very adjective macroeconomic itself is thrown around in ways that make economists, much less professional macroeconomists, cringe. Whether the subject matter of macroeconomics proves useful to scholarship on antiquity must be left to the judgment of specialists on antiquity, but without at least a passing familiarity with that subject matter, how would they know?

This chapter is a very broad-brush overview, hitting all of the major topics of contemporary macroeconomics that I have thought might find some applicability at some time and place in antiquity. It aims to give the determined reader (it's frankly not a chapter for casual readers) a working familiarity with the basic concepts of the field and a substantive feel for how the various concepts relate to one another. The lengthy intermediate textbooks noted above typically involve an academic year of course work. Practicing professionals in another field generally cannot spare the time or mental energy to such an endeavor, especially when it may have such a speculative payoff. This chapter is intended to lower the entry cost to macroeconomics to Classical archaeologists, ancient historians, and philologists. For those who find the material useful to their research, the references in the footnotes offer guidance to a number of options for more intensive study, which this chapter should make more productive.

5.1.1 What is Macroeconomics?

Macroeconomics is the study of national income, employment and unemployment, the price level and inflation, and interest rates, and how these quantities behave and interact over long periods of growth and during short-run fluctuations around long-run trends.[1]

While microeconomics, or price theory, undergirds macroeconomic theories, macroeconomics differs greatly from microeconomic analysis. First, any national economy is comprised of many goods markets, possibly a number of distinct labor markets, and markets for many different assets. To compress all these markets into a small enough number to let their behavior be understood requires considerable aggregation. Many of the characteristics of individual markets that would be necessary to account for in studies of those particular markets must be assumed away. Second, microeconomics always analyzes relative prices—the price of one or more goods relative to that of some numeraire good. Macroeconomics analyzes both relative prices and absolute prices, the latter being the prices of (aggregated) goods and assets denominated ordinarily in some currency. Third, macroeconomics necessarily introduces money into an analysis of markets, whereas money is generally absent from price-theoretic studies, although relative prices in empirical microeconomic studies are often denominated in a currency. The introduction of money necessarily brings along with it the distinction between nominal and real prices, with inflation being the link between those two concepts. Inflation is the change in a price level over time. A price level is a weighted average of all goods and services prices in an economy. A change in a single price is sometimes referred to, erroneously and misleadingly, as "inflation" in the price

[1] I have used many sources for both information and pedagogical examples. In many parts of the chapter it is difficult to identify exactly which sources have exerted what influences, but in some sections in which my debts are more pinpointed, I offer specific citations from among the following and others: Abel and Bernanke (1998); Abel et al. (2011); Arnold (2002); Azariadis (1993); Barro (1997; 2008); Bénassy (2011); Blanchard (1997; 2000; 2011); Blanchard and Fischer (1989); de la Croix and Michel (2002); Dornbusch, Fischer and Startz (1998; 2008); Farmer (1999); Galí (2008); Flaschel et al. (1997); Heijdra (2009); Krugman and Wells (2009); Mankiw (2006; 2010; 2018); Friedman and Woodford (2011, various chapters); Laidler (1993); Ljungqvist and Sargent (2004); McCandless (2008); Candless, with Wallace (1991); Patinkin (1965); Romer (1993; 2006); Sargent (1979; 1987); Snowdon and Vane (2005); Taylor and Woodford (1999, various chapters); Turnovsky (1977; 2000); Woodford (1999; 2003).

of that good. You will do yourself a service by dismissing that expression from your mind and never using it. Inflation is the change in the level of an entire array of prices. When a single price goes up or down, that price just changed—a relative price change. When inflation is negative, i.e., when the price level declines, it is called deflation. Fourth, macroeconomics deals with departures from full employment; full employment is a standard assumption of microeconomic analyses, particularly general equilibrium analyses. In price-theoretic analyses, product and factor prices adjust rapidly to reallocate resources so that they all remain fully employed—known as assuming that all markets clear—that supply equals demand when the day is done. This is fine for many types of analysis, in which unemployment of some factors of production, or failure of some products to be sold, is not the focus of analysis. Fifth, macroeconomics always deals with intertemporal situations, whereas static (i.e., atemporal) analysis is satisfactory for many microeconomic analyses. Interest rates are relative prices of consumption at different dates, and people hold assets in one period so that they may convert them into consumption at a later date. Even when the analysis is only implicitly intertemporal, macroeconomics always deals with time paths of its major variables.

Macroeconomics is intensely practical. In fact, its sole reason for existence is to offer policy makers guidance on fiscal, monetary, exchange rate, and related national policies. Accordingly, the models build in particular institutions. For example, in macroeconomic models, monetary policy is generally implemented by a central bank through the purchase or sale of assets, transactions that simply did not occur in antiquity.[2] The focus of analysis in short- and medium-run macroeconomic general equilibrium models is on policies to compensate for a particular type of disturbance (stabilization policies) or the consequences of a type of government action. Again, ancient governments generally wouldn't have thought of stabilization policies as we understand them today, although the Roman government is thought to have responded to cash shortages and financial panics by increasing the money supply.[3] However, this contemporary, practical focus of macroeconomic theory need not channel the student of antiquity into senseless analyses of policies which didn't exist, or into ignoring a body of theory thought to be irrelevant. Governments undertook fiscal and monetary policies in antiquity without thinking of them as such, but the results, which macroeconomic theory addresses, would have been largely the same as they would under similar circumstances today, with allowances for differences in some markets. Long-run macroeconomics, which is largely growth theory, is not highly policy oriented, and the present chapter will not address that material.

While a number of the issues that macroeconomics deals with can be traced back to analysis several hundred years ago (for instance, what didn't Adam Smith discuss?), it is a relatively new field of economics, arguably being born out of the failure of economic policies worldwide during the Great Depression of the 1930s. Without dragging readers through a history of thought on national income and business cycles, it will be helpful for them to know about major schools of macroeconomic thought which they might encounter in their separate study. A body of theory relating the money stock, the price level and national income existed at the time of the Great Depression, theory which has subsequently become known as Classical (since it was the only one around at the time, it didn't call itself Classical) macroeconomics, but with its emphasis on rapid, even instantaneous price adjustment, it had difficulty understanding unemployment, the salient social and economic feature of the Great Depression. Keynesian theory, entering the scene in 1936, was developed on the substrate of Classical theory and offered a coherent theory of short-run fluctuations (business cycles) focused on demand, which included unemployment and the failure of prices and wages to adjust downward to clear markets. By the early 1950s, Keynesian ideas had been incorporated with parts of the pre-existing theory to form a body of macroeconomics known as the Neoclassical Synthesis about which emerged a broad, although not universal, consensus which lasted into the early 1970s, when it was overtaken by the combination of unemployment and high inflation, which the Keynesian theory of the time had trouble understanding. In the background, from the early 1950s, a monetarist intellectual movement, centered on Milton Friedman and his students, developed at the University of Chicago. It eventually convinced the macroeconomic community of the continuing importance of money, which Keynes' 1936 model had de-emphasized, but also brought to the fore the importance of expectations, which culminated in the rational expectations movement that swept the field in the '70s. The monetarist and Keynesian strands of macroeconomics coalesced to a great extent by the late '70s, just in time to get buffeted by new approaches (although some might call it old wine in new bottles). During the early 1970s and mid-1980s, two new approaches to macroeconomics developed, to a great extent seeing how far the pre-Keynesian approach, with its emphasis on flexible prices, might be revived—New Classical Economics and Real Business Cycle (RBC) Theory. Both challenged the microeconomic underpinnings of Keynesian macroeconomics as being ad hoc, and both took up the rational expectations formulations brought in by the monetarists during the 1960s. Whereas Keynes had introduced the concept of shocks to demand, the New Classical and RBC theorists focused on shocks to supply. Neither New Classical macroeconomics nor RBC Theory gained wide acceptance—neither proved able to generate movements in major variables that looked like empirical business cycles—but each made

[2] That said, during the 5th century B.C.E. the Athenian mint implemented a policy that acted effectively as a central bank adjusting interest rates to maintain full employment. Depending on conditions in currency markets, the mint would adjust the price of minting worn-out coins for re-striking or minting private bullion: when currency seemed to be in a shortage, the mint lowered the price of minting, and when it seemed in excess supply, it increased the price (Bitros et al. 2021, 62.)

[3] See, for example, Barlow (1980) and Lo Cascio (1981).

methodological contributions which the mainstream of macroeconomics incorporated. From the mid-1970s through the '90s, challenged to produce stronger microeconomic underpinnings for the major components of the Keynesian model, macroeconomists working in that tradition made major strides in those topics, developing better—if yet incomplete—understanding of wage and price setting, which is so critical to the Keynesian approach to macroeconomics with its emphasis on failure of markets to clear. This revitalized body of theory, which is based firmly on microeconomic utility and profit maximization, is called New Keynesian macroeconomics. By the end of the first decade of the 2000s, wide areas of agreement exist among New Keynesians and broadly associated Classicals, although important differences of belief remain regarding the speed of price adjustment, a fulcrum of business cycle theory with wide-ranging implications.

Pedagogically, most introductory and intermediate textbooks present the Keynesian model but show how several differences in key assumptions yield the Classical model within the same overall framework. Research in macroeconomics has long departed from the diagrammatic, or even algebraic, IS-LM curves of early Keynesian theory, but that approach still dominates textbooks. In fact, much of the results of the simpler, textbook models is not modified substantively by the increased complications brought by incorporating the microeconomic optimizations, and the intuition of the older approach is much clearer than what the frontier models provide. Additionally, much of the substance of the most recent macroeconomic modeling addresses sophisticated markets and institutions, with accessible information and continuous transactions, leaving these advances largely irrelevant to situations in antiquity. Accordingly, this chapter presents a simple version of the New Keynesian macroeconomics, with occasional adaptations to earlier institutional conditions, and treatments of supply shocks as well as demand shocks.

One such adaptation in this chapter is a relatively sparing use of expectations, particularly endogenous expectations, in the models presented in this section. Contemporary macroeconomics has found expectations of the future values of variables to be critical influences on the current levels of those variables, and many models, even some in intermediate textbooks. There are cases in which the introduction of expectations can't, and in fact shouldn't, be avoided, such as in the Phillips curve, which is involved in the determination of equilibrium unemployment, and the international interest-rate parity condition. Beyond those cases, I do not emphasize expectations of variables as endogenous variables themselves because I do not think most ancient macroeconomic events moved quickly enough to justify the additional effort and complexity. In the present-day industrialized societies that contemporary macroeconomics studies, and even those societies over the past century, electronic communications, extensive reflection on economic events, and sophisticated thinking on economic relationships have made the formation of expectations very important to how macroeconomic variables such as real and financial investment choices evolve. The values of macroeconomic variables such as inflation rates and exchange rates did not change sufficiently rapidly or often to provide a data base for systematic reflection about their interactions, so that even the more reflective and experienced thinkers in antiquity appear not to have had the depth of experience on which to base ideas which would lead to well-thought-out expectations of how those variables would respond to various events. Undoubtedly business people formed expectations regarding prospects for their own activities, but they had repeated observations of related situations, and that is taken account of in the brief refresher on investment necessary for the introduction to macroeconomic models. Expectations played a more central role in the models presented in Chapter 2 on agriculture, for the very reason that the ancients undoubtedly formed expectations regarding agronomic outcomes and their economic (daily life) correlates because they had so many observations of them.

5.1.2 Why a Chapter on Macroeconomics for Two to Five Millennia Ago?

Why include a chapter on macroeconomics in a handbook targeted at the Eastern Mediterranean and Aegean of 3,000 B.C.E. to ca. 400 CE? Macroeconomics deals with economies with myriads of employers and well-formed financial markets. Even in the most commercially advanced of the economies discovered to date in this region and time period, there's nothing like even the Dacca Stock Exchange, much less the NYSE.

Consider several possible reasons for a chapter. First, the information may be completely unusable, but at least knowing the content of the subject may help you avoid errors in describing some issues that are relevant as "macroeconomic." Second, and somewhat more optimistically, there may have been some times and places where at least some of the conditions required for the development of a macroeconomic model might have been present . . . maybe in Middle and New Kingdom Egypt, some of the Mesopotamian city-states and empires, some Classical Greek city states, surely Imperial Rome, and probably even Republican Rome. Third, conceptualizing the economy of one of these ancient societies in terms of the three aggregated markets typical of macroeconomics—the labor market, the goods market, and the asset market—might actually yield some unexpected insights on issues that are either reported in texts or seem to emerge in the archaeological remains.

Some grounds for optimism about the utility of this information might be found in the foundations of macroeconomic theory. The aggregate labor market model is developed from decisions of individuals to seek work and of firms to hire employees. The consumption model is developed from individual decisions to either consume the fruits of their current labor or save them . . . or dip into the stored-up fruits of previous labor. The asset market model is developed from individuals' decisions regarding how to hold their wealth among assets that could grow in value but at some risk and other assets that would be unexpected to change in value quickly but would be immediately useful as an exchange mechanism. Thinking of macroeconomics at this level, there are considerably wider grounds for optimism regarding the usefulness of the theory for the analysis of many of these ancient economies.

Some further grounds for optimism might be found in actions that we know ancient governments took. Consider some fiscal actions: raising armies (how did they pay for the food to feed men and horses, and what were the consequences?), building fleets (think of Themistocles and the Laureion silver mines), feeding the poor (the Roman plebs), construction projects (Egyptian pyramids, Mesopotamian ziggurats, Greek temples, Roman aqueducts, to name just a few prominent examples). On monetary actions, Themistocles' fiscal policy of building an Athenian navy was implemented by his monetary policy of coining the silver coming out of Laureion. Rome experienced a number of financial crises, from the early 2nd century B.C.E. through the 1st century C.E., during which the government undertook monetary actions to ease conditions in financial markets, even though the causes sometimes remain obscure and the specifics of the government's actions can be debated.

It may be argued reasonably that a number of the phenomena and conditions analyzed by macroeconomic models did not exist or existed only in partial form. Money is a prime example. Until coins came into use around the mid-7th century B.C.E., what served as money was not issued by governments with a monopoly on issue. Media that did serve as money were not always the only unit of account in use, when such units of account even existed. For example, hacksilber was used commonly and extensively in ancient Mesopotamia for medium of exchange, unit of account and store of wealth, but sometimes grain was used as a unit of account as well. Pharaonic Egyptians frequently referred to values in terms of deben, which had both silver and copper weights, but most transactions appear to have been executed without the use of any medium of exchange, the deben remaining conceptual; stores of value, at least for common people, appear to have been largely household odds and ends. Mycenaean Greeks appear to have operated a government taxation system and their largely invisible private economy with neither a unit of account nor a medium of exchange, and their stores of value appear to have included luxury products, raw materials and utilitarian consumables, none with any apparent uniform metric.[4] With this range of variation in one major component of the basic macroeconomic model, how can the theory be applied? One major task of the financial market in a macroeconomic model is to determine the interest rate that equates the supply and demand for various assets. As will be shown below, macroeconomic models simplify financial markets considerably, often classifying financial assets into two types—money and everything else—so that when the market for one of them is in equilibrium, the other is as well, so that only one of them need be modeled. An ancient financial market can be modeled even if money does not exist or is used only for a limited array of purposes, focusing on the market for loans or stores of wealth. If money is privately created, such as the Mesopotamian hacksilber, rather than issued by a government, changes in its supply relative to the demand for it will still change its value and may alter the willingness of market participants to extend loans (i.e., affect the interest rate). Focusing on "the" interest rate rather than money, one might argue that interest rates did not change, so modeling how they do change is irrelevant. Whether interest rates at some time and place were changeable or not is a factual question about which various opinions may be held, but even if they were unchanging, these models can illuminate various consequences of their fixity.

5.2 National Income Accounting

National income accounting helps answer three questions. First, what is the output of an economy—its size, composition and uses? Second, what are the sources and uses of national income? And third, what are the sources of saving, which determine future income?

The broadest measure of the total economic activity of a country in a time period is Gross Domestic Product (GDP). GDP measures current production in an economy, not current sales, and it includes the value of final goods and services only, not intermediate goods. GDP as an aggregate national income concept has become familiar to ancient historians in the past several decades, as several estimates have been made of Roman GDP, one has been made for 4th Century B.C.E. Athens, and one recent estimate for Babylonia in the second half of the 1st millennium B.C.E.—all, of course, single snapshots rather than time series.[5]

There are three approaches to national income accounting: the production or value-added approach, the income approach, and the expenditure approach. The production approach sums value added, or the value of a producer's output minus the value of inputs purchased from other producers, across all activities. The income approach sums all income received by producers, the bulk of which is wages of workers and profits of firm owners. The expenditure approach sums the amounts spent by all ultimate users of products. All three approaches can be used to measure GDP, and will yield the same answer, which implies that total production equals total income which in turn equals total expenditure, a relationship that forms the

[4] Schaps (2004, Chapters 3 and 4) provides a useful overview.

[5] Hopkins (1980, 116–120) was a pioneering effort to estimate gross product. Goldsmith (1984) was the initial effort by an economist. The first revision of Goldsmith's estimate was Temin (2006b). Several subsequent estimates have been published: Maddison (2007, Ch. 1); Scheidel and Friesen (2009); Lo Cascio and Melanima (2009). For Babylonia, Foldvari and van Leeuwen (2010); for Greece, Amemiya (2007, 106–111).

basis of national income accounting. Each approach gives a different view of the structure of an economy, and all three together will yield the most insight.

Gross National Product (GNP) differs from GDP in its inclusion of output produced by labor and capital working outside the country, called net factor payments from abroad (NFP). GNP is the value of final goods and services produced by a country's factors of production during the period wherever they are located, while GDP measures production that occurs within the country itself. Thus GNP = GDP + NFP. NFP can be of considerable importance to a country that has many of its citizens working abroad.

GDP measured with the production approach values output at the prices at which it is sold. Government services are not priced, salaries paid to government workers and goods and services purchased by the government being used instead to measure government production. GDP excludes goods produced in previous periods; for example, a house built in the current period would be included, but the value of an existing house that is sold in the current period would not be. Intermediate goods are used in the production of other goods and services and are not accounted in GDP. However, a capital good used to produce other goods is not accounted as an intermediate good because it is not fully used up during the current period; thus the production of a capital good is included in GDP. Goods that are produced in the current period but remain unsold by the end of the period are accounted as added to inventories, even if such goods ultimately are used as intermediate goods. Additions to inventories are treated as inventory investment; if inventories are drawn down in a period, the inventory investment would receive a negative entry.

The expenditure approach to GDP introduces a number of concepts that are widely used in macroeconomic analysis: production or GDP (Y), private consumption (C), investment, (I), government purchases (G), and net exports (NX). Within the category of government purchases, transfer payments, such as disability payments, and interest payments on debt are excluded from GDP. Although there are a number of variants on it, which will be introduced subsequently, the basic income-expenditure identity is $Y \equiv C + I + G + NX$. For rough orders of magnitude, in recent years in the United States, private consumption has accounted for roughly 70 percent of income, investment for around 15 percent, government purchases for about 20 percent and net exports negative 5 percent (other countries, which have been running trade surpluses—value of exports greater than value of imports—will have positive shares for NX, which will require one or more of the other expenditure categories to shrink).

The income approach yields the measure known as National Income, which includes the compensation of employees, incomes or proprietors, individuals' rental incomes, profits of businesses, net interest (interest received minus interest paid), taxes on domestic production and imports, subsidies (which are subtracted), current transfer payments of businesses (e.g., donations of one kind or another and legal settlements), and surpluses of government enterprises. Adding statistical discrepancy to National Income yields Net National Product (NNP); adding consumption of fixed capital (depreciation) to NNP yields GNP. Finally, subtracting NFP from GNP yields GDP.

It is useful to explore further details of several of these major national income accounting relationships. First, consider the private and government components of aggregate income. The major accounting components can be used to express private disposable income (PDI) and net government income (NGI). Private disposable income is the sum of GDP (Y), net factor payments from abroad (NFP), transfers from the government (TR), and receipts of interest payments on government debt (INT_G), minus taxes (T): $PDI = Y + NFP + TR + INT_G - T$. Net government income is tax receipts (T) minus transfers to the private sector (TR) and interest payments on government debt (INT_G): $NGI = T - TR - INT_G$. Summing private disposable income and net government income, which involves canceling a number of the terms in these two identities, yields GNP: $PDI + NGI = Y + NFP = GNP$.

Next, since saving will play such an important role in macroeconomic analysis, it is useful to delve a little more deeply into private and public saving. Saving is simply income less consumption. Therefore, private saving is private disposable income minus consumption: $S_p = PDI - C = Y + NFP + TR + INT_G - T - C$. Similarly, government saving is simply government's income minus its expenditures: $S_g = NGI - G = T - TR - INT_G - G$. An entire national economy's saving is the sum of private and government saving. Again, adding the two sources of saving together cancels a number of the terms and leaves a simpler expression: $S = S_p + S_g = Y + NFP - C - G$, or national saving is GNP minus private consumption and government expenditure. To examine how saving is used, begin with the income-expenditure identity and substitute the full decomposition of GDP ($C + I + G + NX$) for Y in the expression for national saving: $S = (C + I + G + NX) + NFP - C - G = I + (NX + NFP)$. In international accounts, the sum of net exports, net factor payments from abroad, and net unilateral transfers ($NX + NFP + NTR$) is called the current account balance (CA), or the net payments received from abroad for currently produced goods and services, including factor (labor and capital) services. In the end, $S = I + CA$, which is a critically important accounting relationship. Now, the "uses of saving" identity can be derived by subtracting government savings from both sides of this savings-equals-investment-plus-current-account-balance identity: $S_p = I - S_g + CA$, in which S_g is the government budget surplus (and $-S_g$ is the budget deficit). This uses of saving identity shows that an economy's private savings are used in three ways: investment by firms (I), government borrowings from the private sector (the government budget deficit), and the current account balance in which residents of the home country either lend to ($CA > 0$) or borrow from ($CA < 0$) foreigners. Thus, financing a negative current account balance is one use of a country's aggregate private savings. National savings, when positive, adds to national wealth. National wealth can also be changed by changes in the values of existing assets, be they land, structures, capital equipment, or precious metals.

In the international accounts, the other major component besides the current account is the capital and financial account (KFA). Within the KFA are a financial account, which dominates the transactions in magnitude, and a capital account, which covers unilateral transfers of assets (not to be confounded with the net unilateral transfer payments in the current account, which are payments that do not involve the purchase of a good, service or asset; capital account items are largely gifts in one form or another). A non-zero balance on the current account is financed by a corresponding balance of opposite sign on the KFA: CA + KFA = 0. The intuition of this relationship is that, when a country runs a current account surplus (CA > 0), its residents have sold more goods to foreigners than foreigners have sold to its residents, so in order to finance the difference in value, foreigners must sell assets to home-country residents to raise the funds to cover the difference between the value of their imports and the value of their exports. The purchase of the foreign asset by home-country residents is recorded as a financial outflow (a debit item) since the home-country's funds flow out of the country to purchase the foreign asset. Expressed somewhat more boldly, when residents of a country buy more goods and services than they sell, they have to sell part of the family farm (an asset) to cover the difference.

GDP and GNP are annual measurements (they are also measured quarterly in contemporary national accounts for most countries), so as the level of prices changes over time, an adjustment must be made to their values to be able to distinguish between changes in the real quantities of goods and services an economy produces and changes in their monetary value, which may involve no real change at all. Real GDP is constructed by dividing nominal GDP (GDP of a particular year measured in the prices of that year) by a price index, which is a weighted average of prices in one year relative to those in some base year. There is no unique price index. Different indexes can be constructed with different goods included, depending on what particular level of prices one wants to measure; they can use different weighting schemes (fixed or varying over time to match substitution by consumers as relative prices change); they can have a fixed base period or can have a rolling base period such as a chain-weighted index does. Two common price indexes in use currently are the GDP deflator and the Consumer Price Index (CPI). The GDP deflator weights prices according to the quantities of goods and services produced in a country, whereas a CPI weights them according to the quantities of goods and services consumed in the same country. When exports and imports represent sizeable proportions of output and consumption, the GDP deflator and the CPI can have somewhat different paths over time. The price index used to construct real GDP from nominal GDP is the GDP deflator (which may need to be divided by 100, depending on how one has constructed it).

As simple as price indexes may seem, they are far from simple, and their full treatment is well beyond the scope or needs of the current exposition. That said, two particular intricacies should be pointed out. First, when covering periods of rapid technological change in products or when covering long periods of time when less rapid changes may cumulate materially, some adjustments may need to be made for quality changes. Second, quality changes aside, the GDP deflator is not a cost of living index, as a CPI is.

Price indices allow GDP of a particular economy to be compared at different dates. Another comparison that scholars are inclined to make is between economies—countries—either at the same date or at different dates. These comparisons also introduce complications. First, people in different countries may have widely divergent tastes, leaving it unclear what set of weights to use in constructing indexes that would let them be compared meaningfully: their consumption baskets might be quite different. Second, when income levels differ the distinction between tradable and non-tradable goods becomes very important. Tradable goods are priced pretty much the same in poor and wealthy countries, their prices being largely equalized (within transport costs) by trade. Non-tradable goods are predominantly housing and services. Services are quite labor-intensive, and when poor workers provide those services in a poor country, much the same service may be delivered at a price that is considerably lower than would occur in a higher-income country. GDP at home prices in the poor country will understate that country's real GDP relative to the wealthier country's. One method of constructing GDP for such comparisons is to value nontradable goods and services in lower-income countries at their prices in the highest-income country in the comparison group. This procedure yields what is called purchasing-power-parity-adjusted GDP. Use of PPP-adjusted GDP also affects estimates of economic growth. Goods can change from nontraded to traded over time, and changes in their prices in low-income countries as they become priced at world prices can give the appearance of more rapid growth than is actually the case unless the PPP adjustment is made. Third, GDP, even PPP-adjusted GDP, is not a measure of welfare or well-being, so comparing GDP per capita across countries at a given date or between countries at different dates leaves the question of what the comparison means. There does not appear to be a remedy for this perplexity. Fourth, inter-country comparisons, or comparisons of a single country over time, of the composition of GDP measured in any of the three ways—product, expenditure, or income, can be quite informative: percents of GDP produced by particular industries or industry groups in the first method; shares of consumption, investment, and government expenditures by the second; and shares of income by source in the third.

Of course, while these comparisons of sources and uses of GDP are more informative than comparisons of GDP per capita, they are also more difficult to develop for most periods of antiquity.

5.3 The Length of Run: Business Cycles and Long Run Growth

As has been seen in the analysis of many price-theoretic topics, the length of time involved in a phenomenon under study makes a difference in results and sometimes even requires different models. With the emergence of the sub-discipline of macroeconomics from the Great Depression, the new models it developed early in its separate life focused on short- and medium-run problems. The long-run results of the pre-Keynesian Classical theory remained in the background in the form primarily of the long-run neutrality of money (see Jones 2014, Chapter 9) and the full employment of all factors of production in the long run: the new models acknowledged that these results emerged in the long run but focused on explanations of why they did not hold during shorter periods, which occasionally could be quite lengthy as the Great Depression demonstrated.

The intellectual counter-revolution(s) of the 1970s and 1980s, having been absorbed in the mainstream of macroeconomics—to the extent that a Venn diagram of broad consensus could be called a mainstream—left macroeconomists generally doubting the efficacy of trying to fine-tune a nation's economy with fiscal and monetary policies and encouraged greater attention to issues of longer-run economic growth. Business cycles, and policies for alleviating the worst of them, nonetheless continued to be a concern in macroeconomics, and the most commonly known macroeconomic models—the IS-LM and AS-AD models are designed for analysis of short- to medium-run issues, although long-run restrictions can be imposed on both. Before embarking on expositions of those shorter-run models, this section offers an overview of what business cycles are in the first sub-section, then relates very informally some results of newer economic growth theory that may be useful for the study of economic behavior and economic outcomes in antiquity.

One of the primary results of modern macroeconomics is that, while in the long run, the Classical result of the neutrality of money—changes in its supply affect only the price level, not the magnitudes of any real variables—holds, in the short and medium terms, changes in the money supply have temporary real effects. Much of the research in macroeconomics in the past several decades has focused on discovering the microeconomic mechanisms which produce this non-neutrality. Fortunately, it is not necessary for the present purposes to delve deeply into those models. Instead, sluggish, or "sticky" movements of prices and wages can be assumed for the working of the major macroeconomic models over periods of one to several years.

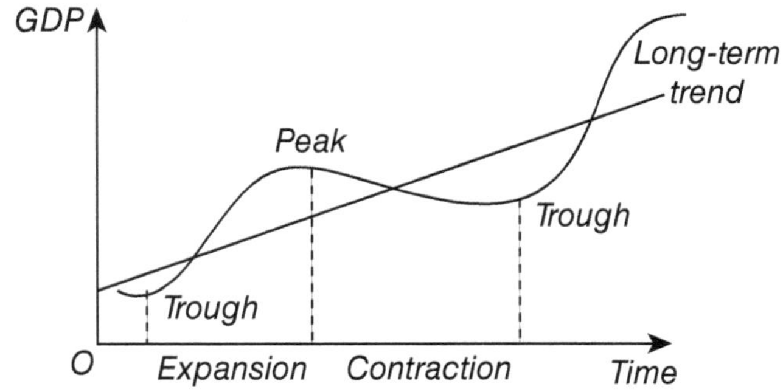

Figure 5.1. Cycles along a long-term growth trend.

5.3.1 The Short and Medium Run: Business Cycles

Contemporary and recent economies have experience growth in per capita income as well as aggregate growth (constant per capita income and increasing population), but they also have experienced periods when business boomed and other periods when it lagged seriously. While some recent research has created some reservations about calling these periods fluctuations about the trend of growth, that nomenclature is surely a reasonable shorthand. This brief sub-section addresses some of their salient characteristics, so that the reader might acquire a sense of the issues the ensuing models are preparing him or her to analyze, then reports on ideas about their causes.

Business cycles are periodic deviations from trend (either growth or constancy) that involve declining production and periods of greater-than-usual unemployment. Business cycles affect all sectors of an economy, not just a single sector or a few. These cycles involve periods of economic expansion above the long-term trend (boom periods), culminating in a peak level of activity, followed by a period of contraction, which eventually reaches a trough, and the entire cycle—irregular and episodic as business cycles are—resumes. These fluctuations recur, but not at predictable intervals. They can last from less than a year to a decade or more. Figure 5.1 offers a stylized illustration of such fluctuations around a trend of growing GDP. The GDP that is growing in Figure 5.1 is total GDP, not per capita, so the figure could, qualitatively, represent even economies in antiquity experiencing population growth with no discernible per capita growth.

Business cycles share many common features with one another, despite their differences in severity and duration. These commonalities are captured in a number of variables that move in the same direction and in the same relative timing over many cycles. Some nomenclature is available that helps describe these variables' movements compactly. Variables that move in the same direction as GDP, such as investment, are said to move procyclically; those that move in the opposite direction, such as unemployment, are said to move countercyclically. In timing, some variables move before GDP, reaching their turning points before GDP turns either down from a peak or up from a trough; these are called leading variables. Those that follow GDP in time are called lagging, and those that move more or less simultaneously are called coincidental. Whether such fine timing could ever be discerned in information from antiquity is an open question, but on the possibility that some glimmers may be available here and there, the vocabulary may prove useful, and the leading and lagging concepts may carry over antiquity quite well on theoretical grounds.

Now, what are the variables that possess these properties of movement relative to GDP over business cycles? Industrial production may be the variable of most potential observability from antiquity; it moves procyclically and is coincident with GDP. Consumption experiences less variability over the business cycle than does production—people live off their savings—but the degree of variability depends on the degree of durability. Consumption of nondurable goods and services experiences the least fluctuation, and to the extent it does move over the business cycle, it is procyclical and coincident. Consumption of durables, as might be expected, shows greater fluctuation than does that of nondurables—most investments, which consumption of durables surely is, can be postponed. Business investment is highly volatile, considerably more so than GDP; it is strongly procyclical and coincident. Inventory investment is even more volatile—after all, it is what couldn't be sold in the current and previous few periods, but it is a small percentage of GDP; it is procyclical and leading. Employment is procyclical and coincident—after all, labor produces industrial output. The unemployment rate is strongly countercyclical but behaves asymmetrically over the business cycle, rising sharply in contractions but falling more gradually in expansions. The unemployment rate is a contemporary measurement of the proportion of the labor force looking unsuccessfully for work. The loose variable in that calculation is the labor force, which has the modern definition of people currently working, either full- or part-time, and unemployed people who have looked for work within the past month or some such relatively short period. When people go long enough without being able to find work, they tend to look less frequently and consequently eventually get dropped from the measure of the labor force, artificially depressing the measured unemployment rate relative to what it is intended to measure. The real wage is modestly procyclical, and average labor productivity—output per worker, regardless of wage—is procyclical and leading. In the financial markets, the money supply, inflation, and nominal interest rates are procyclical, the money supply leading and inflation and nominal interest rates lagging.

The causes of business cycles are many and varied. Theories of the trade cycle abounded prior to the Great Depression, but they were by and large unable to offer an understanding of the forces at work in that economic disaster.[6] Keynesian theory focused on events disturbing the demand side of the economy, events that current terminology would call shocks—unanticipated disturbances to equilibrium. Keynes's famous reference to "animal spirits" being prime motivators of sudden shifts in investment demand finds its contemporary counterpart in Alan Greenspan's irrational exuberance—bandwagons leading to speculative bubbles that burst with ensuing losses spread widely. Financial crises, sometimes called banking panics, are another possible source of business cycles, although distinguishing truly exogenous banking crises from prior animal spirits or irrational exuberance can be difficult. Counterproductive monetary policy has been cited as a cause of business cycles, although ancient monetary authorities may not have possessed adequate technology to inflict great damage with monetary actions. The oil price shocks of the 1970s returned attention to supply-side disturbances, and since then the concept of technology shocks—exogenous changes in productivity, introductions of a new technology—have been recommended as the primary source of business cycles, although with a small number of converts. Nonetheless, supply-side shocks such as severe droughts, earthquakes, floods, wars may have been prime suspects for causes of business cycles in antiquity, although allowance must be made for some of the Roman banking and financial crises.

This said for causes of business cycles, research on business cycles has changed dramatically since the heyday of business cycle theories. Current macroeconomic research sees an economy as on a long-run growth path and experiencing irregular and unanticipated shocks to one of the major equations of a general equilibrium model, either the demand-consumption equation, representing demand shocks, or the production function, representing supply shocks. Since these shocks cannot be anticipated (although some observers cry wolf for years and occasionally can claim they were right all along, at least that one time, and others say they saw it all coming), macroeconomics, being a practical science, has devoted its attention to the best ways of counteracting shocks when they occur—getting an economy back on its long-run growth path and minimizing damage—rather than to theorizing about why they happen, since those theories don't typically do a lot of good. A number of demand shocks can be avoided by better practice of banking and monetary policy, and much research has been devoted to better understanding those subjects for that reason. Supply shocks seem to be by-and-large unavoidable, and research has been devoted to what the best responses to them may be—as it turns out, there's not a lot macroeconomic policy (monetary and fiscal actions) can do to help in the event of supply shocks without making things worse.

5.3.2 The Long Run: Growth

Long-run growth has become part of macroeconomics, but that subject will not be addressed here. Some lessons of more recent extensions of the Solow growth model are pertinent to thinking about how government policies

[6] Haberler (1937; 1941) provides a survey of non-Keynesian theories of the time. A Committee of the American Economic Association (published under the chairmanship of Haberler 1944), provides additional selections, in addition to early Keynesian models.

affect long-run growth rather than how they either precipitate business cycles or how economies respond to their interventions in business cycles. Infinite-horizon models and overlapping generations models of growth offer insights in particular into how consumers respond to changes in government activity. These models yield time paths of household or per capita consumption and of the capital-labor ratio and, in contrast to the Solow model, allow for endogenous savings rates as consumption and saving (capital accumulation) are both determined at the household level. Both types of model distinguish between expected and unexpected changes in government activity and permanent and temporary changes. Consumer responses to expected changes can begin before the government action occurs but must respond following unexpected actions. Of particular interest is the consumer response to an increase in government spending paid for by an increase in taxation (paid for by taxation or debt makes little difference). In the case of a permanent increase in government spending, consumption takes a discrete downward jump, but the optimal path of the capital-labor ratio is unaffected. With temporary increases, consumers are governed by their intertemporal substitution possibilities in consumption and do not reduce their consumption by the full amount of the government's spending (and the exaction of taxes from their income / consumption). Consequently, saving falls and the capital-labor ratio falls, causing the real interest rate to rise. When the government returns to its pre-increase level of spending, while consumption rises, so does saving and consequently the capital-labor ratio, and the real interest rate turns to its pre-existing level.

The recent literature on endogenous economic growth has emphasized the accumulation of knowledge and has derived the result that knowledge production (knowledge itself produced with knowledge) is increased by larger populations. One long-standing question has been why technological change over long periods extending from antiquity to probably the 17th or 18th century C.E. tended to increase population up to the Malthusian limit of sustenance rather than increasing per capita income.[7] While it may be premature to take the results of this research to the bank, one possibility emerging involves the endogenous rate of technological progress finally increasing sufficiently beyond the endogenous population growth rate—itself possibly a consequence of previous population growth resulting in a larger population)—to allow per capita income growth as well as population growth. The per capita income growth sufficiently outweighs population growth long enough for changes in fertility behavior to emerge from the higher incomes and reduce the population growth rate. It's a nice story, but much work is in progress on the subject.

[7] Literature has emerged recently regarding technological progress and per capita income growth during the Roman era and even between the Greek Dark Age and the Hellenistic era. On the possibility of early Greek economic growth—following the nadir of the Mycenaean collapse, an easy point from which to grow, see Morris (2004). For Rome, see the papers in Cascio (2006); Silver (2007); Scheidel (2008).

5.4 The Aggregate Markets: Goods, Financial, Labor

Macroeconomics aggregates markets far beyond those used for study of individual markets, be they markets for goods such as wheat of a certain quality or loans for certain purposes and of various risks, and labor of particular skills. Some nuances are lost in these aggregations, but for the most part the details are not especially important to the operation of an aggregate economy, which is defined contemporarily on the basis of nationality, which can be defined on the extent of sovereignty of a government. Following this definition of nationality, we can extend the application of these models far into antiquity.

5.4.1 Goods

The composition of the goods market can be represented by the income-expenditure identity from national income accounting: $Y \equiv C + I + G + NX$. As an accounting identity, this expression is always true by definition. Analysis of the goods market deals with income and spending as a behavioral relationship, which need not always be true, resulting in the innocuous-looking but significant substitution of the two-line "equals" sign for the three-line identity symbol: $Y = C + I + G + NX$. This section begins with a reminder discussion of the components of the income-expenditure relationship and then turns to the determination of equilibrium output. A brief word about NX, net exports, first however. At this stage in the presentation of the basic models, the economy will be assumed closed, i.e., there is no international trade. I have left NX in the income-expenditure expression just as a reminder that it really is there in a more complete exposition, which will be offered in section 5.7.

The Components of the Goods Market. The macroeconomic goods market contains goods produced by both the private and public sectors and goods for current and continuing consumption. For example, both agricultural and manufactured goods are combined as well as both private (the agricultural and manufactured) goods and public goods (current expenditures on, say, courts and law enforcement).

Consumption. Consumption is something like demand but is more highly aggregated, in fact distinguishing only between goods consumed in the current period and durable goods which last several periods, such as housing and farm equipment, and are considered investment goods. Consumption is related to saving, as noted in the accounting relationships detailed in section 5.2, and in fact, any theory of consumption is a theory of saving and vice versa: given income, if we know what happens to consumption, we know what happens to saving. The permanent income hypothesis of consumption is a microeconomic theory, i.e., a model that begins with the behavior of the utility-maximizing individual. The consumption function in macroeconomics can be linked to such price theoretic models, but by the time the model was built up to the aggregation of an entire economy and linked with other price-theoretic components, it would be too cumbersome to yield insights readily. Consequently, current textbook treatments of the consumption function rely on aggregate models which have been in use for a number of decades. These models rely on a number of simplifications which are not innocuous when one tries to explain the reams of data available on business cycles today but are not bad as heuristic first approximations. Whether ancient data are sufficient to make use of the relaxation of these simplifications is probably a matter of time, place and issue.

At its simplest, consumption is specified as a function of income, $C = C(Y)$, $C_Y > 0$.[8] The next step recognizes that consumption is a function of disposable income, or income gross of transfers and net of taxes: $Y_D = Y + TR - T$, and $C = C(Y_D)$ or $C = C(Y + TR - T)$. Y_D is close to private disposable income introduced in section 5.2 (PDI), but excludes net factor payments from abroad and receipts of interest payments on government debt. This method of specifying the determinants of consumption assumes that changes in income, transfers and taxes all have the same unit effect on consumption, which is known to not be the case, but it is an acceptable heuristic simplification. Additionally, consumption is known to be responsive to the real interest rate (saving is obviously related to the real interest rate, and since changes in saving are equal and opposite in sign to changes in consumption, it should be no surprise that the real interest rate affects consumption). A more general specification of an aggregate consumption function is $C = C(Y, TR, T, r)$, with $C_Y > 0$, $C_{TR} > 0$, $C_T < 0$, and $C_r < 0$.

Returning to a simplified specification of the consumption function, the consumption multiplier can be derived. Let consumption be represented by $c_0 + c_1 Y_D$, in which c_0 is called autonomous consumption, i.e., consumption that is not influenced by variations in income. Figure 5.2 shows the relationship between consumption and disposable income, in which c_0 is the intercept and c_1 is the slope of the consumption line. The coefficient c_1 is the marginal propensity to consume, sometimes called just the propensity to consume; it is the change in consumption induced by a unit change in income, with values between zero and one. Substituting this specification of consumption for C in the income-expenditure relationship yields $Y = c_0 + c_1(Y + \overline{TR} - \overline{T}) + \overline{I} + \overline{G} + \overline{NX}$, in which the bars over some of the terms indicate that these categories of expenditure are being considered exogenous at the moment, an assumption which will be relaxed later. Rearranging to place all the Y terms on the left-hand side of the expression yields $Y = (1/1 - c_1)(c_0 + c_1\overline{TR} - c_1\overline{T} + \overline{I} + \overline{G} + \overline{NX})$ in which $1/1 - c_1$, which can be represented by m_C, is the consumption multiplier. The larger is the propensity to consume, the larger is the consumption multiplier, which is always greater than 1 in magnitude. The multiplier indicates

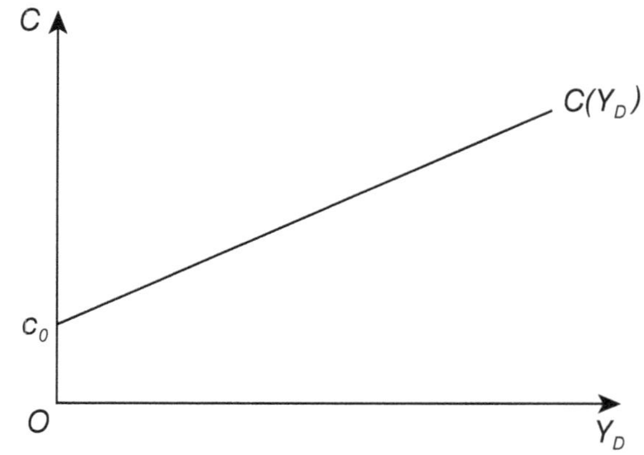

Figure 5.2. Consumption as a function of income.

that a change in autonomous spending (spending not related to income or production, the terms with bars over them in the income-expenditure relationship) has an effect on income that is greater than the initial change in spending. The structure of a multiplier depends on the specifications of the relationship being modeled, and the composition of the multiplier m_C is not immutable. Instead, it depends on the assumption about the taxes and transfers (not to mention investment and government spending, which will not be considered further at this moment). Both are considered exogenous: the government makes transfers and exacts taxes in fixed amounts, independently of how much income the economy is producing, as denoted by the bars over their symbols. If instead taxes contain an element that is proportional to income (keeping transfers exogenous or autonomous), such as $T = t_0 + t_1 Y$, the income expenditure relationship is $Y = c_0 + c_1(Y + \overline{TR} - t_0 - t_1 Y) + \overline{I} + \overline{G} + \overline{NX} = [1/1 - c_1(1 - t_1)][c_0 + c_1(\overline{TR} - t_0) + \overline{I} + \overline{G} + \overline{NX}]$, and the multiplier, designated by m_{Ct}, is smaller than the multiplier with completely autonomous taxes. With the autonomous taxes, tax payments did not increase as income increased, but with partially endogenous taxes, tax payments do increase as income increases, cutting into the expansionary effect of increases in consumption spending.

Investment and Saving. The price-theoretic, profit-maximizing theory of investment will be presented only in the barest details here (see Jones 2014, Chapter 8, section 5). In the introduction to the consumption function above, investment was treated as exogenous, or part of autonomous spending; that was a purely heuristic simplification. Investment is anything but exogenous. As with the consumption function, aggregate investment is often represented in greatly simplified form as a function of the real interest rate, $I = I(r)$, $I_r < 0$, or as a function of the real interest rate and income, $I = I(r, Y)$, $I_r < 0$, $I_Y > 0$.[9]

Investment is a forward-looking activity. It is undertaken for what it can produce in a number of future periods

[8] As a reminder for the reader, the notation C_Y represents the more cumbersome expression $\Delta C/\Delta Y$, which in turn means "the change in C induced by a small (or unit) change in Y.

[9] Recall that the distinction between nominal and real interest rates was treated in Jones (Chapter 9, section 3.3). The nominal interest rate, commonly designated by i, is the real interest rate, commonly designated by r, plus the expected rate of inflation, commonly designated by π^e: $i = r + \pi^e$.

rather than for the satisfaction it can yield today alone. The motivating question behind the choice of how much to invest in the current period is how large a capital stock is desired in future periods. Recalling the distinction between stocks and flows, a stock of capital provides a flow of capital services which, when combined with other inputs, yield output. The production function describes the technical relationships between the services of various inputs and the product they combine to make. Using the law of variable proportions (Jones, Chapter 1, section 2), and the demand for factors of production (e.g., capital and labor), the role of factor costs, and the allocation of factors across activities (Jones 2014, Chapter 2, sections 6 through 8), the reader will find it obvious that the amount of capital a producer chooses to employ is the amount that, given the production technology, will equate the marginal product of capital with its marginal cost. Now we just have to figure out what a producer has in mind about when the anticipated marginal product will occur and what the marginal cost of capital is.

The marginal product of capital is only an expected marginal product; what actually emerges from the new installation depends on how well it works and what the business conditions are in the future. In times of particularly slow technological change such as apparently characterized much of antiquity, the performance of a well-understood piece of equipment or type of building surely could have been anticipated quite closely. Additionally, except for wars and weather anomalies, business conditions also may not have changed as rapidly as they are like to do in contemporary times, so altogether, there may not have been exceptional risk in forecasting the marginal product of new capital. The marginal cost of capital requires us to use the stock-flow distinction (see Jones, Chapter 1, section 10) and applied to the pricing of capital goods in Jones (Chapter 8, section 1). The real interest rate relates the marginal product of a capital good to the price of that good. Roughly, $p_K = MP_K/r^e$, where p_K is the price of a capital good, MP_K is its marginal product, which for simplicity is expected to stay constant over the good's economic life (the one-hoss shay assumption), and r^e is the real interest rate the producer expects to prevail over the life of the capital good. As with the expectations of the As a concession to reality, the owner of a capital good can expect it to depreciate, literally wear out, with use over time. Then the user cost of capital can be considered as the sum of the expected marginal product of capital and the depreciation of the stock: $c_K = (r^e + d)p_K$, where c_K is the user cost and d is the annual depreciation rate of the stock.

Now, assuming that there is a linear relationship between the magnitude of a capital stock (say, a number of plows or shovels or kilns of given dimensions), we can relate the expected marginal product of capital to the size of the stock, assuming that the quantity of cooperating factors of production is taken into consideration. By the law of variable proportions, the marginal product of a stock of capital (and the flow of capital services coming from it) will decrease as more of it is applied to a fixed array of other factors. The magnitude of flows (and correspondingly

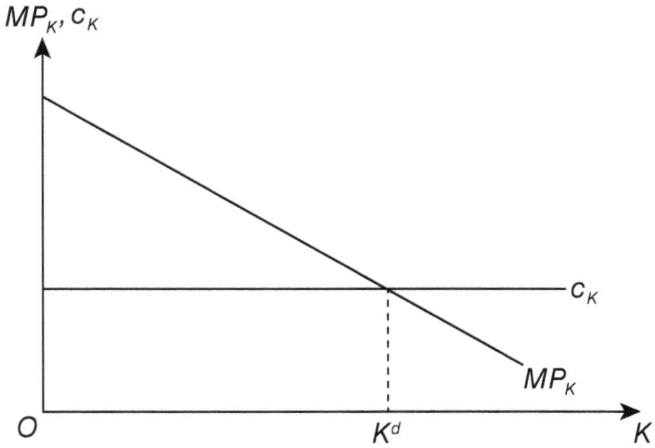

Figure 5.3. Declining marginal product of capital.

the desired size of the stock, K^d) that equates the expected marginal product (effectively the demand function for that input) and the user cost of capital. Figure 5.3 shows this relationship.

We are almost all the way to the magnitude of investment desired in the current period. Net investment is gross investment minus depreciation. That is, some amount of current investment simply replaces capital that wore out during the last period. Since investment this period yields a larger capital stock next period, current investment is added to this year's capital stock to expand the capital stock next period: $I_t - dK_t = K_{t+1} - K_t$, or, gross investment minus the part of the current period's capital stock that wears out this period constitutes the change in the size of the capital stock between this period and next. If the desired capital stock next period is K^d_{t+1}, this period's investment is $I_t = K^d_{t+1}, - K_t + dK_t$, or the investment must replace what wore out and still amount to the difference between the capital stock at the beginning of the current period (before the fraction d of it wore out) and the amount the producer wants to have in place at the beginning of next period.

Now, where do the resources to acquire the new capital stock come from? They come from savings. The amount an individual chooses to save in a period is a function of the real interest rate, current income, expected future income (the life-cycle savings hypothesis), wealth, and taxes. The real interest rate affects the relative price of current and future consumption. An increase in the interest rate loosens the budget constraint a consumer faces next period, making current consumption more expensive relative to current consumption. This is the substitution effect of a change in the real interest rate. It also has an income effect. If an individual is a net borrower, the higher interest rate will force larger interest payments, diverting some current income away from both current consumption and savings. For net borrowers, the income effect of an increase in the real interest rate on savings is negative. For net lenders, the reverse is the case. At the level of the aggregate closed economy, the income effect of an increase in the real interest rate on aggregate savings will be largely a wash, and the substitution effect will prevail. As current income increases, with a marginal propensity to consume less than one, savings will increase. If expected future income increases, the need to save to maintain a target (intertemporal equilibrium) level of consumption in the future is reduced and current saving will fall. Similarly with an increase in wealth, which can provide an incremental flow of consumption in the future. Saving contributes to wealth, so an exogenous increase in wealth can substitute for some current saving. Tax policy can affect the earnings a saver obtains by altering the after-tax real interest rate on savings, defined as $r_{at} = (1 - t)i - \pi^e$, an increase in the tax rate depressing the after-tax earnings. At the aggregate national level, government fiscal policy can affect national savings by absorbing some of the funds that would otherwise be saved. As shown in the national income accounting of section 5.2, a government budget surplus, $G - T < 0$, contributes to national savings whereas a budget deficit, $G - T > 0$, squeezes out savings. The savings function can be expressed as $S = S(r, Y, Y_f, W, T)$, where $S_r > 0$, $S_Y > 0$, $S_{Y_f} < 0$, $S_W < 0$, $S_T < 0$.

Government Expenditure. Unlike the case with consumption, investment and saving, government expenditures are not guided by any optimizing theory.[10] Governments may very well have objective functions; they may change abruptly. Government expenditures may be for public consumption such as festivals or public investment such as transportation infrastructure. Fiscal policies can be characterized by combinations of government expenditures, G, and taxation, T, as well as other activities in which governments may engage. Tax revenues typically decline more than government expenditures during business downturns, and during boom periods they tend to grow more than government expenditures. In general, anything that increases income, Y, will increase a government budget surplus or reduce a budget deficit. While an expansionary fiscal policy may create a government budget deficit, changes in private spending also can contribute to a deficit, so the state of a government's budget surplus is not a clear indicator of policy.

Government expenditures have major and pervasive effects throughout an economy. First, the public goods and services these expenditures provide enter the utility functions of individuals throughout the economy, and the taxes levied to pay for them enter their budget constraints. From the perspective of the aggregate economy, the government's activities both provide spending on both consumption and investment goods and absorb resources that otherwise could be available to the private economy. These government activities, and raising the revenue to pay for them can change the intertemporal pattern of both private consumption and private production. In an open economy, which virtually all of these ancient economies were—the theoretical treatment of that aspect of their activities is being deferred, not the facts of their impacts—government activities transmit consequences throughout the world of their trading partners.

The income-expenditure relationship and the multiplier m_{Ct} can be used to show the effects of changes in fiscal policies on aggregate income. Begin with the full income-expenditure equation: $Y = C + TR - T + I + G + NX$. Substituting the expressions relating consumption and tax payments to income, $Y = c_0 + c_1(Y + TR - T) + I + G = c_0 + c_1(Y + TR - t_0 - t_1 Y) + I + G = c_0 + c_1 t_0 + c_1(1 - t_1)Y + c_1 TR + I + G$ (assuming transfers are not taxed). Now, let government expenditure change, represented by ΔG. Then the change in income is $\Delta Y = c_1(1 - t_1)\Delta Y + \Delta G$. Since transfers, investment, and net exports don't change, they drop out of this change expression. Rearranging yields $\Delta Y = [1/1 - c_1(1 - t1)]\Delta G = m_{Ct}\Delta G$. Now, suppose that the government holds expenditures constant but increases transfers to consumers. The change expression is $\Delta Y = \Delta TR + c_1(1 - t_1)\Delta Y = [c_1/1 - c_1(1 - t_1)]\Delta TR$, which is smaller than the effect of government expenditures because only a portion $c < 1$ of transfers are spent (the remainder is saved).

While there is a government expenditure multiplier, there is no corresponding taxation multiplier because consumers' responses to changes in taxation are more difficult to predict by virtue of the possible operation of a phenomenon known as Ricardian equivalence, named after David Ricardo who first wrote about it in 1820. Although the analytics are intricate, the intuition of the effect is that consumers with good foresight, observing a decrease in taxation without a corresponding reduction in government expenditure, know that at some point they will have to pay for the government spending, which has simply been put on their tab. Accordingly, they will not, or may not, increase their spending when faced with a tax reduction that they know must be temporary either because the government has announced that it is or because they can see the divergent government revenue and expenditure streams.

While there is no positive (as contrasted to normative) theory of government expenditure, theory can offer guidance to what governments can and cannot do economically. A government has a budget constraint just as households do, and it has an analogous structure: the present discounted value of expenditures minus the present discounted value of revenues (tax receipts plus the real rate of return on government capital stock, seigniorage on issuing money, revenues from government-owned natural resources, sale of government assets;[11] other sources could be included as appropriate) must be no less than its current stock of debt.[12] A government budget deficit adds to the stock of debt and a surplus can reduce it. This implies that the ratio of debt to GDP must grow at a rate less than the real interest rate minus the growth rate of GDP, or equivalently

[10] For this section, I have drawn on Romer (2006, Chapter 11); Buiter (1990, Chapter 5); and Frenkel and Razin (1987, Chapter 7).

[11] To the extent that the sale price is greater than the present discounted value of their real returns, otherwise the government incurs a loss in the sale.

[12] Cf. the array of revenue sources of the Seleukid Empire reported in Aperghis (2004, 137–166).

that the real debt must grow at a rate less than the real interest rate. A government could be said to be insolvent if there is no politically feasible set of spending, tax, and other operational plans, including seigniorage from debasing a coinage, that would permit the existing stock of debt to be serviced. Ancient governments seem not to have issued debt on more than a short-term basis and to a great extent current expenditures tended to be financed by current levies of one sort or another, so this formulation of a government budget constraint may seem misplaced. However, zeroing out government debt from the budget constraint leaves the condition that the present value of expenditures, which conceivably could be anticipated for an extended future (thinking of the Peloponnesian and Second Punic Wars), must be able to be covered by resources a government could tap without wrecking the economy or precipitating revolt or civil war.

Net Exports. Explanation of the theory of net exports will be reserved until section 5.7, on the open economy. Since the NX term has been sitting in the income-expenditure equation as a reminder of a national economy's external relations, a few words should be said. First, net exports is the difference between the value of exports, X, and imports, M. Second, a complication which will not be dealt with further here is that exports and imports are priced in different currencies, an intricate subject in itself. Third, as a reminder of how events abroad can affect a nation's economy, foreign income, not home-country income, determines gross exports.

The Determination of Equilibrium Output. The switch from an accounting identity to a behavioral equation for the income-expenditure relationship provides the basis for the determination of equilibrium in the goods market. As has come up in the preceding parts of this section, the basic income-expenditure equation provides one method of determining equilibrium between production and demand, while the saving-investment relationship implied by the accounting in the income-expenditure relationship provides an alternative but equivalent method. Each is presented in turn below.

Income and Spending. Begin by distinguishing between aggregate demand, D^A, and income, Y. Both are composed of the same expenditure components, $D^A = C^d + I^d + G + NX$ and $Y = C^d + I^d + G + NX$. When $D^A = Y$, the goods market is in equilibrium. When $D^A \neq Y$, there is unplanned inventory investment, $I^u = Y - D^A$. When this expression is positive, more goods have been produced than can be sold, so they are added to inventories to be sold at a later date; when it is negative, demand exceeds current production, and inventories must be drawn down to satisfy demand.

Consider the consumption function $C = c_0 + c_1(Y - \overline{T}) = c_0 - \overline{T} + c_1 Y$ and plot it in aggregate demand-income space in Figure 5.4. The first two terms are autonomous components of spending. The 45° line from the origin labeled $D^A = Y$ is the locus of points at which aggregate demand equals income (production or GDP). The slope of

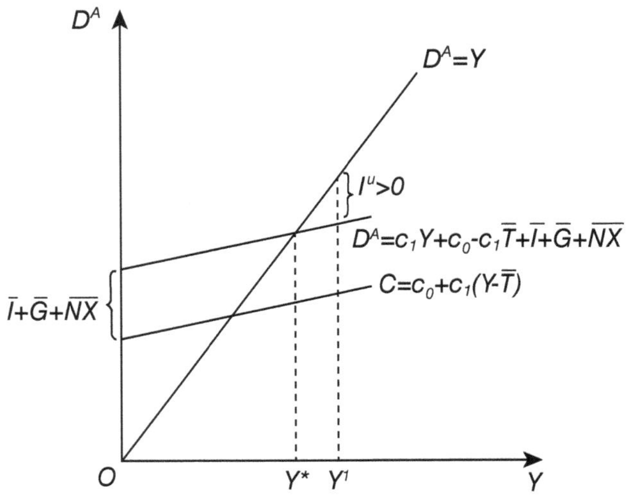

Figure 5.4. The consumption function.

the $D^A = Y$ locus is 1 while the slope of the consumption function is less than 1. Now, add in the other components of autonomous spending, $\overline{I}+\overline{G}+\overline{NX}$ to obtain the full aggregate demand, $D^A = c_0 - c_1\overline{T} + \overline{I} + \overline{G} + \overline{NX}$, which intersects the $D^A = Y$ locus at E, the equilibrium of income and spending, where the demand for goods is equal to the goods produced at income Y*. If income were somewhat greater than Y*, say at Y^1, $I^u > 0$, an unplanned addition to inventories must absorb production that cannot be sold at current levels of demand.

In sum, one way of expressing the equilibrium condition in the goods market is that production equals demand.

Saving and Investment. Savings is not one of the components of the income-expenditure relationship, but as was shown in section 5.2, it is a source of funds that is implicit in the accounts. Taking a different view of how income can be spent, it can go to consumption, it can be saved, or it can be paid in taxes: Y = C + S + T. Using a superscript d to indicated the desired level of a component, the income-expenditure relationship is $Y = C^d + I^d + G + NX$. Since this is not the accounting identity but the behavioral relationship, it is the equilibrium condition in the goods market. Equating these two expression, $C^d + I^d + G + NX = C_d + S + T$. Canceling desired consumption from both sides yields $I^d = S^d + (T - G) - NX$, which says that investment is equal to private saving, S, plus government saving—tax revenue minus government spending—minus net exports. The intuition behind the negative sign on net exports in the investment-saving equilibrium condition is that net exports are a component of national saving, so to avoid double-counting, they must be subtracted from saving. With a balanced government budget and a zero trade balance amounts to $I^d = S^d$, which is simply another way of expressing the equilibrium condition in the goods market. This condition does not have to hold, but when it doesn't, the economy is in disequilibrium, a fundamental insight of Keynesian economics.[13]

[13] Temin (2004, 708) notes that one of Keynes' central contributions to macroeconomics was the observation that disequilibrium—hence

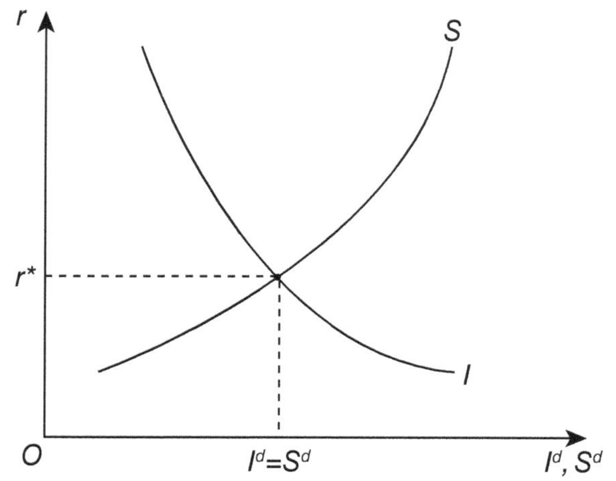

Figure 5.5. Equilibrium of investment and saving.

So, bringing desired saving into equality with planned investment is equivalent to bringing aggregate demand into equality with production. Returning to Figure 5.5, suppose for a moment that trade is balanced so that $\overline{NX} = 0$ and there is no government spending, leaving the distance between the aggregate demand (expenditure) line and the consumption line equal to $\overline{I}$. However, income minus consumption is saving, $Y - C^d = S^d$. The only level of output at which these two distances are equal is Y*, where aggregate demand equals income. So if $S^d = I^d$, $D^A = Y$. Adding back in government expenditure and allowing for $NX \neq 0$ gives a more complete picture of saving and investment in equilibrium. Thus, an alternative way of expressing the equilibrium condition in the goods market is that investment equals savings.

The savings-investment equilibrium in a closed economy can be shown as in Figure 5.5, in which desired investment is a decreasing function of the real interest rate and desired saving is an increasing function of the real interest rate. In a closed economy, equalization of desired saving and desired investment determines the equilibrium real interest rate, r*. At real interest rates higher than r*, businesses will want to invest less than consumers want to save: consumers will not find businesses willing to borrow all their savings at interest rates $r > r^*$ and will consume some of what they had thought to save, working back down the S curve until all they want to save can be placed with willing borrowers. Correspondingly, at real interest rates below r*, businesses will want to borrow (to invest) more than consumers are willing to lend (i.e., save), so they will have to offer a higher interest rate which draws forth more savings.

5.4.2 The Financial Market

Were there financial systems in the economies of the ancient Mediterranean and Aegean? Goldsmith would not admit full-weight commodity money and what he calls "occasional seed loans" as constituting a financial system.[14] Fiduciary money—e.g., coins whose intrinsic value was less than their accepted face value, which would include primarily the lower-denomination, non-precious-metal coins—and various types of loans—trade credit, manufacturers' advances, consumption loans, the occasional real property mortgage, and so on—do qualify as constituting a financial system, along with the full-weight money, which would be equivalent to contemporary high-powered or base money, even if its expansion by a banking system might be quite limited. The extent to which any of the above loans circulated beyond the initially contracting parties as acceptable, if discounted, instruments of value such as the bill of exchange developed in Renaissance Italy, I do not know. Cohen's documentation of extensive and varied loans by both banks and non-bank lenders does not establish whether any of these debt instruments circulated further as transaction devices, able to settle further debts or purchases (Cohen 2008, 69–82).

The Asset Markets. The financial market is the market for assets, which can take many forms. Money, bonds (corresponds most closely to loans in antiquity), stocks (equity in antiquity), and physical goods and structures are all assets. Each has different properties, the primary ones being expected return, risk, and liquidity. Money is the most liquid asset; money held as cash earns no interest while money held as a bank deposit may or may not earn the nominal rate of interest; it can be used for transactions. The risks involved with money are the prospect of physical loss for cash and the possibility of inflation for either form. Bonds (loans in antiquity) earn the real rate of interest (with compensation for risk), can take time to sell even when a secondary market for them exists, and run the risk of not being repaid in full, but cannot be used in transactions. Equity has an expected rate of return equal to the real interest rate (also with compensation for risk), but like bonds, can take time to sell and cannot be used in transactions, and faces risks deriving from the markets in which the assets operate. Physical goods and structures are produced by investment, treated in section 5.2, but once produced, the demand for their ownership is transacted in financial markets. Their expected rate of return is the real interest rate, and they are generally the most illiquid of

---

unemployment—results from the failure of this savings-investment / goods-market equilibrium condition to hold, but also contends that in "mostly agricultural societies" large savers typically are large investors and that there is consequently little possibility for the kind of mismatch, and the attendant unemployment, that can occur in modern industrial societies. In the penultimate section of his paper, Temin presents evidence on Roman financial intermediation and banking practices but without coming down with a clear opinion regarding the relative magnitudes of what he calls (709, Table 1) informal external sources of capital and lending by deposit banks. Cohen (2008) contends that commercial deposit banking (Temin's financial intermediation) was extensive in Classical Athens, with frequent and large loans, of 5 to 7 talents, made for production purposes rather than consumption loans. Cohen notes that, "Maintenance of a bank account was expected of an individual purporting to be of substance" (80). As to Temin's claim (708) that savings-investment "mismatches would not lead to Keynesian unemployment; they would make the economy function less efficiently than if a financial system could eliminate or reduce the mismatches," the ability of non-agricultural workers to shift back into a family's agricultural operation is probably a substitute for outright, observed unemployment in traditional agricultural economies has been noted above. The existence of involuntary unemployment in ancient settings, particularly cities, is an empirical matter rather than a theoretical one.

[14] Goldsmith (1987, 3, Chapters 2–4) on the ancient Near East, Periclean Athens, and Augustan Rome.

the asset classes. The relationship between the price of a non-monetary asset and the interest rate is inverse: $p_A = R_A/r$, where p_A is the price of the asset, R_A is its per-period return, and r is the real interest rate.

It is customary in pedagogic macroeconomic models to aggregate all classes of assets other than money into a single "other financial assets" category and rely on Walras' Law to reduce analysis to only the money market. Aggregating the non-monetary assets into a single class, total nominal wealth demanded is $M^d + A^d$, with the supply $M^s + A^s$, where M is nominal money, A is the nominal value of all other assets, and superscripts d and s represent demand and supply. For equilibrium in each of these markets, supply must equal demand. Subtract the supply of each asset from its demand to obtain $(M_d - M_s) + A_d - A_s) = 0$, from which it is clear that if the money market is in equilibrium, the market for other assets will be in equilibrium also. Consequently, the equilibrium condition for the asset market can be simplified to equilibrium in the money market.

Equilibrium in the Financial Market. The demand for money can be represented as $M^d = P \cdot L(Y, i) = P \cdot L(Y, r + \pi^e)$, where P is the price level and $L_Y > 0$, $L_i < 0$ indicate that money demand increases with higher aggregate income and decreases with a higher nominal interest rate (see Jones Chapter 9, section 4). The demand for money is a function of the nominal interest rate rather than the real interest rate because the cost of holding money is the loss in real value due to expected inflation while the return on other assets—loans (bonds) and physical capital—is the real interest rate. Holding assets in the form of money requires foregoing the difference between these two returns, $r - (-\pi_e) = r + \pi_e = i$. In real terms $(M/P)^d = L(Y, r + \pi^e)$. A useful expression for inflation can be derived by rearranging the money demand equation as $P = M/L(Y, r + \pi^e)$, which says that the price level is the ratio of nominal money supply to nominal money demand. Expressing this in rate-of-change form yields $\dot{P} = \dot{M} + \eta_Y \dot{Y}$, where the dot over a variable indicates a rate of change and $\eta_Y > 0$ is the income elasticity of demand for money derived from L_Y. This expression says that an increase in the nominal money supply will produce a proportional increase in the price level, allowing for increases in the demand for money deriving from growth in income. If the growth rate of the nominal money supply just exactly accommodates the growth in the economy's income and the attendant increase in the demand for money, the price level will remain unchanged. If the money supply remains constant and the economy's aggregate income continues to grow, possibly from growth in population alone, the price level will fall.

The condition for equilibrium in the money market, and hence in the financial market of a macroeconomic model, is $M^d = M^s$. An increase in the money supply, with the demand for money unchanged, will reduce the nominal interest rate, as shown in panel a of Figure 5.6. An increase in the demand for money, as could be caused by an increase in aggregate income, with the money supply unchanged, will increase the equilibrium interest rate, as shown in panel b of Figure 5.6. In both figures, the nominal interest rate is drawn on the vertical axis, whereas the investment-saving relationship depended on the real interest rate, $r = i - \pi^e$, a relationship between the real interest rate, expected inflation, and the nominal interest rate known as the Fisher equation. If the expected rate of inflation, π^e, does not change with either the change in money supply in panel a or the change in income in panel b, the real interest rate will move in tandem with the nominal rate.

Two principal lessons of the monetary theory are that inflation is a purely monetary phenomenon and that money is neutral in the sense that an increase in the supply of money simply increases all prices proportionally and has no effects on real variables. One of the points of contention in contemporary macroeconomics is how long it takes an increase in the money supply to achieve neutrality. During short-run periods of adjustment, when the quantities of goods may change without corresponding changes in money supply, price levels can change—i.e., inflation occurs—without the necessity of a change in the money supply.

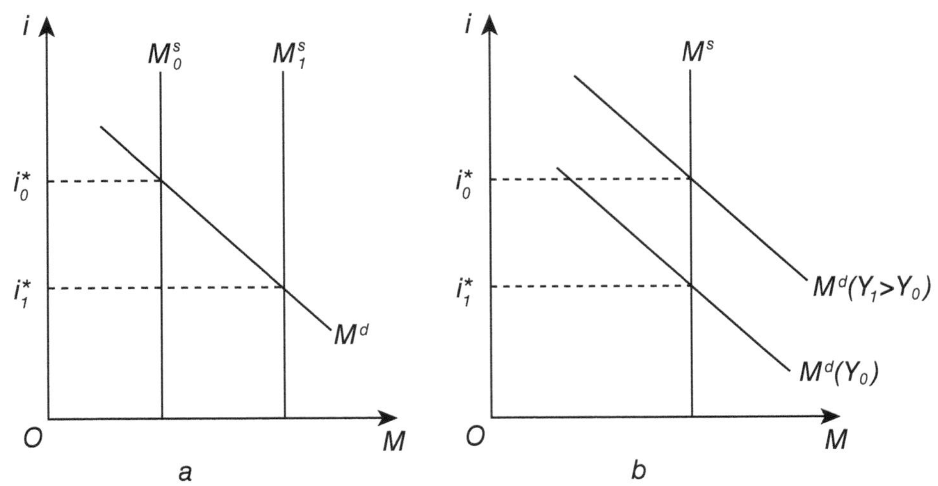

Figure 5.6. Supply and demand in the money market.

5.4.3 Labor

The macroeconomic analysis of the aggregated labor market involves the microeconomic issue of supply and demand as well as why the aggregate labor market often fails to employ these resources.

Labor Supply and Demand. Labor supply from households is a positive function of the real wage and a negative function of wealth: $L^s = L(w, W)$, $L_w > 0$, $L_W < 0$. The real wage is the nominal wage—the wage a worker is actually paid in money terms—divided by the price level. The demand for labor derives from production functions of businesses, and is the marginal product of labor curve. If a production function is $Q = F(K, L)$, the marginal product of labor is $F_L > 0$ (with $F_{LL} < 0$, indicating that as more labor is hired to work with fixed quantities of other inputs, its marginal product will decrease), and the wage is the output price times the marginal product of labor, $pF_L = w$. To see the inverse relationship between the wage rate and the demand for labor emerging from this relationship, consider a simple Cobb-Douglas production function, $Q = AK^{\alpha}L^{1-\alpha}$, with marginal product of labor $F_L = s_L A(K/L)^{\alpha}$, where $s_L = 1 - \alpha$ is labor's share of costs. The wage will be $p_Q s_L A(K/L)^{\alpha}$, where p_Q is the price of the product. Rearranging, $N^d = [p_Q s_L A/w]^{1/\alpha}K$, in which the demand for labor is an increasing function of the product price p_Q and the levels of cooperating factors represented by K and a decreasing function of the wage w. Although this production function does not have a price level in it, it does have a product price, so the demand for labor is a negative function of the wage relative to the product price, a real wage in price-theoretic terms.

Unemployment. First of all, what is unemployment?[15] The price theoretic models used in most of the chapters of Jones (2014) let prices adjust quickly so that no resource goes utilized less than fully in a supply-demand equilibrium. We're not in price-theoretic Kansas anymore. At the risk of some simplification, let's say that involuntary unemployment is the inability to find work at a wage a person is willing to accept. This may mean that the wage a person would accept is the prevailing wage, but available offers are insufficient to give jobs to all who want to work at that wage. Alternatively, it could mean that offers are available at wages below a person's reservation wage, and the person is holding out in hopes of finding a more suitable job. Remember that unemployment is generally a temporary phenomenon, and that wage hold-outs may simply take longer to find a job at their reservation wage, or with experience of not finding employment at that wage, they may revise their expectations or simply get desperate enough to accept a lower wage.

The Walrasian (price adjustments until quantities are in equilibrium) or Marshallian (quantity adjustments until prices are in equilibrium) equilibrium concept is replaced in Keynesian macroeconomic models with the concept of full employment in the long run, which allows for some frictional unemployment—people in between jobs and looking—at what is called the natural rate of unemployment, a concept that needs considerable refinement itself. The natural rate will vary from economy to economy at any given date, and in any given economy over time: it might be 4% in one country and 8% in another; in any given country, it might be 4% at one time and 6% a decade or so later. The magnitude of the natural rate depends on labor market institutions, including provision for income support during unemployment, behavioral limitations such as restrictions on firing, the technology of job search, mobility costs, wage and price flexibility, and so on.

At full employment, the capital stock of an economy is fully employed and is being operated at what could be considered its nameplate capacity. With a given capital stock, there is a particular amount of labor that can be employed, at its usual pace of work (say ten hours a day), which will produce what is called full-employment output. This is the normal productive capacity of an economy, with everyone working full-time and all other inputs being used at their capacity rates of application. This full-employment output is invariant to prices, either goods prices in the form of the overall price level or factor prices such as the interest rate. In real interest rate-output space, this full-employment output, which implies full employment of labor, is a vertical line, as shown in Figure 5.7. During the short-run departures from full employment represented by boom periods, both the capital stock and the labor force may be operated at rates above capacity. The unemployment rate will fall below the natural rate. During the short-run departures represented by recessions or depressions, the reverse is the case. The long run of macroeconomic models differs from that of price theoretic models, in which it is the period required for full adjustment of the capital stock to demand and supply decisions; in the short run, the capital stock is fixed and non-fixed factors of production adjust to full employment. In macroeconomic

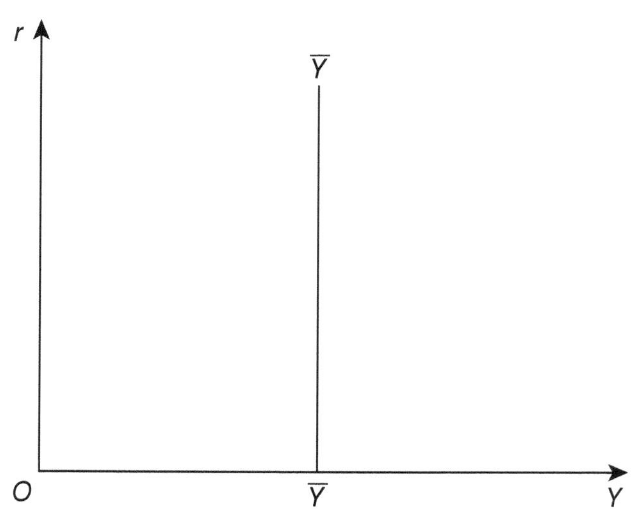

Figure 5.7. Full-employment output.

[15] For this section, I have relied, in addition to the references cited in footnote 1 of this chapter, the following: Blanchard and Katz (1997); Pissarides (2000); Layard, Nickell, and Jackman (2005); and Phelps (1994, Chapters 3–4).

models, we need to distinguish between growth models and static models. The only treatment I will give of growth was in section 5.3.2; the macroeconomic models presented below are static models, distinguished by the degree of price adjustment which they characterize. The long run in a static macroeconomic model keeps the capital stock fixed and represents the period required for prices and the price level to adjust to return the economy to full-employment equilibrium with its natural rate of unemployment. When output in a macroeconomic model is below full capacity or full employment, unemployment exceeds the natural rate. When it exceeds full employment, unemployment is below the natural rate.

But let's back up a moment and ask why even frictional unemployment exists, particularly in a condition we would be willing to call an equilibrium. (We're not questioning whether unemployment exists, just how to understand it with our theory which has focused so heavily on full employment in equilibrium.) During any given period, say a quarter or a year, firms are always in flux. The demands for their products experience random shocks, as some of their customers are pulled away by other suppliers or even other products; tastes of some customers may change; and some may simply die and stop coming around. The firms' technologies may experience some shocks—equipment may break down, a facility may burn down, externally supplied inputs may be interrupted. These events happen randomly, and they affect the quantity, and occasionally skills, of labor that can be fully employed. When demand or production capacity falls off temporarily, some firms may retain some labor that cannot be fully employed because the owners expect to be able to employ them again before long and it would be costly to replace them if they were let go—they might not be available for recall when demand picked back up. But at some point, a firm will decide it is optimal to let some of its employees go—lay them off. And of course, a firm may decide to sack some employee for slacking off. Both sorts of event send workers into the ranks of the unemployed. So workers get unemployed mostly through the vagaries of events in product markets, some of garden-variety magnitude, sometimes tsunamis. For the origins of these fluctuations, go back to section 5.3.1 on the business cycle. A final possible contributor to unemployment appeals to a context of growth: when a labor force is growing faster than aggregate demand is growing, there can be more new entrants into the labor force than there are new job openings during some period. This source of unemployment might find limited application to ancient situations, although a rapid influx of slaves into a labor force could represent such a case.

Exchanges in the labor market, as unemployed workers look for jobs and firms look for workers, are decentralized, uncoordinated, and time consuming for both workers and firms. The time consumed by these exchanges is nontrivial economically because of the multiple dimensions of heterogeneity involved: workers' skills, skill requirements of firms, the timing of opportunities at various locations, the locations of both workers and firms. Each of these variations raises questions without answers, which produces uncertainty and risks for both firms and workers. Workers and firms alike are forced to devote real resources to finding suitable employment and employees.

The length of time unemployed workers remain without a job is a socially interesting and important subject, but is highly variable and doesn't lend itself to a simple, compact summary. The theory guiding thought on the subject deals with the characteristics of the worker (age, skills), the institutional supports available for sustenance while sans income, the reasons for separation, the magnitude of a demand or technology shock involved, the physical setting—population and employment density, and so on. One important consequence of length of unemployment is that a worker's skills can erode. This is a more important consideration during periods of technological change, and may have been less of a consideration during much of antiquity than at present. Nonetheless, even without technological change, a worker's reputation may be affected by an extended period of unemployment. Extended periods of unemployment can induce people to take work in an industry different from that in which he or she has had experience.

5.4.4 Labor Market Equilibration and Wage Adjustment

The immediate question that emerges, and that has roiled macroeconomics since the time of Keynes, is "Why doesn't the real wage fall to maintain full employment?" A change in the real wage would involve the nominal wage changing at a rate different from the change in the price level, or the price of goods. Since workers make decisions about working, and businesses make decisions about hiring, on the basis of the real wage, the proper adjustment of it should clear the labor market—that is, ensure that everyone is employed. Business cycles and their attendant unemployment appear to involve non-Walrasian[16] quantity adjustments in the labor market rather than price adjustments. The current theories of why nominal wages adjust sluggishly and the theories of why wages real may also be inflexible in the short run suggest that the nominal and real inflexibilities[17] interact in ways more complicated than need occupy readers here, and it will suffice to say that a number of costs of adjustment of both wages and product prices have been identified, if not necessarily to the satisfaction of macroeconomists of all convictions, to quite a few. One important underpinning of nominal wage stickiness,

[16] The celebrated – or alternately lamented - Walrasian "auctioneer" (a fictional construct of course) calls out prices until excess demands for all commodities are zero.

[17] The terms nominal and real inflexibilities or rigidities are unfortunate in that they sound parallel but are not. Nominal rigidity or inflexibility simply means that nominal prices don't change instantly when production or demand conditions change, for whatever reason. Real rigidities are not consequences of adjustment costs, parallel to nominal rigidities, but are consequences of production and demand functions, such that marginal products or marginal utilities don't change much when the quantities of factors are altered, i.e., supply is very elastic.

which through product pricing decisions, affects goods price stickiness, is that the labor market is comprised of many different skills, leaving workers imperfect substitutes for one another; consequently, wage changes work their way through the entire labor market rather slowly. The stickiness of goods prices, and the consequent short-run non-neutrality of money, is an important component of Keynesian macroeconomic models as well. Firms changing their prices at different dates also will slow down aggregate price level adjustment, and will even retard the extent of price changes that firms changing their prices do make. Without these features, it is difficult to get a model to yield the result of involuntary unemployment (despite some alternative theories involving misperceptions by both workers and firms of real versus nominal price changes). However, it is not necessary to assume (or to model) that all goods prices are sticky; it is possible to get a considerable degree of overall price-level sluggishness with many prices adjusting quite rapidly.[18]

Currently, the principal, broad explanations for the sluggishness of wage adjustment are the efficiency wage model, appeal to unionization and so-called insider-outsider models. The extent to which either of these models has applicability to ancient labor markets is a question others are better placed to address than I am, but to provide some guidance to those better-placed scholars on what to think about, I offer just the briefest of overviews. The efficiency wage model hypothesizes that employers (at least some, if not necessarily all) will find it optimal to pay their employees more than they absolutely have to in order to secure loyalty, enhance productivity and retard slacking—after all, if a job pays a worker more than he or she could expect to earn elsewhere, that worker will think twice before goldbricking. During downturns, when a firm's demand for labor declines, firms avoid reducing nominal wages to avoid morale problems, letting some of their labor force go but continuing to pay their remaining workers their customary wages. Since the efficiency wage is paid to increase productivity, reducing the wage during a downturn could decrease a firm's output by more than the savings in the wage. To the extent that it emphasizes the rewarding of hard-to-replace skills and specialized activities in businesses, the efficiency wage model might not find especially wide application in antiquity, especially in situations of largely interchangeable workers. Unionization and union bargaining are just what the names imply: an organization of workers that centralize their bargaining efforts over wages and working conditions to enhance their leverage vis-à-vis an employer or group of employers who would otherwise have greater leverage than individual workers would. The outcomes of such bargaining tend to raise wages for union members and depress them for non-unionized workers, result in contracts that extend beyond a single period, and may index wages to changes in the price level. When firms employing unionized workers face a reduction in their demands for labor, their ability to cut wages may be restricted by contract, so they let some workers go, usually those with less seniority. Insider-outsider models of sluggish wage adjustment start with the fact that current employees effectively sit at the bargaining table with employers during a downturn in demand, while unemployed workers who would like to find a job with the firm at a lower wage than the current employees make, do not. They can bargain for layoffs, particularly of less senior employees, rather than wage cuts, whereas the unemployed would prefer wage cuts so they can get a job making something rather than stay unemployed, making nothing.

When prices are sticky, firms adjust to changes in demand by adjusting production since price adjustment is not an economic option in the short run. The market theory behind this adjustment procedure is monopolistic competition (Jones 2014, Chapter 4, section 5). A mark-up over marginal cost, which characterizes monopolistic competition, allows a producer some padding to expand production profitably without increasing price, even if production costs increase somewhat. Firms may be reluctant to change prices in either direction because they may find themselves faced with competition from other firms that choose not to change their prices, and with less than perfect competition, including some brand or supplier loyalty among customers, even price reductions by a firm will not be expected to draw all the market's customers to a firm; leaving price unchanged and accepting some reduction in sales may be more profitable than reducing price and not attracting enough additional sales to make up for the price reduction. This non-price interaction among firms is a type of externality in the product market.

Against this backdrop of heterogeneity, uncertainty, and non-instantaneous price adjustment, there are several approaches to modeling aggregate equilibrium unemployment. Two of the most prominent are the expectational Phillips curve approach, which relates unemployment to expected inflation, and search-matching models, which focus on the resources devoted to locating suitable jobs and workers. It is likely that both approaches would be difficult to apply to ancient situations, for different reasons, but in my judgment the Phillips curve approach is a more suitable approach with which to think about ancient labor markets.

The building blocks of the Phillips curve approach to labor market equilibrium with unemployment are a wage-setting function of agents who set wages and a price-setting function of agents who set goods prices.[19] The wage setters set wages relative to their expectations of goods prices, and the price setters set their goods prices relative to their expectations of wages. If the real wage, w/p, desired by wage setters equals that desired by price setters, inflation will be stable (but not necessarily zero; it just won't change). Otherwise, one price will chase changes in the other. The unemployment rate brings about the equality

[18] A useful, but frankly difficult, discussion is provided by Woodford (2003, 158–173).

[19] This version of the model is adapted from Layard, Nickell, and Jakman (2009, 12–21, 56–58).

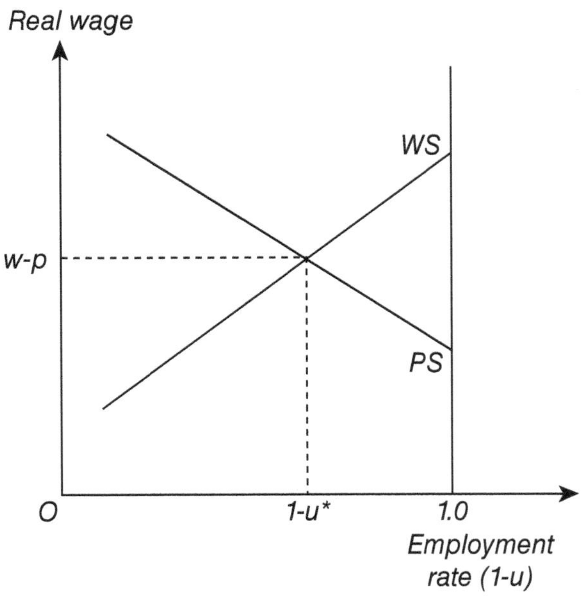

Figure 5.8. Labor market equilibrium with wage setting (WS) and price setting (PS) (Adapted from Layard, Nickell and Jackman, 2005, figure 6A, p. 14, by permission of Richard Layard, Steven Nickell, and Richard Jackman.)

of the real wage desired by both wage and price setters. The price setting relationship is, in logarithmic terms, $p - w^e = \beta_0 - \beta_1 u$, $\beta_0 > 0$, $\beta_1 \geq 0$, where p and w^e are the logarithms of the price and the expected wage and u is the unemployment rate.[20] The left-hand side is the product price mark-up over wage costs, and it rises with the level of activity (i.e., as the unemployment rate falls); it is the line that declines from left to right in Figure 5.8. (Notice that the left-hand side of the price setting relationship is the inverse of the real wage.) The price setting relationship tells the maximum real wage price setters (producers) are willing to offer, given productivity. The wage setting relationship asks for a nominal wage given an expectation of prices: $w - p^e = \gamma_0 - \gamma_1 u$, $\gamma_0 > 0$, $\gamma_1 > 0$, which describes a target real wage sought by wage setters. The target real wage sought by wage setters decreases as the unemployment increase; this is represented by the line that increases from left to right in Figure 5.8.[21] Not included in this particular model, but an important feature of other models of wage and price setting, the amount of non-labor income workers have available, either in the form of asset income (savings) or unemployment benefits such as unemployment insurance in contemporary industrial countries, the dole ancient Rome, or access to family support systems more generally in antiquity, will shift the wage-setting curve vertically. Access to more non-labor income will require employers to offer higher wages to attract workers. If the actual wage and price are at their expected levels, i.e., $p = p^e$ and $w = w^e$, these two relationships can be solved for the non-accelerating inflation rate of unemployment (NAIRU, one of economics' more arresting acronyms): $u^* = \beta_0 + \gamma_0/\beta_1 + \gamma_1$.[22] The parameters subscripted zero are exogenous influences on the wage and the price, known as price-push (β_0) and wage-push (γ_0) factors. The parameters subscripted one represent the degree of flexibility of the price (β_1) and the wage (γ_1) to changes in the unemployment rate. Larger values of β_0 and γ_0 increase the NAIRU (u^*), and larger values of the flexibility parameters β_1 and γ_1 decrease it. If $p \neq p^e$ and $w \neq w^e$, then the unemployment rate is $u = [\beta_0 + \gamma_0 - (p - p^e) - (w - w^e)]/(\beta_1 + \gamma_1)$ or $u = u^* - [(p - p^e) + (w - w^e)]/(\beta_1 + \gamma_1)$. Thus the actual unemployment rate can be characterized as the difference between the NAIRU and a function of the difference between the actual and expected prices and wages, the function being a weight of the flexibility of the unemployment rate with respect to those differences.

If unexpected changes in wages and prices are similar, the last relationship can be written as $u - u^* = (p^e - p)/\theta$, where $\theta = (\beta_1 + \gamma_1)/2$, which is a measure of the flexibility of real prices and wages. According to this relationship, low unemployment is associated with positive price surprises, which is a somewhat more sophisticated interpretation of the earliest Phillips curve relationship, which gave a negative relationship between the unemployment and the inflation rate (actually, the rate of change of the wage rate). If inflation, represented by Δp, has no long-term trend, a rational forecast of inflation is $p^e - p_{t-1} = \Delta p_{t-1}$, where the subscript $t - 1$ indicates the previous period, and unexpected changes in prices are equivalent to increases in inflation. The same is true for wages. Then the last expression for the unemployment rate when expected prices and wages are not equal to actual values implies that $\Delta p - \Delta p_{t-1} = \theta(u^* - u)$, which is a Phillips curve.[23] This relationship says that change in the inflation rate is a function of the difference between the NAIRU and the current actual unemployment rate; the further below the NAIRU is the actual unemployment rate, the higher is inflation, and vice versa. When $u = u^*$, the inflation rate is unchanging, hence the name NAIRU. There is an inertia in this relationship in that inflation in one year is influenced by the previous period's inflation.

Persistence in both unemployment and inflation longer than a pair of adjoining years can be incorporated into the model

[20] Since the expression is in logarithms, the left-hand side of the relationship, non-lograithmically, is p/w^e, or the inverse of the (expected) real wage.

[21] There is broader agreement on the slope of the wage setting relation than there is on the slope of the price setting relation. Macroeconomists who believe in more rapid price adjustment tend to believe β_1 is close to or zero, yielding a horizontal price setting schedule; those who believe that prices adjust more sluggishly work with $\beta_1 > 0$ and a downward sloping price setting schedule. The linearity of the price-setting and wage-setting schedules in Figure 5.8 are the product of this particular model. More generally, the wage setting schedule will bend upward as it approaches lower unemployment rates, as firms must offer yet higher wages to obtain and retain workers.

[22] NAIRU is the current name and theoretical construction of what has been referred to less formally as the natural rate of unemployment.

[23] It is not difficult to see another expression of the Phillips curve that expresses inflation as a function of an output gap in production—the difference between current output and full-employment output. Output is a function of labor inputs; the natural rate of unemployment can be associated with a corresponding natural rate of employment, and the current unemployment rate with a different employment. The employment levels map to output levels, full-employment output, and current output, so $u^* - u$ is equivalent to $Y_f - Y$, for an alternative expression of the Phillips curve.

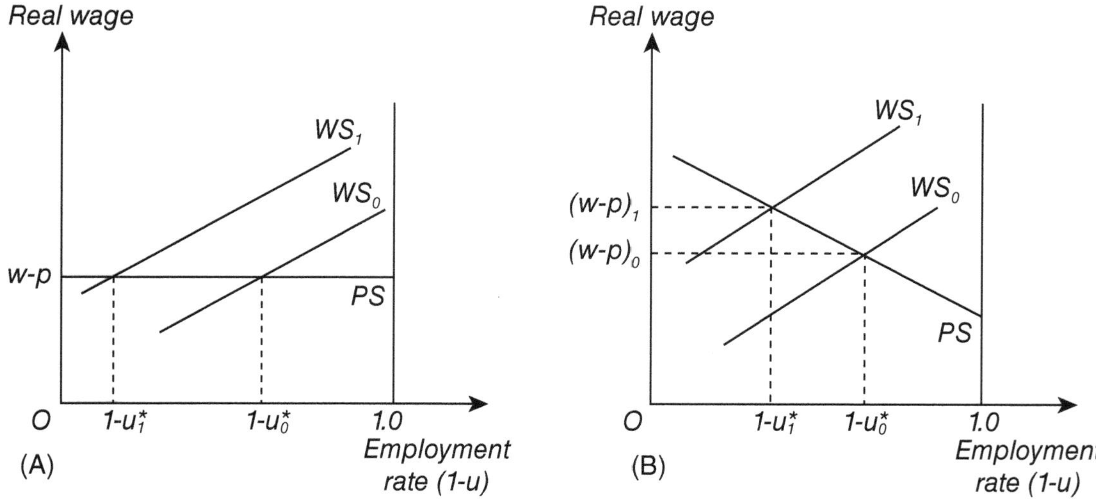

Figure 5.9. (A) Labor market equilibrium and unemployment with flat price-setting mechanism (Adapted from Layard, Nickell and Jackman, 2005, figure 8, p. 19.). (B) Labor market equilibrium and unemployment with declining price-setting mechanism (Adapted from Layard, Nickell and Jackman, 2005, figure 8, p. 19, by permission of Richard Layard, Steven Nickell, and Richard Jackman.)

with some additional terms. If the behavior of wages and prices depends on the change in the unemployment rate as well as its level, the last relationship becomes $\Delta p - \Delta p_{t-1} = \theta(u^* - u) - \theta_{11}(u - u_{t-1})$, where $\theta_{11} > 0$ is the effect of a change in the unemployment rate. Then the short-run NAIRU becomes $u^*_{sr} = \theta_1 u^*/(\theta_1 + \theta_{11}) + \theta_{11} u_{t-1}/(\theta_1 + \theta_{11})$, which says that the short run NAIRU lies between the long-run NAIRU and the last period's unemployment rate. The higher is θ_{11} relative to θ_1, i.e., the stronger the effect of the change in the unemployment rate to the effect of its level, the closer is the short-run NAIRU to last year's unemployment rate.

Whether the real wage is related to unemployment depends in the long run on the slope of the price setting relation, i.e., whether $\beta_1 > 0$ and the line slopes down to the right, or $\beta_1 = 0$ and it is flat. In the latter case, a displacement of the wage setting relation, caused by $\Delta\gamma_0 > 0$, shown in Figure 5.9A, increases the unemployment rate but has no effect on the real wage; it simply increases workers' reservation wage. If, as in Figure 5.9B, $\beta_1 > 0$ and the price setting line slopes downward to the right, the disturbance to the wage-setting relation will cause some increase in the real wage as well as an increase in unemployment. In the short run, whether a demand shock that reduces unemployment increases or decreases the real wage depends on the relative sensitivity of the target wage and the price mark-up to unemployment. If the target wage is more sensitive, the real wage will increase.

Suppose there is considerable reluctance to change prices and wages in the face of inflation. This is called nominal rigidity. In contemporary economies, it could result from staggered long-term wage contracts without indexation of the nominal wages for inflation; in antiquity, it could result from alleged custom in pricing. To model this, a term could be added to the price setting and wage setting relations to incorporate a drag from changes in inflation. The price setting relation would then be $p - w = \beta_0 - \beta_1 u - \beta_2 \Delta^2 p$, where $\Delta^2 p = \Delta p - \Delta p_{t-1}$. The corresponding wage setting relation would be $w - p = \gamma_0 - \gamma_1 u - \gamma_2 \Delta^2 p$. Setting these two relations equal and solving for $\Delta^2 p$ gives another Phillips curve relation, $\Delta^2 p = -(\beta_1 + \gamma_1)/(\beta_2 + \gamma_2)\ [u - (\beta_0 + \gamma_0)/(\beta_1 + \gamma_1)]$. As in the previous case, when $\Delta^2 p = 0$, the NAIRU is $u^* = \beta_0 + \gamma_0/\beta_1 + \gamma_1$, where $\beta_1 + \gamma_1$ represents the degree of real wage flexibility, the degree to which additional unemployment reduces the gap between target and feasible wages. The inverse of this quantity, $1/\beta_1 + \gamma_1$, represents the degree of real wage rigidity, which tells how the NAIRU responds to a supply shock. u* will rise more the greater the degree of real wage rigidity, which can be seen from the previous expression for NAIRU.

The last version of the Phillips curve can be rearranged and manipulated to show the effect of a supply shock on wages, such as might come from a bad crop season or the interruption of imported supplies for manufactured goods. The wage shock can be represented by a change in γ_0, what was called the wage-push factor in the wage setting relation. Thn, where Δs represent "change in," the response in unemployment to a such a supply shock is $\Delta u = -[(\beta_2 + \gamma_2)/(\beta_1 + \gamma_1)]\Delta(\Delta^2 p) + (1/\beta_1 + \gamma_1)\Delta\gamma_0$. This expression says that the more rigid the real wages are, the greater any given supply shock will have on the unemployment rate, while a corresponding surprise increase in the inflation rate (which could be zero) would dampen this effect.

Before leaving the discussion of unemployment, the natural unemployment rate, or NAIRU, concept should be addressed somewhat further. The natural rate is not a fixed magnitude, even in a single country over, say, a decade time period. In general, a more efficient labor market, i.e., one in which workers wanting a job and firms looking for employees can find one another and reach an agreement more quickly, will yield a lower natural rate of unemployment. For example, more generous unemployment benefits tend to raise the natural rate through the effect noted above of increasing the wage employers must pay for a given level of productivity. Nonetheless, a number of factors affect both the wage-setting and price-setting schedules that affect the natural rate emerging as an equilibrium from those relationships, but by affecting both schedules yield an indeterminate effect on the natural rate. Destruction of the capital stock will reduce both workers' nonlabor (capital) income and employers' demand for labor, with an indeterminate result. Public expenditures on consumption goods for which the public competes tend to increase the natural rate (it creates an excess demand for consumer goods which requires an increase in interest rates—and a corresponding drop in asset prices to correct), but public expenditures on capital goods that are not used in the private economy—think war equipment—increases the price of capital goods, reduces the interest rate, and has an expansionary effect, reducing the natural rate. Thus the natural rate of unemployment will move around over time, in response to both government policies and exogenous events.

Ending this section on a more empirical note, let's turn to thoughts on unemployment and inflation in antiquity.Unemployment in antiquity may have borne considerable differences from its contemporary counterpart. In larger, urbanized environments, from ancient Mesopotamia to Imperial Rome, however, the relative anonymity of cities may have lent itself to people looking for work, which is a rough definition of unemployment. However, as suggested earlier, many people out of work may have been able to fall back into family agricultural pursuits, even if they were not fully employed in those activities, leaving unemployment more difficult to observe than it is today—for all the difficulty in arriving at accurate measures of unemployment today. The Greek mercenary armies of the 6th through the 4th centuries B.C.E. have been considered at least partially products of not enough to do at home, and piracy throughout the ages has been associated with periods of slack demand for experienced military or civilian seamen.[24] The notorious army of unemployed in Imperial Rome may have been the product of a unique combination of labor market institutions (ample supply of slave labor depressing the market wage and government unemployment support sustaining reservation wages).

Consider further, nevertheless, the possible structure of unemployment in many ancient urban settings. Think of a furniture maker in, say Periclean Athens. The owner is the chief furniture maker. His employees are his two grown sons and three slaves. The plague of 431 B.C.E. arrives and reduces consumption, which reduces the demand for furniture, and in particular this manufacturer's furniture. What's he going to do with his employees—his two sons and the three slaves? Give them their pink slips? Probably not. The two kids, the fellow is pretty much stuck with. He could take his slaves to the slave market, but he might consider that a drastic solution for what he thinks could be a short-term fall-off in demand. And besides, they're trained to make furniture, and they're not bad; it could be hard to replace them with anybody comparable when the market picks back up. The contemporary term for hanging onto these workers is called labor hoarding: holding onto more workers than would be justified by a strict adherence to a rule of thumb that equated marginal cost to marginal productivity. He could have them whitewash the walls, fix up the roof, sharpen the tools, and so on. So what happens to employment or unemployment. Strictly speaking, neither the two sons nor the three slaves are fully employed right now, so they do fit the concept of unemployment, at least in some sense. However, they haven't been let go, because to the relationship structure of the labor market (family and slave property), so considering them underemployed rather than unemployed—without any job at all—might be more useful. As far as insiders versus outsiders goes, the concept that was introduced above to help explain the stickiness of nominal wages during the business cycle, they're all insiders. The nominal wage very well may have adjusted more quickly than the nominal product prices in a situation like this. But does the concept of unemployment, of people discharged from their jobs and out looking for work, as opposed to less-than-fully-employed workers still showing up to work at least now and then, still apply in such a situation? Maybe, maybe not. That may be a research question. Does it make any difference to the movements of the behavioral schedules of the IS-LM and AD-AS models to be developed in the following sections? Not really. But returning to the structure of the labor market envisioned above in this 4th Century B.C.E. Athenian firm, were there unattached (free non-family) workers in the city's business establishments, and in those of other ancient cities in the Aegean-Mediterranean area? Undoubtedly, and in varying proportions depending on place and period. Certainly not as high a proportion as today. The use of the macroeconomic models developed below, as well as those developed already, will survive this difference by and large.

Several closing points bring us back to applications of the models of this section to the ancient world. First, the differences in unemployment and inflation rates appealed to implicitly in these models are generally small. The difference between a 4% unemployment and an 8% unemployment rate is enormous socially in contemporary societies. The Western world nearly collapsed when unemployment rates reached 25–30% during the Great Depression, and the experience is still with much of the world eight decades later. Differences this small may be very difficult to discern in ancient data, be they textual references or archaeological remains. Whether these changes can be identified or not may be less important than an understanding that something of the sort must have been going on for other things which may be documented to have occurred. The knowledge of the relationships may help contemporary scholars sharpen their interpretations of ancient events, and possibly suggest other places to look for corroboration.

[24] On the economics of piracy, emphasizing human capital (skills) and aggregate demand, see Jones (2000, 23–34).

Second, and closely related to the first point, inflation with (mostly) commodity currencies (allowing for some multiplier capacity of bank money in some ancient societies), is considerably more restricted and less highly variable than it is with fiat currencies. Hyperinflations such as rocked some European countries in the aftermath of World War I, or even Latin American inflations during the 1950s and 1960s, simply are out of the question. In a long unpublished manuscript from the early 1920s, Keynes estimated annual inflation of the Athenian drachma at around one-third of one percent a year for two hundred fifty years.[25] For much of Roman history, inflation was quite low, by all appearances. References by Harl to price level increases during the Republic amount to average annual rates of inflation between $\frac{1}{2}$% per year and about 1%.[26] However, the Roman inflation of the 3rd and 4th centuries C.E. evidently was substantially greater, but still no competitor for major 20th century C.E. inflationary experiences. As bad as Diocletian's revaluation of the nummus upward to five times its initial notional value twice within eight years sounds to the ear, that amounts to an average 29% per year inflation rate. Eight-fold price level increases, if such were actually the case, spread over as little as four years, amount to only 52% per year. Granted, these are inflations substantial enough to seriously disrupt an economy, but they were not sustained for lengthy periods. Rather the nummus devaluations under Diocletian were more discrete price level jumps which did not continue after the devaluations. A sustained inflation would have required either continuing devaluations or increasing coinage above the rate of growth in money demand. The period of Roman Imperial history from the mid- or late 3rd century C.E. through the 4th or into the late 5th century apparently was a period of monetary instability, including some periods of higher inflation, likely well beyond the experience of the population at the time, but overall, the record of Roman inflation is consistent with the limited expansibility of commodity currencies. This quick review of the record, such as it is, of Greek and Roman inflation suggests that variations in inflation appealed to in the equilibrium unemployment model, as well as the other macroeconomic models to follow, like the variations in unemployment, may be, on the one hand, too small to be picked out of ancient evidence, yet on the other, much larger than may have been experienced from year to year in much of antiquity. Again, as with the comments on variations in the unemployment rate, recognition of the relationships between short-term changes in unemployment and short-term changes in price levels may be of use in more clearly understanding some aspects of ancient evidence.

Third, and less an issue of application to antiquity than a clarification, the reader who absorbed the lesson that inflation is a monetary phenomenon may wonder how the equilibrium unemployment model can produce inflation when neither the nominal nor real money supply has changed. Quite a fair question. Macroeconomists agree that inflation, or price-level change, in the long run is a purely monetary phenomenon, and in fact that real variables in the economy are unaffected by the money supply—the fact of the long run neutrality of money to which reference is made constantly. In short periods, given a constant rate of growth of the money supply (which may be zero), the behavior of economic agents in pursuing various goals can involve spending at different rates on quantities of goods and services that are in fixed or modestly expansible supply, essentially altering circulation velocity in the quantity equation of money demand ($MV = PT$, or $M/P = T/V$, in which T is equivalent to aggregate demand denoted by Y throughout this chapter). With M constant and T moving little or not at all, an increase in the velocity of money, V, will increase the price level, which is the definition of inflation: $P = MV/T$.

5.5 The IS-LM Model

The IS-LM model is very much the Keynesian model, as interpreted mathematically and diagrammatically by John Hicks (1937) shortly after the publication of *The General Theory* and subsequently employed as the workhorse of Keynesian macroeconomic analysis to the present date, at least in textbooks, if the forefront of research has looked well beyond its curves. With the price level fixed, it deals with the short run. Letting the price level change allows the IS-LM model to analyze the medium and long runs. The IS curve describes equilibrium in the goods market, and the LM curve equilibrium in the financial market.

5.5.1 The IS Relation

The IS curve can be derived diagrammatically from the equilibrium of the saving and investment curves of Figure 5.10. In fact, the IS curve traces out saving-investment equilibria in r-Y (real interest rate-aggregate income) space as aggregate income Y changes, as shown in Figure 5.10. An increase in income from Y_1 to Y_2 shifts desired savings to the right in the left panel of Figure 5.10, but the investment demand curve is not affected by changes in income (as assumed in this specification; that is a complication that could be handled easily). This outward shift of the saving curve along the investment curve gives savers lower returns on their savings as they attempt to save more, the real interest rate that equilibrates desired saving and desired investment falling from r_1 to r_2. The left panel of Figure 5.10 traces out the saving-investment

[25] Moggridge (1982, 229–230). Keynes appears to have relied on Boeckh and a spotty assortment of ancient writers (see the third footnote on 229). Not dissimilar conclusions are reached on the basis of far more extensive, primary research on ancient prices by Loomis (1998, Chapter 15), who identifies periods of possible inflation as well as deflation during the Classical Period, but with the limitation (not without reason) of relying only on public sector wages.

[26] Harl (1996, 48, 271–274 on the Republican Period; 8, 18, 282, 288–289 on the 3rd to 5th century experiences). Temin (2006a, 149) believes that the Roman inflation rate was generally under 1% per year for the first two centuries C.E., but attributes the demise of banks during the 3rd century to a burst of unaccustomed inflation prior to Diocletian's nummus devaluations and his Edict of Maximum Prices in 301 C.E., as bankers had yet had the opportunity to acquire an understanding of the difference between nominal and real interest rates. Howgego (1995, Chapter 6) offers succinct accounts of debasements and price level increases with both Athenian and Roman currencies.

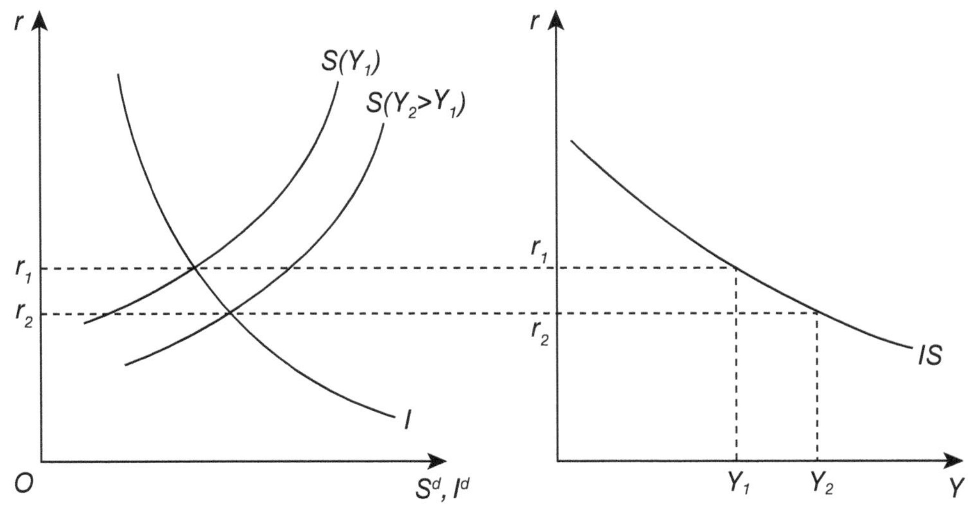

Figure 5.10. Derivation of the IS curve from investment and saving relationships.

equilibria of the right panel in real interest rate-aggregate income space, yielding a downward sloping curve in the interest rate. The locus of equilibria in the goods market shows equilibria as combinations of a higher interest rate and lower aggregate income and a lower interest rate and higher aggregate income.

Because equalization of desired saving and desired investment is equivalent to equalization of equalization of aggregate demand and production (aggregate income), the IS curve can be derived also from shifts in the income-expenditure diagram, Figure 5.4. Figure 5.11, panel a shows

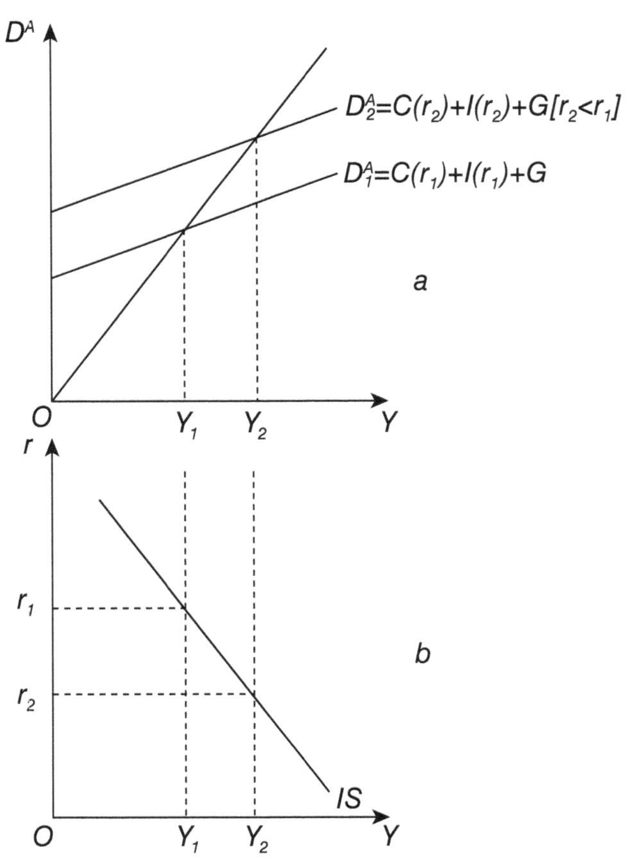

Figure 5.11. Deriving the IS curve from aggregate demand.

the aggregate demand curve at real interest rate r_1 as $D_1^A = C(r_1) + I(r_1) + G$, yielding equilibrium aggregate income Y_1. The consumption function heretofore has been written as a function of income Y or disposable income Y − T, but here it is written as a function of the real interest rate r, relying on the relationship S = Y − C; whatever changes S changes C. Let the real interest rate fall from r_1 to r_2. $D^A = Y$ at Y_1. Now let the real interest rate fall to r_2, and the consumption component of D^A increases to $C(r_2)$, the investment component falls to $I(r_2)$, and $D^A = Y$ at $Y_2 > Y_1$.

An increase in government expenditures shifts the IS curve up and to the right. With the saving and investment curves, because the increase in government spending shifts the saving curve to the left (recall the income accounting) while leaving the investment curve unaffected, as shown in Figure 5.12. Panel a shows the increase in G shift the desired saving curve up and to the right, increasing the real interest rate from r_1 to r_2 as it slides along the desired investment curve. In panel b, the initial IS curve, IS_1, includes the initial equilibrium at (r_1, Y), crowding out investment by the same amount as saving is reduced. The higher real interest rate intersects unchanged aggregate income at a higher IS curve, IS_2. Alternatively, using the income-expenditure diagram offers less transparency: with the D^A line unchanged, the C and I components of D^A must change in compensating amounts as G increases. Clearly, this is a thought experiment in which a given aggregate income Y is composed of different proportions of G, C and I rather than a scenario of a government increasing its expenditures and aggregate income somehow remaining unchanged. The difference in G must be distributed between differences in C and I so as to keep Y constant. The responsiveness of the interest rate to the increase in government spending determines the allocation of the compensating reduction in other spending between consumption and investment. The less sensitive is investment to the interest rate, which will increase as G increases, the small the reduction in investment; at the limit of zero interest rate sensitivity of investment, saving will not change and the entire increase in

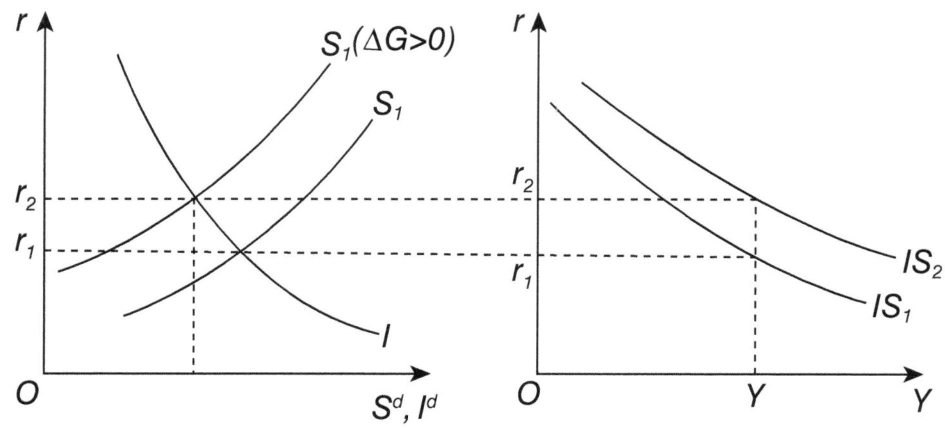

Figure 5.12. Changes in saving behavior shift the IS curve.

government spending must come out of consumption. The increase in the interest rate does not encourage more saving by consumers because investors are unwilling to absorb further funds. At an infinite interest elasticity of investment (a horizontal desired investment curve; admittedly an unlikely prospect), the entire increase in government spending will come out of saving and consumption will be unchanged. While a decrease in taxes may not reliably shift the IS curve in the same direction as an increase in government spending, an increase in taxes shifts it down and to the left.

With the addition of a functional form for the investment component of the income-expenditure equilibrium condition, a simple expression for the IS relation can be obtained. Since investment is a negative function of the real interest rate, and the concept of an autonomous, or non-income-related portion of both consumption and investment has been introduced above, let $I(r) = i_0 + i_1 r$, $i_1 < 0$. Then equilibrium income can be expressed as $Y = c_0 + i_0 - t_0 + G + NX + c_1(1 - t_1)Y + i_1 r$, or $Y = A + c_1(1 - t_1)Y + i_1 r$, where A is the autonomous components. Simplifying yields $Y = m_{ct}(A + i_1 r)$, in which m_{ct} is the post-tax consumption multiplier. Since the real interest rate is on the vertical axis of the IS diagram, this expression can be rearranged as $r = - A/i_1 + Y/m_{ct}i_1$.

From this expression, it is easy to see that greater sensitivity of investment to the real interest rate, a larger consumption multiplier, and a lower tax rate each will impart a flatter slope to the IS curve. The tax rate works through the multiplier, a higher tax rate reducing the magnitude of the multiplier and flattening the slope of the aggregate demand / expenditure line in the income-expenditure graph.

5.5.2 The LM Relation[27]

The LM curve is constructed analogously from the intersections of the money demand and money supply curves of Figure 5.6 as changes in income shift the money demand curve. Panel a of Figure 5.13 shows an increase in aggregate income increasing the demand for real money balances, pushing up the nominal interest rate from i_1 to i_2 along a fixed supply curve of real balances. Panel b translates the intersections of the shifting money demand curve and the fixed money supply curve into $i - Y$ space as was done with the IS relation. In the case of real money demand, however, the higher interest rates are associated with higher incomes, and the LM curve slopes upward in $i - Y$ space. While consumption, saving and investment depend on the real interest rate, the demand for money depends on the nominal interest rate, which is related to the real rate through the expected inflation rate: $i = r + \pi^e$, as noted above. Accordingly, to bring the LM and IS curves together in a single graph to determine general equilibrium, it is necessary to express either the real interest rate as $i - \pi e$ or the nominal interest rate as $r + \pi^e$. As long as $\pi_e = 0$, which will be the case in the very short run, the two interest rates are interchangeable. In longer-run analyses, if the IS and LM curves are graphed in $r - Y$ space, the IS curve will be a function of π_e as well as its non-price shifters, as the investment function becomes $I = I(i - \pi^e)$.

[27] The LM curve has become somewhere between passé and controversial, and although it is still widely taught in intermediate-level macroeconomics courses and texts, the foundation for the LM relationship is a money supply under the control of the monetary authority, an assumption no longer warranted with the innovations in banking and non-banking financial intermediation over the past three decades or so. Central banks no longer target the money supply because their control over it is too loose, depending now as it does on profit maximization behavior of various financial firms and even the money-holding public. Instead, central banks have adopted interest rate targeting as a more effective tool for controlling inflation. What has become known as the Taylor rule, with which a central bank adjusts the nominal interest rate according to departures of actual from desired inflation and the output gap, the difference between potential (full-employment) and actual GDP, has become the general guide to contemporary practice of monetary policy, and this relationship is simply not contained in the LM curve. Woodford's entire treatise (2003) is directed at how to use interest rate targeting for effective monetary policy. On the teaching consequences of jettisoning the LM curve, see Romer (2000) and the articles in Fontana and Setterfield (2009). This said, to a first order, results of the basic macroeconomic models are not materially affected by this substitution of characterizations of equilibrium in the money and financial markets, and the older LM relationship is probably quite satisfactory for the analysis of ancient macroeconomies because those economies' banking and financial intermediation sectors provided for much less expansiveness of the money supply, although some, probably modest, degree of elasticity evidently existed; see Cohen (2008). The monetary authority, or government, had firm control over the money supply in most instances, and interest rate policies simply did not exist.

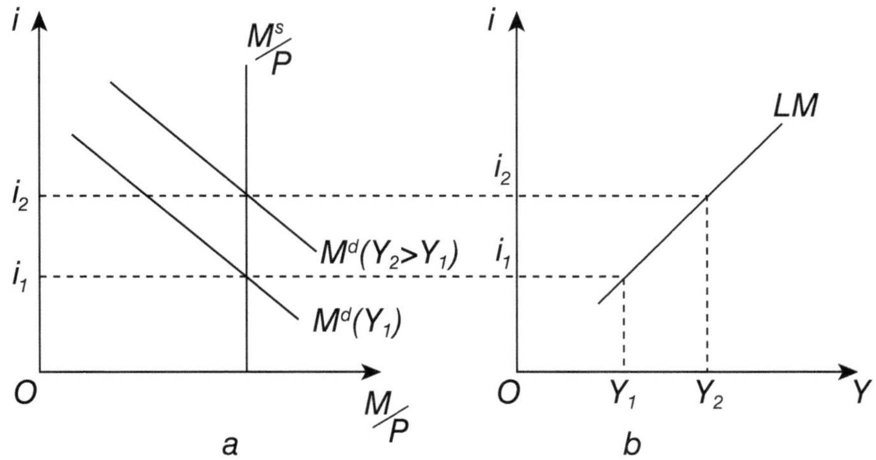

Figure 5.13. Deriving the LM curve from the money supply and demand functions.

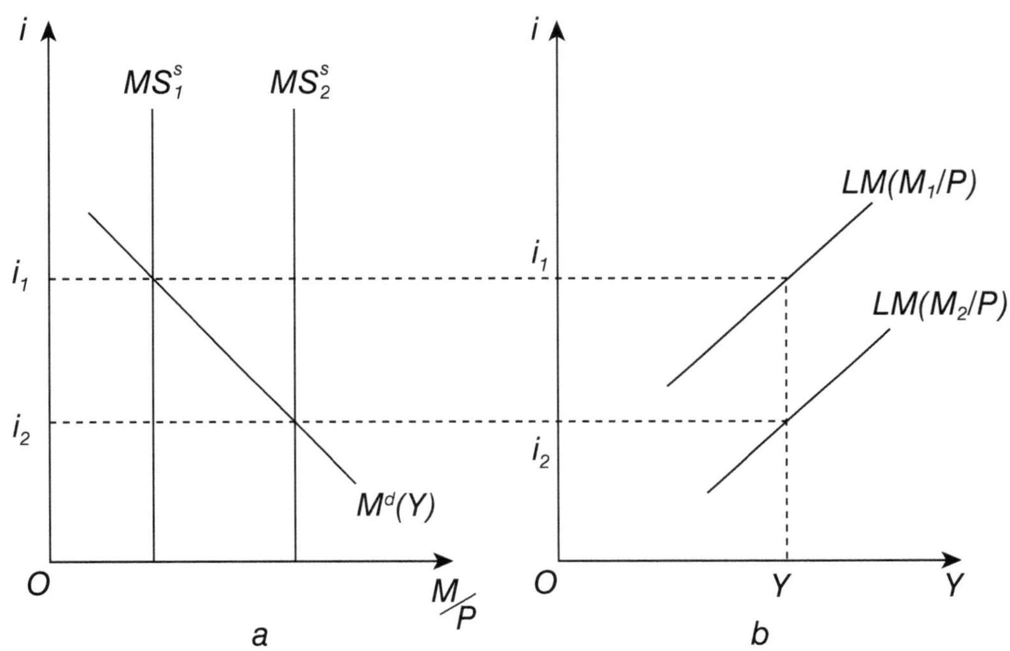

Figure 5.14. An increase in the money supply shifts the LM curve down.

Given the money demand function of section 5.5.2, a functional form, an expression for the LM curve, can be derived. Specify the money demand function $(M/P)^d = L(Y, r + \pi^e)$ as $(M/P)^d = \ell_1 Y + \ell_2 r + \ell_3 \pi^e$, in which $\ell_1 > 0$, $\ell_2 < 0$, and $\ell_3 < 0$. In equilibrium, money demand equals money supply, so $(M/P)^d = M^s/P = \ell_1 Y + \ell_2 r + \ell_3 \pi^e$. Again, since the real interest rate is on the vertical axis of the LM graph, this expression can be rearranged as $r = (M^s/P - \ell_1 Y - \ell_3 \pi^e)/\ell_2$, which yields a curve sloping upward in the real interest rate.

The variables that shift the LM curve include the nominal money supply, the price level, wealth, the riskiness of alternative assets, and the independent components of the nominal interest rate—the real rate and expected inflation. Working with $\pi^e = 0$ simplifies exposition, so the next several diagrams work with the real interest rate.

Figure 5.14 shows the effect of an increase in the real money supply on the LM curve. With the price level fixed ($\pi^e = 0$), an increase in the nominal money stock, M^s, is equivalent to an increase in the real money stock, M^s/P. The increase in the money stock shifts the money supply curve to the right, from M_1^s to M_2^s. With unchanged income, the money demand curve is unchanged, and the interest rate falls from i_1 to i_2 in panel a. In panel b of the figure, at unchanged aggregate income Y, the combination of the lower interest rate r_2 and unchanged Y is a locus below and to the right of the initial LM curve, forming a point on the new LM_2. An increase in the demand for money, caused by an increase in aggregate income Y shifts out the money demand curve, leaving the money supply curve unaffected, and raising the real interest rate from i_1 to i_2 in panel a of Figure 5.15 and shifting the LM curve up and to the left in panel b. An increase in the price level P reduces the real

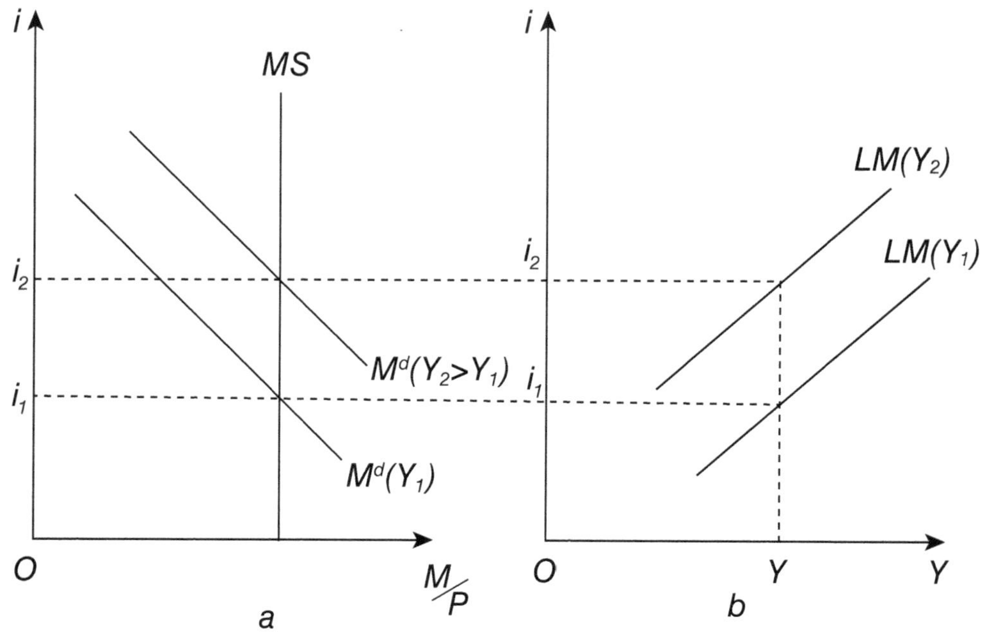

Figure 5.15. Changes in money demand shift the LM curve.

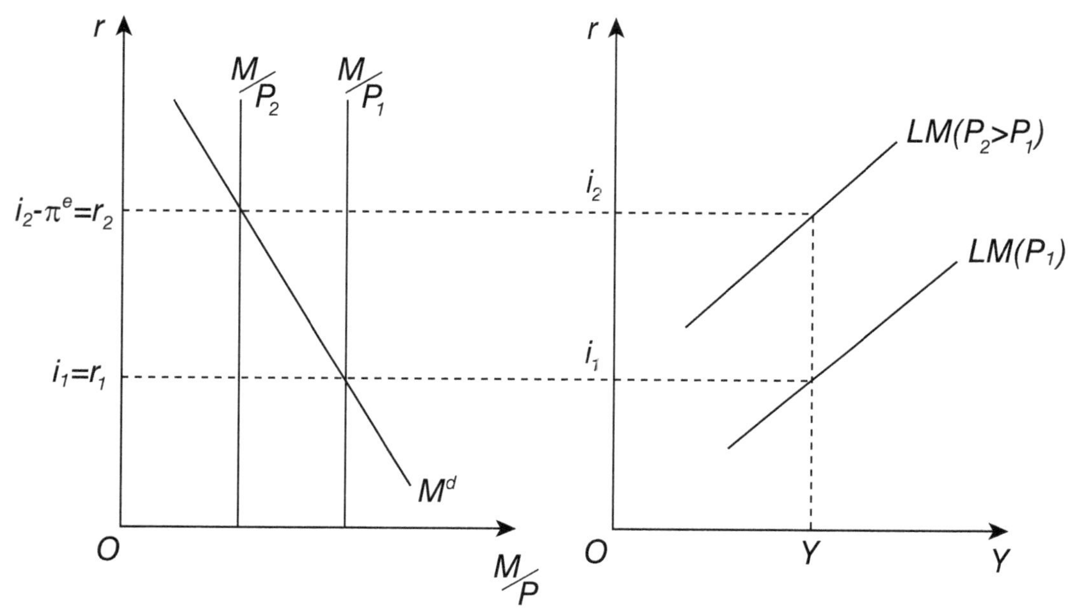

Figure 5.16. A decrease in the money supply shifts the LM curve up.

money supply, shifting the real money supply live to the left in Figure 5.16. The real interest rate increases from $r_1 = i_1$ to r_2, which may be equal to or less than the nominal interest rate i_2, depending on whether the rate of inflation that increased the price level from P_1 to P_2 is expected to continue or not.

5.5.3 Equilibrium and Some Analyses

Begin by assuming that the price level is constant, an innocuous-sounding but critical assumption. This assumption underpins the quantity adjustments that are the hallmark of the Keynesian approach to short-run macroeconomics and the business cycle. For various reasons, on which there is a considerable literature, many producers in imperfectly competitive markets find that, considering other producers' prices, there is little cost to changing their own prices infrequently, a phenomenon referred to as nominal rigidities. Given this proclivity to not change prices in the face of fluctuations in demand (or supplies of inputs), quantity adjustments are more common than competitive conditions would predict. Consequently, producers accommodate shifts in demands for goods more commonly with output changes than with changes in mark-ups of price over marginal cost, while shifts in the demand for labor lead to little change in the real wage and larger changes in employment, phenomena known as real rigidities. These are short-run phenomena, which allow for non-neutrality of money in the short run, but

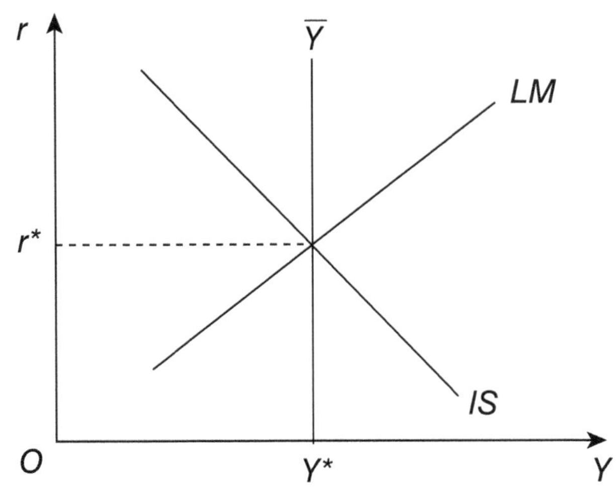

Figure 5.17. Full-employment equilibrium with IS and LM curves.

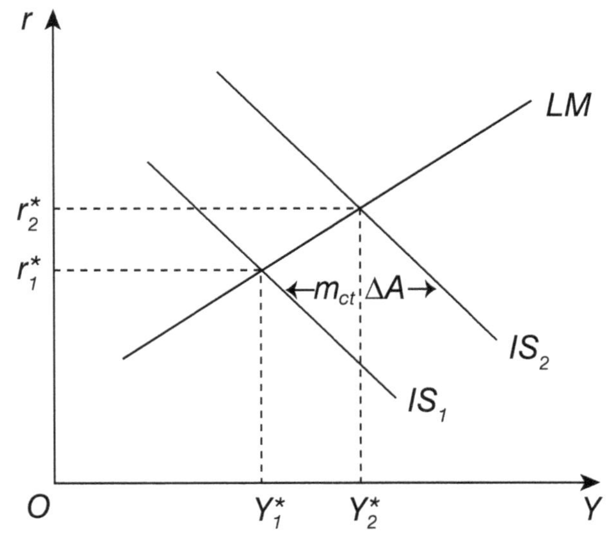

Figure 5.18. An increase in autonomous spending shifts the IS curve to the right.

they disappear in the long run, when prices have finally adjusted, all product and factor markets are in equilibrium, and changes in the money supply find their only impact in a change in the price level.

In the two equations offered for the IS-LM model, there are three variables, the interest rate, aggregate demand and the price level. For determinacy, a third equation is needed, and various candidates have been proposed. The simplest version of the Keynesian approach, as just described, assumes that prices are fixed in the short run, and the third equation could be said to be $P = \overline{P}$, and the interest rate and output adjust to satisfy the IS and LM relationships. The Classical approach, which Keynesian macroeconomics proposes to supplant for analysis of the short run, assumes that prices adjust so rapidly that output is essentially fixed, so that the third equation becomes $Y = \overline{Y}$ and unemployment ceases to exist. In the long run, the Classical assumption is a better description, and in the short run the Keynesian is superior.

Assuming a constant price level and that producers are willing to supply whatever output is demanded at that price level, equilibrium in the goods and money markets is shown by overlaying the IS and LM curves on a single graph in either r – Y or i – Y space. Figure 5.17 uses the real interest rate, assuming $\pi^e = 0$. Equilibrium output is Y* and the equilibrium real interest rate is r*. Full employment at this equilibrium is determined by the intersection of a vertical line representing full-employment output $\overline{Y}$ at the intersection of the IS and LM schedules. The IS and LM curves need not intersect at $Y^* = \overline{Y}$. An intersection to the right of $\overline{Y}$ describes a short-run expansionary period in which production is in excess of full-capacity output. Intersections to the left of $\overline{Y}$ are contractionary periods with unemployment.

To see how exogenous changes work in the model, consider an increase in autonomous spending in Figure 5.18. The change could be an increase in government spending, in the autonomous component of investment or consumption, or in net exports. The IS curve moves to the right by the amount of the direct autonomous increase in spending, times the multiplier m_{ct}, or $m_{ct}\Delta A$, but because of the upward slope of the LM curve, the increase in equilibrium income is less than that amount. If the exogenous change in spending had been negative instead of positive, the LM curve would have shifted to the left by a corresponding magnitude, resulting in a temporary unemployment equilibrium. Such a change might be a pause in investment spending in anticipation of warfare.

Figure 5.19 shows the effect of an increase in the money supply, starting from a long-run equilibrium at $\overline{Y}_1^* = \overline{Y}$, and equilibrium real interest rate r_1^* equal to a nominal interest rate (not shown in the diagram) of i_1^*. The increase in the money supply shifts the LM curve to the right, pushing down the real interest rate from r_1^* to r_2^* and creating a temporary expansion of output to $\overline{Y}_2^*$ where production is greater than full-employment output. Not shown in the diagram is a gradual increase in the price level as the short-run fixed prices are increased, causing the LM curve to shift

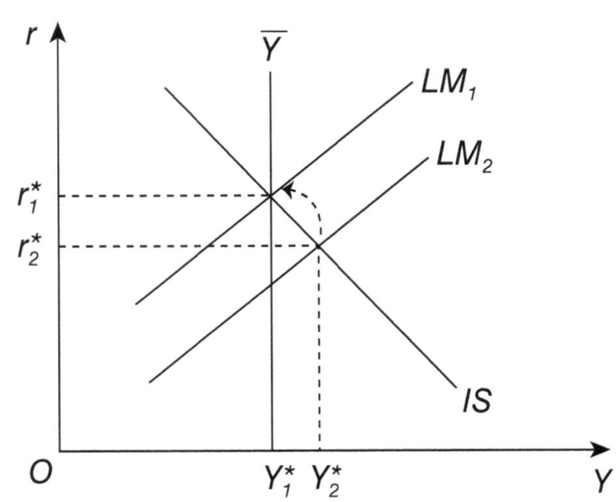

Figure 5.19. The effect of an increase in the money supply on long-run, full-employment equilibrium.

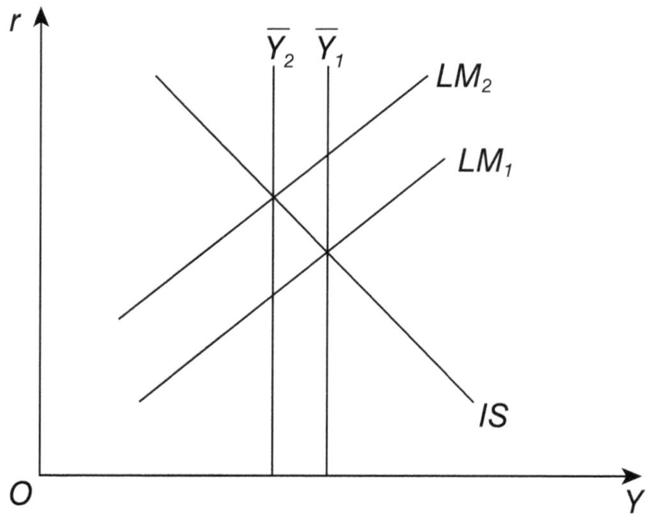

Figure 5.20. Studying supply and demand shocks with the IS-LM framework.

back up the IS curve to the original equilibrium at (r_1^*, Y_1^*), at which point the inflation required to increase the price level has resulted in a nominal interest rate i_3^* above the real rate r_1^*.

Both of these changes using the IS-LM model have acted on the demand side, for which the Keynesian model was originally developed. However, supply shocks can be analyzed with the framework as well. Consider the impact of a severe drought, which reduces the supply of food by such a large amount that suppliers cannot avoid raising the price. Since food comprises a large part of the budget of workers in the typical ancient setting, the cost of labor rises and the food price increase extends to other products as well. In other words, the price level rises, which reduces the real money stock. In Figure 5.20, the reduction in the real money stock is represented by a leftward shift of the LM curve. The reduction in food supply also represents a temporary reduction in the real productive capacity of the economy, shifting the $\overline{Y}$ curve to the left. As drawn, the LM curve shifts up the IS curve beyond the intersection with the new full-employment line $\overline{Y}_2$, indicating unemployment even at the temporarily reduced capacity. Assuming the following season brings normal crops, the full-employment line will shift back to its original position (or some position between $\overline{Y}_2$ and $\overline{Y}_1$), and the LM curve will gradually return to its original position.

5.6 The AD-AS Model

The aggregate demand-aggregate supply model can be derived from the IS-LM model, and in fact is simply an alternative presentation of the same theory expressing the relationship between the price level and output rather than between the interest rate and output.[28] The aggregate

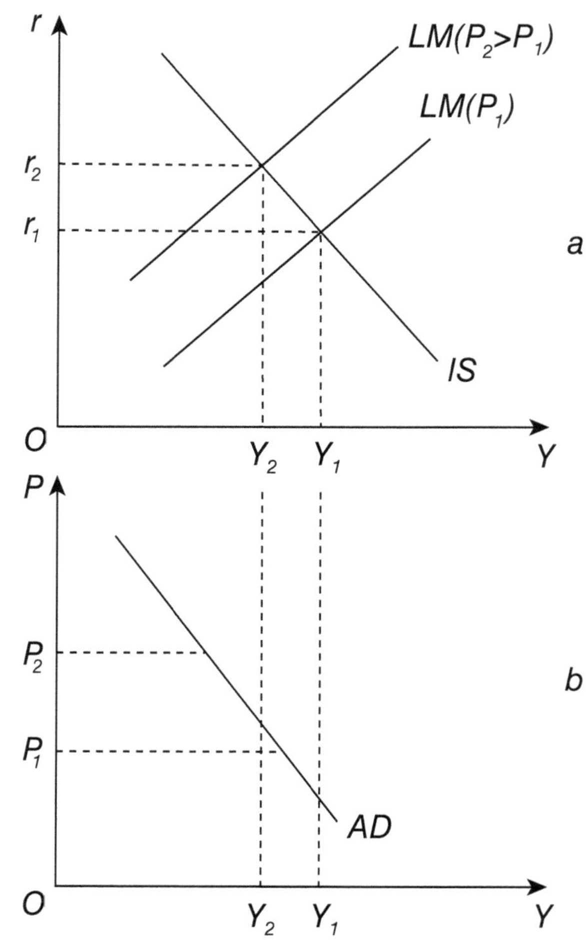

Figure 5.21. Translating the IS-LM framework into the Aggregate Demand (AD) curve.

demand relationship is the same across Classical and Keynesian models, but the aggregate supply relationship both differs across models and remains a subject of research and controversy.

5.6.1 Aggregate Demand

The aggregate demand curve is the locus of intersections of the IS and LM curves as the price level is changed in the LM curve. As a general function, the AD curve can be expressed as $Y = Y^d(M/P, G, T, NX, \Omega)$, $Y^d_{M/P} > 0$, $Y^d_G > 0$, $Y^d_T < 0$, $Y^d_{NX} > 0$, where Ω is other exogenous variables. Using specific functional forms, equating the expressions for IS and LM above and eliminating the real interest rate yields the AD curve relating output to the price level: $Y = \theta A + (\theta i_1/\ell_2)M^s/P + (\theta i_1 \ell_3/\ell_2)\pi^e$, where $\theta = m_{ct}/(1 + m_{ct} i_1 \ell_1/\ell_2) > 0$. Graphically, the translation of the IS-LM intersections into the AD curve is shown in Figure 5.21, in which an increase in the price level reduces real money balances, shifting the LM curve up and to the left along the unchanged IS curve. The increase in the

[28] There are several alternative derivations of the AD-AS model, particularly of the aggregate supply curve, and these alternatives analyze in alternative spaces. Deriving the AS curve from the Phillips curve, the AD-AS model can be developed in inflation-output space rather than price level-output space; e.g., Romer (1996, 228–231). Another derivation from the Phillips curve develops the model in inflation-employment rate space; e.g., Layard, Nickell, and Jackman (2009, 16–20). One advantage of expressing the model in terms of inflation rather than the price level is that, at least in contemporary times, deflation rarely occurs, although the movements of the AD curve along either a short-run or long-run AS curve implies deflation as well as inflation. However, for intermediate-level heuristic purposes, the price level-output presentation is satisfactory.

price level from P_1 to P_2 reduces real money balances and raises the real interest rate necessary to make satisfied with holding these reduced balances.

Like an ordinary demand curve for an individual product, the aggregate demand curve slopes downward in price-output space. The similarities between the aggregate demand curve and individual demand curves end with this superficial appearance. The demand curve for a product slopes downward in price-output space because of decreasing marginal utility and the consumer's budget constraint. The aggregate demand curve slopes downward for several reasons. The first reason is the wealth or real balance effect, commonly known as the Pigou effect after the economist who first proposed it. As the price level decreases, the purchasing power of money increases and consumers are wealthier, spend more, and push up aggregate demand. Once thought to be of considerable magnitude, empirical research has shown it to be fairly small. Another reason, known as the Keynes effect, works through interest rates. For any given quantity of nominal money in circulation, a lower price level will induce consumers to save more, which reduces the interest rate and encourages investment, thus expanding expenditure and output. A third effect derives from an economy's international connections. As the domestic interest rate falls with the lower price level, domestic investors seek higher interest rates overseas, sending more of their country's currency abroad, decreasing the country's real exchange rate (which will be explained in more detail in section 8 below) and increasing net exports as the country's export goods get cheaper in terms of foreign currencies. And there is no substitution among products along the AD curve as there is in individual demand curves.

Influences that shift IS-LM intersections shift the AD curve. Consider, for example, a shift in government purchases, shown in Figure 5.22, which shifts the IS curve out at unchanged prices in panel a. In panel b, the increase in income at the unchanged price level P* entails an outward shift of the AD curve. An increase in the money supply would work in the same direction.

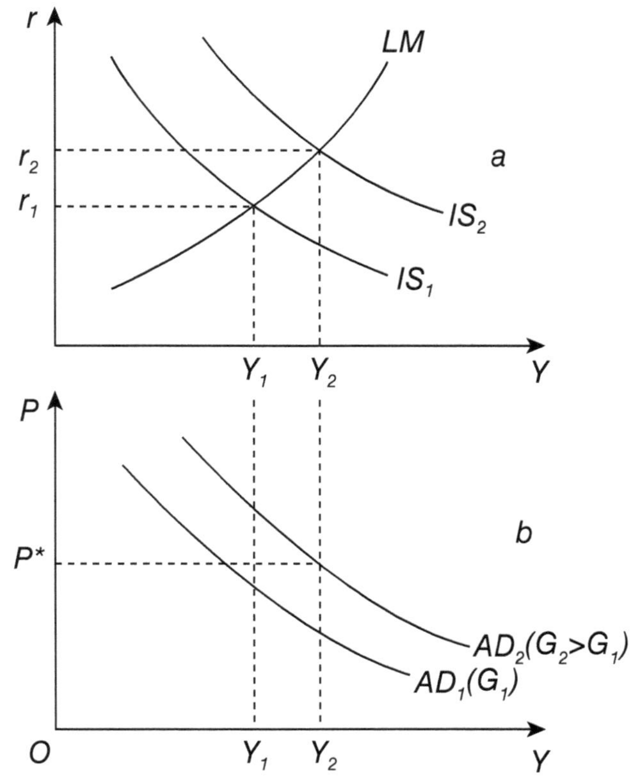

Figure 5.22. IS-LM changes shift the AD curve.

5.6.2 Aggregate Supply

The pure Classical aggregate supply curve is vertical: with fixed factor supplies and full employment assured by flexible prices, increases in demand affect only prices, not output. The pure Keynesian aggregate supply curve is horizontal, implying that firms will supply whatever goods are demanded at a constant price level. Macroeconomists agree that in the long run, the Classical vertical aggregate supply curve is correct. In the very short run, many macroeconomists concede that the aggregate supply curve is flat or nearly so.To understand how the AS curve moves from horizontal to vertical, three relationships are brought into play, an aggregate production function, typically specified as a function of only one variable factor, labor, all other factors being tucked inside a coefficient relating labor to output, Y = aL, where a is labor productivity; a relationship describing how firms set prices in relation to wages; and a relationship between unemployment and wages. The general functional relationship is $Y = Y^s(w/P, P/P^e, K, T)$, $Y^S_{w/P} < 0$, $Y^S_{P/P^e} > 0$, $Y^S_K > 0$, $Y^S_T > 0$, where w/P is the real wage, P and P^e are the actual and expected price levels, K is the physical capital stock, and T is the level of technology.

The simplified production function, letting labor productivity equal one, implies that the marginal cost of output is the cost of hiring one more worker, or the wage rate w. Assuming imperfectly competitive markets that do not drive the price of output P down to its marginal cost w results in a pricing relationship with a mark-up over marginal cost: $P = (1 + \lambda)w$, where λ is the mark-up.

The wage setting relationship is based on what has been learned about the Phillips curve, originally an empirical relationship between the rate of change of wages and the unemployment rate published in 1958. The original concept was expanded in the late 1960s to represent a relationship between changes in inflation (the change in the price level, not simply in the wage) and departures of the unemployment rate from the natural rate of unemployment. The natural rate of unemployment is the rate of unemployment consistent with equality of the price level P and the expected price level P^e, and is consistent with full-employment output Y*. This relationship can be captured, with much detail buried, in a relationship between the wage and the unemployment rate, $w = P^e f(u, \omega)$, $f_u < 0$, where ω represents additional factors that may

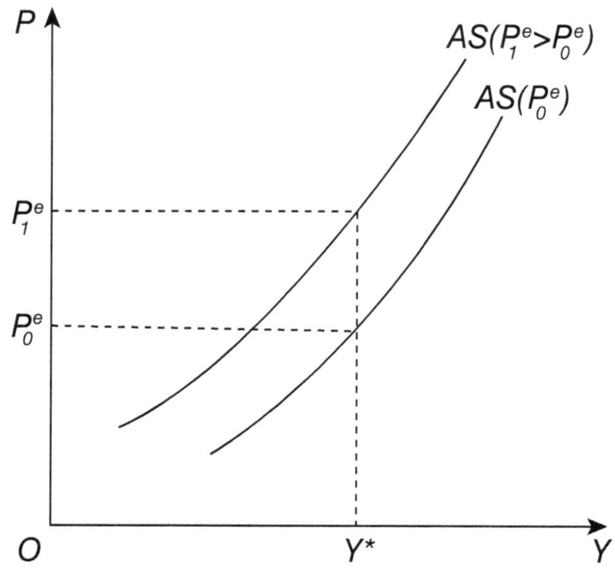

Figure 5.23. The Aggregate Supply (AS) curve in price level-output space.

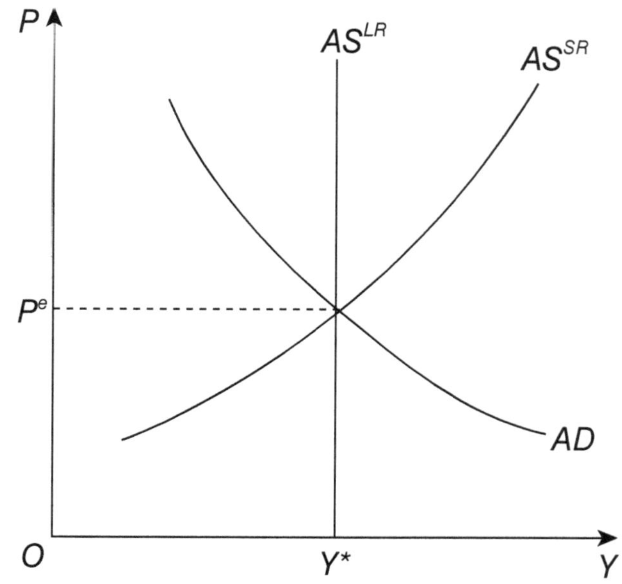

Figure 5.24. Long- and short-run AS curves in long-run equilibrium.

affect the wage. As the unemployment rate gets lower, higher wages must be offered to attract workers. Define the unemployment rate as $1 - L/L^*$, where L^* is the labor force and L is the labor employed. Substituting from the production function with labor productivity set to 1 offers a definition of the unemployment in terms of output, $u = 1 - Y/L^*$. Replace u in the wage-setting function with this expression and substitute the wage expression in the price determination relation to obtain $P = P^e(1 + \lambda)f(1 - Y/L, \omega)$, which is one version of the aggregate supply relation.[29] Since $f_{1-Y/L} \equiv f_u < 0$, the relation between the price level P and output Y is positive, as shown in Figure 5.23. The short-run AS curve passes through the long-run equilibrium point of (P^e, Y^*). he long-run AS curve is vertical at output level Y*, but does not involve a length of time sufficient for the capital stock to adjust optimally, as the long run implies in price theoretic analyses, but rather to the length of time for wages to equilibrate the labor market.

An increase in output leads to an increase in the price level. This occurs through an increase in employment, which is equivalent to a decrease in the unemployment rate, which pushes up the nominal wage, which in turn leads to an increase in the price level through the price-wage mark-up relationship. From the wage relationship, an increase in the expected price level leads to a corresponding increase in the actual price level, operating through the price-wage mark-up relationship again, shifting the AS curve up and to the left, as shown in Figure 5.23.

5.6.3 Equilibrium and Some Analyses

Figure 5.24 shows the AD and AS curves determining a short-run equilibrium output and price level. The short-run AS curve is labeled AS^{SR}. The corresponding equilibrium interest rate can be backed out from the IS-LM diagram underpinning the AD-AS diagram. The long-run AS curve, AS^{LR}, is vertical at full-employment output level Y*, and the price level is at the expected level.

The supply shock of the drought analyzed with the IS-LM model can be addressed quite directly with the AD-AS model. In Figure 5.25, the drought shifts the full-employment long-run AS curve back to the left from Y* to Y_1^*, and shifts the short-run AS curve up and to the left

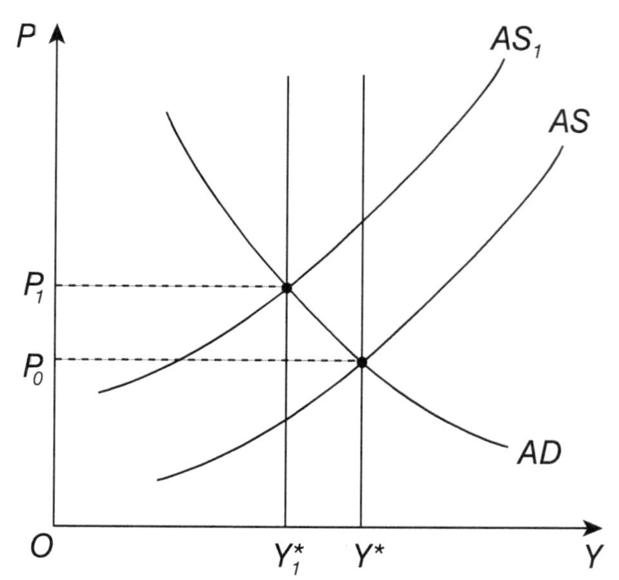

Figure 5.25. Studying a supply shock with the AD-AS model.

29 Various versions of the aggregate supply curve are derived and used, but all relate price-level to output via the Phillips-curve relationship between prices or wages and unemployment. Some, and their corresponding AD curves, use the price level or its logarithm, some use price levels at different dates, some use the inflation rate π instead of the price level P, which is more realistic, particularly for contemporary economies, since movements in π need not involve deflations, which downward movements in P represent. Detecting slight differences in inflation rates in antiquity seems implausible, which favors using one of the price-level representations of the AD and AS relations. Some versions of the AS curve develop the output side of the equation as functions of the difference between actual and full employment. All contain the same basic information.

to AS_1. Since output falls but the money supply stays the same, the price level increases from P_0 to P_1. The fall in output implies an increase in unemployment, so we have an instance of increasing inflation (increasing implicitly from zero) and rising unemployment, a combination of economic ills long uncontemplated by Keynesian macroeconomics—not until the oil price shock of 1973, which was an impetus for major re-thinking of the Keynesian paradigm. If the drought event were more like the Irish Potato Famine and were a permanent new condition, the new long-run equilibrium would be at (P_1, Y_1^*). If the weather returns to what was previously considered normal the following season, the long-run AS curve will shift back to Y* and the short-run AS curve will return to AS. The AD curve has been considered invariant in this simple exercise, but that is just a convenience. If investors decide to hold back on plans under the influence of the drought, the AD curve would shift down and to the left as part of the temporary movements.

A money supply increase, essentially a demand shock, is depicted in Figure 5.26, shown by an outward shift in the AD curve. Initially, the AD curve shifts out the short-run AS curve and reaches a temporary equilibrium at $Y^1 > Y^*$, which pushes the price level up to P_1. However, Y^1 involves production at rates greater than the full-employment rate, and it gradually returns to the full-employment rate. The AS curve rotates from its short-run upward slope to its vertical long-run slope, and the economy shifts back up the AD' curve until it reaches the intersection with the long-run AS curve at price level P_2. In the short run, money affects output, but in the long run it is neutral, the increase in its supply having influenced nothing but the price level. This case illustrates the major difference between positive demand shocks and negative supply shocks: the positive demand shock results in increasing inflation and falling unemployment, while the negative supply shock results in increasing inflation and rising unemployment—known less than technically as stagflation.

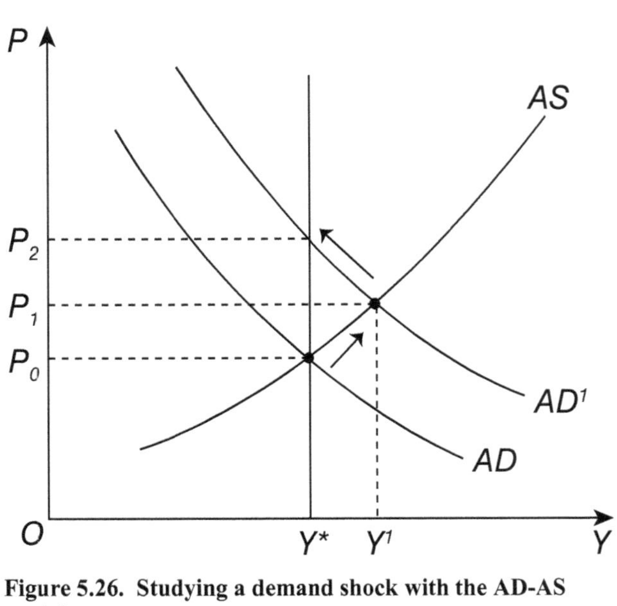

Figure 5.26. Studying a demand shock with the AD-AS model.

5.7 The Open Macroeconomy[30]

So far, the analysis has assumed a closed economy, i.e., no international economic relationships. That is a very constrained case, as the subsequent analysis shows. First, "large" economies have more influence when available to other, "smaller" economies than do "small" economies. Large economies determine terms of trade, as we saw in Chapter 3, and this influence carries over to aggregate inter-country exchanges. First off, countries have different currencies, and their international exchanges need to convert these currencies. Second, national income accounts must incorporate external exchanges, which are especially important in accounting for the relationship between domestic saving-and-investment and net exports. Third, that relationship involves the inter-country exchange and transfer of real and financial capital and the determination on international interest rates.

5.7.1 The Variety of Cases

Analysis of aggregate economies in their international contexts if complicated by the variety of cases that can exist. First, a country can be "small" or it can be "large." A "small" country is too small to affect the interest rate it faces, so IS-LM intersections do not determine its interest rate. A "large" economy is a big enough actor on the international stage to affect the world interest rate. Second, capital can have various degrees of mobility internationally. It could be completely immobile, leaving all international transactions to the goods market. It could be perfectly mobile, simplifying a lot of analysis since a country's interest rate will equal the world interest rate. Or there could be some degree of mobility but still sufficient barriers to leave a country's interest rate different from the world interest rate. Third, a country could fix the value of its currency relative to other countries' currencies (or a basket of them) or it could let the market determine its currency's value relative to other currencies. The former case is called fixed exchange rates, and the latter is called flexible or floating exchange rates. Not all combinations of these three possibilities are plausible empirically (e.g., a large country with immobile capital), but in antiquity, the most plausible cases appear to be some degree of capital mobility and fixed exchange rates, in cases of both small and large countries. A country's monetary authority takes actions to maintain its currency's value at a given level relative to other currencies (or in terms of gold), and there is no evidence of any ancient treasury or other arm of a government undertaking such actions. There is evidence of borrowing and lending across countries in antiquity, or what we would call countries today, whether in currencies such as in Roman times or in contracts denominated in commonly agreed-upon metals in earlier times. There may well have been times and places

[30] In addition to various works referenced in footnote 1 of this chapter, for this section I have relied on the following works: Argy (1994); Dornbusch (1980); Fleming (1962), Frenkel and Razin (1987a; 1987b); Gandolfo (2002); Isard (1995); Krueger (1983); McCallum (1996); Montiel (2009); Mundell (1968); Niehans (1984); Obstfeld and Rogoff (1996); Purvis (1985); Taylor (1995); Turnovsky (1997) .

when no capital moved internationally, and that case will be noted briefly in passing at the appropriate place.

5.7.2 Exchange Rates

Excepting the cases of pure barter economies trading with one another, dealing with an international sector of an ancient, but still sophisticated, economy requires introducing the concepts of foreign exchange and foreign exchange rates. Foreign exchange, from the perspective of any country, is just foreign currencies—other countries' moneys. A foreign exchange rate is simply the price of one currency in terms of another; it can be measured either way: as the price of the home country's currency in terms of a foreign currency or a foreign currency in terms of the home country's currency, e.g., as drachmas per daric or darics per drachma. For an example using contemporary currencies with which readers will be familiar, a nominal exchange rate between the U.S. dollar and the Japanese yen could be expressed as 90 yen per dollar. You will see exchange rates expressed both ways, so be careful which definition you are dealing with: it reverses the signs on a lot of relationships. If the dollar lost value against the yen, the exchange rate expressed this way would fall, from 90 yen per dollar to, say, 88 yen per dollar. In the changed circumstances, one dollar will buy only 88 yen, whereas prior to the change, it would buy 90. Yen have become more expensive in terms of dollars; the dollar has lost value in terms of the number of yen it will purchase.

Whether currencies are fiduciary (i.e., paper) or metallic, their prices are determined by their supplies and the demands for them, just like any other good. Since currencies in the ancient world were metallic, and could be issued in varying degrees of fineness (even plated with a precious metal over a base-metal core), exchange rate determination is simplified to some extent. The exchange rate between two currencies of the same metal would be determined by their relative metal contents. If two ancient currencies used the same metal and same fineness, and the government issuing one of them expanded its money supply (minted more coins, or minted them at a faster rate), both currencies would change (lose) value at the same rate since they would be perfect substitutes because the world supply of that monetized metal had increased. The exchange rate between currencies of different precious metals would be determined by the overall supplies of the two metals, the demands for them, and the metallic content of each currency. Of course, in an ancient urban exchange market that dealt in many different currencies and individual coins rather than large magnitudes of coinage, the rate between any pair of coins might also be influenced by the condition of each (degree of wear, shaving, etc.), although at times and places, coins were accepted at market exchange rates irrespective of wear, an indication of confidence in the acceptability of the currency.

Exchange rates are nominal prices, so the price of one in terms of another doesn't necessarily tell how much each will purchase. The real exchange rate between two currencies is the nominal exchange rate times the ratios of the two countries' price levels: $\varepsilon = eP_h/P_f$, where e is the nominal exchange rate expressed as units of foreign currency per unit of home-country currency,[31] P_h is the home country's price level, and P_f is the foreign country's price level. The real exchange rate tells how much, say, wheat a trader from the home country could secure in the foreign country with a unit of olive oil from his or her own country. The real exchange rate will be the operational variable in international macroeconomic analysis. One complication that international trade introduces at this point is the difference between P_h defined as a price index of goods produced in the home country versus goods consumed in the home country, which now include imported goods. To price the imported goods in terms of the domestically produced goods to calculate the price index, the prices of the imported goods, which are denominated in the foreign country's currency, must be converted to home-country prices, which requires using the nominal exchange rate. So, the consumption price level, which helps determine the real exchange rate, is a function of the nominal exchange rate. When the share of imports in consumption is small, this difference in price index levels will be correspondingly small. For a small city state dependent on trade with a possibly independent hinterland for food, as may have been the case with some of the sites on the Levantine coast, such as Ugarit during the Late Bronze Age and Tyre in the Early Iron Age and into the Hellenistic period, the effect could have been larger.

A characteristic of foreign exchange that complicates modeling how currencies are priced (the determination of nominal exchange rates) is that they are used to purchase both current goods and capital assets denominated in foreign currencies, and to hold as an asset in their own right. There a number of theories of exchange rate determination, some of them offering different predictions from others. Testing has been difficult, particularly in trying to control for real-world violations of simplifying, but crucial, assumptions of the various models. Rather than confuse the disinterested reader with a plethora of them, a simple model of the determination of the real exchange rate will be offered in a subsequent sub-section, following the introduction of several other international financial concepts.

5.7.3 Balance of Payments Accounting Revisited

Section 5.2 introduced the international components of the national accounts, but now that exchange rates have been introduced, it's possible to be a little more explicit, and a brief refresher probably wouldn't hurt either. The international accounts are comprised of the Current Account (CA) and the Capital and Financial Account (KFA), the sum of which equals zero: CA + KFA = 0. The Current Account includes net exports,

[31] This is the most common mode of expressing an exchange rate in American publications. European practice tends to reverse this ratio.

the difference in value between exports and imports, net factor payments from abroad (earnings of nationals working abroad and payments to home-owned capital used abroad), and net unilateral transfers (gifts). The sum of these components may be positive or negative. To this point in the chapter, the variable net exports has been left as simply NX, without disaggregating into exports and imports in either the treatment of the national accounts or in the consumption-expenditure (aggregate demand) relation. With the use of the exchange rate, the disaggregation can be expressed as $NX = X(Y^f, r, \varepsilon) - IM(Y^h, \varepsilon)/\varepsilon$, where ε is the real exchange rate and $X_{Y^f} > 0$, $X_r < 0$, $X_\varepsilon < 0$, $IM_{Y^h} > 0$, $IM_\varepsilon > 0$. The relationships $X_\varepsilon < 0$ and $IM_\varepsilon > 0$ can be explained as simple relative price effects: when the real exchange rate increases, by the definition used here, it takes more domestic currency to purchase a unit of foreign currency, and correspondingly, foreign goods denominated in that currency become more expensive relative to domestically produced goods priced in the home country's currency, so home country consumers substitute domestic goods for imports; and the reverse is the case for exports bought by foreigners. The effect of the real interest rate on exports occurs because an increase in the home country's interest rate attracts investment in the home country from foreigners, which increases the demand for the home country's currency and drives up the exchange rate. Accordingly, net exports can be characterized as a function $NX(Y^h, Y^f, r, \varepsilon)$, with $NX_{Y^h} > 0$, $NX_{Y^f} < 0$, $NX_r < 0$, and $NX_\varepsilon < 0$.

Assuming net factor payments and net unilateral transfers to be zero for the moment, if the value of exports exceeds the value of imports, then the Capital and Financial Account must be negative and equal absolute magnitude to the value of net exports. What does a negative KFA balance mean? Positive net exports means that the home country is producing more than it is spending, which implies that it's saving the difference. How does it accomplish this saving other than through finding domestic investment opportunities? It can find overseas investment opportunities, lending to residents of foreign countries so they can pay the difference between their own export and import bills. Capital in the form of financial instruments—loans or purchases of foreign assets—flows out of the home country, registered as a negative entry in the KFA account.

5.7.4 Saving and Investment in the Open Economy

In a closed economy (more precisely, in a closed economy model, since most actual economies are open to some extent; we shouldn't confuse the models with the reality although the hope is that the models are adequate guides to reality), saving equals investment in equilibrium. In the open-economy case, saving equals investment plus the current account surplus (which may be a deficit): $S^d = I^d + CA = I_d + X - IM/\varepsilon + NFP$ (the "d" superscripts are a reminder that this expression is used as a behavioral relation here rather than an accounting identity). So, letting NFP = 0, $S^d - I^d = NX$ is the goods market equilibrium condition in the open-economy model. Introducing another term widely used in the literature, net exports equals income minus absorption. From the aggregate demand (income-expenditure) relation, $Y = C^d + I^d + G + NX$, or $NX = Y - (C^d + I^d + G)$, the three variables in parentheses being absorption, of the part of domestic production that the domestic economy actually absorbs through some combination of private consumption, investment and government spending. The particularly useful implication of the absorption concept is that, if absorption increases, there is less domestic production left over to export, so net exports fall.

Diagrammatically, the saving-investment equilibrium graphs change accordingly, but they depend on whether our home country is "small" or "large," i.e., whether it's a price-taker in the international economy or is large enough to influence world prices. Figure 5.27 shows the small-economy case, in which the home country, assuming perfect capital mobility, faces a given world interest rate, r^W. Given the positions of the country's saving and investment functions, at a world interest rate of r_1^w, the country runs

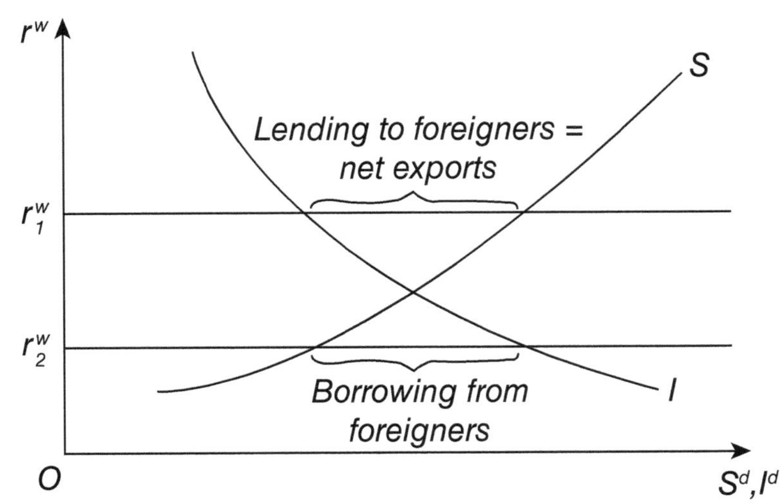

Figure 5.27. International borrowing and lending: small-country case.

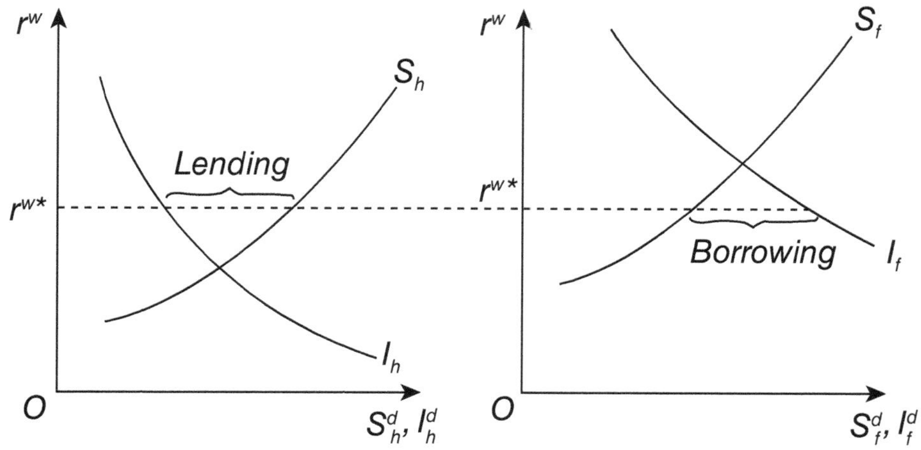

Figure 5.28. International borrowing and lending: large-country case.

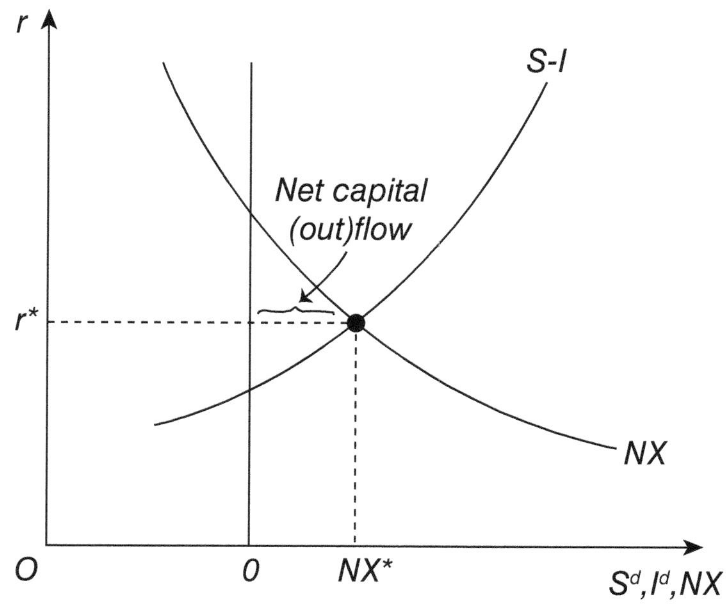

Figure 5.29. The relationship between domestic saving and net exports.

a current account surplus, effectively lending to foreigners an amount equal to the value of its net exports. At a lower world interest rate, r_2^w, this same country would be a net borrower from foreigners, with its businesses wanting to invest more than its consumers want to save at that interest rate, the slack, so to speak, taken up by borrowing from foreigners to pay for the excess value of imports over exports. Figure 5.28 relates the large-country case, in which the world interest rate moves up or down to equilibrate the borrowing of one country (assuming a 2-country world) and the lending of the other country. If either country's saving or investment curve shifted, the world interest rate would have to change to equilibrate the world's demands for investment and for saving, or equivalently, to equilibrate the world capital market.

The relationship between savings, investment, and the current account can be expressed in a different graphical form, relying on the open-economy goods market equilibrium condition $S^d(r) - I^d(r) = NX(r)$. $S_r^d > 0$ and $I_r^d < 0$, rendering $NX_r > 0$. But, assuming zero net factor payments from abroad, net exports is equivalent to the current account, which is the negative of the capital and financial account, so $S^d - I^d = NX = CA = -KFA$. Figure 5.29 shows the equilibrium of the difference between the domestic investment shortfall (relative to desired domestic saving) and net exports in a large country (which can affect the interest rate), with net capital flows preserving the external balance.

It is but a step from the relationship between saving minus investment and net exports to the open-economy IS curve. As the closed-economy IS curve was developed in section 5.5.1, varying aggregate income and tracing its effects on saving minus investment, net exports and the interest rate reveals the open-economy IS curve, as shown in Figure 5.30. At an initial level of aggregate demand, Y_0, saving minus investment is $S(Y_0) - I$ and net exports is represented by $NX(Y_0)$. Equilibrium is reached at interest rate r_0, with a trade surplus. Suppose government spending increases, raising aggregate income from Y_0 to Y_1. Desired saving is increased to $S(Y_1 > Y_0)$ but desired investment

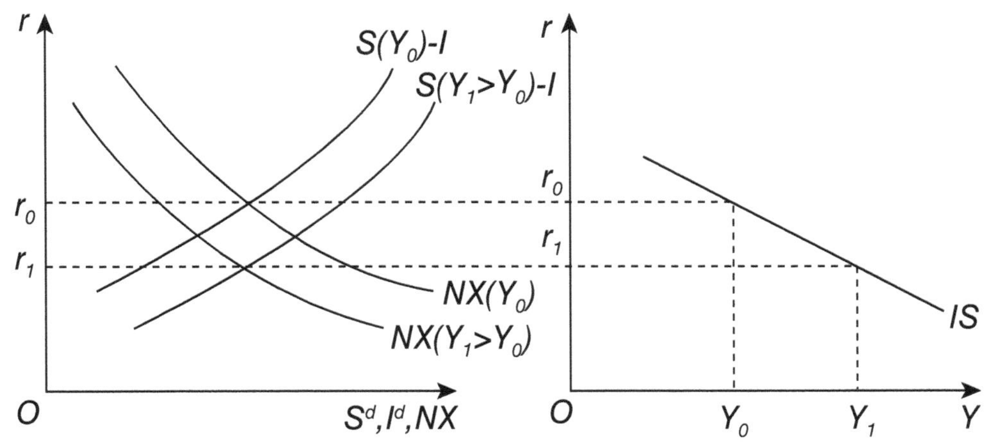

Figure 5.30. The IS curve in an international setting with capital flows.

is unchanged, shifting the saving minus investment curve to $S(Y_1 > Y_0) - I$. The increased income also increases the demand for imports but does not affect exports, so NX shifts to the left. The new equilibrium is established at interest rate $r_1 < r_2$, with a smaller trade surplus.

5.7.5 Capital Mobility and Interest Rate Parity

Capital mobility is a condition of capital markets. In a world of perfect capital mobility, capital flows will equalize interest rates in all countries, and a single world interest rate will prevail, as was used for simplification in the previous section on saving and investment in open economies. These flows are not continuing movements of capital, but are stock adjustments which are completed over some time period, with flows going to zero thereafter. Small countries take this world interest rate as given; large ones can affect it. The process of equilibration is called interest arbitrage. The institutional and technological assumptions underpinning the theory as it is applied to contemporary economies involve much more information about opportunities at various locations and much more rapid communication than were even conceivable in antiquity, but the forces at work in international interest arbitrage, although at much greater speed, are relevant to ancient economies. Imperfect capital mobility could have numerous causes: poor or expensive information which in turn could result from communication difficulties; legal restrictions or deficiencies in legal property rights; differences in national customs which hamper mutual trust; and so on. With zero capital mobility, i.e., perfectly immobile capital, NX will always be zero; trade will always be balanced.

Suppose that domestic and foreign assets are perfect substitutes for one another; if the interest rate on one diverges from that of the other, investors would switch immediately to the higher-yielding asset, driving their interest rates together again. To buy some foreign capital, either in the form of a loan to a foreigner or the purchase of some physical capital in another country, a home-country investor has to buy some of the foreign country's currency at the nominal exchange rate. A unit of the foreign currency next year would yield $e_t(1 + i_t^f)$, where e_t is the nominal exchange rate at present and i_t^f is the nominal interest rate in the foreign country at the date of the lending, abstracting from risk, which would put risk premiums in one or both nominal interest rates. If the lender expects the nominal exchange rate next year to be e_{t+1}^e, each unit of the foreign currency he buys now will be worth $1/e_{t+1}^e$ then, so the investor can expect $e_t(1 + i_t^f)/e_{t+1}^e$ units of domestic currency next year for every unit invested this year. As investors look for the best opportunities, the condition must hold that $i_t = (1 + i_t^f)(e_t/e_{t+1}^e) - 1 \approx i_t^f - (e_{t-1}^e - e_t)/e_t$, which says that the nominal interest rate in the home country must equal the interest rate in the foreign country minus the expected appreciation of the nominal exchange rate over the previous year. Differential risk premiums would add to the differential between nominal interest rates based on expected exchange rate changes, as would imperfect substitutability of assets. One might wonder why the interest parity condition, as it is called, operates on nominal interest rates rather than real rates. To quickly see why, recall the relationship between the nominal and real exchange rates from section 5.7.2 and the relationship presented long ago and in several places between the nominal and real interest rates, and you will see that the real interest rates are implied by the price level changes that govern the relationship between the nominal and real interest rates; the nominal interest rates can be derived from the real interest rates, the relative inflation rates and the real exchange rate.

Now, turning to the degree of capital mobility, return to the equilibrium condition for the international accounts: the balance of payments = $NX(Y^h, Y^f, r, \varepsilon) + KFA(i - i^f) = 0$. The capital flows in the KFA account move in response to interest-rate differentials. With perfect capital mobility, perfect substitutability among assets, and no expected exchange rate change, at any departure of domestic rate i from the foreign rate i^f, capital moves quickly enough between countries, small or large, from the lower-rate country to the higher-rate country, to always keep the nominal interest rates at levels consistent with the interest parity condition, effectively at $i = i^f$. There are plenty of reasons why capital would stop flowing before $i = i^f$ was reached, however, attributable to desires to diversify against risk rather than having all one's assets in a single place or non-comparabilities among assets that lead to less than perfect substitutability. So a small country, even under conditions of perfect capital mobility, can have an interest rate different from the "world" interest rate.

5.8 Cases from Antiquity: The Financial Crisis of 33 C.E.

The sudden enforcement of a law passed during Julius Caesar's reign requiring cash backing for real estate loans sent much of Rome's senatorial class scrambling for cash, with both debtors and lenders trying to sell their land. Naturally, land prices fell precipitously, threatening to reduce Rome's aristocracy to penury. At their request, Tiberius gave them eighteen months to settle their accounts, and the Senate passed an ordinance requiring everyone to invest two-thirds of their money on loan on land in Italy and to discharge two-thirds of their debts immediately. Creditors, however, demanded one hundred percent payment. Such immediate liquidation of assets led to a sharply increased demand for cash but with no elasticity in its supply. Then the government reduced interest rates on real estate loans by directing immediate renegotiation of mortgages, sending money fleeing land. Tiberius came to the rescue with 100 million sestercii from his own resources in interest-free loans for up to three years, relieving the crisis.[32]

Such are the facts in the case, to the extent that they can be determined. The exact content of Julius Caesar's usury law of 49 B.C.E. is unknown, but appears to have been familiar to the contemporaries of 33 C.E., although most of the senators and many others had failed to follow it (Frederiksen 1966). As straightforward as the event sounds, there have been various interpretations of it. Early studies focused on the availability of cash by looking at coin hoards. Had cash been flowing out of Italy to pay for imports with insufficient exports to maintain cash balances in Italy – i.e., was there a balance-of-payments problem (Frank 1935, 340)? Apparently not (Rodewalt 1971, 67–70). While most students of the episode have concentrated on the year of the crisis, Thornton and Thornton (1990) have taken a longer perspective, reaching back into the reign of Augustus and the earlier years of Tiberius' reign.

The Thorntons (1983) constructed a measure of labor inputs on government construction projects stretching from 30 B.C.E. to 70 C.E. Although Elliott (2015, 275–276) has criticized their labor input measure for being based on information from a single, small temple in Gaul dated to 16 B.C.E., the measure shows starkly enough what they propose to show to override errors (Thornton and Thornton 1983, 376, Figure 1; 1990, 658, Figure 1). There are two major spikes in government construction employment, the first under Augustus, tailing off around 12 B.C.E., the second under Caligula, immediately following Tiberius' assassination in 37 C.E. Tiberius was actually in charge of Augustus' public construction program after the death of Agrippa in 12 B.C.E. and was responsible for the extended lull from that date through the end of his reign. Public construction was the Roman government's method of putting purchasing power (money) back in the hands of the Roman populace, and this extended period of exceptionally low expenditures was the equivalent of the government running an extended budget surplus, squeezing the money supply. Construction is a major driver of economic activity, and unemployment would have emerged visibly had not a large proportion of the construction labor force been slaves. Slave owners would have had to either continue feeding their slaves or sell them during this extended period of scarce public construction, which would have extended to private construction through Keynesian multiplier effects. Selling them would have been a last resort, and feeding them would have caused them to draw down their cash reserves. Public construction was especially low and flat from 25 C.E. through the crisis year of 33 C.E., putting additional pressure on slave owners' cash reserves as they and others went into the cash crunch. When Tiberius opened his fiscus with the 100 million sestercii, Thornton and Thornton (1990, 659) contend that, "Obviously Tiberius knew what the problem was and how to solve it."

Elliott contests the accounting of the crisis as it has emerged in recent decades as a boom-and-bust cycle cured by a Keynesian-style monetary injection, although that is clearly what happened. Following Michael Crawford's explanation of Tiberius' opening of his coffers (1970, 46–47) as simply an effort to sustain the aristocracy rather than an effort to relieve the cash crisis, Elliot contends that the recent literature's explanation of the crisis and its alleviation as an example of the timelessness of contemporary macroeconomics is misplaced. According to this view, Tiberius' loans were not a deliberate monetary policy but an effort to save the Roman social structure.

Thornton and Thornton (1990, 657, 660) detail Tiberius' long-standing fiscal tight-fistedness, beginning with an inheritance from Augustus of 100 million sestercii and ending with 2.7 billion, and declining to conduct more than some minimal maintenance on public works. I doubt T&T's conclusion that Tiberius knew what needed to be done when he extended his loans in 33 C.E. I think he was clueless – and the effectiveness in alleviating the crisis was simply the principle that even a blind squirrel gets an occasional nut. Some contemporary politicians suffer from the same ignorance of economic causes and effects, mistaking the economy of a nation for the economy of a household. However, T&T (1990, 660) describe Tiberius' socially and fiscally conservative reign as an extended period of contention between rigid fiscal tightness and fiscal responsiveness and point to Caligula's initiation of construction on two aqueducts immediately on his accession to widespread recognition of long-standing government fiscal error. Tiberius did indeed conduct the

32 Frank (1935), Rodewalt (1971), Thornton and Thornton (1990), and Elliott (2015) offer detailed accounts of the crisis. Duncan-Jones (1994. 23–25), Katsari (2011, 53), and Temin (2013, 142) offer compressed reports.

correct action, whether it was intended to relieve a general credit crisis or to save the aristocracy. The macroeconomic theory of today can explain aggregate economic events of two millennia ago.

5.9 Using this Chapter's Information: Historical, Philological, and Archaeological Applications

As with the material of the agriculture chapter, my ancient studies friends ask, "How can I use this information?" In the discussion of possible applications of the agricultural models, the potential uses of that material in situations when written evidence is available seemed obvious to me, so I focused exclusively on potential archaeological applications. The applications I suggested there generally involved qualitative modifications to how archaeologists approach their finds rather than direct quantitative adjustments. The approach here is similar. The applications of the models of this chapter involve asking different questions of familiar material, sometimes associating information that may not have been brought together previously. I offer suggestions below for both the text-rich disciplines, ancient history and philology, and the text poor discipline of archaeology. As with the corresponding section of the agriculture chapter, I go lightly on citations to avoid unfairly holding a few randomly chosen scholars up for what might seem like apparent criticism which I do not intend.

Some of the ensuing discussion targets tools and their application to particular topics. Some identifies topics that might be illuminated by the tools introduced in the chapter. I don't intend for the discussion to sound like a series of review questions at the end of a chapter in a text book, but rather to identify a few types of application that I can see standing at the outer edges of the disciplines. With luck, the applications I can identify may strike others as structurally similar to issues with which they are familiar.

5.9.1 Accounting Systems

Possibly the most powerful, while in some senses the simplest, tools in this chapter are accounting systems, the national income and product accounts introduced in section 5.2, and the less formal accounting of government revenues in section 5.4.1. The widespread estimations of gross domestic product (GDP) of various countries and time periods (Classical Athens, Early Imperial Rome, the Seleucid Empire) have relied on the GDP concept, sometimes even dipping as far into the accounting system as trying to account for government revenues and expenditures. I realize I have been less than excited by the results, as well as a number of the methods, of these ancient GDP estimates, so that my recommendation of these accounting systems as a powerful tool for archaeologists, ancient historians and philologists may strike a discordant note, so I explain my reasoning, which comes in several parts.

As a prelude, I note some of the "notwithstandings." First, I realize the difficulties in estimating the magnitudes of many of these accounts for antiquity. Although Amemiya (2007, 108–111) has managed to produce estimates of some of the major national income accounts for Classical Athens,[33] the estimates made so far for Imperial Rome have produced error bounds that are wide enough to leave reasonable scholars wondering whether the result was worth the effort, as well as the possible dangers of some people taking the magnitudes too seriously. Second, the proportions of GDP in each of these accounts, at the level of C + I + G + NX may vary by little enough across national experiences that proportions from fifteen or twenty centuries in the future could be considered a laugh test for results for estimates of those proportions from 1st Century C.E. Rome. The potential exists for empirical circularity. With these difficulties, what is left for the applicability of accounting systems to ancient economies?

A very useful aspect of these accounting systems is that there is a good bit of broadly accepted theory regarding how the transactions within the individual accounts interact with the transactions in other accounts, and even with events outside the accounting system. While levels of the magnitudes of these accounts may be difficult to estimate, insights may be more readily available on changes in their magnitudes, which could imply changes in the magnitudes of other accounts. The absolute magnitude of, say imports or exports, from some place at a particular time may be of little import, but changes in those imports or exports give an idea of something behind them causing them as well as other quantities in front of them, so to speak, changing in consequence.

Another useful aspect of the accounting systems derives from the fact that some of the accounts, or combinations of them, are alternative views of other magnitudes of interest. For instance, a trade deficit tells us that domestic saving is smaller than domestic investment and that a country is effectively borrowing from foreigners. Viewed alternatively from the concept of absorption, a trade deficit suggests that a country is spending enough on the goods it produces that there aren't enough of those goods left to export and balance their trade. In neither case is there any presumption that a country should or should not be running a trade deficit or that doing so is in any way abnormal or counterproductive to its economic health.

The suggestions above have been aimed primarily, but not exclusively, at ancient historians and philologists, who ordinarily can depend on finding more written evidence than archaeologists typically can. For the archaeologists, the accounting along the same lines of government revenues and expenditures can be recommended for its simplicity, discipline, and again, the associated theory that can develop additional information from scattered observations. Analysis of what Mycenaean palaces'

[33] He estimates C + G + NX, presumably wrapping investment into one or more of the other accounts.

occupants (i.e., the various governments) did to obtain resources and what they did with the resources they acquired has long rested on the concepts of staple finance and wealth finance, which together have pushed forward only in a limited way the understanding of the interactions of those governments in their economies. Staple finance sounds very much like taxation, which the Pharaonic Egyptian governments have long been known to collect primarily, if not exclusively, in grain which they somehow turned into ships, armies and monumental architecture. Wealth finance sounds very much like government enterprises (see Jones 2014, Chapter 6, section 5). Both are revenue sources, even if the craft activities characterized as wealth finance operated at a negative profit. Aperghis (2004, Chapter 8), in his study of the Seleukid economy, used the government revenue classification of pseudo-Aristotle's *Oikonomika* to considerable benefit, granted that he had the benefit of considerably more informative written evidence on the activities.

But returning to the Mycenaean governments (or palaces or whatever we decide to call the people whose employees wrote the Linear B tablets found at such abundance at Pylos and in scatterings elsewhere), two gross revenue sources appear to have been identified, one taxation, one production for subsequent sale. Some of the in-kind tax revenue was used to support the people engaged in the craft production activities, as well as probably the scribes who kept track of it all on the Linear B tablets. Whether these workers were reduced to receiving simple rations (think of a soldier who gets fed but no "pay") or whether they got a "wage" or "salary" in grain, some of which they ate, the rest of which they traded on for something else they wanted, is open to speculation or empirical examination or both. Did the Mycenaean government have any other sources of revenue? Harbor fees? Mines? Forests for coppicing or running pigs in for fees? Then, what did they do with the revenues? Build fortification walls between 1400 and 1200 B.C.E.? Build bridges over streams? Dams? Equip soldiers such as are depicted in vase paintings (or did the soldiers pay for their own equipment)? Consume game hunting as depicted in frescoes? Import luxury items such as ivories, gold and amber? Did they draw everything that was produced in the entire country into the palace and then ship it out again? Did they own the drayage industry? Which of these putative expenditures were investment and which were consumption? Evidence for all of them exists in the archaeological record.

5.9.2 Roman Unemployment—A Natural Rate?

Sadly or otherwise for the industry of scholarship, ancient Rome did not have a Bureau of Labor Statistics, and evidence on both population and employment is weak, particularly regarding people at the lower end of the income distribution. A long-standing account, which is not entirely without doubt presently, has it that as slaves began to pile up in Late Republican and Early Imperial Rome, Roman citizen farmers were displaced by the lower-cost competition from slave-operated farms. Whatever the precise cause, unemployed and under-employed people were drawn to Rome from areas within the Italian Peninsula and eventually resulted in a sizeable unemployed population in the city itself, although the attractions of potentially higher lifetime earnings in the economically vibrant city could have been an attraction in the simpler form of higher real wages, even adjusted for the probability of obtaining reasonably constant employment. Nonetheless, in this setting, the dole (the *annona*) established during the Late Republic and continuing well into Imperial times, is well known. It provided food at subsidized prices, or sometimes free, to qualifying citizens, although it would not have covered full living expenses. At a time when the population of Rome is estimated to have been between 400,000 and 500,000, between 150,000 and 200,000 people were on the dole (Brunt 1980; Morley 2001). They were not all fully unemployed, but apparently a substantial, if unknown, proportion of them were employed only periodically or seasonally. If sixty percent of the population were adults, 175,000 adults on the dole would amount to some 58 percent of the resident adult population. If the adults on the dole worked only half-time, that would amount to just under a 30-percent unemployment rate, which apparently lasted for decades if not centuries. How does the concept of the natural rate of unemployment, and the theory associated with it, illuminate the components of the Roman labor market required to sustain it? This unemployed army existed for a considerable length of time, so the short-run models of the chapter will not shed light on either its causes or consequences. The analysis would be complicated by the attractiveness of the Eternal City for migrants seeking a better life than the countryside offered, even in light of the prospects of employment which would have been governed by the structural unemployment rate.

5.9.3 The Macroeconomics of the Peloponnesian War

The Peloponnesian War, or Wars, dragged on for nearly three decades. The pestilence of 431 B.C.E. ravaged the city of Athens to an extent comparable to the depredations of the Bubonic Plague in Western Europe nearly nineteen centuries later. Athens lost an entire army in the Sicilian expedition. It lost the use of the northern extent of its homeland, Attica, to Spartan occupation for an extended period of time. In territory it was able to reclaim, much of its agricultural capital stock was destroyed. It financed its military operations with silver tribute paid by League associates, in proportions to real transactions that are not easily measured; it collected taxes episodically through liturgies on its own upper-income citizens, but still ended up reducing the nominal remuneration of various categories of functionaries important to the war effort: there is little reason not to expect price-level change, or inflation, a short-run phenomenon. With the destruction of substantial parts of the country's agricultural capital stock, what happened to other private investment during the Wars? To what extent did military expenditures crowd out private investment? These wars were across the narrow Aegean from the Persian

Empire, with which the Greeks had had less than amicable relations in the recent past. To what extent was foreign trade with Persian Anatolia disrupted by naval or privateer (i.e., commissioned pirates) activity in the Aegean? Was the trade important enough to create a noticeable feedback on the economy of Athens and its allies? The Persian Empire, probably being a considerably larger economy than that of the Greek city states combined, may have been minimally affected by the internecine hostilities among the Greeks, but some of its coastal cities may have either suffered from reduced demand or benefited from opportunities for selling more goods to one or both Greek sides in the conflict. Coin hoards have been found from the period, suggesting that individuals were taking precautions (Figueira 1998, Chapter 1). Do these coin hoards indicate a lower interest rate, letting the demand for money rise, or simply increased risks and (quite successful) hiding places for a proportion of an unchanged demand for money during uncertain periods? If manufacturing expanded in the face of the destruction of a goodly proportion of the agricultural capital stock, where did the savings come from to fund the investment?

5.9.4 The Economics of Enduring National Puzzles

Some of the great destructions at the end of the Late Bronze Age can be attributed fairly securely to military actions. Ugarit apparently succumbed to a group of central or western Mediterranean nations we know as various Sea Peoples today. Some city states on Cyprus may have succumbed similarly. The Sea Peoples continued south from Ugarit until they met with Ramesses III who stopped them on the northeastern outskirts of the Egyptian Delta round 1175 B.C.E. (or possibly considerably further north, in Syria). But Ramesses III's dynasty, and the series of dynasties of which it was one of the last, did not survive long thereafter. Further north, the Mycenaean Greeks were suffering declines in their fortunes as well, but without the explicit depredations of the Sea Peoples on which to blame the trends. Within the last several generations, we of the 20th century C.E. have seen the decline of several long-standing empires in the wakes of devastating wars or series of wars, even though some nations have risen literally from the ashes of the same wars: winners sank and losers re-emerged. The macroeconomics of these 20th century events have been studied extensively, and in fact, the development of the macroeconomic theory presented in this chapter received a powerful fillip from the aftermath of those wars. It may be useful to apply some of the macroeconomic models of this chapter to the economy-wide events of the end of the Bronze Age, as well possibly as to other cases with which I am less familiar.

The End of the Egyptian New Kingdom. In an intriguing suggestion, David Warburton (1998, Chapter 1) raised the possibility that the collapse of the Egyptian 20th Dynasty, ending the New Kingdom and plunging Egypt into the Third Intermediate Period, may have resulted from the withdrawal of the government's long-established fiscal contribution to aggregate demand. The scenario is not developed in detail, but the concept is that withdrawal of government expenditure on pyramid building and other monumental construction toward the end of the 20th Dynasty was the equivalent of a massive reduction in government spending.[34] Regardless whether tax collections fell in parallel, a condition that the country had known for the past two millennia and surely come to accept as a part of its economic backdrop, changed within a few years, a decade or so, and the population's limited entrepreneurial capacity to redirect the resources previously hired by the government resulted in a major dislocation of the economy. This scenario could be cranked through the short-run models with eminently predictable results except for the length of time required for recovery and without a government stimulus package.

The End of the Mycenaean Palace Civilization. Several broad brushes of explanation for the collapse of the Mycenaean palatial civilization, or at least its descent into a less well-to-do period that ushered in the Greek Protogeometric Period, have been offered. There is the putative Dorian Invasion, the primary evidence of which is linguistic; blowback from the Sea Peoples' invasions of other Eastern Mediterranean regions during the 13th and 12th Centuries B.C.E.; earthquakes, peasant revolts; and internecine warfare.[35] One undeniable fact is the series of physical destructions of citadels in the Argolid around the same time. Of course, Mycenaean palaces or comparable edifices existed in the western Peloponnese, Thebes, Thessaly, and probably Athens, not to mention the relatively new entrants from the mainland on Crete, and their declines corresponded in time.

The limited ability of the economies of these city states (for want of a better term) to recover from whatever hit around the end of the 12th century, be it an invasion or consequences of invasions elsewhere, or localized natural disasters or a combination of all of these, has been suggested as a cause for non-recovery. But what would the "limited ability" have consisted of? Whatever occurred toward the end of the 12th century would have hit an economy (or economies, if they had separate governments) with a rudimentary financial system, probably with very limited capability of shifting consumption from one period to another to compensate for lost infrastructure, and as in the Egyptian case, little experience in seeking economic opportunities not circumscribed or otherwise

[34] Although Athenian state financial regulations required balanced budgets, by the time of Euboulos and Lycourgos in the 4th century B.C.E., policymakers had recognized that employment on public works projects to keep in check temporary spells of unemployment could help maintain social peace during such times (Bitros et al. 2021, 56–67). Their description of the Athenian state fiscal system is the most comprehensive I have seen (Bitros et al. 2021, Chapter 3).

[35] Dickinson (2006, 41–57) reviews the long-standing and more recent hypotheses for the collapse, all of which remain inconclusive. A similar assessment is offered by Deger-Jalkotzy (2008), although she allows greater weight to reports of suspected environmental degradation in decades leading up to the early 12th century collapse (389–390). Dickinson (2010) offers a particularly nuanced interpretation of the evidence and review of previous explanations, concluding that no single or simple explanation appears to exist.

overseen by various government agencies—to use modern terms. Considering the likely rudimentary character of the financial system of these economies, the infrastructure destroyed probably was paid for pretty much as it was built, out of current revenue collections. Correspondingly, the ability to borrow from future earnings streams to rebuild was probably equally lacking, and destruction may have been severe enough to reduce full-capacity output too much to permit the government to pull sufficient resources from the economy's current consumption to rebuild. In the lexicon of the models presented here, the long-run, or full- employment output levels would have fallen sharply, resulting in what would be termed unemployment today but may have been experienced simply as nothing to do to earn a living.

Population decline may have resulted from a combination of deaths from dislocation, famine and accompanying disease as well as reduced (below already low) birth rates for a number of generations, to bring the population into line with a fixed capital stock (largely land by then, together with what may have been left of hydraulic and transport infrastructure of previous generations). The movement of interest rates, the demand for assets, consumption, and aggregate output over the lengthy time required to find a new equilibrium might be illuminated by some of the models of this chapter. Archaeological correspondences to some of these changes might also be observable.

A somewhat more fundamental suggestion for research based on this chapter is to construct an aggregate economic (macroeconomic) model specifically tailored to the market structure of the Mycenaean economy (and similarly for the Egyptian New Kingdom economy). I have stretched and bent the IS-LM model somewhat in this chapter to accommodate major differences between the institutional structures of contemporary times and various periods and regions in antiquity, but at some point, the logical subsequent step is to explicitly modify that model to the institutional circumstances of various economies of Mediterranean antiquity. That shouldn't prove too difficult, as demonstrated by the plethora of alternatives to the conventional IS-LM framework put forward in response to recent institutional changes in the contemporary industrialized world,[36] but it is a research task outside the scope of the present endeavor.

[36] Such as suggested in a number of the chapters of Fontana and Setterfield (2009) and references therein.

References

Abel, Andrew B., and Ben S. Bernanke.1998. *Macroeconomics*, 3rd Ed. Boston: Addison-Wesley.

Abel, Andrew B., Ben S. Bernanke, and Dean Croushore. 2011. *Macroeconomics*, 7th Ed. Boston: Addison-Wesley.

Amemiya, Takeshi. 2007. *Economy and Economics of Ancient Greece*. London: Routledge.

Aperghis, G. G. 2004. *The Seleukid Royal Economy; The Finances and Financial Administration of the Seleukid Empire*. Cambridge: Cambridge University Press.

Arnold, Lutz G. 2002. *Business Cycle Theory.* Oxford: Oxford University Press.

Argy, Victor. 1994. *International Macroeconomics; Theory and Policy*. London: Routledge.

Azariadis, Costis. 1993. *Intertemporal Macroeconomics*. Cambridge, Mass.: Blackwell.

Barlow, Charles T. 1980. "The Roman Government and the Roman Economy, 92–80 B.C.," *American Journal of Philology* 101: 212–217.

Barro, Robert J. 1997. *Macroeconomics*, 5th Ed. Cambridge, Mass.: MIT Press.

Barro, Robert J. 2008. *Macroeconomics; A Modern Approach.* Mason, Oh.: Thomson South-Western.

Bénassy, Jean-Pascal. 2011. *Macroeconomic Theory.* Oxford: Oxford University Press.

Bitros, George C., Emmanouil M. L. Economou, and Nicholas C. Kyriazis. 2021. *Democracy and Money: Lessons for Today from Athens in Classical Times*. London: Routledge.

Blanchard, Olivier. 1997. *Macroeconomics*. Boston: Prentice Hall.

Blanchard, Olivier. 2000. "What Do We Know about Macroeconomics that Fisher and Wicksell Did Not?" *Quarterly Journal of Economics* 115: 1375–1409.

Blanchard, Olivier. 2011. *Macroeconomics*, 5th Ed., updated. Boston: Prentice Hall.

Blanchard, Olivier Jean, and Stanley Fischer.1989. *Lectures on Macroeconomics*. Cambridge, Mass.: MIT Press.

Blanchard, Olivier, and Lawrence J. Katz. 1997. "What We Know and Do Not Know About the Natural Rate of Unemployment," *Journal of Economic Perspectives* 11 No. 1: 51–72.

Boeckh, Augustus. 1842. *The Public Economy of Athens*, 2nd Ed., revised, translated by George Corewall Lewis. London: John W. Parker.

Brunt, P. A. 1980. "Free Labour and Public Works at Rome," *Journal of Roman Studies* 70: 81–100.

Buiter, Willem H. 1990. *Principles of Budgetary and Financial Policy*. Cambridge, Mass.: MIT Press.

Cohen, Edward E. 2008. "The Elasticity of the Money-Supply at Athens," in *The Monetary Systems of the Greeks and Romans*, edited by W.V. Harris, 76–81. Oxford: Oxford University Press.

Crawford, Michael. 1970. "Money and Exchange in the Roman World." *Journal of Roman Studies* 60: 40–48.

de la Croix, David, and Philippe Michel. 2002. *A Theory of Economic Growth; Dynamics and Policy in Overlapping Generations*. New York: Cambridge University Press.

Deger-Jalkotzy, Sigrid. 2008. "Decline, Destruction, Aftermath," in *The Cambridge Companion to the Aegean Bronze Age*, edited by Cynthia W. Shelmerdine, 387–415. Cambridge: Cambridge University Press.

Dickinson, Oliver. 2006. *The Aegean from Bronze Age to the Iron Age; Continuity and Change between the Twelfth and Eighth Centuries BC*. London: Routledge.

Dickinson, Oliver. 2010. "The Collapse at the End of the Bronze Age," in *The Oxford Handbook of the Bronze Age Aegean (ca. 3000–1000 BC)*, edited by Eric H. Cline, 483–490. Oxford: Oxford University Press.

Dornbusch, Rudiger. 1980. *Open Economy Macroeconomics*. New York: Basic Books.

Dornbusch, Rudiger, Stanley Fischer, and Richard Startz. 1998. *Macroeconomics*, 7th Ed. Boston: Irwin McGraw-Hill.

Dornbusch, Rudiger, Stanley Fischer, and Richard Startz. 2008. *Macroeconomics*, 10th Ed. Boston: McGraw-Hill Irwin.

Duncan-Jones, Richard. 1994. *Money and Government in the Roman Empire*. Cambridge: Cambridge University Press.

Farmer, Roger E. A. 1999. *Macroeconomics of Self-fulfilling Prophesies*, 2nd Ed. Cambridge, Mass.: MIT Press.

Figueira, Thomas. 1998. *The Power of Money; Coinage and Politics in the Athenian Empire*. Philadelphia: University of Pennsylvania Press.

Flaschel, Peter, Reiner Franke, and Willi Semmler. 1997. *Dynamic Macroeconomics: Instability, Fluctuations and Growth in Monetary Economies*. Cambridge, Mass.: MIT Press.

Fleming, J. Marcus. 1962. "Domestic Financial Policies Under Fixed and Under Floating Exchange Rates," *International Monetary Fund Staff Papers* 9: 369–380.

Foldvari, Peter, and Bas van Leeuwen. 2010. "Comparing per Capita Income in the Hellenistic World: The Case of Mesopotamia," mimeo, University of Debrecen and Utrecht University / Free University / University of Warwick, July.

Fontana, Guiseppe, and Mark Setterfield, eds. 2009. *Macroeconomic Theory and Pedagogy*. New York: Palgrave Macmillan.

Frank, Tenney. 1935. "The Financial Crisis of 33 A.D." *American Journal of Philology* 56: 336–341.

Frederiksen, M. W. 1966. "Caesar, Cicero and the Problem of Debt." *Journal of Roman Studies* 56: 128–141.

Frenkel, Jacob A., and Assaf Razin. 1987. "The Mundell-Fleming Model a Quarter Century Later: A Unified Exposition," *International Monetary Fund Staff Papers* 34: 567–620.

Frenkel, Jacob A., and Assaf Razin. 1987. *Fiscal Policies and the World Economy; An Intertemporal Approach*. Cambridge, Mass.: MIT Press.

Friedman, Benjamin M., and Michael Woodford, eds. 2011. *Handbook of Monetary Economics*, Volume 3A. Amsterdam: Elsevier.

Galí, Jordi. 2008. *Monetary Policy, Inflation, and the Business Cycle; An Introduction to the New Keynesian Framework*. Princeton: Princeton University Press.

Gandolfo, Giancarlo. 2002. *International Finance and Open-Economy Macro-economics*. Berlin: Springer.

Goldsmith, Raymond W. 1984. "An Estimate of the Size and Structure of the National Product of the Early Roman Empire," *Review of Income and Wealth* 30: 263–288.

Goldsmith, Raymond W. 1987. *Premodern Financial Systems; A Historical Comparative Study*. Cambridge: Cambridge University Press.

Haberler, Gottfried von. 1937, 1941. *Prosperity and Depression; A Theoretical Analysis of Cyclical Movements*, 1st Ed. Geneva: League of Nations; 1st Edition reprinted by University Press of the Pacific, Honolulu, 2001.

Haberler, Gottfried. 1944. *Readings in Business Cycle Theory*. Philadelphia: Blakiston.

Harl, Kenneth W. 1996. *Coinage in the Roman Economy, 300 B.C. to A.D. 700*. Baltimore: Johns Hopkins University Press.

Heijdra, Ben. 2009. *The Foundations of Modern Macroeconomics*, 2nd Ed. Oxford: Oxford University Press.

Hicks, J. R. 1937. "Mr. Keynes and the 'Classics,' A Suggested Interpretation," *Econometrica* 5: 147–159.

Hopkins, Keith. 1980. "Taxes and Trade in the Roman Empire (200 B.C.-A.D. 400)," *Journal of Roman Studies* 70: 101–125.

Howgego, Christopher. 1995. *Ancient History from Coins*. London: Routledge.

Isard, Peter. 1995. *Exchange Rate Economics*. Cambridge: Cambridge University Press.

Jones, Donald W. 2000. *External Relations of Early Iron Age Crete, 1100–600 B.C.*, Archaeological Institute of America Monographs New Series, No. 4. Philadelphia: The University Museum, University of Pennsylvania.

Katsari, Constantina. 2011. *The Roman Monetary System: The Eastern Provinces from the First to the Third Century AD*. Cambridge: Cambridge University Press.

Krueger, Anne O. 1983. *Exchange-Rate Determination*. Cambridge: Cambridge University Press.

Krugman, Paul, and Robin Wells. 2009. *Macroeconomics*, 2nd Ed. New York: Worth.

Laidler, David E. W. 1993. *The Demand for Money; Theories, Evidence, and Problems*, 4th Ed. New York: Harper Collins.

Layard, Richard, Stephen Nickell, and Richard Jackman. 2005. *Unemployment; Macroeconomic Performance and the Labour Market*, 2nd Ed. Oxford: Oxford University Press.

Ljungqvist, Lars, and Thomas J. Sargent. 2004. *Recursive Macroeconomic Theory*, 2nd Ed. Cambridge, Mass.: MIT Press.

Lo Cascio, Elio. 1981. "State and Coinage in the Late Republic and Early Empire," *Journal of Roman Studies* 71: 76–86.

Lo Cascio, Elio, ed. 2006. *Innovazione tecnica e progresso economic nel mondo romano; Atti degli Incontri capresi di storia dell'economia antica (Capri 13–16 aprile 2003)*. Bari: Edipuglia.

Lo Cascio, Elio, and Paolo Melanima. 2009. "GDP in Pre-Modern Agrarian Economies (1–1820 AD): A Revision of the Estimates," *Rivista di Storia Economia* 25: 387–415.

Loomis, William T. 1998. *Wages, Welfare Costs and Inflation in Classical Athens*. Ann Arbor: University of Michigan Press.

Lutz, Arnold G. 2002. *Business Cycle Theory*. Oxford: Oxford University Press

Maddison, Angus. 2007. *Contours of the World Economy, 1–2030 AD. Essays in Macro-Economic History*. Oxford: Oxford University Press.

Mankiw, N. Gregory. 2006. "The Macroeconomist as Scientist and Engineer," *Journal of Economic Perspectives* 20, No. 4: 29–46.

Mankiw, N. Gregory. 2010. *Macroeconomics*, 7th Ed. New York: Worth.

Mankiw, N. Gregory. 2018. *Brief Principles of Macroeconomics*, 8th Ed. Boston: Cengage.

McCallum, Bennett T. 1996. *International Monetary Economics*. New York: Oxford University Press.

McCandless, George. 2008. *The ABCs of RBCs; An Introduction to Dynamic Macroeconomic Models*. Cambridge, Mass.: Harvard University Press.

McCandless, Jr., George T., with Neil Wallace. 1991. *Introduction to Dynamic Macroeconomic Theory; An Overlapping Generations Approach*. Cambridge, Mass.: Harvard University Press.

Moggridge, Donald, ed. 1982. *The Collected Writings of John Maynard Keynes, Volume XXVIII, Social, Political and Literary Writings*. London: Macmillan and Cambridge University Press.

Montiel, Peter J. 2009. *International Macroeconomics*. Malden, Mass.: Wiley-Blackwell.

Morley, Neville. 2001. "The Transformation of Italy, 225–28 B.C.," *Journal of Roman Studies* 91: 50–62.

Morris, Ian. 2004. "Economic Growth in Ancient Greece," *Journal of Institutional and Theoretical Economics* 160: 709–742.

Mundell, Robert A. 1968. *International Economics*. New York: Macmillan.

Niehans, Jürg. 1984. *International Monetary Economics*. Baltimore: Johns Hopkins University Press.

Obstfeld, Maurice, and Kenneth Rogoff. 1996. *Foundations of International Macroeconomics*. Cambridge, Mass.: MIT Press.

Patinkin, Don. 1965. *Money, Interest, and Prices; An Integration of Monetary and Value Theory*, 2nd Ed. New York: Harper & Row.

Phelps, Edmund S., in collaboration with Hian Teck Hoon, George Kanaginis, and Gylfi Zoega. 1994. *Structural Slumps; The Modern Equilibrium Theory of Unemployment, Interest, and Assets*. Cambridge, Mass.: Harvard University Press.

Pissarides, Christopher A. 2000. *Equilibrium Unemployment Theory*, 2nd Ed. Cambridge, Mass.: MIT Press.

Purvis, Douglas D. 1985. "Public Sector Deficits, International Capital Movements, and the Domestic Economy: The Medium-Term is the Message," *Canadian Journal of Economics* 18: 723–742.

Rodewald, Cosmo. 1976. *Money in the Age of Tiberius*. Manchester: Manchester University Press.

Romer, David. 1993. "The New Keynesian Synthesis," *Journal of Economic Perspectives* 7, No. 1: 5–22.

Romer, David. 2000. "Keynesian Macroeconomics without the LM Curve," *Journal of Economic Perspectives* 14, No. 2: 149–169.

Romer, David. 2006. *Advanced Macroeconomics*, 3rd Ed. Boston: McGraw Hill Irwin.

Sargent, Thomas J. 1979. *Macroeconomic Theory*. Cambridge, Mass.: Harvard University Press.

Sargent, Thomas J. 1987. *Macroeconomic Theory*, 2nd Ed. Boston: Academic Press.

Schaps, David M. 2004. *The Invention of Coinage and the Monetization of Ancient Greece*. Ann Arbor: University of Michigan Press.

Scheidel, Walter. 2008. "In Search of Roman Economic Growth," version 1.0, Princeton/Stanford Working Papers in Classics, June.

Scheidel, Walter, and Steven J. Friesen, 2009. "The Size of the Economy and the Distribution of Income in the Roman Empire," *Journal of Roman Studies* 99: 61–91.

Silver, Morris. 2007. "Roman Economic Growth and Living Standards: Perceptions versus Evidence," *Ancient Society*: 191–252;

Snowdon Brian, and Howard R. Vane, 2005. *Modern Macroeconomics; Its Origins, Development and Current State*. Cheltenham, U.K.: Edward Elgar.

Taylor, John B., and Michael Woodford, eds. 1999. *Handbook of Macroeconomics*, Volumes 1A, 1B, 1C. Amsterdam: Elsevier.

Taylor, Mark P. 1995. "The Economics of Exchange Rates," *Journal of Economic Literature* 33: 13–47.

Temin, Peter. 2004. "Financial Intermediation in the Early Roman Empire," *Journal of Economic History* 64: 705–733.

Temin, Peter. 2006a. "The Economy of the Early Roman Empire," *Journal of Economic Perspectives* 20 No. 1: 133–151.

Temin, Peter. 2006b. "Estimating GDP in the Early Roman Empire," in *Innovazione tecnica e progresso economico nel mondo romano*, edited by Elio Lo Cascio, 31–54. Rome: Bari.

Turnovsky, Stephen J. 1977. *Macroeconomic Analysis and Stabilization Policies*. Cambridge: Cambridge University Press.

Turnovsky, Stephen J. 1997. *International Macroeconomic Dynamics*. Cambridge, Mass.: MIT Press.

Turnovsky, Stephen J. 2000. *Methods of Macroeconomic Dynamics*. Cambridge, Mass.: MIT Press.

Warburton, David A. 1998. *State and Economy in Ancient Egypt; Fiscal Vocabulary of the New Kingdom*, Orbis Biblicus et Orientalis 151. Fribourg and Göttingen: University Press Fribourg and Vandenhoeck & Ruprecht.

Woodford, Michael. 1999. "Revolution and Evolution in Twentieth-Century Macroeconomics," Paper presented at the conference, "Frontiers of the Mind in the Twenty-First Century," U.S. Library of Congress, Washington, D.C., June.

Woodford, Michael. 2003. *Interest and Prices; Foundations of a Theory of Monetary Policy*. Princeton: Princeton University Press.

www.ingramcontent.com/pod-product-compliance
Ingram Content Group UK Ltd.
Pitfield, Milton Keynes, MK11 3LW, UK
UKHW052302280926
15471UKWH00007B/1060

9 781407 357683